KINGS

or

PEOPLE

KINGS

OR

PEOPLE

Power and the Mandate to Rule

REINHARD BENDIX

UNIVERSITY OF CALIFORNIA PRESS

Berkeley   Los Angeles   London

University of California Press
Berkeley and Los Angeles, California

University of California Press, Ltd.
London, England

Copyright © 1978 by
The Regents of the University of California

ISBN 0-520-02302-1
Library of Congress Catalog Card Number: 72-85525
Printed in the United States of America

1 2 3 4 5 6 7 8 9

For life to be large and full, it must con-
tain the care of the past and of the future
in every passing moment of the present.

Joseph Conrad, *Nostromo*

Contents

Part I: THE AUTHORITY OF KINGS

Part II: TOWARD A MANDATE OF THE PEOPLE

Maps

Preface

The world in which we live has its roots far back in history, and as a world power America must come to terms with countries which were formed in their present mold long before the American revolution. All those to whom an exploration of this historical background will appeal probably share with me an immediate empathy with the anguish of nation-building around the world. This book is a study of what that anguish meant in times past when countries were first developing their political institutions and when they turned more recently from royal authority to a popular mandate. The problems of developing such institutions are formidable, then as well as now. A scholarly concern with these problems must touch on many subjects in social stratification, religion, political sociology, and the history of ideas, and the book treats these and related themes in their specific historical contexts.

This interpretive work is addressed not only to students of political development but also to the general reader who is interested in a large view of history. That reader is provided with sufficient detail and annotation so that the many diverse contexts with which this study deals can be understood. A thematic outline of the book is presented on the first pages of the introduction, which deals as well with the reasons for my approach to historical sociology.

I acknowledge with thanks the research assistance of Theodore Bogacz, Audrey Ichinose, and Neda Tomasovich. The maps were prepared by my wife, Jane Bendix. The long process of revision and editing was much facilitated by my wife, my sons John and Erik Bendix, and by Dr. James Hughes who helped prepare the final draft. In addition, I thank several colleagues for their critique of parts of this study: Professor Robert Darnton, Princeton University; the late Professor Lloyd Fallers, University of Chicago; Professor Toru Haga, University of Tokyo; Professors Elbaki Hermassi, David Keightley, and Martin Malia, University of California, Berkeley; Professor David Riesman, Harvard University; Professor S. Frederick Starr, Executive Director, Kennan Institute of

Russian Studies, Woodrow Wilson Center, Washington, D.C.; and Professor Lawrence Stone, Princeton University.

The second part of the book was first sketched during a leave of absence (1972/73) at the Institute for Advanced Study, Princeton, under Grant GS-31370X of the National Science Foundation. The manuscript was completed at the Woodrow Wilson International Center for Scholars, Smithsonian Institution, Washington, D.C. This work was facilitated by a fellowship from the Center and a Guggenheim fellowship for 1975/76. The support received over many years from the University of California, Berkeley, and specifically from the Institutes of Industrial Relations and of International Studies at Berkeley, has been of great assistance.

A few technical details may be added. When kings or other rulers are mentioned, the years stated in parentheses refer to their reigns, unless *b*(orn) and *d*(ied) have been added. (Some reigns began during the minority of the ruler.) The years added to the names of persons other than rulers indicate their life span. Where it seemed appropriate, I have repeated dates mentioned earlier in order to avoid confusion and aid the reader's sense of chronology. A glossary of terms, maps and illustrations, and a detailed name- and subject-index should facilitate the use of this book. In a work of this kind, footnotes present a problem. My debt to the scholarly work of others has been acknowledged wherever appropriate, but I have not footnoted general information. Some explanatory notes have been inserted in the text, but all footnotes and specialized comments (for example, on terminology) are placed at the end of the book. In this way, the general reader has an uncluttered page while the student can find specialized information without difficulty. Concerning the larger design of the study, my footnotes probably err on the side of parsimony, since I have learned much more from the works of Max Weber, Otto Hintze, and other comparativists than my sparse references indicate. Occasionally, I have added references to further readings.

The footnotes to each chapter contain full publication references for every book or article cited in that chapter. Accordingly, in the interest of saving space, a bibliography of all references cited has not been added to the volume.

Finally, I thank my many colleagues at the University of California, Berkeley, who have provided me with their intellectual fellowship and friendship for over a quarter of a century.

Goldern-Hasliberg
August 1976   Reinhard Bendix

KINGS

or

PEOPLE

1

INTRODUCTION

THIS BOOK is about authority. Its first part deals with the formation of structures of authority in medieval history. Its second part deals with the transformation of these structures beginning in the sixteenth century. A concluding chapter deals more briefly with the problems of state-building in the twentieth century.*

This study of the historical foundations of authority begins in Part 1 with a discussion of the religious bases of royal authority in Western, Islamic, and Chinese civilizations. Subsequent chapters deal with kingship and aristocracy in Japan, Russia, Imperial Germany and Prussia, and England, from roughly 500 A.D. to the sixteenth century.

Kings have ruled human communities from the beginning of recorded history. Through the rule of kingship, political traditions were established which have influenced mankind to the present. The English parliament, German political fragmentation, or Russian autocracy long antedate the development of modern societies. Every country develops its own culture and social structure, but once the basic pattern of institutions is formed under the circumstances of early kingship, it is difficult to change. In order to understand the modern world, one must take into account the traditional practices of a nation and their unique elaborations. Japan, Russia, Germany, and England have always been very different societies, and the formation of their political traditions helps to explain these differences.

At the same time, technical innovations (such as printing or the modern computer) can spread to every country, just as social and economic developments (such as European overseas expansion in the sixteenth century or the industrial revolutions of the eighteenth and nineteenth centuries) cut across national lines. However, as each country encounters sweeping developments of technology and social change, it must adapt them to its own history and long-established practices.

* An early version of this chapter was first published under the title "The Mandate to Rule: An Introduction," *Social Forces* 55 (December, 1976): 242–56.

This study combines an understanding of a country's historical particularity with its participation in a general movement of history.

The *principle* of hereditary monarchy was challenged only some two centuries ago. Since then, governments in one country after another have ruled their communities in the name of the people. Part 2 of this study deals with the transformation of authority as the rule of kings was replaced by governments of the people. In our time, not only democracies but military regimes, dictatorships, and even constitutional monarchies are legitimized by claims of popular mandate. Indeed, other ways of justifying authority have become inconceivable. The leaders and ideas of this great movement toward a popular mandate as it has developed from the English and French revolutions of the seventeenth and eighteenth centuries to the present are the subject of Part 2.

England, France, Germany, Japan, and Russia are today among the most industrialized nations of the world. Historically, these countries represent successive turning points from the medieval to the modern world. Each development—the revolutions of seventeenth-century England, the French revolution, the English industrial revolution, the reform movements in Germany and Japan during the nineteenth century, and the Bolshevik revolution in the twentieth century—had an effect on the next development and on the rest of the world. Together they provide a scenario of the "modern revolution."

My study advances five main themes:

1. The authority of kings depended on religious sanction as well as on internal and external struggles for power. In the course of long and varied histories, royal authority was centralized, expanded, and eventually destroyed. From ancient times, kingship was constituted in divergent ways, and the unity or integration of traditional societies seems largely mythical. Although kingship was sacrosanct and endured for long periods, the authority of any one king was always in jeopardy and had to be manifested continuously to remain effective.

2. Kings governed their realm with the aid of magnates or notables to whom they delegated authority. Aristocratic governance depended on the terms and circumstances of that delegation, which over time helped to form the character of the aristocracy. Though royal supremacy and aristocratic dependence was the norm, the centralization and decentralization of authority varied in practice. If it was true of kings that they delegated authority but wished to control its exercise, it was true of aristocrats that they accepted such authority but sought to make it autonomous. This tension between central authority and local government must be continually managed but is never resolved. Part 1 of this book contains four case studies of this "management" over time.

3. Authority in the name of the people only gradually became an alternative to the authority of kings. Established practices of royal au-

thority were undermined by the commercialization of land and government offices, and by the increasing role of educated commoners in high places. The countries considered here already had fully formed political structures by the time they advanced to popular sovereignty. Each of the countries had several educated elites which hoped to catch up with developments abroad through state action and intellectual mobilization. Under these conditions, specific educated elites advanced ideas concerning the reconstitution of authority in the name of the people.

4. The countries examined here undertook the reconstitution of authority in their early modern periods. Authority in the name of the people has proven as varied in practice as the authority of kings. In each case, the institutionalization of popular sovereignty showed the effects of the way in which the authority of kings was left behind. In turn, each institutionalization created a model which other countries adapted for their own ends.

5. England, France, Germany, Japan, Russia, and China have participated in a worldwide movement of nationalism and of government by popular mandate, though each country has done so in its own way. My account attempts to show that nationalism has become a universal condition in our world because the sense of backwardness in one's own country has led to ever new encounters with the "advanced model" or development of another country. I wish to show that the problems faced by each modernizing country were largely unique. Even the countries which had been building their political institutions for centuries had to cope with unprecedented problems in the process of modernization. Today, new states looking for analogues or precedents in other countries have more models to choose from than ever before, but their histories and the earlier development of other countries have hardly prepared them for the tasks of state-building.[1] As the concluding chapter suggests, this process of historical models and their demonstration effects continues to the present, and I cannot see an end to its further ramifications.

THE AUTHORITY OF KINGS

The major societies of the world before the era of European expansion overseas (roughly before 1500) had some features in common. More than 80 percent of the people lived on the land, close to the subsistence level. Population was checked by frequent wars and epidemics but nevertheless increased slowly. There was some development of technology, of urban centers with specialized crafts, and of a considerable military establishment. The population generally produced at a level which allowed rulers to maintain relatively large political units by means of exploitation and taxation.[2] These societies were marked by a concen-

Frederick I Barbarossa, Henry VI, and Frederick of Swabia in 1185

The central figure, Frederick I, Holy Roman Emperor of the German Nation from 1152 to 1190, holds the imperial staff and globe. The globe or orb is surmounted by a cross which symbolizes the domination of Christianity over the world. These insignia were used by the German emperors from 936 until the dissolution of the empire in 1806. Frederick's son Henry, who succeeded him in 1190, wears an unadorned crown but is placed to the emperor's right. A second son, Frederick Duke of Swabia, who was not in the line of succession, wears only an embroidered cap. (Forschungsinstitut für Kunstgeschichte, Bildarchiv Photo Marburg) tration of wealth, status, and authority in the hands of the governing class, which comprised between 1 or 2 percent of the population but appropriated at least one-half of the society's income above bare subsistence.³ To us, widespread inequality may suggest unremitting coercion and continuous, latent rebellion. But for many centuries, the vast mass of people acquiesced in the established order out of religious awe, a desire for peace and security, and the inability to unite in a common political action.⁴ In those earlier times, the rule of the privileged few appeared to the many as if it were a force of nature; it was to be enjoyed when it was benign and endured when it was not. And where wars and feuds were common, rulers could protect and thus benefit the people over whom they ruled.

For millennia, rulers rested their claims on divine sanction; other grounds of rule such as tradition or law also required and received their warrant from the divine. A deity or spirit was believed to sanctify rule, and the rights of the ruler could not be questioned, lest sacrilege jeopardize the welfare of all. But since the authority of kings required holy sanction, based on the prevailing religious institutions, consecration of rule entailed political liabilities in the relations between the king and the religious functionaries.

The exercise of royal authority also depended on the balance of power among the members and most important retainers of the royal house. In theory, the ruler owned the whole realm, but in practice the territorial possessions of the royal house were the main source of revenue and of favors in peace and war. These possessions were scattered, and the realm as a whole was governed through various forms of delegated authority. Rulers were typically torn between the need to delegate authority and the desire not to lose it. They were frequently driven to appeal to the personal loyalty or consecrated obligation of those to whom they had delegated authority in order to buttress their own position. The internal balance of forces was also influenced by alliances or conflicts with outside powers, a condition greatly affected in early times by the absence of stable, clearly defined frontiers.

All three factors—religious sanction of royal authority, internal contentions over the distribution of authority, and intrusion of outside powers—helped to shape medieval governance.

Until the revolutions of the seventeenth and eighteenth centuries, European rulers assumed that the general population would quietly allow itself to be ruled. Popular uprisings were regarded as violating the divine order and were suppressed by force. Kings, aristocrats, and magnates of the church made claims against one another. In these conflicts, each manipulated appeals to the transcendent powers without fear of seriously undermining the exclusive hold on authority they all enjoyed. The general populace was excluded from the political arena. If some questioned this practice, it was without much effect. However, this questioning spread in the early modern period, first in the religious sphere during the Reformation and subsequently in the political sphere in the seventeenth and eighteenth centuries. The good fortune of the few became a matter of controversy. In *The Social Contract,* Rousseau wrote that "the strongest are still never sufficiently strong to ensure them continual mastership, unless they find means of transforming force into right, and obedience into duty."[5] In France during the eighteenth century, it became more and more difficult for people to distinguish authority from oppression, or right from might. The old religious appeals lost their force; secular appeals on behalf of the status quo were of little avail. The right to rule by and for the few had come into doubt.

Throughout history, the weak had appealed to the deities or other higher powers to bear witness to their suffering. On occasion they had challenged the strong to live up to their own pronouncements. But with the Reformation, the persuasiveness of the ruler's old appeal to divine sanction was irreparably weakened. And since the French revolution, the right to rule has come to depend increasingly on a mandate of the people.

AUTHORITY IN THE NAME OF THE PEOPLE

The French revolution marked the end of an era in which the ruling few monopolized political life. Since 1789, political transactions have become increasingly public. In modern society, unless measures are taken to prevent it, rulers and ruled alike must advance their claims in public and hence with an eye to the public reactions that are likely to follow. *Vox populi, vox dei.*

The Western idea of authority in the name of the people owes something to classical Greek and Roman ideas of what it means to be a citizen in the community. At one time, the Greek city-state and the Roman republic practiced a type of governance in which all male heads of households actively participated in political decision-making for the entire community. This has appealed strongly to the Western imagination. Despite its known association with oligarchic rule, slavery, and conquest, and despite the many centuries during which it lost all political significance, the classical idea of citizenship helped to inspire the leaders of the French revolution.

The idea of popular sovereignty also has roots in the role which consent played in Germanic tribes. This role became known to Roman observers in the first century A.D. The tribes were governed by chieftains who ruled with the aid of a council of elders. Such chieftains succeeded one another on the basis of hereditary claims, provided that their accession to the throne was confirmed through an act of acclamation by the leading warriors of the tribe. During the fourth and fifth centuries A.D., these practices affected the Roman empire directly: Successive emperors were elevated to the imperial throne by the acclamation of frontier armies largely composed of Germanic warriors. As the settlement of Germanic tribes in the Western parts of the Roman empire became stabilized, the relation between the ruler and his warriors was transformed into the contractual obligations between lord and vassal. Hence, the idea of a contract between rulers and ruled has very early antecedents.

The idea of popular mandate owes something to the Christian belief that all men are equal before God. This idea makes rulers and ruled alike part of one community. As baptized members of the church, *all* have access to the sacraments, and all are subject to divine law. Such equality prevailed in the early Christian communities but declined during the long supremacy of the Catholic church, for the pope and through him the whole hierarchy of the priesthood stood in the direct line of apostolic succession. The church alone was the consecrated vessel of divine grace. With the coming of the Reformation, the beliefs of early Christianity were revived, and emphasis shifted from the hierarchic conception of the church to one centering on the Bible as the repository of the divine word. Thus, the Protestant idea emerged that every believer stands in direct relation to God. Some Protestant denominations came to redefine the Christian community as a "brotherhood of all believers," in which responsibility for spiritual welfare was shared alike by all baptized members of the congregation.

Authority in the name of the people also came to the fore in the municipal communities of Western Europe in the twelfth and thirteenth centuries. However, the major modern development of popular mandate dates from the English and French revolutions in the seventeenth and eighteenth centuries. The idea of popular sovereignty has had its greatest impact since that time. Participation by the public in national affairs has widened; the earlier dichotomy between rulers and ruled has become blurred. Noble birth and inherited wealth have ceased to guarantee authority. At the same time, nation-states have emerged with frontiers that are clearly defined and relatively stable.

THE GREAT SOCIAL AND INTELLECTUAL TRANSFORMATION

The fifteenth and sixteenth centuries witnessed a great transformation of European societies. Preconditions of this transformation date back to the growth of towns in the tenth to twelfth centuries, when urban communities developed their economies rapidly and achieved political autonomy. But the turn from the authority of kings to government by popular mandate had its more immediate social and intellectual antecedents in the decades around 1500.

The history of population provides a simple index. In the period between 1000 and 1340 A.D., the population of Europe more than doubled, reaching at least 80 million. During the next century and a half wars, famines, and especially epidemics struck intermittently with such severity that by 1500 the total European population was still 80 million. Thereafter, the causes of catastrophic death remained but became less virulent, with the worst type of epidemic, the plague, disappearing in the seventeenth century. By 1600 Europe probably had 105 million and by 1700 about 115 million people. The growth of population was a main factor in the commercialization of land, labor, and capital, the rapid development of towns, and European expansion overseas.

Before 1500, authority and inequality were linked. Men of wealth and noble birth exercised the functions of government. They had a monopoly over political matters which was challenged in Western Europe only by the church. The people provided services, and if they rebelled they were put in their place. After 1500, however, this rigid bond between authority and inequality loosened. Commoners made inroads on the bastions of privilege through trade, the secularization of learning, and the rise of secular professions in government employment. It became more difficult to contain these social and economic changes in the old political framework after the great reformers challenged the spiritual monopoly of the Catholic church, for that challenge emphasized the spiritual worth of the individual and hence made it easier to question political monopolies which denied the rights of man.

The decades around 1500 witnessed not only economic growth, European expansion overseas, and the Reformation; they also witnessed the rise of Humanism, the invention of printing, and the early development of modern science. The number of educated people increased, as did the number of those whose livelihood depended on teaching, writing, or some other intellectual vocation. The stage was set for a rapid diffusion of ideas.

In one country after another, intellectual elites formulated ideas in conscious response to what they learned from abroad. The belief in government in the name of the people spread during and after the seventeenth century. As countries achieved a breakthrough to authority by popular mandate, they provided models which were imitated, transformed, or rejected by the latecomers to the process of nation-building.

WHAT IS MODERNIZATION?

It is easiest to define modernization as a breakdown of the ideal-typical traditional order: Authority loses its sanctity, monarchy declines, hierarchical social order is disrupted. Secular authority, rule in the name of the people, and an equalitarian ethos are typical attributes of modern society. The eighteenth-century writers who reflected on this transformation were among the first to articulate the contrast between tradition and modernity.[6]

To the theorists of the day, the division of labor appeared as a key factor in this transformation. In his *Essay on the History of Civil Society* (1767), Adam Ferguson attributed the progress of a people to the subdivision of tasks; his discussion formulated a way of looking at modern society which has since become commonplace. The division of labor increases the productivity of those who specialize, and hence the wealth of their country. Private ends and lack of conscious concern for public welfare ironically yield public benefits.

Ferguson portrayed society as divided into a leisured ruling minority and a working majority. Members of the higher class are bound to no task and are free to follow their whims. At the same time, Ferguson suggested that those who eke out a mere subsistence are degraded by the "objects they pursue, and by the means they employ to attain" those objects. Production, he said, is increased as a result of such degradation. In his view, the economic ends of society are best promoted by mechanical arts requiring little capacity and thriving best "under a total suppression of sentiment and reason."[7]

Karl Marx used the insights of Ferguson's work as a guide for action. Marx believed he had discovered the "laws of capitalist development"; knowledge of these laws would help reorganize society to better meet human needs. He also believed that the time was ripe for radical reorganization. Capitalism would spread everywhere and create the preconditions for its own overthrow.

Max Weber wanted to preserve what men valued in the Western cultural tradition. This was one reason why he looked to the religious and ethical beliefs bound up with the capitalist mode of production. His discovery that purely materialistic striving also had spiritual roots made him skeptical of interpretations of the modern transformation which emphasized the division of labor alone. But he was also convinced that the imperatives of capitalist production and bureaucratic organization would suppress the individual and obliterate much cultural diversity.

More recently, theories of modernization have focused on the necessary and sufficient conditions for this great transformation. Once the prerequisites of modernization are acquired, the change toward a modern society appears inevitable. This categorizing approach has tended to replace both Marx's and Weber's concern with historical factors, probably in the hope that a causal analysis based on the isolation of dependent and independent variables would facilitate the management of social change.[8]

In my view, Marx was right to anticipate worldwide repercussions of capitalism and to see a revolutionary potential in its spread. But he was wrong in confining this potential to the economic sphere and to the increasing class struggle in developed capitalist societies. I believe that the chances of revolution increase wherever the new industrial way of life and ideas of popular sovereignty disrupt an old social order. Thus, society is ripe for revolution in the *early* phase of industrialization and democratization, however protracted that phase may be. The term *modernization* is applied best where nonindustrial ways of life and hierarchic social orders are threatened by industrial ways and egalitarian social norms.[9]

UNEVEN DEVELOPMENT

The division of labor is a cause of change especially in economically developing societies, but it is not the only cause in all societies. Historically, many agricultural societies have had little division of labor yet have proved open to change, for example, through the infusion or development of religious ideas.

Naturally, observers were impressed—and rightly so—by the role the division of labor played in the economic development of all Western European societies, especially of England. Since the modern industrial revolution had *begun* in England, other countries followed the English model when they began to develop their own industry. But they wanted to follow the *latest* English development to which they could gain access, not the English practices of the 1760s with which English industrialization began. Countries were, therefore, less and less able or willing to repeat each other's development.

Nor were they likely to become the same kind of society as a result of successful industrialization. Continued political and cultural differentiation is the more likely outcome. The "demonstration effect" itself prevents societies from repeating one another's development, and so tends to prevent industrial societies from converging culturally and institutionally. In *Medieval Cities,* Henri Pirenne showed how this demonstration effect worked in the past. The merchant and craft guilds of a few cities used force (in the eleventh century) to win recognition of their independent jurisdiction from feudal overlords. A good many other rulers took the hint and negotiated a settlement with their own towns before armed conflict occurred.

But these events took place prior to the modern revolution in communications. With the invention of printing in the fifteenth century, ideas spread more quickly. The growth of an educated public provided an audience for writers and artists. This development coincided in turn with the rise of modern science. In each country, the "great transformation" encouraged the growth of an elite which was sensitive to the new ideas developed elsewhere and ready to apply them at home. Countries became examples to one another. Nevertheless, what appeared highly desirable from the point of view of progress often appeared as a danger to national independence or self-respect. Every idea taken from elsewhere can be both an asset to the development of a country and a reminder of its comparative backwardness—both a challenge to be emulated and, whatever its utility, a threat to national identity. The period since 1500 has also been the period of rising nationalism.

The contemporary world has made us familiar with the tension between progress and national identity. Each country must cope socially and politically with the disruptive impact of ideas and industrial practices taken from abroad. Its ability or inability to do so depends on its own history, on the cumulative peculiarities of each affected civilization. Old societies that become new states look back on centuries of historical experience involving a mixture of languages, economic patterns, and religious beliefs. This is the base from which they must master the impact of the "advanced world." The advanced countries of today have had their own periods of underdevelopment and of responding to the "advanced world" of their day, and they still struggle (as all countries must) with the unresolved legacies of their several histories.

PRESENTATION AND TYPES OF EVIDENCE

To bring the large themes set forth in this introduction together in one book, I have divided the discussion into two parts—the authority of kings and movements toward a mandate of the people. The cultural formation of political institutions dates back to an early time, since the religious consecration of royal authority took place in the distant past. This early formation of political institutions foreshadowed the emergence of government in the name of the people, and this long-run effect can be studied by following the development of each country's aristocratic culture forward into the early modern period.

The countries considered here are arranged in a triple sequence from West to East (in Chapter 2), from East to West (in Chapters 3 through 6), and again from West to East (in Chapters 9 through 13), though in the interest of chronology I have placed the discussion of Japan before Russia in Part 2. One reason for the arrangement is to begin with what Western readers will find relatively familiar. A second reason is that I wish to present the "modern revolution" in its chronological sequence. A concluding chapter deals briefly with twentieth-century problems of building nation-states.

This study draws much of its evidence from social and political history. It differs from inquiries in economics, sociology, and psychology, which frequently examine the record of human behavior for the hidden forces which cause that behavior. Such inquiry into underlying structures has been a dominant theme in recent intellectual history. Marxists and Freudians are at one in their attempt to discern the underlying cause of manifest discontents, even if they differ in what they purport to find. Some anthropologists and psychologists have turned their attention from behavioral studies to the analysis of myths in searching for the underlying constants of the human condition. And some sociologists and political scientists engage in a search for universals when they analyze the functional prerequisites of all social and political structures.

Such a search for structural forces can yield insights into motivation, ideological assumptions, and hidden interrelations. I am indebted to this intellectual tendency. But with so many scholars engaged in searching for underlying structures, there is space for an inquiry which focuses attention on structures that lie more open to view. The roots of historically developed structures, of the culture and political institutions of any present-day society, reach far into the past. In studying these roots, I am striving to free our understanding of the stereotyped contrast between tradition and modernity.

The ideas and actions of those in positions of power or authority are the best documented part of the human record. By comparing societies over long spans of time, and by choosing to look at social structures from the top down, one can take advantage of this extensive material. Major aspects of the social structure can be revealed if those in authority are studied in terms of the disunity and dilemmas they face as they advance their claims to legitimacy.

LIMITATIONS

The countries included in this book are those which I have studied for a number of years. They are among the most industrialized countries of the world and are also those in which the great revolutions and restoration movements have occurred since the seventeenth century. Inevitably there are omissions, and some of these deserve comment.

Small countries like Switzerland and the Netherlands have achieved stable authority structures through federation and the delegation of authority rather than through royalty and conquest. They also provide important models. Modern nation-states like the Americas, Australia, or New Zealand present problems of their own. Unlike England or Russia in their early development, the political institutions of the modern state were available at the time of European settlement; thus these institutions (or parts of them) could be adapted at will under the new conditions.[10] Other states like Italy or Spain were omitted simply because I have not mastered their historical experience. Perhaps the most serious omissions are those numerous societies in which state- and nation-building must occur under twentieth-century conditions. Some countries of Asia and Africa have had state institutions in the past but today must rebuild them on new foundations. Other countries have emerged from centuries of cultural cross-currents and recent colonial subjection and must begin the task of building an independent state centuries after the task has been completed by all the major powers of the world. I touch on this question in the concluding chapter but am more acutely aware now than when I began that the "new states" of the twentieth century represent novel conditions of political development.

THE PURPOSES OF COMPARISON

In any scholarly discipline, the advance of knowledge depends on specialization. Hence, over the years there has been a drift toward confining overall presentations to introductory courses in the universities. At the same time, most teaching and research has been devoted to specialized topics. The burden of integrating the knowledge received in different specialties often falls on the student. Even if he is willing, he has little assistance in his efforts to encompass different fields of study. The risks of such integration are great, but one must not expect of students what one is unwilling to undertake oneself.

Comparative analysis should sharpen our understanding of the contexts in which more detailed causal inferences can be drawn. Without a knowledge of contexts, causal inference may pretend to a level of generality to which it is not entitled. On the other hand, comparative studies should not attempt to replace causal analysis, because they can deal only with a few cases and cannot easily isolate the variables (as causal analysis must).

In order to preserve a sense of historical particularity while comparing different countries, I ask the same or at least similar questions of very different contexts and thus allow for divergent answers. Structures of authority in different countries do vary; societies have responded differently to challenges prompted by advances from abroad. The value of this study depends on the illumination obtained from the questions asked and from a sustained comparative perspective. Chapters 2, 7, 8, and 14 elaborate the principal questions; these chapters introduce and conclude the two parts of this book.

My approach to social history differs from mere reportage as well as from the more theoretical approaches to comparative studies. To compare, for example, kingship in Western and Chinese civilization, or intellectual mobilization in sixteenth-century England and eighteenth-century Germany, one must ask questions broad enough for comparison to be possible. Such questions rest on concepts absent from mere reportage. But the concepts suitable for comparisons which preserve a sense of historical particularity are also less comprehensive than the more abstract and systematic concepts of social theory. For purposes of the comparisons here envisaged, a solution is not found by making the concepts either more precise or more comprehensive. On the one hand, concepts become inapplicable to a number of diverse cases as they become more strictly applicable to any one of them. On the other, concepts become inapplicable to any specific case as they become applicable to all cases. Logically, all concepts begin with universals. But once these are stated, it becomes necessary to provide links between such universals and the case materials to be studied, as I try to do in Chapters 2, 7, 8, and 14.

Comparative studies depend on qualitative judgments and illustrative uses of the evidence. I have relied on the judgments of historians but primarily on my own sense of how much illustrative material is needed to give the reader a vivid impression of the point to be made. In practice, I have found it necessary to make the best judgments I can and then warn the reader, as I do here, that these judgments remain tentative and may have to be modified by further scholarly work or by the judgments of scholars more expert in a given field than I can hope to be.

POWER AND THE MANDATE TO RULE

Authority and inequality are basic dimensions of all social structures. Societies are governed by the few, because the few can reach an understanding among themselves and use that understanding to facilitate decision-making. This is a universal condition of all complex societies; only tribal societies are not governed in this manner. Whether a society is under the authority of a king or under a government in the name of the people, the few will be distinguished from the many. Thus, where authority is present, inequality between rulers and ruled will occur.

This book deals with power and the mandate to rule, that is, the use of force as an attribute of authority and the justifications which attempt to make the use of force legitimate. It may be objected that concern with the purposes of rule and the legitimation of power merely assuage the conscience of the powerful and that force alone really matters. I think this view is mistaken.

Power needs ideas and legitimation the way a conventional bank needs investment policies and the confidence of its depositors. Rulers are always few in number and could never obtain compliance if each command were purely random and had to be backed by force sufficient to compel obedience. Likewise, banks rely on the confidence of their depositors, which allows them to retain only a small fraction of their assets in liquid funds in order to meet the expected rate of withdrawal by depositors. All is well as long as depositors believe that the bank will cash their checks on demand, and part of that trust depends on a vague knowledge about the bank's adherence to certain accepted business standards. In the nation-state, all is well as long as citizens believe that the government knows what it is about, has the ability to deliver on some of its promises, and has sufficient force to back up its commands when necessary. Psychologically, bank credit and governmental legitimacy rest on an amalgam of convenient commonplaces, inarticulate assumptions, and a willingness to let others take the lead and to leave well enough alone. But once the trust based on such feelings is disturbed, conditions can change quickly. A run on the bank is like a massive challenge to state authority, for each may demonstrate that the bank's and the state's resources are insufficient to withstand such a loss of confidence. Legitimation achieves what power alone cannot, for it establishes the belief in the rightness of rule which, as long as it endures, precludes massive challenges. Thus, the emphasis of this study is on power and the mandate to rule, not on one to the exclusion of the other.

Like the polarities so frequently used in Max Weber's work, one phrase combines the use of force with the belief in legitimacy. As Otto Hintze has stated,

> All human activity, political and religious, stems from an undivided root. As a rule, the first impulse for . . . social action comes from tangible interests, political or economic. . . . Ideal interests elevate and animate these tangible interests and lend them justification. Man does not live by bread alone; he wants to have a good conscience when he pursues his vital interests; and in pursuing them he develops his powers fully only if he is conscious of simultaneously serving purposes higher than purely egotistical ones. Interests without such spiritual elevation are lame; on the other hand, ideas can succeed in history only when and to the extent that they attach themselves to tangible interests.[11]

Thus, wherever power is vigorously pursued and exercised, ideas of legitimacy tend to develop to give meaning, reinforcement, and justification to that power. Conversely, wherever a mandate to rule is to sway the minds and hearts of men, it requires the exercise of force or the awareness that those who rule are able, and will not hesitate, to use force if that is needed to assert their will.

The authority of kings—their power and mandate to rule—often weaken. When that occurs,

Criticism and propaganda expose the *arcana imperii* to the light of common day. Subjects ask if they should obey, and whom, and why. Authority is constrained to plead its case with reasons or impose itself by violence. In either instance it has lost its virtue: for while authority remains itself, it neither argues nor coerces, but merely speaks and is accepted. Upon the complex scene already charged with tense uncertainties, unexpected fresh initiatives supervene.[12]

These initiatives accompany the decline of royal authority and often anticipate its actual downfall. But sacred authority is more easily destroyed than reconstructed, or perhaps one should say that critics of royal authority have seldom been conscious that the new authority they propose requires a sacred foundation as well. These comments anticipate the prominence of inviolate symbols like "the people" or "the nation" in all efforts to reconstitute authority since the decline of kingship.

Part I

THE AUTHORITY OF KINGS

The heavens themselves, the planets, and this centre,
Observe degree, priority, and place . . .
. . . but when the planets,
In evil mixture, to disorder wander . . .
What raging of the sea, shaking of earth, . . .
Divert and crack, . . .
The unity and married calm of states
Quite from their fixture! . . . How could communities,
Degrees in schools, and brotherhoods in cities, . . .
The primogenity and due of birth,
Prerogative of age, crowns, sceptres, laurels,
But by degree, stand in authentic place?
Take but degree away, untune that string,
And, hark, what discord follows!

SHAKESPEARE,
Troilus and Cressida, I, iii

2

SACRED AND SECULAR
FOUNDATIONS
OF KINGSHIP

IN THE PAST, one ruler stood at
the summit of the social hierarchy. Rulers possessed supreme status,
great wealth, and commanding authority. For the exercise of rule, they
depended on retainers, personal confidants, and magnates of more independent position. Collectively, sovereign rulers and their agents constituted an oligarchy or government by the few. Such government provides one of the best documented records of inequality.[1]

Kings do not necessarily wield effective authority. In some Asian
societies, kingship consisted of pomp and circumstance rather than governance, while actual authority was exercised at local or regional levels.[2]
Even when kings and oligarchs have ruled at the outset, the rise of provincial governors and military forces may erode that central authority
later.[3] Nevertheless, royal authority has endured for the greater part of
human history. This would not have been the case if kings, officials, and
the mass of the people had not to some degree believed the authority
of kings to be inviolate.

We do not know how the belief in kingship originated. Weber
suggests,

> Kingship is preceded by all those charismatic forms which assure relief in the
> face of extraordinary external or internal distress or which promise success
> in risky undertakings. In early history, the precursor of the king, the chief-
> tain, often has a double function: he is the patriarch of the family or sib, but
> also the charismatic leader in hunt and war, the magician, rainmaker, med-
> icine man—hence priest and doctor—and finally, the arbiter. Frequently,
> each of these kinds of charisma has a special bearer.[4]

People have a strong desire to perpetuate a leader's success in dealing with extraordinary misfortunes or great risks. The leader himself
feels inspired by his success. His followers and the community at large

21

naturally want to benefit from the wonders they have attributed to his charismatic powers. As long as his undertakings are successful, his actions legitimate the social and political establishment he heads. Conversely, doubts arise concerning his legitimacy when poor harvests or defeat in war suggest that his mission has failed and that he has lost his charisma.

A rudimentary or contingent exchange, therefore, is built into the function of leadership. The ruler's supreme authority and endorsement of the hierarchy of rank are accepted as long as the people believe in the charismatic gifts of the king and in the social order as divinely established.

The success of a ruler may be as uncertain as the people's satisfaction. The leader often has little control over the vicissitudes that befall him and his people. Since he wants to stay in power, his magical or divinatory practice may incorporate ambiguity or uncertainty concerning the future, thus safeguarding his own position while adhering to the beliefs of those involved in state affairs. The people themselves are perhaps aware of contingencies and may credit their ruler for attempting to contact the spirits, even if these spirits prove malevolent. As long as the ruler and his people share the belief in the ruler's intercession with the spirits on behalf of the community, the exchange relation of authority is sustained. Such a belief would be weak indeed were it to crumble the moment the ruler is uncertain or adversity befalls his realm. But beliefs of this kind are seldom so strong that they cannot be discredited when misfortune becomes too massive and doubts concerning the ruler's capacity cumulate.[5]

Despite these hazards, a ruler can represent the whole society and conjoin the greatest physical and spiritual powers available to man. Since every community desires to perpetuate the benefits attributed to such powers, a king's claim to supreme authority will be acknowledged by the people's belief in his god-descended powers. Patterns of royal authority have varied from civilization to civilization depending on the way in which the royal person has been designated, consecrated, and acknowledged.

The religious authentication of the king usually has depended on experts in esoteric knowledge, that is, knowledge of the mysteries and ritual which are believed capable of validating the act of consecration. Such experts are the guardians of a country's cultural heritage which rulers disregard at their peril. But experts in esoteric knowledge also have much secular influence and participate—along with the members of the governing class—in the internal contentions for power. Thus, royal authority is often constrained by its own religious and secular foundations.

GERMANIC TRADITIONS AND
CHRISTIAN CONSECRATION

In the West, kingship arose in two different patterns, both under the influence of Christianity. In the eastern part of the Roman empire, Hellenistic and Oriental influences merged, giving rise to a conception of the emperor as the Expected One of Christian prophecy, representing God on earth, the symbol of the Kingdom of Heaven. By invoking the authentic power of Christ's name, the king or autocrat could ensure prosperity and victory in war. This Byzantine conception of kingship became a dominant influence in Russia and will be discussed in Chapter 4.

In the western part of the Roman empire, kingship arose from a conjunction of Germanic tribal traditions and the expanding influence of the Catholic church. The Germanic tribal chiefs represented the principle of inherited charisma and election by acclamation. The Catholic church represented the principle of hierarchy and law. The two principles merged when the Carolingian kings were consecrated by the Pope in Rome. These principles will be examined in their historical context.

A sporadic migration of Germanic tribesmen into the western part of the Roman empire began during the first century of our era. The migration took on a massive character two and a half centuries later when whole tribes sought refuge before the onslaught of the Huns. At that time, the Roman empire's need to defend its extended frontiers greatly strained the available manpower. Epidemics and war casualties reduced the agricultural population further. The pressure on slave laborers to produce more food increased, rural unrest became endemic, and land went out of cultivation. In rural areas and in the Roman armies, the demand for manpower mounted just when Germanic tribes arrived in search of land and food. These tribesmen settled on deserted properties, filled the ranks of the Roman legions, and proceeded to elect and unseat emperors. In the century between 180 and 285 A.D., thirty different emperors were put on the throne, and few of them died a natural death. By 376 A.D. these scattered movements had turned into full-scale invasions. Many of the remaining native settlers were displaced, and Germanic kingdoms were established in lieu of imperial Roman authority.[6]

All of Europe, especially its western part, was affected. The Visigoths swept from the northern Balkan area into Macedonia, Greece, and Italy where their king, Alaric, conquered Rome in 410 A.D. From Italy, the Visigoths returned north to southern Gaul where they established a kingdom from 418 to 507. Finally, they moved into Spain where they ruled between 507 and 711. The Vandals started from the middle of

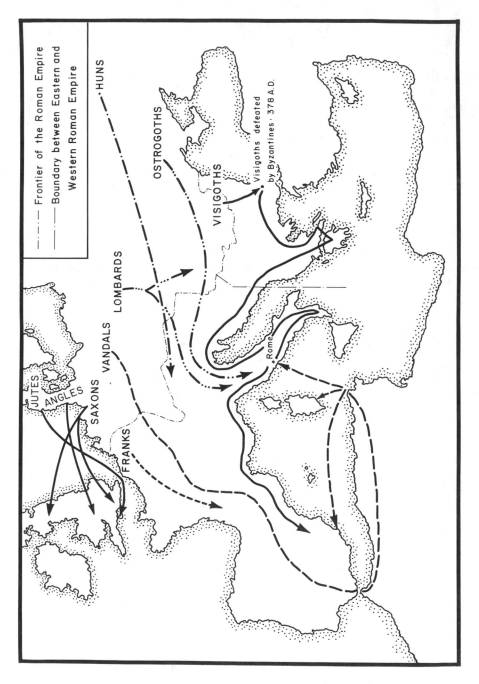

OSTROGOTHS

VISIGOTHS

Visigoths defeated
by Byzantines · 378 A.D.

LOMBARDS

JUTES

ANGLES

SAXONS

VANDALS

FRANKS

Rome

1. Barbarian Invasions of the Fifth Century A.D.

Germany, went into central France, moved into Spain and North Africa, then to Sardinia and Rome, and finally back to a more permanent settlement in North Africa—all in less than a century. By conquering North Africa, the Vandals occupied the area which supplied the bulk of food staples such as grain and oil for major cities of the empire. They also occupied some harbors along the Mediterranean coastline, thus breaking the Byzantine monopoly of the seafaring trade. The Vandals ruled in North Africa (429–534) and the Ostrogoths in Italy (493–553) until both were conquered and made part of the Byzantine empire under Justinian (527–565).

Through the *Germania* of Tacitus (98 A.D.), we have an early report on the Germanic tribes and their military leaders and war bands (*comitatus*). The problem for the Romans was how to contain these roving German bands. The Romans hoped that the countryside could be stabilized by negotiation. The Germanic war-leaders were thought to be kings with whom the Romans could negotiate, for these leaders appeared able to speak for their fellow tribesmen. However, the Germanic leaders were much more diverse than the Romans assumed in terms of title, authority, and the scope of their military activities. Some warbands were merely intent on vendettas and loot. Others involved whole tribes (including women and children, dependents, and slaves) which desired to conquer new lands and settle them. In a period of migration, the many leaders and heirs of a charismatic lineage group were more useful than a single king would have been, whatever might be true under more settled conditions.[7]

The Germanic word for king developed from the word for kindred. Kingship emerged as the supreme authority of a clan rather than of an individual ruler. Ancient pantheistic beliefs attributed supernatural powers to nature and within society to a kin group or clan (*Sippe*) endowed with special capacities that were attributed to blood relationships. The whole clan was thought to possess a god-descended power or *mana* which ensured good crops, victory in battle, and the power to heal certain diseases. Chieftains or rulers were distinguished by the singular luck associated with their clan.[8] As in the Homeric epic, the early Germanic sagas told of how "gods often walked the earth and mingled in the affairs of rulers."[9] The divine descent of a clan therefore suggested itself readily. All descendants of that clan could be charismatic mediators with the divine and thus repositories of the tribal "luck." This religious idea of "kin-right" or "blood-right" gave a sacral character to the rightful incumbent even when his power was greatly reduced.[10]

A ruler's function was at once military, political, and religious: He was expected to lead in war, settle disputes, and make sacrifices for victory, good crops, and peace. The "people," but more specifically the heads of the clans composing the tribe, looked to the charisma of the ruler's clan for intercession with the gods. The beliefs which attributed supernatural gifts to an entire clan presumably depended on the hope or expectation of preserving the benefits which these gifts bestowed on the people. When usurpers came to power, their rule would endure only if by success and appropriate genealogical constructions they were found to be "related" to the charismatic kindred.

Practices which were advantageous under conditions of migration became disadvantageous under more settled conditions. When all members of a clan were believed to be endowed with charisma, succession to the throne presented special problems. Succession was decided by inheritance when an incumbent ruler divided the realm among his legitimate heirs. The lineage was preserved, but at the price of dispersing the resources of the realm and fostering internal strife. The Frankish rule of the Merovingian (482–714) and Carolingian (714–911) houses was marked by these divisive characteristics.[11] On the other hand, a choice could be made among the many legitimate descendants of the charismatic clan. Such a choice was usually based on the recognition of superior military leadership, thus combining hereditary charisma with the principle of election by acclamation. The incumbent ruler would publicly choose the most promising successor among his heirs, and the notables of other clans would confirm the choice by acclamation.[a]

Problems arose when legitimate heirs were unsuitable, when more than one suitable heir had legitimate claims, or when the clan appeared bereft of its charismatic power, its "tribal luck." The god-descended claims of the clan with their emphasis on the right of inheritance would clash with the pragmatic political interests of other clans and their emphasis on the right of "election" or consent. In these uncertain situations, the Catholic church began to assert its influence.

For Germanic chieftains in England and on the Continent, the influence of the church had certain advantages. Their main task was to stabilize their authority in recently conquered territories in which the church was already established. From a pagan perspective, conversion meant that another especially powerful god was added to the native pantheon. Tribal chieftains saw in this a further buttress to their authority, especially if their title was insecure in the eyes of the "people." The danger of dependence on the church did not yet loom large: power still seemed largely a matter of military prowess and "luck." Where rule was insecure, "consecration could strengthen the claims of heredity, sanction a usurpation, incline God to make queens fruitful, and bind the clergy

---

[a]*Acclamation* and *election* are used interchangeably because the act of acclamation was probably preceded by some kind of deliberation among the notables. It would be misleading, however, to call such deliberation and acclamation an election in our sense.

to a king. . . . " Indeed, consecration may have seemed to "distracted and threatened churchmen" much the same as it did to the chieftains themselves—as a way of "enhancing the power of the king" and thereby stabilizing the social order.[12]

Christianity had been a religious movement in all parts of the Roman empire long before the Germanic invasions. Missions had spread to towns and settlements but reached the vast countryside only after considerable delay. Many Germanic tribes had been converted before their migrations began, but they often continued to adhere to pagan beliefs and practices. Moreover, the missionaries were generally converts to the Arian doctrine, espousing the deity of the Father but not of the Son, and as a result many German tribesmen became Arians. The Church Council of Nicaea declared the Arian doctrine heretical in 325 A.D., but it was some time before the orthodox Catholic creed became dominant in the Christian West.[13] In 330 A.D., Constantinople was consecrated as the capital of the Roman empire, and by the end of the fourth century Christianity was declared the state religion. However, pagan beliefs and practices continued in the Germanic kingdoms.

Christianity gradually became a force in the defense of the empire, because the organization of the church was strengthening local government while the institutions of Roman government were foundering. The church was organized into dioceses (under patriarchs), provinces (under metropolitans), and cities (under bishops), paralleling the administrative subdivisions of the empire. Emperor Constantine's (306–337) secular control of religion permitted the church a privileged position in several respects. The Christian clergy was exempted from certain taxes on the basis of their charity and professional contribution. The church was treated as a corporation capable of receiving donations and bequests. As early as 314 A.D., an imperial decree declared that judicial sentences of bishops were to be regarded like the judgments of Christ himself. Episcopal courts (handling cases that touched on the consecrated functions of the church) were recognized as part of the judicial system, and the civil authority enforced their decisions. The right of intercession on behalf of clients passed from wealthy patrons or hired pleaders into the hands of bishops. Closely connected with this episcopal intercession was the church's right of asylum, which allowed fugitives to seek the protection of bishops instead of the old pagan temples of Rome.[14]

These rights of the church were compatible with civil government, though with rather different results in the eastern and western parts of the empire. In the East, the imperial government was headed by an emperor who reigned supreme in both secular and religious affairs. The institutions of the church were safeguarded in the sense that the emperor protected the church politically, although he was not a member of the hierarchy. As Constantine told the bishops at Nicaea, they were in charge of "internal church matters" while he, the emperor, had the legal and administrative management of Christianity in his safekeeping. In these "external matters" there was no limit to the emperor's authority over the church. Moreover, the eastern part of the empire remained militarily and politically intact. The Huns, who had caused the Germanic migrations toward the West, failed in their attacks on the frontiers of the eastern empire (Thrace, Armenia, Syria) and the Visigoths were defeated by Byzantium in 378 A.D. In the course of the fifth century, the position of the Byzantine emperor became formalized: He was crowned by the patriarch of Constantinople, a ceremony which in the Eastern church symbolized the divine derivation of the emperor's authority.[15]

In the West, on the other hand, Roman political authority disinte-

Christ Crowning the Byzantine Emperor
The concentration of both spiritual authority and temporal power in the person of the East Roman emperor is symbolized in this Byzantine ivory (from about 944) showing Christ crowning Emperor Constantine VII Porphyrogenitus (912–959). The ruler is thus the direct successor to Christ on earth. (Museum of Fine Arts, Moscow)

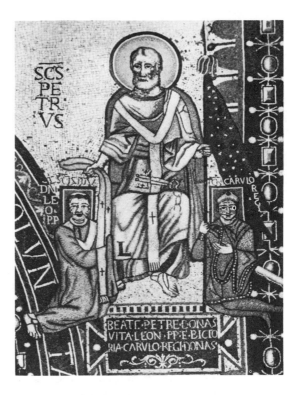

St. Peter Conferring Spiritual Authority and Temporal Power

This restored eighth-century mosaic in the Church of St. John Lateran, Rome, shows St. Peter conferring spiritual authority on Pope Leo III, symbolized by the pallium or stole, and temporal power on Charlemagne, symbolized by the imperial banner. Catholicism derives its authority from the apostle, not from Christ directly as in the Greek Orthodox conception. According to this belief in the apostolic succession of the papacy, St. Peter elevates the spiritual pope over the temporal king. Later representations, as in the Sachsenspiegel of 1230, show St. Peter handing the keys of the kingdom of heaven to the pope while the king with the insignia of temporal power merely looks on. (The Granger Collection; Sachsenspiegel)

grated as Italy, Gaul, and Spain were conquered by successive waves of Germanic tribes. Under the empire, local administration had been entrusted to magistrates and could survive changes at the center of power. But during the great migrations, local authority was not able to cope with the conflicts resulting from the Germanic settlement of lands belonging to the native population. The authority of the local bishop, therefore, tended to take the place of secular government, in part because the church attracted abler men than the Roman provincial government. As Momigliano has stated,

> Much can be said about the internal conflicts, the worldly ambitions, the intolerance of the Church. Yet the conclusion remains that while the political organization of the empire became increasingly rigid, unimaginative, and unsuccessful, the Church was mobile and resilient and provided space for those whom the State was unable to absorb. The bishops were the centres of large voluntary organizations. They founded and controlled charitable institutions. They defended their flocks against the state officials. When the military situation of the empire grew worse, they often organized armed resistance against the barbarians. . . . People escaped from the state into the Church and weakened the state by giving their best to the Church. . . . The best men were working for the Church, not for the state.[16]

At the local level, the church had a mission as civil officials did not. But these local or provincial functions did nothing to bolster the central hierarchy of the church. How then did the papacy establish its ecclesiastical supremacy?

The bishops of Rome possessed considerable wealth in land. In the West they were confronted with pagans and heretics who had overrun the empire, while in the East they faced the rival spiritual claims of an emerging Eastern Christianity which was backed by the great power of the Byzantine empire. In this fifth-century setting, the Roman bishops had no political authority to support them. Yet, by a combination of political and doctrinal strategies, the bishops achieved ascendancy in the church hierarchy and established the medieval papacy. Rome elaborated its doctrinal position against the Eastern church, even though it could not challenge the secular authority of Byzantium. And in western and northern Europe, the Roman bishops sponsored missionary activities which succeeded in part because the Byzantine empire could not interfere effectively.

The Roman papal claims rested in the first place on the cult of St. Peter, the first bishop of Rome, a martyr to his faith, and the apostle to whom Christ had given "the keys to the kingdom of heaven" (Matthew 16: 18–19). The popes made the most of their primacy as the direct successors of Peter. They cited a letter in which Pope Clement described how Peter in the presence of the Roman community had handed his power over to the bishop of Rome and his successors. This testamentary deposition became available in a Latin translation around 400 A.D. It was a forgery, but the *Epistola Clementis* was cited throughout the Middle Ages because it appeared to authenticate the doctrine of papal monarchy. The implications of this doctrine were spelled out by Pope Leo I (440–461) and Pope Gelasius (492–496). Leo distinguished between the unique merit of Peter, which Christ had recognized, and the Petrine powers which could be transmitted. God had given His gift of grace to the pope as the direct successor of Peter; therefore, the pope could not be judged or deposed by anyone. But the person holding that office was distinguished from the powers of the office. The unworthiness of the incumbent could not invalidate the binding authority either of God's gift of grace to the pope or of the pope's gifts of grace to his flock. All powers exercised by members of the church (the pope, archbishops, bishops, monks, priests) were not based on right, but possessed as a matter of grace, as in the Pauline doctrine, "What I am, I am by the grace of God." Such favor of grace could not be compelled; it could only be freely given. Every office of the church was a *beneficium* in this sense. It could be taken away as freely as it had been given.

This papal interpretation challenged the claims of imperial authority over the church, espoused in Byzantium. According to St. Ambrose (340?–397), bishop of Milan, "the emperor is within the church, not above it": he does not possess autonomous powers. In this early Catholic view, the king had been called by God to his high office, but as a Christian he was the son of the church, not its master. In the view of Pope Gelasius I, the king's duty was to carry out the divine plan. But who was to have authority to lay down faith and doctrine and hence to give the law to the entire corporate body of Christianity? Gelasius answered that only the pope as the successor of St. Peter possesses authority or *auctoritas* (moral influence); only he has the faculty of shaping things in a manner that is binding on all. By contrast, the emperor possessed a *regia potestas* (royal executive power)—the power to execute what had been laid down as binding authority under God.[17]

Authority and power had already been distinguished in Roman law, and the popes in the West used the distinction for their own purposes. In the East, the Byzantine emperors prevailed over the church because they had defeated the Germanic invaders and were in full political control. By contrast, conditions were so unsettled in the West that secular rulers often welcomed the added strength derived from church support. The difference in the relative positions of secular rulers and the church was reflected in the forms of address used by the pope in Rome. A century after Gelasius I, Pope Gregory I (590–603) continued to address the ruler in Constantinople as "Lord Emperor," whereas he addressed the kings of western and northern Europe as "Dearest sons." The papal doctrine that kings were sons of the church became part of the Christian mission only in western Europe, especially among the Franks.

Conversion of the Franks had begun at the end of the fifth century. By the end of the sixth century, they had become in turn Christian missionaries, converting the Germanic tribes east of the Rhine and south of the Loire as they conquered them. At the same time, the Franks adhered to their tribal traditions. The rulers divided territories equally among their legitimate heirs, thus increasing political instability at almost every succession.[18] Merovingian and Carolingian rulership was precarious despite military successes, and the church utilized this opportunity to play a greater role in determining the succession.

The Merovingian house continued to reign, but in name only. Actual power had passed to the chief ministers of the court, who were illegitimate descendants of earlier Merovingian rulers. These regents were the first representatives of the Carolingian dynasty, but they lacked legitimacy. In 751–752, however, the Carolingian regent Pepin was elected king by an assembly of nobles *and then anointed by Bishop Bonifacius*. In this way, the Merovingian house was deposed with the formal approval of the church. The act of consecrating the king added a new dimension of authority to the earlier, conventional method of spreading the Gospel by converting kings to the Christian faith. The Western church had assumed the function of consecrating, and hence of authenticating, the royal succession in contrast to the Eastern church which by crowning the emperor symbolized the divine origin of his authority. The Western church put the king under God's law as interpreted by the church; the Eastern church accepted the emperor as representing Christ on earth.[19]

Consecration endowed kings with a new sacral character which helped to weaken the old pagan belief in charismatic blood-right. The unction through which the king became "God's Anointed" on earth was a visible symbol of divine sanction which replaced the earlier belief in the divine origin of the charismatic lineage. To this symbol, Charlemagne (768–814) added the formula "by the Grace of God" (*Dei gratia*), thus appearing to give the monarch a position based on divine inspiration. At the time, the church seemed to give unequivocal support to this conception of kingship, which at the very least implied the king's direct relation to God.[20]

In practice, the church was not consistent. From the Catholic standpoint, the pagan idea of a God-descended, sacred lineage was anathema, yet claims to legitimacy based on hereditary succession were generally accepted because they supported the sacred inviolability of marriage. However, though minors might have an hereditary right to the throne,

the church combated their claims, presumably because of the danger of
dynastic instability. Even adult heirs with a legitimate claim were opposed if they belonged to dynasties hostile to the church. Similarly, the
church opposed bastards because they made a mockery of the sanctity
of marriage, but it also favored them when this seemed to further the
interests of the church. In these various positions, the main doctrinal
point was that kingship is an office and duty (*ministerium*), not a proprietary right. Hence, the suitability of an individual candidate was more
important than the preservation of a dynastic lineage, or a consistent
policy. To the church, its act of consecration authenticated the king's
mandate from God. In this way, political stability was increased. Rulers
were independent of the "popular will" (the consent of the notables of
the realm), but to a degree dependent on the church.[21]

But absolute royal control also became a hazard against which the
church had to be on guard. Once political stability was achieved, the
main mission of the church would come to the fore. Then churchmen
would reemphasize what they had always said, namely, that the king was
under God and subject to His law. As Archbishop Hincmar told his king
in 860, "You have not created me archbishop of Rheims, but I, together
with my colleagues, have elected you to the government of the kingdom,
on condition that you observe the laws."[22] From the perspective of the
papacy, the consecration of kings meant that the ruler was a member
of the congregation and must fulfill the singular mandate he had received as "God's Anointed." Kings on earth reflected the Heavenly King,
and secular authority was legitimate to the extent that it implemented
God's purposes. Accordingly, a main part of the king's task was to uphold the Christian religion by protecting priests and monks, encouraging their work, and exhorting the faithful through his personal example.
Moreover, kings were duty-bound to carry the message of the Gospel
to the heathens, by fire and sword if necessary. Kings *and* people were
under God. Only if kings walked the ways of the righteous, as the church
interpreted those ways, could they obtain felicity, good harvests, and
victory over their enemies.[23]

The monarchies of Western Europe amalgamated divine right acquired through consecration with hereditary right acquired through
birth. That amalgamation helped to authenticate the legitimacy of a
ruler, in his own eyes as well as in those of the people. At the same time,
the church increased its secular role. Personal links with the clergy increased as members of royal houses and aristocratic families took monastic vows. Through pious gifts, rulers and magnates sought solace for
their troubled souls even as they advanced more mundane ambitions.
Such acts enlarged the land and resources under ecclesiastical jurisdiction. In the great councils of the realm, church spokesmen could influ-

Ecclesiastical and Secular Hierarchies
In the ideal conception of the medieval world the institutions of church and state should
parallel each other, the church in the sphere of spiritual authority and government in the
sphere of temporal power. In this fourteenth-century fresco (attributed to Andrea di
Firenze) the two hierarchies are ranged on opposite sides: pope and emperor, cardinal
and king, archbishop and count, clerics and clerks. (Alinari/Scala)

ence the exercise of authority and even give weight to their choice of a
royal successor by claiming inspiration from divine authority in the
name of His law, to which all mortals were subject.

The church was transformed, though not in a straightforward manner, from speaking only in the name of God to championing electoral
rights as well.[24] In its struggle against paganism, the church had supported theocracy. Even after the success of the Christianizing mission
and the stabilization of secular rule, kings remained important as protectors and patrons of the church. Kings also were potential allies in
balancing the competing claims not only of feudal lords but also of
church dignitaries whose local or national interests might deviate from

the interests of the Roman church. But at the same time, the church was bound to compete with kings whenever the exercise of secular authority touched the realm of the sacred, and few matters were entirely outside this realm. The church insisted on its exclusive claim to interpret the word of God. It opposed the sacralization of kingship which was strongly sustained by pagan beliefs and popular sentiment.[25]

Western European kingship thus owed its pattern to the confluence among pagan practices of a Germanic origin, the legal heritage of Rome (as in concepts like *auctoritas* and *ministerium*), and the interpretations and institutional interests of the Catholic church.

NOMADIC TRIBES, RELIGIOUS PROPHECY, AND THE PATRIARCHAL CALIPHATE IN ISLAM

In the Arabic world, kingship arose from a conjunction of pre-Islamic tribal traditions, the religious message of Muhammad the Prophet (c. 570–632 A.D.), and the traditions of rule established under Muhammad and his immediate successors.

The Arabian peninsula was roughly divided into a sedentary, economically thriving area in the south and a vast, arid or semi-arid interior to the north, containing nomadic Bedouins and a few settlements in oases and along caravan routes. Kingship existed only in the south.

The only recognized social units among the Bedouins were the tribe and its clans; survival depended on a high degree of social solidarity. The *lex talionis* or blood-revenge is the best known practice of this tribal culture.

> [If the member of a kinship group] is killed, the others will at once take steps to avenge him; if he is attacked, they will spring to his support without asking about the rights or wrongs of the matter. It was a sacred duty for each member of the group to give "help" to another member of the group and, if necessary, to avenge his death. Since there could be no police force in the conditions of the Arabian desert, public security required the highest regard for the [sacred and imperative] duty of revenge and "help."[26]

Later, it became acceptable to settle blood-feuds by payment of compensation (a hundred camels for an adult male was customary in Muhammad's time), though a strict interpretation of the code of honor scorned this substitution of "milk for blood." Blood-feuds sometimes continued for generations, during which tribes would avenge wrongs committed against them, feud over access to grazing and water, raid the herds of others, and prey on caravans. One safeguard against constant depredations were the holy months and holy places which provided protection by tacit consent. When a kin-group was weak, it might seek help from a stronger one; when an individual required protection, he might become the client of a respected elder. Likewise, pledges of alliance between kin-groups or tribes, based on mutual obligations, might provide protection. The tribal community (*gawm* or *umma*) was clearly of major significance, and the idea of a federation of tribes has remained a principal tenet of Islamic civilization.[27]

In the nomadic tribes, each adult male was considered an equal; the chieftain (*sayyid*), therefore, had limited powers. Leadership in war, soothsaying, and the arbitration of disputes might be in the hands of others than the chieftain; hence, they could curtail his powers. The noble qualities required for these several functions of leadership were believed to be hereditary, so the choice of leaders was restricted to charismatically qualified lineages. Since lavish generosity was expected of a chieftain, only a man from a rich clan qualified. Chieftains were chosen from the heads of clans but depended on the counsel of the tribal elders. Even though chieftainship was hereditary, it required a continual proof of courage and cunning, prudence and discretion in council, and a highly developed sense of honor. While an incumbent could designate his successor, he would do so only with due regard to the judgment of the council of elders.[28]

The whole Arabian peninsula was an isolated and inhospitable area which was connected with the outside world through trade routes leading from the southern kingdoms adjoining the Indian Ocean along the western coast through Mecca to Syria and Byzantium in the north and to the Persian empire in the northeast. For a long time, incense, spices, and precious artifacts had been carried along these routes. The southern kingdoms where the routes originated or where goods were transshipped became an object of contention among rival powers. Politics, conquest, and religion were so intertwined that the peninsula also became the scene of several competing creeds, among them Judaism and the Christian mission. The situation was compounded further by the great struggles in the second half of the sixth century between the Byzantine and Persian empires. In this setting of mounting conflicts, the prime interest of Arab traders was to preserve their neutrality.

Nothing in the situation suggested that a generation later Arab tribes would be unified under Muhammad and initiate wars of conquest. Mecca was the birthplace of Muhammad. Though it lay in an infertile valley, the city was located at the crossroads of four major trade routes, and many holy places were within its walls and immediate surroundings. Mecca was settled by the Quraysh, a single tribe which was relatively free of feuds, despite its division into clans. Community affairs were regulated by an assembly composed of representatives of the rich and aristocratic clans. The relative peace contrasted with other settled areas like

Medina, the oasis to the north where many tribes competed for dominance. Trade interests, the peace ensured by holy places (the Ka'ba, a Meccan sanctuary devoted to the God Hubal, protected the whole city), and the absence of blood-feuds combined to make the city a haven of tranquility in a world of conflicts.

The whole life of the city revolved around its markets. Townspeople, pilgrims visiting the holy places, and tribesmen from the surrounding areas depended on these markets. The city's merchants invested in the great caravans which supplied all the needs of the inhabitants and transported precious cargoes of native and foreign products to the empires in the north. The great wealth of the city testified to the success with which leading Mecca merchants negotiated with Bedouin tribes and with foreign powers for the safe conduct of their caravans. A commercial mentality was fostered which gave due respect to the holy places and ancient practices since they were good for business. What Irfan Shahid said of Southern Arabia applies to Mecca as well:

> Theirs was a business culture, and their ideal was materialistic, the acquisition of wealth, which they relentlessly pursued, as the Carthaginians did, with similar results. The remains of their material culture are uninspiring, more interesting archeologically than artistically, lacking that significant form which differentiates an artefact from a work of art. . . . But the very same isolation which possibly operated to their disadvantage in the cultural sphere was their salvation politically. . . . [29]

The peace of Mecca made it a crossroad of spiritual influences as well as of trade. To understand the character of royal authority in Islamic civilization, we must understand the manner in which Muhammad's prophecy emerged and became the unifying force over the whole peninsula and beyond. Max Weber has said that great religious innovations tend to occur not in "culturally satiated areas" where people are preoccupied with the routines of a complex society, but in areas adjacent to these centers where men still preserve "the capacity to be astonished about the course of events."[30] Something like this was probably true of Mecca and Medina in relation to the Persian and Byzantine empires.

Among the Quraysh within Mecca, social and cultural divisions had developed between successful merchants who had become rather indifferent to the religious and moral traditions of their tribe and those who did not share in the wealth and power of the dominant groups. The Umayyad clan belonged to the merchants of the first rank, but Muhammad's clan, the Hashim, did not. Compared with the stark life of Bedouin tribesmen, the misfortunes of Mecca citizens were probably moderate. But Muhammad's clan headed a league of families opposed to the most successful merchants of the city.

About 610 A.D., Muhammad began telling of his religious experiences. A few fellow-citizens of Mecca were converted by his message. Muhammad and his initial flock of believers were certainly overcome by a religious experience. But it is significant nonetheless that the earliest parts of the Qur'an warn of an all-powerful God who not only will judge each man and community on the Last Day, but who also expects men of wealth to help the poor and the unfortunate. Among the prophet's first followers were disadvantaged younger brothers and sons, leaders of kin-groups that had lost out in the competitive struggle, and foreigners who had failed to obtain protection from the powerful.[31]

Muhammad's message began by recalling the people to the purity of ancient traditions in pointed contrast to the good living and conventional religiosity common in Mecca. But the prophet's monotheistic creed also led to contentions with the polytheistic, nomadic tribes of the peninsula, and with the monotheistic Jewish communities of Medina. Muhammad had initially found protection from his adversaries through his own clan in Mecca, but eventually he fled to Medina. There he won new adherents and gradually built up a military force with which he raided the herds and caravans venturing too close to his base of operations.

Muhammad's message was an extraordinary blend of charismatic prophecy with elements from the nomadic tradition. His great break with that tradition consisted in the idea of one God, Allah, who had sent His messenger, Muhammad, to warn the people of the judgment to come. In addition, he enjoined on all believers a new form of worship which must be observed with punctilious regularity. In the Constitution of Medina, however, Muhammad also drew on tribal traditions. There Muhammad is depicted as the Messenger of God, as the chief of Meccan emigrants, and as an arbiter (*hakam*) of disputes. Prophecy, chieftainship, and arbitration were all familiar aspects of the pre-Islamic tribes, and the constitution portrays other traditions characteristic of a tribal community.

In Medina, the emigrants from the Meccan tribe of Quraysh were regarded as one of nine tribes, so initially Muhammad did not outrank the chiefs of the other tribes. But as the prophet gained adherents to the new faith, the traditional, tribal solidarity was broadened to all those "who follow them [the believers] and are attached to them and who crusade along with them. They are a single community (*umma*) distinct from [other] people."[32] This appeal to faith rather than kinship as the basis of the community represents the other great break with tradition. But again, this new precept was embedded in ancient practices. The believers were exhorted to the same standards of conduct as the members of tribes had been, including blood-revenge, mutual assistance, protection of the poor, and patron-client relations. In this way, Muhammad extended tribal beliefs and practices to the entire community of believers.

The doctrine of the umma, the community of Muslims, is the basic political concept of Islam. All members of that community are bound together by ties of religion rather than race or kinship, since all profess their belief in Allah and in the mission of His prophet. While differences of function within the umma are recognized, all members are equal in their relation to God. They are charged with the duty to bear witness to Allah, to uphold the true faith, and to instruct people in the ways of God. Allah alone is the head of the umma. His commands, as revealed to Muhammad, embody the Holy Law. In this conception, God Himself is the sole legislator; therefore, the *Shari'a* exists before the state, and the sole purpose of the state is to maintain God's law. The Qur'an and the sayings of the prophet are the sole constitutional authority within the Muslim community, yet they contain no precise instructions concerning the political organization of the umma. Historical precedents associated with the prophet and his successors provided what the direct expression of God's will failed to provide—guidelines for the political constitution of the Muslim community. It is for this reason that knowledge of the early history of Islam is essential for an understanding of its concept of royal authority.

With hindsight one can read into the Constitution of Medina the basic political precepts of Islam as they were formulated later: that the purpose of man is the service of God, that this service requires an organized community of true believers, and that it is impossible for a non-Muslim to be a full member of the community.[33] During the last years of his life, Muhammad launched a successful military campaign against Mecca, his hometown. Once established there, he proceeded to range across the peninsula, combining religious conversion with military pressure and inducing one tribe after another to acknowledge him as the "messenger of God" and sole ruler over the Arab people.

The Germanic and the Arab experience may be seen in parallel and contrasting terms. The migration and conquests of Germanic tribes, coming to a head late in the fourth century A.D., helped to precipitate the downfall of the Roman empire in the West. The migration and conquests of Arab tribes, following the death of Muhammad in 632 A.D., made great inroads on the Byzantine empire and helped to establish an Islamic empire reaching at its height from the Indian subcontinent to Spain. The battle at Tours and Poitiers (732 A.D.) finally halted the Muslim advance in France, just a century after the death of the prophet.

By way of contrast, the Germanic tribes were converted to Christianity before they conquered and settled agricultural land, whereas the

Arab tribes spread their faith as they conquered vast territories, exacted tribute from the native populations, and settled in urban areas. To a degree, the Germanic tribes were unified and pacified by their common religious conversion; by contrast, the tribes of the Arabian peninsula were pacified and unified among themselves only by joining in a holy war (*jihad*) against the infidel. For the Germanic tribes, migration toward the west was a response to the invasions of Europe by the Huns from the east; for the tribes of the Arabian peninsula, migration and conquest toward the north, the east, and the west resulted from initial conquests and conversions under the leadership of Muhammad, the prophet, followed by a holy war under his successors beyond the confines of the peninsula.

In western Europe, kingship arose from a blending of Germanic and Christian elements. Charismatic lineage, with its belief in bloodright and acclamation by the community, Roman legal conceptions, and consecration by the church as the repository of divine grace all blended into a single tradition. Of these elements, only acclamation by the community played a role in the emergence of Islam. Ideas of blood-right had existed also, but did not prevail against the call to a new faith by a charismatic prophet. Nor was this faith compatible with the organization of a church. Charismatic prophecy was bound up with one man, Muhammad, the messenger of God. When he died, no one else could step into his place as a prophet. Since he left no male descendants, we do not know whether his heirs could have established a dynasty of prophets. After Muhammad's death there was a revolt of several tribes; other prophets appeared. Abu Bakr (632–634), Muhammad's successor by acclamation, had to first subdue these rebellious tribes before he ordered them to carry war beyond the borders of the realm the prophet had founded.

Muhammad's rule was followed by the patriarchal caliphate, consisting of Abu Bakr, Umar (634–644), Uthman (644–656), and Ali (656–661); all four were in-laws of the prophet, members of the Quraysh tribe, and companions of his rise as a religious and political leader. Abu Bakr had been chosen because Umar paid him homage in an assembly. Abu Bakr designated Umar. When Umar lay dying he appointed a committee of electors whose choice fell on Uthman (an early convert, but a member of the Umayyad clan). And when Uthman was murdered, the choice fell on Ali, the prophet's cousin, the husband of Muhammad's favorite daughter Fatima, but unlike the other three also a descendant of Muhammad's own clan, the Hashim.

In Islam there is no agreement on the religious significance of this account and perhaps there cannot be. For the true believer, access to the truth of God's word can be had only through the Qur'an and the sayings of the prophet. Although these sources provide no guidance concerning the succession, the true faith and man's fate depend absolutely on preserving Muhammad's prophetic charisma by finding the one right line of succession.

In a strictly spiritual sense, Muhammad could have no successors.[34] This is the reason why an "objective" history of the caliphate (caliph means lieutenant, companion, or successor, at least originally) cannot be written. There are two main branches of the Islamic tradition which began after Muhammad's death and continue to the present. The majority group (Sunni), which calls itself "the people of the tradition," gives preference to Abu Bakr, Umar, Uthman, the five electors chosen by Umar, and those who fought alongside the prophet at the battle of Badr. Emphasis is placed on the *companionship* with Muhammad as the criterion best suited to preserve his charisma for the benefit of the community. Hence, successors were chosen by acclamation of the companions. This principle of acclamation was inherited from the pre-Islamic tribal traditions. But the companions of the prophet included Uthman, who belonged to the Umayyad clan which was suspect in the eyes of believers. For this clan had opposed the prophet during his lifetime and accepted the new faith only belatedly and under military pressure.

The minority group (Shi'ites) is the *Shi'at Ali* or the party of Ali. Shi'ite Muslims feel that members of the prophet's clan, the Hashim, possess special powers which set them above other men; hence, the leader of the community should be chosen from among the descendants of that clan. Among the patriarchal caliphs, only Ali possessed this qualification, and there are various versions how and why Ali was passed over when the first three caliphs were chosen. Here the emphasis is placed on the *inheritance of charisma* as the criterion best suited to preserve its benefit for the community. This approach accentuates the principle of blood-right also derived from pre-Islamic tribal traditions. But it quietly ignores the controversial role of Ali himself.

The early history of the caliphate is marked by two struggles for power. In the first, Ali associated himself with opposition to Uthman, the descendant of the merchant Umayyad clan and therefore suspect to those who upheld the tribal traditions. Uthman was murdered, and this murder probably reflected conflicts between merchants and nomadic tribesmen. (Merchants were sedentary and interested primarily in the safety of trading. By contrast, the nomadic tribes stood in the forefront of Islamic conquests, inspired by traditions of militancy.) There is no evidence of Ali's direct involvement in the murder of Uthman, but his enemies attributed to him guilt by association. The second struggle for power was precipitated when Ali as the newly chosen caliph pressed his claim against Mu'awiya, the Umayyad governor of Syria. Mu'awiya re-

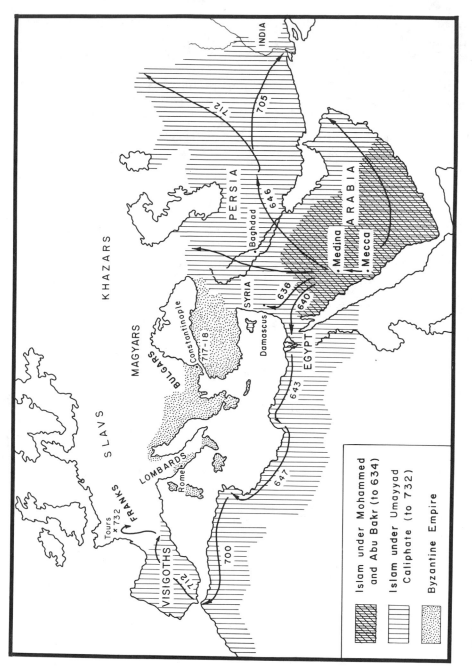

2. Expansion of Islam, 630–732

sisted Ali and demanded vengeance for the murder of Uthman. Both parties believed the Sacred Law to be on their side and agreed to arbitration. Traditionally, such arbitration was considered binding, but Ali protested when the verdict went against him. The standoff between the two contenders ended when Ali was murdered in 661.[b] In the same year, Mu'awiya was recognized as caliph, beginning the Umayyad dynasty (661–749).

Under this dynasty, Islamic conquests reached from the Indus to the Pyrenees, and on the surface the Umayyad caliphs possessed an abundance of authority. But problems of government mounted with expansion, demanding new administrative measures and the application of the Sacred Law (Shari'a) to ever-changing circumstances. Gradually, the task of interpreting the principles laid down by the Prophet passed into the hands of specialists. By 700 A.D., formal teaching had emerged, and in the circles of the learned (*ulema,* or teachers of the Shari'a), the Umayyad dynasts were perceived increasingly as autocrats. Eventually, opposition to the Umayyad dynasty mounted, and a revolution under Abbasid leadership occurred.

Under the Abbasid dynasty (750–1258), the center of power shifted from the Umayyad capital of Damascus to Baghdad. In the new capital, the caliphate came under the intellectual and political influence of the Persian imperial tradition. The Abbasids hired Persian secretaries who advocated an autocratic exercise of power. At the same time, the "constitutionalist" Islamic school under the leadership of the *ulema* had the support of the Muslim community. The Abbasid caliphate was stabilized for a time. The caliph and his deputies exercised political and (to an extent) judicial authority, while all religious matters were put under the scriptural authority of the ulema.

Yet Abbasid rule remained stable only briefly. Early in the ninth century, warlords appeared in various parts of the empire whose subordination to the caliphate became nominal. By the early tenth century, the Abbasid caliphate had weakened even in Baghdad. Turkish mercenaries were hired in lieu of Arab tribesmen and civilians. By 935 the caliphs were forced to accept the warlord dynasty of the Buwayhids (935–1058) in Baghdad. The Abbasid caliphate lost much of its temporal power when these military leaders came to rule in its name or even without its sanction and when Turkish forces replaced the Arabs as the politically dominant group in Islam. These events had far-reaching implications for the Islamic interpretation of royal authority.[35]

In practice, the caliphs became increasingly preoccupied with reli-

---

[b]Some of Ali's supporters rejected the idea of arbitration since according to the Qur'an rebels must be fought until they return to obedience. The so-called Kharijites (from the verb meaning *to go out*) withdrew their allegiance to Ali and when they refused to listen to his appeals, he massacred them. In 661, Ali was stabbed to death by a Kharijite fanatic.

gious matters while real power passed into the hands of warlords. Under the rule of these warlords, Persian secretaries supported autocracy and attacked the orthodox Islamic insistence on the supremacy of the Sacred Law. By the tenth century, the Abbasid caliphs had to accept the effective rule of successive warlords; Islamic jurists were thus confronted in practice with a system in which military rulers were accepted by the caliph and exercised all authority. Under these conditions, secular government concerned with mundane affairs was severed from the caliphate concerned with upholding the religious practices of the people. This separation is evident in a passage from Ibn Khaldun (d. 1406).

> Natural kingship [i.e., the kingship of the warlords] forces the people to conform to the private ambitions and uncontrolled desires of the ruler. Political government induces the people to conform to the dictates of reason for the promotion of worldly interests and the warding off of evils. [By contrast,] the Caliphate leads the people to conform to the insights of the Revealed Law in regard to their interests both in the world to come and those in this world which relate to it, since all the affairs of this world are assessed in the light of their relation to the interests of the future life.[36]

In this formulation the caliphate is concerned only with those worldly interests which relate to the future life. By contrast, the military rulers were not concerned with the preservation of the Shari'a. Gibb documents that Islamic jurists increasingly tended to interpret rule seized by force as legitimate, and that religious scholars sought to preserve intact the spiritual heritage and hence the ideal of a community of believers, even if this meant a more or less complete separation between temporal affairs and spiritual concerns. This separation had itself a religious foundation.[37]

The differences between the Islamic and Christian traditions should be noted. Both were characterized by factionalism in their early periods. But in Christianity, conflicts between the Western Catholic and the Eastern Orthodox church occurred over the proper *theological* interpretation of the nature of Christ and over the proper relation between kings and the church as successors to Christ's mission on earth. By contrast, the conflicts within Islam referred to a legitimation of royal authority derived from *historical events*.

The caliph was an absolute ruler whose duty it was to watch over the people and, if necessary, compel them to obey the Law. Islamic jurists enjoined on the people the duty of complete obedience to the ruler.

> The Prophet said, "Do not abuse those who bear rule. If they act uprightly, they shall have their reward, and your duty is to show gratitude. If they do evil, they shall bear the burden, and your duty is to endure patiently.

They are a chastisement which God inflicts upon those whom He will; therefore accept the chastisement of God, not with indignation and wrath, but with humility and meekness."[38]

There was little dispute concerning the necessity of absolute rule under God. People are weak, and Sacred Law must limit their liberty of action. A governor is needed to restrain them and protect the faith. In theory, the caliph was subject to the Sacred Law and had to rule in accord with it, for the Law existed independently of him. As successors to the prophet, their authority was derived directly from God, "who as sole Head of the Community has alone the power to confer authority of any kind; and this authority rests primarily on religious obligation . . . in accordance with the verse: 'Oh God, the possessor of the kingly rule, Thou givest the rule to whom Thou wilt and withdrawest the rule from whom Thou wilt' (Q. III, 25–27)."[39] Thus, orthodox doctrine justified the caliph's actions, whatever they might be, as automatically in accord with the Law laid down in the Qur'an. As long as the caliphs upheld the faith, their actual wrongdoing was a chastisement from God which no religious institution or human agency should attempt to control.

The Umayyad dynasty followed the precedents established in Muhammad's lifetime. Muhammad had acted as arbiter of disputes. The Umayyads continued this practice, and under their aegis the special office of judge (*qadi*) developed. The caliphs controlled the public treasury and performed certain religious functions, such as leading public worship and delivering the Friday sermon. In these ways, the caliphs fulfilled their sacred duty of upholding the faith and thus legitimized their absolute rule in accord with the Shari'a.

These accepted principles were nevertheless subject to divergent interpretations because contending parties cited one or another historical precedent to support their cause. A legitimation of royal authority that depended on the actual successors to the prophet (rather than on theological argument as in Christianity) had only precedent to rely on. For example, the Sunni doctrine of the caliphate emphasized that caliphs must be descended from Muhammad's tribe, the Quraysh, and must be chosen by consensus, but the caliphate cannot be passed to a successor through inheritance. This was an argument directed against the Shi'ites by emphasizing the conditions under which Abu Bakr, Umar, and Uthman (but not Ali) had succeeded the prophet, thus upholding the principle of companionship at the expense of charismatic inheritance.[40]

On an imperial scale, the Islamic community of believers replaced the solidary community of the pre-Islamic tribe. In the empire as in the tribe, the community (umma) embodied the values which the individual cherished and enjoyed solely by virtue of his membership. The word of

The Revelation Brought to Muhammad by the Archangel Gabriel
The depiction of the prophet and the archangel is contrary to Islamic tradition and suggests the great tasks of religious conversion and cultural assimilation confronting the religious teachers, jurists, scholars, and dignitaries (*ulema*) of the Abbasid caliphate after the Mongol conquest. This miniature is taken from Rashid al-Din's World History. The author (c. 1247–1317) was a Persian Jew who converted to Islam and rose to great wealth and power under Mongol overlordship, following the Mongol capture of Baghdad in 1258. (Edinburgh University Library)

God as vouchsafed in the Qur'an and the teachings of Muhammad provided the bond of brotherhood which allowed the Abbasids to destroy invidious distinctions between Arab and non-Arab Muslims, albeit at the price of loosening (if not losing) the unity between ethnic and religious identification. The preservation of the Sacred Law as the foundation of that brotherhood was the purpose of the ulema and the basis of their central, spiritual position in Islamic society, even though in the later Abbasid caliphate they lost what influence on temporal authority they had possessed before. In turn, the caliphs began as protectors of the Sacred Law and for a time enjoyed the spiritual support of the believers, as interpreted by the ulema. But *no* caliph was a prophet himself, and none was believed able to receive further revelations. The tradition established by Muhammad was considered perfect and final.

One root of the contrast between the Islamic and early Christian conceptions of kingship lies in the difference between the charismatic prophecy of Muhammad and the charisma of Christ as the Son of God. Muhammad was the inspired messenger of God, whose utterances represented God's word and must be preserved in their purity. Hence, the Islamic emphasis was on the finality of this written and oral tradition in accord with which the community of believers had to be governed. Therefore, the task of protecting the Sacred Law was the supreme obligation of the ruler.

In the early Christian tradition, the sayings of Christ did not have a comparable significance. The suffering of Christ provided a more compelling symbol than his words: through His death the Son of God suffered for our sins. Believers were purified by partaking of His body through the sacrament. Through the apostolic succession, the church was empowered to administer this sacrament and interpret the Scriptures. The church fathers were, therefore, not as bound by the written word as were their Muslim counterparts.[c]

Western European kingship and the church were greater counterweights to each other than was the case of the Islamic caliphate and the *ulema*. Western European kings were bound by a customary law whose interpretation was *not* in the sole keeping of the church. The sacral character of Western kingship was also ensured by the charisma of blood-right and hereditary succession. At the same time, the kings did not stand in a direct line of succession to Christ. Only the church made that claim and as the sole interpreter of Scriptures declared God's law to which even kings as mere mortals were subject. Yet this claim was also limited by the secular dependence of the church on the Western kings and especially on the success of their military defense against invasions from the East. By contrast, the Umayyad and Abbasid caliphs were unable to defend their empire against Turkish and Mongol invasions. Their secular power quickly declined, but they were successors of Muhammad to whom God had spoken directly and were thus literally the representatives of God on earth. The caliphs had the task of defending the faith in its charismatic purity, yet they had little secular power with which to discharge that sacred trust. Under these conditions, they used what influence remained to them on behalf of Islam and its leading

---

[c]In the Protestant tradition of Christianity, the word of the Bible is clearly more important than in the Catholic and thus there is a superficial similarity between Protestantism and Islam. But for Protestantism, the word of the Bible is the rock upon which the *individual* believer bases his faith, whereas for Islam the word of the Qur'an is the utterance of God which is the *Law* that is binding on the *community* of Muslim believers. The Protestant emphasis on the Bible allows the individual to find and express his faith; the Islamic emphasis on the Qur'an makes God's word the literal obligation of all true believers.

Mongol Conquest of a Town

The commander of the conquering forces carries a scepter and appears together with a warrior on a bridge crossing the river. Groups of warriors appear on the walls of the town (Baghdad?); two catapults are shown, as well as three female figures witnessing the scene from walled enclosures. No enemy is shown and the sense of catastrophe is strangely absent. Perhaps this reflects the Mongol's own sense of divine vengeance. The historian Juvaini tells that after the conquest of Bokhara Genghiz Khan rode his horse into the mosque and said to the people of the city, "I am the punishment of God. If you had not committed great sins, God would not have sent a punishment like me upon you." Juvaini mentions the figure of 1,300,000 dead after the capture of Merv; even allowing for much exaggeration the Mongol campaigns were of the utmost savagery, using terror and devastation to achieve their ends. (Staatsbibliothek, Preussischer Kulturbesitz, Berlin. Juvaini is quoted in *Times Literary Supplement*, April 15, 1977, p. 465.)

teachers and functionaries. The purity of the faith was preserved, but at the price of abandoning efforts to make secular rulers abide by the Sacred Law.

ANCESTORS, KINGS, AND OFFICIALS IN ANCIENT CHINA

The formation of Chinese kingship goes back to the Shang dynasty, conventionally dated from 1766 to 1122 B.C., a period coinciding with the later Egyptian dynasties. This major Bronze Age civilization of North China was based on specialized agriculture. Nature and ancestor worship were dominant practices and have remained important in Chinese culture throughout history. They have had a bearing on the legitimation of royal authority, because they signify an interdependence between the cosmos and the world of man.

> . . . Humanity is constantly under the influence of forces emanating from the directions of the compass and from stars and planets. These forces may produce welfare and prosperity or work havoc, according to whether or not individuals and social groups, above all the state, succeed in bringing their lives and activities in harmony with the universe. Individuals may attain such harmony by following the indications offered by astrology, the lore of lucky and unlucky days, and many other minor rules. Harmony between the empire and the universe is achieved by organizing the former as an image of the latter, as a universe on a smaller scale.[41]

Cities were built in accord with the design of the universe. This cosmological parallelism was not only an interpretation of how things are; it was a call to action to ensure the desired harmony.

> The need to maintain harmony between the world of the gods and the world of men required that man should participate in cosmic events by accompanying them with appropriate rituals. Such ceremonies, either actual or idealized, are well documented in China from Shang times onward, being epitomized in the saying of *Li-Chi* that "in ceremonies of the grandest form there is the same hierarchical relationship as that which exists between Heaven and Earth."[42]

The favorable outcome of human affairs depended on whether men performed the proper ceremonies and made the required sacrifices to the higher spiritual forces. Warfare, alliances, tribute payments, the selection of personnel, agriculture, the weather, hunting, sickness, dreams, child-bearing, travel plans, and other matters were subject to divination. Much attention was devoted to the propitiation of the ancestral spirits. The dead were believed to continue their existence in the form of the soul, and all existence was marked by the mutual dependence between the dead and the living.[43]

Since all aspects of life were believed to possess spiritual significance, special importance was attributed to the religious functions of the king. In Shang China, the king's ancestors were believed able to intercede with the High God (Ti) whose blessings could bring prosperity and success. By means of rituals, sacrifices, and divination, the king was believed capable of influencing his ancestral spirits. Hence, the king embodied authority because he alone could "appeal for the ancestral blessing, or dissipate the ancestral curses, which affected the commonality."[44]

In ancient China, a tacit exchange was believed to exist between the king and his ancestors. The king depended on his ancestors to legitimize his rule; the strength of the ancestors depended in the eyes of the people on the rituals and sacrifices which the king offered. The powers of the ancestors increased in proportion to the sacrifices offered them, just as in the secular world the power of the king increased in proportion to the tribute and taxes which his agents collected from the people.[45]

Though this function of kingship tends to occur wherever the worship of ancestors and of nature prevails, the practices of Shang China were distinctive. A diviner addressed a prediction, wish, or intention to a turtle shell or cattle bone, in which hollows had been bored or chiseled and in which cracks appeared when heat was applied. By interpreting the ensuing cracks, the diviner judged whether or not the projected event or action had the ancestral blessing.

As diviner, the king served as intermediary between the people and the powerful spirits of his ancestors. His divinations were believed to increase the likelihood that crops would be plentiful and military campaigns victorious. His proper attention to ceremonies at least showed him to be worthy of the favorable regard of his ancestral spirits. Good crops and victories in battle were thus spiritually significant and served to strengthen the legitimacy of the king.

But the inscriptions on the shells and bones typically appeared in complementary fashion, allowing for a positive as well as a negative outcome. Positive predictions served as a ritual incantation because emphasis on the desirable course of events was thought to help bring it about. But negative predictions were made in the interest of realism. As Keightley explains,

Only by facing both possibilities, by giving each possibility, as it were, a fair chance, could the divination itself be fair, in accord with reality, and thus valid. The inscribed divinations documented the fact that fair chance had been given, that the divination itself had been metaphysically realistic. Divination, and hence legitimation, was effective to the degree that it accorded with the nature of reality. The divining king had to immerse himself, as it were, in the forces of the universe, before he could emerge, triumphant, as the validated king. And by "risking" the outcome in this way, the king made the eventual validation,—such as abundant harvest, or victory in battle,—all the greater, because all the more founded in reality.[46]

Adversity by itself probably did not undermine the king's authority, as long as he observed the proper rituals. Nevertheless, times of human or natural misfortune might eventually be considered evidence that the Mandate of Heaven had been withdrawn and that the king had forfeited his right to rule. This Mandate theory seems to have developed during the Western Chou empire (1122–771 B.C.), when the overthrow of the ruling Shang dynasty was justified on the ground that "heaven . . . sent down this ruin" on the last Shang king, so that the conquering "Chou merely assisted by carrying out [the Heavenly] Mandate. . . . "[47] Here the self-contained system of Shang beliefs seems to have been used as the simple justification of conquest. But the Mandate theory could be used in the same manner to justify subsequent conquests or revolts. It could also be used to apply a theory of responsible government to the rule of Chinese emperors generally.

Evidence for autocracy can be cited from all periods of Chinese history and finds ready assent among experts in the field.[48] Nor is there much doubt that Chinese emperors were as autocratic as they could manage to be in practice. But Creel has assembled evidence for the Western Chou dynasty which suggests that the theory of supreme imperial rule was at times difficult to implement. Conquering as large a territory as the Chou did was one thing, governing it another. The Western Chou kings employed the whole arsenal of political controls through imperial supremacy, the delegation of authority, and quasi-feudal relations. As many as one thousand feudal "states" may have existed between 1122 and 221 B.C., and many of these vassal states were only nominally subordinate to the emperor.[49] Extremes of autocratic centralism and near anarchy apparently existed side by side.

As in other times and places, the struggles of the powerful were "sustained" by a mass of exploited peasants who suffered the ravages of war and gained little from the temporary victories of their rulers.[50] Amid this nearly universal insecurity, descendants of aristocratic families (like younger brothers, sons of concubines, distant kin) came to form a motley, impoverished class of mercenaries, scribes for hire, and itinerant teachers in search of employment. Confucius (551–479 B.C.) belonged to this class. During his lifetime, he was a man of prominence only among his disciples. He spent much of his life wandering from one noble household to another, returning to his native state of Lu in his later years. He was apparently reduced to the role of a freelance teacher and philosopher by his failure to secure an official position for any length of time.[51]

A good many scribes and teachers were competing for employment and produced a welter of conflicting doctrines which a later literary convention referred to as "the hundred schools." The times were out of joint. Then as now scholars had three typical alternatives for coming to terms with such conditions. They could withdraw from all worldly affairs, as did the founder of Taoism, Lao Tzu, whose object was "the regulation of one's own person . . . in accord with the natural order of things," admitting no selfish consideration.[52] This mystical sense of oneness with nature had enormous appeal, for it was in accord with the fundamental belief in a parallelism between the universe and the world of man. Taoism influenced the adherents of many other doctrines, perhaps also because it glossed over the modest opportunities of men from prominent families who had lost out in the competition for fame and office.

A second alternative was for scholars to ingratiate themselves with a local ruler, the more powerful the better, because power promised rich rewards and some security against ill fortune. Scholars could offer such rulers their skills as scribes and teachers, their knowledge of ancient texts, and their advice (although by definition scholars were men without administrative experience). Rulers were beset by the insecurity of anarchic conditions, and every failure in peace or war jeopardized their title to rule. Hence, scholars had a certain utility if by appropriate ceremonies, by interpretations, and by emphasis on rules and penalties they helped to legitimize a ruler. Scholars performing these functions came to be called Legalists or Realists.

There was also a third alternative, albeit the most difficult of the three. Scholars could attempt the way of reform. One can speculate that it was difficult for them to gain access to the rulers, especially those of larger states who would accept a scholar's services only on their own terms. Access to the heads of noble households may have been more promising. Scholars themselves were often descendants of such houses, and their services as scribes, teachers, and would-be administrators were in some demand at the level of officialdom. Even here, however, reforms were difficult to make, as Confucius and his followers discovered. But teaching and reform at this level appeared possible, since the more successful dynastic rulers of the time needed skilled men to govern large territories.

In the long run, "Confucianism" affected Chinese rulership to the degree that the many doctrines which went under the name of the great teacher became the ideology of Chinese dynastic bureaucracies. But in the first instance, Confucius addressed himself to officials and to those who aspired to government office. His attitude toward the religious beliefs of his time had special importance for his teaching.

Under the Western and Eastern Chou dynasty (1122–256 B.C.), traditional religious practices—the sacrifices to Heaven and the ancestral spirits—had done nothing to ensure peace and prosperity. One consequence was a rise of skepticism among the Chinese aristocracy along with the proliferation of omens and spirits which people hoped would ensure good fortune. In this setting, Confucius aimed at a decrease in political anarchy and the restoration of social norms. He supported the conventional religious practices of the day; to have challenged them would have jeopardized basic beliefs of his time and thus added to instability. But Confucius refrained from raising religious issues. He would serve people and understand life rather than serve the spirits and be concerned with death. One should do for the ancestral spirits all that was proper, but Confucius did not recommend either sacrifices or any other religious practice in order to deal with the world's ills.

Confucius was not an irreligious man. In his view, Heaven sanctioned his great mission. Heaven was the source of truth, of protection against enemies, and of comfort in adversity. But Confucius' own attitude was detached. Making sacrifices was only proper, but to expect Heaven's reward in return was not. The proper attitude was the practice of virtue without thought of reward. Confucius instructed by example and by appeals to the understanding, not by charismatic appeals as the messenger of God, let alone of a single God. Later generations attributed charismatic powers to him and to his teaching, but he himself disclaimed them.[53]

His ethical teaching called for a fundamental reorientation. Indirectly, at least, it challenged the ancient notion that religious observances would be conducive to well-being and a long life in this world. Though he permitted such beliefs among the common people, Confucius told the rulers of his time in effect that fitness to rule depended on virtue and ability.[d] This advice was offered to warring nobles who thought the fortunes of their house depended on the military arts; it was offered to men of humble origin who conquered power and tried to rule by force alone. Such men vied with one another in a war of all against all in which life was indeed nasty, brutish, and short. In this setting, it made sense to emphasize self-control and tell the rulers that good ministers could secure prosperity and keep the people content.

[d]The elitism of the doctrine was expressed by Hsün Tzu, about the middle of the third century B.C.: "Sacrificial rites are the expression of man's affectionate longings. They represent the height of altruism, faithfulness, love, and reverence. They represent the completion of propriety and refinement. If there were no Sages, no one could understand this. The Sage plainly understands it; the scholar and superior man accordingly performs it; the official observes it; and among the people it becomes an established custom. Among Superior Men it is considered to be a *human practice*; among the common people it is considered to be a *serving of the spirits....*" (Quoted in C. K. Yang, *Religion in Chinese Society,* p. 48).

> If one is able to correct himself, what difficulty will he find in carrying on government? But if a man cannot govern himself, what has he to do with governing others?

But these admonitions to the powerful could be ignored. For years Confucius failed to secure an appointment. This experience may be reflected in the teaching he addressed to aspiring officials:

> Do not be concerned that you are not in office, but only about making yourself fit for one. Do not be concerned if you win no recognition; only seek to make yourself worthy of it.

That advice was especially suitable for men who enjoyed a genteel way of life. However, it emphasized virtue rather than hereditary status or wealth, and it minimized ritual observances designed to enlist Heavenly blessings in matters that were beyond one's control.[54] Confucius attached a comprehensive meaning to the single principle or Way (*Tao*) which should govern the conduct of a gentleman or person of high character:

> Death and life are as decreed, wealth and rank depend upon Heaven; the gentleman is serious and does not fail in his duties, he behaves courteously to others and accords with *li*.

Originally, *li* referred to religious ritual. As Creel observes, the decorum observed in ritual became the ideal standard of conduct. Confucius extended the meaning of the term by emphasizing the spirit in which sacrifices were made. As he said, "I cannot bear to see the forms of *li* gone through by those who have no reverence in their hearts." The proper forms of conduct animated by a sincere spirit were applied beyond ritual to other spheres of behavior:

> Courtesy, if not regulated by *li*, becomes labored effort; caution, if not regulated by *li*, becomes mere timidity; courage, if not regulated by *li*, becomes mere unruliness; frankness, if not regulated by *li*, becomes mere effrontery.[55]

This principle of decorum or propriety (li) was a guide to action. Confucius called not only for sincerity, but for the virtues of an aristocrat without the vices. Poise and flexibility were to come from self-reliance and independence. Self-cultivation was to induce peace of mind. These qualities allowed one to admit his mistakes and correct them openly; it also allowed him to say, "If upon looking into my heart I find that I am right, I will go forward though those that oppose me number thousands and tens of thousands."[56]

Nothing in the career of Confucius or the circumstances of his day suggests that some three centuries after his death Confucianism would begin its ascendance as a major belief-system in Chinese civilization. We must not confuse Confucianism with the original teachings of the master, nor impute to the Confucian interpretation of kingship a consistency it did not possess.

In an era of great political fragmentation and almost continuous vendettas, it was unlikely that itinerant teachers in search of employment would have much influence. A main condition for the rise of Confucianism as a state doctrine was an alliance of its disciples with the victorious contenders in one of the many dynastic struggles of the period. For centuries after the death of Confucius, that prospect seemed dim. However, one should not underestimate the inconspicuous but widespread influence of moral teaching itself, for when China was unified for the first time under the Ch'in dynasty (221–206 B.C.) the emperor Shih Huang-ti in part adhered to Confucian principles. Morality was by that time conceived in Confucian terms, and no ruler would forego appeals to morality.

In practice, Shih Huang-ti favored the teachers and scribes disposed to support his despotic rule. Prominent among his officials were followers of the School of Law (Fa-chia), which dated back to the fourth century B.C. The Legalists identified with the ruler and his problems. They taught that laws were binding not for reasons of justice, but solely because violations would diminish when they were punished quickly and with utmost severity. The people did not understand public affairs and could only be expected to fear the ruler and the state. Legalist doctrine was strictly utilitarian: many crimes and punishments were costly and could be avoided if punishments were so severe that only a few crimes were committed. Many laws and severe punishments were the main method to unify the country and benefit it as a whole.

These methods must have appeared useful for the consolidation of power, but it is doubtful whether the first emperor completely agreed with Legalist doctrine. Though Shih Huang-ti is notorious for ordering the burning of Confucian books and the execution of scholars, he also sponsored the collection of books and their study by Confucians and others. His despotic rule helped to create a unified empire, and he utilized *all* the ideas of his age to legitimize his regime. He sponsored the Legalists when they served his purposes but probably rejected their purely utilitarian attitude toward governance and did not forego the moral support of Confucian teaching.[57] In practice, Shih Huang-ti's rule was extremely punitive and eventually provoked widespread rebellions leading to the overthrow of the Ch'in dynasty. Confucian scholars were associated with the rebels, the founders of the Han dynasty. The position of Confucianism was officially consolidated through sponsorship by the Han emperor, Wu Ti (140–87 B.C.).[58]

This outward ascendance of Confucianism did not terminate the "battle of the books" among rival schools of thought and contenders for office. By the first century B.C., "Confucianism" had become an amalgam of many elements derived from interpretations of ancient texts and the ideas of Confucius. Modern scholars must try to unscramble the texts to discover the probable date of composition and the most likely intent behind the apparent textual manipulation.[59] These manipulations had their root not only in the ambitions of rival scholars, but in the conflicting imperatives of imperial rule.

In a unified China, the emperor sought to concentrate authority in his hands and enhance it by exploiting the people and resources of the country. But the emperor also sought to avert rebellion and retain the throne for himself and his descendants. Thus, he might temper his ambition and exploitation by responding to popular grievances. Under the Han dynasty, both alternatives found their scholarly champions *within* Confucianism, which by then had melded inextricably the various traditions of Lao Tzu, Confucius, and the Legalist school.

The early Han dynasty was founded in 206 B.C. and the first two rulers seemed to abide by the original precepts of Confucius. Han Kaotzu (202–195 B.C.), who was the son of a farmer, sought counsel from elders and officials and even yielded to their advice on the question of succession. His eldest son, Emperor Wen, is depicted in the Annals as the ideal Confucian ruler. Whatever the facts may have been, the purposes of a new dynasty, which originated in rebellion, as well as of Confucian scholars were served by praising Wen's exemplary conduct, which did not arise from laws or punishment.

> Confucius said, "Lead the people with governmental measures and regulate them by law and punishment, and they will avoid wrongdoing but will have no sense of honor and shame. Lead them with virtue and regulate them by the rules of propriety (*li*), and they will have a sense of shame and, moreover, set themselves right" [*Analects* 2:3].[60]

However, Confucianism in its more Legalist modes also contained the opposite precepts, formulated in the *Han Fei Tzu*. This collection of writings shared the Master's distrust of superstition, but not his benign view of human nature. In the opinion of those who followed the teachings of the *Han Fei Tzu*, behavior must be regulated by law. The ruler must have at his disposal a "succinct, easily understood, and consistent" language so that his statutes will be accepted by the people as right and true.

> Scholars are always telling us that punishments should be light. This is the way to bring about confusion and ruin. The object of rewards is to encourage; that of punishment, to prevent. If rewards are high, then what the

ruler wants will be quickly effected; if punishments are heavy, what he does not want will be swiftly prevented.[61]

Government by virtuous example and government by rules and punishment were the two ideologies corresponding to the conflicting imperatives of imperial rule.

The government of the Han emperor Wu Ti illustrates that in practice it was easy to combine what seemed logically distinct, and indeed contradictory. In view of the anti-Confucian tendencies of the Ch'in dynasty, Wu made a great show of supporting Confucian precepts, but in practice he employed men who defended or assisted his autocratic rule. In this way, Confucianism became the state-subsidized doctrine of the empire, while ambitious officials assisted autocratic rule. Much of the government was run on Legalist principles, including the examination system, but the teaching of Confucianism continued to allow for some influence of the original teachings with their ethical and anti-statist tendencies.[62] Whenever the one principle resulted in cumulative difficulties, the other could provide the needed ideological corrective.

CONCLUSION

The Western, Islamic, and Chinese traditions have in common an appeal to a higher power to legitimize secular rulers. They differ in their conception of the believer's obligations, in their idea of the higher power, and in the specialists who interpreted the meaning of transcendent forces in relation to royal authority.

Earlier I noted the contrast between the Christian belief in the Son of God as the sole redeemer of mankind and the Islamic belief in Muhammad the Prophet as the sole transmitter of God's word to mankind. For the early Christian believer, the most significant means of identification with God is to partake of the sacraments, the transsubstantiated representation of Christ's flesh and blood. For the Muslim believer, the most significant means of identification with God is each individual's strict observance of prescribed prayer and of adherence to the Sacred Law, as the Prophet transmitted it directly from God. For the Confucian believer (if that is quite the word), the most significant means of identification with the ancestral spirits and the cosmological order they inhabit is to observe the rules of proper conduct. These rules bear on the "five relationships" of ruler to subject, father to son, husband to wife, elder to younger brother, and friend to friend.

Religion has its own logic. Special acts of worship or prescribed conduct relate the believer to a transcendent power. Knowledge of this power is sacred. It is by reference to this knowledge of the sacred that people have attempted to curtail claims to unlimited royal authority.

In the early Christian tradition, the believer worships the Creator as His works have revealed Him and as He has shown His special mercy to mankind through the coming, the message, and the sacrificial death of His own Son. This conception of one omnipotent and omniscient God represents an ultimate mystery which the believer approaches through an act of faith, subsequently mediated by the church. In the Western tradition, the church came to oppose royal succession on the basis of blood-right because belief in the divine descent of kings was incompatible with belief in the Son of God as the sole redeemer of mankind. The popes claimed, and were believed, to be the direct successors of Christ's mission on earth. In this capacity they claimed ultimate jurisdiction in all matters pertaining to the salvation of souls. In practice, these matters impinged on secular affairs at many points; hence, the papal claim imparted a tension between the sacred and the profane to all aspects of life. Not only the family, but state affairs and royal authority were affected by this tension. The king was indeed the supreme ruler subject to none, but still he was a man and as such subject to God's Law as interpreted by the church. That Law was itself part of the divine mystery, and royal violation of it condemned the king to eternal damnation. This ultimate subjection of the royal will to God's Law rested on the spiritual claim of the church as the sole repository of divine grace and the only authentic interpreter of the divine word. But in a more practical sense, the royal will was limited as well by the wealth and influence of the church hierarchy, at least when opportunity arose to bring that influence to bear.

In the Islamic tradition, the believer worships the Creator as His words have revealed Him through Muhammad, the messenger of God. In contrast to Catholicism, Islamic religion knows no ultimate mystery because God has revealed himself through the Qur'an and the sayings of the Prophet. Hence, the believer's task is to worship as he has been taught, for God's truth is known, at least to those learned in the Sacred Law. Kings stand in the same relation to God's revealed truth as all other Muslim believers, even though their high position imposes special obligations on them. They must use their secular power to protect God's truth as embodied in Sacred Law, and they must be a model to the Muslim community in endowing and adorning the places of worship sanctified by tradition. Ultimately, rulers are subject to God's law, but only in the sense that as successors to the Prophet their authority is directly derived from God. This direct authentication has failed to impart to Islamic kingship a tension similar to that of the Western tradition. Kings worship like other Muslim believers. And in practice the ulema are individual interpreters of the sacred texts, often at odds with one another, and without the hierarchic organization, secular strength, and monopolistic claims of the Catholic church. The caliphs have had to cope only with the spiritual hazards common to all Muslim believers, because their rule was a mere instrument of God who was the sole head of the Islamic community.

In the Confucian tradition, the head of the family performs the religious rites on behalf of all members much as the emperor as the Son of Heaven performs the rites on behalf of the whole society. The object of these rites at all social levels is to "maintain harmony between the world of the gods and the world of men" (Wheatley). In this system, there are no institutional checks on the supreme authority of the hereditary monarch. Nevertheless, his actions *can* be circumscribed not only by social precedents, but by the suggestions and advice of officials whose primary allegiance is to the preservation of the Way. During the early Han dynasty, the Confucian literati developed as a status group distinguished from priests precisely because their expertise concerning ritual observances cast them in the role of advisors to heads of families from the emperor on down, not in the role of religious functionaries marked off by an act of ordination. In the Confucian interpretation of Hsün Tzu, the emperor's authority is unquestioned as long as the state prospers. But loss of social harmony is *prima facie* evidence that the monarch has not been an effective mediator between heaven and earth, and a ruler who does not follow the Way may be replaced by one who does. In this interpretation, influence and political power must be wielded by those who know how to conduct themselves so as to preserve the desired harmony between the world of man and the cosmos. Wealth and birth are irrelevant considerations. All those who possess the requisite knowledge are entitled to rule.[63]

Thus, in Chinese civilization, the ideal of kingship is not formulated by an elite of experts in holy writ who circumscribe royal authority—at least theoretically—through an appeal to divine revelation. Theoretically again, Chinese royal authority is circumscribed by an elite of scholars and officials learned in the Way, who conduct the affairs of government or aspire to do so. Skepticism is certainly in order concerning the efficacy of such teaching by, and largely for, government officials. But I doubt that complete cynicism is realistic. Even though scholars agree that China has been characterized by two thousand years of autocracy, they can hardly mean that all autocrats were equally effective. Nor is it wise to neglect the opportunities of influence open to subordinates even under effective imperial rule. The ideal Chinese emperor was a projection of his own subordinates, and I believe that even strong rulers had moments of weakness or indecision when the whispered counsel of an aide could make a difference, even aside from the more overt political functions of astronomers.[64] These aides and advisors of Chinese emperors were influenced greatly by a hallowed cultural tradition of rich texture and ancient origin. Rarely, if ever, have the rulers of great empires been confronted for two millennia by a class of subordinates so steeped in a cultural mode of expression that it could affect every bit of court intrigue and even the most self-possessed autocrat.

This comparative study of kingship has been concerned with a universal aspect of the human condition. Legitimation calls for reasons. Even in ages of faith, reasons provoke arguments, and appeals to a higher power can be used by the weak as well as the strong. Therefore, authority relations are bilateral, involving an "exchange" between ruler and ruled that creates dilemmas and contradictions for the rulers.

This chapter has shown that the authority of kings became differentiated in an early age of religious creativity, when the kinship-based sources of tribal authority were supplemented or replaced by types of charismatic authentication unrelated to kinship. The early patterns of royal authority necessarily developed in the context of internal political struggles and relations with foreign powers. At the same time, kings always rule with the assistance of their entourages, and their consecration and social supremacy buttress the rank-order of society. For this reason I refer to kingship and oligarchy as a type of rule, and the following chapters (3–6) are roughly divided into a discussion of royal authority on the one hand and aristocratic (oligarchic) governance on the other.

3

JAPAN

RIVAL CLANS AND IMPERIAL AUTHORITY

THE EARLIEST Japanese chronicles were composed in the eighth century A.D. The Record of Ancient Matters (*Kojiki*) and the Chronicles of Japan (*Nihon-shoki* or *Nihongi*) contain legends or myths describing the genesis of the Japanese islands, the life of the gods, the foundation of the imperial house, and the history of the Japanese empire up to 697 A.D. The legends are mingled with historical accounts describing contentions among rival clans. Fortunately, Chinese chronicles concerning Japan composed before the eighth century provide additional information which allows us to examine the gradual transformation both of clan organization into an imperial state and of nature and ancestor worship into a dynastic cult.

Early Japanese society was divided into three classes. An upper or ruling class consisted of large clans of families (*Uji*) related in fact or fiction to main-descent lineages.[1] A second class of common workers (*be*) was grouped by locale or occupation. A third class of slaves (*nuhi*) —approximately 5 percent of the population—was attached to the households of the upper class.

Each ruling clan was united by a common ancestor cult and ancestral myths, and its leaders claimed descent from an ancestral god. Hence, the political unification among clans depended on a merging of cults. Such mergers were probably promoted by the necessity of organizing for defense against native tribes and against the possibility of a Chinese invasion.

> It was chiefly through the spread of an extended kinship system and the tightening of marriage and fictive kinship bonds with an increasingly large body of subservient family lines that the authority of the Yamato chieftain was extended. . . .
>
> One of the strongest continuing methods of cementing close but subservient ties was the taking of wives and "tribute" men and women from the families of subordinate chiefs. Tribute females frequently found their way into the

61

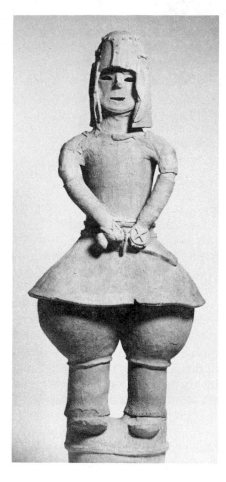

Haniwa Warrior
People buried their eminent dead in huge earthen mounds (tumuli) which contained colored pottery and clay figures of animals and people known as *haniwa*. This figure of a warrior from a late tumulus (c. sixth century A.D.) comes from Fujioka, Gumma Prefecture. These tumuli and their contents represent part of the evidence for the existence of rival clans during the third to sixth centuries A.D. (Asian Art Museum of San Francisco, The Avery Brundage Collection)

group of recognized wives of the Yamato chieftains. Tribute males served as guards and servants of the sovereign. While in the service of the sovereign, such individuals must also have remained as hostages on behalf of their own family.[2]

Familial consolidation through real or fictive kinship ties was supported at an early time by the popular nature worship (*Shinto*). All aspects of life, including inanimate objects, were seen as harboring a spiritual presence and were worshiped accordingly. In Japanese, this presence was designated by the word *kami*.

The great ancestors and the great heroes have it. So have certain objects, like rocks and trees, and certain places like groves and springs, and certain important things like tools and weapons and boundary stones between fields. The quality may be conferred by rarity, or by beauty, or by exceptional shape or size, or by great utility or by past history, or only by the feeling of the worshipper.[3]

To ward off calamities and ensure the good life, it was important to make the kami favorably inclined and thereby avoid the contamination or pollution that would arise from its ill will. The earliest records refer to an "abstainer" whose duty was to maintain ceremonial purity on behalf of the community. In a world in which that purity was considered the main condition of human welfare, all ceremonies which removed impurities gave extraordinary importance to a ruler capable of interceding with the spirits on behalf of the people.[4] These Shinto beliefs retained an unbroken hold on Japanese culture for centuries. They were anonymous in the sense that they were not associated with the name of an early religious leader. Their continuity with folk beliefs stands in marked contrast to Christianity, Islam, and Confucianism, since these other belief-systems arose through a revolution of ethical ideas, whether inspired by the Son of God, the messenger of God, or a great teacher of morals.

The Japanese chronicles of the eighth century relate the rise of kingship to contentions among the gods. In these contentions the Sun Goddess (*Amaterasu-omikami*) was victorious. The legendary first emperor of Japan, Jimmu (660 B.C.), was said to be of divine descent. This idea of divine descent contrasts with the charismatic personality and message of Christ and Muhammad, whose claims of divine inspiration undermined the old gods. The continuity of the Japanese imperial tradition with earlier beliefs is striking even when compared with the Chinese experience. Confucius emphasized the practice of virtue while merely tolerating folk-beliefs, and his disciples taught that such beliefs were for the masses, while virtue was for the rulers. Among the countries considered in this study, Japan is the only one in which political unity and royal authority were justified by ancestor-worship in times prior to recorded history. The Japanese emperor was believed to be the descendant of deities and to be a deity himself.

The Chronicles record that the Sun Goddess sent the God-child Jimmu to rule Japan and that he descended to the island of Kyushu. It is also stated that this first emperor started from Kyushu, and proceeded to conquer the east. After much fighting, he established his rule in Yamato, which became the center of Japan. Thereafter, the earliest rulers of Japan were grouped together under the Yamato dynasty, and while much remains nebulous, a few details emerge which shed light on the rise of Japanese kingship.

The political consolidation under the Yamato consisted of struggles with other clans, sporadic fighting against tribes on the expanding fron-

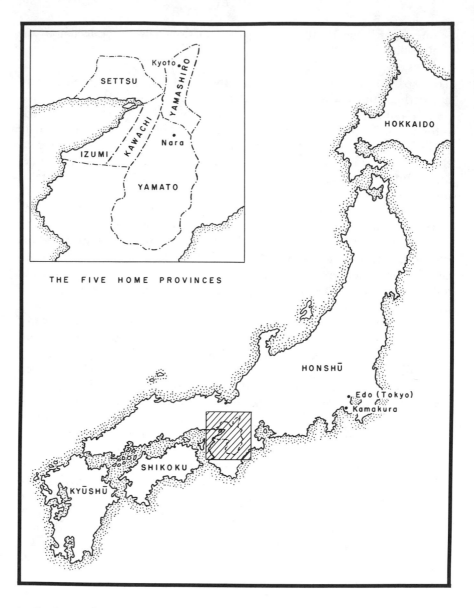

THE FIVE HOME PROVINCES

3. Japan in 900 A.D.

tiers of the realm, and expansion to the Korean peninsula.[a] Priestly functions were performed by the head of each clan; thus, each claimed access to the ancestral spirits of his house. If a divinely descended, imperial lineage was to emerge from among many rival clans, it had to make special claims based not only on its esoteric knowledge of ceremony, like the "abstainers" of old, but also on its wealth and recognition by others. In the early period, the house of the Yamato was only one great clan among many, and the other clans also possessed hereditary, priestly functions. Claims to divine descent were presumably a factor in the rise of one clan over others, but with all clans practicing ancestor-worship the descent of any one could be rather insignificant.

In the case of the Yamato dynasty, the emperor possessed the sacred regalia and represented the people in Japan's relations with China, where much importance was attached to dynastic claims. The Yamato house also increased its wealth by sponsoring the establishment of hereditary occupations. Many of the workers were skilled artisans, scribes, and scholars from Korea whose work was highly valued. But neither the regalia, nor foreign recognition, nor increasing wealth were sufficient. The position of the Yamato throne depended in the long run on recognition by the great territorial chieftains who were leaders of other clans, ruled their own domains, had their own corporations of hereditary workers, and commanded the loyalty of all those united with them in a common worship. In the provinces, these clan-chieftains were the effective local rulers. Gradually they accepted the mythological and ceremonial supremacy of the Yamato house, which increasingly had functioned as an arbiter among the clans. Real or fictive kinship ties with the dynasty facilitated acceptance of imperial rule.[5]

At the court of the Yamato dynasty, formal subservience to the emperor by the heads of other clans did little to mitigate the murderous rivalries among them. They wanted power for themselves even though they recognized the primacy of the Yamato house. They sought power by acting as the senior ministers or protectors of the throne. As in the early history of monarchies elsewhere, early Japanese history is a story of rivalries, intrigues, assassinations, and military campaigns among the

[a]The Japanese established an enclave in Korea in the middle of the fourth century but were finally ousted from Korea by the Chinese in 622. The sixteenth century witnessed another Japanese attempt to gain a foothold in Korea which also ended in military defeat. A third expansion on the mainland was the Japanese "co-prosperity sphere" in 1939–1945. In fifteen hundred years, there were only three direct threats against Japan from abroad: the unsuccessful Mongol invasions of the thirteenth century, Western trading and missionary intrusions which ended in the seventeenth and only resumed in the nineteenth century, and the American occupation after World War II. Japan probably enjoyed longer periods of immunity from outside interference than any other civilization.

great nobles, who desired access to positions close to the throne. Disputes over succession were used to enhance the cause of one clan over another. In these struggles surrounding the throne, the Soga family was the first to achieve ascendance.

A multiple hierarchy of government is characteristic of all monarchical rule. Even a king who rules as well as reigns relies on men who are strong-willed and powerful in their own right. Such men usurp some functions of management and thus multiply the hierarchies of authority. Traditional Japanese society shows this phenomenon in a marked degree, for where the ruler is believed to be a god, it is easy to so exalt the incumbent that he cannot concern himself with the management of affairs in the country. The emperor either retains decision-making powers and controls the chief ministers who manage in his behalf, or he will become a mere figurehead in whose name the ministers make all important decisions.

Imperial rule in Japan was divided into two hierarchies. One hierarchy consisted of the imperial family with its largely ceremonial functions, attended by a court nobility. Maintenance of these noble families and of the imperial household depended on extensive estates. Although government was conducted in the name of the emperor, neither he nor his court was directly involved with public affairs—except in two respects. Since all elevations in rank formally depended on the imperial sanction, there was much manipulation of etiquette and rank. Inevitably, the court was also involved in disputes over the succession.

The second hierarchy consisted of a regent (*sessho*) and various high offices of government under him. In 830 A.D., the position of civil dictator (*kampaku*) was created in place of the office of regent and made hereditary in the Fujiwara family. The creation of this office marked the ascendance of a governing executive over the emperor. The man appointed as dictator acted as head of his clan, as manager of governmental affairs, and as chief "advisor" to the throne. In the first capacity, leaders of the Soga and then of the Fujiwara families managed the extensive lands and hereditary corporations of workers which belonged to their respective clans. At court, they buttressed their commanding positions by marrying their daughters or other closely related women to the emperor or descendants of the imperial family. As the effective head of government and recognized "advisor" to the throne, the kampaku exercised dictatorial powers. Thus, the fusion of wealth and authority was largely located in this paragovernment, while the fusion of wealth and status remained with the imperial house.

The rising prominence of the imperial institution and the ascendance of a governing clan, the Soga, at the side of the imperial family in the sixth and early seventh centuries seem—at least for a time—to have been two aspects of the same development. Both were part of a political consolidation marked by the increase of estates (*miyake*) held under direct ownership of the Yamato rulers and managed by the head of the Soga family.[6] But at the same time, disunity among the leading clans was rife and disloyalty to the reigning emperor quite common. The struggles for hegemony within Japan may account for the early occupation of Korea, since foreign conquests could tip the balance of forces at home. Japan's military involvement in Korea required a central organization and considerable resources at the disposal of the Yamato rulers.

The introduction of Buddhism aided the consolidation of Yamato rule. Monks traveling with foreign merchants from India had brought Buddhism to China in the later Han dynasty (25–220 A.D.). Confucian scholars and members of the Chinese gentry regarded these monks with contempt as belonging to the lower class. But Buddhism came to have a popular appeal. Its doctrine of reincarnation suggested that the officials oppressing the people would receive their just punishment, for they would be reborn disfigured and in a lowly position. And the deprived who suffered unjustly in this life could be reborn in a high position in the next. The temples were relatively secure from attack because of their religious mission, and this security prompted poor peasants to settle nearby. However, Buddhism appealed not only to the common people of China; it also appealed to merchants who used the Buddhist monasteries as banks, warehouses, and places of exchange and therefore donated money and land to Buddhist temples.[7] By the sixth century A.D. Buddhism had spread to Japan, and between 624 and 692 the number of Buddhist monasteries and shrines increased from 46 to 545. The most prominent Buddhist shrine was located in Nara, where the imperial court established its capital in 710.[b]

In Japan, certain prominent clans sponsored Buddhist temples much as they did Shinto shrines. In these temples, various scriptures (*sutras*) were recited for their supposed power to bring health, good fortune, and long life. Buddhism acquired a universal appeal with its de-

---

[b]Japanese history is divided into named periods. Our knowledge of the early history is largely based on the artifacts found in earthen mounds erected over the tombs of Uji chieftains. This period is, therefore, called Shizoku, or sometimes Uji, and extended from about 50 B.C. to 552 A.D. The Yamato state (ca. 300–645) overlaps with this period. Subsequent periods are named after the Taika reforms (552–710), the capital of Nara (710–784), and the second capital of Heian (Kyoto), which is divided into an early (784–857) and later (857–1160) Heian period. The later Heian period is also called Fujiwara after the family of regents (later civil dictators) who ruled the country in the name of the emperor.

veloped art, rituals, and voluminous scriptural literature. Buddhism as a common faith could help overcome the political and religious divisions among the clans because it was not bound up with ancestor worship. Under the leadership of Shotoku Taishi (574–622), Buddhism received its patronage increasingly from the imperial court, and the importance of clan-sponsored Buddhist temples declined.[c] Accordingly, the Buddhist establishment focused its attention on the performance of official ceremonies in the imperial capital, while in the provinces the Buddhist clergy and Buddhist temples were subjected to governmental controls.[8] Whereas Shinto was related to the authority structure of the clans, Buddhism helped turn the attention of the people toward the capital and the imperial court.[9] It should be added, of course, that the increase of land controlled by Buddhist monasteries and their close ties with court affairs increased the secular involvements of Buddhism. Withdrawal into a monastery even at an early age became a highly esteemed form of retirement for the court nobility.

The initial rise of imperial power was also aided by the adaptation of Chinese principles of administration to Japanese conditions. Through the Taika reforms of 646 and subsequent codifications, the imperial government claimed sovereignty over all privately held land. Based on a national survey, incomplete population and tax registers were drawn up and laws enacted which would distribute rice lands and tax liabilities accordingly.

> Let men of skill and intelligence with ability at writing and arithmetic be selected as administrative chiefs and record keepers.[10]

Here was a concerted effort to strengthen the central government by the appointment of government officials, the adoption of codes of law, and the central organization of local government, taxation, and military recruitment. Historians are unanimous that these reforms failed to establish an effective, nationwide administrative system. Such a system did not exist in China either, but the *ideal* imperial bureaucracy of China was used as the model for Japan. In practice, the Taika reforms fused a central administrative system with the locally dominant clans. The

---

[c]There were probably other reasons why Buddhism was received differently in China and Japan. On the surface, the main difference was that the Chinese gentry rejected Buddhism, while in Japan the high society at court and the heads of leading clans accepted it. One reason may be that in China, Buddhism challenged the Confucian monopoly of learning, whereas in Japan Buddhist teaching was added to the Shinto cults and the elaborate ceremonial life at court. Buddhist teaching did not discourage a union of different beliefs and practices, and Japanese high culture favored such union. Most important perhaps, there was no status group in Japan equivalent to the Confucian scholars in China. Learning and the arts were cultivated by all adult members of the aristocratic society.

Yamato rulers had overwhelming power to enforce the new governmental structure, and local leaders could not resist this power. At the same time, these local leaders did not lose much of their wealth or influence. Their local preeminence was now guaranteed not so much by the traditional, familial authority, as by imperial rule; henceforward, they would administer in the name of the emperor.[11]

The reforms of the seventh and eighth centuries initiated one of Japan's most impressive cultural periods. The court at Nara became a center of fashion and etiquette, of religious and artistic cultivation. In Nara, the position of Buddhism was especially privileged. But while a high aristocratic culture continued to flourish, the military power of the emperor waned. Buddhism taught that all life is inviolate. There seemed no need to maintain a regular army, for friendly relations with China diminished the danger of foreign invasion. With the reclamation of new land and increasing production, city life and especially imperial court society became luxurious, the Buddhist temples flourished, and for a time the new administrative system under the Taiho Code (702) appeared to work.

In 701 the possession of weapons by private persons had been forbidden, the uniform of officers of state included no deadly implements to symbolize their powers, and the profession of arms was not respected. In the capital the only military personnel were members of the Imperial Guard, commanded by officers principally interested in ceremony and appointed to their posts on the basis of family connections, wealth, and court rank. No capital punishment was meted out to courtiers or officials, although the codes made treason and similar crimes punishable by death.[12] The culture of the imperial court under the Fujiwara regents (858–1184) thus flourished for some three centuries.

However, the imperial house found it necessary to extricate itself from the influences of Buddhism and moved the capital from Nara to Heian (Kyoto) in 794. There were sporadic disturbances in the new capital and in the provinces, and paradoxically Buddhism contributed to these disturbances. Secular ties meant that the important Buddhist monasteries used political devices and armed monks to defend their great wealth—despite the Buddhist belief in the inviolability of life. Buddhism had been important for the consolidation of Yamato rule, but by the Heian period (794–1160) some Buddhist monasteries had become a military threat to the imperial court itself. To cope with these religious as well as other civilian disturbances, the Fujiwara established a special metropolitan police force in 810, and eventually this force became permanent and acquired additional judicial and military functions.[13] This and other expedients served to maintain the court society of the Heian emperors and the Fujiwara dictators until the middle of the twelfth cen-

tury, despite the steady decline of imperial authority. This decline and
the replacement of the imperial court by a military government (*sho-*
gunate) as the center of power must be described if we are to understand
the ascendance of a feudal society in the provinces.

The Yamato rulers had not pacified the whole of Japan, and raids
by aboriginal tribes (Ainu) continued on the frontiers. There were sporadic peasant revolts and, perhaps most important, competing clans of
the same lineage group engaged in numerous armed clashes over the
distribution and inheritance of land-rights. The government proved itself ill-equipped to cope with these disorders. The Taika reforms (646)
had established a national recruitment system which imposed a tremendous burden on the small cultivators. Conscription drained away much
of the agricultural work force, and the additional services and goods
required by the military proved ruinous. While well-to-do peasants and
the aristocracy evaded conscription or were given various exemptions,
ordinary peasants could best evade governmental requisitions by entering the service of a locally powerful clan. The system of national recruitment proved unworkable and was revoked in 792. Various substi-
tutes for this system were tried but did not work either. In the provinces,
civilian officials were incapable of organizing a police force and hence
unable to curb local outbreaks of violence. The need for local military
forces remained acute. In practice, the imperial government came to
rely on military forces organized by heads of locally dominant clans who
had both the resources and the manpower to keep the peace. Thus,
armed clashes were considered a local affair, unless their escalation became a threat to the established order. Then the imperial government
relied on the extralegal police force (*Kebiishi*) organized by the Fujiwara
dictators or on provincial leaders who were given an explicit mandate
to organize a special military campaign on behalf of the emperor.

Under the Taika reforms, the imperial authority to collect taxes had
never been fully implemented.[14] An effective regulation of tax assessments and collection depended on periodic audits and foreclosures
when taxes were unpaid. Such a system called for administrative skills
and personnel which did not exist. Moreover, the imperial government
allowed several exemptions from the taxes it had formally imposed.
Many religious establishments were exempted from the grain tax. Tax
exemptions were used as an incentive to open up new tracts of land for
cultivation and to settle frontier areas exposed to raids by aboriginal
tribes. Thus, the earlier and partial appropriation of land by the imperial government was gradually replaced by private appropriations.[15]
The landholdings of local clans increased in size, and private authority
relations replaced the imperial claim to governmental authority over the

land. The attempt of the Taika reforms to assert the emperor's local authority despite the wealth and status of local clans had failed.

Japanese landed estates were governed by the several ranks of owners, managers, cultivators, and tenants in accord with rules based on personal agreements. The Fujiwara regents, the court aristocracy, and locally powerful clans used such agreements to organize their household management. In the provinces, the Fujiwara, especially, administered their extensive holdings autonomously. Thus, the large landholdings of the leading clans became exempt from governmental regulation, with the result that administrative, military, and fiscal functions devolved upon household management. The central direction of local affairs by the imperial government became superfluous.

Eventually, this process reached the imperial house itself.

> Behind the gradual abandonment of the Sinified bureaucratic machinery and of the idea of the state as an extension of the imperial person, we find the imperial *uji* (lineage group) working to secure a private hold over the elements of political influence and wealth which had once been its by definition. Increasingly, the imperial house was obliged to protect its position as a familial power bloc in competition with the Fujiwara, Minamoto, and other court interests. . . . [16]

This is the explanation of the "cloistered emperors" of the eleventh and twelfth centuries. Incumbent emperors abdicated in favor of a chosen successor, both to escape from the cauldron of rivalries surrounding the throne and to exercise real authority from the protected position of a monastery. By discarding the machinery of government and converting large pieces of public domain into landholdings of the imperial family administered by its own household offices, the cloistered emperors entered into competition against the Fujiwara. In this way, they obtained a foundation for the continued preeminence of the imperial house despite the emergence of Japan's feudal order.

During the later Heian period from 857 to 1160, the expansion of private rights at the expense of imperial rights occurred together with the private organization of armed forces and hence the emergence of a class of professional mercenaries. Confusion and insecurity were so extreme that small and even well-to-do owners often found it advantageous to commend their land to a family of notables, which was strong enough to defend them against both the civil authority and other powerful clans. As a result, disputes over rights to the land and over the obligation to pay taxes in goods and services frequently changed from a legal case involving the government into a private vendetta involving the interests of rival landowning families.

Among these families, the Fujiwara dictators played the leading role, at least for a time. They "maintained the peace" in the provinces by calling on local notables to organize military forces to defend the frontiers and enforce the law. Since relatives of the Fujiwara were prominent local notables in many parts of the country, the distinction inevitably blurred between the military force of the imperial government under the direction of the Fujiwara dictators and privately organized bands of warriors under other Fujiwara clans.[17] In addition, the wealthier provincial notables also established private armed forces to defend the frontier, organize defensive or offensive operations against rival clans, and last but not least "enforce the law"—sometimes at the behest of the government and sometimes not.

> By the middle of the Heian era (say 950) the Court could no longer keep the peace in the capital, nor could the aristocratic absentee landlords, whether nobles or abbots, protect their own property without the assistance of armed forces maintained by local magnates who did not fail to exact a price for their services.[18]

In 946 a government constable, after suppressing a local revolt, reported as follows:

> Many make lawless use of power and authority; form confederations; engage daily in military exercises; collect and maintain men and horses under pretext of hunting game; menace district governors; plunder the common people; violate their wives and daughters; and steal their beasts of burden and employ them for their own purposes. Thus interrupting agricultural operations. . . . My appeal is that, with the exception of provincial governors' envoys, any who enter the province at the head of parties carrying bows and arrows . . . shall be recognized as common bandits and thrown into prison on apprehension.[19]

These developments occurred quite gradually, but one can date the definite ascendance of the warrior class (out of scattered groups of professional mercenaries) from the Hogen disturbance of 1156. For the first time since the Taika reforms an issue of dynastic policy involving the imperial succession was resolved by warriors playing a leading role in the center of affairs.[20]

To summarize, Japanese imperial authority emerged directly from a tribal society composed of lineage-groups. The origin-myth of direct descent from the Sun-Goddess signified the importance of the reigning emperor's religious and ceremonial functions. It also established the principle that the historical continuity of the god-descended imperial house must be preserved, lest the well-being of the whole community be endangered. Through the introduction of the Taika reforms (646) and the Taiho Code (702), the emperors achieved considerable power as well. But this imperial rule was relatively short-lived, and the reigning emperor was increasingly confined to his ceremonial and religious functions. The ascendance of the Fujiwara regents by the middle of the ninth century was directly connected with the incapacity of the court to function administratively so that real power was exercised through the household management of the regent.

By the end of the twelfth century, the Fujiwara regents were replaced in turn by the formal establishment of the Kamakura shogunate (1185–1333). From that time on, the imperial institution and the court nobility surrounding the throne in Kyoto were separated permanently from the effective military government (shogunate) in Kamakura and, later on, in Edo (Tokyo). Shogunal authority was authenticated by an imperial mandate. The shogunate derived its power from its command over the warrior class or military gentry in the provinces. This class had emerged from the privatization of land and of military force by the great landowning families. From the time of the Kamakura shogunate until the middle of the nineteenth century, the Japanese aristocracy remained divided between a nobility associated with the ceremonious life of the imperial court and a military aristocracy involved in the government and warfare of the shogunate.[21] But by the beginning of the seventeenth century, with the foundation of the Tokugawa shogunate, the political and social structure of Japan would be transformed for the next two hundred and fifty years. I will consider the Tokugawa shogunate and the Meiji restoration in Chapter 12.

HOUSEHOLD AND MILITARY GOVERNMENT AS THE BASIS OF ARISTOCRACY

The seventh and eighth centuries may be considered the formative period of the Japanese aristocracy. The ancient lineage-groups of the island constituted the ruling class. The Taiho Code (702) established four superior orders reserved for princes of the blood and ten court ranks with various subdivisions, resulting in some thirty grades altogether. High court nobles (*kugyo*), appointed by the emperor, comprised the top three ranks under the members of the imperial family. The fourth and fifth ranks constituted a second subdivision of court nobles, also appointed by the emperor. All remaining ranks were considered inferior. Members of these relatively inferior ranks were appointed by the Great Council of State rather than the emperor, and they were debarred from many important privileges.

Access to the ranks of the court nobility depended on family connections. The highest court nobles were derived from the junior branches of the imperial family and the great clans of the Yamato region. The fourth and fifth ranks drew their membership from the lesser clans and from distinguished families that had immigrated during the previous centuries. The remaining ranks were recruited from prominent provincial clans. Family origin, court rank, government position, and wealth were closely related.

The privileges accruing to the top ranks were substantial. Each court noble received a grant of rice land, and members of the first five ranks received especially generous grants. The number and size of peasant households allotted to the noble, and the taxes in kind due from them, likewise varied with his rank. Other privileges consisted of exclusive access to education, the inheritance of rank when children came of age, rigidly differentiated ceremonial dress, and permission to be present at the imperial audience, as well as such humbler accoutrements as having guards and messengers, burial privileges, and special exemptions from penalties, taxes, forced labor, and conscription. At the top of the rank-hierarchy, privileges were sumptuous indeed; but at the same time, patrician life was rigidly circumscribed down to the type of fan appropriate for each of the main rank-categories. Naturally, preoccupation with rank governed every move in this closed world of a tiny segment of Japanese society. Promotion depended almost entirely on family connections with the imperial house and the favors dispensed by the dominant faction of the Fujiwaras.

For a short period, this rank-conscious and inbred court nobility was also the administrative center of Heian Japan.[22] The Taika reforms had adopted the administrative structure of China, but not the Chinese examination system. Critics of the Chinese system have commented on its self-serving inefficiencies and the cultivation of decorous learning for its own sake. But in Japan, the substitution of birth for learning as a condition of appointment quickly turned the central administration at the imperial court into a quagmire of overlapping offices and circuitous procedures. The political function of the imperial court was shortlived, but its cultural preeminence proved lasting. In his *World of the Shining Prince,* Professor Ivan Morris has described this cultural achievement in detail. The refinement of esthetic sensibility in music and poetry and the discriminating appreciation of painting, ceramics, dress, and other decorative arts by the court nobility of Heian Japan set as distinctive a pattern for the country's culture as the divine descent of its emperors did for the legitimation of authority. For it imparted to nature-worship and to the cultivation of esthetic sensibility the very highest social prestige, a fact that has left its mark on Japanese culture to the present day.

Such cultural achievements exact their price. Esthetic sensibility and an elaborate stylization of manners became attributes of aristocratic conduct that were incompatible with the military skill and prowess usually associated with aristocracy. First in Nara and then in Kyoto military duties at court were turned into decorous ceremonies so that the capital and the court became an easy prey to military depredations emanating from the countryside (or from the Buddhist monasteries adjacent to the capital). Indeed, the demilitarization of the court was one reason why the exercise of authority slipped so quickly out of the hands of the emperor and his entourage. However, some allowance must be made for the fact that much information about Heian Japan is derived from the writings of court ladies who were not only remote from the countryside and its frequent upheavals but even from the administrative affairs at the court itself. For this reason, one may have a somewhat exaggerated picture of the political weakness of the imperial court at the height of its power.

In any case, the emperor failed to establish a patrimonial bureau-

Minamoto Yoritomo
This wood sculpture dates from the thirteenth century, shortly after Yoritomo's forces defeated the Fujiwara regents and the Taira clan. Yoritomo's victory also marked the ascendance of provincial warriors who came to be organized under the Kamakura shogunate. The legitimacy of this military government was secured by its formal subordination to the emperor. (National Museum, Tokyo)

cracy after the Chinese model. Instead, the Japanese aristocracy was formed by the feudal system established under the Fujiwara regents and the Kamakura shogunate. As the imperial house weakened, provincial society became increasingly warlike. At first, military bands were organized by local notables and they were nominally subordinate to the emperor. Then they became subject to strong shogunal authority under the Kamakura. Later they developed considerable local autonomy from the shogunate as well so that these provincial forces became as nominally subordinate to the shogun as they had earlier been to the emperor.

Under the Fujiwara regents, the new military leaders in the provinces were often men descended from prominent families of the court nobility. As the unrest in the country increased, members of the nobility had moved into the provinces to protect their lands, and the combination of formal authority and social prestige was naturally attractive to the men who had become professional fighters (*bushi*). As military forces grew in size, a new dimension was added to the traditional Japanese reliance on kinship relations: personal military service was rendered in return for a grant of land.[23] Hall adds a characteristic example of the privatization of governmental authority. When in 1088 Minamoto Yo-

The Burning of the Sanjo Palace during the Heiji Rising of 1159
A celebrated episode from the power struggle between the Fujiwara, Taira, and Minamoto clans taken from the picture scroll called the Heiji Monogatari, painted in the mid-thirteenth century. The Fujiwara and Taira families had vied with one another for acquisition of high posts in the central government and intermarriage with the imperial family. The Taira ascendancy lasted only twenty years and came to an end in the Gempei war (1180–1185) in which the Minamoto forces were victorious. This chapter of Japanese history also marked the ascendance of provincial warriors (*bushi*) and the establishment under the Minamoto of a national military hegemony (Kamakura shogunate). (Museum of Fine Arts, Boston)

shiie found himself unrewarded by the court, he used some of his own landholdings to reward his followers. This action induced other bushi to commend their land to him for protection, a development which prompted the court to prohibit such commendations (1091), albeit without success. On this basis, some families like the Taira and the Minamoto were able to build up both large landholdings in many provinces and a large following of fighting men bound to them by ties of loyalty as compensation for grants of land.[24]

The second half of the twelfth century was marked by almost continuous fighting in many parts of Japan, but the eventual military success of the Minamoto clan still had to be transformed into a legitimate political order. Minamoto Yoritomo's establishment of Kamakura as his governmental headquarters signified the clan's ascendance and independence from Kyoto. His gesture of asking the throne's approval for his actions signified his formal submission to the emperor, which did not preclude the manipulation or defiance of the throne on substantive points. Submission served to secure the legitimacy of the shogunal order at Kamakura, while the emperor lacked the military force to withhold the imperial sanction. In turn, the military gentry in the provinces were loyal vassals of the shogun at Kamakura and had to obtain his permission in all matters affecting their social and economic position.

In the model of "traditional society" used here, I have assumed that wealth, status, and authority are fused in the hands of powerful heads of households. Kingship is the most conspicuous example of such fusion. But there are societies without kingship and societies in which the king's supreme privileges are made nominal by the burdens and restrictions placed on him. When kings reign but do not rule, anarchic tendencies will militate against strong government, for it is difficult for landowning aristocracies to create a stable political order in the absence of an effective and consecrated leader. Poland and the Holy Roman Empire of the German Nation are examples, but Japan is an exception. Here we have the case of a feudal aristocracy which developed an effective government through prolonged military campaigns, resulting in the establishment of the Kamakura shogunate. As the authority of the imperial house and the power of the Fujiwara regents declined, a warrior class stepped into the breach and was led to final success by the Minamoto clan under the leadership of Minamoto Yoritomo (1147–1199).

Specific measures were taken to guard against the divisive tendencies of a feudal regime.

> The chieftain of the Minamoto clan was to be the ruler of the eastern provinces, the leader of all warriors wherever situated, and at the same time the guardian of the Throne and the protector of the state. For these reasons Yoritomo was careful to limit his relations with the aristocratic Court to formal interchanges. He was firm in his determination to make Kamakura the permanent seat of feudal government. His vassals were strictly forbidden to enter Court society or take any office from the Crown without his approval; and he himself would accept no appointment or title other than that of Commander-in-Chief (*Sei-i-Tai-Shogun*), apart from honorary military ranks.[25]

Other measures were taken to provide for a strict enforcement of authority. Under the Kamakura shogunate three special offices were created: one supervised all the affairs of the military (*samurai-dokoro*); a second handled disputes between vassals (*monchujo*); and a third was an enlarged replica of a great noble's household office (*mandokoro*) handling the private and public business of the Minamoto. These offices were put into the hands of civilian officials and run in accordance with strict official procedures; thus, even in this early phase, Japanese feudalism took over a measure of the bureaucratization which had been introduced by the Taika reforms of the seventh century. More effectively than in feudal Europe, the Kamakura shogunate exercised very close control over the personal life of the vassal, his privileges and obligations, his property and rank, and his family affairs, including marriages and friendships.

This administrative consolidation shows the success with which Yoritomo "always contended that loyalty to himself was loyalty to the Throne, and he would not tolerate any direct relation of service to the Throne by his vassals."[26] To a degree not found elsewhere, this policy reflected a social and political order in which, under titular imperial authority, the inequalities among people were organized and administered by a governor who supposed that persons of all social ranks were the dependents of his own supreme household. To be sure, personal ties to the shogun became more nominal as his authority extended over the whole country. Nevertheless, the shogun's authority retained its patriarchal character, and the offices of his household at Kamakura provided the administrative means to enforce the shogunal will.

At the top of the shogunal dependents, the honorific rank of housemen (*kenin*) was granted to leading vassals of the Minamoto. Much attention was given to their property interests. Many applicants were refused, and the rank could be revoked easily for behavior subversive of feudal discipline. Fighting men (*samurai*) ranked below the kenin in whose service they stood. Here again rank was bestowed carefully; mere fighting ability did not suffice, and the right to grant this rank belonged to the shogun rather than the immediate lord. Below the samurai, the followers or attendants were ranked by various grades, and below them were several ranks of cultivators, skilled and unskilled workers, artists, and Buddhist clergy. Relatively little is known of these people except that they were distinguished as freemen (*ryomin* or good people) from the "base people" (*semmin*) consisting of servants, slaves, and workers in despised occupations.[27]

Thus, by the thirteenth century the Kamakura shogunate had established a feudal regime noteworthy for the strength of its central government and the tight organization of feudal dependencies, an unusual case since feudal regimes are generally more decentralized. The shogunate governed under imperial sanction. Seldom were wealth, status, and effective authority fused as completely as they were in this period of Japanese history.

Yet this concentration of military and symbolic power proved fragile.[28] Where all legitimacy was concentrated in the emperor and all military and administrative power in the shogun, every succession dispute placed the whole structure in jeopardy.[d] Between 1272 and 1318, two court factions continued a dispute over succession to the imperial throne which the shogun was unable to settle. The accession of Emperor Go-Daigo (1318) brought no relief, since he attempted to restore imperial authority, culminating in the Kemmu restoration of 1334–1336. In 1337 a renewed succession dispute turned into civil war which continued until 1392, when a settlement was finally achieved. Meanwhile, some fifty years of organizing the country against the Mongol invasion threat had depleted the resources of the Kamakura shoguns, who were replaced by the Ashikaga in 1338. But order was not restored. After ending the civil wars over the succession in 1392, the Ashikaga were confronted with insubordinate warlords from one end of the country to the other. In all, Japan witnessed recurrent civil war from the 1330s until national unification was achieved late in the sixteenth century, a period of over two centuries.[29]

Little is known of the size of Japanese fighting forces before the sixteenth century. In over fifty years of civil war between contending claimants to the imperial throne (1337–1392), large bodies of men moved to and fro across the country. Circumstantial evidence suggests that in Japan, medieval warfare, though greatly disrupting the political structure, was not overly destructive. The warriors were supplied with food and arms, and there is evidence of a relatively flourishing economy. Marketplaces developed, market days were held more frequently, peasants who sold their surplus produce for cash improved their position, and the diversity and quality of crops increased. Towns grew and traffic along the highways became more frequent.

This growth of the economy was linked with the changing character of the provincial aristocracy. Specifically, the inheritance of land was changed and local government was restructured.

The strength of the Kamakura shogunate had been based in part on the practice of primogeniture. When the oldest son alone had title to the land, families could preserve their inheritance. As a result, relations became stabilized between these families and the headquarters of the shogun (bakufu). But from the late thirteenth and during the fourteenth centuries, the practice of sole inheritance was abandoned gradually, and estates were divided equally among the sons of the family. As the size of single holdings declined, the number of yeoman peasants (ji-samurai) increased as well as efforts to increase the productivity of

---

[d]A striking example is the period following Minamoto Yoritomo's death, when a titular shogun and regents acting for him appeared in Kamakura just as earlier a titular emperor, a regent, and a "cloistered emperor" had appeared simultaneously in Kyoto.

agriculture. These yeomen were of warrior descent. They did not owe allegiance to a great lord and hence were conscious of their independence in contrast to an earlier time when many peasants had "commended" their services to obtain protection.

Itinerant military forces depended on local supplies to keep moving. In specific situations, warriors might force the peasants to do their bidding. But the agrarian uprisings of the period testify to the self-confidence of the yeomen, who were determined to defend their interests by force of arms if necessary. For a time, yeomen combined in mutual defense leagues (*ikki*) and attacked landlords, moneylenders, and even local governors to obtain relief from specific debts and taxes. Nevertheless, these burdens frequently became too heavy to bear, and self-defense proved insufficient. Peasants would then escape by taking up military service. This in turn would add to the destructiveness of the civil wars by increasing the number of foot soldiers and reducing the agricultural labor force. In the late fifteenth and early sixteenth centuries, neighboring territorial rulers (*daimyo*) agreed to surrender fugitive peasants in an effort to arrest this militarization of the peasantry. On the other hand, warriors turned increasingly to the conscription of peasants as the struggle for political consolidation of the country intensified. During the Ashikaga shogunate (1338–1573), peasants appear to have regained—at least temporarily—some of their earlier independence. To understand these changing fortunes of the peasants, we must turn to the restructuring of local government and the transformation of the aristocracy.

At the summit, the imperial throne and its court nobility in Kyoto had existed side by side with the shogunal establishment and its service-aristocracy at Kamakura. The shogunal system was capable of assuming the whole burden of local government. Specifically, the Kamakura shogunate stabilized its rule by appointing Minamoto housemen to positions as military governors (*shugo*) and land stewards (*jito*) throughout the country. For a time, this network of military deputies existed alongside the local authority which was appointed by the imperial court. But gradually the military governors and land stewards of the Kamakura shogun made inroads on imperial civil authority and the proprietary rights nominally protected by that authority. By the beginning of the fourteenth century, this development had become irreversible. An attempt to restore the old imperial authority precipitated fifty years of civil war, in the course of which both the imperial civil authority and the power of the Kamakura shogunate declined. Eventually a new balance of power developed in which the weight of influence shifted once more, this time away from the center of shogunal power toward the provinces.

The local deputies of the Kamakura and, after 1338, of the Ashi-

kaga shogunates usurped the authority previously exercised by the shoguns on behalf of the emperor, by combining civil with military functions in the provinces. These local "deputies" weakened the shogunate,
because they retained local revenues and obliged the Ashigaka to depend entirely on the income and military forces drawn from the shogun's own territories. The shogunate, therefore, was confronted with a
varied assortment of provincial military governors (*shugo-daimyo*), each
with his own base of income and military force and only nominally under the authority of the shogunate. Still, the shogunate was the only
countrywide authority remaining, though it was now often forced to
establish precarious alliances with powerful provincial families. The
move of the Ashikaga shoguns from Kamakura to Kyoto was symbolic
of the new dispensation. In Kyoto, shogunal rule was unquestioned however weak it had become in the provinces, because the shogun had received the emperor's mandate. But with much of the taxing power in
the hands of the provincial governors, financial resources were now
dwindling rapidly for the shogun *and* the imperial court.

The provincial rulers exercised military and civil authority in their
area on the basis of their own extensive landholdings. When the need
arose, they would make military alliances with their own branch families
and various military vassals. But their wealth, status, and authority were
not consolidated. Though their territories were extensive, they were also
scattered. Their rights over the land varied from one location to another, often falling short of full ownership. Naturally, these provincial
rulers (shugo-daimyo) sought to enlarge their wealth and power by using military pressure, marriage alliances, and grants of land in return
for loyal service. They were often successful at the expense of absentee
proprietors, such as members of the court nobility and even of the imperial family. But these efforts at expansion and consolidation of provincial power frequently collided with the competing interests of other
provincial rulers. Since now the shogunate and the imperial court resided in Kyoto, one after another of the provincial governors sought to
strengthen his position by establishing his own residence there as well.
Provincial vendettas and armed clashes, therefore, were supplemented
by a competition for favors at the shogunal headquarters.

The imperial house, the court nobility, and the Kamakura shoguns
had earlier sent their sons, deputies, or housemen to dominate local affairs in the interest of their respective centers. Now a provincial gentry
sought to strengthen its position at the local level by manifesting its
newly won local preeminence through its presence in the capital.[30]

These developments took place in an era of unceasing civil strife in
which the shugo-daimyo were a rising power, though not in secure command. Once they had acquired legitimate title from the shogun, they

still had to enforce that sanctioned authority locally in recurrent struggles with competing claimants. In an era of conflicting rights and divided loyalties, with their scattered holdings in the hands of rear-vassals or other agents and with the scene of the struggle often shifting to Kyoto, the shugo-daimyo found themselves increasingly at the mercy of their own subordinates.

Scholars of Japanese history distinguish between the shugo-daimyo who rose to prominence roughly in the century following the Kemmu restoration (1334–1336) and the *sengoku-daimyo*, their former subordinates, who rose to prominence during the period from the Onin war (1467–1477) to Nobunaga's entry into Kyoto in 1568. Typically, the new claimants to power (sengoku-daimyo) advanced their position by ruthless exploitation of the peasants and by treacherous intervention in the succession disputes among their own masters. The two strategies were closely related. By exacting more from the peasants, these deputies and vassals increased their own fortunes, often to the point where peasants joined military bands to escape oppression. On the basis of increased wealth, the former subordinates could intervene more effectively in the disputes among their masters, the shugo-daimyo. "Every great feudal house was plagued by succession quarrels, often instigated and planned by subordinates who sought to improve their own condition."[31]

Medieval Japan thus witnessed periodic turnovers in the composition and administrative functions of its aristocracy. In a crude approximation one can speak of successive phases of this governing class and status group: (1) a conglomerate of clans; (2) the Yamato state with its first unification of Japan's central provinces; (3) the early division among imperial family, court nobility, the Soga or Fujiwara regents, and the attempted bureaucratization of imperial rule under the Taika reforms; (4) the Kamakura shogunate with its centrally controlled restoration of local clan authority; and (5) the two phases of Ashikaga rule under the shugo-daimyo and the sengoku-daimyo. Such a regrouping is a continuous process which the social historian divides into phases and categories for the sake of convenience and comprehension. Nonetheless, some changes of the historical context can be at least approximately dated.

Reference has been made to the evidence of economic advance during the fourteenth and fifteenth centuries, a development which Sansom attributes to the decline of inheritance by the oldest son (primogeniture), the rise of yeomen peasants of warrior descent, and the relatively low level of destruction in Japanese medieval warfare. How else, he asks, could the country have sustained the incessant strife of rival claimants to the throne and the continual vendettas for local supremacy among families of the provincial aristocracy? Nevertheless, a time came when the burdens of warfare began to exceed what the peasants were willing to accept as an inevitable fate. Sansom cites a major peasant uprising of 1428 in Omi, and Hall refers to another during the following year in Harima.[32] The number of such uprisings mounted during this period, and it is certain that many local incidents were unrecorded. Thus, some time before the period of 1467 to 1568, which Japanese historians designate as "the country at war" (sengoku), the earlier compatibility of civil strife with economic growth was diminishing. In the later fifteenth century, civil war interfered with the economy, though the incidence of war remained local and sporadic so that in many places trade, the arts, and agriculture continued to flourish.

By this time, measures had been taken to counteract the destructive effects of the fighting. The sengoku-daimyo found time to devote to the management of their estates, despite their recurrent preoccupation with vendettas and wars. Consolidated landholdings replaced the old administrative subdivisions. The simplification of land rights during the fifteenth century was the conscious policy of these new landlords, and while it was often accomplished by force, the policy eliminated the "long chain of privileges and claims" which had left little "for the man who tilled the soil."[33] In an effort to protect the countryside, the number of forts and castles increased rapidly. Where the shugo-daimyo had begun with a formal title to certain lands and rights which they then endeavored to free from shogunal control, the sengoku-daimyo apparently began with the forced occupation of the land and then endeavored to obtain an ex post facto legitimation of their holdings by shogunal edict.[34]

In the late fifteenth century, the sengoku-daimyo began to expand their local control from fortified headquarters, resulting in struggles for regional hegemony in many parts of Japan. Gradually, leagues of daimyo formed locally. New families rose to power whose leaders turned their vassals into a military command system, held together by oaths of allegiance. The most successful sengoku-daimyo induced their warriors to leave the land and take up residence in or around their own main estate and stronghold. Here they were ready for instant service and all the more easily controlled. As this warrior aristocracy of samurai was urbanized, peasant communities became free to develop organizations of their own and to increase their productivity. Taxes were put on a regular basis; thus, villages had an inducement to develop irrigation systems and programs of land reclamation, sometimes with and sometimes without the assistance of the local daimyo.[35]

The whole development may be summarized. In their castle-towns, the sengoku-daimyo developed a superior organization based on the strategic military placement of their strongholds. Simultaneously, the samurai were transformed from landed and dispersed warriors into an urbanized force of retainers, dependent on a rentier existence based on rice stipends, and thus instantly available for military action. Finally, the sengoku-daimyo strengthened their own direct authority over the peasants by means of land surveys which restabilized the rights to the land.

This local consolidation of power led to a prolonged period of further fighting, but by the middle of the sixteenth century the methods of consolidation were applied on a larger and eventually on a national scale. Under the leadership of Oda Nobunaga (1559–1582), Toyotomi Hideyoshi (1582–1598), and Tokugawa Ieyasu (1603–1616), the country became politically unified.[e] The chronology of unification and of changes in military technology should be kept in mind. Firearms were introduced in Japan in 1543. By 1556 some 300,000 guns were available. Nobunaga became master of Owari province in 1559. By 1560 eight great families controlled one-third of the country. By 1572 thirteen warrior families controlled two-thirds of the country. By 1582 one-third of the soldiers of the leading military contenders were gunners, and the destructiveness of long-range weapons had led to the massive construction of stone castles in locations that took advantage of the terrain. Nobunaga was assassinated in 1582, and Hideyoshi assumed power, beginning his reign with land surveys (which lasted for sixteen years) and with the great castle construction in Osaka.[36]

For the second time since the Taika reforms a thousand years earlier, all the land of Japan was placed under the direct authority of the government. Overcoming considerable resistance and evasion, Hideyoshi increased the taxed land area (roughly from 2.5 to 3.75 million acres), but also benefited the peasants by eliminating multiple rights to the same land and unpredictable exactions. Moreover, agricultural productivity was greatly increased by the gradual pacification of the country, as Hideyoshi systematically demolished the fortifications of his enemies and rewarded his followers. By shifting local ruling clans away from their original areas of dominance, he prevented the rise of new centers of opposition to his government.[f] To this must be added the famous sword hunt of 1588 which disarmed the soldier-monks and the

[e]In Japanese, the family name comes first and the given name second. Usually it is sufficient to give only the family name to identify the person concerned, but in the case of large ruling houses it is often more practical to provide only the given name, or both names, for purposes of identification. Thus, *Oda* Nobunaga, *Toyotomi* Hideyoshi, and *Tokugawa* Ieyasu are customarily referred to as Nobunaga, Hideyoshi, and Ieyasu.

[f]The assignment of the Kanto region to Tokugawa Ieyasu, away from his home base in Mikawa and Totomi, was one such move. Its effect was contrary to Hideyoshi's intention, since it enabled Ieyasu to perfect the organization of his domains and the cohesion of his followers in an entirely new area. This was the basis for his later ascendance to supreme power.

peasants, bound the latter firmly to the land, and henceforth distinguished clearly between the civilian population of peasants, merchants, and craftsmen and the military aristocracy which alone had the privilege to bear arms.[37]

All these results were achieved with much bloodshed, treachery, and murder, though like many victorious warriors before them these powerful leaders were careful to preserve the semblance of legitimate succession under the imperial throne. Through grand displays and the patronage of the arts, they reproduced as their own the refinement of taste and manners which had been cultivated for so long by the imperial house and the court nobility. Nobunaga and Hideyoshi were followed by Ieyasu as the third great unifier of Japan, who not only completed their work but also established a system of governance which endured until the Meiji Restoration of 1868. In Chapter 12, I return to this era of internal peace under the Tokugawa shogunate. For the moment, I shall summarize the preceding survey of the Japanese aristocracy in preparation for the discussion of aristocratic culture-patterns in Russia, Germany, and England.

Japanese history appears to have followed periodic phases of centralization and devolution of power. The early Yamato, Nara, and Heian periods had their phases of centralized rule under successive emperors who were soon overshadowed by the household power of the Soga and then the Fujiwara regential families. With the rise of the Kamakura shogunate in the late twelfth century, an enduring division emerged between shogunal rule and the religious and ceremonial culture of the imperial house. Effective government was centralized as it had not been even under the Taika reforms, since the vassals of the Kamakura shoguns were not granted seignorial rights to the land. Nevertheless, the power of these provincial vassals increased at the expense of the Kamakura shogunate. Under the Ashikaga, local authority was preempted first by the shugo-daimyo and subsequently by their own subvassals, the sengoku-daimyo. One puzzle is that as shogunal authority and hence personal fealty weakened, the quest for shogunal support continued. Contests for local or regional hegemony turned time and again into a competition for favors and sanctions at the Ashikaga headquarters in Kyoto—despite their reduced power. Perhaps the explanation is that throughout the history of the shogunate these military governors had been punctilious in observing the formal legitimation of their position through the emperor, and so the new provincial leaders may likewise have continued to observe the old forms of legitimation.

A second puzzle is that the society did not disintegrate. The long-standing separation between the legitimate authority of the emperor and the effective authority of the shogun, the proliferation of authoritative figures like "cloistered emperors" and regents at the center, and finally the recurring contests for military power in the provinces certainly increased the number of feuds. It could be that the very multiplicity of such feuds at so many levels helped to blunt the impact of any one of them. At any rate, tolerance for violence had a high threshold in a society in which not only aristocrats, but monks, peasants, and merchants fought to enhance their collective interests. Many ranks of the social hierarchy engaged in massive fencing matches and prevented any group from gaining the upper hand for long, except locally. Above all, there was no outside pressure which might have forced the issue or presented opportunities for forcing the issue. Japan's freedom from foreign intervention enabled the society to endure prolonged periods of civil strife just as the Tokugawa policy of exclusion (to be discussed in Chapter 12) made the political unification by force of arms into an enduring social order.

The cultivation of arts and manners by the court nobility was a symbol of the highest status from the earliest period. Recourse to arms was confined to the aristocracy in the provinces and at shogunal headquarters. High culture and militancy were two sides of the aristocratic way of life, much as emperor and shogun were two aspects of authority. The link between these two sides was maintained throughout: the shugo-daimyo established lavish residences in Kyoto, and the neglect of their home base facilitated the rise of the sengoku-daimyo who also cultivated the arts. In addition to imperial authority, shogunal sanction, and court rank, high culture legitimized aristocratic privilege through the identification of culture with the imperial court. Warfare repeatedly engulfed this cultural center of Japanese society, but each time rebuilding was resumed promptly on a more lavish scale. In the provinces, the local ascendancy of leading families was marked regularly by patronage of arts, learning, and religious establishments, despite the treachery and bloodshed which marked each road to power; indeed, such action was probably a means of atoning for these ways of the world. In Japan cultural refinement clearly did nothing to limit aggression, perhaps because the imperial center of culture was divorced from the shogunal center of authority.

4

RUSSIA

THE RISE OF THE MUSCOVITE DYNASTY

THE FIRST Russian historical source, the *Primary Chronicle,* was compiled in 1110 or 1112. The first date mentioned in the *Chronicle* is 852, and the few pages preceding this date refer to the Biblical division of the earth, the Tower of Babel, and the reputed settlement of tribes related to the early Slavs. Historical events before the ninth century must be reconstructed from scattered foreign sources and from archeological evidence. By contrast, the first chronicles of Japan were compiled in 712 and 720. In addition to a legendary history going back to 660 B.C., these Japanese accounts refer to historical events dating from about 600 A.D.

Geographically, the area of what is now modern European Russia was divided between a densely forested and rather primitive region in the north and an economically more developed region in the south where agriculture and various handicrafts were practiced and remained virtually unchanged until the later medieval period. There is archeological evidence that towns of the ninth century like Tver', Novgorod, or Kiev go back to earlier and smaller settlements. The most important of these settlements were located on the main rivers and were also markets for overland trade. The bulk of the population was rural, divided into settled, agricultural and nomadic, pastoral peoples who lived uneasily side by side. There was no discernible political structure for the whole area; rather, there were instances of tributary dependence of certain peoples on a more powerful state, such as the Khazar Khanate in the area northeast of the Black Sea.

The *Primary Chronicle* refers to such tributary dependence in its account of the establishment of the Russian state. Scandinavian traders had been active along the Russian rivers, and by 862 these Varangians were well-established in the trading and military communities which had sprung up. The *Chronicle* tells a half-legendary story that Slavic and other tribes around Novgorod managed to expel the Varagians to whom they had been paying tribute. But when internal discord ensued, the tribes invited new rulers from Scandinavia. In 862 Rurik, the founder of the new dynasty, became prince of Novgorod.

A state controlled by these Norsemen seems to have existed in northwestern Russia for some time prior to 862. A mission representing a people who called themselves Rhos appeared in Constantinople in 839, but members of the mission described themselves as Swedes. The emissaries offered the Byzantine emperor a treaty of friendship but asked for protection on their way home, which suggests that they represented a state to the north but had not yet subdued the south. By 860 a Russian army under Scandinavian leadership appeared at the gates of Constantinople. In the interval between the two dates, the Norsemen seem to have overcome the resistance of Slavic tribes and other peoples dwelling along the Dnieper.

The account of the *Chronicle* and even the existence of Rurik have been questioned, but part of the account has a factual basis. In the early Russian principalities,

> commercial and military cities . . . controlled the adjoining territories. . . . The Norsemen played an important part both in the promotion of trade and in the creation of the city-states. Since the slave trade and the collection of tribute were among the functions of the new ruling group, it was only natural that relations with the populations under its control should lead to conflict. The leadership of the merchant soldiers in the struggle against the neighboring tribes and the nomads of the steppes might . . . have made their harsh rule more palatable. Moreover, the Varangians not infrequently made their first appearance as hired defenders against the outside enemy. Nevertheless, the abuse of power . . . could not but result in occasional popular uprisings against the oppressors. It is probable that it was one of these occurrences that led to the expulsion of the Varangians from Novgorod and to the subsequent arrival of a new group of Norsemen. . . .[1]

In this interpretation, the main function of the Scandinavian overlords was the promotion of trade and the defense of territories from their base in the main towns. Both functions probably account for the rising importance of Kiev, from where trade to the south could be defended against various Asiatic tribes.

The protection of trade and the exaction of tribute from the subject population were probably indistinguishable from unprovoked raids and the distribution of booty as a means of organizing campaigns. There is little doubt that the early Kievan princes engaged in concerted military expeditions to extend their domain, which reached for a time from the Khazars in the east to the Bulgars in the west and the Patzinacs in the south. Murderous struggles over the succession together with almost constant campaigning made princely authority precarious. The testament of Vladimir II (Monomakh, 1113–1125) refers to a grand total of eighty-three major campaigns in which he participated during his life. And according to one calculation, wars occurred during eighty out of one hundred and seventy years following the death of Yaroslav the Wise in 1054.[2]

The Kievan principality lasted roughly from the late ninth to the middle of the thirteenth century. It was a precarious political structure not only for the reasons cited, but also because tradition called for the division of the realm among members of the Rurik dynasty under the nominal leadership of the Grand Prince of Kiev. Kievan Russia as a whole included such towns and territories as Polotsk, Pskov, Novgorod, Suzdal, Smolensk, and Vladimir. The rather large number of towns reflects the significance of long-distance trade. The route went from the north along the rivers to Kiev, and beyond to the Byzantine empire at Constantinople and other areas of the Middle East. The treaties between Kiev and Byzantium attest to the importance of this trading relationship. There is also independent evidence of pasturage and agriculture as well as of trade in agricultural products.

By the eleventh century, the prosperity of Kievan Russia began to decline, in part because the international trade routes from Europe to Byzantium shifted away from the Russian rivers toward the Italian cities and the Mediterranean. To this must be added the wholesale destruction of Kievan Russia at the hands of the Mongols during the thirteenth century and the prolonged subjection of the area to Mongol overlordship thereafter. The Russian territories became a physically remote and economically backward area, as some of the towns lost their earlier economic prominence. Only Novgorod remained an important principality under an urban patriciate. These major transformations bear on the eventual emergence of the Muscovite dynasty. But before explaining that emergence, something more needs to be said concerning princely authority and social rank in Kievan Russia as a forerunner of later institutional developments.

One speaks of Kievan Russia and Kievan society, but not of a Kievan state. The country consisted of some ten principalities (including the patrician city-state of Novgorod) named after their major towns which became princely residences. In each of these territories of Kievan Russia, a prince exercised personal rule, he was the chief judge and military leader, and he collected tribute to maintain order and defend his realm. The princely domains were managed by his servants, while retainers of high status administered the principality. The army organization of Kievan Russia shows a social division among these retainers. One group consisted of individual warriors who were princely servitors, another of landed notables of considerable influence who brought their own armed following with them when they joined the prince in his military campaigns. Both groups consisted of men enjoying high status, but there was already some difference between the service obligations of the first

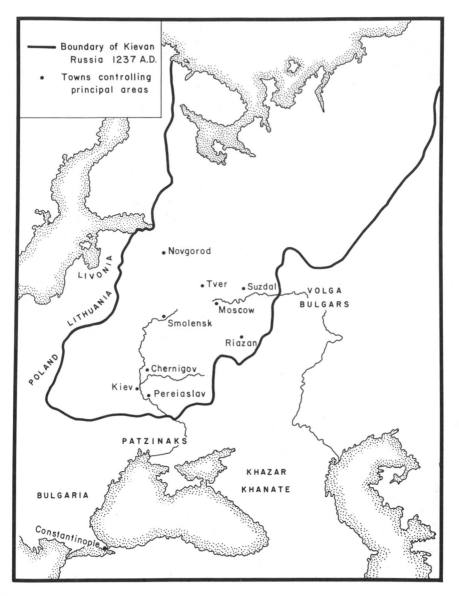

Boundary of Kievan
Russia 1237 A.D.
Towns controlling
principal areas

Novgorod

LIVONIA

Tver • Suzdal

LITHUANIA

Moscow

VOLGA
BULGARS

Smolensk

POLAND

Riazan

Chernigov

Kiev •
Pereiaslav

PATZINAKS

KHAZAR
KHANATE

BULGARIA

Constantinople

4. Russia in the Kievan Period

and the greater independence of the second group, a difference which became much more marked later on. The second rank of Kievan society (*liudi*) was formed by the prominent merchants and artisans of the towns. These people were important for the trade with Byzantium and the Middle East, and their number was considerable. The bulk of the population consisted of peasants (*smerdy*). Most of them were originally freemen, but many became clients because they needed protection, or slaves due to indebtedness.

Political institutions corresponded to this rank-hierarchy of Kievan society. The retainers of the prince served him in an official capacity; their functions included dispute settlement, administration, and military campaigns. But princely government also had to come to terms with local political institutions, such as councils of notables which resembled the councils of elders or heads of households we have encountered in the case of Germanic tribes and of Arab nomads. In practice, such councils (*veche*) assembled mostly in the towns, their importance increasing primarily when princely rule weakened. The later councils of landed notables (*boyar duma*) probably also developed out of the tribal councils. The prince could call on the veche or boyar duma for aid and advice when he considered such action expedient. Like other autocratic rulers,

Russian Town Assemblies
Town assemblies or *veche* played an important role in Kievan Russia and after 1240 in the city-republic of Novgorod. This fourteenth-century woodcut shows the substantial citizens being summoned by bell to a meeting of the *veche*. The importance of these town assemblies declined with the rise of Muscovite autocracy. (New York Public Library)

a Kievan prince had ways of assuring that the good will of the assembled notables was forthcoming, but he still depended on them for assistance in raids, military campaigns, and special contributions. This dependence is reflected in the *Primary Chronicle*, which praises good and denounces bad princes:

> The good prince reveres law and justice and establishes his administration along these lines. The bad prince . . . neglects the administration and lets his agents plunder the people. To prevent misrule the prince must rely on the advice of experienced "councillors"—that is, on the council, or Duma, of the boyars. . . . This amounts to a mild approval of the aristocratic element in government.[3]

Customary practices rather than formal rights were the basis of cooperation among prince, boyars, and merchants. It may be added that the town meetings (*veche*) of freemen came to play an important role in the later history of Novgorod.

The conversion of Kievan society to Greek Orthodox Christianity was a gradual process that is impossible to separate from the foreign relations and the political ideas of the period. Georgia and Armenia had been among the first Christian states, and Christian missions were active in the Crimea and the Khazar Khanate from an early time. We also have a record of a Greek Orthodox mission to Kievan Russia in the ninth century. The area was subject to many religious influences, and paganism was clearly on the wane.

> In the nine-eighties Russia was surrounded by nations of Christian, Jewish, and Moslem faith. The Khazars had been converted to Judaism around 865; the Volga Bulgars accepted Islam in 922. Simultaneously, Christianity made rapid progress among Russia's western neighbors.
>
> In the period between 942 and 968 several tribes of the Baltic Slavs were converted; in 966 Prince Mieszko of Poland was baptized and in 974 King Harold Blotand of Denmark. Olaf Trygvasson, king of Norway since 955, had become a Christian in 976. In 986 Duke Geza of Hungary accepted the faith.[4]

In the middle of the tenth century, the Kievan princess Olga (945–964) converted to the Greek Orthodox faith, though only after she had ceased to be regent. Before her conversion, however, she had sent requests for missionaries not only to Constantinople but also to the German emperor, Otto I (936–973). Apparently she sought terms from Constantinople or Rome that would favor an autonomous Russian church. Later exploratory missions examined both Islam and the Judaism of the Khazars.

The final conversion of Kievan Russia to the Greek Orthodox faith occurred under the rule of Vladimir (978–1015). At the time, the Byzantine emperor Basileios (976–1025) appealed for Kievan aid in his simultaneous struggle against the Bulgars in the west and the claims of Bordas Phokas, a rival emperor within Byzantium. Vladimir agreed to help on condition that Anna, the sister of the Byzantine emperor, would become his wife. This condition was granted, provided that Vladimir would convert to the Greek Orthodox faith. Vladimir was baptized in 988. For Kievan Russia, the marriage alliance with Byzantium meant an important gain in its foreign relations and henceforth Greek Orthodox influence was established in Russia.

The towns of Kievan Russia were the first to convert to the Orthodox faith, while for some centuries the people in the countryside remained pagan. Nevertheless, the spread of the faith and a certain amalgamation of Christian and pagan practices were favored by the circumstances of Christianization. Cyril (826–869) and Methodius (815?–885), the first Byzantine missionaries to the Slavs, had translated the Bible and the church service into Church Slavonic. Unlike the Western church with its insistence on Latin, the Orthodox church presented the Slavs with a gospel and liturgy which many people could understand. More importantly, the conversion of the Slavs began at a time when the period of the great controversies had ended.[a] Thus, the main Christian doctrines came to Russia in their definitive form. As a result, the Orthodox church and its members took on the obligation of preserving unchanged the original Doctrine of the Lord as a spiritual treasure which must not be blemished or diminished in any way; Orthodoxy did not encourage preaching, doctrinal disputes, or theological speculation. Illiteracy as well as ignorance of doctrine were widespread among the clergy, especially in its lower ranks; but this did not matter because the proper ritual of worship by itself was at the heart of Russian religiosity. Since church and people believed that they possessed the only true faith, it was sufficient to practice that faith as the ritual of the church prescribed. In this sense, the orthodox faith became identified as the culture of the whole people.

What bearing did Greek Orthodox influence have on princely (and later tsarist) authority? Francis Dvornik has examined the documentary evidence regarding the Byzantine conception of kingship which was part of the Greek Orthodox faith and its doctrinal elaborations.

[a]The reference is to the great church councils of the early Middle Ages. The council of Nicaea of 325 was mentioned in Chapter 2, and seven councils followed (Constantinople, 381; Ephesus, 431; Chalcedon, 451; Constantinople, 553, 680–681; Nicaea, 787; Constantinople, 869–870). At these councils major doctrinal issues were resolved dealing with the nature of Christ, the divinity of the Holy Spirit, and the proper worship of images. Such heresies as Arianism, Nestorianism, and others were condemned. Though other councils followed which dealt with issues of doctrine and church organization, these eight early councils defined the basic tenets of Christianity.

The main ideas of Byzantine political philosophy are clearly set out . . . by the representatives of the Byzantine Church: The Emperor is appointed by God as master of the Universe, he represents Christ on earth, his duty is not only to take care of earthly things, but above all, of heavenly things. Like Christ, he has to go after the strayed sheep—the heretics and sinners—and bring them back to the fold of the Church. . . . As a representative of God, he has to take care of the Church, convoke the councils of bishops, confirm their decrees and enforce their application to the life of the faithful.[5]

The documents containing these and related ideas became available in Slavonic translations, beginning in the ninth century. They extolled the divine nature, if not the divinity, of the all-powerful ruler, enjoined utter obedience on all his subjects, and explained tyrannical rule as just punishment sent by the Lord God who was angered by the people's sins. The Kievan clergy (many of them Greek monks) espoused the idea that the Byzantine emperor (not the patriarch of Constantinople) was the representative of God on earth—that is, the supreme legislator for the Christian commonwealth and the protector of the church. Members of the clergy also wrote idolizing biographies of the Kievan princes. The admonition that "the true ruler is one who governs himself and is not a slave of his passions" even had an oddly Confucian ring.[6]

The Kievan princes accepted the ecclesiastical supremacy of the Byzantine emperor and allowed the adoption of Orthodox canon law, actions which satisfied the Byzantine rulers. There is also some indication of compromise concerning church affairs between Kiev and Byzantium. Occasionally, a native Russian priest rather than a Greek prelate would be appointed to the office of metropolitan, as the chief dignitary of the Kievan church was called, though all appointees required final approval from Constantinople. But this arrangement was not a token of political or even ecclesiastical submission. The Kievan princes were not the vassals of the Byzantine emperor, and even though they acknowledged his religious supremacy, Byzantium allowed for considerable ecclesiastical decentralization.

The Byzantine and Orthodox outlook of the Kievan clergy made them partisans of ecclesiastical and political unity, while the equal division of inheritance adhered to by the Kievan princes made for territorial fragmentation. From the beginning, the Russian Orthodox church lacked that institutional independence which made the Catholic church such a formidable counterweight to secular rulership in Western Europe. In keeping with Byzantine example, though contrary to Kievan practice, Russia's Orthodox church gave ideological support to autocratic rule over a unified realm, and Orthodox doctrine demanded the subordination of all clerics to the prince as the secular ruler. But Kievan practices of inheritance encouraged political fragmentation. The clerical spokesmen of the Orthodox church probably played no political role in Kievan Russia.[7]

In the thirteenth century, sporadic raids from the steppes became a concerted drive. The Russian territories were conquered by the Mongols, central Asian tribesmen who had initiated their transcontinental conquests in 1215 with the seizure of Peking. A mere eight years later, the Mongols defeated a Russian force at the Battle of Kalka (1223), northeast of the Crimea. This battle appeared as just another engagement with the nomads of the steppe; there had been many such engagements in the past. The rise of the Mongol empire was unknown in Russia. Fourteen years later (1237/38), however, the Mongols conquered all the Russian principalities, beginning in the northeast and fanning out toward the west and south. Kiev was sacked in 1240, and its prominence declined thereafter. The westward march of the Mongols came to a halt in Hungary in 1241, not because superior forces opposed them, but because the Great Khan had died and the Mongol commanders broke off their campaign. Henceforth, all Russian princes were obliged to pay obeisance and tribute to the Khan of the Golden Horde, in his capital of Sarai.

Mongol overlordship over the Russian principalities meant the collection of tribute and the use of these territories as a buffer zone against Lithuania and the Teutonic Order in the West. This political situation is illustrated by reference to the principalities of Vladimir and Novgorod, located in the center of European Russia. In 1240, when Kiev fell to the Mongols, Prince Alexander of Vladimir defeated the Swedes at the Neva in the north and came to be known as Alexander Nevski. Two years later, the leading families (boyars) of Novgorod asked Alexander's aid, and he successfully defended the city against the Livonian Knights of the Sword, an affiliate of the Teutonic Order. (The embattled condition of the Russian principalities on their western frontiers is indicated by a calculation of two Soviet specialists: between 1142 and 1466 Novgorod fought the Swedes twenty-six times, the Lithuanians fourteen times, the German knights eleven times, and the Norwegians five times.[8]) This victory over the Catholic crusaders from the West was achieved at the price of submission to the Mongol infidels in the East. Alexander seems to have justified this choice as necessary for the preservation of Russian Orthodoxy, which had less to fear from the Mongols than from the Catholicism of the Teutonic Order. Alexander's defense of his inherited territories against attacks from the West served Mongol interests as well, and in 1252 the Mongol overlord conferred the title of Grand Prince of Vladimir on Alexander Nevski. (That title had been used for centuries to designate supremacy over other Russian princes). The political price of this ascendance and of defending the Orthodox church against Catholicism was great. When Alexander was installed as Grand Prince, his brothers rose against him and were defeated with the help of Mongol troops.

Novgorod occupied a special position. Throughout the Mongol period, the city controlled five provinces in northwestern Russia. Its autonomy as a major commercial center was protected by the Mongols, because the city served them not only with its own tribute but as a collector of taxes from the subject population. Yet in 1257, fifteen years after he had successfully defended the city against incursions from the West, Alexander Nevski forced the boyars, at the request of the khan, to accept the tax survey drawn up by Mongol officials. This measure obviously was designed to curb tax evasion and reduce the pocketing of taxes by Novgorod notables. The local autonomy of Russia's most important city-state was curtailed at a time when Western European towns were successfully expanding their local jurisdiction.

Alexander Nevski's position was typical of the Russian princes under Mongol rule. All their territories were caught between the contending powers of East and West. Economic decline was aggravated by the payment of tribute to the Mongol overlords which made money scarce and by sporadic raids from the steppe which threatened the trade routes.[9] Territorial aggrandizement and struggles over inheritance existed in Russia as they did everywhere else. But in Russia such conflicts among princely families were especially hazardous, because foreign powers like the Mongols in the East and Poland and Lithuania in the West used the conquest of Russian territories to resolve their own internal conflicts.

The resulting political situation was precarious for the Russian princes. Internal peace in a territory was only as secure as a ruler could make it by utilizing his military forces and political opportunities. Initial success would attract people in search of security; they would add to the sparse rural labor force, increase the ruler's resources, and thus indirectly help him provide more security for his people. Marriage alliances among the ruling families also could extend peace over a larger territory. On the other hand, disputes over inheritance among the heirs of a ruling house increased the likelihood of armed conflict. Inheritance might be governed by the rule of "lateral succession," according to which the title of grand prince (instead of passing to the son) passed from the incumbent to his oldest brother, or if he was deceased to the second oldest brother, and so on. Alternatively, the inheritance might be divided among the sons, as in Moscow where the title of prince and authority over the principality went to one son, while the other sons received only land to maintain them and no authority (*appanage*). Rival claimants proliferated under both systems and aggravated divisive tendencies unchecked by family solidarity.[10]

Geographically, the open-steppe frontier in the east and south also made strong princely rule difficult. Where settlement was sparse, transportation difficult, and the border areas subject to marauding nomads, the hereditary owners of land had to be self-sufficient to survive, and only emergencies induced them to band together. Early documentation is fragmentary, but by the eleventh century the ruling princes and leading notables of Kievan Russia possessed large landholdings. Their rights of hunting, grazing, and fishing as well as their rights to the land were hereditary (*votchina*). (The Russian term for patrimony, *votchina*, means the same as allodial holdings in Western Europe. Marc Bloch defines the latter term as "a holding absolutely free, over which no superior had rights, which owed dues or services to no one, the possession of which involved no loyalty or obedience to any individual.")[11] There were also estates granted on condition of service (later called *pomestie*). The distinction between the two types of holdings was to play a large role in the development of the Russian aristocracy, but neither of these titles to land was tied to the exercise of authority on behalf of the ruler. The hereditary landowners under a ruling prince could terminate their service without loss of property, in part because their local power was entirely personal rather than political. As the number of appanage princes increased, so did the number of hereditary notables (*boyars*) who left the service of one prince for that of another. In the period of appanage principalities after 1240, the division of property among the legitimate heirs of ruling princes prevailed over efforts at territorial and political consolidation.[b]

The ease with which boyars could change their allegiance was reflected lower down in the social hierarchy by the relative freedom of the peasantry. Large numbers of freeholders lived in village communities of their own, beholden only to the princely ruler. Aristocratic landown-

---

[b]The division of property by princely families and the freedom of hereditary landowners went hand-in-hand, just as later on political consolidation depended in good part on increasing the number of pomestie estates. But the heirs of votchina estates, originally belonging to princes, appanage princes, and boyars, continued their claims to superior status compared with the heirs of servitors who at one time had held pomestie estates, long after the former had lost their earlier independence and freedom of movement by having come under the protection of the rising Muscovite dynasty. The prestige distinction between the owners of votchina and pomestie estates continued to divide the Russian aristocracy until the late seventeenth century, although by then that distinction had often become a genealogical fiction.

ers relied on a work force of slaves or of persons who had become dependent due to debts or the need for protection. Peasants could better their condition by seeking their fortunes elsewhere, although usually they could do so only with the aid of another landlord, who would offer easier terms and/or pay off the peasant's obligations.[12] This relative freedom of movement by many peasants was facilitated by the scarcity of agricultural labor in the remoter areas and hence by the chance to escape there, or by the interest of landowners in attracting peasants to their estates.[c] While the details of this picture are unclear, there is some evidence that during the Kievan period and for some time after the thirteenth century, both landlords and peasants enjoyed a degree of independence which was the counterpart of weak princely rule. In later years, that freedom acquired a powerful symbolic appeal.

The organization, but not the ideology, of the Orthodox church also increased the difficulties of political consolidation. In all clerical affairs, the church depended on decisions by the head of the church, the patriarch of Constantinople. He alone could confirm the metropolitan, the highest single dignitary of the Russian church. But in a country fragmented by rival princely families, the appointment of the metropolitan became an issue of political importance. Every Russian ruler was interested in having a priest from his realm appointed head of the Russian church so that the religious authority of the metropolitan would be physically and symbolically present in his domain. For example, Lithuanian and other west Russian rulers sought to promote their political aims by urging the appointment of a metropolitan from their areas, sometimes under the threat of converting to Catholicism if their demands were rejected. Under these conditions, almost every new appointment of a metropolitan accentuated the political divisions of the country.[13] At the same time, the Russian church was ideologically the foremost advocate of political unity under one dynasty. The church was the repository of Russia's religious culture. It was also a promoter of trade: a statute of Grand Prince Vladimir (980–1015) regularized the tithes to be paid to the church and made the bishops responsible for the supervision of weights and measures.[14]

How, then, did the Muscovite rulers gradually achieve a political and military ascendance over rival principalities and eventually succeed in establishing a unified state? Under Mongol leadership, superiority of rank among the Russian princes depended on the title of grand prince,

---

[c]Note in this connection that peasants could seek greater freedom only under another and more lenient lord, rather than by moving into the towns as the peasants did in Western Europe.

conferred by the Mongol khans at Sarai. On the death of an incumbent, a charter (*yarlyk*) had to be obtained at the Mongol court by the prince who was next in the line of succession. Every grand prince returning from Sarai with the khan's confirmation did so in the company of a Mongol plenipotentiary and of Mongol troops which guaranteed his investiture and helped to support the new incumbent against his Russian enemies. Accordingly, the relative position of Russian rulers depended on the success with which they maneuvered against each other at the Mongol court. The Russian word *pchelobitie* which means both petition and "forehead beating" gives an apt description of Russian efforts to obtain favors from their Mongol overlords. The later Muscovite empire applied similar practices to conquered territories of its own.

Like other conquerors, the Mongols fostered internal divisions among the Russian princes, but the Mongols also had some interest in political stability. They wanted at least enough stability to secure payments of tribute to themselves and to preserve the defensive capability of the Russian princes against attacks from the West. The Mongol rulers did not have "a policy": they had to contend with their own internal divisions. But the effect of their actions was to allow the Russians to pursue their own political practices, even when these led to territorial consolidation, as in the case of Moscow.

In the later thirteenth century, Mongol rulers permitted the consolidation of territories and a measure of prosperity in two principalities: Moscow and Tver'. Both cities were located near trade routes and waterways, while forests, marshes, and rivers protected them against enemy attacks. Since much trade had shifted to the Mediterranean and raids on Russian territories increased, many people migrated into the sparsely settled areas around Moscow and Tver' in search of more security, and their presence contributed to the prosperity of the two areas. In the fourteenth century, Tver' was in the ascendance and the Mongol rulers tended to support Moscow, probably to maintain a balance between the two.[15] That support was increased when the princes of Tver' appeared to lean toward an alliance with Lithuania. In 1327 Ivan Kalita of Moscow gained support at Sarai by denouncing Tver' and returned with a Mongol army that razed the cities of Tver' to the ground. Thereupon the Mongols began to sponsor the Russian principality of Suzdal' as a new counterweight to Moscow. But the mounting threat of eastward expansion on the part of Lithuania made it appear important to support Moscow's defense against the West. While Ivan Kalita's reign (1325–1341) was marked by subservience to the Mongol rulers, shortly before his death Ivan secured the khan's endorsement of his will, which reserved the title of grand prince to Moscow. From then on, only the heirs of the Muscovite rulers could claim the grand-princely title.[16] Ivan had turned his opportunities as principal collector of tribute for the Mongols into permanent political gain.

Moscow's rise and Mongol sponsorship of the Russian church were also closely connected. The Mongol overlords exempted the Orthodox church from taxation, protected its property, and avoided religious persecution, policies which allowed the church to support autocracy and political consolidation. Mongol charters (*yarlyki*) were granted to the metropolitan of the church, and the wealth of the church increased enormously after the 1270s. Since pious gifts of territorial holdings to the church were legally protected, church lands were at peace, and this attracted agricultural laborers. Secular landowners lost peasants because they lacked comparable privileges. One can infer that the Mongols sought to obtain the support of the church so as to counteract anti-Mongol sentiments and to limit the political and economic power of the secular rulers. It is possible that the church appeared as a safe ally since it commanded no military forces of its own. Yet by enriching and protecting the church, the Mongols aided an organization that was inviolable in the eyes of the Russian people.

The church transcended political boundaries and by its spiritual sanctions was capable of aiding the political unification of the country. After the Mongols had razed Kiev once more in 1299, Maximus, the metropolitan of the Russian church, removed his supreme office from Kiev to Perejaslavl in the north. Perejaslavl then came into the possession of the princes of Moscow through inheritance. This accidental identification of the church with Moscow was followed during the early fourteenth century by maneuvers which involved the princes of Moscow, Tver', and Volhynia, their rival nominees for the position of metropolitan, several patriarchs at Constantinople, and the Mongol rulers.[17] By 1328 the head of the Russian Orthodox church had firmly sided with the Muscovite rulers, and this identification of the church with Moscow was sanctioned by the Mongol khans at Sarai.

The late fourteenth and fifteenth centuries witnessed a temporary decline of Mongol power, a major Lithuanian expansion toward the east, then a new consolidation of Mongol rule. At the same time, there were mounting internal struggles within Moscow, Tver', and several other Russian principalities. With these complex developments, the political and military fortunes of the Muscovite rulers were repeatedly at a low ebb. In 1368, 1370, 1372, 1382, and 1408, Moscow itself was beleaguered or conquered. But the fifteenth century saw the ascendance of Moscow. The city's advantageous location, Ivan Kalita's maneuvers at the Mongol court, and the identification of the Orthodox church with Muscovite rule contributed to Moscow's success. Lithuanian expansion toward the east drew to a close and Mongol interference in Russian affairs declined.[d] The exploitation of these international opportunities was the work of Ivan III (1462–1505).

Perhaps it is easiest to contrast princely authority in Kievan Russia and its successor principalities under the Mongols with the imperial institution in Japan. The Japanese emperor was initially the first among several heads of major clans, all of whom performed the ritual ceremonies and sacrifices of ancestor worship. This native religious culture continued uninterrupted for centuries. Although the emperor lost his governmental powers rather early, native legend ascribed divine descent to him and his successors, and he continued to retain his religious functions. This fundamental continuity may be one reason why the Japanese imperial court could provide the country with cultural leadership of a high order, even when the Yamato dynasty adapted the ancient and highly sophisticated model of China. The cultural influence of Japanese kingship remained very great throughout, although the emperor's secular authority virtually disappeared.

Contrast this position with that of the Russian princes before the ascendance of the Muscovite dynasty. Originally, they were conquerors from Scandinavia who vanquished Slavic and other tribes and rose to prominence as traders and defenders against nomadic attacks from the east and south. Even though the permanent settlement of these Norse conquerors led to their assimilation, the contrast to Japanese rulership remains. In the Russian case, princely authority was based on conquest and for a time there was little cultural affinity between rulers and ruled, since the Norsemen came from a different native tradition. In Russia as in the West, the chronicles recounting early historical events are clearly separated from the creation myths and legends which reflect tribal cultural conditions. By contrast, the earliest Japanese records blend the creation myths of their tribal past with the chronicle of historical events so that the Japanese emperors seem to emerge from among the native clans. This continuity of the Japanese tradi-

---

[d]Mongol raids into Russian territories continued during the fifteenth century and later, but by then the power of the original Mongol conquerors was diminished. Competing successor-states of the Mongols developed in the southern and eastern frontier regions of the Russian territories. These were composed of remnants of the Golden Horde and of Russian peasants who sought their fortunes away from their homeland because of its conditions of mounting servitude. Accordingly, Mongol overlordship was superseded by several Mongol and Cossack border states, which posed a threat from time to time but were too divided to dominate the Russian rulers as the Mongol khans had done. (See Günther Stökl, *Russische Geschichte*, pp. 173–4, and the same author's *Die Entstehung des Kosakentums* [vol. 3 of Veröffentlichungen des Osteuropainstituts; Munich: Isar Verlag, 1953]. The latter work contains an analysis of the social structure of these "frontier societies.")

tion differs from the adoption of Christianity by Grand Prince Vladimir of Kiev in 987 or 988, which represented a break with native traditions.

Preaching the Christian doctrine in Kievan Russia was so difficult that the Christian faith itself was transformed. As elsewhere, the people had their own pagan beliefs and no background for understanding the new message. In addition, all the higher clergy and some of the lower clergy were Greeks whose command of Russian was imperfect. Vladimir and his successors embarked on campaigns to spread the new faith. They destroyed pagan images and proceeded to build churches. When persuasion did not work, the mission was accomplished by fire and sword, which occasionally led to popular uprisings but more often to a quiet submission. Among the masses, paganism and Christianity existed side by side for centuries. Illiterate village priests encouraged this blending of different creeds, since their income derived in good part from offerings to miracle-working icons and to the charismatic remnants of Christian saints. The worship of holy images helps to account for the fact that the Russian church became the repository of popular feeling and culture despite forced conversions, the influence of alien clerics, and the great wealth of ecclesiastical institutions.[e]

Relations between royal authority and the church in Russia differed strikingly from those in Western Europe. The head of the Russian church, the metropolitan, was nominated and consecrated by the patriarch of Constantinople. All the Russian principalities constituted a single church domain, subdivided into a number of dioceses, each headed by a bishop. Each diocese extended into several principalities and was consequently large. Each bishopric was a highly prized office within the gift of the princes, though requiring confirmation by the metropolitan. Bishops were entitled to a special tax from the population and to a variety of fees which the lower clergy had to pay in return for their privileged functions. In addition, judicial fees accrued from the church's jurisdiction not only in ecclesiastical matters but in all cases involving people residing on church estates. Some metropolitans and bishops even supplemented their income by lending money at high interest. The church became very wealthy, especially when Mongol protection made it a haven of peace amid devastation, but the church remained subordinate to secular rule. This subordination was symbolized by a fairly common practice going back to the twelfth century. Princes and wealthy boyars would seek eternal peace by taking monastic vows toward the end of

[e]To an observer outside the Greek Orthodox tradition, the worship of images may appear as a survival of pagan practices. However, in the Greek Orthodox view, images are literally believed to represent the holy.

their lives, often only a few hours before death. Clerical writers then embellished the practice in their accounts, providing the most notable Russian rulers with a retrospective sanctification of their secular authority.[18] The princely rulers of Russia thus derived their authority directly from God and did not look elsewhere for their mandate to rule. But they and their entourages were Christians who were well aware of the discrepancy between autocratic practice and the Ten Commandments. Monastic vows a few hours before death provided Russian rulers with spiritual legitimation as an afterthought.

This was not the pattern in Western Europe. In the early centuries of the Christian era, the bishops of Rome had favored theocracy in order to strengthen political order in a disturbed period. Converted Germanic chieftains needed support against followers who still adhered to pagan beliefs of blood-right and charismatic lineage. But after the consecration of the Carolingian ruler Pepin in 751, the church began to elaborate its doctrine of the king as a Christian prince who was under the law and obliged to protect the church and abide by its edicts in ecclesiastical matters. Though in later years the line dividing secular from clerical jurisdiction was much disputed, there was no ambiguity about the ambitions of the church. As Pope Gelasius stated in his letter of 496 to Emperor Anastasius I,

> There are two things, most august emperor, by which this world is chiefly ruled: the sacred authority of the priesthood, and the royal power. Of these two, the priests carry the greater weight, because they will have to render account in the divine judgment even for the kings of men.[19]

This doctrine differed from the Orthodox emphasis on the supremacy of the emperor, as did the political circumstances of the Christian mission in the West and in Russia.

When Vladimir converted to Orthodoxy late in the tenth century, Byzantium was beset by enemies, and the separation (in 1054) between the patriarchate in Constantinople and the papacy in Rome was at hand. In the preceding centuries, the Roman popes had been a spiritual and organizational force, but until the eighth century there was no imperial force to back them up. The papacy in Rome favored royal authority in order to combat paganism and attempted to politically circumscribe that authority primarily through alliance with its opponents. By contrast, the

Patriarch blesses the Tsar on a Dais before St. Basil's Cathedral
This ceremony marks the beginning of a holiday in the Russian Orthodox church. Though the tsar is shown bending down before the patriarch, the tsar was in practice superior to the hierarchy of the church. Only a patriarch acceptable to the tsar could become head of the Orthodox church. (Olearius, *Voyages* (1662))

Byzantine state and the Greek Orthodox church had been united under the leadership of the emperor. To the Byzantine empire, Russia was important as a potential ally against its many enemies, and to the patriarchate of Constantinople Russia was part of its religious domain and a source of revenue. Byzantine political and clerical interests converged as they had not in the West. State and church favored Russian unity.

After the conversion of Vladimir in the tenth century, the Russian church remained formally subordinate to the patriarchate of the Greek Orthodox church in Constantinople. The metropolitan of the Russian church had to be confirmed by the Byzantine patriarch, and Greeks rather than Russians predominated among the metropolitans appointed in this manner. The Byzantine empire weakened under the onslaught of the Ottoman Turks, and by the early fifteenth century the empire was reduced to the environs of Constantinople and the Peleponnesian peninsula of Greece. The predominance of the patriarchate also declined. The final breach between the Russian church and the patriarchate in Constantinople occurred in 1448 when a synod of Russian bishops elected a new metropolitan of the Russian church. Efforts to obtain patriarchal confirmation were delayed and came to nothing after Constantinople was conquered by the Turks in 1453. Thereafter, heads of the Russian church were elected by a synod of Russian bishops provided the candidate was acceptable to the grand prince of Moscow. The independence of the Russian church from the patriarchate and the unity of church and state under the overlordship of the Muscovite rulers were accomplished facts by the middle of the fifteenth century.

PRINCES, BOYARS, AND TSARIST SERVITORS

Aristocrats have usually possessed prestige and wealth. Their privileges consist in a title of nobility, freedom from taxation, and special rights associated with the control of land. Aristocrats also constitute a hierarchy of honor in which different degrees or ranks are marked by special insignia, the right to bear arms, and the preemption of activities that are believed to confer prestige. A good many of these marks of prestige (though not all) remain valid—at least in the eyes of other aristocrats—even when a family loses its wealth. The reason is that aristocratic privileges and conventions help to define the circle of those considered eligible for marriage and social intercourse.

One way of avoiding a misconception of "aristocracy," and of the Russian aristocracy in particular, is to employ a twofold definition of authority. Authority may be exercised either by peremptory commands or by grants of rights in return for services. Taken as the extremes of a continuum, the two categories cover the range from a tyrant whose

grants of delegated authority are temporary, willful, and closely supervised, to a king who reigns but does not rule because he has sanctioned
a delegation of rights that remain his in name only. There is a parallel
range among the subordinates who, on the one hand, may be subject to
exacting demands and personal humiliation or, on the other, enjoy an
autonomy which is not diminished by formal acts of homage.

In the case of Russia, tsarist rule increasingly tended toward peremptory commands and hence the Russian aristocrats came to derive
their prestige and wealth from proximity to the ruler. Their local power
over the serfs went together with an often degrading subjection to the
arbitrary will of the autocrat. The terms *Russian aristocracy* or *Russian
gentry* designate this group because its members served the ruling tsar
and had privileged access to positions of government.[20] But the term
nobility is best avoided, because distinctions of birth derived from a family's independent status declined in importance with the rise of Moscow.

As the Muscovite dynasty rose to preeminence in the fourteenth
and fifteenth centuries, Russia's tsarist rule and aristocracy came closer
to the first of these alternatives, though the struggle against the inherited privileges of boyar and princely families continued until the seventeenth century. Muscovite ascendance was related to Russia's international position. In contrast to Japan, which was almost immune to
outside attacks, Russia was exposed to foreign invasions or marauding
raids for the better part of its recorded history. In Russia, recurrent
warfare led to the concentration of Muscovite authority, the increasing
subordination of all social ranks, and the persistent neglect of local government and estate management. By contrast, Japan's greater immunity
to attack was accompanied (during the Ashikaga period) by the gradual
decline of shogunal, and a corresponding growth of local, authority as
well as the rise of a class of small, independent landowners. Russia's embattled condition led to more, not less, centralized power, and time and
again the country was like an armed camp. The following discussion
examines an aristocratic governance which was shaped by this militarization of society. The development of the Russian aristocracy is discussed in terms of (1) the initial freedom of princes and boyars in the
Kievan and appanage periods, (2) the military aspects of Moscow's rise
to power, and (3) the effects of this rise on the aristocracy. I shall further
describe (4) the *mestnichestvo* system (see glossary) as it developed in the
fifteenth century, and (5) the resulting composition and functions of the
Russian aristocracy. The chapter concludes with (6) a description of
Russia's "aristocratic culture pattern" and its reaffirmation in the legal
codes of the seventeenth century.

1. In Kievan Russia and the subsequent period of appanage principalities, central authority was rather nominal. Russia was sparsely pop-

ulated, and trade was a more important source of wealth than land. In the frontier areas of the open steppe, peasants retained their freedom of movement, and large landowners were free to change their allegiance from one prince to another without losing their patrimony. One should bear in mind that the princes and boyars of the time were independent, self-equipped warriors who made up the fighting forces of the several principalities, a condition which changed only as the Muscovite dynasty gradually subdued one after another of the Russian principalities. The absence of primogeniture made for the frequent division of estates and the repeated weakening of aristocratic dominance at the local level, so that landed aristocrats became more willing to enter the services of a strong ruler.[21] As the Grand Duchy of Muscovy achieved ascendance during the fourteenth century, the freedom of boyars to change their allegiance from one ruler to another was curtailed.

2. Moscow's initial rise to power occurred under Ivan Kalita (1325–1341). Still another century of subordination to the Mongol overlords was to pass before the weakening of Mongol power in the east and of Lithuanian power in the west resulted in the rise of the Muscovite dynasty under Ivan III (1462–1505). At the beginning of the fourteenth century, Muscovy extended over only 47,000 square kilometers. By the mid-fifteenth century, the state's territories had increased to 430,000 square kilometers, and by 1600 they had reached 5,400,000 square kilometers.[22] Yet the decline of Mongol and the rise of Moscow's power only meant the end of Russia's direct subservience, not the security of its domain. Even though the Khanates of Kazan and Astrakhan were annexed to Moscow by Ivan IV (The Terrible, 1533–1584) in the 1550s, the Crimean Tartars continued to harass Russian borderlands throughout the sixteenth and seventeenth centuries, often with the support of Poland or the Ottoman empire. Every raid exacted its toll in looting and burning. Men, women, and children were captured and sold as slave laborers or held for ransom. One estimate puts the number of captives in the period 1600–1650 at 200,000, but the actual total was probably much higher. During this period, total income from the slave trade and related transactions probably amounted to several million rubles, and Moscow's expenditures solely for the conduct of its "diplomatic" relations with the Crimea have been estimated at some 900,000 rubles. If expenditures for fortified defense lines and the annual conscription of recruits are added, it is clear that under Ivan IV and his successors Russia underwent an almost continuous mobilization for war.[23]

The record of Moscow's ascendancy must be put alongside a survey of its military activity. One compilation records that in the 234 years between 1228 and 1462, northern Russia witnessed a total of 133 foreign invasions and 90 feuds among rival principalities.[24] These repeated on-

FINLAND

NOVGOROD
REPUBLIC

TEUTONIC
ORDER

• Novgorod

MUSCOVY

TVER

KAZAN

Smolensk

• Moscow

RIAZAN

POLAND

LITHUANIA

Volga R.

• Kiev

GOLDEN
HORDE

Dnieper R.

CRIMEAN TARTARS

Don R.

• Sarai

———— Boundary of Russia

— · — · Boundary of Lithuania

5. Russia, Lithuania, and the Mongols in the Fifteenth Century

Ivan the Terrible
Ivan is depicted on his throne flanked by churchmen and boyars. The churchmen are turned away from the tsar engrossed in prayers and the contemplation of icons. Officially, neither churchmen nor boyars are counsellors of the ruler. (New York Public Library)

slaughts and feuds were part of the struggle against the Tartars and other nomads of the steppe, while Russia's later militarization was part of a Europeanwide phenomenon. During the two centuries between 1500 and 1700, the major European powers were at war for more than half the period. In the comparison in Table 1, Russia ranks very high except in the first half of the seventeenth century—a period during which the better part of Siberia was explored and conquered from Tomsk in the west (1604) to the coastal regions of eastern Siberia (1647–1648).[25] One hundred and thirty-three invasions up to 1462 and one hundred and thirty-six years of war in the two centuries after 1500 obviously represented an enormous strain on Russia's undeveloped economy, probably more so than the even greater military efforts of more developed countries like Spain and Austria. After 1689 the strain increased further: during the thirty-five years of Peter the Great's active reign, Russia was at peace for only two years.[26]

    3. During the Mongol overlordship, Moscow had initially been one

TABLE 1
NUMBER OF YEARS IN WHICH EUROPEAN POWERS WERE
AT WAR, BY FIFTY-YEAR PERIODS

Country	1500–1549	1550–1599	1600–1649	1650–1699	Total
France	29.5	31.0	24.0	22.5	107
Austria	36.0	39.5	40.5	33.0	149
Great Britain	16.0	38.5	17.5	26.0	98
Spain	27.5	45.5	48.0	34.0	155
Turkey	33.0	47.5	47.0	42.0	169.5
Russia	42.5	36.0	18.0	39.5	136.0

SOURCE: Quincy Wright, *A Study of War* (Chicago: University of Chicago Press, 1965), p. 653.

principality among others. Its ascendancy depended in part on the allegiance of princes, boyars, and court servitors to the grand dukes of Moscow.

Differences of interest emerged early among the several ranks of the aristocracy. When the descendants of princely and boyar families from other principalities entered the Muscovite service, they sought to preserve the prestige of their lineage and the hereditary claim to their lands (votchina). Similarly, as borderlands were annexed to Moscow, the resident princes and boyars sought to exchange their pledge of loyalty for tsarist guarantees of property rights and status. Naturally, aristocratic families from the older Russian territories claimed priority of status over families from more recently acquired lands. In addition, the grand duke of Moscow had important retainers whose families had risen to high status in his service and who now saw their claims to precedence challenged by aristocratic families of formerly independent status, that is, families which had been in Moscow's service for generations now pitted their claims based on long service against the claims of princely descent and hereditary rights.

From the early fourteenth until the mid fifteenth century, the Muscovite grand dukes could not free themselves of these conflicting claims. Their rise depended on the collaboration of princes and boyars from other principalities who had been induced to throw in their lot with Moscow.[27] The strength of these notables lay in their patrimonial estates and the proximity of their lands to centers of power other than Moscow. There were many such centers, though with the exception of Suzdal and Lithuania, they had become rather weak. The right of boyars to shift allegiance from one ruler to another was traditional, but conditions had changed. For the most part, the Moscow rulers respected that right only as long as they could use it to Moscow's advantage. Appanage principalities were confiscated whenever a case of "treason" could be made, and not much evidence was needed to do so. Gradually, Moscow's wealth and authority increased.

The widely scattered territories of the emerging state had to be administered. Princes and boyars who supported the grand duke helped him rule his realm through a state council (boyar duma). The bulk of the officer corps consisted of the sons of Moscow boyars and court servitors (*dvoriane*), supplemented during campaigns by princes, boyars, and Mongol notables from elsewhere who declared their allegiance to Moscow. At the local level, judges were appointed as administrators and tax collectors, without salary; they were entitled to receive maintenance cost and a share of the taxes from the people of their district (*kormlenie*). In this way, an early division developed between a court and a provincial aristocracy, the first consisting of several ranks of notables at the tsarist court, the second composed of local administrators appointed by the tsar or reinstated by him after appropriate declarations of loyalty. In the borderlands of the growing state, these local notables had to fend for themselves, compounding the insecurity of Moscow's boundaries by their own uncertain loyalty and military position.

Under the circumstances, conquest of new territories appeared the safest way of adding to the strength of the emerging state. In conquered territories, the Muscovite rulers could ignore the hereditary rights of aristocratic landowners and local rulers with relative impunity. Earlier, the Mongols had secured invaded areas not only by looting and burning, but by the deportation of people to sparsely populated areas in order to increase the work force and tap new sources of revenue. Muscovite practices of this kind date back to the reign of Ivan Kalita in the fourteenth century; they became of major importance under Ivan III, especially with the conquest of Novgorod in the 1480s and 1490s. One estimate states that by 1500 Ivan III had conquered and confiscated over 2.5 million acres of boyar and church land. The conquered territory was treated as state land. The original owners were dispossessed and deported, enrolled in the Muscovite army, and given lands in the vicinity of Moscow. At the same time, the conquered lands of Novgorod were distributed to deserving servitors of Ivan III. But neither the Novgorodian settlers in the Moscow area nor the Muscovite settlers in the Novgorod area were full owners of the land. All were army officers whose title to the land depended on their service to the state. By conquest and forced resettlement, the Moscow ruler undermined the claims of old families to their patrimony.

The conquest of Novgorod was the first fully documented case in which, by a combination of forcible expropriation and the establishment of military fiefs in the conquered territory, the Moscow ruler greatly increased his power and his independence from princes and boyars with hereditary claims to their land.[28] The conquest of Pskov (1509), of Smolensk (1514), and of Riasan (1520) followed a similar pattern, as did a generation later the conquest of the Khanate of Kazan (1552) and a number of Livonian cities in the late sixteenth and early seventeenth centuries. The annexation of borderlands was facilitated by giving families from these areas a preferred position at the tsarist court. The ethnic composition of the aristocracy reflects this policy. In 1682 a new register of aristocratic families was prepared which showed that less than 10 percent of the top ranks of Moscow's servitor-aristocracy were of purely Russian descent, while some 80 percent were of Polish-Lithuanian, Western European, or Tartar extraction.[29]

Annexations of the borderlands of Muscovy shaded off imperceptibly into strategies of internal politics designed to shift the balance of power away from princes and boyars whose hereditary claims limited the power of the tsar. In the course of the sixteenth century, the importance of unencumbered hereditary possession of land (votchina) declined.

> Up to the latter part of the fifteenth century, it had been by far the most common way by which members of the upper classes held their land. Then starting in the reign of Ivan III it began to yield preeminence to the *pomestye,* hitherto a relatively exceptional form of tenure. The explanation for this shift lay in the state-making policies of the Muscovite tsars. Ivan and his successors were intent upon building up the military forces they needed to conquer their brother princes, to crush the oligarchic ambitions of their own boyars, to stave off foreign invasions, and to expand their realm. They needed an army that was as dependent as possible upon them, and upon whose loyalty, therefore, they could themselves depend. But they lacked the money to buy the men and the allegiance they required. So they decided to use land. Their conquests and their confiscations of aloidal properties, beginning with Novgorod in Ivan III's reign and culminating in Ivan IV's *Oprichnina,* provided them with the necessary resources and brought about a decrease in the number of *votchinas.* For they distributed the land they seized as *pomestyes,* and not as *votchinas.*[30]

This shift in tsarist policy toward landholding entailed major conflicts. Moscow was often engaged in wars to the south against the Crimean Tartars and in the west against Poland and Lithuania. In these wars on two fronts, the state relied on the new military fiefholders (*pomeshchiki*). The old, established families of boyars watched the growing number and power of these men with apprehension. Boyars, fearful for their established status, sought further guarantees. Pomeshchiki, envious of boyar claims, attempted to obtain more security for their families than a revokable grant provided. In disputed border areas, bargaining for advantage verged on blackmail and treason. In addition, the country's resources were strained to the utmost, and Ivan IV showed markedly paranoid features. To cope with these mounting internal struggles, the strain of frequent wars, and not least his own fears, real and imagined, the tsar established a personal police force and military guard "of Nobility and Gentry" (*oprichnina*), directly loyal to himself and based on landholdings in districts around Moscow, from which other "Noblemen and Gentlemen" had been evicted. Although Ivan eventually abolished this "general schism, and public division among the subjects of his realm," Giles Fletcher's report of 1591 makes clear that the policy had resulted from the tsar's "extreme doubt and desperate fear, which he had conceived of most of his Nobility and Gentlemen—in his wars with Poland and the Crim Tartar."[31]

Given the desperate need of the rising state for a reliable corps of officers and administrators, these fears had some foundation. Descendants of princes and boyars, while pledging their loyalty, still wanted to retain their privileges. The claims of ancient lineage and the obligation to serve did pull in opposite directions. Those landowners who held both votchina and pomestie lands were in a deep quandary, and much the same came to be true of the pomeshchiki. The granting of military fiefs in conquered territories was a means of increasing the number of dependent servitors without hereditary rights. Or so it seemed. But the pomeshchiki were free to own or purchase other lands as well and wanted to will their benefices to their heirs. This was allowed sporadically, probably in part to ensure the continued loyalty of these servitors; but to the extent that it was allowed, pomeshchiki became hereditary landowners. This also occurred with regard to Ivan the Terrible's special military guard. In the 1560s, Ivan made the landholdings of these oprichniki hereditary, presumably in an effort to ensure that this personal police force would remain loyal to him. Thus, the legal distinction between military fiefs (pomestie) and hereditary lands (votchina) became blurred, as boyars came to hold service lands while servitors held hereditary properties.[32] The status distinctions among princes, boyars, and military fiefholders were jeopardized, as all ranks of the aristocracy pledged their loyal service to the tsar and the obligation to serve him became universal.

To summarize, the families of princes and boyars had enjoyed considerable independence in Kievan Russia and the appanage period that followed. Under the reign of Ivan III (1462–1505), this independence declined, and the status and wealth of Russia's aristocrats came to depend increasingly on service to the tsar as officers and high-ranking administrators.[33] When a member of this class exercised authority, he did so at the behest of the tsar, not on the basis of rights which he possessed or which had been granted to him. Eventually, military or administrative service became the Russian aristocrat's way of life. For leading segments of the Russian aristocracy, that way of life remained characteristic until well into the nineteenth century. Honor came to depend on service at a high rank.

4. Families vied with one another for higher prestige, basing their claims on having served the tsar for a longer period and at a higher rank than others. Eventually, this competition hardened into a system of preferment based on the relative position of families of servitor aristocrats (mestnichestvo).

> The fundamental principle of the system was that no one need serve under another person if he could show that one of his ancestors had held a higher position than had the ancestors of his proposed superior. Moreover, each servitor was responsible for the honor of all his living kinsmen and of all his descendants, for if he accepted a rank inferior to that warranted by his pedigree he set a precedent that would damage the careers of all his present and future relatives.[34]

Infighting among noble families was an obvious consequence of this system. To uphold the family honor, much energy was expended on "*mestnichestvo* arithmetic" (Kluchevsky), litigation, feuds, and personal combat. According to the then prevailing view, death itself was preferable to the unspeakable disgrace of being placed "below" a man whose ancestors' record did not entitle him to the higher position either at court or in the army.[35] Such intense competition for preferment added to the prestige of the court by its implicit acknowledgment that aristocratic honor depended on service to the tsar. No concerted opposition to autocratic encroachments could be organized on this basis. But the mestnichestvo system also imposed limits on the autocrat, who had to abide by genealogical precedence if he wished to uphold the established rank-order of society. And since competition for status and wealth turned on questions of genealogy, servitors of middle rank were ever anxious to convert their pomestie holdings into hereditary grants for the benefit of their descendants.

5. By the sixteenth century, Russia's aristocrats were divided into three broad service cadres. There was an upper service class, concentrated in Moscow and supported by hereditary lands and service land-grants from the government. This Moscow power elite served as judges, heads of governmental chancelleries, generals in the army, ambassadors, and provincial governors. Most of these men were descendants of the ancient princely houses and boyar families (whether of Russian or for-

eign descent). They were members of the boyar duma, some were very wealthy, and most had substantial holdings, including lavish residences in the capital. In addition there was a second echelon of this upper service class, men who ranked lower in wealth and service but still derived mostly from the old aristocratic families. The two groups of the upper service class together comprised some 6,400 individuals by the end of the seventeenth century, more than half of them officers in regiments of the provincial gentry and the remainder officers in the tsar's regiment. The position of this upper-service class was protected by the mestnichestvo system.

A middle service class comprised a second rank of servitors, who were based in the provinces and lived on land grants (pomestie) from the government and some irregularly paid stipends. In its period of major influence (ca. 1550–1650), this class comprised some 25,000 men, many of whom constituted a cavalry force of great importance in defending the rising Muscovite state against attacks from the steppe. Every pomestie holder was responsible for a contingent of equipped fighting men, who were charged with garrison or field duty, but whose obligation ceased with the end of each military campaign.

The lower service class was comprised of professional soldiers (streltsy), who were paid a small annual salary and denied the right to exploit peasant labor. The streltsy were usually garrisoned outside the towns. They were recruited from townsmen and peasants and in times of peace supplemented their meagre (and often irregular) salary as traders and craftsmen. But in the seventeenth century, this standing army of professional soldiers became hereditary, developed a strong *esprit de corps,* and for a time constituted a crucial physical power in Moscow despite the overall decline of its military importance.[36]

A characteristic aristocratic culture-pattern had formed in the course of Moscow's rise to preeminence.[37] The tsarist capital and the provinces had become separate worlds in a manner that is characteristic of predominantly agricultural societies. This cleavage had already appeared in the early phase of Muscovite ascendancy. Appanage princes, who pledged their allegiance to the grand duke of Moscow, lost touch with the region they had ruled, in part because Moscow had an interest in loosening their patrimonial ties. As the principle of a service aristocracy gained ground, the Moscow rulers saw to it that the fortunes of old aristocratic families declined if they evaded their obligations to serve. The cleavage between the capital and provinces was also manifested in the *kormlenie* system of local administration by centrally appointed officials, for it appeared to the local population as little different from a foreign occupation since the officials had short tenure and tended to exploit the people.[38] True, many provincial nobles remained on their estates if they were allowed to perform their lifelong service obligation on a seasonal basis. But up to the end of the seventeenth century, most of these nobles were illiterate, the life of the small provincial towns extremely dull, and chances for advancement nonexistent. If provincial nobles wanted to do better, they had to go to Moscow where they could do regular garrison duty and serve permanently at the court. Moscow service men were a privileged group. Chances for advancement depended on the distribution of favors by the tsar (or through his intimates), and many of these favors took the form of land grants. But the men so favored could visit their estates only on rare occasions, and their holdings were apt to be widely dispersed, depending on the availability of land and the tsar's convenience.

Since the mestnichestvo system tied a man's status at court to the service record of his ancestors, infighting for precedence at court often decided a family's fortune and could be more important than the service actually rendered.[39] Moreover, the claims to preferment were inflated by the absence of primogeniture, for each inheritance tended to increase both the dispersal of landholdings and the number of servitors with a prima facie claim on the tsar's largesse.

With service either at court or in a centrally organized army as the basis of aristocratic status, armed might based on hereditary landownership did not provide a foundation of local power that endured. Developments in this direction in Kievan Russia were probably cut short by declining economic conditions during the period of Mongol overlordship and by Moscow's ascendancy in the fourteenth and fifteenth centuries. Estate assemblies (boyar duma) developed, as they did in Western Europe. Tsarist rule was not sheer autocracy, without consultation or concessions. Like all rulers, the Russian tsars required assistance to help them govern the whole realm. Aristocratic rank depended on service to the tsar, but service also provided access to his person. Every tsar had his favorites whose counsel he sought when it suited him and who in turn could induce him to make special grants to themselves and their friends. Neither the functions of the boyar duma (which was only gradually replaced by a bureaucracy) nor the strong defense of rank through mestnichestvo would have been possible without this uncertain but important influence on the ruler.

The "estate assemblies" (*zemskie sobory*), which met during the sixteenth and seventeenth centuries, also had some importance and influence. Composed of "delegates" coopted from the various strata of society, these assemblies were convoked from time to time to rally the whole community behind momentous military decisions, to vote the required taxes, and on occasion to endorse the legitimacy of a successor to the throne by acclamation.[40] Such assemblies provided opportunities to present petitions to the tsar, though requests for relief or special consideration did not have to await these special occasions. The patriarchal claim of the tsar as the father of his people prompted the people as "his children" to appeal to his paternal benevolence and protection. Such appeals were frequently repudiated; then grievances would fester, resulting in riots or revolts. But while assemblies could be dismissed, petitions denied, and revolts suppressed, they were also evidence of unresolved problems and of calls for remedial action.

In this dialectic of an autocratic will above and anguished voices from below, the tsar did not always prevail even though his supremacy was rarely in doubt. On occasion, the tsarist government had to make concessions to the boyars, the middle service class, and the streltsy if it desired compliance or cooperation rather than risk sullen withdrawal or tacit resistance. Even under the tsarist regime something like "opposition" was possible through formal assemblies, petitions, and this "withdrawal of efficiency" (Veblen), though much depended on circumstance and infighting at court. One certainly must not think of opposition in constitutional terms.

The tsarist court was the main institutional basis for the distribution of wealth and status. Pleas for favors or petitions containing grievances had to be put forward at court. Capital and court were the state and society of Russia, combining the work of administrators, the outlook and manners of an officers' club, and a luxurious round of festive gatherings for the members of Russia's high society. Provincial society was a pale reflection of these activities in Moscow and, later on, Petersburg. In effect, the bulk of the country was "merely" a source of taxes and recruits that could sustain the social and military activities of the center.

6. This culture pattern of the Russian aristocracy was affected, though not basically altered, by developments of the seventeenth century. To understand these developments, some account must be taken of the events following the reign of Ivan IV (1533–1584) which are known as the "Time of Troubles."

With the reign of Fedor I (1584–1598), the Rurik dynasty died out. In the absence of a law of succession, many claimants to the throne appeared, giving rise to fantastic intrigues. This uncertainty at the very center of autocratic rule was exploited by Poland and Sweden. Their military campaigns led to the occupation of large parts of Western Russia, the conquest of Moscow, and their participation in the struggles over the succession. Droughts, famines, and epidemics scourged the country from 1601 to 1603, further compounding the political and military debacle. All these setbacks came on the heels of the terrorist methods (oprichnina) with which Ivan IV had expanded his state and made the aristocracy subservient to his will. The country had been forced to un-

dertake military campaigns which greatly outstripped its available resources. The mounting demands on the aristocracy to provide peasants
who would perform military service had meant that fewer peasants were
available to work the land, and the pressure for production on the peasants who remained increased accordingly. As a result, many peasants
escaped the burdens of serfdom, military recruitment, and requisitions
by illegally migrating to the steppe. This drain of manpower helped to
undermine the economic foundations of the landed gentry. The period
of great upheaval extended from Boris Godunov's accession to the
throne in 1598 to the establishment of the Romanov dynasty in 1613.

In the first decades of the Romanov dynasty, further threats developed to the position of the upper- and middle-service classes. Cavalry
officers from these classes had been vitally important in defending the
country against raids and concerted attacks from the south and the west;
they were essential in reconquering the territories lost to the Poles during the Time of Troubles. Their high social position at court was an
expression of this vital role. At the end of the sixteenth century, Russia's
armed forces had consisted of about 110,000 men, of whom about half
were serfs. Twenty-nine thousand belonged to the upper- and middle-
service class (among them 4,000 foreigners), and varied military units
made up the rest. The streltsy around Moscow were the most important
of these other units; they served as an internal security force rather than
in a military capacity. By the end of the seventeenth century, the country's military forces were greatly increased and their composition altered. In 1681, Russia's armies totaled some 215,000 men. Officers from
the upper- and middle-service class had been cut to 10 percent of the
total force. The streltsy and other lower class servitors now comprised
an internal security force of well over 100,000 men. At the same time,
over eighty-nine new regiments had been formed, equipped with firearms and trained by foreign officers or their Russian students. These
new regiments comprised more than half of the total military force and
completely overshadowed the remnants of the old army.

The techniques of warfare had changed with the introduction of
gunpowder in Russia in the 1620s and 1630s. As Hellie interprets his
findings,

> [In the mid-seventeenth century] the gunpowder revolution finally overtook
> Muscovy almost completely. By this time the Tartars had ceased to be the
> major threat to the Muscovite state. The result was that, in warfare for the
> control of huge fortresses, the middle service class cavalryman with his bow
> and arrow was technologically obsolete in the face of infantry outfitted with
> firearms. . . . Beginning in the reign of Boris Godunov (1598–1605), the ser-
> vicemen took advantage of the Tsar's weak position to get the government
> to restrict access to their increasingly privileged position. . . . They were a

group with no technical skill or genuine specialization to support claims to exclusiveness, so they built on their historically legitimate base to achieve privilege. . . . [Faced with a technically superior, but lower class infantry] this caste had to rule out competition artificially, by having the government codify the caste's privileged position in the law.[41]

It certainly makes sense that a privileged class whose services become obsolete for technical reasons looks for new reasons to support its privileged position. But it is equally relevant to point out that a newly formed army recruited from the lower classes and equipped with firearms would be considered a potential threat to social stability by any conservative government. Larger security forces were needed because the widespread unrest of the succession struggles and military campaigns during the Time of Troubles could have spilled over into far more dangerous uprisings, if the newly armed riflemen had joined that unrest. Hence, the tsarist legislation reasserting aristocratic privileges in 1649 was probably as much protection against this potential threat as it was a response to aristocratic demands for more concessions.

Legislative developments of the seventeenth century reflect this entire political and military background. Almost a century of upheaval had resulted in great disarray. Specifically, the upper- and middle-service classes had been undermined first by mounting service obligations, second by arbitrary elevations in rank due to emergency needs of the ruling tsar, third by diminution of income from estates because peasant escapes had decreased the available work force, and fourth by the obsolescence of their military function. With the return of some stability, leading representatives of the aristocracy pressed for restoration and confirmation of their privileges, and the early years of Alexis' reign (1645–1676) provided them with a welcome opportunity. Comprehensive legislation of *any* kind ran counter to the supremacy of the ruler's will. Even when it occurred (as it had in 1550), it had not been printed, thus encouraging abuses of all kinds. Now order was to be substituted for arbitrariness, and in the process the government and the servitor aristocracy were strengthened at the expense of the church, the boyars, and the peasants.

Two pieces of legislation in the seventeenth century represented attempts at a complete legal ordering of Russian society from the top down: the Code of Law of 1649 (*Ulozhenie*) and the formal abolition of the mestnichestvo system in 1682. The code of 1649 reflected the long-standing struggle of the tsar and his servitors against all those landed aristocrats who were descended from the old princely and boyar families and who on that account retained some of their inherited privileges. Among these were special rights to proceed against peasants who ran away and thus weakened the work force available to till the soil.[f] The tsar's servitors did not possess such rights. The old princely and boyar families also enjoyed exemption from taxes while residing on estates just outside the towns; thus, the products of their serf economy had a competitive advantage over the products of the tax-burdened town residents. The Ulozhenie abolished such privileges by binding the peasants and their families yet more firmly to the land, and by abolishing tax privileges of boyar families in the suburbs. This time two thousand copies of the new legal code were printed—a gesture of legality in connection with a code of law that embodied the most systematic deprivation of privileges (rights) enacted so far. Implementation might fall short of what the law called for, but the principle was clear. Peasants were losing what little freedom had remained to them, while boyars were also losing their remaining privileges.[42] The Ulozhenie also established a special office in charge of overseeing claims and litigation involving the church. All land acquired by the church between 1580 and 1648 was surveyed, despite the protests of church leaders. Further land acquisitions by the church were prohibited, and the church was subjected to ministerial control.

Aristocratic servitors of the tsar (*pomeshchiki*) actually gained more status than benefits by the new code, for the destruction of remaining boyar privileges did not lighten their own burdens. There had been mounting opposition to these privileges during the seventeenth century, especially opposition to the mestnichestvo system. Claims to genealogical preferment were incompatible with military promotions based on performance in battle, and indeed that preferment interfered with the tsar's own prerogative of promoting the most deserving. Finally, when the gentry militia was formally replaced by a standing army, a rank-order based on hereditary privileges became altogether obsolete, and in 1682 the old mestnichestvo records were destroyed. But while the tsar ordered the destruction of the registers through which the genealogical seniority of the old aristocratic families could be traced, he also ordered

[f]The earlier discussion of Kievan Russia indicated that hereditary landowners had personal rather than political rights over their estates. That is, in managing these estates and ruling over the peasants they were acting as personal owners of the land, not as administrators appointed by the prince and acting on his behalf. These personal rights over the peasants were extensive, including not only the right to settle disputes and collect taxes but also far-reaching police powers which included corporal punishment, the right to banish peasants for wrongdoing, and indeed the right to execute them for crimes. The provincial governors of the princes and later of the tsars did not interfere with this private jurisdiction as long as "peace" was maintained and taxes were collected. Even where revolts broke out and military force was needed to collect taxes, that interference was not systematic.

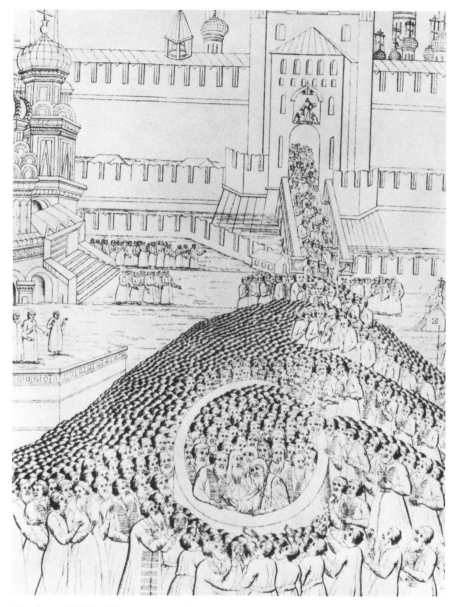

Election of Mikhail Romanov as Russia's Tsar in 1613

This miniature from the contemporary *Book of the Election of Mikhail Fedorovich* shows a large circular enclosure where a priest announces the unanimous election of the new tsar by the zemsky sobor to the large crowd gathered outside the walls of the Kremlin. Coming at the end of the Time of Troubles, the "election" was an act of acclamation by a body of representatives whose main concern was the stability of autocratic rule. Participation by dignitaries of the church consecrated the new dynasty in the eyes of the people.

the preparation of new records based on the universal obligation of all aristocrats to serve the tsar.[43]

A main task of the Code of 1649 was to create order where foreign occupation and peasant revolts during the Time of Troubles had created chaos. Grants of land made during this period of upheaval were confirmed whenever the beneficiaries had supported the new Romanov dynasty, which began with the reign of Michael (1613–1645). The Ulozhenie facilitated the inheritance of land where the titleholders had been confirmed, and it provided the pomestie holder's family with considerable security after his death. The result was that the remaining distinctions between boyars and servitors were obliterated, while control over all lands remained in the hands of the government and the obligation of military service continued. No private ownership of land existed in Siberia, where the whole territory belonged to the government.

From the standpoint of upholding authority and the rank-order of society, the stabilization of the labor supply on the land was the most important part of the code. Guarantees of land rights to the aristocracy already dated back to the reign of Ivan IV, but they meant little without control over the mobility of the rural labor force. Earlier, the movements of peasants had been curbed only in certain years, whereas the Ulozhenie met the desires of the aristocracy by a total abolition of peasant movements. Henceforth, the peasant was permanently bound to the estate, and while he retained some residual rights distinguishing him from a slave, the main point is that permanent serfdom was instituted just at the time when the old families of princes and boyars lost the last vestiges of their hereditary privileges.

How can one compare and contrast the Russian and the Japanese aristocracies? The history of Russia shows a definite break between the late twelfth century when foreign trade shifted away from the Russian river towns and the mid fifteenth century when Russian tribute payments to the Mongols became irregular and the ascendancy of the Muscovite state was well on its way. The history of Japan shows no comparable discontinuity, for even the establishment of the Tokugawa shogunate in the early 1600s has only superficial similarities with the Muscovite rise to supremacy a century earlier.

The different fates of the two aristocracies appear to be directly associated with this major contrast. There was some continuity between the Kievan aristocracy and its tribal past. The early boyar duma, the freedom of boyars to change their allegiance with impunity, and the town assemblies (veche) seem like echoes of an earlier condition in which tribal chieftains were assisted by the heads of households. In theory, these freedoms were already incompatible with the princely authority

established by the Varangian rulers and with the theocratic doctrines of
Byzantium. In practice, freedom was crushed by economic decline,
Mongol conquest, and Muscovite ascendancy.

In Japan, the central authority of emperor and regential family
emerged out of the warlike contentions among armed lineage groups.
These groups may have been similar to the Slavic and Germanic tribes
of Eastern Europe. In any case, Japan's central authority resulted from
wars among tribes or extended kinship groups and not from foreign
conquest, as in ninth-century Russia. Once this central imperial and regential authority was established, its continuity was preserved in fact and
in myth through all the vicissitudes that followed. Such a major change
as the destruction of the Fujiwara regency and the establishment of the
Kamakura shogunate (1185) was accomplished with the imperial supremacy in religious and ceremonial matters formally intact. Under the
cultural shelter of that supremacy, a highly centralized political order
like the Kamakura or a greatly decentralized one like the Ashikaga shogunates could be established, apparently with equal facility. One may
call the two kinds of regimes centralized and decentralized feudalism,
respectively. Both depended on the reciprocal obligations between the
shogunal ruler and his landed and armed vassals in the provinces,
though under the Kamakura, the shoguns and under the Ashikaga, the
vassals dominated this relationship. Throughout the centuries of internal conflict in Japan, the armed might of local rulers remained unimpaired, even though their identity and social composition changed from
time to time. In Russia, by contrast, it was above all this armed might
at the local level which was crushed first by the Mongol conquest and
subsequently by the systematic deportation and resettlement policies of
the Muscovite rulers from Ivan Kalita to Ivan the Terrible.

This preservation or destruction of armed might at the local level
is the clue to the difference between the Tokugawa shogunate, on the
one hand, and the rise of Muscovy, on the other. In seventeenth-century
Japan, the Tokugawa established a type of centralized rule which divided the country into some two hundred and fifty domains (han). Each
of these domains was under a vassal (daimyo) who depended on the
shogun for the welfare of his family and himself, but who at the same
time exercised absolute authority over his domain. (The details of this
sociopolitical structure are discussed in Chapter 12.) Centralized as Tokugawa rule was, it preserved to a remarkable degree the autonomy of
local rule which had been characteristic of the Japanese social structure
for centuries past. To be sure, the Tokugawa shoguns enlarged or decreased the size of a daimyo's holdings depending on his family's initial
relation to the founder of the Tokugawa shogunate. They also reas-
signed domains at will when they saw signs of disloyalty to their house.

But none of these methods of ensuring Tokugawa supremacy can be likened to the Russian case, because such redistribution or reassignment of landholdings never challenged the underlying principle that loyalty to the shogun would be rewarded by nearly complete autonomy within each daimyo domain. This differs strikingly from Russia, where a comparable centralization of authority under Ivan IV depended on deportation and resettlement policies which were designed to destroy the remaining vestiges of local independence.

The difference in military and political organization shows one important consequence of this contrast in structures of authority. In Japan, the Tokugawa military forces were organized on a regional basis. Tokugawa supremacy depended on political organization as much as on armed might, for the superiority of Tokugawa forces was based on the imperial mandate and the relatively greater wealth of the Tokugawa domains. The Tokugawa shogunate could have been destroyed easily if the major daimyo domains had banded together in opposing the shogunate. The shogun saw to it that they did not, and this policy of "divide and rule" was effective for over two hundred years. The same policy showed its great weakness in the 1850s when the Tokugawa were unable to deal militarily with the threat of Western intrusion. Now they needed but could not command the political and military support of the major daimyo domains. This changed balance of power led to the fall of the Tokugawa house and the emergence of a political arena in the Meiji Restoration.

By contrast, tsarist military forces were organized on a centralized basis. Tsarist supremacy depended on armed might in the sense that all provincial government was under centrally appointed officials whose tax collection and military recruitment were backed up by military force. The superiority of this force was based on the prior destruction of local independence and, conversely, on the centralization of social and political opportunities and of economic favors (land grants) in the hands of the autocrat. The tsarist regime did not depend on a divide-and-rule policy. After Moscow's supremacy had been established, the highest circles of the Russian aristocracy came to compete for place and favors at court. In a good many cases, Russian aristocrats competed for handouts instead of paying attention to the management of their estates. We shall see (in Chapter 13) that the great crisis of tsarist rule came when the military forces based on this structure of authority met defeat in the Crimean War (1856), only a few years after the arrival of an American flotilla in Japan (1853) had undermined the political structure of the Tokugawa shogunate.

In both countries, defeat or the threat of invasion occasioned major political reassessments. Since in Russia all authority was concentrated in the person of the autocrat, he alone could set reforms in motion, and after 1856 he addressed the crucial issue of serfdom. In Japan, the Tokugawa regime had encouraged considerable initiative at the local level since the eighteenth century. When the regime proved unable to cope with the threat of intrusion, the bureaucratic politics of the Tokugawa were replaced by an emerging political participation from the provinces. In the end, tsarist autocracy was overthrown because neither the tsar nor his officials knew whether or not to repress independent initiative entirely or, if they permitted it, how to combine the central exercise of authority with the development of such initiative. Nor did they appreciate the urgency of this task for their own survival.

One can consider other dimensions of this comparison. The bulk of the aristocracy resided in the provinces in both countries. In Japan, the samurai were removed from the land and became urban rentiers and administrators in the castle towns of the han. In Russia, most landed gentry remained on their estates, while the leading minority flocked to Moscow and, later, to Petersburg. Since in both countries the whole aristocracy consisted of servitors, the two aristocracies have important similarities in contrast to the greater independence of the English or French aristocracies considered in the following chapters. But the Japanese and Russian servitor aristocrats were not alike. In Japan, the Tokugawa regime distinguished the landed notables in terms of their relative affinity and reliability in relation to the ruling house. In Russia, the tsarist regime eventually suppressed the old differences in rank between votchina and pomestie holders so that all aristocrats were obliged to serve. When that universal service-obligation was removed, all Russian aristocrats were given their freedom, but it was a freedom from service rather than a right.

We shall see in Chapter 13 that freedom without rights is not a propitious basis for the development of self-government and individual initiative. In the course of its rise to supremacy, Muscovite autocracy proved inimical to local autonomy and to the public institution (boyar duma) in which such initiative could express itself politically. The oprichnina of Ivan IV (in the 1560s), the abolition of mestnichestvo in 1682, and Peter the Great's imposition of service as the sole criterion of rank show that much resistance had to be overcome. The great severity of Peter's rule was relaxed under his successors, but individual initiative on a broader scale developed only after Alexander II's proposal of serf-emancipation in 1856. It is symptomatic of a regime which concentrated all authority in one ruler and his administrative and military staff that the defeats in the Crimean War (1856), the Russo-Japanese War (1905), and World War I (1917) ended in inadequate reforms and partial or total revolution.

In the preceding summation I have run far ahead of my "story" in order to outline the social and political differences between Russia and Japan over the major part of their history.[44] In turning now to Germany and Prussia, I begin once again in the medieval period when in these territories of Central Europe the authority of kings was established on an enduring though insecure basis.

5

IMPERIAL GERMANY
AND PRUSSIA

In JAPAN, imperial authority emerged from a past dominated by rival lineage groups. Historically, authority under the emperor fluctuated from the strong Kamakura to the weak Ashikaga and then back to the strong Tokugawa shogunates. Struggles over the imperial and shogunal succession as well as long internal wars gave Japanese history a sanguinary aspect, but the endless vendettas also left room for the independence of local rulers and even of peasants. One reason why amid civil strife local rulers could remain independent was the absence of foreign invasions for fourteen hundred years. In Russia, princely authority emerged when armed traders from the north, intent on defending their areas of settlement, had to come to terms with independent local notables and town assemblies. Their independence was gradually lost as a centralized autocracy was established at Moscow. The rulers of both Japan and Russia faced the delicate problem of asserting central authority while allowing leading aristocrats to increase their status and power. As seen from a very long time perspective, central authority prevailed in both Japan and Russia, but only in Japan did it remain compatible with a high degree of local independence. The relation between central and local authority was the issue on which the internal politics of the two countries turned for much of their histories.

In the case of the Central European countries, which subsequently became Germany, the record of rulership is considerably more complex. For that reason I will first refer to Imperial Germany and then deal with the emergence of rulership in Brandenburg and Prussia and with the development of the Prussian aristocracy.[a] I choose this format because in Central Europe, royal authority did not prevail over the centrifugal

[a]*Imperial Germany* is an unavoidable terminological shortcut. The Roman Empire of the German Nation (later the Holy Roman Empire) is the designation commonly given to a changing complex of lands, ruled over by Frankish and later by German kings from

authorities of princes, dukes, margraves, and others at the regional or provincial level. Some of the provinces (*Länder*) of the present Federal Republic of Germany have a very long prehistory. In order to examine kingship and aristocracy at this regional level it seems useful to focus attention on rulership in Prussia, the most important constituent state of early modern Germany (seventeenth century), rather than discuss the increasingly shadowy presence of the Roman Empire of the German Nation, or the Holy Roman Empire as it was called by the Hohenstaufen emperor, Frederick I (Barbarossa) in 1157.

EMPERORS, GERMAN PRINCES, AND PAPAL AUTHORITY

Imperial Germany had its beginning in the Frankish empire. In 751 or 752, the pope, or bishop of Rome, gave his consent to the discontinuation of the Merovingian house and authorized Bishop Bonifacius to anoint the Carolingian ruler, Pepin, king of the Franks. At that time, the pope was a subject of the Byzantine empire, confirmed in his jurisdiction, like other bishops, by the Byzantine emperor. This control of Rome and of Italy weakened when the Byzantine emperor turned to the East to combat the rising power of Islam. The Lombards, one of the Germanic tribes that had earlier settled in Italy, used this opportunity to invade the lands belonging to Byzantium, and Pope Stephen II appealed to Pepin III to help stop their encroachment. The Frankish king defeated the Lombards in 754 and bestowed the Italian possessions of Byzantium on the papacy, thus establishing the temporal power of the papacy and its close alliance with the Frankish kingdom. This first extension of Frankish rule into Italy proved to be an antecedent of later conflicts between the Roman Empire of the German Nation and the papacy. But these consequences could not be foreseen in the eighth century.

---

the coronation of Charlemagne in 800 until its formal dissolution by Napoleon in 1806. The extent as well as the designation of this empire changed from time to time. I shall refer to Imperial Germany when the discussion deals with the German empire rather than its constituent units, and to the emperor as the ruler of that empire regardless of whether or not he was formally designated "emperor" at the given time. Some emperors of Germany were not consecrated by the pope and hence not emperors in the strict sense, but it became the German custom to refer to the king of Germany as emperor (*Kaiser*). The absence of papal consecration did not change the emperor's own claim to exercise authority under God. All the Frankish and German emperors were chosen from among the rulers of the constituent parts of Imperial Germany and also remained rulers of their inherited lands, like the duke of Saxony or the count of Habsburg. The title of Margrave referred to the military ruler of a German border province, appointed to that position by the emperor. The rulers of Brandenburg and later of Prussia were margraves and electors (*Kurfürsten*) of the emperor before they became kings of Prussia in 1701. The election of the emperor and the changing meaning of "Prussia" are discussed further on.

The Frankish defender of the papacy could become as dangerous to the pope as the Lombards had been. By 774 Pepin's successor, Charlemagne (768–814), had defeated the last independent king of the Lombards. This campaign in Italy was part of Frankish expansion on many fronts. After his accession to the throne, the conquest of the Saxons occupied Charlemagne, on and off, for thirty years. In 778 and again in 795 he campaigned in Spain. In 791 and again in 796 he campaigned against the Avars on the Danube, and in 800 against the Byzantine forces south of Rome. By the end of his reign in 814 most of Europe west of the Elbe had been united under Frankish rule. This record of expansion is the context of Charlemagne's coronation as emperor.

When Pope Leo III (795–816) came in conflict with the Roman nobility in 800, he called on Charlemagne to intervene. Charlemagne traveled to Rome to judge the dispute and also witness the consecration of his son. At the ceremony, Pope Leo suddenly placed a crown on Charlemagne's head and abased himself before the king, while the assembly of Roman notables acclaimed him emperor. Since the pope had no legal right to confer the title, the action was apparently designed to secure the pope's position against his adversaries. The new title of emperor added tensions to the relations between the Carolingian dynasty and the Byzantine emperors. Frankish rule over Lombardy and acceptance of the title of emperor thus involved Charlemagne and his successors irrevocably in the temporal and ecclesiastical interests of the papacy.

These interests were directly linked to the legitimation of rule. The consecration of the Carolingian dynasty may have originated in political exigencies which induced the popes to seek Frankish assistance against the Lombards and other Italian adversaries; but according to papal theory, the empire was the secular arm of the church, charged with the task of protecting and enhancing its mission, and hence ultimately accountable for its actions to the pope. Naturally, the Frankish or imperial theory of kingship placed greater emphasis on the emperor's direct mandate from God as the ultimate justification of his authority and of his right to designate his successor. The two positions were destined to come into open conflict in the investiture controversy of the eleventh century.

Charlemagne ruled a divided empire.[1] In the West, the Franks had inherited the provincial organization of Rome. Authority was concentrated above and devolved downward through regional or provincial counts to the individual localities. No such provincial organization existed in the East, which we now call Central Europe, but which was then frontier territory barely reached by religious missions and political authority. For a time, the Frankish empire was strong enough to impose its rule on hundreds of local rulers, but such imposition was achieved only after protracted struggle. Even then most local communities and estates retained much of their independence.

Charlemagne died in 814, and under the Treaty of Verdun (843), the empire was peacefully divided into a western, middle, and eastern part, each ruled by a son of the deceased ruler. This compromise was of short duration. The royal domains, which were the principal material basis of government, had been reduced; hence, the authority of the three kings was weakened. By 887 one of Charlemagne's successors was already paying tribute to the Vikings, who were besieging Paris. In 911 the Carolingian line died out, and during the ninth and tenth centuries Viking, Magyar, and Saracen invasions devastated much of Europe. Land under cultivation decreased as population declined, and famine and disease spread. Everywhere people looked for local rulers who were strong enough to protect them. In what had been the East Frankish empire, five great duchies (Saxony, Franconia, Lorraine, Swabia, and Bavaria) emerged. They were organized on a military basis in an effort to halt invasions from the north and east. The men who rose to power in these duchies were descendants of Carolingian administrators, counts, and margraves (*Markgrafen*), who had no tribal or other mandate to rule but became powerful as military leaders. In part because of their lack of legitimation, these leaders chose Duke Conrad of Franconia in 911 to inherit the crown from the extinct Carolingian line.

Conrad I was the first ruler of this eastern frontier area to be anointed, a token of his alliance with the church. He sought to strengthen his internal position against the aristocracy by his campaigns against Lorraine in the west and the Magyars in the east. His main support came from great magnates of the church who were also wealthy landed proprietors. However, Conrad failed in his campaigns against the Magyars and died in 918. During his reign, the leaders in the several duchies consolidated their own authority by assuring themselves of support from the local aristocracy and asserting their control over the local churches. As yet, kingship was based on little more than the agreement by the rulers of the duchies to have one of their number lead them in war. The crown passed to the dukes of Saxony who were more successful militarily than Conrad had been. Military success was important for consolidating the rule of a dynasty. By a combination of meeting this test and receiving the acclamation of other ducal leaders, the Saxon dynasty became hereditary.

The Saxon kings (919–1024) attempted to reassert the authority of the crown. At critical junctures they appointed members of the royal family to leading positions in the duchies; they insisted on nominating successors to the ducal title where they could; and they undermined control of the church by the secular rulers in the duchies. But in achieving greater political authority, the Saxon kings had to rely on allies that were relatively independent of the particular interests in each duchy. The church, with its extensive organization in many lands, was the most suit-

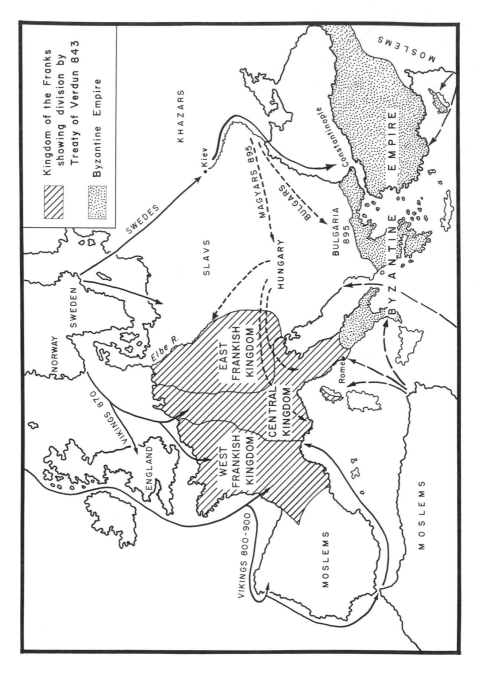

6. Europe, 800–900: Political Divisions and Invasions

able ally in this undertaking and became the mainstay of imperial government. A succession of Saxon rulers exempted the churches from the ordinary authority of local rulers and placed them directly under the crown. At the same time, the churches were made into an instrument of government by investing their bishops and abbots with secular authority over the areas under their jurisdiction. On the eastern frontiers the churches acted as agents of government and centers of missionary work among the Slavs, though not without provoking occasional rebellions against themselves. In 937 the Saxon king Otto I (936–973) enlarged his domain by establishing his overlordship in Burgundy and Provence. In his Italian campaign of 951–952, he then secured the Marks of Verona, Friuli, and Istria (roughly the areas of northeastern Italy and Trieste) for his son Henry, Duke of Bavaria. In 955 Otto defeated the Magyars at Lechfeld, and in 960 he defended the papacy against an attempt to seize its lands. Pope John XII bestowed on Otto the title *Imperator et Augustus* in 962, confirming the reestablishment of the empire which had been in abeyance for more than a century. The successors of Otto I continued his work of expansion and consolidation in alliance with the church. For example, in Otto II's (973–983) Italian campaign of 981, three quarters of his forces were provided by German abbeys and bishoprics, only one quarter by lay magnates. But this alliance did not last. When Otto I died in 973, all the German monasteries (over 100) were attached to the crown. But by the beginning of the eleventh century, ecclesiastical jurisdictions had proliferated (there were over 700 monasteries) under the sponsorship of the aristocracy, and from that time on the church tended to accentuate the political fragmentation of the empire.

Nevertheless, by the eleventh century, the principle of an hereditary monarchy was accepted for the whole Roman Empire of the German Nation—that is, the right of the reigning emperor to nominate his son for the succession was considered axiomatic, although his choice had to be confirmed through an election by the princes. The whole Roman empire in 1000 extended from the North Sea coast to the Mediterranean, including present-day Germany, Holland, Czechoslovakia, Switzerland, Austria, eastern France, and most of Italy. For a time, even the consecration by the pope became a formality; thus, the ruling dynasty's supremacy countered most tendencies toward decentralized rule. However, the emperor's supremacy depended on his personal presence, and this limited the durability of his rule. In his absence, the administration either of Italy or of the German territories would weaken, resulting in the reassertion of the authority of the princes or of the church.

Emperors from the Salian Franks (hence the Salian dynasty, 1024–1125) followed the Saxon kings and attempted to cope with the unresolved problem of the mandate to rule. The new dynasty turned to the

Otto III (983–1002) Receiving the Homage of the Nations

This painting from the Reichenau gospels of the tenth century shows (on the left) the Slavs, Germans, Franks, and Romans bringing presents to emperor Otto III, who is seated on the right. Wearing a Roman imperial costume, the emperor is represented as heir of the Caesars, surrounded by archbishops and nobles carrying the stole and sword signifying spiritual and temporal authority. The emperor himself holds the imperial staff and globe. The scene emphasizes the symbolic continuity between the Roman empire and the Holy Roman Empire of the German Nation. (Clm 4453, fol. 23v and fol. 24r, Bayerische Staatsbibliothek, Munich) upper ranks of dependent retainers and knights for the support which the princes and the magnates of the church withheld. In this frontier area of East Central Europe, ties of vassalage were as weak as they were in Kievan Russia and for many of the same reasons. Administrative officers and armed knights were drawn from social ranks below the aristocracy, because such men depended directly on the ruler for advancement. With the aid of this class of *ministeriales,* the Salian emperors embarked on their campaign of recovering crown lands which had been usurped by local rulers. The reign of Henry IV (1056–1106) is most notable in this respect. He built royal fortresses in Saxony and Thuringia and wanted to establish a permanent capital in Goslar. By restoring the economy of the royal domains with the aid of the *ministeriales,* he hoped to create a material base that would be sufficient to make royal authority independent of the German princes.[b]

Yet the strength of the Salian dynasty proved brittle. The minority of Henry IV lasted for fourteen years (1056–1070), and during this interval the papacy sought to emancipate itself from its dependence on imperial authority.[c] Many monasteries were reformed in order to assert papal authority: since 910, the Cluniac reform movement had prepared the ground for a revival of the church by freeing all monastic houses of feudal control and placing them directly under the papacy. In addition, Cluniac reforms strengthened the church by insisting on the celibacy of the clergy and by condemning lay investiture of church offices and the sale of such offices and of ecclesiastical pardons (*simony*). The Lateran Council of 1059 then abolished both lay investiture and simony. The council particularly condemned the imperial practice of appointing selected bishops to local jurisdictions in order to obtain their aid in combating the autonomy of local rulers. Thus, the reform movements encouraged representatives of the church to make common cause with antiroyalist aristocrats in lieu of the earlier alliance between the emperor and the church against princes and other local secular rulers. Although the Saxon and Salian emperors had strengthened royal authority, they

[b]The term *prince* is used throughout in its generic sense as the sovereign ruler of a territory, not as a junior member of a royal house. Chapter 2 referred to papal support of the electoral principle for political and theological reasons and to the Germanic tradition of "electing" an heir to the chieftainship by acclamation. The importance of this principle in the history of Imperial Germany was due in part to the frequency with which German kings died without heir or left a minor to succeed them. As the following discussion indicates, this circumstance was powerfully reinforced by the contest with the papacy which gave further impetus to existing divisions among the German princes.

[c]That dependence had increased under Otto I, who at first had been refused the imperial coronation by the pope, but who had given military assistance to the papacy subsequently. After being crowned in 962, Otto deposed one pope, nominated another, and compelled the pope to recognize the emperor's right to approve or reject papal nominations.

had not crushed the autonomy of the duchies or the traditional freedom which landowners claimed as their ancient inheritance. In some areas, the landed aristocracy and the monasteries now formed an alliance and came to oppose royal authority.[d]

The issue of imperial and papal jurisdiction came to a head when riots broke out in Milan in a conflict between an episcopal and an imperial candidate for the office of the Milanese bishop. Henry IV quelled these riots and installed his own candidate by force of arms. Moves and countermoves followed, and in 1075 Pope Gregory VII challenged the very authority of the German emperor by excommunicating him. In the ensuing controversy, the emperor sought support against the pope from his own ecclesiastical appointees, while the pope in turn tried to form an alliance with the many German enemies of Henry IV. Both alliances were unstable. A number of Henry's ecclesiastical supporters were divided in their loyalty between the emperor and the pope. A number of the pope's German supporters joined him only because they opposed the emperor, but meanwhile they deprived German churches and monasteries of their lands wherever they had the upper hand. It was in the early phases of this great controversy that Henry IV was forced to free himself from the papal ban of excommunication by making his famous journey to Italy, where he did penance and received absolution at Canossa in 1077. But the emperor did not thereby relinquish his claims to legitimate royal authority; rather he purged himself of the papal ban in order to ensure the support of his German followers.

Henry's submission to, and reconciliation with, the church disappointed the German princes who had allied themselves with the pope. They had wanted to depose the emperor, and the pope's absolution deprived them of a convenient pretext. Now, following the journey to Canossa, a faction of German princes elected a rival king, Rudolf of Rheinfelden. The church took an ambiguous position, with Pope Gregory's legates approving this election but in the absence of papal confirmation, presumably because the church opposed and feared the emperor's resurgence of authority. A civil war ensued in which Henry, supported by the towns, defeated Rudolf (d. 1080). The pope again excommunicated and "deposed" the emperor, but a synod of German and Italian bishops then deposed Pope Gregory. Still, Gregory did not yield, Henry undertook a series of expeditions to Italy (1081–1082), the pope called in his Norman allies (from Sicily), and the conflict continued. The papal theory maintained that an evil ruler who violates the contract with

---

[d]In other areas rivalries developed between them. Thus the Saxon dukes were opposed by the archbishop of Bremen favored by the Salian house. Eventually, the Saxons rebelled against the ruling dynasty, but they were defeated by Henry IV in 1075.

REX ROGAT ABBATEM. MATHILDIM SUPPLICAT ATQ.

Henry IV and Countess Mathilda at Canossa
This miniature from the *Vita Mathildis* by the Monk Denis (1114) shows the German emperor in the garments of a penitent humbly asking Countess Mathilda of Tuscany and St. Hugh, the abbott of Cluny and the emperor's godfather, to intercede for him with Pope Gregory VII. They did so, and Henry was admitted into the presence of the pope on January 28, 1077. (Biblioteca Apostolica Vaticana, Rome)

his subjects may be deposed by the pope, who is responsible for the salvation of mankind. On this basis, Gregory's successors continued their opposition to Henry IV by supporting the revolts of Henry's sons against their father. But when Henry V (1106–1125) succeeded his father, he continued the policies of lay investiture, opposition to papal interference in Germany, and reliance on the towns and ministeriales while pretend-

The Aftermath of Canossa
The pope's triumph over Henry IV was only an episode in the struggle between the German emperors and the papacy. This contemporary miniature shows Pope Gregory in flight while the emperor sits side by side with Guibert, archbishop of Ravenna, whom Henry IV had installed as the anti-pope Clementis III. In 1084 the Normans freed Gregory and conducted him to Salerno, where he died in exile the next year. Henry IV was crowned emperor in Rome by Clementis III in 1084. (Chronicum libri, VIII ab origine mundi (1156) by Otto von Freising)

ing to depend on the princes. By 1122 the Synod at Worms sought to settle the great conflict through a concordat between pope and emperor, but in practice the rivalry between the two continued.

The journey to Canossa was but one incident in a controversy that resulted in further political fragmentation which subsequent intervals of imperial centralization could interrupt but not undo. To some extent, the "investiture controversy" is a misnomer. Pope Gregory VII had attacked the claim of the Salian dynasty to rule over the German church by divine right. In the interpretation of the Roman Curia, the emperor, like any other king, was a removable official if he violated God's law as interpreted by the church. Suitability alone was the test of kingship. At this time in the history of the church, the popes chose to emphasize the principle of an elective monarchy; hence, the princes who elected the emperor were the real source of authority, a fact which revitalized old Germanic traditions of election.

The result was further political particularism and anarchic conditions which could be exploited by the German aristocracy.

> The aristocracy, a class of locally powerful landowners, took advantage of the stress of civil war and the dissolution of old social classes to strengthen its hold by reducing large elements of the population to dependence. It multiplied its clients and affirmed its control by deft exploitation of the bonds of feudalism. It used the pretext that for thirty years, from 1076 to 1106, there was no lawful universally recognized German king as an excuse for exercising powers of government without royal assent and for extending the powers it was already exercising.[2]

Castles sprang up everywhere, and formerly free peasants who had been uprooted by civil war flocked to them for protection. Poor freemen became serfs and rich ones became knights and ministeriales. Weak nobles sought out stronger ones. Generally, then, men of lower rank came to be bound to those of higher rank by ties of vassalage and homage. As civil wars repeatedly swept the country, the demand for armed knights increased rapidly, and even bishops or abbots were recruiting trained warriors to defend their estates. Minor nobles and many freemen escaped ruin or the degradation of serfdom by abandoning their liberty and entering the ranks of the ministeriales. In that position they were maintained and armed at the lord's expense. Since the demand for such men was great, the conditions of the ministeriales became attractive; they were free of personal bondage, free to leave their lord, and able to transform their lands from servile tenures into manorial estates. The most successful of them built castles on their land and employed armed knights in turn, a case of upward mobility similar to the case of the Japanese warriors who eventually replaced their own masters. Thus, in the course of the civil wars following the investiture controversy, German society was transformed. Old noble families died out, while a new class of armed knights and ministeriales allied itself through marriage with older dynastic families, inheriting their estates and franchises and occupying the high offices in church and state which had once been the prerogative of ancient lineage.

The rise of the Hohenstaufen empire (1152–1272) achieved a degree of political unity similar to that of the Saxon and Salian dynasties. Royal domains again were consolidated with the help of the ministeriales, and for a time the many secular and ecclesiastical rulers together with their local landed aristocracies submitted to imperial authority. But even gifted rulers foundered on the administrative and political problems arising from the size and heterogeneity of a realm extending during its greatest expansion from the North Sea and the Baltic to the Mediterranean.

The Hohenstaufen emperors were concerned with reasserting their dominion in Italy, which through intermarriage and inheritance came to include the Norman kingdom of Sicily (after 1189). But the very success of enforcing and enlarging their authority in Italy brought on a new conflict with the papacy as well as indirectly strengthening the German princes. In the eighth century, the popes had called on Pepin and Charlemagne for protection against the Lombards. Now, in the twelfth century, the popes allied themselves with Lombard communities in a common opposition to the Hohenstaufen. When the Hohenstaufen emperor Henry VI (1190–1197) left a three-year-old son as his heir, the German princes split into two factions, each with its own candidate for the throne. The popes sided with one faction against the other and thus again became a party to the electoral struggles among the German princes. The contest between the Hohenstaufen rulers and the papacy continued under Frederick II (1215–1250).[e] Emperor Frederick was preoccupied with the effort to exercise his dominion over Italy, and this left the German princes and archbishops free to fight one another for territorial gain. In his charters of 1220 and 1232, he gave ecclesiastical and secular rulers written guarantees against the activities of royal domain officials and limited the expansion of imperial towns at the expense of territories belonging to the church (that is, archbishoprics, bishoprics, and monasteries). In the short run, stabilization was achieved despite the two anti-kings sponsored by the papacy. But the emperor died in 1250, and his son Conrad IV died in 1254. Their passing gave rise to the same feudal fragmentation and proliferation of local wars which had followed the investiture controversy in 1076–1077.

With the demise of Hohenstaufen rule, central authority disappeared from Germany altogether. The office of dukes, margraves, and others had been indivisible under imperial rule because they were at the disposal of the emperor. Now, the political integrity of these offices was in jeopardy. Between the close of the Hohenstaufen dynasty and the inception of Habsburg rule (1254–1273), princes were free to increase their domains and often threatened the possessions of the church. The papacy had hastened the downfall of the Hohenstaufen, but now that the church was threatened, Pope Gregory X intervened to restore imperial authority. In 1273 the electors raised the Swabian count Rudolf of Habsburg (1273–1291) to the throne.

[e]The year of Frederick II's imperial coronation (1215) coincided both with Magna Carta and with the Mongols' conquest of Peking and the start of their movement westward.

Rudolf of Habsburg quickly added to his realm by defending the empire against the aggressive policies of the king of Bohemia and by annexing the king's territories outside Bohemia. Rudolf also obtained the consent of the German princes when he granted Austria, Styria, and Western Slovenia (Carniola) to his two sons. But when Rudolf died in 1291, the electors feared the power he had amassed and chose Adolf (1291–1298), count of Nassau, as the next king. Adolf's policies aroused much opposition. He was deposed in 1298, and Albert of Habsburg (1298–1308) was elected in his stead. When Albert was murdered, the electors chose Count Henry of Luxemburg (1308–1313), a brother of the archbishop of Trier, one of the electors. Henry's reign was followed by a double election in which one group of electors chose Louis of Wittelsbach (1314–1347), duke of Upper Bavaria, while another chose Frederick of Habsburg (1314–1325), duke of Austria. Eight years of war followed which ended in the defeat of Frederick and the ascendance of the Wittelsbach house. But a feud between the two houses had begun which would last until the seventeenth century. On Louis' death in 1347, the German crown was bestowed once more on the Luxemburg house. The electors chose Charles IV (1349–1378), who was Margrave of Moravia and King of Bohemia. Charles was enormously successful in increasing his royal domain at the expense of the Wittelsbach and Habsburg houses. In the end, he wore the crowns of the Empire, Bohemia, Lombardy, and Burgundy, and in addition to other acquisitions he secured the Margraviate of Brandenburg for his son Wenceslas in 1373. When Charles died in 1378, his son Wenceslas was unopposed as heir to the throne, a succession from father to son that had not occurred in two hundred years.

Under the Saxon, Salian, and Hohenstaufen dynasties, the emperor had possessed royal authority in the conventional sense of that day. The empire's principalities had been fiefs over which dukes, counts, margraves, and others could not rule without imperial consent. The most important functions of the emperor were the defense of the eastern frontiers against the Magyars (and later the Turks), the adjudication of disputes among territorial rulers, and, when he required funds for common defense beyond the resources of his own domains, the imposition of extraordinary levies. There were weak as well as strong emperors, and changing political conditions inevitably affected what any one emperor could accomplish. But the principle of imperial sovereignty based on election was universally recognized and still further enhanced by papal consecration. The fact that Henry IV could assume that his position as emperor would be intact once he had purged himself of the ban of excommunication testifies to this general acceptance of imperial sovereignty and the revered authority of papal consecration.

These general assumptions became invalid during the thirteenth century. Three different dynasties (Habsburg, Wittelsbach, Luxemburg) occupied the German throne between 1273 and 1356, when a new settlement was reached. Despite the brief period of political consolidation which was achieved by Charles IV, imperial rule had seriously weakened. Before 1250, the emperor had possessed the right to exercise his imperial authority with or without the consent of the princes. After 1250, an era of princely rule began which extended from that time to the unification of Germany in 1871. Although imperial rule did not disappear, the emperor now depended both de facto and de jure on the willing cooperation of the princes.

Hereditary succession was unequivocally recognized only at the territorial level, whereas the electoral principle governed the selection of the emperor. The composition of the electoral body was at first uncertain, but during the twelfth century the three Rhenish archbishops (of Mainz, Cologne, and Trier) and the rulers of the great duchies emerged as the electors (*Kurfürsten*) to whose choice the other rulers gave their assent. But elections continued to be contested, and the papacy intervened from time to time. Legally, the Golden Bull of Charles IV (1356) marked the turning point. By this edict, the emperor determined that the three archbishops, the ruler of the Palatinate, the duke of Saxony, the margrave (later elector) of Brandenburg, and the king of Bohemia would decide by majority vote the successor to the imperial crown. The Golden Bull added the proviso that the candidate receiving a majority should be regarded as unanimously elected. Once elected, the king and emperor was immediately entitled to exercise his royal prerogatives. Both provisions put a stop to earlier claims of the pope that he had the right to examine rival candidates and then choose the one on whom he would bestow imperial authority by an act of consecration. With these and related provisions, the Golden Bull effectively terminated disputed elections and papal interventions. But this unity in the face of the papacy was achieved only by according full recognition to the prerogatives of the princes. From this time forward, dynasties might change, but the electors would remain, for the partition of electoral territories was prohibited. The electors were also granted rights of coinage and the monopoly of precious metals, which gave them a quasi-regal position. Furthermore, crown lands could not be transferred without the consent of the electors. The emperor became in effect the mouthpiece of the electors and the representative of the consensus which the electors had organized among the princes. Henceforth, the principalities were anchored in the Golden Bull, which legally precluded a revival of the imperial monarchy at the expense of the princes.

The elections in the period after 1250 showed that the princes had

Charles IV and the Seven Electors
This manuscript illustration depicts the settlement under the Golden Bull of 1356. It shows Charles IV wearing the crown, sword, and imperial scepter with the archbishops of Mainz, Cologne, and Trier to his right, and the king of Bohemia, the duke of Saxony, the margrave of Brandenburg, and the court of Palatinate to his left. Although the Golden Bull regularized the succession to the imperial throne, it also marked the decline of the emperor's effective authority. (Bibliothèque Royale Albert Iᵉʳ, Brussels)

only a qualified interest in the imperial institution. The electors probably reflected the opinions of other territorial rulers when they changed their preferences. Rudolf of Habsburg's initial popularity was due to his success against Bohemia, and his skill in dealing with the princes accounts for their consent to the territorial grants to his sons. But the emperor could perform only the imperial functions on which the princes agreed, provided that he possessed sufficiently extensive territories so that he himself could finance the costs of the imperial government. He could then induce the princes to grant the additional funds and materiel needed for recognized emergencies, such as the struggle against the Turks. Some part of the emperor's authority was still due to that mixture of awe and hope for peace which attached itself to the imperial throne even in the midst of family feuds and ruthless bids for power. But as soon as an emperor had amassed sufficient resources to give weight to his formal authority, he was also seen by many princes as endangering their autonomy—a dilemma which helps to account for the chronic instability of imperial rule.[3]

In the aftermath of Hohenstaufen rule, two of the four houses competing for the crown, Wittelsbach and Luxemburg, had ruled over the

Margraviate of Brandenburg (among their many other domains). I turn now to this frontier area of medieval Germany, the territorial nucleus of the future kingdom of Prussia.

FROM THE BRANDENBURG ELECTORATE TO THE KINGDOM OF PRUSSIA

The Saxon emperor, Otto I, founded the bishoprics of Havelberg and Brandenburg in 948 in an attempt to support Christian missions to the Slavic tribes living these areas. As with previous attempts at German settlement, this one was unsuccessful, and it was not until the twelfth century that German rulers defeated the Slavs and established permanent settlements. Lothair, duke of Saxony, and Albert I (the Bear), count of Ballerstadt and founder of the Ascanian house, renewed the attack on the Slavs in 1106. When Lothair was elected emperor in 1133, he invested Albert as margrave of the North Mark, a major area of Brandenburg east of the Elbe River. Albert followed his campaign against the Slavs by bringing Frisian, Saxon, and Rhenish settlers to the area. In this work of colonization he had the assistance of two missionary orders, the Cistercians and Premonstratensians. Albert and his successors entrusted these orders with large tracts of territory, which were farmed by lay brethren and subsequently by tenants. The clearing of forests, swamp drainage, and the development of agriculture went hand in hand. Though the first moves of colonization had been military, the major expansion of German settlement in the twelfth and early thirteenth centuries was peaceful. Slav settlements were sparse, and the development of the land allowed Slav residents and German settlers to prosper together, the two peoples gradually merging.

During the twelfth and thirteenth centuries, conditions in western Germany and the Low Countries furthered migration to the east, for with the decline of the Hohenstaufen dynasty the fragmentation of princely rule was accompanied by much armed conflict. Beyond the Elbe River, vast and thinly populated areas not only required pioneering activities of settling and cultivation, but also encouraged—once the area was pacified—a peasantry free of onerous burdens. Villages and towns enjoyed considerable autonomy. The weakness of territorial princes and of the landed nobility resulted in good part from their dependence on peasants and town-dwellers, created by conditions of labor scarcity and relative economic prosperity.[4]

But while conditions of settlement were favorable, the political and military situation was highly unstable. The same freedom which attracted settlers to develop the land could also encourage local rulers and landowners to enlarge their possessions and oppose restrictions by higher authority. Yet the involvement of German princes in the dynastic struggles of the empire drew their resources away from the duchies, margraviates, and other polities over which they ruled. Thus, the princes were stronger at the imperial level than on their home ground. For while the emperor depended on the consent of the princes obtained by negotiation, in the frontier regions of the empire princely authority itself was not strong either. An example from thirteenth-century Brandenburg illustrates this weakness.

In 1280 the incumbent ruler of Brandenburg, the Ascanian margrave Otto IV, was imprisoned in a clash with the archbishop of Magdeburg.[f] To obtain Otto's release, a ransom was collected by special levy on his vassals as well as on the towns in his domain. Such a levy was a conventional part of the feudal contract which made the payment of ransom money for the imprisoned ruler a legal obligation of his vassals. But in this case, the towns and aristocratic estates of Brandenburg would agree to the ransom payment only after prolonged negotiations. Eventually, a settlement was reached (1280–1283) which obliged the margrave to swear under oath that in the future he would call for special levies only when the country was endangered. For the margrave, such an agreement greatly curtailed his effectiveness as a ruler, since special levies to meet political or military emergencies were an essential part of princely authority at a time when even the wealthiest rulers often found the costs of government beyond their financial capacity. In addition, the margrave was forced to concede to his vassals the *right* of armed resistance if this oath were broken. That concession gave retroactive legal force to the resistance of the towns and estates. Henceforth, the margrave had to live within the means which his own domains provided for the support of government. These means were of course substantial; but his political moves would be greatly hampered if he had to anticipate armed resistance from his own notables whenever his policies led to expenses beyond his means. Finally, the margrave's right to impose special levies was made a part of his vassals' jurisdiction over their peasants; that is, the vassals were entitled to pass special burdens on to their own dependents, thus strengthening the vassals financially at the expense of both the margrave and the peasants.[5]

The story characterizes political conditions from the thirteenth to the fifteenth centuries, not only in Brandenburg but in many parts of the empire.[6] Duchies, margraviates, and other formally subordinate territories had earlier consolidated their rule at the expense of the emperor. Now, a similar transference of power was occurring at the ter-

---

[f] The territory of the archbishopric Magdeburg formed a sizable wedge in the southwestern part of Brandenburg. At the time, Magdeburg was a power in its own right because six other bishoprics were subordinate to it.

ritorial level, from the dukes, counts, and margraves to the towns and estate assemblies of aristocratic landowners. In the case of Brandenburg, this ascendance of local over territorial rulership was hastened by the dynastic struggle between the Wittelsbach and Luxemburg houses. Central rule over the margraviate weakened, in part because the Luxemburg rulers found it necessary to sell or pawn portions of Brandenburg and its adjacent possessions, a policy facilitated by the extinction of the Ascanian line. Between 1320 and 1415, the margraviate lost approximately half of its territories to the Teutonic Order in the east, to Saxony and Bohemia in the south, and to various other polities in the west and southwest.[7]

When central authority weakens and local rule becomes fragmented among an increasing number of relatively small competitors, a vacuum of authority is created. During the thirteenth and fourteenth centuries, many towns in Brandenburg and elsewhere in northern Germany succeeded in having the castles of formerly powerful, landed aristocrats razed to the ground. Formal settlements often guaranteed the towns their local autonomy, and various territorial magnates declared under oath that they would not reconstruct castles in or near the towns. To protect this newly won autonomy, the towns of Brandenburg and also of Pomerania to the north allied themselves with the Hanseatic League, and for a time this defensive alliance protected the urban jurisdictions against encroachments by local rulers and members of the landed aristocracy. The Hanseatic League was an association of north German and Baltic towns with agents and branch offices in many other countries. The league had developed in the twelfth and flourished from the thirteenth to the fifteenth century. Its monopoly of the Baltic trade made it powerful enough during the fourteenth century to aid the towns' opposition to local rulers and the special exactions resulting from dynastic struggles. At the same time, towns and mercantile associations supported the empire in the hope that a strong emperor could defend them against the territorial princes. However, in the fifteenth century, the economic importance of the Hanseatic League declined, and so did the political support which the league had given to the towns allied with it.

A more enduring rise to power was characteristic of the knightly class. The dependent ministeriales originally had aided the consolidation of imperial and of princely rule, each in its own domains. But the social status of these dependent men rose quickly with the demand for their administrative services. They received offices, lands, and rights. The distinction between the old aristocracy, which had been composed of free vassals of the prince (or the emperor), and these "new men" gradually diminished as the latter became warriors and landlords (*Ritter*) in their own right.

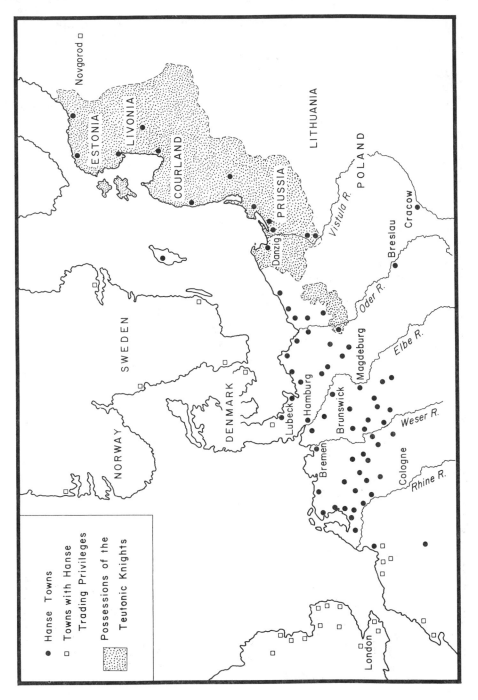

Novgorod

ESTONIA

LIVONIA

COURLAND

PRUSSIA

LITHUANIA

POLAND

Vistula R.

Danzig

Breslau

Cracow

Oder R.

Elbe R.

SWEDEN

Magdeburg

NORWAY

DENMARK

Lubeck

Hamburg

Brunswick

Weser R.

Bremen

Cologne

Rhine R.

London

● Hanse Towns

□ Towns with Hanse
  Trading Privileges

  Possessions of the
  Teutonic Knights

7. The Hanseatic League and the Teutonic Knights

This meant a greater freedom, and all the advantages accruing from a place in the feudal hierarchy including the right to enfeoff vassals of their own, to hold courts, and even in certain districts—for example, Mecklenburg, Holstein and the march of Brandenburg—to tax their dependents. Thus the rise of the *ministeriales*, which in its early stages was sponsored by the princes, finally came to endanger the cohesion of the German territories. Proceeding in exactly the same way as the princes themselves, who had made feudalism an instrument for weakening the crown and securing their own rise to power, the knightly class within the territorial states set out to undermine the strict feudal rules governing felony, escheat, division and alienation of fiefs, to shake off personal obligations, and to stabilize and consolidate their own hold over their fiefs and offices.[8]

Thus, landed warriors rose to aristocratic status and developed common interests in opposing the special levies which territorial princes periodically made to finance their dynastic struggles in the empire. To press these interests on the ruler, they formed estate assemblies which remained a formidable challenge to sovereign authority until the seventeenth century.

The corporate state (*Ständestaat*) of Brandenburg was very different from a constitutional state. The people were subjects, not citizens, and hence without any political rights. The mass of the peasants were hereditary serfs rendering compulsory services on the estates of their lords, while the townspeople—though formally free—were excluded from all political rights. Representation was the exclusive privilege of the landed squirearchy and an oligarchy of town magistrates. The ruler's authority as well as that of the landed squires consisted in patrimonial domination over the land and its people. Hence, all governmental functions were usable rights which could be sold or leased at will. For example, judicial authority was a type of property. The person who bought or leased that property was entitled to adjudicate disputes *and* receive the fees and penalties incident to such adjudication. In the corporate principality, the estates represented their own interests and privileges. They were literally the owners of local government in town and country. Landowners owned the power to police their estates and to settle disputes among their tenants, just as the members of the town patriciate governed their communities as if these were private property. Thus, the ruling class of the corporate state in the margraviate (later electorate) of Brandenburg consisted of two parts. All owners of local patrimonial authority on the land and in the towns represented the "country," while the elector with his court and government was the hereditary overlord.

The so-called era of princely rule began, then, with a period of social transformation in which not only the emperor but also the territorial rulers lost much of their former power. Dynastic struggles and the fortunes of the house of Luxemburg, however, continued to affect the fate of Brandenburg. In 1373 Emperor Charles IV had strengthened imperial rule and secured Brandenburg for his son Wenceslas. When Charles died in 1378, Wenceslas (1378–1400) was elected emperor and Brandenburg passed to Wenceslas' half-brother Sigismund. In 1410 Sigismund (1410–1437) was elected emperor in turn. Under these sons of Charles IV, imperial rule weakened once more, and in Brandenburg internal disputes became endemic. Feuding aristocratic families made the area so unsafe that an estate assembly in Berlin petitioned Emperor Sigismund for relief. In 1411 he appointed Frederick of Hohenzollern, imperial burgrave of Nuremberg, to represent the Luxemburg house as ruler of Brandenburg.[9] Four years later, Sigismund invested Frederick (1415–1440) and his heirs with Brandenburg and the electoral privilege in return for a payment of 400,000 gold gulden. Given the anarchic conditions of Brandenburg, it is not surprising that cash seemed more important to the emperor than a retention of the Luxemburg claim.

The right of sovereign authority over the electorate of Brandenburg seemed a dubious gain. Frederick I "found the princely estate practically denuded of its goods and rights and all the castles, with the sole exception of Spandau, in the possession of his subjects."[10] Nevertheless, the new elector had considerable means at his disposal. He used diplomacy and strategic force in order to assert his authority. But his attempt to claim all the rights of the Ascanian house provoked resistance, which led to his defeat by local lords in alliance with the Pomeranians in 1425. Frederick left Brandenburg in the hands of his sons, who engaged in protracted struggles with the towns, which were not effectively subdued until the mid-fifteenth century. Against the estate assemblies of the landed aristocracy, Frederick's successors were much less successful, and highway robbery by armed knights as well as periodic invasions by neighboring powers left the country in almost perpetual turmoil. Time and again, the Hohenzollern were obliged to pawn or sell their possessions and prerogatives in order to buy arms and men with whose help they could establish a semblance of order.[11]

This great strength of the local aristocracy was due in part to the changing position of the peasants. Under the exigencies of colonization, landowners had vied with one another to attract peasants by offering them favorable conditions. However, during the fifteenth century the peasantry suffered major reverses as wars, plagues, and famines depopulated the area and brought widespread poverty. Gradually, the landlords enlarged their domains, appropriating peasant freeholds by eviction or purchase. Where peasants were prevented from moving elsewhere, they saw their proprietary rights revoked and their freedom curtailed until they were bound to the soil, forced to render increasingly burdensome services and completely subjected to the jurisdiction of their lords.[12] These measures partly made up for the difficulties arising from the sparse settlement of the land. At the same time, the price of corn rose and the export of grains increased so that the landowners improved their economic position. The landed aristocracy of northeastern Germany had been formidable warriors earlier. Now they became grain-exporting landowners, the *Junkers*, who combined local administrative power with a businesslike management of their estates. This combination of increasing wealth and local power buttressed their opposition to the Hohenzollern rulers.

Through their estate assemblies, these landed notables circumscribed the power of the electors of Brandenburg, just as the towns had limited the powers of local rulers during the peak of the Hanseatic League's influence.[13] As the wealth derived from agriculture gradually increased, the landed aristocracy also began to intervene in urban affairs; the Hohenzollern electors did the same when they supported the small urban patriciate in its struggles with the middle-class or lower-class urban population. By the end of the fifteenth century, the electors with the aid of the squirearchy succeeded in curbing the privileges of taxation and jurisdiction which the towns of Brandenburg and Pomerania had enjoyed.[14] Yet during the sixteenth century, the Hohenzollern rulers fought unsuccessfully against the dominant position of the landed aristocracy. These large landowners preempted all local authority and enjoyed a growing economic prosperity, often won at the expense of the peasantry and of the economic and political position of the towns.[15] To be sure, the Hohenzollern rulers profited from their own extensive holdings as conditions improved, and they were as willing to gain at the expense of peasants and towns as the other landowners of the electorate. But the latter had won such a strong position economically, and through their estate assemblies politically, that until the beginning of the seventeenth century the Hohenzollern dynasty could achieve only negotiated settlements with these local magnates.

During the sixteenth and seventeenth centuries, the Hohenzollern rulers were the largest landowners in their realm and managed their domains like all other estate-owners. The working assumption was that the prince finances his court from the yield of his domains and from the income accruing through governmental functions such as coinage, customs dues, and related princely prerogatives. Under ordinary circumstances, the court budget and the "state budget" were indistinguishable. Only in emergencies or on special state occassions was it customary that the "country" (the estate assemblies and the towns) would grant the ruler special levies, such as those required by the empire to fight the Turks, or those occasioned by the marriage of a princess. The theoretical balance between rulers and estates did not function smoothly, and in the early sixteenth century it hardly functioned at all. Under Joachim

Emperor Sigismund Invests Burgrave Frederick of Nürnberg
Emperor Sigismund is surrounded by Duke Ludwig of Saxony with a scepter, Duke Ludwig of Bavaria-Heidelberg with a sword, and Duke Henry of Bavaria with the imperial globe. Burgrave Frederick of Nürnberg, flag in hand, kneels opposite the emperor, at the head of his entourage. Below, the forces of the burgrave with their horses and standards are shown. This formal act of investiture with the electorate of Brandenburg occurred in 1417 in Konstanz. (Chronicle of Ulrich von Richenthal, Rosgartenmuseum, Konstanz)

II (1535–1571), the ruling house was near bankruptcy, and the estates agreed to assume its debts on condition that they would be entitled to administer the tax system; the ruler retained the administration of his domains. Under these circumstances, Brandenburg, like most other German territories, was incapable of political action on the international scene. Instead, these corporate principalities were preoccupied with family alliances and feuds, dispute settlements, and the maintenance of a hierarchic social order.[16]

In the history of Brandenburg and the other Hohenzollern possessions, the Reformation and the Thirty Years' War (1618–1648) proved to be the dividing line between the particularism of a petty principality and the emergence of the country as a European power. The Reformation had special significance for the concept of authority in the Hohenzollern domains.

By the end of the fifteenth century, the rulers and the estates of Brandenburg had achieved a precarious balance of forces, but the empire was in complete disarray. Frequent political crises and armed conflicts as well as widespread poverty throughout the empire engendered attacks on the papacy, the great archbishops, and the higher social classes whether they were princes, aristocrats, or rich merchants. Since political conditions had approached anarchy for more than a century, men yearned for spiritual comfort as well as civil peace. These desires as well as increasing poverty helped to focus general hostility on the Roman church and its wealth. This sentiment reverberated throughout the empire despite its territorial divisions, a first intimation of national feeling.

Luther challenged Rome in the Wittenberg theses of 1517. His own concerns originated in a profound religious experience. At the same time, Luther appealed to every man, from the princes to the common people, by espousing a religion of inward experience against such merely human institutions as the papacy, church councils, and canon law. By translating the Bible from Latin into vernacular German, he brought religion close to the people, and his program of religious reform was applicable to all parts of the empire. Luther's manifesto of 1520, "To the Christian nobility of the German Nation on the improvement of the Christian condition," called for a return to religious fundamentals and transcended special political interests. The reigning emperor, however, was in no position to respond to these appeals. As head of the house of Habsburg based in Austria and as king of Spain, Charles V (1519–1558) would have had to compromise his position outside Germany if he had placed himself at the head of a German opposition to Rome. Hence, the emperor was determined to suppress the reform movement.

In 1521 Luther was placed under an imperial ban, which provoked the protest of some very influential territorial rulers. Efforts to restore unity failed, and a League of Protestant Princes was formed. In 1526 the Diet in Speyer declared that every principality in the empire should follow its conscience on the ecclesiastical issue; thus, decisions concerning the religious question were turned over to each separate territory. This resolution of 1526 was accepted as the basis of the compromise of 1555 in the Peace of Augsburg. Henceforth, each prince was given the right to decide the religion of his principality; only heads of ecclesiastical states were not permitted to change to the reformed faith.

The principle that each subject must adopt the religion of his prince (*cuius regio, eius religio*) transformed the old conception of kingship. Luther probably had not intended to subordinate the church to secular power, but the opposition of Charles V and the social unrest of the peasants forced him to seek the help of the princes. By opposing the juridical institutions of Rome and preaching a purely spiritual church, he conceded that under God's will the state is the form in which the world exists. The great magnates of the church were great territorial rulers as well, and princes frequently had enlisted the resources of the church in support of their territorial power. But while the relations between princes and the church had always been close, Luther now endowed the authority of the state with a religious halo it had previously lacked. By holding the secular ruler responsible for the organization of the church, Luther made the individual's submission to authority into a religious obligation and thus added an aura of sanctity to the authority of the prince.

In its own way, however, the Lutheran position was as equivocal as the Catholic. Pope Gelasius had argued for the supremacy of the church over all secular power, and that claim had been given a spiritual basis by "documenting" the apostolic succession from St. Peter to the bishop of Rome. Thereafter, the problem had been how kings could be consecrated as God's Anointed and yet subordinate their supreme authority in all matters affecting the sacred (such as baptism, marriage, and death) to the jurisdiction of the church. Protestant kingship posed a different dilemma. All affairs of this world exist under God's will, including the state under the authority of kings. Yet Luther was no more willing than the papacy to abandon spiritual matters to a merely secular jurisdiction. In his view there were two kingdoms, one of mercy and love, the other of anger and punishment.

But since they were both willed by God, a Christian had to fulfill his duty in both realms. The contrast was eased by knowledge that the secular order was not only a penalty for sin, but also contained promise of ultimate mercy. Since government made dissemination of the Word possible, and thereby access to salvation, this instrument of God's world rule was surrounded by a certain Christian aura after all. The whole conception led to a characteristic dichotomy in ethics. A true Christian was bound by his conscience to an ethics of

Martin Luther and the Wittenberg Reformers
This 1543 painting by Lucas Cranach the Younger shows in the foreground (from left to right) Luther, the elector of Saxony, Zwingli, and Melanchton. The most prominent figure is that of the elector John Frederick, an apt symbol of the Reformer's dependence on secular power. John Frederick and his family protected Luther personally, sheltering him in their castles after he refused to recant his heretical Wittenberg theses. (Gift of Edward Drummond Libbey, Toledo Museum of Art)

love, but as a prince or ordinary officeholder he had to adhere to the secular law. The ensuing conflict of heart was harmonized by the assurance that preservation of the natural order was ordained by God, and consequently adhering to the secular order was a service to Him and to one's neighbor. In this perspective Luther could call strict execution of the law by a prince, or relentless fighting on the part of a soldier, true worship of God.[17]

The king or soldier was enjoined to do God's work by facilitating the church's efforts to guide and sustain each individual's abiding faith in his God.[g]

The Lutheran faith of the people provided the Hohenzollern rulers with a religious justification of their authority, but the actual assertion of that authority was the indirect result of war. Imperial Germany had been engulfed by religious and political controversies during the sixteenth century, and by 1618 a war broke out that was to last for thirty years and involve the major European powers. The economic and political dislocations caused by the war greatly weakened all segments of the population, and the whole period was marked by economic depression. Brandenburg was alternately occupied by Imperial German or by Swedish mercenaries as the fortunes of war fluctuated. In many towns, one-half to one-third of the houses were destroyed. Destruction in much of the Electorate was so severe that it took a century for the population to regain its prewar size.[18] Economically, the most damaging aspect of this destruction was the widespread devastation of peasant holdings. Many peasant families disappeared, and after the war their unoccupied holdings were absorbed by the large estates.[19]

These upheavals inadvertently favored administrative centralization. The Hohenzollern territories were scattered (except for Brandenburg), but during the sixteenth century the Hohenzollern rulers had added to their holdings by a series of dynastic marriages which involved them in relations with the major powers. Even then, they did not assume an active role in European power politics as long as the Thirty Years' War engulfed their territories. The elector George William (1619–1640) resided in faraway (East) Prussia, while his home province of Brandenburg was occupied by Swedish troops from 1627 onward.[h] He actually

---

[g]In 1613 one of the Hohenzollern rulers of Brandenburg converted to the Reformed (Calvinist) faith, while the population of his domains remained predominantly Lutheran. When Elector Johann Sigismund of Brandenburg (1608–1619) made his Calvinist faith public, his step aroused considerable discontent and the elector conceded religious liberty to his subjects by abandoning the attempt to proselytize. For an analysis of the political and religious ramifications of Johann Sigismund's conversion, see Otto Hintze, "Calvinism and Raison d'Etat in Early Seventeenth Century Brandenburg," in *Historical Essays,* pp. 88–154.

[h]The term *Prussia* was originally the name of a tribal country on the southeastern coast of the Baltic Sea, roughly between the Vistula and the Memel. Prussians were the pagan settlers in this area who resisted Christianization until the thirteenth century, when the knights of the Teutonic Order were invited to assist the Christian mission and were authorized by the Hohenstaufen emperor to settle the country. As noted earlier, the order, based on the disciplined development and organization of its territories, became a major contender for power with Muscovy. The order suffered a major defeat in 1410 and declined thereafter; it was formally dissolved in 1525. As the order declined, parts of Prussia came under Polish sovereignty, while other parts were held as a fief of the Polish crown

benefited from this military occupation, because the political and economic position of the landed aristocracy declined and its power to oppose him weakened. The elector also increased his military preparations,
and his successor Frederick William (1640–1688) used his emergency
powers due to participation in the war between Sweden and Poland
from 1655 to 1660 to raise the revenues needed for the military
establishment.[20]

These strategies were eminently successful. In 1640, when the
"Great Elector" Frederick William came to power, total revenue
amounted to one million Taler; by the time of his death in 1688 it had
tripled. During the same period the size of his standing army increased
from 4,500 to 30,000.[21] Prior to these developments, armies had been
recruited only in wartime and disbanded when hostilities ceased. Frederick William introduced the principle of a standing army in peacetime.
To meet the cost of that army and other increased expenses, a *regular*
tax was imposed—in place of the *special* levies for the maintenance of
troops which had sufficed prior to the seventeenth century.[i]

By these changes, the Hohenzollern rulers initiated the creation of
a unified state which was accomplished against the will of the estate assemblies.[22] The Thirty Years' War had undermined the ability of the
estates to resist this "revolution from above." Eventually, the estate assemblies condoned the elector's unilateral actions in the military and
fiscal fields, and "in return" Frederick William reconfirmed and increased the status privileges and local authority of the squirearchy at the
expense of the towns. At the same time, he firmly excluded the estates
from their previous preemption of such sovereign functions as control
of the tax system, participation in foreign affairs, and others. In 1701
Prussia became a kingdom, and by 1704 the new political system was
complete. That year marked the last meeting in which a Prussian assem-

---

by the Teutonic Order under its grand master, Albert of Hohenzollern. In 1618 Ducal
Prussia passed through inheritance to the Hohenzollern elector of Brandenburg, contrib-
uting to the rise of the Hohenzollern monarchy as a great European power. By military
intervention in the Swedish-Polish war of 1655–1660, Frederic William of Brandenburg
("The Great Elector") ended Polish sovereignty over Ducal Prussia at the Peace of Oliva.
In this way, the Hohenzollern rulers became sovereigns of Ducal Prussia, which formally
remained outside the German empire. Prussia subsequently became the name of all the
Hohenzollern possessions throughout Germany. I shall use the term in this last extended
sense for the period after 1618.

[i]A few details will help to underscore the significance of foreign relations for these
major changes in the internal distribution of power. During the 1640s and 1650s, the
estates of Cleve-Mark still retained their right to enter into direct diplomatic negotiations
with foreign powers. This right was formally abolished in 1661. Similarly, the right of the
estates to convoke assemblies on their own initiative was abolished at various times during
this period. The Great Elector used the standing army as a major weapon to achieve this
victory over the estates, but in doing so he depended on financial subsidies from *foreign*
powers in order to maintain that army. See Otto Hintze, *Hohenzollern und ihr Werk*, p. 221.

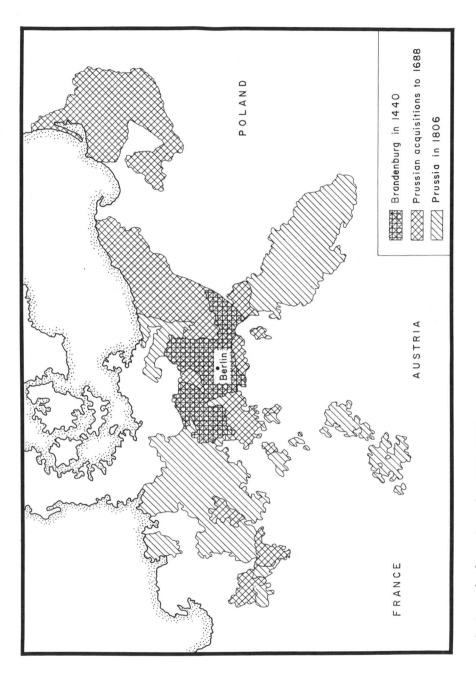

POLAND

AUSTRIA

FRANCE

Berlin

8. Brandenburg-Prussia, 1440–1806

bly (*Landtag*) gave its formal consent to the revenue to be assessed in the rural areas. Thereafter, taxes were assessed and collected without formal consent. Subsequent measures of administrative reorganization and centralization consolidated monarchical rule. The standing army had become the prime instrument of the ruler's authority.[23]

This new militarism left an enduring imprint on Prussian society. Most cities became garrison towns; the cavalry was often quartered in the countryside. Compulsory billeting of military personnel became a permanent burden. A standing army meant regular taxation, a major factor in undermining the earlier independence of estate assemblies which had been based on their ability to grant or withhold special levies. In the towns as well as the countryside, the local administration of tax collection and of the police was replaced by centrally organized war-commissariats. On royal initiative, the old-fashioned regional patriarchalism was replaced by a central bureaucracy and its agents, who abruptly disregarded local traditions. The result was a growing antagonism between the old squirearchy and the new monarchy, lasting through the first decades of the eighteenth century. In his political testament of 1722, Frederick William I still called the Junkers the most dangerous foes of the monarchy, but by the accession of Frederick II in 1740 an accommodation had been reached. The estate assemblies no longer asserted an independent political position, and members of the aristocracy entered state service in increasing numbers. At the same time, the monarchy supported the privileged position of the aristocracy in state and society. The compatibility of that support with royal prerogative increased because the Prussian rulers as well as their aristocratic followers accepted the personal obligation to serve the state.

This accommodation between monarchy and aristocracy was assisted by the Reformed faith, which inculcated a sense of duty. The Prussian territories were predominantly Lutheran, and the Hohenzollern rulers upheld the principle of religious toleration. An undogmatic, inward piety became popular and ensured that religious questions would remain nonpolitical, while the idea of service to a Higher Power buttressed the social order. Perhaps nothing shows this political quiescence as well as the literature of the eighteenth century in which the idealization of pious feeling and moral rectitude precluded all assertion of individuality, even against the most blatant injustice.[24]

Under Frederick William I (1713–1740), the build-up of Prussia's military might, administrative organization, and budgetary surplus were impressive, though the country's policies remained peaceful. In 1740 this situation changed abruptly when Frederick II (1740–1786) occupied Silesia and precipitated the first Silesian war (1740–1742). The alliances between Prussia and France against Austria and England indicated that Prussia had become a major European power. Subsequently,

Austria, France, and Russia formed a defensive alliance against Prussia, but Frederick retained the initiative by invading Saxony and thus precipitated the Seven Years' War (1756–1763). The peace of Hubertusburg (1763) confirmed Prussia's possession of Silesia but not of Saxony. Although this assured its new position as a great power, the prolonged war had impoverished the country. Henceforth, Prussia's position depended on its standing army of 200,000 men, and all efforts to increase the prosperity of the country were designed to support this military establishment. Frederick II introduced measures of reconstruction. He settled 300,000 colonists in the sparsely populated eastern parts of his territories. He sought to further the manufacture of textiles, pottery, and glass; he promoted trade and banking, tightened up taxation, and regularized the judiciary by foregoing all personal interference with it. He also sought to reconcile conflicting interests between rich and poor by regulations designed to keep the price of grains at a middle level. Under Frederick's reign, the Prussian state was based on a legally defined division of labor:

> The aristocracy furnished the officers for the army; therefore it was allowed exclusive possession of knightly estates (*Rittergüter*). The peasantry furnished the footsoldiers and paid the land tax (*Kontribution*); therefore the enclosure of peasant holdings was prohibited and care was taken to give administrative protection to the peasants. Town-residents had the exclusive right to engage in trade and manufacture: this was the source of the sales tax (*Akzise*); therefore all trade and manufacture was restricted to the towns and competition in the countryside was prohibited.[25]

Under the reign of Frederick William II (1786–1797), this spirit of a fully regulated social order was articulated in a comprehensive legal code (*Allgemeine Landrecht*, 1794). But the successors of Frederick II were unable to maintain the momentum he had imparted to the cumbersome machinery of the state. Without this central impulse, Prussia stagnated until it collapsed under the onslaught of Napoleon's armies in 1806.

These antecedents of Imperial Germany and the Hohenzollern domains can be compared with the developments considered thus far.

1. The legitimation of authority offers the most striking contrasts, both within Christianity and between the Western and Japanese conceptions of kingship. The rulers of the Holy Roman Empire acquired their imperial title through consecration by the pope. By this act, the church claimed and the emperor acknowledged the supremacy of the pope in all matters pertaining to God's law. Since the church was a great secular power, it could press this claim in political affairs whenever its institutional interests were involved. The Reformation rejected this Catholic claim to supremacy by putting the organization of God's min-

istry into the hands of the secular ruler. All rulers of the Reformed faith were still under God's law and obliged to abide by His word, but now their own secular rule was itself evidence of faith. They were charged with protection of the ministry, but the Protestant church did not claim a spiritual supremacy over the secular ruler. The Greek Orthodox faith resembles the Protestant in some respects, for it also put the organization of God's ministry into the hands of the secular ruler. But the Protestant emphasis on the Bible, the individual's faith, and the community of believers was closer to early Christianity and its controversies. By contrast, the Greek Orthodox emphasis on the received faith underscored the blessings of holiness and the sacredness of tradition, which discouraged theological argument. Both interpretations allowed for a religious justification of unchecked secular rule, but German Protestant rulers also allowed for the emergence of religious toleration.

All three Christian interpretations are quite different from the religion of Japan. Shintoism sought man's harmony with nature through the mediation of ancestral spirits. In Japan, the starting-point of rulership was the appeal to these spirits on behalf of the clan and the community as a whole. In Western Christianity, the starting-point of rulership was the claim to be the secular representative of Christ on earth, however differently that claim was authenticated. Japanese religious beliefs permitted the idea of one divine imperial lineage throughout the country's history; the Christian tradition precluded this fiction, since a continuous presence throughout nature and history is solely an attribute of God. Finally, the Japanese emperor remained the symbol of worship and artistic excellence even after he lost all secular authority; by contrast, the German emperor became a shadowy figure as he lost authority, for the center of Catholic culture remained in Rome while German culture became as fragmented and derivative from foreign models as its political order.

2. The German empire never achieved political unity. Imperial Germany lacked the forces that promoted political unification in Russia. The Mongols had an interest in a Russian capability of defending the western frontiers against Teutonic and Lithuanian attacks. The Mongols also favored the Orthodox church, which gave its ideological and eventually its institutional support to unified rule. These forces counteracted the tendency toward political fragmentation which had been present in the steppe areas of Kievan Russia. Political fragmentation was endemic in feudalism, especially in underpopulated frontier areas, and Imperial Germany was no exception. For six centuries, from Pepin's anointment in 751 to the Golden Bull of 1356, the papacy encouraged divisive forces in German society, while the German emperors divided their attention between their Italian and German possessions. These papal and imperial policies militated against the unity of the Holy Roman empire.

3. By the beginning of the eighteenth century, the Hohenzollern rulers had eliminated the estate assemblies of the aristocracy, while safeguarding its local preeminence. In Prussia, aristocratic landlords remained masters over their own domains. To some extent, this development paralleled the Russian, where the *boyar duma* had played a major role in the Kievan period but where this assembly and the independence of princes and boyars had declined with the final ascendance of Muscovite rule. In both countries, a servitor aristocracy developed. But whereas in Russia, local authority increasingly came into the hands of military commanders, provincial governors, or their corrupt agents, Prussian local government retained a greater degree of autonomy. In the early unification of the Hohenzollern domains, the duties of local administration had been assigned to war commissars. But as these duties were expanded by royal edict, a new office of *Landrat* was inaugurated to which such duties were assigned. The Landrat depended on instructions from the central government, but he was also a local notable elected by the estate assembly of the county (*Kreis*) and then appointed by the king. Moreover, in the fields of credit policy and justice, local estate assemblies (*Kreistage*) continued to have influence, even after autocratic power had destroyed their earlier political functions.[26]

4. The Hohenzollern rulers favored the aristocracy at the expense of the towns and the peasants, but imposed considerable burdens of military service on the aristocracy as well. In the seventeenth and eighteenth centuries, the Prussian rulers also imposed austerity on their own household which legitimated the service demanded of the aristocracy —an attitude derived in part from the Calvinism of the Hohenzollern. Such austerity stood in striking contrast to the conspicuous luxuries characteristic of court life in other countries. In Prussia, austerity at the court was for a time as much a symbol of national identity as the cultivation of art and manners had been at Kyoto.

5. By the beginning of the eighteenth century, the Prussian rulers had developed a new corps of officials of heterogeneous origins. They were primarily dependent on the king and assisted him in harnessing the country's resources for military purposes, including the personal and financial contributions of the aristocracy. As a result, Prussian society was characterized by institutionalized opposition between autocratic, monarchical government and the locally dominant, landed aristocracy. In Russia, by contrast, all major governmental positions were staffed by aristocratic placemen, whose social and political position (if not also their wealth) depended on their hereditary service-rank in the government. In this case there was less institutionalized opposition between monarchical government and aristocracy, because in the course of its rise the Muscovite state had destroyed the hereditary independence of princes and boyars.

Central authority emerged in Prussia only in the seventeenth century, a development long delayed by autonomous estate assemblies. For a time, the subordination of towns and aristocrats to their princely ruler was largely nominal. In a second phase, the Hohenzollern dynasty established military and political supremacy over the estates by exploiting international involvements, especially the devastation of the Thirty Years' War. Henceforth, the landed aristocracy enjoyed *local* authority, but was strictly excluded from national affairs. Moreover, aristocratic status came to be associated directly with service in the officer corps of a large and powerful military establishment. Until about 1740, aristocratic status was *not* tied to positions in the civil service, since officials under the Hohenzollern rulers were frequently recruited from bourgeois families, often from areas outside Prussia and with special emphasis on their Calvinist faith in contrast to the Lutheran persuasion of the Prussian population generally.[27]

FROM INDEPENDENT KNIGHTS TO LANDED ARMY OFFICERS

The Hohenzollern rule of Brandenburg had begun in 1415 when the new rulers were confronted with a country dominated by armed warriors who made the country unsafe for towns and merchants and who were quite unwilling to submit to higher authority. Political disorder continued for much of the fifteenth and sixteenth centuries until changes in economic conditions, the Reformation, and the impact of the Thirty Years' War weakened the aristocracy and facilitated Hohenzollern supremacy. Thereafter, the Prussian military establishment became the mainstay of monarchical rule and a major instrument in making dynastic interest prevail over the interest of the provincial aristocracy.

The army increased from 40,000 in 1713 to 235,000 in 1806, when it comprised some 16 percent of the eligible male population. In 1740 the army included every twenty-fifth person in the population, in contrast to France whose army included one of every one hundred and fifty. In terms of the size of its army, Prussia ranked third or fourth among the European powers, but tenth in terms of territory and thirteenth in terms of population.[28]

With a standing army as a prime instrument of dynastic policy, the Hohenzollern ruler saw to it that the officers were largely recruited from aristocratic families. In the early eighteenth century, when elsewhere in Europe an aristocratic education included the "grand tour" of European capitals, the sons of the Prussian aristocracy were denied the right to travel abroad, let alone to enter the service of a foreign ruler. Violators were threatened with confiscation of their property and stigmatized as deserters. Even retired army officers were barred from foreign travel,

and petitions for exemption from service by young aristocrats were rejected summarily.[29] Attendance at foreign universities was prohibited
on penalty of being denied employment in Prussia, and parents of sons
eligible for military service, who were abroad before the prohibition,
were instructed to request their return. The monarchy was symbolically
identified with the ideal of military service. The king personally determined which young aristocrats were to be called up from lists of eligible
officer candidates prepared for each area. The Hohenzollern rulers also
made it their practice to don a military uniform and enter personally
into many details of military organization.

The consequences of these policies for the aristocracy are reflected
in the changing size and composition of the Prussian officer corps. From
1,030 in 1688, the number of officers increased to 3,116 in 1740, 5,511
in 1786, and between 7,000 and 8,000 in the first decade of the nineteenth century. In 1739 all generals were from aristocratic families, and
out of 211 staff officers only 11 were commoners. At a time when the
military forces of Europe were largely mercenary and of motley com-

Prussian Militarism Personified
Frederick William I (1713–1740) gave his special attention to a guard regiment of 2,400
men who had to be at least six feet tall. Young peasants meeting this qualification were often
recruited by force and the annual cost of maintaining the guard regiment equaled the cost
of 10,000 ordinary soldiers. When the king was ill or depressed, he would have two or three
hundred of these grenadiers march through his bedroom to cheer him up. (Archiv Deutscher
Militärverlag)

position, Frederick William I (1713–1740) had succeeded in making the officer corps exclusively Prussian and aristocratic. By 1740 even two-thirds of the enlisted men were native Prussians, while the rest were foreign mercenaries. The fact that half the staff officers of the corps of engineers were of bourgeois origin only reflected the aristocratic disdain for learning and technical work. Officers of nonaristocratic background remained in separate, "lower class" units even when their number increased temporarily, as it did during the Seven Years' War (1756–1763). By the beginning of the nineteenth century, there were only 695 non-aristocratic officers in a corps of over 7,000.[30]

The aristocracy of the officer corps represented the top rank of Prussian society, symbolized by the uniform worn by officers and ruler alike. Officers were favored over civilians in matters of precedence, even low-ranking officers who were aristocrats over high-ranking civilian officials who were also aristocrats. Moreover, officers were expressly forbidden to have social relations with persons of lower status than themselves. Officers enjoyed the privilege that they would be judged only by their peers, a right which separated them from the population at large. Moreover, under Frederick II (1740–1786), special edicts forbade aristocrats to establish a business in the towns or enter a profession; thus, the only careers available to them were in the officer corps, the civil service, and landownership. Service in the military was the most tempting, in part because distinguished service in wartime was considered a basis for promotion in rank, and indeed for elevation to the aristocracy in the case of noncommissioned officers from middle-class families. An ideology of "honor" made the officer corps the supreme embodiment of an aristocratic way of life.

The military establishment imposed a great burden on the society as a whole. In the seventeenth century, the Prussian territories with a population of one million people paid nearly twice as much per head to support the military establishment as their more prosperous French contemporaries.[31] In the course of the eighteenth century, these expenditures rose to two-thirds of total public revenue.[32] To help meet the cost of his policies, Frederick William I greatly extended the royal domains and increased their productivity. Royal purchases of encumbered estates diminished the total holdings of the aristocracy, and tenancy on the royal domains specifically excluded aristocrats in favor of commoners, both measures continuing that monarchical encroachment on aristocratic privilege which had characterized the seventeenth century. By 1740 the royal domains constituted one-third of the arable lands and forested areas of the state; income from them had almost doubled since 1713. Income from the royal domains contributed about one-half of total public revenue, but the remaining burden on the population was severe, amounting to some 40 percent of the net income of peasant holdings. To avoid internal debts or external political liabilities, a considerable portion of this income was saved. By 1740 some eight million Taler had accumulated, more than one million in excess of the total annual budget of the state.[33]

The military establishment imposed heavy direct and indirect burdens on the aristocracy. To be sure, knightly estates (*Rittergüter*) were exempted from the land tax, except in a province like East Prussia where Frederick William I consolidated various direct taxes and eliminated the tax exemptions of the aristocracy. In Brandenburg and Magdeburg, despite substantial resistance, he managed to enforce a new tax which was calculated in terms of the number of horses due from each estate. When aristocrats had added indebted or deserted peasant lands to their own estates, these lands were taxable. Perhaps more important were the indirect burdens which the aristocracy could not evade. Landowners were held liable for the required contributions of their peasants if the latter defaulted. A heavy sales tax imposed on the cities greatly increased the price of goods bought by the aristocracy. Payments to officers on active duty were so minimal that they required considerable supplementation from their families if they were to compete successfully in advancing their military careers. Finally, the heavy demands made on the peasants became a major economic liability for the economy of landed estates. Large numbers of peasants were recruited for military service, and the peasants who remained on the land were required to perform a great many personal services in connection with military supplies and the billeting of soldiers. Both practices diminished the available work force, especially in times of war. It is not surprising that these policies caused resistance or evasion, prompting Frederick William I to denounce the thickheaded recalcitrance of the aristocracy in his political testament of 1722.

The cultural impact of militarism was far-reaching. Young aristocrats who were called to the colors could expect to remain on military duty for decades. To advance in rank required so many years that a captain or colonel would return to his estate only at the age of fifty. In times of war, even retired officers had to serve with the militia. In 1724 the landed aristocracy of Pomerania consisted with few exceptions of officers or former officers, and in two counties (*Kreise*) of East Prussia, officers and former officers represented 57 and 63 percent of the total number of aristocrats.[34] In England, as we shall see, the squirearchy became urbanized to a certain extent with the development of a London "season" and the establishment of town residences by leading families of the rural gentry. In Prussia some urbanization also occurred, but without comparable effects on manners and outlook. Aristocrats who spent part or all of their lives as urban residents did so as officers or civil servants. In the Prussian towns, the economy depended to such an extent on the presence of military personnel stationed in garrisons that public revenue derived from a tax on consumer goods (*Akzise*) declined by one-third whenever the army was on the march. Among the population of Berlin during the eighteenth century, the proportion of military personnel was never less than 20 percent. And if recruits and officers on leave are included, the military constituted over 40 percent of the Berlin residents.[35]

Under these circumstances, the urban residence of Prussian aristocrats did little to encourage the urbane manners which characterized the court society of England and France. Not that intrigues, influence peddling, and fierce competition were wanting. But in the Prussian towns, aristocratic officers encouraged a military bearing, an authoritarian manner, and at best an idealization of service which would have been out of place in the polite society of London or Versailles. The urbanization of the Prussian and the English aristocracies differed as much as dynastic militarism and administrative centralization differed from parliamentary supremacy and oligarchic place-hunting at court.

In the course of the eighteenth century, Prussian militarism undermined the economic fortunes of many aristocratic landowners, even when dynastic policies came to their aid as under the reign of Frederick II (1740–1786). The economic decline of the landed aristocracy would result in a changing social composition of the army, the bureaucracy, and the class of landowners. By the middle of the nineteenth century, the Prussian governing class would be transformed socially, but unified ideologically.

The economic fortunes of landowners were in jeopardy as a result of policies designed to pay for a rapidly growing military establishment. Under Frederick William I, the crown encroached on earlier aristocratic prerogatives. The purchase of encumbered manorial estates, short-term leases of royal lands to bourgeois estate-managers, and an edict prohibiting the sale of royal domains are instances of this kind. By contrast, Frederick II instructed his officials not to press legal claims in disputes with aristocratic landowners. He curtailed the sale of manorial estates to commoners, restricted the number of hereditary claims against these estates, and encouraged rural credit institutions that would grant aristocratic landowners long-term loans at low interest rates. Yet these policies did not achieve their purpose. Many aristocratic families had been decimated and their estates laid waste or rendered unprofitable during the Seven Years' War (1756–1763) and the economic crisis that followed. Just at this time new techniques for improving agricultural productivity had become available, but the cost of these new methods was high and increased the need for long-term credit. Even with governmental assistance many impoverished aristocratic landowners were unable to improve their estates.

Moreover, the Prussian aristocracy often proved unwilling to take advantage of the facilities the government placed at its disposal. The *fidei commissum* was a legal instrument for confining the inheritance of manorial estates to a single heir and restricting the sale, though not necessarily the mortgaging, of the family estate. But this instrument did not prove an effective vehicle for the preservation of unencumbered estates. The landed squires wanted to maintain their estates intact, but they also wanted to preserve the right of all male heirs to an equal share in the property. To realize both goals often meant encumbering the estate by raising loans, which required the prior consent of all male descendants. Such consent was difficult to obtain, especially in periods of economic recession. Hence, loans were hard to raise and expensive and legal disputes numerous. Frequently, the very principle of equal inheritance resulted in family disunity. The crown sought to relieve these difficulties by facilitating the conversion of estates into fidei commissa, but the Prussian aristocracy made limited use of this device because they preferred equal inheritance. During the last decades of the eighteenth century, economic conditions worsened and the need for credit increased. Lenders exploited these difficulties, and with the rise of land values many aristocratic families liquidated parts of their landed property.[36]

A proportion of the aristocracy was in actual need during the last part of the eighteenth century. We noted earlier that the low pay of officers made them dependent on financial assistance from their families. A rough estimate from one study suggests that some 10 percent of the officer corps did not receive such assistance and therefore found it impossible to pay for the education of their children.[37] Moreover, Frederick's officers were prohibited from marrying without the consent of higher military authority. It was feared that marriages would lead to large, indigent families with pension claims on the state and large numbers of children with hereditary rights. Also, marriages without a proper economic foundation might prompt officers to petition for release from military service. Special assistance was given to the needy widows and daughters of officers and to impoverished members of old, aristocratic families, for whom quite menial public offices were found. Comments on the indigence and outright begging of aristocrats suggest that such measures did not relieve the situation. Indeed, a good many aristocrats relinquished their title to escape the prohibition against entering a trade or profession. As commoners, they would be able to recoup their fortune.[38]

The prestige and economic fortunes of the aristocracy declined. Deaths in battle as well as economic adversity had thinned the ranks of titled families at a time when the Prussian rulers required more officers and civil servants. Accordingly, it became royal policy to confer new titles and to renew titles that had been allowed to lapse. Frederick II conferred twice as many titles as his father, and Frederick William II (1786–1797) five times as many as Frederick II. In the ten years between 1797 and 1807, Frederick William III (1797–1840) conferred two-and-a-half times as many titles as Frederick II had conferred in forty-six years. The rapid increase of titles quickly devalued their prestige. Also, many titles were based on recognition of conspicuous service and conferred without reference to the ownership of land. Finally, since many noble immigrants sought service in the army and the bureaucracy, the relationship of titles to landownership became attenuated. Clearly, native aristocrats in straitened circumstances faced increasing competition despite the policies designed to assist them.[39]

A case study of the Electoral Mark (*Kurmark*) Brandenburg allows insight into the conditions of the aristocracy around 1800. In that year there were 409 aristocratic landowners in the province, while their 133 brothers and 116 sons did not own land. More than one-third of these 658 men were in military service in 1800, and a little less than one-third had seen service earlier. Altogether, almost 60 percent of the landowners had seen military service, while of their brothers and sons who did not own land more than 80 percent had served in the army.[40] Taking the 409 landowners by themselves, we find that in 1800 290 (71 percent) resided on their estates, but that 178 of them had previously lived in the towns as officers or civil servants for an average of eighteen years. Since the remaining 119 landowners lived in the towns either as officers or simply as absentee landowners, more than 70 percent of the landed aristocracy in Brandenburg were or had been urban residents for considerable periods. Only 27.4 percent of this Prussian squirearchy lived on the land throughout.[41]

This overwhelming record of service to the state was itself a cause of the deteriorating position of the aristocracy. Frederick William I had favored natives over foreigners in his recruitment of officers and men. When their ranks were decimated during the Seven Years' War, Prussian aristocrats lost their exclusive priority as officer candidates. Frederick II resorted to the recruitment of titled foreigners in order to maintain the aristocratic officer corps at its proper strength. By 1804–1806 over one thousand Prussian officers had French or Polish names in a corps of over seven thousand men. But the education of these officers was poor and a significant proportion of the higher officers were between fifty and eighty years old—two defects related to the restrictive recruitment policies of the Hohenzollern rulers. (At a time when the proportion of nonaristocratic officers in the Prussian army was less than 10 percent, the proportion of middle-class officers in the British army amounted to 60 percent.)[42] Frederick II also determined that native army recruits should not exceed 3 percent of the male population, since a large number of recruits impaired the productive capacity of the estates. Consequently, entire regiments came to consist of foreign mercenaries. At the same time, exemptions from military service were granted as an inducement to immigrants and to the people in conquered territories. Such measures, along with the liberalization of furloughs, sought to preserve the agricultural work force and its tax-paying capacity. In some cases, this boost to the estates of the landed aristocracy may have been effective, but it was obtained at the price of military weakness.[43]

The Prussian army was defeated by Napoleon in the Battle of Jena and Auerbach in 1806. This defeat brought on a popular outcry against militarism which had embittered human relations and now had proved futile as well. The principal official warrant of aristocratic privilege was undermined. The inflation of titles had already lessened the prestige of social rank, and policies intended to support the landed aristocracy had often been ineffective. During the decades around 1800, Prussia's aristocracy lost status and wealth in addition to the demise of the estate assemblies in the sixteenth and seventeenth centuries.

However, the aristocracy eventually recovered from this decline, though its character was transformed in the process. During the nineteenth century, aristocratic status rose once more by identification with the army and the bureaucracy as the main supports of the state. The military debacle of 1806 was followed by reform legislation which failed in many respects. But some of the successful reforms helped to restore the preeminent position of the aristocracy on a new basis. The Prussian Junkers of the nineteenth century became successful as capitalists, while a good many wealthy merchants and industrialists purchased estates east of the Elbe and became pseudo-aristocrats.[44] This transformation of the Prussian governing class had far-reaching ideological implications which were related to the social redistribution of the officer corps, the bureaucracy, and the class of landowners.

In 1813 the Prussian army stood at 280,000 men. In 1808 a new system of selection had opened officer candidacy to all young men of seventeen, with admission and promotion dependent on regimental examinations. In the same year, new articles of war were promulgated, designed to reduce the civilian repugnance toward military life. The war of liberation against Napoleon kindled widespread enthusiasm. By 1819 there were as many middle-class as aristocratic officers. Despite some fluctuations, this proportion of middle-class officers increased during the nineteenth century, reaching 70 percent before World War I. How is it that under these circumstances the officer corps remained a bastion of aristocratic influence?

Part of the answer is suggested by an analysis of officer candidates for the years 1862–1864 and 1866–1867. Among 2,516 candidates, 49 percent were aristocrats, and 51 percent commoners, but 79 percent were the sons of officers, higher civil servants, and landowners—that is, almost 80 percent came from families whose occupations strongly identified them with the prevailing monarchic regime, whether they were aristocratic or middle-class. After 1819 the education of officers was disparaged once again; emphasis was placed on technical training while participation in public affairs was considered a source of corruption. Accordingly, officers from middle-class families like their aristocratic colleagues were drawn into a warrior estate "requiring its own honor, its own justice, and its own way of thinking. . . . This conception of the military vocation [was] recognized as a higher form of life that is superior to bourgeois customs" and accepted as such by major sections of society.[45]

The changing character of the Prussian aristocracy is also evident from the history of the Prussian civil service. Since the seventeenth century, the social background of officials had been diverse. There were indigenous nobles, legally trained commoners, foreign-born career bureaucrats, administrators elevated to aristocratic rank, and others. Under Frederick William I, the numbers of jurists and "civilian" aristocrats declined, while merchants, petty officials, and aristocratic army officers increased. At the center of government commoners were favored, because they were dependent on the ruler and dependable in conflicts with the aristocracy. Even Frederick II, who favored the nobility, allowed only men of low birth direct access to himself.[46] This mixed social background of the civil service showed the diversity of dynastic personnel "policies." Aristocrats were often favored, but their aspirations and independent status might prove dangerous and therefore called for vigilance. Commoners and foreigners were probably more dependable, but they also carried less weight with native aristocrats which could impair their effectiveness. Expertise of some kind was needed, but it was ill-defined, and autocratic rulers were uncomfortable with book-learning and preferred compliance as proof of loyalty. Yet compliant courtiers were suspect also, because their motives and accomplishments were in doubt. In an era of government through court politics, royal servants would presumably use their influence for personal gain. That assumption imparted an atmosphere of suspicion to the conduct of administration, beginning with the ruler himself. While government office might open great opportunities to men of ambition, the risks were great and personal insecurity endemic.

Eventually, a bureaucratic culture pattern formed in response to these conditions. Though Frederick II favored officials from the Junker squirearchy, he also conferred many new titles in recognition of long service. A new service aristocracy formed which acquired a degree of solidarity in its struggles against royal arbitrariness. As the size of the government increased, so did the dependence of the ruler on the advice of leading officials. As the latter gradually acquired control over admissions and promotions, they achieved the mutual protection of a colleagial interest group.[47] When interests are vigorously pursued, an ideology tends to develop, and in the late eighteenth century Prussian officials fused the ideal of service to the Prussian state with the ideal of self-cultivation or *Bildung*. Criteria of human worth competed with the criteria of militarism and aristocratic privilege.[48]

Bildung became a prestigious attribute of officials at once loyal to the ruler and concerned with their own rights, critical of inherited privilege without commensurate service and also of selfish commercial dealings. Praise of cultivated sensitivity and moral perfection became linked with attacks on the unearned pretensions of "the aristocrat" and the demeaning money-making of "the bourgeois." Those who championed this "aristocracy of mind and heart" promoted a fraternal feeling among the educated which claimed to transcend all rank differences based on birth, status, office, or wealth. This spirit came to influence leading segments of the Prussian bureaucracy during the later eighteenth century, aiding their moral and intellectual emancipation from royal autocracy *and* from the class-egotism of the landed aristocracy.[49]

Changes in land ownership also provide clues to the character of the Prussian aristocracy. Prior to 1805, the sale of manorial estates had been greatly restricted. Commoners were forbidden to purchase such estates, and even when exceptions were made, aristocrats retained their exclusive rights of private jurisdiction.[j] In 1800 only 18 percent of the aristocratic landowners of Brandenburg had bought or sold land, and in a five-year period their total landholding declined by only 11 percent. Commoners owned 13 percent of the estates, but these were relatively small holdings since they represented only about 5 percent of the value of landed property in the province.[50] The edict of 1807 and subsequent reform legislation produced major changes. Henceforth, aristocrats were allowed to enter trade and the professions without thereby relinquishing their titles, while commoners were permitted to purchase manorial estates even though this did not involve the acquisition of a title.

The effects of these changes were immediate. In East Prussia, between 1806 and 1829, 510 of 888 estates changed hands, and more than half of the new owners acquired their property through foreclosure.

---

[j]Rights of private jurisdiction refer to the privilege of participating in provincial or county assemblies, of patrimonial jurisdiction, of hunting, and so forth. Still other rights involved tax exemptions as well as claims to extensive *corvée* services, often requiring manual labor and teams of horses. The abolition of these privileges occurred only in piecemeal fashion; it was delayed until the second half of the nineteenth century, and peasants were required to pay large amounts or provide extensive services to acquire title to their land.

Though less rapid in other provinces, the transfer of landed properties was substantial everywhere. Many aristocrats quickly took advantage of the new opportunities by buying land which now came on the market. These were affluent families capable of hardheaded management and of improving their estates. Others did not survive this period of commercialization for familial and ideological reasons. By 1857 a major redistribution of landownership had occurred: of 12,399 manorial estates, 7,023 (57.3 percent) remained in the hands of aristocrats, while 5,296 (42.7 percent) belonged to middle-class owners.[51] Data for 1885 indicate that the proportion of middle-class owners (53 percent) was larger than that of aristocratic owners (47 percent). Nevertheless, the aristocratic dominance remained. Three-fourths of the aristocratic but only one-fourth of the bourgeois owners had estates of over forty acres.[52] Therefore, the commercialization of land led in effect to an "aristocratization" of the Prussian bourgeoisie in much the same way as had parallel changes in the composition of the officer corps. Commoners who purchased manorial estates also acquired the more intangible habits and attitudes of the landed aristocracy, hoping to obtain some of the most cherished privileges of the aristocracy. (Bourgeois landowners petitioned the king to consent to the establishment of their property as a fidei commissum, a designation of aristocratic status as well as a legal instrument. By 1898 only ninety bourgeois landowners had succeeded in this respect.[53])

By the mid-nineteenth century, the distinction between aristocrat and bourgeois had lost much of its earlier significance. Middle-class families had become landed proprietors and had adapted themselves ideologically to their quasi-aristocratic status, while landed aristocrats had become rural capitalists once again. Between aristocrats and "persons of higher or more educated estate," the legal enforcement of differences in rank steadily diminished. With regard to civil or criminal penalties, the law of libel, tax exemption, and marital eligibility, the aristocracy and the higher bourgeoisie came to be treated as social equals. The special legal privileges of public officials made it clear that their higher ranks also belonged to this newly amalgamated elite. To be sure, invidious distinctions within this elite remained, but they cannot compare with the legal enforcement of class differences existing in the eighteenth century. Under the monarchy, military rank, office, education, and wealth had become related attributes of upper-class status, though in this altered setting the aristocracy continued to enjoy the advantages of a generally recognized distinction.[54]

In conclusion, the common ideology of this governing class should be noted. In the early nineteenth century, liberal reform legislation had been inspired by an enlightened ideal of self-cultivation (Bildung), which cut across social distinctions. However, the reforms themselves were confined to establishing the freedom of the market and the principle of self-government in municipal administration. Next to nothing had been accomplished in the field of constitutional reform, and in the countryside the bastion of aristocratic privilege remained as entrenched as ever. For decades public officials inspired by liberal ideals had to cope with the determined resistance of landed interests at the local level. One can speculate that this frustration in the political realm intensified the idealization of governmental authority as the embodiment of reason and national purpose against the selfishness of class and locality. Bildung and service could become a prized possession of an elite of officials much as the idealization of honor and service had become the ideology of the officer corps. Emphasis on loyal service in a hierarchical organization under the aegis of royal authority was combined with a cultivation of inwardness that recalled the humanistic inspiration of the Enlightenment.

Nevertheless, the context of Enlightenment values had changed. The libertarian protest against the pretensions of rank had become an idealization of service as a means of self-cultivation. The ideal of inwardness was placed at the disposal of military discipline and governmental power. As Ernst Troeltsch expressed it,

> The political thought of Germany is marked by a curious dilemma. . . . Look at one of its sides, and you will see an abundance of remnants of Romanticism and lofty idealism; look at the other, and you will see a realism which goes to the verge of cynicism and of utter indifference to all ideals and all morality. But what you will see above all is an inclination to make an astonishing combination of the two elements—in a word to brutalize romance, and to romanticize cynicism.[55]

It was in this combination of various idealisms with service in the army and the bureaucracy that aristocrats and well-to-do commoners (whether they were landowners, industrialists, or professionals) achieved a general unity of outlook as the "governing class" of an emerging industrial society.

6

ENGLAND

ENGLAND IS physically related to the European continent much as Japan is related to the Asian mainland. In ancient times, the native British population was Celtic, the native Japanese, Ainu. In Japan, rulership arose through the gradual emergence of a dominant lineage, the Yamato, which eventually won supremacy in struggles against rival clans and hostile native tribes. Thereafter, Japanese rulership developed through many internal struggles, but without military conquest by outside forces. At the same time, Chinese civilization became an ideal model which the Japanese adapted in developing their own culture.

In England, central rulership arose through foreign conquest of the Celtic population. The islands were attacked and then occupied by Roman legions from 55 B.C. to 450 A.D. The Roman occupation was followed by successive waves of Germanic settlers who founded a number of Anglo-Saxon kingdoms. Beginning in the late eighth century, Scandinavian raids initiated a third period of invasions. The Norman conquest of 1066 completed the settlement of the English Isles and established unified rule where none had existed since the Roman occupation.

The Romans called the country Britannia, the Anglo-Saxon settlers called their several kingdoms by names reflecting their continental origins, and the Danes and Normans left their own linguistic imprint. The proliferation of terms for the country and its several regions as well as the many place names originating in different languages attest to a thousand-year history of conquest and a corresponding diversity of cultural influences.[1]

TRIBES, CONQUESTS, AND KINGS

The Roman occupation of England dates from 43 A.D., though Roman raids of the islands began a century earlier. The conquest occurred in response to an appeal by a native chieftain, and the Roman army landed in Kent with forty thousand men. The military advance of the Roman legions encountered fierce resistance from the native population, and sporadic revolts disrupted the Roman occupation for another two centuries. Nevertheless, the Romans succeeded in stabilizing their authority through an elaborate system of fortifications extending in the north to Hadrian's wall (ca. 122 A.D.), which stretched from modern Newcastle on the North Sea to the Irish Sea near Carlisle.

Outside the areas of Roman military occupation unrest flared up periodically, but south of Hadrian's wall the country became Romanized. Towns were founded and settled by discharged Roman legionaries; these towns were endowed with franchises and constitutions similar to the municipalities in Italy. Under their own tribal leaders, the native Celtic population came to accept Roman civilization, a process which can be partially traced through the remains of town settlements like Colchester, Lincoln, and others. In a major, though unsuccessful, Celtic revolt against foreign rule (61 A.D.), many Romanized natives were massacred along with the Romans themselves. Roman civilization was widely, though unevenly, spread over England, and by the fourth century there was evidence of considerable prosperity as exemplified in the remains of country houses and the work of skilled artisans.

The administration of the occupied part of the island was subject to a Roman governor, but in practice entrusted to local authorities. Each municipality ruled itself as well as its surrounding territory. Some districts were set aside as part of the imperial domains, but the larger portion of the country was divided among ten or twelve tribes, each grouped around a town where the tribal council met to conduct the business of the district. This type of decentralized rule was known from Roman Gaul, and it was compatible with tribal practice which emphasized joint government by a chieftain and a council of elders.

Many additional fortifications built in the fourth century testify to increased barbarian assaults from the north and west, and early in the fifth century the Germanic conquests of Gaul cut the island off from Rome. Roman troops were withdrawn, and the Romanized Celtic population found itself under increasing attack not only from the north and west where Roman fortifications were located, but also from Anglo-Saxon invaders in the unfortified east and south. These Anglo-Saxon invaders eventually succeeded in occupying England, in repelling the attacks of Scots and Picts in the north, and in pacifying the rest of the country by establishing a number of kingdoms. One of these kingdoms, Kent, was unified under one ruler; another, Northumbria, was ruled by four leaders; still others, like Wessex and Mercia, consisted of an overlord and lesser kings who were local rulers with their own dependents. These lesser kings were frequently only nominally subordinate to the overlord.

The difference between unified and decentralized kingdoms probably arose from the manner of settlement. England was sometimes invaded by a tribe under one king, but more often by groups of conquerors who brought with them the idea of chieftainship based on charismatic lineage and "election" by the tribal notables. A leader claiming such descent could establish himself as the king of an area if he was successful in his undertakings and provided security to those who followed him. There was no tradition that a lesser king had to give allegiance to the dead overlord's son, or adhere to a ruler whose luck had deserted him.[2] A "confederacy" of lesser kings under an overlord was often formed, which was similar to tribal practices on the continent as well as to those found among the native peoples of the British Isles.

The circumstances of Anglo-Saxon occupation (beginning in the fifth century) reinforced the earlier Roman tendency to establish loose authority which allowed for considerable regional and local autonomy. Under the Roman occupation, this had been the imperial practice in the first and second centuries. In the case of the Anglo-Saxon kingdoms of the seventh century, decentralized rule was most likely a tribal legacy. The Mercian king Penda (633–654?)

> . . . could claim ancestral right, but . . . the mechanics of government had yet to be worked out. . . . Like an Irish king, he exacted hostages and enforced tribute; he impressed British [meaning native Celtic] tradition by a distribution of gifts to his subordinate rulers. . . . He did not dethrone conquered kings and annex their kingdoms. . . . He expelled Cenwalh from Wessex, but he left the regional kings alone; . . . and though he twice killed rebellious kings of the East Angles, he permitted their heirs to succeed them as his subordinate allies. . . .
>
> The Mercian monarchs retained their subjects' loyalty and increased their majesty because they continued the forms of government they inherited from the past, tolerating and encouraging the autonomy of dependent rulers, and leaving large areas of administrative and judicial and political decision in the hands of periodical local representative assemblies.[3]

The Romans and several Anglo-Saxon kings established precedents which eventually hardened into the English tradition of balancing monarchical with local authority. That tradition was to be reinforced by the Norman conquest. But the dominant fact of Anglo-Saxon rule was political fragmentation and frequent fighting among Northumbrians, Mercians, East Angles, the several Saxon kingdoms, and Kent.

Anglo-Saxon kingship replicated the Germanic customs of the continent. The king was attended by a bodyguard of well-born companions, who had the duty to defend and avenge their lord, and were disgraced if they survived him in battle. (These companions often included men of royal descent.) The most admired virtue of a king was his generosity, a view no doubt diligently cultivated by his followers. At an early time, a follower was endowed with land in newly conquered territories; he and his household were maintained by the food rents and services of the native population. Later, the king's gift often took the form of entitling the recipient not to the land itself, but to the goods and services due from the cultivators. In this way, the king retained title to the land, while his companions received part or all of the tribute that was assessed. These were matters of political opportunity and calculation. The Anglo-Saxon kings could enlarge their domains and authority only with the help of followers and hence at the price of rewarding them. Land and the tribute derived from the land were the main sources of wealth and power. Kings tried to make sure that the gains they made through the services of their followers were worth the loss of wealth and power which grants to them represented.

The power of the Anglo-Saxon kings often faltered, although the principle of royal authority was generally upheld.[4] The lesser kings and earls (or *ealdormen*) were the effective rulers over the constituent units (the shires) of England, governing in the name of the king. They and the diocesan bishops (who were installed throughout the country in the late seventh century) would sit as joint presidents of the shire court, and in times of war the earls would command the shire militia. The primary function of the earls was political, and since this was a period of much internal strife, these great provincial rulers would often be away on campaigns. However, their presence was required in all controversial cases before the shire court, for only the full authority of the state could deal with recalcitrant local magnates. Much routine business was nevertheless transacted in their absence, and as affairs became more complex, the king (with the consent of the earls) created the new office of sheriff to take charge of local government, local finance, and the execution of justice. The earl was a great lord with whom the ordinary man had few contacts, but the sheriff was the man known to be in touch with local affairs as the representative of the king.

For the king's rule to be effective, he also had to have the cooperation of local leaders of opinion who held no official position. These were the freemen, the king's *thegns*, on whose services and taxes in kind the wealth and power of the Anglo-Saxon kingdoms depended. Their obligation included military service, the food rent (*feorm*) levied for the maintenance of the king's household, cartage services and provision of labor for the king's works, and charges for the entertainment of strangers coming to court. In the early Anglo-Saxon period, the freemen owed these services directly to the king, though by the seventh century they were rendering their dues to a lord who was the king's vassal. Some of these freemen were substantial landholders who might obtain positions at court or be raised to an earldom by special favor, but who would ordinarily come in contact with public affairs only through their duty of attending the great council of the realm (*witena gemot*). The early councils appear to have been composed of the king's immediate followers and officials, both lay and ecclesiastical; by the tenth century, this council was composed of earls, churchmen, and important thegns, all owing direct allegiance to the king.

Our knowledge of these councils comes largely from the royal charters in which the king's grants were witnessed by members of the council.

> There were very few matters of importance to the state on which an Anglo-Saxon king cannot be shown to have consulted his council. During the century before the Conquest its assent is recorded to the issue of laws and the imposition of taxes, to negotiations with foreign powers, and to measures undertaken for the defense of the land. It was in his council that a king would prosecute suspected traitors against whom he felt strongly enough to take legal action. That he was expected to secure its assent before creating privileged estates in land is made clear by the innumerable charters which assert that a royal gift of such an estate has been approved by the magnates of the kingdom.[5]

The instability of royal succession also strengthened the king's council, stimulating its elective function. Of the eight kings who reigned between 899 and 1016, only three were immediate heirs to an uncontested kingdom; in the other cases, the deceased king's council took the initiative in the choice of a successor. One must guard against the modern notion that the attestation of royal writs or even deliberations concerning the succession represented acts of voting. Bishops, abbots, and earls attended the council because of the offices they held by a royal grant, while thegns attended in obedience to a royal summons. Few individuals would directly oppose the king's declared will, but at the same time many earls and thegns were men who possessed much local influence and were not easily coerced.[6] The authority of Anglo-Saxon kingship depended in practice on at least intermittent negotiation with the great magnates of the realm whose power had increased through administrative consolidation in the shires.

Amid the prevailing political fragmentation one can see the process by which royal authority was periodically consolidated. Such consolidation depended on bringing lesser kings into allegiance with their overlord.

> The creation of the great Mercian kingdom of the eighth century meant that the heirs of many lesser dynasties were brought to seek the court of the Mercian king, to take gifts from him, and to promise him fidelity. It is sometimes possible to trace the actual course of their decline into subordination. Sigered,

the last king of Essex, attests many charters of Cenwulf, king of the Mercians: at first as *rex*, then as *subregulus*, and finally as *dux* or *ealdorman*.[a] Men of this type may often have been allowed to rule their own people under their lord's ultimate authority. But a king who was strong enough could always ignore the claims of a local dynasty, and in the course of time men with no hereditary title to rule appear as *ealdormen* of provinces which had once been kingdoms.[7]

Overlords would assert their authority whenever disloyalty or local revolt put the hereditary succession of an earldom in question. Moreover, an appeal to sentiment and faith was invoked by the claims of divine descent which suggested the sacred foundation and potential expansion of Anglo-Saxon kingship. (The early reference to *Bretwalda* or ruler over Britain probably expressed the political aspirations of Celtic and Irish kings, since otherwise such an imperial title was only used with reference to the Roman empire.)[8]

The Christianization of England contributed to the stabilization of royal authority, though not at first and not always directly. King Aethelberht of Kent (560–616) married the daughter of the king of Paris, presumably in order to strengthen the Kentish position in relation to the other Anglo-Saxon kingdoms. In 596 Aethelberht gave a friendly reception to a Christian mission, which Pope Gregory I sent to England. Neither the king's marriage nor his protection of the mission actually strengthened Aethelberht's rule. Kentish supremacy did not even last during the king's lifetime; indeed, Stenton states that "no confederacy of this period survived the king who had brought it into being."[9] England was still a pagan country, and Christian missions required royal support. In this context, grants to the church had special significance for the consolidation of royal authority. The church benefited from the protection of the king and tended to support his authority. The king could also benefit from the countrywide organization of dioceses which the church introduced under Archbishop Theodore (668–690). This stabilizing influence of the church coincided with the regularization of land tenures on the basis of charters written by clerics. Since clerical appointments remained in the jurisdiction of Anglo-Saxon kings, the

[a]The Mercian kingdom rose to preeminence in the early eighth century and declined a century later. Its two outstanding rulers were Aethelbald (716–757) and Offa (757–796), who influenced the contemporary Carolingian rulers on the continent. *Rex* and *subregulus* are the Latin equivalents of overlord and lesser (or under-) king. *Dux* or *ealdorman* are the Latin and Old English equivalents of earl. The term *gesith* and its later equivalent *thegn* originally meant "one who serves another"; the standing of these men was largely determined by the rank of the man they served, though such service itself was a mark of aristocratic status. Titles and terms like these changed their meaning in the course of time, an indication that the delegation of authority was a continuous process.

church was not only an ally, but at times a willing subordinate of royal authority.

This position of the church was reflected in the clerical interpretation of secular rule. For some four centuries, the clerics who wrote the land charters reiterated the idea that the king reigns by the grace of God. Anglo-Saxon churchmen insisted that the Christian king is the representative of Christ among a Christian people, a view more in accord with the Byzantine than the later papal conception of kingship. In their laws, the kings themselves often addressed their people not only as the secular ruler, but as the spiritual leader. English churchmen did not challenge the king's ecclesiastical patronage: if the king protected the church, he had the right to appoint its chief ministers. Both lay and ecclesiastical powers were subordinated to the authority of the Anglo-Saxon kings only decades before the Norman conquest of 1066. This was only a short time before the investiture controversy between the Holy Roman emperor and the pope. But England was very distant from continental affairs, and under frontier conditions the church naturally favored strong kings who would support its mission.

The authority of English kingship was also strengthened in the course of protracted fighting with the Danes and eventually through the unity imposed by the Norman conquest. It is sufficient here to give a bare outline of the Danish invasions which began in earnest in 835 and resulted in Danish overlordship of much of eastern England. Although the Anglo-Saxon kings were nearly defeated a number of times, they

Three Anglo-Saxon Kings
Following five hundred years of Roman occupation, Anglo-Saxon England achieved a high level of civilization despite its political fragmentation. These three coins show stages of Anglo-Saxon political development. Offa (757–796), king of Mercia, at least claimed dominion over the whole of England. Alfred (871–899) won back territories which had been conquered by the Vikings. Edgar (959–975) achieved considerable stability and was a patron of the arts and learning. (British Museum)

gained the upper hand when Alfred, King of Wessex (871–899), and his son, Edward the Elder (899–924), effected a virtual union between Wessex and Mercia. Aethelstan (924–939) further unified the English realm and was successful in his campaigns against the Danes and Norwegians north of the Humber estuary. Under Aethelstan's successor, the Danish settlers accepted the king of Wessex as their sovereign. By the middle of the tenth century, the West Saxon royal house ruled England. The entire settled population, including the descendants of Danish conquerors, had been converted to Christianity, and further Norse invasions from Ireland had failed. England was a unified kingdom, but internal rule remained weak and the threat of invasions did not abate.

King Athelred (978–1016) took into his service a large force of Viking mercenaries who remained loyal to the Danish king. That loyalty facilitated the Danish invasion of England in 1013. As the Danish king consolidated his English conquest, Athelred went into exile at the court of his brother-in-law, Richard, duke of Normandy. The Danish king died in 1014, and although Athelred was recalled to England, he in turn died in 1016. Thereafter, England was ruled by Cnut (1016–1035), who was simultaneously king of England and Denmark.

A few years after the death of Cnut, the English aristocracy recalled the West Saxon dynasty in the person of Edward the Confessor (1042–1066). Edward had grown up at the Norman court during his father's (King Athelred's) exile. After succeeding to the English throne, Edward sponsored the spread of Norman influences in England by granting estates to Norman knights and patronizing Norman churchmen. His reign also saw the ascendance to great power of a number of wealthy aristocratic families who had been influential in recalling the West Saxon dynasty and who now challenged the will, and sometimes the authority, of the king. The threat of new Scandinavian invasions made these challenges seem treasonous and Edward responded by designating as his successor his cousin, William of Normandy. But the great influence of the English aristocracy did not diminish, and when Edward died some years later the succession to the throne was in much dispute. The kings of Denmark and of Norway, two members of the English royal family (one a minor, the other an exile distantly related to Edward), as well as two or three powerful English earls could make some claim to the English succession. The Norman conquest of 1066 settled the question by force of arms, and William the Conqueror (1066–1087) became king of England.

The conquest resulted in the subordination of the English aristocracy. By 1086 only about 8 percent of the land remained in English hands, although many native aristocratic families survived as subtenants on their former property. However, the highest ranks of the English

Danish Rule in England

The Danish king Sweyn I raided England in 982 and 994. Subsequently he was declared king of England and forced Ethelred (978–1016) to flee the country. This eleventh-century manuscript illustration shows the crowning of Sweyn's son King Canute (Cnut) and his queen Aelgifu, as the king grasps the cross and his sword while one angel bestows the crown of temporal rule and another the pallium of spiritual authority. Above, the scene is sanctified by Christ's image in the company of Mary and St. Peter with the key to the kingdom of heaven. Below, monks are witnesses in an attitude of adoration. Danish rule lasted from Canute's reign (1016–1035) to 1042, when the Saxon ruler Edward the Confessor was restored to the throne. (British Museum)

aristocracy, the men who had held positions of great responsibility under Edward, were purged and replaced by Norman notables.[10] About one-fifth of the land was held by the king, about one-quarter by the church, and nearly one-half by the Norman followers of the king. (Two of these followers were the king's half-brothers. If we add these last possessions to those of the king, then the royal family owned about half the land of England, although any disputes within the royal family diminished this royal concentration of power.)[11] In a native population well in excess of one million, total immigration as a result of the conquest probably did not exceed ten thousand, which may be compared with the forty thousand men the Romans had used a thousand years earlier to conquer and occupy England. The number of Norman knights who were granted land during William's reign was probably less than two thousand.[12] These figures suggest that English institutions could preserve their continuity despite the replacement of a native by a foreign ruling class.

A main result of the conquest was the division of English landed property among a Norman aristocracy organized for war. In the first years after the conquest, William required military service from his Norman barons and tenants-in-chief, and a major task of government consisted in assessing the service obligations of each fief. The Domesday Book of 1086 assessed each landed estate up to the limit of, and frequently well beyond, its economic capacity. For the time, these assessments were an extraordinary political achievement, indicating the subordination even of the great lords to William the Conqueror in contrast to the relative autonomy of local rulers and landed notables not only in Anglo-Saxon England but also in Normandy, France, and other continental countries.[13] The effectiveness of the Norman rule was due less to the Domesday record of landholding tenures (remarkable as a census, even if not too effective as a basis of administration) than to the solidarity of a conquering group of foreign warriors who could take over an existing government and leave its subordinate positions in native hands. However, this initial concentration of power soon gave way to further struggles between the English kings and the magnates of their realm.

The Norman occupation contributed to the English tradition of balancing monarchical with local authority. Conditions of organization and transport did not favor centralized government even by an occupying force as ruthless as that of William the Conqueror. Roman imperial practice, the Anglo-Saxon tribal traditions, and the practicalities of governing a conquered country with only two thousand Norman knights obliged the successive rulers of England to rely on the authority and uncertain collaboration of local notables.

Norman rule required that the barons and tenants-in-chief supply the king with armed knights on horseback. This military service obligation provided the magnates of the realm with several options. They could serve their king loyally as he required, they could use their military might to oppose him at their own risk, or they could pass the burden of military service onto others. This last alternative meant that either they could maintain household knights from their own revenue, or they could give these knights fiefs in return for the required military service to the king. From the standpoint of the English king, the military service obligation of his magnates had certain disadvantages. These autonomous rural lords were a potential threat to the king, and in campaigns on the Continent many soldiering tasks could be better performed by mercenaries than by armed knights. The great wealth of the royal family made it possible to hire these mercenaries. Hence, the king would often accept payment (*scutage*) in lieu of service, a substitution which was at his discretion and not a baronial privilege. The king could use such fees to pay for mercenaries, and he could further add to his treasury by imposing a fine for permission to substitute payment for service. He could also favor his supporters by lowering the military service or scutage required of their estates while increasing such assessments where he suspected opposition.

Obligations other than military service were significant because they allowed the king to increase his revenue *and* exercise personal control over his leading subjects. Family fortunes were affected whenever a fief was left to a minor, for the crown enjoyed the revenues until the heir came of age, and it could sell the custody of the heir or the use of his lands in order to reward loyal followers. The value of the king's right of wardship was great, since revenues during the minority of an heir derived directly from the land. Wardship remained an important part of royal revenue until the seventeenth century. The king also reserved the right of consent when the daughters of his tenants-in-chief married, or when the widow of a tenant-in-chief wished to remarry or remain single:

> The political aspects of the right of marriage were extremely significant. It enabled the crown to control the family alliances formed among the barons. Then every marriage involved the transfer of a marriage portion, and many governed the future possession of a barony or part of one. . . . The crown could make the fortune of a feudal house by permitting it to make good marriages. . . . On the other hand, great baronies could be broken into insignificant fragments by marrying heiresses to men of little position. In short, through its right of marriage the crown could to a great extent control the accumulation and dispersion of great feudal estates. [14]

Finally, when a king's tenant died, his heir would pay "relief" to the crown so that he was "relieved" from the obligation (incident to most royal grants of land) to return the fief to the king. Such payments often involved as much as an entire year's income from an estate. Since these payments were at the crown's discretion, the king could "reward the loyal with low relief and punish the disaffected with high ones."[15] Naturally, the great barons of Norman England endeavored to circumscribe the king's discretion and thus stabilize their own position in the social hierarchy.

In theory, the relationship between William the Conqueror and his vassals was based on mutual agreement and trust; in practice, it was characterized by considerable tension. The Norman aristocrats exploited their new opportunities and prepared to defend themselves against renewed opposition from the native population and the competing claims of rival magnates. Over five thousand castles had been built in England a generation after the conquest. Though the king had encouraged the building of private strongholds as a defense against the native population, he wanted his vassals to help him rule the land without encroaching upon his own rights. That danger arose partly from the practice of subinfeudation. The magnates would meet their obligations to the king through granting fiefs to rear-vassals who would then substitute for the magnates and render the service required by the king. In this arrangement, it was not clear whether the rear-vassals would be loyal to the lord from whom they held their fief or to the king for whom they rendered service on behalf of their lord. In his council of 1086, at Salisbury, the king made the rear-vassals do homage to himself in order to forestall the growth of power centers independent of his will.[16] The oath at Salisbury demonstrated William's ample authority in England, but his control of Normandy was more precarious. He could demand a far greater number of knights from his vassals in England than he could in Normandy. For a time, the English magnates could barely meet their obligations to the king, while William's Norman vassals were easily able to maintain private military forces in addition to the number of knights they owed to their ruler.[17]

The reign of William the Conqueror exemplified the strength of English kingship. William died in 1087, and the succession crisis which followed led to a reassessment of the relations between king and vassals. The crisis also revealed some of the underlying issues of medieval kingship in England. Inheritance concerned every landowner and especially the notables of the realm who wanted to preserve the wealth and status of their houses. There had been open opposition between William and his oldest son, Robert, for more than two decades, but on his deathbed William gave him the duchy of Normandy, realizing that he could not deprive Robert of his hereditary right without jeopardizing the political support of his vassals and hence the continued rule of his house. At the same time, William considered the English crown at his disposal because he had conquered it. He bequeathed England to his second son, William Rufus, who was crowned as William II (1087–1100) and given an oath of allegiance. Nevertheless, many English barons sympathized with Robert for being deprived of the English crown. Barons with holdings in both England and Normandy were placed simultaneously under the harsh rule of William and the mild rule of Robert. On his deathbed William had also ordered that royal funds be distributed to the English churches and that political prisoners be freed. When William II followed these instructions, he probably sought to strengthen his political support in England, but he also impoverished the royal treasury and facilitated a rebellion against his own rule.

William II was able to put down the rebellion which his uncle Odo organized against him, and he established a regime noted for its rigorous control of the vassals.

> Private war and disturbance were not allowed. . . . The financial obligations
> of a vassal were rigorously enforced. Rufus emphasized the original precar-
> iousness and revocability of the fief. . . . On the death of a baron he selected
> the successor—not always the eldest son—and made him buy back the land.
> He insisted on his right to the fief and the wardship of the children when a
> vassal died without leaving a mature heir, and he disposed of the marriages
> of the widow and of the children to his profit. He restricted the right of the
> laity to leave money by will, and confiscated the chattels of dead prelates.[18]

In this way, the new king limited the transformation of fiefs and offices
into hereditary holdings, though the severity of his rule also prepared
the ground for later opposition.

Norman rule stabilized conditions in England at a time when anarchic tendencies prevailed in Imperial Germany and elsewhere on the
Continent. But in addition to the many strengths of English kingship,
there were also conditions which weakened it. The domains of the English kings were very large, but still not large enough to simultaneously
meet the demands of household expenses, the financing of government,
and the costs of military campaigns. The incessant competition for royal
favors was a further drain on the king's resources. Nor did the king have
the organization or resources needed for the work of local government;
he had to leave his tenants-in-chief free to make their own arrangements. In addition, the papacy exerted continuing pressure for the recognition and extension of ecclesiastical rights. Finally, the English royal
house and many English magnates held fiefs in Normandy and elsewhere as vassals of the king of France. Indeed, the kings of England
were Frenchmen in language, culture, and political interests, and a number of them spent the greater part of their reign of the Continent. The
result was that English domestic disputes within the royal family and
between the English kings and their barons were frequently aggravated
by disputes involving English interests in "French" territories.

Under these conditions, the chief barons of England attempted to
circumscribe royal prerogatives even as they accepted the king's legitimate authority. In part, this opposition involved the *executive power* of
the king. The great magnates of the realm acted as official agents of the
crown in the king's name. The king preferred to choose his officials
outside the ranks of these great lords, but often found himself obliged
to ask their assistance. In the long run, the king's executive power declined in administrative and judicial matters whenever his personally
dependent officials were replaced by these more independent notables.
Opposition to royal prerogatives also involved the *issue of representation*
in the king's council and eventually in other deliberative bodies of government. Did the barons have the duty of attending the council at the
king's pleasure, or did they have the right to attend by virtue of their

position? Was the crown obliged to call a meeting of the council, and if so at what intervals? When the council met, could the king simply demand the assent of those assembled to the measures put before them? Was he obliged to listen to the counsel of those assembled, and only with reference to issues he had raised, or also to those raised by some of the assembled notables? The answers to these and related questions in effect constitute the history of royal authority in relation to the English parliament. Problems like these can be formulated only in retrospect; therefore, to speak of opposition to royal prerogatives is only a convenient shorthand for the piecemeal process of delimiting the authority of the English king.

In practice, the relationship between kings and barons alternated between periods of central control and periods of tacit resistance or outright opposition. These were different phases not of right against wrong, but of the king's rights against the rights of his vassals, and it is important to realize that each side upheld the rights of the other—in principle. Vassals often began as personal retainers of high status who had become independent notables as their services led to a cumulation of royal favors. They were obliged to use their resources at the behest of the king in return for grants of land and of rights, and they derived part of their own upkeep from the performance of administrative and judicial functions. Such notables could become a threat to the king's power even if they did not challenge his authority. But then the king could favor a new echelon of vassals who depended more on him than his erstwhile followers—at least until the replacement of vassals was repeated.

For twenty years after the death of William the Conqueror, the duchy of Normandy under Robert and the English kingdom under William II followed their independent ways, but in 1106 the Conqueror's third son, Henry I (1100–1135), was involved in a war against his brother Robert. Henry conquered Normandy and reestablished the Anglo-Norman state which endured for a century thereafter. In 1128 Matilda, the only surviving child of the last Norman king, married Geoffrey Plantagenet, son of the Count of Anjou. After years of civil war and disputes over the succession to the Norman dynasty, stability was achieved in 1135 under the early Plantagenets. Matilda's son, Henry II (1154–1189), achieved the greatest extension of English rule, combining the kingdom of England with sovereignty over Scotland and Ireland and with control of the fiefs which he held as vassal to the king of France. These fiefs comprised not only Normandy and Brittany, but the kingdom of Aquitaine. Thus, English continental possessions extended from the channel coast to the Pyrenees. This great realm disintegrated under Henry's successors, leading to the loss not only of the Angevin fiefs but also of Normandy. However, claims to this inheritance, especially those

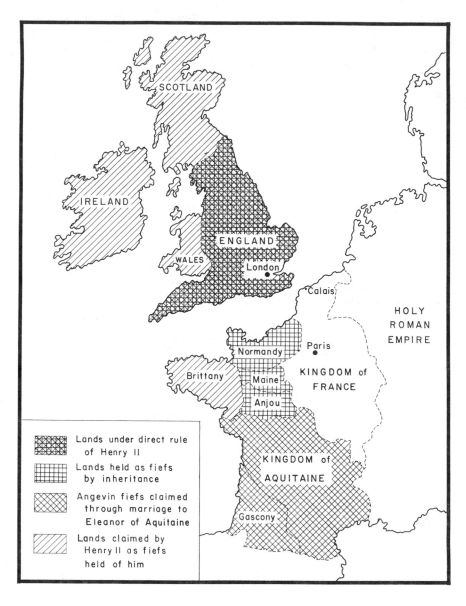

SCOTLAND

IRELAND

ENGLAND

WALES

London

Calais

HOLY
ROMAN
EMPIRE

Normandy

Paris

Brittany

Maine

KINGDOM of
FRANCE

Anjou

KINGDOM of
AQUITAINE

Gascony

Lands under direct rule
of Henry II

Lands held as fiefs
by inheritance

Angevin fiefs claimed
through marriage to
Eleanor of Aquitaine

Lands claimed by
Henry II as fiefs
held of him

9. Dominions of Henry II, 1154–1189

relating to Gascony, the southern part of Aquitaine, remained a major issue of Anglo-French relations until the sixteenth century.

The rule of Henry II was a high point of royal authority, similar in this respect to the earlier reign of William the Conqueror and to the latter part of the reign of Henry III (1216–1272). All three reigns were marked by legal recognition of the royal claim that each man owed his main loyalty to the king rather than to his immediate lord.[19] It was a clear sign of strength that during their frequent absences from England, the Norman and Plantagenet kings delegated their authority to high officials (*justiciars*) as their personal appointees who were able to consolidate the financial and judicial business of the crown.

The delimitation of royal authority may be set against these cases of powerful monarchical rule. The coronation charters issued by the successors of William the Conqueror provide us with examples. When the reign of William II was followed by that of his youngest brother Henry I, the new king was challenged by his oldest brother Robert, duke of Normandy. To strengthen his position in the war against Normandy, Henry I gave solemn promises of protecting the rights of his barons, which were laid down in a charter authenticated by the king's great seal. Stephen's (1135–1154) succession was challenged by Henry I's daughter, Matilda, and a new charter (1136) containing promises of good government was issued. In 1154 Matilda's son, Henry II, also began his reign with a charter promising to restore and confirm the liberties which his grandfather, Henry I, had granted to the church and the baronage. These coronation oaths became a tradition during the twelfth century: every reign had to begin with the new king's solemn affirmation of established rights. In the reign of John I (1199–1216), the king's position was further weakened, partly through rival claims to the throne, partly through conflicts with Pope Innocent III, and partly through the determination of the French king, Philip II (1180–1223), to end English possession of Normandy. As early as 1201, English earls refused to cross the sea in the king's service unless he promised them "their rights." After the loss of Normandy in 1204, the king had to rely on English resources alone in defending his realm against a threatened French invasion. The text of *Magna Carta* (1215), which eventuated from this conflict, enumerates the rights the king promises to uphold and sets up procedures by which the barons could force the king to comply. The specific threat to take the king's "castles, lands, and possessions" if he violated the terms of the charter may have been the work of extremists, but the assertion of baronial and ecclesiastical rights was well within the established framework.

King John died in 1216. His son Henry, the heir apparent, was a boy of nine, and a group of rebellious barons allied itself with Louis of

The Norman Kings
William the Conqueror, William Rufus, Henry I, and Stephen are shown as benefactors
of Westminster Abbey in this thirteenth-century illustration from the *Historia* of Matthew.
(British Museum)

France who was preparing to invade England. Effective authority over England passed to the Regent William the Marshall and his council, who reaffirmed Magna Carta but were also determined to maintain the position of the king and the realm. Baronial opposition to King John in defense of their own established rights was thus combined with the protection of the king's estate by leading magnates in the interest of repelling enemies of the country and maintaining good order.[20] By the time of Magna Carta, the rights of the king were matched by the rights of the barons under the king, and the two were linked by mutual recognition.

Convincing evidence of such reciprocity comes from the reign of Edward I (1272–1307), in the course of which over £400,000 were raised from subsidies which the barons provided in support of Edward's wars against Wales and Scotland and in defense of his interests as duke of Aquitaine. There was strikingly little local opposition to these subsidies, since Edward was an exceptionally strong and adroit ruler who pursued a policy of taxation by consent.

> Without surrendering his right to impose a tallage[b] on his boroughs and demesne, he merged it in a request for general subsidies which required consent. He made the subsidy on movables a normal source of revenue, and so prepared the way for parliamentary taxation granted by lords and commons. This is not to say that he and his competent advisers created parliament. . . . [Rather] in a time of need they adjusted circumstances to existing methods by a series of expedients. They exploited, on the one hand, the negotiable element in the compulsory tallage and on the other hand invested the ancient right of the magnates to consent to or refuse taxation with the dignity of an obligation, common to all, to serve the common good by providing the means for the defense of the realm.[21]

To be sure, this policy of enlisting consent through protoparliamentary assemblies existed elsewhere in Europe. But by the beginning of the fourteenth century, the English polity had become singular in the degree to which even strong kings shared the tasks of national and local administration with the estates. On the Continent, strong royal authority or political fragmentation seemed the only available alternatives. But in England, traveling judges of the king's council came into close touch with the knights of the county courts, while local churches and the shires and boroughs of the land sent their elected representatives to parliament. Gradually, the English kings had come to accept "the necessity of taking the nation into partnership in [the] administration" of the country.[22]

Moreover, a countrywide jurisdiction had developed (in addition to local adjudication) as the king's judges handled an increasing number

---

[b]Tallage is a charge levied by a lord on his tenants.

Parliament of Edward I, probably 1279

Edward I in parliament with Alexander, king of Scots, and Llewellyn, prince of Wales. The bishops are seated on benches at the left and in the foreground, the barons on the right. In the center, the judiciary sits on woolsacks, while at the bottom, behind two clerks holding scrolls, are royal officials and representatives of boroughs. (British Museum) of cases brought before them. Such an extended jurisdiction of the king's courts depersonalized the relations between lord and vassal. Also, as wars came to be fought by armies paid from the royal treasury, the English kings stressed the duty of all to defend the realm; thus, the obligation of military service transcended its earlier basis in a personal relationship. At the highest level of society, the transactions between the king and the barons came to depend on political and economic conditions affecting the whole country rather than on a feudal bargain or contract in the narrow sense. Many scholars have become skeptical about the utility of the term *feudalism* because the connection between grants of rights and the obligation to serve became a legal fiction at an early time; however, the idea of a "national contract" between rulers and ruled retained its psychological importance for a long period.

A comparison with Japan under the Ashikaga shogunate suggests the importance of the national community in medieval England. Between the early fourteenth and the late sixteenth century, civil strife became so endemic in Japan that the power of the shogunate was at a low ebb. At the same time, Japan's landed gentry had enormous vitality which expressed itself in the rise of new clans as old ones declined. That vitality was evident in the marked independence of many daimyo families even under the police controls of the late Tokugawa shogunate. In this case, a national polity was created only by the enforced coordination of the great daimyo domains and the expulsion of the Christian missions. The case of England is different. The period from Magna Carta (1215) to the end of the fifteenth century may be described as an uneven seesaw between baronial interests *as represented in parliament* and the authority and power of the English kings. This "balanced" development in England contrasts with the repeated rise of local authority in Japan and its lasting suppression in Russia.[23] The vitality of the English barons certainly compares with that of the Japanese gentry, but there are two marked contrasts between England and Japan. First, in England there was an early emergence of a quasi-parliamentary institution, a collective forum in which the notables of the realm assembled to counsel the king and eventually to oppose him. This provided the English aristocracy with a national forum which was lacking in Japan. Second, English kings intermarried with the French royal family and through inheritance of territorial possessions also became vassals of the king of France. These political ties with the Continent *involved the whole country* in the national defense, especially since France made periodic attempts to gain a foothold in Scotland. By contrast, Japan retained its isolation from the Asian mainland so that neither a common representative body nor a common political involvement overseas restrained internal strife.

To sum up, English possessions and claims on the continent had a marked effect on the developing relationship between English kings and the English aristocracy. That effect was due, among other things, to the frequent absence of the kings from England, their intermarriages with the French royal house, hence the division of their interests between England and France, and the opportunities of bargaining or outright opposition which these continental ties of the kings (and some magnates) provided to the great barons of England. By utilizing these opportunities, the English baronage managed to increase its power position vis-à-vis the English monarchy, though for a long time this was hardly a deliberate process. Events during the fourteenth and fifteenth centuries illustrate how the relationship between the English kings and the baronage developed.

In the medieval world, public order was maintained by the enforcement of the king's rights. The English king's rights included his claims as duke of Aquitaine and vassal to the king of France as well as his claims to authority over Wales, Scotland, and Ireland. After 1290, all partnership in the administration of the country and all balance between the king's rights and the rights of the barons became instead a struggle of contending forces over rights acknowledged in principle but contested in practice.

The barons had supported King Edward I's conquest of Wales and the assertion of his rights in Gascony. But Edward's attempt to extend his authority over Scotland involved him in a war with France when the Scottish barons allied themselves with the French king. Edward thus had to contend with the king of France in Scotland and in Gascony, and the economic burdens resulting from these undertakings provoked a rebellion of the English baronage. When Edward II (1307–1327) inherited the throne, he also inherited the large debt left by his father as well as the baronial opposition which the son now managed to exacerbate further by the favors he bestowed on Piers Gaveston, a courtier from Gascony. The barons opposing the king were magnates who were suspicious of one another but able to unite against a foreign interloper like Gaveston. The Ordinances of 1311 sought to placate baronial opposition, which was especially directed against the king's advisors. Nevertheless, civil war followed, and when the barons were defeated, the Statute of York (1322) codified the king's rights, though it also promulgated the principle that royal government required the consent of the "prelates, earls, barons, and of the community of the realm." But the Statute of 1322 did not settle the matter, for the Scottish war was resumed, as was the dispute with France. Edward II sent his wife, Queen Isabella, to intercede on his behalf with her brother, the French king. She did so successfully, but in the end the queen conspired with her husband's enemies, returned to England with an army commanded by her lover

(Roger Mortimer of Wigmore), and with baronial help deposed Edward II in favor of the heir apparent, Edward III (1327–1377). The new king's reign witnessed the inception (1337) of the "Hundred Years' War" with France (originating in disputes over Gascony and Scotland), the Black Death, and a long-run economic decline with effects that lasted until the late fifteenth century. English kingship declined with the mounting struggles among the baronage, which centered on the rival houses of York and Lancaster and culminated in the War of the Roses (1455–1485).

In these dynastic struggles, leading aristocratic families asserted their rights against one another. Time and again, one of these families would use the weakened position of a king to enlarge its own claims, only to go down to defeat with the revival of the king's fortunes and the mounting envy of other baronial families. However, two important dimensions of domestic stability persisted throughout these centuries of foreign entanglements and internal strife: local government was one; the steady development of royal adjudication and administration was the other. At both levels, legal and administrative affairs were indistinguishable because the safeguarding of rights was tantamount to the collection of payments (fees, fines, dues) as the material equivalents of those rights. Royal as well as aristocratic governance depended essentially on these rights and that collection.

The formative conditions of royal authority are of enduring importance. For example, Imperial German kingship began with the legitimation of the Carolingian dynasty by an act of consecration and the subsequent involvement of the Frankish kings with papal political interests in Italy. Prussian kingship emerged much later, an outgrowth of efforts to overcome political fragmentation in a frontier province and a by-product of dynastic policies which utilized the devastations of the Thirty Years' War. Russian kingship began in two disconnected phases. Princely authority in Kievan Russia was established by armed merchants from Scandinavia, who chose certain towns as trading posts and attracted followers seeking protection and material advantage by organizing the defense against steppe nomads. In a second phase, the Muscovite tsars rose to preeminence under Mongol overlordship as collectors of tribute from other principalities and as a defense force against Lithuania; eventually they consolidated power by means of a systematic resettling of landed aristocrats from conquered territories like Novgorod. What then of England?

English kingship began with Anglo-Saxon war bands (*comitates*) invading and settling the British Isles. This initial condition was unusually favorable to an eventual balance between central and local power. The conditions of conquest and occupation by bands of armed tribesmen made for a solidarity of near equals. The Germanic tradition of equal inheritance among royal descendants quickly circumscribed whatever concentration of power had resulted from the conquest itself. By the time of the Norman conquest, more than a thousand years of Roman rule and Anglo-Saxon kingdoms had given great impetus to a structure of local rule which provided continuity despite much internal political strife and centuries of struggle against foreign invasions.

Of the cases examined here, the foundations of English kingship probably have their closest analogue in the Varangian occupation of early Kievan Russia. But Varangian forces were used in the interest of merchants and trade, not in the interest of warriors and the settlement of land. This mercantile orientation facilitated the acceptance by Kievan princes of native customs such as the town assembly (*veche*) and boyar freedom. The Varangian rulers probably accepted the notables of the Slavic tribes inhabiting the conquered areas because they wanted the collaboration of the native population in the promotion of trade and the organization of defense. By contrast, the Anglo-Saxon settlers competed for land with the native Celtic population and hence imposed their own institutions.

From the Norman conquest until the seventeenth century, English history moved back and forth between strong assertions of royal authority and strong countervailing tendencies of local autonomy and political representation. From the perspective of kingship, English medieval history since the Roman occupation is a record of discontinuity due to centuries of invasions and later to volatile political alliances with European powers. English political involvement with France was particularly important, beginning with the special link between England and Normandy, fostered for centuries by intermarriage between the two royal houses, and continuing with disputes over Gascony until well into the fifteenth century. From the perspective of local institutions, however, the same history shows much continuity.

Here the comparison with Japan is most instructive. Whereas England was unified by *foreign* conquest, first by the Romans and then by the Normans, Japan was unified by *indigenous* forces, first by the Yamato dynasty, later under the Taika reforms (at least formally), and then by the Kamakura shogunate. Chronologically, the Roman political unification of England coincided with the Uji period of ancient clan conflicts in Japan, whereas the decentralized Anglo-Saxon kingdoms coincided with Japanese efforts at centralizing government institutions under the Taika reforms. Five centuries of Roman rule over England as well as the regional and local government of the Anglo-Saxon and Norman invaders had established a balance between local and central rule that was absent from the Japanese experience. This may be the reason why English local institutions could develop gradually, whereas in Japan local institutions were altered a number of times by internal conflicts—by the Taika reforms and later by the repeated turnover of local elites which followed the dismantling of imperial control over the countryside.

The stability and gradual development of English local government were due to the long-established independence of local authorities, going back to Roman times. Oligarchic rule came to prevail in the counties, in parliament, and at court; thus, local influence and participation in national affairs were closely related. In addition, many sons of aristocratic families were appointed to administrative offices through patron-client relations within this oligarchy. One can speak, then, of a "nationalization" of local politics. Political factions within the oligarchy were formed while the crown matched oligarchic influence by using its prerogatives in making local appointments and developing the jurisdiction of the royal courts. One can compare this development with the Prussian, which witnessed the consolidation of princely rule over the provincial estates during the seventeenth century. In this period, the Hohenzollern rulers built a civil and military establishment which ensured their own dominance over the squirearchy. In the countryside, aristocratic landowners introduced the military and authoritarian manner which characterized their own careers in the army. This domination of the countryside had complete royal support. An ideology of honor and service enhanced this local dominance as well as the privileged position of the aristocracy in the army and the civil service. At the same time, "national" affairs were the prerogative of the crown; regular participation by the aristocracy was excluded. Prussia knew little of that combination of local dominance and preponderance in national affairs which characterized English oligarchic rule.

The contrast is reflected in the practice of local government. Both the Prussian rural councillor (*Landrat*) and the English justice of the peace represented the local aristocratic oligarchies. In Prussia, the Landrat was nominated by the local estates and then appointed by the king, although as a disciplinary measure Frederick William I occasionally appointed Landräte by himself. The Landrat was paid, partly by the Treasury and partly by the local estate, but he had no judicial authority. Many duties of the Landrat reflected the militarization of Prussian society. He was charged with the supervision of recruitment, the capture of deserters, the provision and proper care of the required number of horses, the reimbursement of peasants for services rendered, and the handling of military administration and supplies while an army unit was in transit through his district. These duties and the prevalence of former officers among the Landräte reveal the intrusion of dynastic and military interests in the conduct of local affairs. In England, justices of the peace were also appointed by the crown from among the local notables, but they served without salary. These local justices were concerned with work-houses, prisons, roads, bridges, vagrants, and other communal duties along with their several judicial functions. Active leadership was a matter of personal inclination on the part of gentlemen-amateurs who treated these matters in much the same way as they did the management of their own estates. The justices of the peace were above all civilian offi-cials, and although their conduct of office was formally coordinated by the government, their administrative and judicial activities expressed the rule of the local oligarchy.[24] The implications of this contrast for the character of the English aristocracy are discussed in the next section.

FROM THE KING'S COMPANIONS TO PARLIAMENT

Anglo-Saxon law recorded the social distinctions of the time by as-signing different amounts of compensation (*wergild*) owed to the rela-tions of a slain man: 30,000 shillings for a king's life, 1,200 shillings for the life of an earl or a king's companion (*gesith*), 200 shillings for the life of a freeman. The king with his companions, the earls in the shires, the more substantial thegns, and the magnates of the church constituted the Anglo-Saxon aristocracy. And since there were several Anglo-Saxon kingdoms, each overlord and lesser king had his own aristocratic entourage.[25]

After 1066, the authority of one king was recognized throughout the realm. William the Conqueror emphasized the legitimacy of his succession to the English throne, and within a decade after the conquest most landholdings had been expropriated and redistributed.

> William divided England into great fiefs or "honours." The laymen to whom he granted them were his vassals, or as they came to be called in England, his barons. These men, when they rewarded their own vassals, likewise granted them fiefs. In practice, within a relatively short time, certainly by the time of Domesday Book [1086], there had arisen every tenurial complexity which can be imagined: barons holding fiefs of each other, and of their own or of another's vassal; tenants holding fiefs of several lords and of each other.

Each of these relationships was established by homage and fealty. There was a belief that all links would ultimately reach the king, but in practice a tangle of rights and obligations gave rise to disputes which had to be settled.

> The law had to be declared; and through judgments made by the suitors in the honorial courts the law of the honour was formed. There were innu-merable matters which had to be decided: the exact services due from a vassal to his lord, on what terms could a fief or part of it be alienated, who had the

wardship of a vassal's children under age, when could a lord claim an aid or relief, and so on. The influence of the king's court and the interlocking of the honours hindered extreme individuality of custom in the several baronies; but diversity there was. . . . One of the great effects of the Conquest, therefore, was the creation of a new body of law in the kingdom.[26]

New social bonds emerged out of this process of litigation by which the parties to a dispute were involved in a developing network of common rules.

Marc Bloch has distinguished between two phases of feudalism in Western Europe. In the first, population is sparse, communication difficult, and aristocratic society intensely local; the status of a family is directly proportional to its local wealth and authority. This formulation roughly describes the conditions of Anglo-Saxon England. In the second, population increases, and there is a growth of towns and commerce; the fragmentation of political authority gives way to stronger monarchical rule. This process is well exemplified by the Norman and Plantagenet dynasties in England. Bloch describes a society based on the reciprocal bonds between a lord who grants a fief and a vassal who owes loyalty and service in return. This seemingly simple principle was undermined as soon as a fief granted for service became hereditary, for then the grant would no longer be conditional; in fact, inheritance became a fertile source of disputes. The king claimed a right to all the land and hence would demand payment for permitting the heirs to assume legal title to an inherited fief, even when they were quite willing to assume the service obligations incumbent upon it. The king's insistence on his rights was periodically limited by his financial needs; thus, he might consent to sell some part of his rights in particular cases. In turn, the heirs would typically seek out ways of legally construing their payments as entitling them to an inheritance free of additional obligations. Such conflicting constructions were applied not only by the king and his tenants-in-chief, but by other lords and vassals. As the complexities of inheritance increased, the connection became attenuated between grants and the services or payments rendered in return.[27]

After 1066, there was only one king's court at which the king's tenants-in-chief mingled with magnates of the church and earls from the shires. Royal supremacy was unchallenged. Under the protection of the king, however, an aristocracy was formed for which the quasi-parliamentary councils of the medieval period provided a meeting place and eventually a forum for asserting baronial rights. The Norman aristocracy remained organized for war, but the Norman kings were rich and relaxed their inherited claim to the military service of their vassals by accepting a fine (*scutage*) in lieu of service. By the end of the twelfth century, feudal levies based on quotas of armed knights were becoming obsolete.[c] The inadequacy of the old system of armed knights and the need for paid professional soldiers became apparent when countrywide royal authority brought with it military engagements involving large and coordinated forces. For wars on the Continent it was uneconomical to use knights recruited in England, and when the danger from invasions subsided, a standing force of armed knights was dispensable. From the eleventh to the thirteenth centuries, the total number of armed knights which the king's vassals owed to the crown was reduced from about 6,500 to 375.[28]

As a mounted warrior, the armed knight was best adapted to local engagements and individual combat, but ill-suited as an officer coordinating the motley units recruited from the shires and towns. From a military standpoint, discipline was needed in place of the heterogeneous feudal warriors from many different areas. From an administrative standpoint, it was more efficient for the crown to appoint commissioners who surveyed the able-bodied men of each shire and selected the best of them to serve at the king's wages, with the cost of the initial equipment borne by the localities. From a political standpoint, this so-called Commission of Array meant that a military service partly financed by the royal treasury made even the greatest magnates more dependent on the king, although they remained important military leaders of the king's army.

The daily stipends paid to the knights recruited in this way reflected the status distinctions made in the fourteenth century. Edward Balliol, titular king of the Scots, drew 30 shillings a day in peacetime and 50 shillings in wartime. A duke was paid 13s. 4d. per day, while an earl drew 8s. Bannerets, who were general staff officers responsible for commanding units in the field and garrisoning castles, ranked below this level at a rate of 4 shillings a day. The lowest rank of these warriors— all those entitled and wealthy enough to serve as heavily armed knights on horseback—were the knights bachelor paid at a rate of 2s. a day. All these men from different ranks of the aristocracy had to possess sufficient land so that they could afford the expenses for armor and horses, which often exceeded the pay they received. But these expenses might be worthwhile, because the rewards from foreign wars could be substantial due to requisitions, looting, and the additional grants of land and rights which the king would have at his disposal in case of success.[29] No medieval king was rich enough to finance an army of mercenaries by himself; therefore, much depended on the consent of the magnates to grant the king the special levies he requested for his military cam-

[c]The last feudal host was called out by Richard II (1377–1399) for the Scottish campaign of 1385.

paigns. Though the mercenary force began with the substitution of scutage for personal service, the king's military establishment depended not only on the royal treasury but on the financial and personal cooperation of the magnates.

One can date these changes in military organization from the reign of Edward I (1272–1307), who regularized military service for pay, and from the 1330s when Edward III first employed archers in his Scottish campaigns. From that time till the middle of the fifteenth century, one can speak of a "military-commercial complex," for at the behest of the king the great magnates and the lesser gentry organized armies supplied by contractors and sustained by the rich rewards to be obtained through the wars in France. As the power of these magnates increased, that of the king declined. By the end of the fifteenth century, the magnates were embroiled in a struggle for the control of the government. That civil war (the War of the Roses) ended in the victory of the Tudors. Henry VII (1485–1509) not only dismissed the mercenaries who had helped him win the throne, but also reverted to the old institution of the shire militia. However, this was now organized by the king's own officers (sheriffs, justices of the peace) rather than by local magnates. With only a few exceptions, this was the basis on which the Tudor and Stuart kings governed a very turbulent country. The relatively independent role of the great magnates in helping to finance and organize the king's army had become incompatible with the continuation of kingship now that the war in France no longer provided outlets for domestic strife.

Changes of military technique and organization were responsible for the transformation of the aristocratic way of life. The readiness of warriors to serve their king had been one rationale of their privileged position, but this uncoordinated recruitment of armed knights was superseded by countrywide levies financed by the king and the barons.[d] Still, training in the arts of war remained essential to the aristocratic way of life. Militancy was associated with an acute consciousness of rank, a jealous regard for the honor of the family name, and the protection of the rights of family possessions. Moreover, a noble lord was typically surrounded by retainers, personal servants, and tenants who enhanced his standing by marks of deference, by personal service, by military service in times of war, and occasionally by armed support in private quarrels. In this setting, men trained in the arts of war were quick to resort to force in response to provocations, real or imagined, and armed feuds

[d]The following survey is limited to the changing aristocratic life style in England since the sixteenth century. The changing historical setting of the period is presented in Chapter 9.

over rights in times of peace were a regular feature of feudal law. Feuds had a legal aspect insofar as they grew out of the jealous insistence by baronial families on maintaining their rights. But feuds were an obvious threat to the king's peace. King Edward I shared the passion for tournaments, and although he was aware that tournaments encouraged the barons' dangerous impulses of self-help, he was unable to regulate these jousting contests and to forbid illicit assemblies of men at arms.[30]

This cult of personal combat by mounted warriors as a mark of the aristocrat declined in importance as arrows and longbows were introduced in the fourteenth and firearms in the fifteenth and sixteenth centuries. The size of the armies increased from about seven thousand men at the battle of Hastings (1066) to about thirty-five thousand men in the sixteenth century, but in the later period the English forces were notably smaller than the contemporary armies on the Continent. As the task of commanding disciplined troops of foot soldiers increased, the importance of the feudal cavalry declined. Ever since the substitution of payment for personal service, armies had been organized by commission, the king paying a gentleman to raise, equip, officer, and lead his force of soldiers. The wars fought with such armies were affected by changes in military organization as well as technology. In the century between 1550 and 1650, military campaigns became increasingly a problem in logistics, ordinance, transport, and engineering. On the Continent, these changes brought about the establishment of standing armies composed of foreign mercenaries and native troops; England, however, abandoned the system of commissioned troops and instead of a standing army relied on the shire militia, occasional mercenary forces, and a build-up of its navy.[31]

In the course of these transformations, duels began to replace tournaments or individual combat in battle as as the type of militancy most suited to a gentleman. By the middle of the seventeenth century, the old warlike ideals and practices of the aristocracy had virtually disappeared. Forces of private retainers were reduced, and the armories of the aristocracy became obsolete. Personal experience in war waned, though deaths from duels increased rapidly, especially among the young magnates of the realm.[32] (By the nineteenth century, physical violence itself came to be considered a form of vulgarity characteristic of the lower classes.)

A rising interest in higher education may be compared with this decline of combat as the ideal of aristocratic conduct. From the middle of the sixteenth to the middle of the seventeenth century, the old diatribes against clerkly book-learning as unbecoming to a gentleman were superseded by tracts deploring the aristocrats' ignorance and their indifference toward education. By 1630 the proportion of entrants into the university or the Inns of Court had reached a level of 2.48 percent of the annual cohort of males aged seventeen; sons of the gentry represented about one-third of the entering students.[33] The educational background of members of parliament indicates that this development had special significance for the peerage and the squirearchy. In 1563 the proportion of the 420 members who had been at the university or at the Inns of Court stood at 38 percent; by 1640–1642 the membership of parliament had increased to 552, and the proportion of those who had received some higher education had risen to 70 percent.[34]

This expansion of English higher education helped to destroy the old clerical monopoly of culture. The teachings of sixteenth- and seventeenth-century humanists, the Puritan zeal to spread the word of God, and the increasing appeal of the Baconian view of science combined to persuade the landed classes of the importance of learning. In addition, the mounting religious and political controversies in the House of Commons put a premium on eloquence and learning as effective weapons in the struggle for influence.[35] Moreover, the administrative class expanded and opportunities for placement at the disposal of the king were concentrated at the court. The old aristocratic virtues of valor, loyalty, and chivalry as well as the old aristocratic contempt for letters were out of place in this setting.[36] By 1700 education had done its share in transforming the aristocratic way of life.

The expansion of government in the sixteenth and seventeenth centuries put a premium on educational qualifications for those who aspired to public office. As greater demands were made on the organizing capacity of government (in part by a changed pattern of warfare), monarchical government became more bureaucratic and the demand for literary skills increased. English and Japanese aristocrats came to terms with education along parallel lines.

> At a fairly early stage both societies freed education from the monopoly of priests, England in the sixteenth century, Japan in the seventeenth. Both developed schools for their elite in which the children could be taught firstly —and most importantly—the virtue of obedience to superiors in order to preserve social stability; secondly, the art of war, which was the original justification of their privileged status; thirdly, the techniques and skills which would equip them for administrative chores in an increasingly bureaucratic society; fourthly, scholarly appreciation of the classics, in which all wisdom was believed to reside; and fifthly, the manners, skills, and aesthetic interests that distinguished them from the rest of society.[37]

Menial clerical jobs continued to be performed by hirelings, but now aristocrats adapted themselves to play a role in the conduct of affairs. Strict discipline and esoteric learning provided these men with the necessary "domestication" of manners and with a new invidious distinction which set them apart from commoners. The Russian and the Prussian developments were different. In these countries, clerics and commoners continued to fill prominent public offices, while the Russian and Prussian autocrats of the eighteenth century regarded the education of young aristocrats as a matter of dynastic policy. Hence, some members of aristocratic families turned primarily to legal education as a means of competing for public careers in contrast to Japan and England, where esthetic or classical education retained its importance.

The aristocratic ideals of military service or combativeness on points of honor were not abandoned, but the pursuit of these ideals was redirected. During the sixteenth and seventeenth centuries, the age of exploration called for personal valor and national service of a high order. During the eighteenth and nineteenth centuries, colonial conquests and rule provided new challenges for the adaptation of aristocratic ideals. Moreover, service as an officer in the English navy became a mark of aristocratic distinction even before England resumed its military engagements on land in the later seventeenth century. But while England equalled or exceeded the foreign military exploits of continental countries, the retention of the shire militia as the main domestic military force set England apart. This force represented the landed aristocracy and its tenants at the local level. England's militia system arose from the common law obligation of all citizens to defend the country; the system put minimal burdens on the population. For the nation as a whole, however, even eighteen thousand "fighting effectives" were considered dangerous. The seventeenth-century parliament introduced annual budgetary controls over the military establishment in order to forestall the accumulation of military power in the hands of the monarchy.[38]

The aristocracy of sixteenth- and seventeenth-century England, then, underwent a change through education, government service, and a partial demilitarization which accentuated the importance of manners at court and in high society. London became the center of that society, as ties of fear and hope bound peers and gentry to the court.[e] During the period 1590–1730, London was the only city of consequence, pos-

---

[e]Lawrence Stone writes, "In the eyes of the sixteenth century [the peers] were a distinct group of the nobility, *nobilitas major*, as distinct from the *nobilitas minor*, of knights, esquires, and armigerous gentry. . . . The criterion of an English peer of the realm was the right to sit in the House of Lords, a right obtained either by letters patent [see Glossary] or by receipt of a writ of summons. Since in the sixteenth century most peers were created by patent, male succession took on an increased importance. Already in the fourteenth century writs of summons were issued not in respect to legal tenure, but of wealth and political influence, the tenurial barony being ancient, vague, and outdated. . . . Those who could no longer maintain status because of poverty were quietly dropped from the list."[39]

sessing over 300,000 residents while no other city had more than 25,000. The London "season" became a regular practice of the landed aristocracy, facilitated after 1590 by the increased use of the private coach. By 1630 at least three-quarters of the peerage had acquired a permanent residence in London in addition to the residence on their country estates, a practice which was widely imitated by lower-ranking gentry families. The attractions of the city were many. Men of rank could escape the boredom of the countryside and mix their business, lawsuits, personal intrigues, and attendance at court with the pleasures of the city. So many peers and gentry came to London during the social "season" that the crown issued proclamations against this practice and even initiated legal proceedings (in the 1630s) in order to drive peers and gentry back to their estates in the country.[40] Such measures proved to no avail.

The "domestication" of the aristocracy was also a consequence of the increasing wealth of the Tudors and of increasing competition at court. Henry VII (1485–1509) was the first English king in over a century whose wealth and influence were greater than the total resources available to the magnates surrounding him, and under the chancellorship of Thomas Cromwell (1485?–1540) the revenue of Henry VIII (1509–1547) tripled.[41] The reorganization and streamlining of monarchical government under Cromwell's influence, the break with the Roman church (1534), and the resources accruing to the monarchy following the dissolution of the monasteries are related indications of this rise of monarchical authority.[42]

In the English setting, however, this rise was equivocal. For example, prevailing opinion held that the king "must live on his own" and finance the ordinary operations of government, except in times of war. Accordingly, to maintain the king's position at home and abroad, the search for additional revenue was a constant preoccupation. The king and his advisors resorted to all kinds of expedients.[43] By distributing titles, grants, and other favors the Tudors used their wealth to foster competition at court and thus ensure the personal dependence even of the great magnates. But this policy also increased the need for funds, and the means used to obtain them increased the liabilities of the crown, often leading to acute financial difficulty. As a result, Elizabeth I (1558–1603) became very parsimonious in handing out gifts and titles. But the early Stuarts returned again to largesse.[44]

As the court became the major center for the distribution of opportunities, its scale of expenditures became lavish, and every new grant of royal favors further stimulated the demand for preferment. From 1603 to 1641, the gifts and favors distributed by the crown totaled about £3 million. During the same period, the profusion of titles and favors led to an "inflation of honors," cheapening each honor or benefit be-

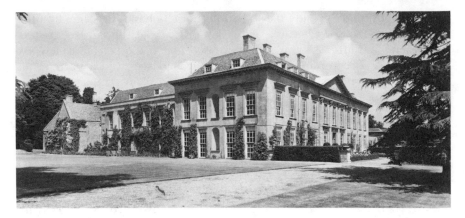

Country and Townhouses
Great families built both townhouses in London, near the center of affairs at court and in parliament, and mansions on their country estates. They moved back and forth between them in accord with the "season." The history of these houses has been associated with many famous names of the English aristocracy. In the seventeenth century Cornbury Park and Clarendon house, London, belonged to Edward Hyde, earl of Clarendon. (*Country Life;* British Museum)

stowed while providing a precedent for still more largesse. Notorious intrigues, mounting corruption, and conspicuous luxuries accompanied this inflation. The wealthiest members of the aristocracy enjoyed a very large indirect income through tax exemptions and gifts or bribes in return for using their influence at court. Largesse in hospitality and a luxurious style of life became attributes of aristocracy with its easygoing or studied contempt for base, material considerations. The monarchy set the pace in this respect, in part as a cultural affirmation of its legitimate supremacy and in part as a means of encouraging competition that often resulted in enormous debts by aristocrats to the crown or to moneylenders. Debts were incurred by the competition for favors and by conspicuous consumption as a mark of high status. Debts were encouraged by moneylenders willing to speculate on the prospective gains of courtiers.[45] These mounting financial obligations could jeopardize the economic foundations of aristocratic wealth and on occasion led to aristocratic revolts sparked by the loss of power and influence. But where one family declined, another rose in its place. The court and parliament were at the center of affairs; what happened there had become of supreme importance and increasingly absorbed the attention of the squirearchy. As personal combat declined while higher education, urban interests, and competition for place at the capital increased, the English aristocracy was brought to acknowledge the supremacy of national over local concerns.[46]

Attention must also be given to the social mobility of the English aristocracy. For all its exclusiveness, this governing class was not a closed group, nor had it been as far back as the twelfth century. After 1066, primogeniture had been introduced with specific reference to the land-holdings of knights, but gradually the principle was applied more generally. By preventing the division of estates, their prosperity was preserved. At the same time, social mobility was facilitated because younger sons dropped into the ranks of commoners, and the king could elevate commoners to aristocratic rank as a reward for services rendered. Social ranks existed in profusion without any neat distinctions among them, save the main distinction between gentlemen and the many who did not count as such. The king's council and later parliaments were recruited from a great diversity of groups. By the end of the thirteenth century, the principles of representation had been laid down. Various chapters, cathedrals, and dioceses of the church were to be represented. Each shire, town, and borough was to elect two representatives. In addition, seven earls and forty-one barons were summoned by name. As Maitland states the position,

> The clergy and baronage are summoned to treat, ordain and execute, the representatives of the commons are to bring full powers from those whom they represent to execute what should be ordained by common counsel. A

body constituted in this manner is a parliament; what the king enacts with
the consent of such a body is a statute. . . . Thus before the end of the thirteenth century the national assembly is ceasing to be a feudal court; it is becoming an assembly of the estates of the realm. . . . The three estates are
clergy, barons, and commons, those who pray, those who fight, those who
work; this seems to have been considered an exhaustive classification of the
diverse conditions of men.[47]

The Lords were an exclusive class assembly, but a large number of barons who belonged to the same class as the Lords were excluded from
that assembly.[48] And in later years the House of Lords was composed
not only of barons but also of bishops who had received a special
summons.

When aristocrats interact with other strata at court, when many of
their sons become commoners while other commoners are raised in
rank, when rank itself is given no firm institutional foundation, one may
expect many overlapping grades of gentility. In the fourteenth and fifteenth centuries, the great majority of landowning squires had very
modest estates; thus, wealth did not mark them off from their nonaristocratic neighbors. Nor was there any other *single* criterion of aristocratic
status. Rather, gentility was recognized by descent as well as by "achievement," by types of household or military service, and negatively by disdain for manual labor, book-learning, and retail trade. In fact, criteria
of rank varied at the different levels of the social hierarchy. For the
peerage and great, nonbaronial landed families, gentility meant an unquestioned enjoyment of status and power based on wealth derived from
land. But in the service of the royal court or the great magnates, gentility
was also derived from the responsible functions performed on behalf
of a great lord. In the case of the landed gentry of moderate or small
means, gentility implied freedom from manual labor and the respect
due to such ranks of governmental or military service as were within
their reach. The lesser gentry still modeled its life style on the patterns
established by the great lords—even if it did not serve the king or barons
directly. In the course of time, criteria of achievement imperceptibly
blended with those of ascription at this middle level. Skill and knowledge
had been considered menial qualities until roughly the fifteenth century.
But during the sixteenth century sons of noble families found classical
education (like philosophy, rhetoric) serviceable in their careers at court,
in parliament, or in the performance of administrative functions. Accordingly, skill and knowledge came to give new overtones to the conception of gentility.[49]

So many overlapping criteria of rank suggest that the English social
hierarchy was relatively flexible. In addition, the composition of the aristocracy changed due to political and economic upheavals. Of the fifty-

three lay lords who had been summoned to parliament before the War of the Roses, only twenty-nine received a summons to the first parliament of Henry VII, in 1485.[50] More important were subsequent changes: as the territorial possessions of the great families declined, so did their influence. In 1559 eighteen out of sixty-two families owned seventy manors or more; by 1641 only six out of one hundred twenty-one families had holdings of that size.[51] Persecution of individual families by the early Tudor kings, infertility, exile, and the failure of the Tudors to create new landed families, meant that by 1620 only one family of peers was left of those who had dominated society and politics in the late fifteenth century. But this decline of old families was more than matched by the rise of new ones. When the Stuarts came to power, they sought to bolster their political and financial position by a profusion of honors bestowed on a large number of new families.

At lower levels, the same flexibility led to relatively close economic and social relations of the gentry with merchant families, London lawyers, and city officials. Members of the gentry showed considerable interest in wholesale trade, though that interest remained intermittent and did not become a regular occupation. But the gentry drew a line at family relations. Even aristocrats of lower rank were evidently reluctant to accept prominent commoners as guardians for their children or to give their daughters in marriage to merchant families without land.[52] Such practices reveal an interesting sense of priorities. The gentry would forego the advantages of birth more readily than those of landownership, and in turn prominent London commoners aspired above all to the great prestige of a life style associated with land ownership and a country residence.[53]

This discussion of the English aristocracy has emphasized its considerable internal mobility. I have not attempted a judgment on the issues raised by the "gentry controversy" in which scholars have assessed the changing economic fortunes of the aristocracy as causes of the English revolution. It is probable that the economic fortunes of the gentry rose from the late sixteenth to the middle of the seventeenth century, while those of the peerage declined. But it is certain that this change did not seriously disturb the ruling ideas of the age which judged people in terms of the honor or dignity attached to their position in society. Social commentators from the time of Henry VIII to the early eighteenth century divided Englishmen into nobility, burgesses, yeomen, and laborers. The nobility was divided, in turn, into the king and the peerage, on the one hand, and the lesser ranks of knights, esquires, and gentlemen, on the other. Unlike the peerage, these lesser ranks of the gentry did not enjoy legally sanctioned privileges. But although peerage and gentry constituted separate ranks, both together comprised an ar-

istocracy that was internally differentiated by age of title, family emi-
nence, size of landed income, opulence of life style, dignity of office,
and regional or neighborhood importance. Legal enactments and common parlance alike labeled men by their recognized social rank and vigorously enforced the elementary distinction between those who were
gentlemen and those who were not. The distinction was crucial, for the
great majority of the people were not gentlemen and were consequently
excluded from all exercise of authority. In 1565 Sir Thomas Smith defined them as having "no voice nor authoritie in our common wealth,
and no account is made of them but onelie to be ruled, and not to rule
other," a sentiment echoed more than two centuries later when Edmund
Burke declared that the state suffers oppression if persons in servile
employment are permitted to rule.[54]

England is our fourth example of a society in which political leadership was restricted to a ruling minority of the population. Political
leadership presupposed economic affluence and the economic and social exploitation of large numbers of people. Only those who could afford not to work had access to court or parliament or the decision-making bodies of local government. But wealth alone was not enough, since
many economically successful men from modest family backgrounds
were excluded from active political participation. Only gentlemen were
recognized as eligible for public functions, though one could advance
into that rank through the purchase of land and adaptation to the life
style of the gentry. When these conditions were met, a modest family
background did not bar a man for long from playing a political role if
he wished, and it certainly did not bar his son. Accordingly, we must
attend to this combination of status attributes, landed wealth, and local
authority which together account for the political predominance of the
English aristocracy.

The authority of government was divided between the crown and
its court society, on the one hand, and the counties, on the other. In a
predominantly agricultural economy, land was the chief source of wealth
and the shire was the most effective unit of government. At this local
level, the English government of the sixteenth century was comparatively active and efficient. R. H. Tawney states that "the ordinary relationships between social classes [at the local level were made] the machinery for executing the mandates of the State, by entrusting
administration . . . to persons who already possessed local authority, and
who were confirmed in it, rather than given it, by the Crown."[55] Inevitably, local politics mirrored the class interests of this group, given the
overwhelming predominance of justices of the peace, sheriffs, and lord

lieutenants recruited from the leading gentry families. At the local level the crown did not exert pressure to alter this state of affairs, though it was capable of intervention in order to mitigate the hardships of local rule.[56]

This juxtaposition of county politics and royal government is a characteristic feature of English society from the sixteenth century onward. The crown's powers of appointment to local office were unchallenged, and all appointments went to local notables on the assumption that public affairs would be in the hands of those who "have some connection with the interests and fortunes of the country."[57] No doubt it was selfish pride to assume that wealth and status were intimately linked with a capacity to judge public affairs. But the same pride was also combined with a willingness to serve without salary and later to spend large sums in election campaigns without promise of immediate reward. There were counties in which a single family's wealth and status were unchallenged. Members of such families would compete for precedence and favors only at the royal court. In many counties, however, rural society was rife with contention among families seeking the honor of unsalaried office in local affairs. Sometimes the repercussion from these local rivalries would reach the court and parliament. By the power of appointment and by new distributions of royal favors, the crown "resolved" those disputes among local gentry families which reached its attention. Thus, in the absence of nationwide and continuous administration, the royal government was linked with local administration in the shires and hundreds (see Glossary).

The social standing of families was expressed in part by the number of liveried retainers who served their lord in his country residence and in London. These retainers would also serve the role of henchmen who occasionally fought pitched battles to settle a personal quarrel in their master's behalf. But the sixteenth and early seventeenth centuries saw a decline in the number of retainers. In part, economic changes were responsible for the commutation of service obligations into rent. The mounting competition for place at court precluded overt aggression. Also, in an effort to curb violence the crown meted out conspicuous punishment to retainers who had committed crimes at the behest of a great lord. These penalties together with the increase of absentee ownership helped to undermine the traditional role of retainers.[58]

But if armed retainers were on the decline, the practice of *clientage* was not. In the counties, most of the gentry families grouped themselves around a few great men, the younger sons often taking service in the patron's household.[59] The patron-client relationship was not confined to such service.

> In a world of dependents, independence was a quixotic luxury. The smaller man found friendship, patronage, and protection in the system. The great man gained reputation and power: he made manifest his greatness by the number of gentlemen whom he could on occasion summon to follow him. . . . Inevitably, this tendency of the gentry to move within the orbit of some magnate provoked or intensified rivalry, which percolated through from the highest to the lowest ranks of the gentry and even to their tenantry.[60]

Here is another reason why in this period sons from aristocratic families increasingly flocked to the Inns of Court. As direct aggression declined, litigation came to be used to annoy one's enemies and perhaps impoverish them. During Elizabeth's reign alone the number of bills lodged in the Star Chamber and in the Court of Requests increased tenfold.

The enlargement of the House of Commons is another indication of mounting contentiousness, arising as it did from local initiative and involving a large number of bitterly fought electoral contests. During the sixteenth century the House increased from 296 to 462 members, to which another 45 members were added under the early Stuarts.[61] With all freeholders worth forty shillings a year entitled to vote, county elections were a "mustering of the community . . . [which] furnished an opportunity . . . of testing the social standing of an individual or the relative strength of rival groups and parties." Though Elizabethan statutes encouraged the parliamentary representation of cities and boroughs over "country gentlemen," in practice the latter were favored four to one.[62] Landed families continued to furnish a substantial majority of the House of Commons until 1868 and still a slight majority in the parliament of 1880.[63]

Lasting dominance did not ensure internal tranquility. From the litigations and electoral contests of the Elizabethan period to the twelve fiercely fought general elections between 1689 and 1715, rivalries of long standing made for political controversy. The convulsions of the Cromwellian revolution resulted in a rapidly increasing number of freeholders entitled to vote at the local level. Aristocratic dominance was partly responsible for this increase in the electorate, because it put a premium on the multiplication of freeholds, commissions, and benefices that were considered property.

> England was littered with them, myriad marks of status, of possession, of profit: stewards of hundreds, precentors of cathedrals, beadles of corporations. Usually these offices were held for life and they all enjoyed standing and status within the community they adorned; most of them carried a vote. Such freeholds bred independence, truculence, a willingness to fight and litigate that bordered on neurosis, and yet when they conglomerated, as in the universities, the cathedral cities, and the Parliamentary boroughs, they could build up into formidable heaps of political influence. Difficult to discipline,

secure in their self-importance, their holders, with the gentry, became the leaders of public opinion outside London and the great towns, an opinion that proved easy to influence—through newspapers, pamphlets, and ballads —but hard to manage.[64]

Plumb emphasizes the contrast between this contentiousness and the political stability of a ruling oligarchy which characterized the later eighteenth and in lesser degree parts of the nineteenth century. Landownership was the key to both aristocratic infighting and the overall stability of the English aristocracy as a governing class.

The family estate was the basis of aristocratic governance. The financial security and social status associated with landownership facilitated the control of tenants in local and parliamentary elections as well as the dominance and deference typical of patron-client relations. In addition, land was made a "vehicle of family purpose" through the "strict settlement" which came into prominence in the late seventeenth century.

> These arrangements were most commonly made at the marriage of the heir, and they secured that the estate, or the greater part of it, descended intact to him, but descended on terms which greatly limited his power to sell and mortgage it. Once the deed of settlement was signed, the descent of the estate was settled for a generation ahead. Except by promoting a private Act of Parliament to break the settlement, there was no way by which the owner could obtain complete control of the estate until the eldest son of the marriage came of age. As a corollary, the settlement provided that the younger children of the marriage should receive annuities or capital sums charged upon the estate. . . . In the longterm interests of the family [the strict settlement thus] limited the immediate interests of its representative for the time being.[65]

With every generation the need to formulate the terms of the settlement arose anew and thus provided an opportunity to define and implement the will of the family as a unit. Although this legal device was used rather flexibly, its effect was to impede the sale or dispersion of estates and hence to buttress the continuity and dominance of old and new aristocratic families.

The country residences of the landed gentry were the social centers of the locality; the enormous number of rooms accommodated large households and the many guests who came frequently. Many prominent families also maintained a London residence to which they would move during the "season." As the new wealth of prominent merchants and lawyers flowed into country residence and landed estates, the old wealth of the landed gentry flowed into the establishment of elaborate urban residences. The London residences facilitated competition for influence at court and the claims to high status manifest in conspicuous hospitality and consumption. The great houses of seventeenth- and eighteenth-century London were the town residences of the landed gentry rather than of an urban patriciate, as in Holland or Italy.[66]

For the English gentry, urban sophistication and the pursuit of preferment at the center of affairs existed side by side with a socially and economically active life in the country. At the end of the "season," the family returned to its country residence, where even the great magnates spent the bulk of their time. While hospitality, hunting, and other diversions absorbed a good deal of their leisure, the head of the house and his wife also devoted time to estate and household management. These landed gentry were rentiers depending on tenants to farm their lands. Unlike many rentiers, however, they took an active interest in their estates, because the payments of their tenants provided the most important source of their income. By 1800 income from urban and mining property also became an important source of revenue for the gentry, and income from officeholding had become a sizable supplement to their land rents.[67]

Prominent writers linked landed property with the right to an active share in government.[68] Since the seventeenth century some landowners had built canals, engaged in wholesale trade, or taken an interest in mining and real estate. With land the main source of their wealth, however, the gentry were predominantly consumers and borrowers.[69] Nevertheless, in their public role these men showed a lively awareness of economic affairs as a whole. During the eighteenth century, parliamentary debates turned largely on financial and commercial questions, indicating an orientation "we should rather have expected in a middle-class Parliament than in a Parliament consisting in a very large measure of the nominees of great families."[70] A number of aristocratic political leaders of the eighteenth century studied trade and finance because they considered competence in these fields a prerequisite of political leadership. The classical learning of the time did not prevent the English gentry from becoming champions of commerce.[71]

Given the customary aristocratic disdain of menial and clerkly occupations, some explanation of this anomaly is required. The interest of some English landowners in wholesale trade can be documented as far back as the fourteenth century. English commerce was closely linked with overseas trade, which benefited from the national prestige of seafaring, exploration, and piracy in past centuries and from the special importance of the navy for the defense of an island nation.[72] At the same time, the English gentry hardly diminished its disdain for trade and continued to use government offices as a social prerogative until well into the nineteenth century. Hence, it is at least plausible to attribute

the gentry's championship of commerce to its longstanding self-identi-
fication as the English ruling class and to its pragmatic identification
with the national interest. Landed gentlemen might profit from trade
and mining, but they advanced commerce and industry as a national
interest in the same way in which they performed the functions of local
government without salary.[73]

The political dominance of the English gentry came to be increasingly at odds with the declining economic significance of landownership
in the course of the nineteenth century.[74] But as the combination of
status *and* wealth based on land was weakened, other means were found
to maintain the gentry's political prestige. An aristocratic way of life increasingly ill-adapted to the values and practices of a business civilization
was transmitted and reinforced through the public school system which
gained special prominence during the nineteenth century.[75] A privileged education now buttressed the continued dominance of the gentry
in English public life, and the spirit inculcated by the public schools facilitated the acceptance of this governing class by a "deferential society."
Following the Reform Act of 1867, Walter Bagehot pointed out that the
mass of householders who were entitled to vote accepted as a matter of
course that they would be represented by their superiors in rank and
wealth, whom a good many also considered their superiors "in the more
intangible qualities of sense and knowledge." Five years later Hippolyte
Taine reported one of the greatest English industrialists as saying that
men of the middle class were ready to leave the government and high
offices in the hands of the aristocracy, because these men were "born
and bred to the work for generations." But there should be no medi-
ocrities and no nepotism: "Let them govern, but let them be fit to govern."[76] If such acknowledgment was grudging or hostile, the aristocracy
met it with a disdain and indifference which have left repercussions in
English society to this day.

7

KINGSHIP AND ARISTOCRACY AS A TYPE OF RULE

THE AUTHORITY OF KINGS

THE COUNTRIES ruled by kings may have been slow to change socially and economically, but politically they were scenes of turmoil and bloodshed. Protracted feuds fill the annals of royal history. Why was this so? What explains the almost universal political instability of these countries? What chronic uncertainties plagued the relations between kings and aristocrats or lay at the bottom of royal attempts to assert effective rule?

Consider the king's predicament. His aim is to rule his land according to his will by relying on others to do his bidding. To this end, he has various means at his disposal, but each of them is flawed and none is ultimately dependable.

The king may seek to enforce his will by awing his subjects with displays of majesty and reminders of his consecrated position. In his defeat, Shakespeare's King Richard expresses these aspects of royalty:

> ... thus long have we stood
> To watch the fearful bending of thy knee,
> Because we thought ourself thy lawful king:
> And if we be, how dare thy joints forget
> To pay their awful duty to our presence?
> If we be not, show us the hand of God
> That hath dismist us from our stewardship;
> For well we know, no hand of blood and bone
> Can gripe the sacred handle of our sceptre,
> Unless he do profane, steal, or usurp.
> And though you think that all, as you have done,
> Have torn their souls by turning them from us,

And we are barren and bereft of friends;
Yet know, my master, God omnipotent,
Is mustering in his clouds, on our behalf,
Armies of pestilence; and they shall strike
Your children yet unborn and unbegot,
That lift your vassal hands against my head,
And threat the glory of my precious crown
                    RICHARD II, ACT III, SCENE iii

The grandeur of the supreme ruler and the appeal to rank, to God's grace, and to the appalling consequences of usurpation have political utility. The threat of force plays a large role in any type of rule, and the king's majesty and consecration symbolize this threat and help preserve political order. Appeals, of course, may be empty, as King Richard's are, and even effective displays of majesty may drain a king's coffers and put him in need of more substantial aids to his rule. Moreover, a king's more wealthy and powerful subjects may so contrive to exalt the majesty of their ruler that he becomes immobilized. Majesty alone is too fickle a servant of a king's will to ensure his effective rule, and neither will consecration dependably serve him.

One is tempted to say that what a king really needs to carry out his rule is force by which he can back up his commands and secure his needed resources. But force, while always needed, is not sufficient, for there is never enough of it to make the king's will prevail in the long run. Nevertheless, kings have resorted to violence so often because the other means of rule are also ineffective or counterproductive.

The bestowal of royal favors has always been a preferred method of luring subjects into obedience. These favors could range from massive grants of land and rights to a mere token of regard, sometimes no more than fleeting access to the royal presence. Kings have had an interest in increasing these personalized assets, though only up to a point. For since the king must have real benefits to distribute if access to his person is to mean anything, he must be sparing with his grants and even with the distribution of honors, lest with proliferation each award be reduced in value.

Of the favors a king has to distribute, those of rank and office are perhaps most intimately connected with the achievement of his purposes. Ideally for a king, the attainment of rank or office within his realm is a privilege, not something to which anyone can acquire a legal claim. The king alone is the arbiter of social rank, and his supremacy is sustained by the overwhelming consent of all those whose position would be impaired if royal supremacy were questioned. We are today unaccustomed to such a clear ordering of social status, but under royal authority status was determined authoritatively. The ruler could change the position of individuals in the rank order to suit his purposes. Ideally, then, the king is able to demote as well as promote, and he must not become bound by obligations arising from his previous favors.

Kings employ servants to execute their will. Such service is a principal avenue of social and economic advancement, both through special rewards and through a portion of the revenue collected in return for the service performed on behalf of the king. A king's rule is probably most secure where the officials appointed by him come from lower and educated social strata. This is one reason why the Ottoman empire staffed its armies and administrative corps with slaves of foreign origin who were educated in special schools and converted to Islam. For much the same reasons, tsarist governments chose to recruit increasing numbers of officials from the ranks of *educated* aristocrats and commoners, thus freeing the regime from the obligation to employ aristocrats without regard to ability. By such methods, it is possible to reject inherited privileges and make social rank and the distribution of wealth (through officeholding) depend primarily on merit.

Thus, a king seeks to maximize his control over the careers of all subordinate officials. Their tenure of office is typically short, depending as it does on a favor granted or withdrawn at will. The ruler can maximize his power only if he can compel incumbent officials to pass on to him a large share of the taxes they collect. Yet temporary officeholding also means that the incumbents will try to enrich themselves as quickly as they can and manipulate the office so as to advance their subsequent careers. They will act toward the population as arbitrarily as the ruler acts toward them.

Arbitrariness is an instrument of rule, for it provides the ruler with an effective test of instant obedience by large numbers of subordinates, even if it fails to accomplish any other end. Arbitrariness creates fear of royal displeasure and may be conducive to obedience. A dictatorial regime cannot achieve stability, because to do so would require that it refrain from being arbitrary. But extreme arbitrariness as a main device of governing is self-defeating, for sooner or later it will provoke either assassinations or the surreptitious manipulation of the ruler by those who purport to do his bidding.[1] Even if the leading subjects of a despotic ruler are unable to do anything against his tyranny, they are sure to seek revenge against his successor.

Every ruler must delegate some of his authority, but he will try to keep such delegation as revocable or provisional as he can. To this end, a king may visit the different parts of his realm and by his repeated presence reinforce his authority over his subjects. He may send judges or administrators on circuit to act in his behalf and make the presence of royal authority felt even in the absence of his person. Or the king may employ various devices to ensure that his will is obeyed. Delegation of authority may be of short duration; officials may be excluded from areas in which they have personal ties; their sons or other relatives may be called on to serve as courtiers, retainers, or hostages at court so that the official must fear for their safety.

Nevertheless, the vassals, retainers, and officials of the king can use their status and resources to develop their own power. Subinfeudation partially removes their own dependents from the control of the crown and adds to their income the payments of their subvassals. At court, successful competition for the king's favor can lead to reductions in the services or payments owed, as well as to advantageous marriages. Royal government is exposed to efforts by subordinates to appropriate the authority delegated or granted to them.

Just as under royal government all rank and office ideally depend on the king's will, so, ideally, no one possesses an inviolable right to property. The king owns all the land. The poor must give their labor, the land and its produce must yield taxes, the rich must serve and pass on a portion of their revenue, and the movable wealth of commerce and industry must be at the government's disposal. When land and commerce show high yields, government confiscation often follows. Officials search constantly for opportunities of taxation which promise high yields to the royal house and its servants. Such rule is as inimical to the free merchant class as it is to an independent aristocracy and for much the same reason: both groups claim private rights.

Royal authority depends in the first place on the king's own resources. Typically, a ruler will try to augment these resources by expanding his domain without weakening control over it. But this double objective becomes more difficult to accomplish with every successful expansion of the realm. More vassals or retainers are needed to administer the new areas, and control may weaken where these notables have independent standing. To be sure, even the great magnates of the realm accept some limitation of their power by virtue of the obligation they have assumed toward their ruler. Moreover, both sides couch their relations in a language of sanctified command and loyal obedience, and these symbols have their own material consequences. But the expansion of a territory, or its intensified exploitation, may not in the end lead to an enduring increase of the ruler's personal authority. For the balance of power between a king and his grantees depends on the resources available to each side and the strategic use they make of them.

The politics of medieval history oscillated with efforts to defend the rights of the household or estate. Such defense was often of a piece with efforts at aggrandizement. Kings and princes looked on conquests of territories, or on their acquisition through marriage alliances, as a means of increasing their resources and hence of obtaining additional services. At the lower end of the social hierarchy, this defensive-offensive posture of the ruler was reflected in the efforts of weaker men, families, or communities to obtain the protection of a master, no doubt frequently a mixture of the desire for security and submission to brute force. As Marc Bloch put it with reference to the Merovingian period,

> Everywhere, the weak man felt the need to be sheltered by someone more powerful. The powerful man, in his turn, could not maintain his prestige or his fortune or even his own safety except by securing for himself, by persuasion or coercion, the support of subordinates bound to his service. On the one hand, there was the urgent quest for a protector; on the other, there were usurpations of authority, often by violent means. And as notions of weakness and strength are always relative, in many cases the same man occupied a dual role—as a dependent of a more powerful man and a protector of humbler ones. Thus there began to be built up a vast system of personal relationships whose intersecting threads ran from one level of the social structure to another.[2]

A ruler's authority depends on implementation of his orders by subordinate jurisdictions. By the same token, such jurisdictions must have their own capacity for action. To an extent, the ruler must accept the autonomy of his dependents. But since his own position requires the collection of taxes in money and kind, he must also control their jurisdictions. The extent and limits of royal authority are thus uncertain, and this uncertainty lies at the root of the protracted feuds which fill the annals of medieval history.

A traditional society which is rent by such feuds is often weakened by uncertain boundaries as well. Frontiers are not easily determined where territorial holdings are at the same time more or less autonomous jurisdictions. The border areas of a kingdom are also a tempting prize for the king's rivals. As a result, the king's rule over these areas may be precarious. Moreover, the king's own lands as well as the territorial and jurisdictional units of his grantees are often widely scattered owing to the vagaries of inheritance, grants, and alliances, so that not only adjacent areas but even the same area may enjoy a variety of rights and owe allegiance to different rulers. Under these conditions it is often possible for territorial jurisdictions to break away when this appears politically promising. There are many instances in which the division between two realms is not marked by a frontier, but by a disputed jurisdiction like Aquitaine and Scotland between England and France, or certain border areas between Muscovy and Lithuania.

Where the fortunes of men wax and wane with the fortunes of the house to which they belong, victory or defeat in jurisdictional feuds bears directly on the well-being of the individual. That well-being depends on the size and productivity of landholdings and on the degree to which political authorities can exact tribute in money or kind. Patriarchal jurisdictions are engaged, therefore, in efforts to better their holdings vis-à-vis their neighbors and to lessen the tribute paid to their ruler. In the absence of stable frontiers, this arena of internal conflict stands exposed to intrusions from the outside.

The result is bloody turmoil which has regularly accompanied the efforts of kings to establish their authority over a country. Witness the rise of the Muscovite dynasty under Mongolian overlordship, the painful assertion of Hohenzollern rule in the emerging state of Prussia, or the role of the Norman conquest in English history. Japan seems to be an exception only because, as far as is known, its early history was free of external threats; nevertheless, the Yamato state was established through prolonged struggles against native tribes and rival clans. In the four societies surveyed, external conditions of early authority formation as well as internal struggles for dominance have had lasting repercussions for the distinctive institutional structure of each country.

It has always proved difficult to stabilize the authority of kings. Monarchical rule does not have a good solution to the problem of succession. Inheritance of the crown is easily upset by biological failure or by rival claims among members of the royal family. Uncertainty is also produced by the necessity to delegate authority, as well as the vagaries of foreign entanglements by means of which the king and his grantees seek to tip the internal balance of power. These and related reasons of political instability undoubtedly impose great burdens on the population at large, and on occasion these burdens lead to popular revolts. Nevertheless, internal political instability mostly affects the ruling groups directly concerned with the affairs of the kingdom, and political instability probably has coexisted with a marked degree of social stability. The bulk of the population lived in isolated communities and households. People could do little to change their condition. Most of the time, life near the level of subsistence discouraged even the most courageous from actions that would jeopardize such security as they enjoyed. Kings and their notables could fight their protracted battles for dominance at home and abroad only on the basis of this politically submerged but economically active population.

Chronic uncertainty and protracted feuds are pervasive features of royal authority, yet patriarchal rule has been found compatible with household government, the delegation of authority, and world empires, as well as various forms of tribal political orders in which authority resides in the heads of lineage groups.[3] The authority of kings may be unstable, but it gives rise to different political structures.

Hereditary Kingship
In Western Europe according to the medieval ideal of hereditary succession, the eldest son would follow his father as the head of the house, and this illustration shows the eldest son associated with the king in power. In France, the Capetian dynasty (987–1328) which followed the Carolingian, had an unbroken line of male descendants for 350 years. Each Capetian king was careful to have his son crowned king before his own death. (British Museum)

During the early development of royal authority, kingship has frequently appeared in two forms, as Machiavelli noted in *The Prince*:

> Kingdoms known to history have been governed in two ways: either by a prince and his servants, who, as ministers by his grace and permission, assist in governing the realm; or by a prince and by barons, who hold their positions not by favor of the ruler but by antiquity of blood.[4]

The distinction points to the patrimonial (autocratic) and the feudal principle of organization. The first emphasizes rule through peremptory commands by the king and his servants in the royal household. The second emphasizes the association between the king and notables whose families possess standing in the community on the basis of ancient lineage, wealth, and the authority which accompanies these attributes. The king recognizes the position of these great families and hence rules through grants of rights in return for service.

In practice, the two forms of kingship have coexisted; thus, the king's servants and the magnates of the realm constitute the "governing class."[5] Patrimonialism is the kind of autocratic rule the king and his great vassals exercise over their households and domains. The emphasis is on the exercise of authority *within* a household. Feudalism means a "type of government . . . which [is] marked by the division of political power among many lords and by the tendency to treat political power as a private possession."[6] Here the emphasis is on the exercise of authority (however tenuous) by the king's court over many patrimonial households, and hence on the *relations between* the court and these many households. Transitions between these two aspects of kingship occur frequently because servants obeying the king's command may acquire rights and turn into feudal vassals, while magnates of high standing may lose their rights despite their ancient lineage. However, the patrimonial and feudal aspects of kingship may be emphasized separately. In Russia, the tsar treated the entire realm and its people as his personally owned domain (autocracy). Under this rule, officials were granted authority only to enable them to implement the will of the tsar. In England, by contrast, the Plantagenet dynasty emphasized feudal rule allowing for much local autonomy. The kings were frequently absent from the country and left the conduct of affairs in the hands of high officials whom they authorized to act in the name of the king.

The patrimonial or autocratic aspect of kingship typically presupposes the exaltation of the ruler, whose majesty stands above mortal law because he is believed to be divine or in privileged contact with the higher powers venerated by the people.

> The most ordinary man becomes awe-inspiring when encased in the riches of a huge realm and all the pomp humans can devise; surrounded by glitter

and jeweled trappings, with color and pageantry infinitely beyond ordinary men, the hallowed autocrat seems superhuman to the simple, and tingles the nerves even of the educated. . . . Power, no matter how come by, is almost equivalent to greatness in the ordinary estimation; when it is made manifest by a brilliant display, few can avoid being at least a little dazzled. The higher one stands over the many, the more easily are mysterious powers attributed to him. . . . Certainly the power of the ruler over their lives is apparent and conducive to deep respect.[7]

It was believed that at the summit of the social order, royal authority reflects cosmic forces. When the realm is in harmony with the universe, peace and prosperity will prevail; when this harmony is lost, ill fate will befall the people. In this perspective, the splendor of kingship serves to propitiate the supernatural forces by symbolic representation. A consecrated ruler is regarded much as one regards the Supreme Being: an authority that cannot be questioned but to whom one can appeal for grace or indulgence. In this religious context there is a direct relation between kings and their people.

Under feudalism, the king's great vassals who help him administer the realm accept the principle that their own power is limited by virtue of the obligation they have assumed toward their ruler. Since the ruler embodies the symbols of highest authority, he alone can legitimize the high rank and privileges of the aristocracy. In the words of Antonio Marongiu,

> [The king] stood out because of his sacerdotal attributes; because he was the first of the great vassals; because he was recognized as head of the state by the pope, the emperor and other foreign powers; because he continued to administer directly large areas within the boundaries of the state, and was in possession of his own force of armed men; because he was the supreme representative of judicial authority, as guarantor of justice and peace, and because fiefs without heirs reverted to him.[8]

But we have seen that the vassals of the king could use their status and resources to develop their own power, sometimes to such an extent that kings and aristocrats became bitter enemies despite all outward signs of majesty and obedience. In Western Europe, the independence of the great lords could develop until

> they were no longer ordinary subjects, but possessed economic and legal privileges, granted or accepted by the sovereign. . . . They were considered outside the "general subordination" of subjects by custom and by the very terms of their investiture. They owed fealty, counsel and aid, but in return were exempt from all other obligations and impositions. They represented and personified both the population of their territories in their relations with the sovereign, and public authority within their territories.[9]

In practice, the king and his vassals attempted to buttress their respective rights; apparently they simultaneously needed and fought one another. Gregory of Tours commented in the seventh century that in the relations of the Merovingian ruler Clovis with his kindred, he "needs them, and yet they are in his way."[10]

There was no reason to assume that some balance would be achieved between these countervailing tendencies. A warrior aristocracy might appropriate all sovereign (or seignorial) rights and consequently eliminate the contractual reciprocity between the king and his vassals, as in Poland. Or the conditions of conquest might facilitate the coexistence of monarchical rule with a high degree of local autonomy, as in England.[11] Conquest could also lead to an absolutist regime, in which land grants were not given on a hereditary basis, vassals were obliged to live at the royal court, and their holdings were supervised by royal agents and subject to confiscation, as in Han China. In other words, different authority structures can arise in an agrarian economy with poorly developed techniques of transport and communication, ranging from federalist or even anarchic to absolutist or despotic tendencies.

Rule through a grant of rights in return for service varies greatly with the conditions of the grant and the social status of the grantees. Max Weber distinguishes among three main types and seven subtypes of feudalism, but his main distinction is between autocratic and free feudalism. Under *autocratic feudalism*, a principal device of governing is the creation of associations like corporations, municipalities, and the like which are collectively liable for specific services but which also have the right to exact these services from their members. For example, residents of border areas, manorial dependents, or hereditary clients may be grouped in compulsory associations which are charged with a collective responsibility for military service, the building of roads and fortifications, the payment of special taxes, or any other task the ruler assigns. Under *free feudalism*, a principal device of governing is the grant of rights to land in return for a service to which the parties have agreed. Here the rights granted vary with the status of the grantee, a matter of great political significance whenever the grant to land includes the right to exercise governmental authority.[12] A feudal aristocracy arises only where personal loyalty (fealty) is combined with the royal recognition of social privileges and hereditary succession, the dependence on the labor of others, the profession of arms, and the exercise of local authority. This combination of the honor of the warrior with the loyalty of the servant was a distinctive feature of Western European and Japanese feudalism.[13]

Government through compulsory associations and through the grant of rights is capable of endless elaborations, nor are the two forms of governing clearly separable. A municipal corporation may be given the right to collect bridge tolls in return for the payment of an annual fee, while membership in that corporation and payment of dues to it are compulsory. A grant of rights to land in return for military service may have been an original form of feudalism, but this principle of obtaining services for the purposes of rule is not confined to land rights or military service.[14] Both principles of governing can be applied to any task which kings want to accomplish but do not have the resources or the will to accomplish under their own direction. In most cases, it is a matter of turning such *tasks* into *rights* or privileges (also called "liberties"), which can be obtained in return for services or payments rendered to the king and his treasury. In this way, the tasks of governing a country can be divided into separate functions like military recruitment, tax collection, trade or craft monopolies, and the construction of fortifications or public works. Indeed, any function of government is a "right" which the king can bestow as a reward for a service, or in return for a payment. The incentive of obtaining such burdensome rights or privileges is that income from taxes, tolls, or services, as well as the rights and status of self-government, are associated with these privileges. When rule through compulsory associations and through grants of rights are elaborated in this manner, household government and "fief," and hence the terms *patrimonialism* and *feudalism*, lose their original meaning.

ARISTOCRATIC SOCIETY

In the past, the exercise of governmental authority was an aspect of family and property. The various functions of government were appropriated on a hereditary basis by a governing class consisting of a king, his high officials, the magnates of the realm, and privileged corporations which controlled their respective territories and thus ruled the country. Typically, states under the authority of kings consisted of competing jurisdictions engaged in efforts to defend the rights of the household or estate. Rights that were not asserted would lapse, revert to the disposal of the king, and eventually be claimed by other grantees; hence, jurisdictional feuds were directly related to the hierarchy of societies in which families and corporations were distinguished by the rights they enjoyed.

In countries ruled by kings, it is reasonable to ask what effect the continual feuds had on the societies in which they took place. Violence, it seems, was built into the very texture of aristocratic life. While it threatened the individual's safety at every turn, it propped up a remarkably rigid system of social inequalities. The great controversies among kings, priests, and notables eventually established stable patterns of domination and submission. By the time we learn of these controversies, the distinctions between rulers and ruled, between rich and poor, are already well established. But it is reasonable to suppose that these distinctions arose from the struggles surrounding the emergence of kingship. Inequality in the early period was probably due to the extreme insecurity of life, which gave an initial advantage to those who could protect themselves and others.

By the tenth and eleventh centuries, an elaborate court life existed at the center of societies governed by kings. The warlike culture of an aristocracy, with its stress on high status, autonomy, and individual strength, was combined with an emphasis on almost filial submission of the vassal to his king. Although this particular combination was fully

Feudal Homage
In medieval times, a personally performed ritual was essential to confirm formal rights and obligations. The illustration shows the citizens of Perpignan presenting themselves to King Alfonso. One citizen performs the act of homage, three vassals are preparing to do so, and one is standing and about to receive investiture. (Archivo de la Corona de Aragón, Barcelona)

developed only in Western Europe and Japan, the culture associated
with this type of feudalism, characterized by Weber, contains elements
found elsewhere.

> In feudal ideology the most important relations in life are pervaded by per-
> sonalized ties, in contrast to all factual and impersonal relationships, which
> are regarded as plebeian and specifically devoid of dignity. This contrast has
> several aspects. Originating in an army of warriors for whom the battle be-
> tween individuals was decisive, feudalism made skillful handling of weapons
> the object of its military education; it had little use for mass discipline to
> perfect a collectively organized military effort. As a result the feudal style of
> life incorporated the game as an important means of training that inculcated
> useful abilities and qualities of character. The game was not a "pastime" but
> the natural medium in which the physical and psychological capacities of the
> human organism came alive and became supple. In this form of "training"
> the spontaneous drives of man found their outlet, irrespective of any division
> between "body" and "soul" and regardless of how conventionalized the games
> often became. The knightly strata of medieval Europe and Japan regarded
> the game as a serious and important aspect of life that had a special affinity
> with spontaneous artistic interests and helped bar the way to all forms of
> utilitarian rationality. The aristocratic sentiment of these feudal strata found
> its expression in pomp and circumstance, in utensils and equipment that dis-
> played the splendour of the household. From this standpoint luxury is not
> a superfluous frill but a means of self-assertion and a weapon in the struggle
> for power. This antiutilitarian attitude towards consumption was of a piece
> with the equally antiutilitarian orientation toward one's life. Aristocratic strata
> specifically rejected any idea of a "mission in life," any suggestion that a man
> should have a purpose or seek to realize an ideal; the value of aristocratic
> existence was self-contained. Thus feudal ideology was contemptuous of a
> businesslike approach to economic affairs, which it saw as sordid greed.
> Aristocrats deliberately cultivated a nonchalance that stemmed from the con-
> ventions of chivalry, a pride of status and a sense of honor. Their orientation
> was more worldly than the idealization of the charismatic warrior, more he-
> roic and belligerent than a literary education, and more playful and artistic
> than professional training.[15]

The feudal ideology emphasizes personal ties and an antiutilitarian
attitude toward life: both have contributed to that bearing under stress
which is an enduring element of aristocratic culture. In Western Europe
and Japan, admiration for noble sacrifice was so strong that even magnates of the realm could submit to the royal will without damage to their
pride, in their own eyes and in those of others. Such conditions did not
exist in Russia, where submission often went together with personal humiliation. The balance between pride and submission was also in jeopardy in seventeenth-century Prussia, where the Great Elector disciplined
a recalcitrant nobility, and in Tokugawa Japan, where daimyos and sa-

murai were put under surveillance and often suffered the debilities of a meagre rentier existence. Still, status pride is a main attribute of aristocratic culture, and efforts to preserve it are made even under the most disadvantageous conditions.

Warfare was a prominent feature of aristocratic culture until well into the sixteenth century. This is one reason why traditional societies appear so much alike despite the differences among them. Each lord jealously guarded his rights, ready to defend them at a moment's notice and to enlarge them when opportunity presented itself. Instant willingness to engage in personal combat required a high level of personal aggression and an absence of normative restraints in the highest strata of society. Not only was personal valor idealized, but bloodletting, mutilation, and the whole ferocity of battle were as well. Some restraint was shown toward social equals, because they could be held for ransom. But ordinary captives were a liability: if retained, they had to be fed; if returned, they would bolster the strength of the enemy. Very often they were killed or sent back mutilated. For similar reasons, the attacker would destroy his enemy's fields, fill his wells, and cut down his trees. These features of war have existed for a long time, but in the societies here considered they were specifically the work and the norm of aristocratic warriors.[16]

What are the psychological consequences of this "violent tenor of life" (Huizinga)? In a Christian context, violence was seen as evidence of divine wrath, provoked by the sinfulness of man. Yet the fighting vigor prized by aristocratic warriors did not prompt them to put fate in the hereafter uppermost in their minds. They would enjoy life to the full while there was time, but they valued honor more than life. "Death is certain," runs a statement of the fifteenth century, "but one does not know one's future.... [Therefore] be of good cheer and don't fear death too much, for if you do, you will have no joy in life."[17] Along with piety, the fear of hell, and contrition there were outbreaks of gaiety and intense enjoyment; arrant pride, outbursts of hatred, and an often prolonged demand for vengeance were commonplace among the upper strata. People acted impulsively and in public and expected others to do the same, in contrast, say, to the Puritan tradition which has taught us to moderate our feelings and guard our privacy. "All things in life were of a proud and cruel publicity" (Huizinga). Hierarchic notions such as honor, loyalty, and vengeance received public display.[18] The most cruel punishments were a source of popular entertainment and edification, dramatizing the sinfulness of man, the mutability of fortunes, and the terrible pains awaiting the sinner. Men were drawn and quartered, and the torture of animals could be amusing. In Paris on St. John's day under Charles IX (1560–1574), the public incineration of two dozen cats brought the king, his court, and the people together for a gay festival with music, the king himself taking a prominent part in the proceedings.[19] Frequent experience with violence and sudden reversals of fortune were likely to evoke passionate reactions, and there is reason to expect people to have been excessively irritable, unless they found some private or institutional haven where they could escape from the world.

Instructions on proper conduct give some intimation of how people tended in fact to behave. In a series of documents on manners at the table, in the bedroom, and in performing various bodily functions, Elias shows that in early medieval times people had little concern with the control of impulse and apparently felt little shame. Men and women bathed together in the nude, housing accommodations allowed for little or no privacy, and bodily functions were performed in public. Manuals on table manners advised against noisy eating, spitting, and direct physical threats against neighbors, which suggests that self-restraint had to be learned. Since aristocratic marriages involved important property transactions, it was considered advisable to make the first copulation of bride and groom an act witnessed by the interested parties.[20] The early manuals were often addressed to people of standing. As the concern with the control of impulse increased and the reactions of others were taken into account, the manuals became more specifically instructions for the young. Types of behavior previously considered natural came to be tabooed as shameful.

An earlier discussion (Chapter 6) dealt with changes in aristocratic life styles in England: the decline of personal combativeness, a turn to higher education, the establishment of a "London season," and the concentration of real and imagined opportunities at court. The behavior appropriate in the early phase of feudalism had come to be out of place in the society of the court. One should note that for the safety of royalty and the preservation of peace among the magnates acts of violence at court were quickly punished. Patterns of interdependence among people had changed due to the more effective centralization of monarchical authority.[21]

By the sixteenth century, court society had become the center of opportunity and fashion. Aristocrats flocked there to make their fortune. A residence near the court had become indispensable to the pursuit of gain and status. For a man at court, impulsiveness and irritability would be injurious and the public display of passion improper. On the other hand, feelings of shame or guilt would stand him in good stead, since they would facilitate the control of impulse. Such a man could maximize his chances by artful maneuvers rather than by physical aggression. "A man who knows the Court," says St. Simon, "is master of his gestures, his eyes, and his expression. . . . He restrains his humor, disguises his passions, speaks and acts against his sentiments."[22]

Tournament with Lances by Lucas Cranach The Elder
This engraving of the early sixteenth century dates from a time when the conditions of medieval warfare had changed. At one time, tournaments had been serious tests of strength and skill and training for them was training for war as well. By the time of Cranach, these tournaments were fought with blunted spears and lances and had become a principal recreational pursuit of the aristocracy. (Metropolitan Museum of Art, Harris Brisbane Dick Fund, 1927)

In his famous *Hand Oracle* of 1647, the Spanish Jesuit Baltasar Gracián provided a code of conduct for the courtier. One should not reveal one's real intentions. A bad manner spoils everything, including justice, reason, and truth. He should learn the weakness of whomever he deals with so that he may put that person under pressure. Think first and deeply and only then act, because some people are like façades with nothing behind them, while with others their inner thoughts exceed their appearance many times over. He should learn to blame others for mistakes and failures, while putting his best foot forward. The circumspect man never acts in a state of passion. Even when alone, he acts as if the eyes of the whole world were upon him.[23] Not all men at court acted in this manner, but by the eighteenth century, after an interval of five hundred years, the culture of European aristocracies had changed due to the influences of court society.

With the concentration of monarchical power and the emergence of court societies, a transition in manners had occurred. Expressive behavior that was impulsive, aggressive, and had a high tolerance for public exposure was superseded very gradually by an orientation which through shame and related forms of self-restraint enabled people to control their impulses and thereby manage their relations with others. "Civilized behavior" emerged at the time when monarchies consolidated their position during the sixteenth and seventeenth centuries.

We have before us now a picture of an initially unstable royal authority and of an aristocratic culture which was at first violent and thrived on instability but became more mannered and courtly with the stabilization and centralization of monarchy. This change in style generally accompanied a political change. In early times, the king had struggled to unite a scattering of feudal baronies through asserting his authority, whereas in the later period unification had largely succeeded and the age-old contest between king and aristocrats was conducted in a more centralized fashion. It is in this context that representative bodies like councils, parliaments, or estate assemblies first came into prominence. These institutions eventually were to pave the way for public participation in government on a broader scale.

The picture just sketched is general and calls for specific examples. For we must look at the different developments of local autonomy and representative assemblies in various countries if we are to make sense of the vastly different developments toward a popular mandate which occurred later. It is true that a king's council and a modern parliament are at opposite ends of a very long development, but there is some affinity between such different institutions in the sense that an implicit "exchange" underlies all exercise of authority. Even in the case of extremely autocratic rule, one may assume the existence of some pressure on the ruler. The authority of kings is subject to the personal influence of subordinates. Petitions to the ruler are typically based on rights he has already granted. To insist on this give and take does not mean that it is equitable, only that it occurs everywhere and provides a useful basis for comparison. Subjects always make "representations" to their masters, although representative institutions are a Western European phenomenon.

REPRESENTATION

It is easiest to trace the development of representative institutions in the case of England, where such institutions have had a continuous history since Anglo-Saxon times. In their earliest form, protorepresentative bodies consisted of the king's court with its household retainers and a few secular and ecclesiastical dignitaries who offered their counsel only at the king's command. When the king sought the weightier counsel of the great men of his realm, he could do so conveniently at the regular gatherings for Christmas, Easter, and Whitsunday. On these occasions he would wear his ceremonial crown for the celebration of mass and the eating of a great feast. No magnate could absent himself from these crown-wearings without affronting the king, but the magnates were not eager to counsel, much less to influence, him. For summons by the king or even requests for advice frequently resulted in a demand for additional services or financial assistance. Thus, attendance was an onerous duty. The phrase *general or unanimous consent* (*commune consilium*) was not the name of a distinct institution, but a reference to the advice or counsel which the king elicited. The Constitution of Clarendon (1164) states explicitly that in the king's view ecclesiastics, like everyone else who held a barony of the king, were duty-bound to take part in the judgments of the court and were excused only in cases involving death or mutilation. (Note that the king's court was a court in the judicial as well as the ceremonial sense and that the counsel and aid asked for by the king were as yet not distinguished from the adjudication of disputes or the management of the king's household.) By the thirteenth century, there is evidence of an assembly of barons which was occasionally summoned, which had no regular function or constitution, but through which the barons were asked to counsel the king on administrative and political issues, on taxation, and on judgments to be rendered by his court. At first an anomalous institution, these special assemblies eventually developed into the English parliament.[24]

Documentation on the early councils reveals little about the nature of this consultation between the king and his barons. The barons may have unanimously consented to the king's wishes, perhaps by an act of acclamation; they may have offered informal advice on request; or they may have stipulated conditions before consenting to the king's imposition of an extraordinary tax. Magna Carta (1215) is unique in part because it put such conditions of consent in writing. In 1258 the Provisions of Oxford called for periodic meetings of parliament, and in 1311 the Lord Ordainers demanded that the king consult and reach agreement with his barons "in matters of consequence." By the early fourteenth century, the membership of parliament no longer depended on the king's discretion, and henceforth the concept "community of the realm" referred to parliament as the institution which represented the country as a whole.[25]

Representation is to be distinguished from government. English medieval parliaments worked slowly, met irregularly, and were of short duration. They never questioned the king's right to govern and primarily met in order to advise and assist.

> Many assemblies . . . witnessed the exchange of mutual pledges between king and subjects on the accession of a new sovereign to the throne. Other assemblies . . . judged controversial questions of a varied nature, and were present at the promulgation of new statutes by the king; they took part in the apportioning of feudal aids, or confirmed the legitimacy of analogous requests for extraordinary subsidies—or in exceptional cases even denied them or granted them on conditions . . . ; they put forward requests and grievances to the king on behalf of groups or individuals against abuses and errors of the administration or of the king himself, and demanded their redress. . . . Although the permanent officials of the court normally exercised such functions, occasionally these assemblies also took part in giving judgment in trials . . . against extortionate officials . . . or over disputed feudal successions.[26]

The king was not obliged to abide by the judgments of the assemblies. But it became unwise for him to ignore them, because he depended on his tenants-in-chief and other subjects to provide the funds necessary for the assertion of his rights, even though that assertion would be at their expense. The size of royal expenditures increased and aroused opposition, and out of that opposition representative institutions eventually emerged.

If we now shift our attention from the 1200s to the seventeenth and eighteenth centuries, we find a greatly altered situation. The peers, gentry, and higher clergy who helped the king rule often disputed his exercise of authority, even though they accepted his title to reign. On their lands, aristocrats and magnates of the church enjoyed a fusion of wealth, status, and authority which at times was almost equal to that of the king and hence allowed them to engage in the struggle for power. Long before the period of the English revolution (1640–1660), Francis Bacon (1561–1626) described the dynamics of this relationship between king and aristocracy.

> A great and potent nobility addeth majesty to a monarch, but diminisheth power; and putteth life and spirit into the people, but presseth their fortune. It is well when nobles are not too great for sovereignty nor for justice; and yet maintained in that height, as the insolency of inferiors may be broken upon them before it come on too fast upon the majesty of kings. A numerous nobility causeth poverty and inconvenience in a state; for it is a surcharge of expense; and besides, it being of necessity that many of the nobility fell in time to be weak in fortune, it maketh a kind of disproportion between honor and means.[27]

Here, with exemplary brevity, is a generalized comment on the English political structure which contained a balance of forces and a social mobility lacking in Prussia, Russia, and Japan.

By the end of the seventeenth century, the "king-in-parliament" had become the sovereign *legislative* power in the state, while the crown was accepted as the head of the *executive* without question. The members of parliament represented the whole realm; there was close interaction and rivalry, but no deep cleavage between these representatives and the crown. The expression "king-in-parliament" referred both to the crown as an independent part of parliament and to the king's friends or court party, a loosely allied group of prominent men who held powerful positions in the Commons and the House of Lords, and contributed to the collaboration between legislature and executive. The balance achieved is suggested by the fact that three prime ministers (Walpole, Pelham, and North) served twenty-one, eleven, and twelve years respectively, enjoying the confidence of both king and Commons. That this balance was precarious is evident from the fact that during these three ministries there were fourteen different First Lords of the Treasury.[28] The king's authority to rule declined as parliament's authority grew, though the court remained the apex of the aristocratic prestige hierarchy and a main center for the distribution of privileges.[29] By the eighteenth century, meetings of parliament had become regular, legal enactments and taxation were decided by the Commons, and parliamentary budgetary controls, even over the crown's expenditures, were gradually expanded.

Both the electorate and its parliamentary representatives were a relatively homogeneous group, consisting for the most part of members of the gentry, in addition to commoners whose economic success and social aspirations made them acceptable to the gentry. In the middle of the eighteenth century, the electorate of the shires amounted to some 160,000 and that of the boroughs to about 85,000 in a population of roughly 7 million. In the six general elections from 1754 to 1784, elections with more than one candidate seeking office occurred in only 452 out of 1,800 possible cases.[30] Parliamentary power was used for private aggrandizement through the enclosure of common pasture land. Government offices were used for personal enrichment or the provisioning of younger sons of the gentry. A parliament so elected and conducted was certainly not likely to take measures that would effectively cope with the problems brought on by industrialization. But on the positive side, this homogeneous ruling group was based on ample practical experience in local self-government. There was a consensus on basic constitutional issues which promoted both the effectiveness of central government and its responsiveness to local concerns.

In one sense, English parliamentary rule during the eighteenth century was similar to the rule of representative bodies in other countries. A survey of such institutions in about 1760 shows that, apart from Russia, oligarchic and hereditary rule of counties and communities by small groups of aristocratic families was the prevailing practice—if "aristocratic" is understood to include not only the titled but also wealthy patrician families and occasionally leading members of urban guilds.[31] Whether the representative assembly or the absolute ruler prevailed in a given instance depended on many factors, including problems of succession, the personal ability of rulers, the cohesion and capability of representatives, and degrees of corruption and extravagance. Still more important was whether the ruler demanded financial support for a standing army, perhaps the principal source of conflict with the estate assemblies of the period.[32] But it is not the mere existence of aristocracies and estate assemblies, but the differences among them which are of interest here.

In the case of Prussia, comparison is made difficult by the scattering of its territories, each of which had a complicated history of its own. For convenience I will consider only the Electoral Mark Brandenburg (*Kurmark*). Before the ascendance of the Hohenzollern dynasty in the fifteenth century, this territory was divided among numerous jurisdictions in the hands of landed nobles, bishoprics, and towns. On occasion these petty rulers would be called on by their local overlords to assemble for a renewal of their pledge, or for advice and consent, or in a juridical capacity. But in the absence of unified rule such occasions were infrequent, they would involve different overlords, and they did not provide a basis for the development of representative institutions. The accession of the Hohenzollern rulers in 1411 unified the country under their sovereignty, though in the fifteenth and sixteenth centuries governance in Brandenburg still meant to a large extent the local autonomy of each lord over his domain.

While Hohenzollern rule became gradually more effective, the local lords and municipalities jealously guarded their prerogatives, and the power of these local jurisdictions militated against the solidarity of the estates. As a result, the estate assemblies met rarely and were politically weak. This condition was not even altered in the sixteenth century following the Reformation, when Joachim II (1535–1571) was heavily in debt while the landed gentry were relatively prosperous, profiting from the dissolution of the monasteries. In the absence of regular estate assemblies, current business was handled through commissions whose composition was greatly influenced by the elector (*Kurfürst*). And while the estates retained an important position in fiscal administration, they were also obliged to assume responsibility for the debts of the ruling house.

In the seventeenth century, the Great Elector completed the subordination of the landed aristocracy. The Prussian rulers emphasized the supremacy of their own position. For example, the Hohenzollern (before Frederick II) allowed bourgeois ownership of landed "knightly" estates (*Rittergüter*), although the practice had been to reserve such estates for members of the aristocracy. In addition, highly placed counselors of bourgeois origin were frequently ennobled on the explicit ground that faithful servants of the ruler deserved such distinction— that is, deserved to belong to the first estate of the realm.[33] In these and related ways the Hohenzollern established the priority of service to their house and to the state over inheritance as the basis of aristocratic status. The contrast should be noted between such social mobility at the king's command and the spontaneous intermingling of commoners and gentry in England, where merchant wealth was freely invested in land and younger sons of the gentry went into trade and the professions without so much as a nod from the king. In his political testament (1667), the Great Elector warned his successor that his authority would be diminished the more he convened estate assemblies, since such assemblies were always encroaching on the will of the sovereign. Frederick William's suspicions had prompted the earlier organization of war commissariats, which were put in charge of the standing army and of a new system of taxation. Henceforth, the self-governing commissions of the estates were allowed only to implement directives; they had lost not only the right to consent to new taxation but also the right to have a voice in the determination of expenditures.

In the administration of public affairs, aristocrats were restricted to the counties (*Kreise*) of the several regions where they resided.[34] But ideologically, the Hohenzollern rulers supported the high status of the aristocrats. The local basis of aristocratic status was left intact, and by his support of established privileges Frederick II laid the groundwork for the political role of this ruling class during the nineteenth century.

It has often been said that in Prussia the hold of the autocracy was never broken because a bourgeois revolution did not materialize, but in our context it seems more accurate to speak of the failure of aristocratic protest. The failure of the Prussian gentry to establish permanent urban residences is a mark of its political subordination, as are the irregular meetings of the estate assemblies and their eventual abolition. In England, an upper class of peers, gentry, and wealthy commoners achieved a partnership-in-rule with the monarchy. Such a partnership was missing in Prussia, where the protest of landed estates as in East Prussia and elsewhere came to nothing. Under the Hohenzollern dynasty, the aristocracy was allowed a voice in ruling only at the local level and under circumscribed conditions. In political affairs, aristocrats served the king and the king claimed to be the first servant of his country.

Yet if the comparison with England shows the weakness of the Prussian aristocracy, the comparison with Russia shows its strength. In Prussia aristocrats had significant liberties of person and property, and they possessed important rights of local authority.[a] The Hohenzollern rulers never encroached upon these individual and local liberties or privileges even when they suppressed the corporate liberties of the estate assemblies. By contrast, the Muscovite rulers did not accept the idea of rights at all, once their own preeminence was assured.

This difference marks the distinction between Prussian absolutism and Russian autocracy. However arbitrary they were in practice, Western European rulers acknowledged that they governed under divine law, that in principle their authority and their rights were limited, although they alone were entitled to specify those limits. Such self-limitation looks like an empty formula until one turns to Ivan IV (1530–1584), who denied it on principle. For Ivan, the tsar was directly inspired by God, his every action an emanation of the divine will; thus, the tsar was free to pardon or punish as he saw fit. There was no recognition of rights. It is true that by the eighteenth century the ideology of tsarist rule had changed. In keeping with the enlightened absolutism of his time, Peter the Great spoke of the duty which God's delegation of power had imposed on him. But by then it had already become established that subjects of *all* ranks have duties but not rights. This view is reflected in the headtax imposed on every male, regardless of age, in 1724. By being taxed at birth, he immediately entered the service of the state.[35]

In the Russian case, the conditions of early monarchical authority militated against the idea of rights even for the aristocracy. As the Muscovite dynasty rose, previously independent boyars and princes became highly placed servitors. Other power centers became less attractive and the Moscow rulers were able to abolish the old aristocratic right of changing one's military and political allegiance. As a result,

> the problems of the old aristocracy [were compounded], for former rulers of the annexed regions and their servitors began to clamor for significant military and administrative positions in the enlarged realm. Descendants of the old untitled Muscovite aristocracy and the princes who had recently enrolled in service found themselves in competition for the influential posts at court and in the army. The animosities that developed over family seniority and personal position caused constant strife and thereby prevented any possibility of a coalescence of interest to resist the growing powers of the crown.[36]

In the fifteenth and sixteenth centuries, the size of aristocratic families increased. In keeping with tradition, property continued to be divided among all male heirs, and with increasing numbers of heirs the economic basis of aristocratic families was weakened. For many of these

---

[a]In Western Europe the privileges granted by a sovereign ruler were termed *liberties* or *rights*, a usage which terminated with the French revolution. For if all men have rights by virtue of being born, the term *privilege* acquires a pejorative meaning which it did not have earlier when an inequality of condition was the prevailing assumption.

families landownership became a dwindling resource, and since very few aristocrats would or could enter trade or the church, they had no alternative to serving either in the army or at court. By contrast, the princes of Moscow tended to resist the division of their domains; for example, in the fifteenth century they bequeathed more than half of their holdings to the oldest son (Ivan III, 1462–1505).

The reforms of Peter I in the early eighteenth century further accentuated the subservience of the aristocracy. When boyars, generals, and officers, as well as merchants, craftsmen, and Tartars, could be forcibly resettled to serve the convenience of autocratic government, all social strata were "equal in their lack of rights" (Platonov). Nor were aristocrats exempt from physical punishment or from censorship of all religious and political matters. Ideological spokesmen for the aristocracy responded by placing their strongest emphasis on the honor and dignity of *a rank based on service* and on the need to protect that rank from contamination through intermarriage with commoners.[37] Peter's reforms were facilitated by this absence of an independent aristocracy such as existed even in Prussia. After the reign of Ivan IV, there was no need to overcome the resistance (or obtain the cooperation) of the estates or of a parliament.

The status of the Russian aristocracy was based on court rank and rank in the officer corps of the army. Its members rarely pursued their social and economic interests at the local level with any determination. When Peter instituted a collegial form of local government, it became necessary to force local aristocrats at gunpoint to participate in the decreed elections. The major objectives of aristocrats during the eighteenth century consisted of demands for reduced service obligations, legal security, tax exemptions, and protection against confiscations and corporal punishment. Some of them were also interested in agricultural improvements. The decree of 1762 freed the aristocracy from compulsory service but failed to provide an alternative to state service. In fact, the legal emancipation of the aristocracy from their former obligations served the interests of the tsarist government and did not create an independent aristocracy. In the eighteenth and nineteenth centuries, successive reform efforts of the tsarist government revealed just how little Russian culture had prepared the aristocracy to act on its own initiative, and just how difficult it was for tsarist officials to allow local initiatives that were not controlled by the center.

In contrast to Russia, the Japanese aristocracy under the Tokugawa shogunate (1600–1868) was quite able to play an effective role in local self-government. Without strength in local government there could be no effective opposition to absolute rule, as the Russian experience shows, though the Prussian case also makes clear that local strength alone was not sufficient for such opposition. The reasons for the relative strength of the Japanese aristocracy go back to the early phases of the country's history. Periods such as the Taika reforms, the Fujiwara regents, and the Kamakura shogunate show a certain similarity. Typically, each period began with a violent struggle over succession from which one clan emerged victorious. The result of that struggle was a notable concentration of power, usually accompanied by a remodeled administrative structure. (The Ashikaga shogunate is a partial exception in this respect.) In time, such centralized authority would weaken as tax collection, dispute settlement, the task of policing, and the organization of defense were in practice taken over by regionally powerful clans. This transfer of authority varied with the prevailing administrative structure. For example, the early phase of the Fujiwara regency was marked by the substitution of household for governmental management. The Fujiwara expanded their landholdings and became for a time the most powerful clan in the country; thus, their central "household" authority increased, even though the organization of the central government was enfeebled. As rival clans eventually increased their own holdings, the authority of the Fujiwara regents weakened. A new centralization occurred under Minamoto Yoritomo when the office of the regent was transformed into a separate shogunate at Kamakura, and household management was replaced by centrally organized feudal rule. In this way, the authority of government was contingent on the landed wealth of one preeminent family. If one looks at the several periods of Japanese history from the standpoint of local rule, as John Hall has done, one observes a succession of regionally powerful clans whose rise parallels the localization of authority and whose fall is accompanied by its recentralization.

As discussed in more detail in Chapter 12, the Tokugawa shogunate represents a stabilization in the relation between central rule and a local aristocracy. For some two hundred and fifty years the Tokugawa hegemony was overwhelming. The territory of the shogunate represented about one-quarter of the entire country. It was located in the central region (*Kanto*) and included the principal cities. Tokugawa supremacy was ensured in part through pledges of loyalty by the daimyos to the shogun. These involved the duty of assistance when called on, and the obligation of each daimyo to administer his realm peacefully and efficiently. The requirement of alternate residence (*sankin-kotai*) ensured personal control over the daimyo and involved expenditures which further increased the great discrepancy in wealth between the Tokugawa shogun and even the wealthiest daimyo. In the period 1600–1651, one hundred and eleven daimyo houses were eliminated. Confiscations and transfers were common practice during the Tokugawa regime, and only a few of the most powerful houses retained their hereditary territories throughout the period. The aristocracy of daimyos and their bands of retainers were moved from domain to domain and gradually became a professional corps of administrators implementing a uniform set of rules under Tokugawa law. In this way, the Tokugawa achieved an unchallengeable supremacy.

However, the local autonomy of the daimyo must not be forgotten. Each daimyo was charged with the full rights of governance over his domain, and he exercised his authority through his band of retainers. Most important among these were vassals of independent status called "elders" (*karo*) who formed a council of advisors to the daimyo, acted as his deputies and judges, and served as his generals in the field. The next level was composed of high-ranking retainers who headed the major divisions of the daimyo's government and military force. Other levels were in charge of more specific tasks from a variety of administrative functions down to menial or routine work. Under the supervision of the daimyo's government, local administrators controlled each village and the several wards of the towns, but their control was indirect because the rural and urban population lived in self-governing units under the authority of their own headmen.[b]

Japan's aristocracy is another case of subordinate preeminence. All daimyo were definitely subject to detailed control by the shogun, and only the direct retainers of the shogun, whose domains were typically small, were admitted to his councils. By careful attention to the strategic location of daimyo domains—the larger and less reliable daimyo were kept "outside" the central Tokugawa domain—their subordination was ensured. But within these carefully defined limits, the daimyo and their major retainers enjoyed wealth, status, and authority. The Tokugawa shogunate treated the larger daimyo with circumspection. The aristocracy was controlled but not crushed, and the obligation of loyalty and service to the shogun proved compatible with considerable initiative at the local level. The leadership of the Meiji restoration was recruited from several outside domains located on the periphery of Tokugawa domination.

I have concluded Part 1 on the authority of kings with this comparative discussion of aristocratic representation. Only landed aristocrats, clerics, and patrician townsmen were represented in the estate assemblies and parliaments of the time. Part 2 will deal with the mandate of the people in a broader sense. The idea of an increased popular participation in church services and eventually in the political process was a result of the wide intellectual mobilization which occurred in the fifteenth and sixteenth centuries. I shall describe this mobilization in the next chapter, which introduces the country-by-country discussion of Part 2.

[b]Fuller discussion regarding Tokugawa Japan is reserved for Chapter 12.

"The people, no."

Part II

TOWARD
A MANDATE
OF THE PEOPLE

*. . . I think that the poorest he that is in England
hath a life to live, as the greatest he;
and therefore . . . that every man that is to live
under a government ought first by his own consent
to put himself under that government. . . .*
—CAPT. RAINBOROUGH, *The Putney Debates* (1647)

*When the inhabitant of a democratic country
compares himself individually with all those about him, he
feels with pride that he is the equal of any one of them;
but when he comes to survey the totality of his fellows he is
instantly overwhelmed by the sense of his own
insignificance and weakness. The same equality that
renders him independent of each of his fellow citizens,
taken severally, exposes him alone and unprotected to the
influence of the greater number. . . . For it would seem
probable that, as they are all endowed with equal means of
judging, the greater truth should go with the greater
number.*
—ALEXIS DE TOCQUEVILLE, *Democracy in America*

8

TRANSFORMATIONS OF WESTERN EUROPEAN SOCIETIES IN THE SIXTEENTH CENTURY

Monarchical authority and its impact on aristocratic culture had repercussions which were felt until well into the nineteenth century. The societies over which a king ruled comprised shires and boroughs, guilds and other corporations, provinces and estates, all possessing different kinds of judicial and executive authority. The further one goes back in history, the more these units of government consisted of communities of households, in which each household was ruled by a master seeking to protect his domain against trespass. When unable to do so, the head of a household would commend himself and his dependents to the protection of a more powerful house. Each of the aristocratic families had to assert its rights, for failure to do so, even by force of arms when necessary, was tantamount to relinquishing those rights. Feuds of the more powerful houses became integral parts of the legal order. This concluded a very complex development from a condition in which feuds were de facto efforts to assert or maintain rights to a later condition in which such feuds had become institutionalized by stipulations marking them as justified (de jure).[1]

The crown eventually succeeded in controlling these feuds by settling disputes through the authority of its military and civilian officials. This development occurred in Imperial Germany as early as the thirteenth century, when Emperor Frederick II (1215–1250) prohibited feuds and established the royal monopoly of legitimate force through a police and bureaucracy. But Frederick's achievement did not last.[2] In England, powerful kings sporadically achieved the same monopoly, but centralized rule became an accomplished fact only under the Tudor monarchy in the sixteenth century. In Russia, the development occurred with the ascendance of the Muscovite dynasty and in Japan with the rise of the Tokugawa shogunate in the early seventeenth century.

We have discussed Marc Bloch's distinction between an early phase of feudalism like that of the Anglo-Saxon kingdoms in which aristocratic society was localized and royal authority weak, and a later phase in which population and commerce increased while political fragmentation gave way to stronger monarchical rule. Following Machiavelli and Weber, I have further distinguished in that second phase between an autocratic and a free feudalism. These two terms refer to two interdependent but countervailing tendencies of rule, one emphasizing peremptory commands to compulsory associations and the other contractual agreements between a king and his vassals. Under favorable conditions these tendencies of Bloch's second phase may give rise to representative institutions under monarchical authority, a social structure that is no longer feudal in the proper sense and has been designated as an "estate (or corporate) society" (*Ständestaat*) in the German literature. These corporate societies developed in many European countries after the thirteenth century, and most successfully in England, where by the end of the seventeenth century the idea of a sovereign "king-in-parliament" achieved a balance between central monarchical authority and the representation of the country in parliament. Elsewhere in Europe and in countries like Russia and Japan, absolutist regimes emerged in which monarchical authority monopolized the use of legitimate force and paved the way for the development of the modern state with its monopolization of functions like taxation and defense in the hands of the central government. These patterns of authority overlapped for long periods, and it is best to consider chronological divisions among them crude approximations.

In the early medieval period, a king governed his country like a giant household. There was little distinction between public revenue and income derived from the royal domains, though with the expansion of government an increasing proportion of revenue was derived from taxation.[3] Members of the royal family participated in affairs of state as a matter of hereditary right. The king was entitled to his throne and the aristocracy to their property by similar hereditary claims. Titles to property were also held by municipal corporations, churches, and monasteries. Such titles typically included not only the ownership of land, but also the exercise of judicial and administrative rights. These rights or liberties were recognized as just and valid by virtue of their antiquity. This view gave rise to numerous forgeries seeking to prove the antiquity of lineage and titles. Rights were recognized as valid because they were old, not because they had been enacted by higher authority.[4] In this way, property ownership, social status, and participation in public affairs were closely linked. The man of high status possessed rights of authority by virtue of ancient lineage or title, and his various privileges (or liberties) were important sources of income.

The second part of this study is concerned with the breakup of the fusion among family, property, and authority. The traditional structure of authority was undermined when land lost its importance as the principal source of wealth and under the laws of inheritance individuals became more autonomous. It was undermined as well when the absolute authority of the king was gradually replaced in practice by the authority of his officials. This bureaucratization of government gradually separated the exercise of authority from its earlier link with a family's property. And as the ties between property and authority weakened, so did the idea that the king personally owned all the resources of his country and indeed his people's productive capacity as well. The delegitimization of kingship has varied from country to country. But where the claim that the king protects the welfare of his people was juxtaposed again and again with abuses of authority and widespread misery, that claim itself could be turned into an argument against kingship. If the welfare of the people was to be uppermost, then kings who did not maintain that welfare lost some of their earlier authority. Eventually, the authority of kings was replaced by government in the name of the people.

The changes which foreshadowed the nation-state, with its concomitant legal recognition of individual rights, go back as far as the thirteenth century. I shall deal in this chapter with some of the early changes which culminated in the breakup of the "traditional social order" during the seventeenth and eighteenth centuries. That breakup became irreversible when even the head of the household lost his preeminent civil status, as social and economic dependents (like wives, children above minimum age, and servants) acquired a civil status of their own. Constituted authority came to be legitimized by appeals to history, nature, and reason rather than to the symbolic inviolability of the king's authority. Under a popular mandate, persuasion was added to the tenuous symbolic sanctity of high office. Today, representative bodies base their legitimacy on a mixture of intellectual constructions, popular mandate, and appeals to specific constituencies. The following chapters will examine the political and intellectual conditions under which these new bases of authority were formulated.

MOBILIZATION

The societies examined in this book have become the most industrialized countries of the world; as nation-states they are among the most developed politically. Each of these countries underwent a revolution or restoration, and each of these transformations influenced the next. In

the sixteenth and seventeenth centuries, England began these great upheavals with the Henrician Reformation and the revolution of 1640–
1660. This was followed by the industrial and the French revolutions of
the eighteenth century, the Prussian reforms (1807–1814) and the unification of Germany under Bismarck (1870–1871), the Meiji restoration
of Japan in 1868, and the transformation of Russia from the emancipation of the serfs in 1861 to the Bolshevik revolution of 1917 and the
Stalinist revolution of 1928.

Each of these revolutions or restorations was a collective response
to both internal conditions *and* external stimuli. Each had repercussions
beyond the frontiers of the country in which it occurred. After each
transformation, the world had changed in Heraclitus' sense that you
cannot step into the same river twice. Once the English king had been
overthrown and parliament was supreme, other monarchies became insecure and the idea of parliamentary government was launched. Once
industrialization was initiated, other economies became backward. Once
the ideal of equality had been proclaimed before a worldwide audience,
inequality became a burden too heavy to bear.

Inequality had been an accepted condition of life. In the household,
masters ruled over their servants as the king ruled over his subjects. In
Tocqueville's view, the "whole course of society" since the eleventh century had been marked by an increasing equality of condition. The hold
of family inheritance weakened. The clergy acquired power and opened
its ranks to all classes. Commoners acquired high positions at court, enriched themselves through commerce, and acquired title by purchase.
Every improvement in trade and manufacture, every acquisition of
property, and every discovery in the arts created "new elements of
equality," as did the great historical events of this long period.

> The Crusades and the English wars decimated the nobles and divided their
> possessions; the municipal corporations introduced democratic liberty into
> the bosom of feudal monarchy; the invention of firearms equalized the vassal
> and the noble on the field of battle; the art of printing opened the same
> resources to the minds of all classes; the post brought knowledge alike to the
> door of the cottage and to the gate of the palace; and Protestantism pro-
> claimed that all men are equally able to find the road to heaven. The dis-
> covery of America opened a thousand new paths to fortune and led obscure
> adventurers to wealth and power.[5]

The elements Tocqueville enumerates are clearly important. But if
equality had been like a rising tide for centuries, then it is hard to understand why revolutions were necessary to establish it. The reason is
that with each rise of equality social distinctions were reasserted. Those
who gained *new* wealth and influence sought to secure it for their fam-

ilies by the acquisition of title, and titles were linked to monarchical authority. With luck, only a generation or two were needed for a rising family to take its place among the magnates of the realm and obscure the fact that this rise had once overcome existing privileges.

Toqueville was right in emphasizing the spread of equalitarian ideas, but he failed to examine the process by which such ideas spread from country to country. The perspective adopted in the following chapters combines a structuralist with a diffusionist approach but gives special emphasis to the demonstration effects through which advances in one part of the world provide impulses for change in others. Since the fifteenth century, the transformation of societies has been accelerated by an overall mobilization which eventuated in the transition from the authority of kings to the mandate of the people. The following discussion describes the mobilization of resources in the fifteenth and sixteenth centuries, with particular attention to "intellectual mobilization." However, the changes to which I refer had remote antecedents.

PRECONDITIONS[6]

One of these antecedents is the changing role of towns. Greco-Roman civilization had prosperous towns, but the decline of the Roman empire left many of them in ruins. Population in Europe was sparse. Even in 1000 A.D. it probably did not exceed thirty to thirty-five million people (including Russia and the Balkans). Education, trade, and production were reduced to a minimal level, and people withdrew into largely self-sufficient manors and monasteries. These conditions changed between 1000 and 1330. By the latter date, Europe's population had increased to eighty million. Urban centers developed rapidly as people migrated from the countryside. The towns offered many attractions: freedom from the personal servitude of the manor, economic opportunities, and an autonomous jurisdiction which provided protection against the armed might of landed magnates. The urban merchants, artisans, and professionals created a culture based on the cooperation of guilds within the municipality. During the eleventh and twelfth centuries, the towns introduced new types of production and exchange and an education and administration which differed from feudal practice. Municipal independence often led to armed conflict with the rulers, whose main source of wealth was based on the rural areas and whose cultural outlook was shaped by hierarchical rather than egalitarian conceptions. In some cases, as in Italy, this conflict led to the dominance of towns over the surrounding countryside; elsewhere it led to an uneasy accommodation with the landed aristocracy. The urban revolution of Western Europe greatly increased the economic and social prominence of merchants and artisans in contrast to Russia, Japan, and many other countries where merchants ranked low and were despised despite their increasing wealth. The Western European towns were centers of education as well as commerce before 1300.

Then a long period of stagnation occurred in Western Europe due to epidemic diseases. The Black Death killed about 25 million people between 1348 and 1350, and from that time epidemics (often greatly aggravating the effects of wars and famines) were endemic in Europe for three centuries. In 1500 the total European population was 80 million, the same as in 1330. However, the sixteenth and seventeenth centuries witnessed a resumption of growth. Europe's population totaled about 105 million in 1600 and 115 million in 1700. This renewed population growth was a necessary condition for the mobilization of economic and intellectual resources in the sixteenth century.

A third precondition of the great transformation was technological. The water mill, the heavy plow, the horseshoe, and new methods of harnessing originated elsewhere, but by the ninth century they were being adapted to productive uses by Europeans. By the thirteenth century water mills were used for the production of iron, the sawing of wood, and the manufacture of paper. This harnessing of water power to replace manual labor was seen as a great technological change. The great inventions facilitating transport date from the same period: the compass, naval charts, the stern rudder, trigonometric tables for navigation, and the waterclock to measure the movement of a ship. Clocks and firearms came in the early fourteenth century. New commercial techniques were also developed. Fairs were organized, manuals of commerce became available, and insurance, the check, new methods of accounting, and bills of exchange were invented. No financial mechanism had been available between the fifth and the eleventh centuries for the transformation of savings into investment. But after the eleventh century, sales credit, forms of partnership (*commenda*, sea loans, mutual-agency partnerships), and other devices made it possible for all members of society to invest their savings, thus diminishing the chronic shortage of capital.

These and related preconditions had a subjective dimension which we can recognize as important even when we do not have adequate explanations for them. Christianity was probably the most important subjective factor which made its influence felt throughout. Religion had special impact in the urban areas, for the medieval towns developed cooperative capabilities which were absent from the feudal emphasis on hierarchy. All Christian believers were equal under God, and this principle put the associations of town residents on the same footing. Religious equality may help to explain the oath-bound associations of European towns, which did not exist outside Europe. Population growth was slow partly because a large number did not marry, others typically married late, and Christian doctrine helped to idealize celibacy in contrast to the belief systems of Oriental societies which condemned it. In technology, Europe was distinguished less by its originality than by its receptivity and capacity for creative adaptation. Western Europe was distinguished by a "mechanization of the world picture" which greatly facilitated technological developments that could be put to use. Carlo Cipolla makes the ingenious point that

> [even the Christian] saints did not take their ease in the hieratic immobility of the oriental holymen, nor did they amuse themselves like the Greek gods by punishing men for their audacity. On the contrary, they were always at work to overcome the adverse forces of nature: they defeated diseases, calmed stormy seas, saved the harvests from storms and locusts, softened the fall for whoever leapt into a ravine, stopped fires, made the drowning float, and guided ships in danger. The saints practiced what the commoners dreamed: they harnessed nature and, far from being condemned for doing so, they lived pleasantly in Paradise in the company of God. Harnessing nature was not regarded as a sin; it was a miracle. A belief in miracles is the first step toward making them possible.[7]

Finally, the whole structure of commercial credit could not have developed without a spirit of mutual trust and standards of honesty which again had a cultural as well as an economic foundation.

These and other preconditions had the cumulative effect of producing a world economy during the sixteenth century. Intellectual mobilization was an aspect of this great sixteenth-century transformation, and neither the causes nor the consequences of that mobilization are adequately explained by economic and political interests alone.[8] In the twentieth century, it has become easy to recognize that the development of science has an economic foundation, that it is a force of production, but that it cannot prosper without a community of scientists at work. This should make it easier to see the social structure which facilitated "intellectual mobilization" at an earlier time and to recognize the influence of ideas on social change as well. For this reason, the present chapter gives special attention to those aspects of sixteenth-century European societies which help to account for "intellectual mobilization." Such mobilization had the eventual effect of creating in many societies an educated public and intellectual leaders who were sensitive to the position of their country in the world and eager to see it enhanced, an attitude that had important repercussions on the successive revolutions and restorations which are examined in Part 2 of this study.

OVERSEAS EXPANSION AND ITS DOMESTIC CORRELATES

Exploration, trade, printing, universities, early modern science, and the Reformation developed concurrently in the fifteenth and sixteenth centuries. All these transformations are instances of "mobilization." Increasing contacts among people and a rapid diffusion of ideas overcame the earlier isolation of households and communities. We may speculate that increased communication is the common element of this pervasive mobilization.

Islamic conquests established new imperial powers on the southern and eastern flanks of Europe from the seventh to the thirteenth centuries. Russia was under Mongol overlordship from the thirteenth to the mid fifteenth century and was to expand into Siberia only after 1580. Turkish invaders of the fifteenth century crushed the Byzantine empire and conquered Constantinople in 1453. The Ottoman empire exerted pressure on central Europe until the late seventeenth century, so that the menace from the Turks was a major preoccupation. Among books printed in France between 1480 and 1609, twice as many titles related to the Turkish empire as to the Americas. It is still an open question whether these invasions from Asia gave the impetus to westward expansion and the great explorations, or whether the prospects of overseas discoveries made Europeans turn away from their eastern frontier and thus facilitated the Mongol and Turkish invasions of the Near East, Africa, Russia, and the Balkans.[9] At any rate, Western advances in sailing and artillery from the fifteenth century onward initiated a period of outward expansion which allowed Europeans to combine the promising adventure of exploration with a circumvention of the mounting obstacles in the East. Portugal and Spain pioneered this expansion, but soon Holland, England, and France followed suit.

Until the fifteenth century, oceangoing vessels had used the seas primarily for trade; their military use was confined to guarding the coastlines, defending ships against pirates, and carrying support for land warfare. However, as gunpowder had revolutionized warfare on land, so cannons mounted on ships changed the balance of power on the high seas.[10] Early European colonization was confined to trading concessions and coastal settlements. Even these limited colonizing ventures, however, preempted the seas, and occupied territories outside Europe were treated in the same way that other conquests within Europe had been customarily treated in the past. The Portuguese initiated their overseas conquests and "sovereignty of the sea" under a papal mandate. The Bull of 1454 granted Prince Henry the Navigator (1394–1460) "the right, total and absolute, to invade, conquer, and subject all the countries which are under the rule of the enemies of Christ," adding the missionary charge that these "perfidious enemies of God" should be brought into the "Catholic fold."[11] The era of Portuguese explorations extended from the discovery of the nearby Madeira islands in 1418–1419 and the initiation of West African trade to the discovery of a direct route to India by Vasco da Gama, who reached the Malabar coast in 1498. Portugal had pioneered this expansion but soon the other European powers vied with Portugal for commercial supremacy on the high seas and in overseas settlements.

Westward expansion to the Americas also began from the Iberian peninsula. Columbus appealed in vain to the Portuguese king, but eventually found a sponsor in Queen Isabella of Spain. His four voyages from 1492 to 1504 led to discoveries of various Caribbean islands and the coast of South America. Explorations in the sixteenth century yielded further discoveries in South America, North America, Africa, and Asia. This enormous geographic expansion was accompanied within Europe by population growth, an intensification of trade, and an intellectual mobilization through printing, education, and the growth of science.

For the countries bordering on the Mediterranean, total population probably doubled between 1500 and 1600, increasing from roughly 30 to 60 million people. Considering the fact that the economies of the time were predominantly agricultural and the bulk of the trade local or regional, some of the totals achieved in international trade are quite striking.

> 102,000 casks of wine were exported from Bordeaux in 1308–9, which looks quite respectable alongside the 270,000 tons of various goods which the same port sent to England in 1961. Some clues also make it possible to see how important the grain trade was. In the first half of the fourteenth century, the total value of English exports was around £250,000, and she exported between 35,000 and 40,000 sacks of wool (weighing 15 million pounds) and 540,000 cloths (each 28 yards long); and this latter figure represents only perhaps one-third of Flemish cloth production at its peak. The taxable value of the goods exported from the principal Hanseatic towns in the 1370's reached 3 million Lübeck marks. . . . In the fifteenth century trade with Lombardy brought Venice 2,800,000 ducats, and through Venice the Lombard cities imported 300,000 ducats-worth of pepper alone.[12]

Braudel gives the example of Constantinople, a city of 700,000, where a grain fleet carrying a million hundredweight (quintals) of cereals arrived annually, or of Naples, where business in the amount of 1,300,000 ducats was transacted on the exchanges in 1559.[13]

To understand the intellectual mobilization of the period, we must describe the means of transport available to carry both goods and mail. Sea-going vessels were small, 30 to 50 tons being more or less standard during the fifteenth century, though 200 to 500 tons were common, especially in Venice. Bulk goods were carried in a few larger boats. An estimate of 350,000 tons of shipping in the Mediterranean and twice that tonnage in the Atlantic meant that sizable fleets were plying the seas. The fastest speeds achieved in the sixteenth century did not much exceed 200 kilometers per day at sea. Speeds on overland routes were necessarily lower, though the fastest postal route between Italy and Brussels covered 764 kilometers in five and a half days, or about 139 kilometers a day. Despite these peak performances, most transport and communication remained irregular and involved many delays.[14]

The foundation of universities is, perhaps, the simplest index of intellectual mobilization in the pre-Reformation period. Precise dating is difficult because corporations of teachers and students often existed before they secured a papal or imperial charter, and some Italian schools of law and medicine date back to the ninth and tenth centuries. If we consider only the formally established universities between 1160 (Paris) and 1900 (Birmingham) and divide this period in half, we find that fifty-three universities were founded before 1530, and sixty-five universities after that year.[15] The early universities were centers of scholastic learning outside the monasteries and provided new opportunities for study; thus, one may well speak of a cultural awakening.

The invention of printing in the mid fifteenth century revolutionized communication. The spread of the facility itself is an impressive indication. Within fifty years after the invention of movable type, 236 European towns had their own printing presses. The number of books printed before 1500 (*incunabula*) is uncertain; estimates of the number of copies of printed books vary between 8 and 20 million at a time when Europe had about seventy million inhabitants. A somewhat better figure comes from the end of the sixteenth century, when different titles printed were estimated to number between 140,000 and 200,000 while the total European population was about one hundred million. If editions averaged 500 copies, the total number of books would be between 70 and 100 million. While these impressive totals remain uncertain, it is quite clear that printing transformed the book trade. In Spain, around 800, a book had cost roughly as much as two cows; in Lombardy, during the fifteenth century, a medical book cost the equivalent of the living costs of a person for three months, and a law book as much as living expenses for sixteen months. Printing brought books suddenly within reach of ordinary persons, although initially production was not on a large scale. Even the largest publisher of the time only produced 236 works between 1473 and 1513, averaging less than 6 works per year.[16] Other publishers produced only 2 works per year, or even less, and many publications were broadsheets of various kinds. Germany seems to rank highest with the publication of 571 books in 1520 and 944 books

(*Opposite page*) **The Art of Bookmaking**
The four woodcuts illustrate the work of the papermaker, the type cutter, the printer, and the bookbinder. The whole work of 114 woodcuts by Jost Amman (1568) is of interest because it shows by its title *Die Stände* or *Ständebuch* that by the sixteenth century the term *estate* was used both in the sense of craft or occupation and in the sense of estate such as nobility or clergy. (*Ständebuch*, Frankfurt 1568)

Chartarius. Der Papyrer.

EX vetuli pannu tenuem contexo papyrum,
Vertitur in gyros dum mola scabra suos:
In tabulis olim sua scripsit verba vetustas,
Quas rudis ex cæra dextra liquente dabat.

Sculptor. Der Formschneider.

EXimias Regum species, hominumq́ Deumq́
Omnia Phidiaca corpora sculpo manu.
Deniq́ pictoris quicquid manus æmula ducit,
Id digiti possunt arte polire mei.

Typographus. Der Buchdrucker.

ARte mea reliquas illustro Typographus artes,
Imprimo dum varios ære micante libros.
Quæ prius aucta situ, quæ puluere plena iacebant,
Vidimus obscura nocte sepulta premi.

Concinnator librorum. Buchbinder.

QVisquis in Aonijs studiosus obambulat hortu,
Et studijs tempus mitibus omne locat.
Huc properet, vigili ferat atq́ volumina dextra,
Edita Calcographus quæ prius ære dedit.

in 1523. England, with an annual production of 100 new books, ranks much lower.[17] An index of the growing interest in science can be constructed from a compilation of scientific books published between 1450 and 1550. A total of 900 books is recorded for this period. Venice published 220 books, Paris published 97, and seventeen other European towns published the remaining 583 scientific titles.[18]

Other aspects of intellectual mobilization cannot be dated or quantified so readily. The Reformation of the sixteenth century had a widespread effect on intellectual life. Lay participation in religious learning and affairs of the church increased as the Scriptures became available in the vernacular, and this in turn increased the habit of reading among the people. Literacy apparently increased during the sixteenth century, and by the end of the seventeenth century between 35 and 45 percent of Protestant adults and between 20 and 30 percent of Catholic adults were literate. Luther's ninety-five theses of 1517 were disseminated with impressive speed. Between 1517 and 1520, Luther's thirty publications sold over 300,000 copies. Printed Bibles and prayer books greatly facilitated family worship and blurred the boundaries between church and home.[19] A market for printed matter which appealed to a general public had emerged.

The developments of urbanization and the commercialization of land, labor, and capital were accompanied by a many-sided intellectual mobilization.[20] Various groups of educated minorities became alerted to the social and cultural position of their own society in relation to the "demonstration of advances" beyond their frontiers, a process which acquired momentum in Europe in the sixteenth century and has since spread to most other countries of the world. I shall sketch this mobilization with reference to England.

INTELLECTUAL MOBILIZATION IN ENGLAND

In his *Novum Organum* (1620), Francis Bacon noted that printing, gunpowder, and the magnet had "changed the whole face and state of things throughout the world."[21] Guns mounted on ships were the technical means by which explorers and conquerors initiated the age of European expansion overseas. The lifetimes of the main explorers (Columbus, 1445–1506; da Gama, 1469?–1524; Magellan, 1480–1521) overlapped with those of Luther (1483–1546) and Copernicus (1473–1543), suggesting a broad concurrence between exploration, overseas expansion, and the transformation of the prevailing religious and scientific world view. All of this had been preceded by the invention of printing, the first Gutenberg Bible appearing sometime before 1456.[22] This new facility explains how overseas exploration, the Reformation, and the early development of science resulted in a burgeoning literature of travelogues, religious pamphlets, and scientific and political tracts. I call this whole process of a more rapid production and diffusion of ideas and the related increase in the number of writers and readers "intellectual mobilization."

The change of social composition in government service is one example of this mobilization. Until roughly the fifteenth century, most civil servants were clergymen, though for the highest positions the king often chose aristocratic laymen as well. These conditions changed under the Tudor "revolution in government" in the sixteenth century, and by the early seventeenth century English "civil service" showed a predominance of laymen.[23]

The case of law is more complex. Originally, litigation was conducted without the aid of lawyers, though litigants could bring a friend to court with whom they took counsel. Such friends were often clerics. However, as legal procedure became formalized in England, the jurisdiction of the ecclesiastical courts was more strictly confined. At the same time, civil courts (in contrast to the Continent) resisted the use of the Roman code and developed a native "common law" outside the range of theological subjects and canon law taught at the universities. Much common law litigation was concentrated in London, where by the middle of the fifteenth century the societies of lawyers developed an organized legal education in the Inns of Court, which perhaps originated in clubs formed to provide lodging and service when legal business brought lawyers to the capital. In this manner, a secular legal education developed outside the universities and unrelated to the church. The legal profession came to play a significant role in the English Reformation and the political revolution which followed in the seventeenth century.[24]

Other ancient professions like medicine, nursing, and teaching were more closely tied to the church. Although occasional lay physicians date back to an early age, physicians regularly entered the priesthood because their professional advancement often depended on appointments to benefices and hence on ecclesiastical status. This practice continued until the Reformation, although the church often looked with disfavor on the study of medicine by beneficed clergy and actively discriminated against surgeons because it did not approve the shedding of blood by ecclesiastics. On the other hand, nursing was an approved activity of the monastic orders, and with their dissolution in sixteenth-century England no lay organizations of caring for the sick arose for a considerable time. Physicians lost their bond with the church when the development of medicine made the profession independent, whereas nursing was for a considerable period literally destroyed by the dissolution of the monasteries.

Teaching was a special province of the church. Grammar schools for boys were established at cathedrals and collegiate churches while others were founded at chantries (endowments for the chanting of masses, commonly for the founder), guilds, and a few hospitals. By 1500 as many as four hundred grammar schools may have existed in England and Wales for a population of 2.5 million people. In addition, the boys and girls of wealthy households were tutored privately. Education consisted primarily of instruction in religion and Latin with a bit of ciphering, household skills, and medical knowledge added for the girls. The boys of high-ranking families served as pages in the halls and castles of the aristocracy, receiving instruction in the courtly arts and knightly skills as well as in reading and writing.

All higher education was under ecclesiastical jurisdiction. Old universities like Oxford and Cambridge owed their primary allegiance to the church, and all students and teachers had the status of clerics, whether or not they were in holy orders. While the teachers (or masters as they were called) were organized as a guild and had jurisdiction over the admission of members, only the bishops had the right to grant licenses to teach and only ecclesiastical courts had authority to discipline the masters. The colleges were organized within the framework of the church, but owing to the privileges or liberties granted by the crown, they soon achieved a considerable autonomy. The students had to adapt themselves to a curriculum dominated by theological and classical learning. In England, university teaching remained a clerical profession until the nineteenth century.[25]

This system of education received a setback during the Reformation of the sixteenth century. The crown's continuous demand for funds probably militated against the private financial endowments needed for grammar schools and universities. Specifically, many grammar schools had been associated with chantries based on private endowments, and the dissolution of the chantries damaged the education available in Tudor England. At the accession of Queen Elizabeth in 1558, complaints were voiced in the House of Commons concerning the lack of schools, the decay of the universities, and the many towns without schools or preachers.[26]

But these trends were reversed during the last decades of the century. Support for education became the fashion as wealthy families and the great town guilds endowed grammar schools as well as loan funds at the universities. Lawyers and the Inns of Court in London also acquired a new prominence as aristocrats increasingly turned from combat to litigation. Privately endowed libraries were established, and education in the vernacular came to the fore. English translations of the Bible and of law books were made available. The fact that private initiative was largely responsible for these educational developments suggests that it is proper to speak of a widespread concern with learning.[27]

In Chapter 6 (pp. 204–206) the increased aristocratic interest in education was examined. Here it will be useful to consider the effects and general causes of English education. Oddly enough, the sentences imposed on criminals give one indication of the impact of learning. Due to the changed outlook of the Reformation, benefit of clergy was extended to laymen who could read. If a man was able to read a sentence from the Bible, he could plead benefit of clergy and have a death sentence reduced to branding. In this roundabout way we get at least a clue to the literacy of the male population of London: between 1612 and 1614, in a group of 204 men sentenced to death, 47 percent successfully pleaded benefit of clergy. Other incentives to literacy arose from the popular preaching of the period which stressed the importance of reading the Bible. Between one-third and two-thirds of the male population could sign their names (according to two studies of the seventeenth century), if this can be used as an indication of literacy. But the most persuasive evidence for the spread of learning comes from a tabulation of entrants to higher education. If attendance at universities, Inns of Court, and private tutorials are added together, the annual total of students increased from about 780 in the 1560s to a peak of 1,240 in the 1630s, the last figure representing about 2.5 percent of the annual male cohort reaching the age of seventeen.[28]

This educational revolution occurred when the demand for lay administrators and professionals was increasing. Stone has suggested a model for analyzing social mobility and the role of learning between 1560 and 1640. Over 90 percent of the population consisted of people whom contemporaries considered outside the rank of gentlemen, such as peasants, laborers, artisans, small traders, and dependents. Surprisingly, opportunities for acquiring an education existed even for sons of the more substantial yeomen, artisans, and shopkeepers at the top of this submerged majority; a number of these became prominent divines. Nevertheless, the major changes in mobility occurred among gentlemen —that is, among the remaining 10 percent. Landed proprietors had always ranked first, although the division between the peerage at the top, the county squirearchy, and the parish gentry was clearly important. But in the course of the sixteenth century, four other groups emerged which constituted social hierarchies of their own—namely, merchants, lawyers, clergy, and government officials (including military officers). As Stone comments, there was a status hierarchy based on land, and there were additional occupational hierarchies whose relation to that standard system of reference was uncertain.[29]

Learning was also stimulated by its manifest utility for merchants and craftsmen and early advances in science responded to these practical interests. Still, royal and aristocratic sponsorship of science was important as well. When the universities resisted the teaching of science, institutions of scientific learning like Gresham College were founded outside the universities. When during the agitation of the 1640s and 1650s

Emblem of the Royal Society, 1661

The foundation of the Royal Society was sponsored by king Charles II, whose bust is displayed on the pedestal. The figure to the left is the first president of the society, who is pointing to the king's sponsorship. The figure to the right is Francis Bacon, the initiator of the new science, who is pointing to some of the scientific instruments (and to a gun) displayed on a wall behind him. Even this early allegory shows that science depends on political sponsorship but also claims independence from it. (Thomas Sprat, *History of the Royal Society,* 1734)

Académie des sciences, 1700
This picture of the French Academy shows the early proliferation of scientific instruments. On the far left are musical instruments for harmonic studies; on the lower shelf in the rear are cannon models for experiments in ballistics. Pulleys, catapults, globes, and geometric instruments are among the articles on display. (British Museum)

science was assailed as dangerous to established beliefs, the king's sponsorship of the Royal Society (1661) helped to dispel popular and ecclesiastical suspicion. Nevertheless, many early scientists and clergymen found it necessary to defend the compatibility among science, religion, and commerce.[30]

During the seventeenth century, religion was probably more important than science for arousing the intellectual interest of the population. Lawrence Stone's estimate that roughly one-half of the total male population of London was literate by the early seventeenth century is best explained by the religious agitation in which laymen supported their arguments by scriptural quotations. In many Puritan congregations, laymen had become active in both the administrative and religious functions of their church. Church livings frequently depended on the financial sponsorship of aristocratic landowners and could be maintained only with their consent. In this way, popular religious interest and aristocratic sponsorship found a basis of common concern despite the social divisions of English society.

The promotion of literacy went beyond the confines of the church, though there was considerable opposition to literacy. An act of 1543 "for the advancement of true religion" expressly prohibited the reading of the English Bible by artificers and journeymen under the rank of yeoman, and by all women of less than noble rank. This concern with the danger of excessive social aspirations among the lower classes existed until well into the eighteenth century, when churchmen still inveighed against the subversive activity of teaching reading in charity schools.[31] Nevertheless, the sixteenth and seventeenth centuries witnessed a rapid growth of a reading public, if one may judge from the sevenfold increase in the number of printers in London during the reign of Queen Elizabeth (1558–1603) and the tripling of printing houses between 1688 and 1757.[32] Though the number of new books published annually remained relatively small until the end of the eighteenth century, the size of editions increased and circulating libraries aided the diffusion of reading matter, offsetting the high price of each volume.

For successful authors this growth of a reading public made freelance writing lucrative enough to provide an independent livelihood. Writers had previously been troubled by the need to defer to their aristocratic patrons. Now, dependence on an anonymous reading public meant freedom from personal subservience and a new social independence from the aristocracy. It meant, however, a new dependence on the taste of the people. Ever since writing developed into a profession, writers have grappled with the distinction between the few and the many. Social distinctions based on titles and inheritance have been supplemented (or even superseded) by the distinction between the few marked off by their education and creativity and "the people" whose numbers give them purchasing power unrelated to taste. Populists see the mass of the people in terms of the virtues of the simple life; elitists see them in terms of vulgar tastes to which a crass commercialism can readily appeal.[33]

Similar cultural changes occurred elsewhere in Western civilization, although the details differ from country to country. Facilitated by the invention of printing in the fifteenth century, old learned occupations turned secular, new professions based on learning developed, governments became bureaucratic, and secular education rose to social esteem and functional importance. Furthermore, the Reformation gave impetus to literacy among the middle and lower strata of the population, and later writing became an independent, secular profession. In the course of these transformations, many people became consumers of secular culture, whereas formerly they had been confined to religious observances and popular amusements. This emergence of a culture-consuming public is the background for the intellectual leadership of an active minority, composed of lawyers, teachers, ministers, writers, and many others.

Beginning in the era of the Reformation and of overseas exploration, each major change of the modern world has had demonstration effects abroad. Once the church was challenged, a king beheaded, or a parliament supreme, once industrialization was initiated and the ideal of equality proclaimed, no country could remain unaffected. Everywhere people were made aware of events and "advances" which served as reference points for the assessment of developments at home. In sixteenth-century England, "intellectual mobilization" was motivated from across frontiers by national rivalries and religious fears. In the eighteenth and nineteenth centuries, "intellectual mobilization" was a by-product of economic development and of the striving for political and social equality. But these distinctions are crude. "Intellectual mobilization" created conditions favoring the cultural leadership of educated minorities, which played a major role in the state- and nation-building efforts of follower societies. An elaboration of this point will outline the framework that has guided the following studies.

AUTHORITY RECONSTITUTED:
A FRAMEWORK FOR STUDY

European explorations and conquests, trade and Christian missions, the diffusion of ideas through printing, the demonstration effects of modern science and of industrial economies, the ideas of the Reformation and of the French revolution—all these had repercussions in most parts of the world. Societies with ancient traditions have been disrupted by this multiple outward thrust of Europe, often through coercion or conquest but frequently also through the demonstration effect itself. This revolutionary process began with the first empires built by Portugal and Spain in the late fifteenth century, a process which Marx aptly described as "primitive accumulation." That process has entered its concluding phase only now with the decolonization of most African and Asian societies, though the effects of overseas expansion were centuries in the making and will not quickly disappear. We are dealing with a protracted revolution which has occurred wherever conquest, commerce, industry, technical innovations, and the spread of ideas have overturned established social relations and political structures.

Commerce and industry were an important part of this overall revolutionary process, but it does not make good sense to attribute all changes of the last four or five hundred years to "capitalism." In recent years we have come to recognize that scientific advance and technological innovation have often developed a momentum of their own. Such advance must have some economic basis, but it often depends as well on the development of a scientific or technical community (that is, a network of communication among qualified people with related intellectual interests). Such communities have a social and psychological capacity for promoting science and technology and are therefore a force of production. Moreover, the era of the "second industrial revolution" (with its vast elaboration of electronics, atomic power, chemical engineering, and so forth) has made us aware that science and technology have unanticipated economic repercussions and that the repercussions of ideas are fully as important as the material interests which play a role in stimulating ideas. These insights should not be confined to the present. For example, the invention of printing and the scientific revolution of the seventeenth century were part of an intellectual mobilization that was facilitated by commercialization in the early modern period, but that also occurred well in advance of commercialization and provided a means to promote commerce and industry.

I propose to treat intellectual mobilization—the growth of a reading public and of an educated secular elite dependent on learned occupations—as an independent cause of social change. Recognition of this cause need not detract from the familiar processes associated with economic development, such as urbanization and the commercialization of land, labor, and capital. But there are some mass movements since 1500, such as the Reformation, nationalism, agitation for ethnic and religious autonomy and for freedom and equality, which do not have a *simple* basis in the division of labor or class interest. Nationalism is noteworthy for its protean reaction to the international position of one's country, whether it is a superpower among nations or a country searching for a new identity. Also, ethnic and religious agitation is rooted in a sense of community, often at the price of economic well-being. Marx saw the human condition as defined by a person's relation to the work process and by the use of his faculties in that process. But in his interactions with others, man's occupational role is only one source of identity among many.

In the seventeenth and eighteenth centuries, England and France underwent major constitutional changes, and new modes of organizing social groups came into being. In England, Tudor and Stuart "absolutism" was superseded by a new, contractual relation between king and parliament in the revolution of 1688. In France, a nation of citizens emerged in place of the division between notables active in and subjects excluded from public affairs. These two reconstituted societies had been affected by the process of intellectual mobilization in an international setting. England felt the challenge of Spanish imperial power and Catholic subversion, while France responded to the challenge of English political institutions and the American war of independence. But once their own reconstitution was effected, these two societies became the reference-point to which follower societies responded by taking them either as models or as an indication of what to avoid in charting their own development. The purpose of the following chapters on England,

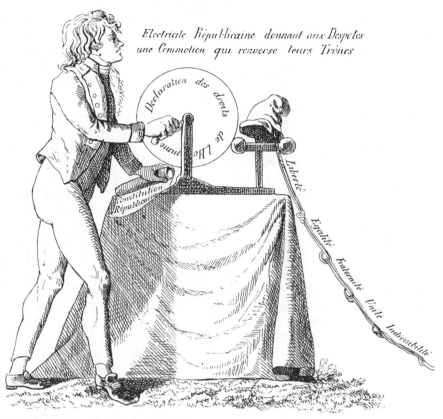

Diffusion of French Revolutionary Ideas
Contemporaries of the French revolution were well aware of the "demonstration effect" and its association with modern means of communication. In this cartoon entitled "Électricité Républicaine donnant aux Despotes une Commotion qui renverse leurs Trônes," a French patriot turns the handle of an electrical machine which sends a current of "liberté, égalité, fraternité, unité, indivisibilité" through the thrones of Europe. (Mansell Collection)

France, Germany, Japan, and Russia is to trace their respective developments away from the authority of kings and toward a mandate of the people. To achieve a proper vantage point for the more detailed studies which follow, it is necessary to broaden the evolutionist framework which we have inherited from the nineteenth century and which still influences modern studies of social change.[34]

That framework originated in Western Europe. It conceived of societies in isolation and saw in economic development and the division of labor the key to social change. This view had a certain plausibility. The social theories of the nineteenth century were developed in societies that pioneered the industrial and democratic revolutions of the modern world. These revolutions occurred in the center of the British empire and in the great state of France, societies which could easily be considered in isolation. The theories developed in England and France depicted societies as self-contained units and focused attention on the major classes striving for social and political recognition. It is true that the main political theories took some limited notice of the international setting. Liberal theory was concerned with international trade. Conservative theory emphasized the inequality of nations as a natural outgrowth of power politics. And radical theory construed international affairs as a continuation of the national class struggle by other means. Yet these considerations remained peripheral extensions of the idea that economic development based on the division of labor was the main determinant of change in the "modernization" of societies.

In addition, nineteenth-century theories were notably selective. Liberal theory emphasized the rise of productivity and market exchange as by-products of the division of labor. Such an approach tended to account only for people directly involved in exchange relations, thereby excluding economic dependents of all kinds. Conservative theory emphasized the division of society into status groups, each with its rights and duties defined as part of the whole. This accounted for people with assured status, but neglected all persons of inferior status, the efforts of such people to gain status, and intellectuals or foreigners whose status was unclear. Nor could conservatives do much with categories like legal equality or citizenship which applied in principle to everyone. Radical theory saw the division of labor in terms of conflicts between exploiters and exploited and thus accounted only for people involved in employment relationships. Women, children, intellectuals, old people, ethnic minorities, and others were subsumed under this archetypical conflict whether or not it pertained to their experience.

To note these deficiencies is not to reject the division of labor as an important agent of social change or the partial insights of these theories. But in the case studies which follow, this agent is slighted in favor of the impact of external events on societies, engendering ideas which have facilitated "modernization." The reasons for this reorientation are stated here in summary form.

1. The political revolutions in England and France and the commercial and industrial revolutions in England had a profound cultural impact in the seventeenth and eighteenth centuries. Men of letters began to formulate pervasive contrasts between a traditional social order which existed before these revolutions, and a modern social order which these revolutions had brought about. But these contrasts were misleading, for tradition and modernity have coexisted throughout. A recent study traces the rise of European individualism back to the twelfth cen-

tury; thus, elements of the modern revolutions since the seventeenth century are found in the remote past.[35] Conversely, the early cultural and political differentiation of kingship traced in the first part of this study still has repercussions today.

2. Since the late eighteenth century, European social theorists have interpreted the commercialization of land, labor, and capital as arising from specifically English, and more broadly Western European, preconditions. The general tendency has been to attribute all other social changes and all ideas about society to this basic cause—the division of labor. Economic change is basic, all other change is derivative, and all basic and derivative change can be best understood by examining what goes on within a society. I maintain against these conceptions that every process of modernization, including the early breakthroughs in England and France, involves causal links that run in both directions, combining tangible and ideal interests as well as indigenous and foreign influences.

3. Industrialization and democratization appear to have certain necessary and sufficient prerequisites without which these types of development cannot occur. And conversely, once these prerequisites are given, the predicted change is considered inevitable. Against this conception of a largely uniform structural change I emphasize the importance of ideas and of government "intervention" for an understanding of change. Once constitutionalism, industrialization, and democratization had been initiated in England and France, both the institutions and the ideas of the advanced country were used in others as a model in order to move ahead more rapidly and avoid, if possible, the problems encountered in the pioneering country.

For these reasons, we should never have assumed that the processes of industrialization and democratization would follow similar sequences of change in any two countries. It is easier to see this now. We know that the pioneering role of a bourgeoisie was not the sole factor in the development of any modern industrial economy. When the strength of the bourgeoisie is wanting, other social groups may come forward to provide political and economic leadership, though there is no assurance of success. The whole past history of uneven development has created mounting, worldwide inequalities for which there is no easy remedy. But ideas travel quickly, and in countries that become aware of their backwardness in comparison with an advanced country, the search for ways to overcome that backwardness often precedes every other kind of change. This insight was formulated early, but has not received the attention it deserves.

In the late 1840s, the German conservative Wilhelm Riehl gave a telling analysis of this correlation between economic backwardness and intellectual mobilization. He entitled his chapter *Die Proletarier der Geistesarbeit* or, literally, the proletarians of mental labor.

In Germany, the intellectual proletariat is the real, fighting church of the fourth estate. It represents the great vanguard of that social stratum which has broken with the traditional social structure, openly and self-consciously. . . .

I think of this group of the fourth estate in the broadest terms. It consists of a proletariat of civil servants, a proletariat of schoolmasters, perennial students of theology, starving academic instructors, literati, journalists, artists of all kinds ranging downwards from the travelling virtuosi to the itinerant comedians, organ-grinders and vaudeville singers. If one examines the legions of this intellectual proletariat in Germany, one can only conclude that this group of the fourth estate is in no country of Europe more numerous and varied than it is with us. This goes to prove that the turnover of the nation's material capital is disproportionately small compared with this wholesale and retail trade, this hawking and profiteering in spiritual goods. Germany produces more mental product than she can use or pay for. This over-production which is not transitory but permanent, and in fact always growing, is a symptom of sickness in the whole national economy, of an unnatural division of labor. The intellectual proletariat is a much more poignant satire of the nation's welfare than all the misery among factory-workers and peasants.

We are confronted with a vicious circle. Intellectual work shoots up like weeds, because economic enterprise does not provide it with sufficiently extensive opportunities for growth, and this growth in turn cannot come to fruition, because every surplus of energy is dissipated in an endless foliage of books. There are various dangers in this for the social conditions of Germany. In other countries the fourth estate was created by the sudden and overwhelming rise of industry. In Germany, the fourth estate is largely the onesided result of an overgrown intellectual uprising. Also, the German bourgeoisie owes its prevailing influence in modern society to the two great facts of an *intellectual* uprising, the Reformation and the classical period of the newer national literature. It is only during the most recent period that industry has begun to weigh the scales in favor of the bourgeoisie. The lush growth of the intellectual proletariat is the reverse side of a spirited development in the bourgeoisie.[36]

Riehl's conservatism put him out of sympathy with the intellectuals he described. But his insight into the inverse relation between an "intellectual proletariat" and a vigorous middle class applies quite generally to follower societies of the nineteenth and twentieth centuries.

As one moves east in Europe during the nineteenth century, or as one observes old societies today that have lain on the periphery of Europe's outward thrust over the centuries, one finds countries in which an economically pioneering bourgeoisie is not an indigenous development, or not a vigorous one. Such countries are arenas of intellectual mobilization, in which officials, teachers, literary people, and other members of Riehl's "intellectual proletariat" tend to coalesce into a class of their own.[37]

This coalescence results from an archetypical experience. In comparison with some or all advanced countries, the educated minority or intelligentsia sees its own country as backward. This is a troubled perception, for it identifies strength if not goodness with alien forces and sees weakness if not evil in the land of one's birth. In this setting, ideas are used to locate and mobilize forces which will be capable of effecting change and thus redressing this psychologically unfavorable accounting. A typical strategy of perception and argument ensues. As viewed by the outsider, the strength of the advanced country is formidable, but it is also sapped by false values, corruption, and spiritual decay and therefore should not or cannot endure. At the same time, the weakness of one's native land is pervasive, but the hidden spiritual values of the people are an untapped source of strength which will prevail in the end. Thus, the dominance of the advanced country carries within it the seeds of its own destruction, while the backward people and the underdeveloped country possess capacities that are signs of a bright future. Behind this strategy lies the simple belief that ultimately the advanced country must be weak because its people are evil, while the backward country must be strong because its people are good.

Such secular prophecy has been an important factor in nationalist efforts to achieve the social and economic development of backward countries by routes other than those which were followed in the West. This archetype of "intellectual mobilization" under conditions of relative backwardness provides only a model. When sensitive and articulate men and women suffer from the weakness and deprivation that is all around them, they will leave no avenue untried to better the fortune of the country and its people. When practical measures to do so are unavailable, free play is given to ideas. The result is a kaleidoscope of responses. The following chapters do not provide a comprehensive account, but focus attention on those intellectual opponents of the status quo who propose a reconstitution of authority.

In the nineteenth century, social thought tended to be divided between those who considered politics and economics from the standpoint of *Realpolitik* and those who considered ideas as a world divested of all crass, materialistic interests. When this second, idealist approach prevailed, it was quite persuasive to oppose it with the first, more tough-minded view of the world. Economists and sociologists tend to agree with the Marxist thesis that governments and ideologies are secondary phenomena, because political maneuvers and any expression of ideas "merely" reflect the more basic interests at work. This materialism is not as realistic as it pretends, even if one accepts the fact that ideas, like political actions, are continuations of the struggle for existence by other means. For the cultural and institutional life (which Marx lumped together under the term *superstructure*) is an extension of the mind and of social relations through which men seek to enhance their opportunities in situations of relative adversity. Men always face such situations, but the significance attributed to ideas seems to increase in roughly inverse proportion to the opportunities for change which are readily available. The history of Marxism is perhaps the best evidence for the limitations of materialism. Marxist theory was modeled on the internal development of English capitalism. But as that theory traveled eastward to countries in which an economically pioneering middle class was not an indigenous development, Marxism was reinterpreted in the interest of achieving socialism in economically backward countries. Societies that still seek to promote their industrialization have seen little value in a Marxism which made the ideal society of the future depend on the economic achievements of advanced capitalism. Economically backward countries have modified Marxism in accord with their national aspirations, even though this nationalism conflicts with the strongly internationalist orientation of Marxism in its original, theoretical formulation.[38]

Each of the case studies begins with the decline of a society's aristocratic culture pattern and follows with a sketch of its international setting in order to characterize the emergence of national aspirations. Each shows the emergence of ideological groups sensitive to developments beyond their country's frontiers and anxious to find a more viable mode of social organization for their native land. The remainder of each chapter is devoted to an analysis of basic political ideas with emphasis on those which have provided the major themes of the country's subsequent development.

Part 1 dealt with the authority of kings and in particular with the early intermingling between consecration and secular struggles for power. The chapters of Part 2 begin at a time when the sacred authority of kingship was being gradually undermined, sometimes through the very assertion of absolute supremacy as under Louis XIV and Peter the Great. Three times in the successive revolutions of the modern world the sacred authority of the king was destroyed by violence: the English king, the French king, and the Russian tsar were executed in 1649, 1793, and 1918, respectively. In all cases, however, the effort to reconstitute authority in the name of the people has involved a search for a new mandate to rule that is more valid than the authority of kings. This is why "the people," the appeal to the nation, and the search for a national identity recur so regularly in the movements of "intellectual mobilization" which are outlined in the following chapters.

9

KINGS AND PEOPLE
IN ENGLAND

THE ENGLISH REFORMATION
AND THE REIGN OF QUEEN ELIZABETH

THE DECADES around 1500 provide a convenient separation between the medieval and the early modern world. The conjunction of European overseas expansion, population increase, trade expansion, the invention of printing, the rise of modern science, and the Reformation heralded a new era. The political scene of that time was also one of intense activity.

In the late fifteenth century, the Iberian peninsula was divided from west to east into the kingdom of Portugal, the kingdom of Castile, and the kingdom of Aragon which included eastern Spain, the Balearic Islands, Sardinia, and Sicily. The small kingdom of Navarre formed a wedge between northern Castile and Aragon. In addition, the southern Emirate of Granada represented the remnant of the once powerful Muslim empire in Spain. In 1469 Prince Ferdinand (b. 1452–d. 1516) and Princess Isabella (b. 1451–d. 1504) were married. Ferdinand succeeded to the throne of Aragon in 1479, Isabella to the throne of Castile in 1474. This union of the two crowns was followed by the conquest of Granada in 1492, of the kingdom of Naples in 1503, and the acquisition of Navarre in 1512. Although this was also a period of Spanish explorations and conquests in the American colonies, the newly united Spanish empire was oriented toward the east as the defender of the Christian faith against the Turks.

In 1516 Ferdinand died, and the crowns of the Spanish kingdoms devolved on his grandson, Charles (1516–1556), ruler of the Netherlands and heir to the Austrian Habsburg dominions. In 1519 the German electors at Frankfurt designated him Holy Roman Emperor and during his reign as Charles V the main focus of the empire shifted to the center of Europe. Charles was a Netherlander at home neither in

Spain nor in Austria. His chief preoccupation was the struggle against France, which was surrounded by the Netherlands in the north, the Holy Roman Empire in the east, and the Spanish kingdoms in the south. France responded to this encirclement by concluding an alliance with the Ottoman Turks (1536). Thus, Charles was simultaneously engaged in Western Europe and the Mediterranean. After secretly ceding his hereditary Austrian domains to his brother Ferdinand (1521), Charles' power primarily depended on his Italian and Dutch possessions. The wealth of the Netherlands and of Naples together with large sums of money from Germany and from the colonies made the political structure under Charles V the most imposing empire of the mid-sixteenth century. After his election as emperor, one courtier wrote to Charles,

> Sire, now that God in His prodigious grace has elevated Your Majesty above all Kings and Princes of Christendom, to a pinnacle of power occupied before by none except your mighty predecessor Charlemagne, you are on the road towards Universal Monarchy and on the point of uniting Christendom under a single shepherd.[1]

One may discount the rhetoric of the courtier without diminishing the real concern with universal monarchy as a bastion of Christianity against the Turks.

The rise of the Ottoman Turks in Anatolia dated back to the early fourteenth century. Their expansion westward proceeded rapidly, both cause and consequence of the declining Byzantine empire. The fall of Constantinople in 1453 was one incident of the expansion which by 1481 had encompassed the whole Greek peninsula and Macedonia, Bulgaria, Wallachia, and Bosnia to the north and west. Wars between the Turks and the Venetian Republic broke out twice, and both wars (1463–1479, 1499–1503) witnessed the defeat of Venice. Under the reign of Suleiman the Magnificent (1520–1566), the Turks captured Belgrade (1521) and Rhodes (1522), conquered the kingdom of Hungary (1526), laid siege to Vienna (1529), and thereafter exerted pressure on central Europe for centuries. Pressure became intermittent when the Ottoman empire also became engaged in conflicts with the Persians in the east. But the Turks remained in control of Hungary until 1699 and of Greece until 1830.

The empire of Charles V had been a main bulwark against the Turks, but under Charles's brother, Ferdinand, who ruled the Habsburg lands after 1521, that central European defense had weakened. Charles's and Ferdinand's cosmopolitan outlook had been reflected in the Flemish, Burgundian, and Italian members of their entourage, and in their encouragement of humanist learning. When Charles V abdicated in 1556, his domains in the Netherlands, Italy, and Spain were inherited by his son, Philip II (1556–1598). Philip was a Spanish and

Catholic traditionalist, concerned with defending the faith against both Protestants and Muslims. As crown prince, Philip had married the Catholic queen Mary Tudor of England in 1554, which led to the persecution of Protestants in England and English participation in the Spanish war with France. In the peace of Cateau-Cambrésis (1559), France confirmed Spanish hegemony in Italy and the Spanish Netherlands, which were still the main bases of the struggle against the Turks. Suleiman died in 1566, and by 1571 Pope Pius V had succeeded in organizing a Holy League against the Turks. In the ensuing battle of Lepanto (1571), the combined Spanish, Venetian, and papal fleets annihilated the Turkish fleet. The victory had few strategic effects since the Turks quickly recovered, but it was of immense symbolic importance because it confirmed Philip in his chosen role as the defender of Christendom against the heretics.

That role was further enhanced when Philip settled the long-standing conflict with Portugal by combining the two crowns of Spain and Portugal while allowing the Portuguese their own jurisdiction at home and abroad. Henceforth, the two Iberian powers possessed a world empire which drew on the treasures of the Orient and the Americas while denying all other powers access to these areas and to the oceans of the world. These large claims were sustained for a time by the greater navigational and geographic knowledge which the pioneering explorers had acquired. To rule this vast empire, Spain and Portugal depended on the many Dutch sailors who were in their employment and on the Dutch commercial fleet, which grew rapidly. But in 1581 the Netherlands declared their independence from Spain, which marked the initial decline of Spanish power in world affairs.

Until the seventeenth century, Spain and France were the dominant world powers. As Richard Koebner has observed, "To Englishmen of the sixteenth and seventeenth centuries ascendancy was a salutary expectation, but it was not one which had been secured. Compared with France and Spain, the country remained a power of the second rank."[2] England's rise to a position of international importance was due initially to the political consolidation which followed a long era of civil wars. The early Tudor monarchs, Henry VII (1485–1509) and Henry VIII (1509–1547), suppressed private feudal armies, established a number of effective courts (of which the Star Chamber, 1487, was one), put down several rebellions, engaged in wars with Scotland and France, and made the English church independent of Rome (Act of Supremacy, 1534). The future domestic and international politics of England were rooted in its dynastic history.

Henry VIII was followed on the throne by his ten-year-old son, Edward VI (1547–1553), who died at sixteen. Complicated intrigues preceded the succession of Henry VIII's daughter, Mary Tudor (1553–

TABLE 2

GENEALOGICAL AFFILIATIONS of MARY TUDOR and MARY STUART, QUEEN of SCOTS

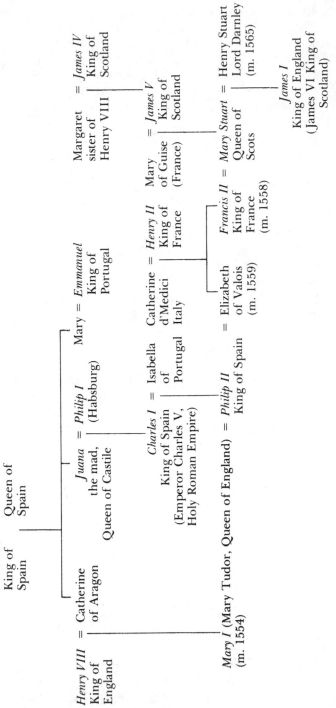

1558), but more importantly, she was a Catholic and out of touch with English affairs. The apparent aberration of Mary Tudor's reign becomes more intelligible when it is recalled that Mary's mother was Catherine of Aragon, the daughter of Ferdinand and Isabella of Spain and the first wife of Henry VIII. Moreover, Mary's aunt, Juana the Mad, married Philip I, king of Castile, and their son and Mary's cousin was Emperor Charles V. Thus, Mary's ties with Catholicism, Spain, and the empire were a natural by-product of her family connections on her mother's side. In 1554 she married her second cousin, Crown Prince Philip of Spain, despite considerable English opposition. Mary Tudor died in 1558, and Elizabeth I ascended the throne soon after France (under the command of the duke of Guise) had conquered Calais, the last remaining English foothold on the Continent. In 1559, when Spain, France, and England concluded their treaty of Cateau-Cambrésis, Philip II married the daughter of Henry II, the king of France, thus consolidating the Spanish-French alliance. But the French king died suddenly, and his crown passed to his son, Francis II, who was married to Mary Stuart. The mother of Mary Stuart was Mary of Guise, who had become regent of Scotland following the death of her husband, James V, in 1542. Consequently, the new queen of France, Mary Stuart, made the house of Guise dominant in France and Scotland. The threat implicit in this French claim to Scotland was enhanced by Mary Stuart's right to the English succession (her grandmother was a sister of Henry VIII) if Elizabeth died childless. The religious question compounded the difficulty. Mary Tudor's ardent Catholicism had led to her unpopular marriage with Philip of Spain; now the Catholicism of Mary Stuart became the focus of Catholic hopes. Real as well as imagined Catholic moves against England became a constant preoccupation during Elizabeth's reign (1558–1603). But despite these apprehensions, England was becoming a power to be reckoned with in international affairs, and in 1588 the English defeated the Spanish Armada.

This outcome had been difficult to foresee at the beginning of the sixteenth century. England was a country on the periphery in comparison with France, Spain, and the Holy Roman and Ottoman empires. In 1500 the English population was two and a half or three million, while that of Spain numbered six million and that of France about twelve million. By 1600 the English and Irish population had increased to four million, but the population of the Iberian peninsula numbered almost twelve million and that of France about sixteen million. Englishmen had hardly participated in the first half-century of exploration and conquest, and the first English book on geography appeared only in 1559. Until the last decades of the sixteenth century, England was a relatively backward island-nation, whose richest merchants could not compare with those of the Continent.

In the absence of comprehensive statistics for the period 1500–1600, descriptive statements veer uneasily between emphasizing the backwardness of the English economy and noting its signs of change.[3] But the growth of London is one clear indication of change after 1500. The city increased from 50,000 in 1500 to 200,000 in 1600, and in the ensuing fifty years the London population doubled to 400,000. This growth alone raised the demand for agricultural products. The sixteenth century is noteworthy for the development of the woolen industry, building construction, coal mining, and some promotion of transport. Rivers were cleared of obstruction so that by the early 1600s the country possessed seven hundred miles of navigable rivers, and by 1700 there were few places more than fifteen miles from access to water transport.[4] Roads remained very poor, since repairs depended on the availability of local labor and supplies; by the 1570s, however, the carrier and postal system had made some headway and benefited from the toll-free land transportation which was carried over from the Middle Ages. To contemporary observers, England appeared as a country of increasing economic opportunities. Religious refugees had other countries open to them, but large numbers of entrepreneurs came to England for its safety, growing market, and cheap labor. Skilled craftsmen in textiles and mining migrated to England, and by the 1570s the country was productive and well-equipped both technically and financially. Though not rich by comparison with the larger continental countries, England was prospering.[5]

Amidst these gradual changes, there were two which had lasting effects on English society: the price revolution and the Henrician Reformation. With expansion, the English economy needed an increasing supply of commercial capital; hence, the demand for money rose. Owing not only to this money shortage, but to the absence of credit facilities, the debasements of the currency and related factors, a long-term inflationary trend resulted. Coins lost their purchasing power; creditors lost and debtors gained as loans could be repaid in less valuable currency. Likewise, traders gained because they could pay their bills in cheaper coins, whereas landowners with fixed rental incomes lost because the same amount of money was worth less than before. These conditions were advantageous for export. Agricultural producers were attracted by profits from an expanding overseas market for grains, dairy products, and wool. The wool trade in particular expanded enormously during the sixteenth century, and many fields were fenced off and turned into sheep runs. Where arable land was turned into pasture, fewer hands were needed. The result was that whole villages declined, musters for the militia dwindled, and parish tithes no longer supported the priests. Villagers, the crown, and literary men were united in their opposition to the growth of sheep-farming, which enriched landlords and the wool traders but impoverished the farmers, especially in the English Midlands. Nevertheless, enclosures also facilitated the consolidation of holdings and—along with new farming techniques—contributed to increased productivity.

The English Reformation of the sixteenth century was the culmination of religious developments which reached far back into the past. Since 1066, the English kings had repeatedly attempted to curtail the connection between Rome and the high officers of the English church, because the bishops were also tenants-in-chief of the king and posed a threat to royal authority if they became too independent. The opposition of prominent ecclesiastics like Archbishop Anselm, Thomas Becket, and others against the English king was in part a struggle for ecclesiastical independence from the crown. Indeed, when royal authority weakened, papal tax collectors took advantage, and this in turn provoked popular as well as official resistance. During the fourteenth century, these controversies gave way to a settlement (the statutes of Provisors and of Praemunire, 1351–1353, 1365, 1390–1393), which preserved the crown's control over appointments to bishoprics, made it more difficult for plaintiffs to carry their appeals from English courts to the papal court in Rome, and forbade under penalty of forfeiture the introduction from Rome of papal bulls and excommunications. The English church was able to maintain this marked independence from Rome because since Norman times the parish clergy had often been appointed by lay landowners. Church benefices, therefore, were treated as secular property, and legal disputes involving such benefices were referred to the royal, rather than the ecclesiastical, courts. The *advowson* or right to appoint to a benefice could be sold or exchanged or bequeathed like a piece of property, just as the incumbent parson possessed his benefice as a freehold. Thus, when Henry VIII formally abolished the papal right of appointment to bishoprics, he legalized conditions that already existed. By abolishing papal jurisdiction, the king prohibited the payment of taxes to the church in Rome and diminished the old conflict between secular and ecclesiastical courts. But he did not claim authority "in the ministration of spiritual things," and his Statute of the Six Articles (1539) largely restated Catholic doctrine. Despite these indications of continuity with the English and Catholic traditions, the Henrician Reformation caused major changes in English society.

Between 1535 and 1540, all the monasteries of England either dissolved themselves or were suppressed under the direction of Henry VIII's minister, Thomas Cromwell. There were at least 825 religious houses in England and Wales with a total collective income of over £160,000 a year, derived from about 25 percent of the country's agricultural land. Royal revenue from land was about £40,000 a year; thus, the landed property taken from the monasteries brought the crown a

fourfold increase in its annual income. Other valuables confiscated from the church added a further £1 million to the royal treasury.[6] Confiscatory policies did not terminate with the reign of Henry VIII. Under Edward VI, lands worth more than £100,000 were confiscated from the endowments for prayers and masses (*chantries*), while Queen Elizabeth appropriated the landed estates (*temporalities*) of some bishops in exchange for tithes transferred to the bishops from the monasteries (*spiritualities*). Military expenditures were certainly a major factor behind this policy of the Tudor monarchy; between 1509 and 1572 the crown spent some £5 million on wars alone. The lands confiscated from the monasteries were sold or leased at current market prices, and crown lands were also sold to pay royal debts. Between 1558 and 1640, monastic and crown lands valued at more than £2 million were sold to meet the expenses of the crown.[7] The sale of monastic lands also had the effect of committing the English upper classes to the Reformation. Whatever the religious sentiment involved, landowning families had a manifest interest in the validity of titles to former monastic estates which they had purchased from the crown.

This massive mobilization of land was paralleled by a religious revival—a mobilization of the spirit. Dynastic and secular motives had prompted Henry VIII to clear "the ground for reformers to attack what seemed the empty ritual of the Mass, the ignorance of the common clergy, the corruption of the monastic and mendicant orders, the worldliness of the hierarchy."[8] Though one effect was to stimulate secular ambitions, another was to intensify religious zeal. In a period of twenty-four years—following the Act of Supremacy of 1534—the government's religious policy veered between the authoritarianism of Henry VIII, the Protestantism of Edward VI, the Catholicism of Mary Tudor, and the religious settlement (1558–1559) under Elizabeth. In the absence of strong religious leadership, issues of church policy were decided by governmental decree. It was partly as a reaction against so much uncertainty that religious groups formed which were determined to preserve the faith as they had come to define it.[9]

There is also considerable circumstantial evidence for a rise of national sentiment. Difficulties at home mounted during the sixteenth cen-

(*Opposite page*) **Title Page of the Great Bible, 1539**
Henry VIII's official version of the Bible was based on English translations of the preceding thirty years and became part of everyday thought and language. The title page shows the king presenting the new work, labeled *verbum dei* or word of God, to Chancellor Thomas Cromwell and Archbishop Thomas Cranmer. These great men distribute the Bible to the clergy who in turn expound it to the laity. In response, the people cry *vivat rex* or long live the king. The use of Latin phrases shows the continued influence of the Catholic tradition, the stress on the Word of God reflects Protestant influences, while the people's glorification of the king confirms Henry VIII as head of the Anglican church. (British Museum)

Dissolution of Monasteries
The aristocracy was interested in the dissolution of monasteries, which enabled them to gain control of church lands. Fountains Abbey, Yorkshire had been built by the Cistercian Order beginning in 1135. At its height the abbey possessed pasture and cornland, game preserves and fisheries, lead mines and quarries. A monk might have walked for thirty miles without leaving the communal property. The last abbot was forced to resign in 1536 and three years later the abbey was dissolved. At the time its 543 acres yielded an annual revenue of £1,000, its moveable wealth was valued at £700, and its assets included over 3,000 heads of cattle. The property was bestowed on a layman, Sir Richard Gresham. By 1540 the church and cloister had been stripped of lead and glass, woodwork and furniture. The ruins of the abbey remain a Yorkshire landmark to this day. After being deserted for over 50 years the estate passed in 1597 into the hands of Stephen Proctor, who in 1611 at the height of his career built Fountains Hall nearby, using the lead and stone of the abandoned abbey. In the 1960s the abbey and hall together with related properties were purchased by the West Riding of Yorkshire County Council. The Hall is still occupied by its last private owners. (British Museum)

tury. Landowners raised rents in order to keep up with inflation and meet the costs of financing land purchases. There was periodic unemployment. Great anxiety was caused by the widespread distress due to enclosures, by vagrancy in the countryside, and by sporadic rebellions. The last decades of the sixteenth century were a period of upheaval which should be seen in conjunction with England's international position.

Uneasy alliances were formed between France, Spain, and the pope based on common opposition to the English heresy. Each move by the pope or by Spain had a potentially divisive effect in England, intensi-

fying the conflicts among Catholics and Protestants. To counter these moves, England formed tacit alliances with the Huguenots in France and the Dutch in their struggles against Spain. Moreover, mounting difficulties led to a psychological mobilization. Threats from abroad linked to subversion at home helped to solidify religious and political sentiments so that along with their rising anti-Catholicism Englishmen developed a sense of national pride.[10] Economic developments also supported a sense of confidence. In the late sixteenth and early seventeenth centuries, despite periodic economic distress, the re-export trade of goods from America and the East Indies as well as English manufacture developed rapidly. Many conditions of the industrial revolution were already present by 1700, although obstacles in the techniques of production had created a lull after 1640.

REFERENCE SOCIETIES: SPANISH DOMINANCE AND CATHOLIC DANGER

In the European world of the sixteenth century, dominated by the Holy Roman Empire of Charles V, by Spain and the Ottoman Turks, a lesser country like England had to achieve its political position in relation to these superpowers. Nevertheless, English self-confidence rose owing to the country's increasingly active role in international affairs.

European explorations overseas had been pioneered by the Portuguese and the Spaniards for two generations before Englishmen began to participate in these ventures. The early English explorations were confined to the Atlantic fisheries and to the search for a northwest passage which would provide access to the spice trade of the East. Spain's maritime strength prevented English explorers from interfering with the Spanish sea routes. However, a major change in English-Spanish relations occurred in the 1550s owing to events in the Netherlands. Philip II succeeded to the throne in 1556 and two years later left the Spanish Netherlands in the hands of a viceroy, Cardinal Granvelle, whose rule provoked a series of local revolts leading to open rebellion by the Netherlands. England favored the Dutch rebels, for undisturbed Spanish control in the Netherlands would make a Spanish invasion of England much easier. Spanish intrigues fomenting a Catholic uprising in England lent support to the fear of invasion. These contentions were linked to England's competition with Spain on the high seas when Queen Elizabeth's secretary, William Cecil, spoke to the Spanish ambassador (1561), directly challenging the right of the pope to partition the world as the papal bull of 1454 to Henry the Navigator had done. English fears of the Spanish threat and of Catholicism were confirmed when the pope excommunicated Queen Elizabeth in 1570, thereby calling for open revolt against the English throne.

During these years John Hawkins launched his trading activities by supplying African Negroes to Spanish planters in Hispaniola (the modern Dominican Republic). At first permitted, if not fully recognized by the Spaniards, this English trade soon came to be interpreted as an invasion of Spanish territories, in part because it coincided with the trouble in the Netherlands. Hawkins's fleet was partly destroyed in 1568 by the Spanish viceroy in San Juan de Ulua, Mexico. Later in the same year, this attack was countered by England's seizure of Spanish bullion ships, which had fled into English ports to escape the channel pirates. In 1571 Francis Drake started his campaign of privateering in the Caribbean. By the time of Drake's famous voyage of circumnavigation (1577–1580), exploration and privateering had become government policy. Drake's search for a Pacific end of the reputed northwest passage, his occupation of the California coast in the queen's name, and the triumphant conclusion of his voyage with its colossal plunder from Spanish settlements and shipping were met with widespread acclaim in England.

Hawkins's privateering had shown that the Spanish sea routes could be plundered. Drake's circumnavigation revealed that Spain and Portugal had to defend widely scattered strongholds in the Mediterranean, the Atlantic, the North Sea, and the Pacific. Against this background, English exploration and privateering, like overseas trade and colonial settlement, were conceived "for the good of the Nation, the terror of Antichrist, the comfort of the Church, the honour of our Prince, the renowne of our kingdom, and the immortality of your owne name," as it says in the preamble of a book dedicated to Sir Francis Drake.[11] Where Spaniards and Portuguese had undertaken a Christian mission with the blessing of the pope, Englishmen sailed forth recalling "legends of booty easily won from Spanish incompetence, and righteously won from torturers of Protestants and oppressors of Indians."[12] No undertaking of the sixteenth and seventeenth centuries was without its religious motive. Through preaching and the printing press, the language of the Gospel and of anti-Spanish feeling had the power to crystallize national sentiment.

English overseas trade had been in the hands of foreign merchants for centuries, despite much English opposition. The alien traders enjoyed royal protection because their prices and customs dues were advantageous to the crown. By the mid sixteenth century, 42 percent of the export of woolen products was still in foreign hands. Moreover, English trade was confined geographically: England's most valuable markets were in Western Europe. Expansion beyond these markets proceeded slowly. The English Muscovy Company was founded in 1555 and explored the possibilities of the Russian market. Some English merchants became engaged in a precarious but lucrative slave trade in Africa, and trading benefits accrued to the mercantile community from the North Atlantic fisheries. But the habitable part of the North American continent remained unexplored by English navigators until Frobisher attempted to find a northwest passage in 1576. Central and South America were under Spanish control, and the Near and Far East were preserves of the Venetians and the Portuguese.[13] Yet much of the world which was closed to ordinary English trade, was "open" to English pirates. Profits from privateering could be so extraordinarily high that financial support of such ventures was often more attractive, despite the risks, than investment in ordinary trade.[a]

In the 1570s and 1580s, the English fleet was considerably expanded, adding yet another impetus to the drift toward war with Spain.[14] Intermittent hostilities had occurred for some fifteen years and in 1585 war broke out, leading to the defeat of the Spanish Armada in 1588. Despite this defeat England was not free from the fear of invasion until Philip II's death ten years later.

Thus, English overseas trade was pursued in a highly charged political setting. If a northwest passage could be found, it would enable England to trade with the Indies and hence compete with Spain. Colonial expansion would secure strongholds for attacks on the Spanish

---

[a]In 1585–1603 the goods brought in by privateers came to 10 to 15 percent of total imports. Also, a large part of the £4.5 million bullion coined during Elizabeth's reign came from plunder of precious metals seized from Spain.

empire and access to precious metals in the Americas. Overseas settlements would provide markets for English products and supply the country with raw materials. Colonial expansion was also desirable for domestic political reasons. There was idleness, crime, and unrest in England, and these social problems were considered the result of unemployment which in turn was attributed to overcrowding. To find outlets for an excess of population was an important argument in favor of colonization.[15] English colonization took on a unique character because in North America there was no docile labor force to be exploited. As a result, the English settlers included laborers as well as masters. Joint stock enterprises and royal charters were required to finance these ventures. The main task of promoters was to attract enough men, capital, and government support to promise rich returns to the investors and the English crown.[16] Colonization, therefore, became a national enterprise rather than one that only promised returns to the king and his favorites.

The crown supported English exploration and colonization at the same time that Queen Elizabeth attempted to conduct a cautious foreign policy. At the beginning of her reign, she contrived to use the Protestant uprisings in Scotland and the religious conflict in France in order to rid herself of the French claims to Scotland and thus of an implicit threat to her throne. But this initial success was temporary. After the treaty of Cateau-Cambrésis of 1559 a new phase of confrontation began,

> . . . dominated by the spy, the assassin, the *agent provocateur*, the Fifth Column, the privateer and the pirate. In England, Spanish agents instigated and supported the plots and risings of the Roman Catholics; in France, Spain promoted the Guise faction. In the Netherlands, as the aristocratic opposition to Philip's centralizing plans hardened, those nobles whose sympathies were Protestant looked to the French Huguenots for support. France herself was plunged into forty years of crippling violence and social chaos, during which she suffered, on a modest count, nine separate civil wars, down to the Peace of Vervins in 1598.[17]

Under these conditions, the queen's attention turned from France to Spain and to the pope's designs against England. English Catholics seemed a potentially subversive group, and some Protestant spokesmen called for their suppression. Elizabeth's own conservative views and the difficulties she faced in minimizing internal divisions led her to steer a wary course, which did not satisfy the believers on either side. Against the Catholicism of Mary Tudor she restored her father's Act of Supremacy with its endorsement of the crown's authority over the church. But with regard to the conduct of religious services—while giving signs of her own Protestant persuasion—she deviated as little as possible from the conventional Anglican pattern with its many Catholic legacies. The

Armada Portrait of Queen Elizabeth I
This majestic portrait was painted shortly after the defeat of the Spanish Armada. On the left the English ships are shown in the light; on the right the Armada is tossed about in the darkness of the storm. Elizabeth's face, set off by the raylike collar of her splendid robe, can be likened to the sun and may have been meant to symbolize "Gloriana," one of many encomiums addressed to her. She rests her hand lightly on the globe and seems to be covering the North American continent. (From the Woburn Abbey Collection by permission of the Marquess of Tavistock and Trustees of the Bedford estates)

queen feared the danger of Protestant extremism both as a threat to her royal authority and as a disruption of popular beliefs.

In affairs of state, she also moved cautiously. When the Netherlands revolted against Spain, Elizabeth held the view that the Spanish crown had the rightful authority over the country; to deny that would put the royal prerogative in question. Later, she supported the Dutch cause, but in her eyes the Dutch merchants were subjects of Spain and as rebels they were questionable allies. She snubbed the middle-class negotiators sent to her court and obviously preferred to deal with aristocrats as the natural leaders of society.[18]

Elizabeth's attitudes grew out of her role as a Protestant sovereign and a ruler without heir with profoundly conservative impulses in all matters touching religious and political affairs. As MacCaffrey has put it,

> While her contemporaries' reactions to politics were cast more and more in the frames of ideology or of policy, the Queen's reactions to any given political situation remained highly personal ones. On some occasions her responses arose almost automatically from . . . her reverence for the prerogatives of royalty. . . . On other occasions she could give way to unexpected impulse. . . .
>
> Since many of the men surrounding her held vigorous and clear-cut ideas about national policy, every major—and most minor—decisions were the culmination of a long, complicated and uncomfortable sequence of maneuvers in which conciliar petition, persuasion, and exhortation alternated with royal hesitation, irritation, and obstinacy. There arose a basic political pattern in which the stubborn biases of the royal mind repeatedly came athwart the harsh circumstances of contemporary politics and counter to the policies, the ambitions, and the fears of her councillors.[19]

Interpretations have alternated between very positive and very negative portrayals of the queen's statecraft, often depending on an estimate of the economic and political problems she faced at home.[20] But there is little dispute about the queen's great caution in her domestic and foreign policies.

Popular opinion was not so moderate. Following the Catholic reign of Mary Tudor, a large number of Protestant Englishmen defined the political situation in terms of their opposition to Spain and the Catholic danger.[21] To them, Spain represented the Catholic church. As a world empire, Spain was a political and commercial threat to England. Catholic subversion in England after 1559 was traced to Spanish influence. Mary Stuart became a focus for religious and political discontent, Catholic missionaries infiltrated the country, and the papal excommunication of Elizabeth in 1570 released English Catholics from their duty of obedience to the queen. Broadsheets and preaching plus hearsay and fantasy added to the tension.[b] This convergence of opinion had been greatly enhanced by the religious issues of the 1550s.

Mary Tudor's accession to the throne in 1553 had reestablished Catholicism, thus reversing the English Reformation initiated by Henry VIII. Under Mary, about eight hundred Protestant nonconformists went into exile on the Continent. The implications of this Catholic interregnum for the emergence of a nonconformist intelligentsia are discussed further on. Here I call attention to the martyrological literature

---

[b]English writers of the period used references to republican ideas from the classics, the Venetian constitutions, the fighting Protestants of France, and the revolt of the Netherlands as political and religious models for reform in England. All these symbols could be united through opposition to Spain.

in which zealous Protestant believers defined England's new aspiration as a world power at a time when the country's prospects seemed in great jeopardy. A large number of annals and histories were published first on the Continent and then in England, after the exiles returned during the first years of Elizabeth's reign. John Foxe's *Actes and Monuments* (1563), commonly called the *Book of Martyrs*, was a classic of this literature and had a lasting impact.

Foxe was one of the Marian exiles. He noted that God's church works not with the sword but with printing, reading, and preaching. The Marian exiles prepared a new translation of the Bible. The Protestant conception of the individual's relation to God emphasized the Bible printed in the language of the congregation in contrast to the Catholic emphasis on a mass conducted in Latin. In addition, Foxe's *Book of Martyrs* helped to identify Protestantism with the national mission of England. The Scriptures contained the record of accomplished fact and revealed truth. The task of history was to retrace events in accord with scriptural authority.

[Foxe's book] provided a circumstantial account of the events which led directly to the queen's accession. In the stories of the Marian martyrs, with Elizabeth's own story for climax, it presented in the most vivid dramatic terms the essence of the faith presumed to have been established in the national Church by her authority.

It framed these stories in an account of ecclesiastical history which purported to show that this faith was the same for which the martyrs of the primitive Church had died, the same which had been brought uncorrupted to Britain in the beginning directly from the apostles. This account of Church history the book also linked to a history of the long succession of native rulers down to Elizabeth, shown as owing their authority directly to divine appointment and prospering or not, and their people with them, according as they heeded their vocation to defend the faith and the people in the faith, or suffered themselves to be misled by false counsellors, or overborne by misbelieving usurpers and invaders. And to conclude, the book made plain that by all the signs to be found in scripture and history the will of God was about to be fulfilled in England by a prince perfect in her obedience to her vocation, ruling a people perfect in their obedience to her authority.[22]

The English church was a body of the elect charged with transmitting this message to the people. The elect and the church were identified with the nation, the nation with the queen, and the queen with the country's mission. The religion of the Word was synonymous with a national community, set apart from all others by God for purposes of His own. The elect were called to cooperate with the Lord, for they were His chosen agents whose enemies were in league with Satan. "God is English," exclaimed John Aylmer in 1559, "for you fight not only in the quarrel of your country but also and chiefly in defense of His true religion and of His dear son Christ." Preaching of this kind appealed to the sentiments of "true believers."[23] The whole nation was elect if it but followed the lead provided by these spokesmen, a sentiment existing side by side with the fact that a great majority of the people were indifferent to questions of church government provided no one interfered drastically with established church practices.[24] However questionable this mixture of anti-Catholicism and conventional religion may have been on theological grounds, it was a bracing doctrine indeed at a time when the country was threatened by subversion and gradually rallying its forces to mount a challenge against the Spanish empire.[25]

The international setting of sixteenth-century England suggests the political and ideological context in which a backward society was transformed into a major European power. For the first time, England became a national society. Following major military defeats during the fifteenth century, the country had lost its great fiefs in France, some of which it had held intermittently since the Norman conquest. Diplomatic reversals under Cardinal Wolsey followed in the early sixteenth century. The English Reformation can be seen as an assertion of English nationalism at a time when several other developments facilitated the growth of national unity. English towns favored a strong central government, for, in contrast to the Continent, they did not dominate the surrounding countryside and therefore could not fend for themselves. Under the Tudors, government administration definitely became more centralized and bureaucratic, thus strengthening the monarchy. At the local level, the Reformation put the administrative organization of the parish at the disposal of justices of the peace who were appointed by the crown. Once again, English society developed a balance between strong central and strong local rule, represented at the national level by a series of accommodations between king and parliament. Perhaps the most important step toward national unification was the subordination of the church to monarchical authority. Since the king was both sovereign of

John Foxe's Book of Martyrs
This elaborate title page of *Actes and Monuments* depicts the main message of the work. The left side shows Protestant martyrs burning at the stake singing or trumpeting their praises of the Lord, and above them those gone to heaven and the angels similarly praising the Lord. The right panel shows the devil and his minions trumpeting their evil works while a Catholic mass below them appears to worship that satanic company. The left bottom panel portrays the Protestant worship of The Word from the pulpit; the Hebrew word for God (Adonai) appears like the sun before which the devout kneel in adoration. The right bottom panel shows a Catholic priest blessing the congregation, some of whom are holding prayer rosaries in their hands. To the right a procession led by priests moves towards an image of the crucified Christ in what is—to the Protestant—a merely ceremonial display of piety. (Folger Shakespeare Library)

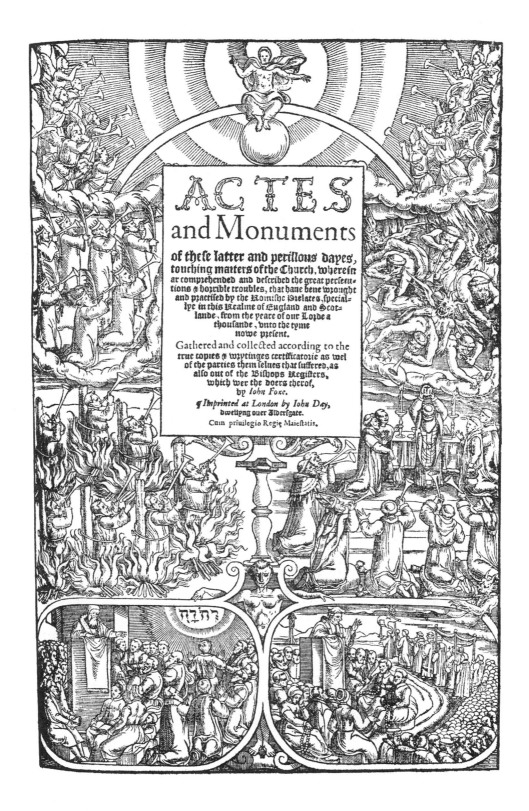

ACTES
and Monuments

of these latter and perillous dayes,
touching matters of the Church, wherein
ar comprehended and described the great persecutions & horrible troubles, that haue bene wrought
and practised by the Romishe Prelates, special-
lye in this Realme of England and Scot-
lande, from the yeare of our Lorde a
thousande, vnto the tyme
nowe present.

Gathered and collected according to the
true copies & wrytinges certificatorie as wel
of the parties them selues that suffered, as
also out of the Bishops Registers,
which wer the doers therof,
by Iohn Foxe.

¶ Imprinted at London by Iohn Day,
dwelling ouer Aldersgate.

Cum priuilegio Regiæ Maiestatis.

his country and head of the church, religious belief and national feeling could merge under a popular sovereign like Queen Elizabeth. The early Protestant reformers were English patriots and strong supporters of the monarchy. In an era of national ascendancy, most of these reformers were politically conservative so that the religious emphasis on individual conscience was not easily transformed into a theoretical right of resistance to constituted authority.[26]

Before turning to the leaders who effected the change toward parliamentary supremacy, a digression on the term *reference society* is in order, for the idea implied by that term recurs in each of the following chapters. Sixteenth-century England was still comparatively slow in the commercialization of labor and capital, but the country witnessed a flourishing trade, a rapid commercialization of land, and a high degree of intellectual mobilization. The awakening of both national awareness and of self-confidence mixed with apprehension was due in good part to English perceptions of French, Spanish, and Catholic intentions. It was due also to English self-perceptions vis-à-vis the Spanish world empire. I shall use the term *reference society* whenever intellectual leaders and an educated public react to the values and institutions of another country with ideas and actions that pertain to their own country.[27]

PURITANS, LAWYERS, AND "THE COUNTRY"

The international, economic, and religious changes of the sixteenth century prepared the way for the reconstitution of English government during the seventeenth century. In the process, the traditional supremacy of the king was gradually replaced by the supremacy of the king-in-parliament (that is, by a sharing of highest authority between king and parliament as representatives of the country). During the reigns of Queen Elizabeth (1558–1603), James I (1603–1625), and Charles I (1625–1649) opposition to the concept of royal supremacy was gradually intensified by three overlapping groups: Puritan preachers, common lawyers, and spokesmen of "the country" in parliament. Each of these groups had a subculture of its own as well as a common meeting ground in parliament, for many members of parliament were themselves Puritans and lawyers, or closely associated with them. The following section discusses the separate settings of the three groups, and the concluding section examines basic ideas of constitutional reform which were promulgated in a religious, legal, and parliamentary framework. My discussion of the religious issues will be confined to the main contrast between Anglicanism and Puritanism, that is, between the principle of an episcopal hierarchy and a presbyterian or congregational election of ministers of the church.

These terms require some explanation since they are difficult to avoid but also difficult to define. The term *Puritan* was frequently used in the seventeenth century to designate particularly rigorous forms of the Protestant persuasion. The term generally designated the intensity of Protestant belief and practice within the Anglican church, while doctrinal nonconformity *and* separation from the church were designated by terms like *Brownist*, *Anabaptist*, and so forth. My use of the word is nonspecific, as suggested by Basil Hall: "Puritan is the regular word for those clergymen and laymen of the established Church of England whose attitude ranged from the tolerably conformable to the downright obstreperous, and to those who sought to presbyterianize that Church from within."[28] Anglicanism or the Anglican church means the Church of England which under Henry VIII and Elizabeth I retained in its doctrine and ritual many Catholic features that were changed only slowly in a Protestant direction. The distinctive feature of the Anglican church is its government by a council of bishops in conference—hence the term *episcopacy*. Presbyterianism as a manner of thinking about the doctrine and government of the Christian church owes its greatest debt to the teaching of Calvin. The term *presbyter* means elected elder and refers to the idea that Christ as the only head of the church moves his people to elect from their midst various persons to discharge the church's functions. The presbyterian principle of election conflicts with the episcopal principle of hierarchy. Congregationalism emphasizes the electoral principle even more than Presbyterianism, since it stresses the autonomy of each congregation as a fellowship of equals and hence rejects all kinds of hierarchical subordination. Even so, Congregationalism is not as radical in this respect as other Protestant groups which derive from the so-called Independents of seventeenth-century England, like the Quakers, some groups of Baptists, and others.

The Religious Aspect

Religious dissent and treasonable disloyalty toward the king were judged severely in the sixteenth century. Contemporary opinion accepted the view that convicted heretics must suffer the penalty of burning at the stake, and treason was likewise punishable by death. In the English Reformation, these views were tested severely. By his Act of Supremacy (1534), Henry VIII confronted his Catholic subjects with the alternative of disobeying their sovereign ruler or betraying their faith. In 1553, twenty years after this Protestant reform, policy was abruptly reversed when Mary Tudor confronted her Protestant subjects with the same alternative of treason or heresy. In practice, most men complied first by obeying the Act of Supremacy and later by obeying the restoration of Catholicism. The Marian government aided this accommodation by permitting determined nonconformists to emigrate.

Yet many nonconformists remained in England. It is estimated that in less than four years of Mary Tudor's reign some 275 persons were convicted of heresy and executed. The largest number of victims were artisans and laborers, which confirms that English Protestantism was a popular movement despite its original, political motivation. Among these martyrs to their faith, there were also high church dignitaries such as the archbishop of Canterbury and the bishop of London. Their martyrdom was publicized instantly by their exiled brethren who had moved to the Continent, where they were allowed to settle in self-governing communities.[29] The exiled group comprised some 800 persons, among them 472 males with a nonconformist core of 186 clergymen, clerics who had not yet been ordained, students of theology, self-styled preachers, and the ex-religious.[30]

Such exile of true believers bred dissent. Among the Protestant refugees, a minority came to reject Anglican church practices altogether because they retained too many Catholic elements. This minority went into a second exile from Frankfurt to Geneva where they formulated their religious commitment, based on an overwhelming sense of mission. They were prophets of the Word who felt personally called to bear witness to the truth of the Lord. By that standard, all mundane affairs and indeed the very structure of constituted authority were matters of no value. In a stream of pamphlets filled with invective and denunciation, these Protestant exiles expressed a radical devaluation of the world. They would recognize authority only if it promoted God's glory. They recognized no distinctions of rank. In the sight of God all men are equal, for all men are equally responsible for the iniquities of this world and equally duty-bound to fulfill His commands.[31] One cannot know what the outcome of this reforming zeal might have been if the exiles had been forced to wander in the wilderness for decades. The death of Mary Tudor allowed the reformers to come home and seemed to vindicate their sense of mission.

> The promptitude with which providence thus brought about their anticipated deliverance confirmed their sense of their selection, and they at once made ready to participate in the fulfillment of its design. . . . And yet that providence should be left to shape its ends as it would, or the new queen her policies, was the last thing to occur to the returning exiles and their partisans. Believing that they had everything to lose if she should fail them, they undertook at once to impose upon her, her government and the public their conception of the role which the Lord expected her to play. They announced at once that a great new age was about to begin for the Church and the nation, and that Elizabeth was the appointed agent for bringing it about.[32]

Michael Walzer has characterized this "revolution of the saints" as the first appearance of radical politics in modern European history. From Elizabeth's accession to the throne in 1558 to the outbreak of the civil war in 1640, elite groups of true believers emerged which were dedicated to reforming the religious life of the country.

To appreciate the impact of these believers, it is necessary to visualize the local role of the church throughout the medieval period. Men and women attended Sunday services regularly and were liable to penalties if they did not. Each householder had to pay one-tenth of his produce (*tithe*) to the parish. The ecclesiastical courts handed out penalties not only for heresy, nonattendance at church, or sexual immorality, but also for working on Sundays or Saint's days, for nonpayment of tithes, and for other transgressions. These courts were an irritant for the well-to-do who could escape sentencing, but a burden for the poorer people who had to suffer the penalties. At the same time, the church was the center of social life, especially in the rural areas. Military training went on in the churchyard. Titles to property were kept in the church. Parish officials managed poor relief and administered corporal punishment for petty crimes. In this setting, the parson played a major role in the political and moral life of his parishioners, and was enjoined to make government announcements from the pulpit and to preach sermons in support of official policies. In many cases, he was the best-educated man in the parish and the only accredited expounder of Christian doctrine. Since the church censored books and determined the content of education, no other authoritative opinions were available. Inevitably, the words of the parson carried great weight. Parsons were nominated regularly by the main landed proprietors of the area, and bishops were legally bound to accept such nominees; thus, the ecclesiastical hierarchy was closely tied to the landed wealth of the country.

All these functions were in jeopardy when the Reformation questioned the legitimacy of the Catholic church. Attacks on church property continued from the dissolution of the monasteries to the reign of Queen Elizabeth. Abbeys, friaries, and other church buildings were converted to secular uses. Penance and the sale of indulgences were abolished. Altars, statues, and other traditional objects of church service were destroyed. Under Mary Tudor and Elizabeth, efforts were made to reverse these developments or prevent abuses, but the main difficulties of the church were economic. By allowing the parson to marry, his financial needs and aspirations increased, while the church had difficulty in making clerical careers financially attractive.[c]

[c]The Anglican church sought to ease its economic problems by selling or leasing rights to tithes and patronage. Such rights to the income of the church, or to its power of appointing ministers to a living, were called "impropriated." The laymen who owned or rented impropriated rights could make a handsome profit by allowing the minister an utterly inadequate income out of their proceeds. In 1603 there were 3,849 impropriated livings out of a total of 9,244, or 41.5 percent. One clergyman often held several livings,

The conditions of the Anglican church gave an impetus to church reform, and for a time that drive was at least tolerated by the Elizabethan government. When the Marian exiles returned to England after 1558, a number of them (along with other nonconformists) were appointed to positions in the church. From the standpoint of the government, these men were needed to reverse the policies of Mary Tudor and ensure a clergy personally loyal to Elizabeth. At the same time, leading Puritans wanted to push reform further and hoped for the queen's support of their cause. However, the queen would not tolerate her authority over the church to be challenged. She demanded "exact order and uniformity," and Archbishop Parker (in his *Book of Advertisements* of 1566) laid down fixed rules for the conduct of public worship. Enforcement of this policy was sporadic because many bishops sympathized with the reformers, as did many landed patrons who controlled parishes. Clergymen who refused to obey were suspended from office, but discipline was hampered because ceremonies of the church were in great disorder. Hence, many clergymen were able to conduct services in accord with their own precepts without risking suspension.[d]

---

because each of them paid very little. Pastoral duties were neglected as a result. Also, nearly 60 percent of the benefices of the church were occupied by persons who had been denied the license to preach, because the church authorities considered them either unqualified or politically unreliable. Only 3,804 licensed preachers had earned a university degree.[33]

[d]Queen Elizabeth and her early Stuart successors were concerned with these questions for reasons of state as much as of religion. They preferred the Book of Prayers to preaching because the latter fostered disputation and encouraged disobedience. The paucity of preachers and their lack of education did not trouble them if only the established form of worship was preserved. Elizabeth preferred the middle way in religious matters: "Protestant doctrine for the intellectuals, Catholic ceremonies for the masses."[34] Hence, resistance to the "religious settlement" of 1558 and other veiled attempts to reform the church were considered a defiance of the law and the royal prerogative. Harsher measures against nonconformists may be dated from 1577, when the queen suspended Archbishop Grindal and ordered the suppression of meetings in which clergymen gathered for the study of Scriptures (so-called "prophesyings"). With the appointment of Archbishop Whitgift in 1583, a period of even greater repression set in. A Court of High Commission was appointed which supplemented the ordinary diocesan controls of the church. Nonconformity as an organized movement was curtailed, but issuance of a penal code against Catholics in 1593 made clear that the queen was determined to maintain her intermediate position. The position remained basically the same under James I (1603–1625), though with a more permissive policy toward Catholics on the one hand and—at least verbally —a more consistent pressure against Puritans on the other. The Millenary Petition (1603), which claimed to express the views of more than a thousand ministers, only urged the abolition of some practices like the ring in marriage or the sign of the cross in baptism, while other matters like the cap and surplice were to be left optional. But even these studiously moderate demands were rejected. James I insisted on conformity because such demands appeared to him as a presbyterian attack on the bishops and through them on his own supremacy.

Yet the intrinsic radicalism of the Puritans could not be disguised, for Puritan spokesmen advanced the claims of Scripture against all external aspects of church organization. In so doing, they tended to discount the sacred character of the priest while elevating the self-respect of the congregation.[35] Preaching of this kind was firmly circumscribed under Elizabeth and James I. But it was not crushed, because the Puritans had powerful sympathizers at court who found the more moderate nonconformists useful in keeping a political balance among conflicting interests, even though they were ready to discipline, imprison, or even hang the most fanatic dissenters.[36] The preaching of the Word was the ideological and organizational mainstay of the Puritan movement within the framework of church and state. Puritans were not separatists; they wanted to reform the church from within.

By 1539 the Bible as the foundation of truth had become available in the vernacular. In his sermons on selected passages from the Scriptures,

> the preacher . . . taught people to see themselves, their own predicaments, the predicaments of their time, mirrored in the scriptural saga of spiritual striving. He demonstrated by what they could not but take for incontrovertible proof the way of escape from frustration, doubt and confusion, and he described the inner process by which such relief would make its coming known, the way of life that must inevitably follow, and the ineffable reward.[37]

Protestant churches became auditoria for the pulpit rather than places for processions and ceremonies with their organ music, prayers, and expositions of the catechism. To Puritans, Archbishop Laud's (1633–1645) emphasis on "the beauty of holiness" in ritual and ceremony seemed little better than popery. The restoration of priests to a position of privilege, the enclosure of the altar, and the insistence on kneeling at communion suggested the doctrine of the real presence of Christ's body and blood in the sacrament and thus a reversal of the Reformation.[38]

Preachers and writers who had been driven into exile or hiding under Mary Tudor found that preaching was an important organizational device, and soon there were more men eager to preach than the church could support. There was a prima facie case for ordaining and licensing recruits capable of preaching, because in 60 percent of the benefices the incumbent did no preaching. As a result, a new institution of lectureships developed:

> [They provided] for regular preaching in addition to the legally required quarterly or monthly sermons and a nexus between the various components of the Puritan connection. The universities provided the training ground and recruiting place for lecturers; the town corporation, gentry patron, or city parish provided not only the pulpit and frequently the financial basis of lectures, but also powerful friends to protect and intercede in the lecturers' behalf.[39]

The Puritan preachers saw themselves as called on to do God's will on earth. Their task was difficult, since congregations were either indifferent, despairing, or overconfident. As William Haller has put it, "They had in the first place to arouse men out of indifference by warning them of the wrath to come. After that they were engrossed with two supreme dangers to morale, the failure of confidence and the excess of confidence."[40] Earnest preachers created an intense atmosphere in which their passionate cultivation of the Christian spirit verged on subversion of the Anglican church.

THE LEGAL ASPECT

Neither then nor today do lawyers fit this image of nonconformist intellectuals. They were men of affairs in contrast to Puritan divines who stood in the service of the Lord. Lawyers were organized in an officially recognized guild and pursued a highly remunerative career as free professionals, whereas Puritan divines were appointed to their livings or lectureships and often enjoyed only a modest subsistence. However, lawyers played an important, perhaps a decisive, role in the great constitutional debates of the seventeenth century. Sir Edward Coke (1552–1634) was the most famous, but still only one of many, legal spokesmen for the view that the ancient law of the land circumscribed the prerogative jurisdiction of the crown. This limitation of royal absolutism resulted from the conservative claims of a profession which was jealously safeguarding its jurisdiction.

There were important affinities between Puritans and lawyers. Puritans sought to reform the church without separating from it. Similarly, English lawyers used a common-law tradition to oppose absolutist claims, but maintained their loyalty to the crown. Lawyers and their clerical brethren stood for hallowed precedent, whether this consisted of Anglo-Saxon antecedents, Magna Carta, or the congregational practices of the primitive church. Lawyers opposed on legal grounds the prerogative claims of the Court of High Commission (the inquisitorial commission under Archbishop Whitgift) which Puritans opposed on grounds of conscience. Ties based on principle, kinship, and policy account for the fact that in a critical period lawyers and Puritans became influential spokesmen in the House of Commons, united in their opposition to royal absolutism.[41]

The legal profession had developed over a long period. A system of courts and a body of law had become established by the thirteenth century. By the early fourteenth century, legal education had become divided between clerical and secular institutions, with the universities teaching Roman and canon law and the four Inns of Court (as well as the associated Inns of Chancery) teaching common law. The contrast between equity and common law proved to be one basis for the constitutional transformation of seventeenth-century England. The common law was essentially the law of the land, handled by the Court of Common Pleas and involving the bulk of the important litigation until well into the sixteenth century.ᵉ In its early form, the common law had considerable flexibility. Cases could move from court to court; the division between different jurisdictions were not hard and fast. Royal intervention and constant contact with the king's council permitted the judges to exercise a good deal of discretion. Their own training as ecclesiastics in Roman and canon law also encouraged them to temper the rigid application of rules by considerations of equity, defined as "the operation of conscience in legal proceedings."⁴³ But after 1316 no ecclesiastic was appointed to a judgeship, and the Statute of Northampton (1328) declared that no royal command shall disturb the course of the common law. By the mid-fourteenth century, equity was disappearing from the practice of common law.

From then on, the role and procedure of the courts were changing. The bench and bar repeatedly declared that cases had to be decided in accord with ancient usage in contrast to the earlier period when the courts could use their discretion in deciding similar cases. When the judges could not make up their minds in difficult cases parliament, lay commissioners, or a group of lords undertook to settle the matter in the

---

ᵉKnowledge and skill were required to formulate the issue to be tried, to present the claims of the litigants, and to aid the court in the application of laws to that issue. Legal knowledge became an object of secular education, for the church increasingly discouraged the clergy from practicing law outside the ecclesiastical courts. The history of legal education is also a history of court procedure which became specialized as the judicial system was elaborated. At successive stages, professional advocates were called narrators, serjeants, barristers, and a variety of other names, designating distinctions of status and function, but by the mid-fifteenth century the legal profession was subdivided into two groups. One group comprised lecturers and students (apprentices) at the Inns of Court and Chancery from whose ranks judges and barristers would eventually be chosen. The other group consisted of attorneys and solicitors who specialized in the drafting of legal documents and had contact with clients, but were not called to the bar and indeed were not members of the Inns of Court.

Sitting judges were at the top of this hierarchy. They alone nominated new judges who were then appointed by the crown. Judges had the right to serve in the Inns of Court as examiners and to call an apprentice to the bar. Only those admitted to the bar had the right to practice law or lecture and argue in the moot courts at the Inns. Ordinarily, the Inns were governed by the lecturers (Masters of the Bench), a self-perpetuating body presided over by a member elected annually. The Masters of the Inns of Court were neither university professors nor jurists writing commentaries, but practicing judges and barristers whose teaching was tied directly to the work of the courts. English legal education retained its empirical character of learning the law as a "craft" rather than as a "science." Practice in the courts was the main foundation of a career in the law, which led to a judicial post or the work of a barrister.⁴²

name of the king. This meant that when the courts gained some independence from the crown, they lost their recourse to the use of discretion. At the local level, rich landowners had little interest in equity, which made it easier for their poorer neighbors to bring them into court and win cases.

> The process by which the final single issue was ultimately arrived at was refined and elaborated by the ruthless application of pure dialectical method, and became an exact science of extraordinarily minute and subtle technicality. . . . Each of the forms of action—i.e., the actions which it was possible to bring under an original writ—required strict adherence to the detailed rules of pleading applicable to it. The choice of the wrong writ on which to base a claim or a mistake in the pleadings . . . meant the instant dismissal of the suit. "Duplicity", which meant not deceitfulness, but pleading or attempting to plead more than one issue, was at once fatal, even though a clear miscarriage of justice would result.[44]

Bench and bar also had an interest in maintaining a hardened system of writ and precedent, and elaboration of technicalities gave overwhelming advantage to those who could afford to pay for the assistance of the most skilled legal practitioners. Moreover, the upper grades of the legal profession were as a rule indistinguishable from the prosperous country gentry—in terms of education, social status, and local or national political office. The disappearance of equity from the common law coincided with the weakening of royal power, and with the ascendance of the baronage since the fourteenth century.

However, the common law had limitations which provided an opening for new developments. During the sixteenth century, the common law courts were denounced for the slowness and costliness of their procedures. The leisurely pace of court schedules was onerous for a growing commercial society. Designed for people who owned land, its writs, pleadings, and weakness in the finding of facts were inadequate in cases involving other kinds of property and different types of litigants. The use of executive methods and more equitable rules were demanded; these were matters best handled by securing prompt personal attendance of the parties and by giving them direct personal commands to act or desist.[45] Accordingly, the principle of the royal prerogative was upheld in certain courts in which the "operation of conscience in legal proceedings" was applied. During the Tudor period, the use of special writs and courts (Star Chamber, Court of Requests, of Chancery, and others) developed swiftly. These courts used various forms of petition between the parties. Proceedings of the crown could be initiated by information, citation, and the like, thus employing the forms used by administrative officers toward their subordinates. The prerogative courts were a means of ensuring the broader judicial use of royal authority.[f]

The courts of the common law were identified with the interests of the landed gentry and the legal profession. Judicial office was considered private property and became the source of immense fortunes. The language of the time referred to such property as pertaining to the liberty of the subject, a usage reminiscent of the earlier identification between privilege and liberty. The common law was thus associated with the rigid defense of privilege. By contrast, the prerogative courts adapted their procedure to the demand for equity in social and economic disputes, especially in the Court of Requests. But this gain in flexibility was partial and temporary. The courts of Star Chamber and High Commission buttressed royal supremacy as they handled religious dissension, economic distress, and domestic sedition. Under the influence of chancellors trained in the common law, other courts like Chancery soon developed delays and intricacies of their own. When such drawbacks mounted, courts of equity became unpopular in turn and the king's privy council took many cases in order to handle them more expeditiously.[47]

The people at large probably stood in fear of the courts generally. There was little chance to prevail against the massive interests of lawyers and landowners. Perhaps men had a better chance in the prerogative courts. The baronial disorders of the fifteenth century had made people anxious to keep the peace, and in that context the king's court of Star Chamber was a popular institution. Moreover, under the royal prerog-

---

[f]In the early Tudor period, there was no fundamental incompatibility between the prerogative courts and the common law courts. Kings and their ministers did not press for a fundamental legal reform. Common lawyers recognized the jurisdiction of the Privy Council and the Court of Chancery in a large number of cases involving mercantile and domestic disputes as well as sedition, heresy, unlicensed printing, perjury, and riot. An exception is found in Cardinal Wolsey's tenure of office (1516–1529), which was marked by an emphasis on equity in hearing poor men's complaints and by a determined assertion of the royal prerogative against the interests associated with the common law. Under Wolsey's successor, Sir Thomas More, conflict was muted, but tension remained. When Henry VIII decided to use parliament in his quarrel with the pope, the king had to compromise since the common lawyers were strongly represented in the House of Commons. When the king sought to forestall legal methods of evading feudal dues, his conflict of interest with the landed parliament became manifest and negotiations were protracted. To some extent, both sides gained. The royal jurisdiction of the Chancery was expanding at the expense of the common law courts, the conciliar tribunals of the crown were popular, and through the prerogative courts the crown handled much legal business. On the other hand, the king appointed common lawyers to the office of chancellor. A decree of 1546 proclaimed that only common lawyers trained in an Inn of Court and appointed by the chancellor and the two chief justices were eligible to plead in the prerogative courts. The study of canon law was forbidden, and law reports came to record judicial decisions rather than pleadings, giving still greater prestige to the judiciary.[46]

ative even a poor man could still hope for the "operation of conscience" in the handling of his complaint. In the perspective of the time, both the common law and the king's prerogative came to be considered parts of the English heritage.

To us, it appears that seventeenth-century England witnessed a struggle for sovereignty between the king and the men of property represented in the House of Commons. Contemporaries did not think in these terms. They were heirs to a tradition in which the king's authority ranked supreme, albeit with the understanding that he take counsel with the great men of his realm.[48] In the seventeenth century that tradition was challenged by the assertion that in certain respects the king's authority was subject to law and the consent of parliament. Yet the lawyers who issued that challenge were traditionalists themselves and had great difficulty freeing themselves from the time-honored acceptance of royal supremacy.

Several cases illustrate this difficulty. Edward Hake (1560?–1604) affirmed the absolute power of the king *and* the freedom of the subject from his duty of obedience when the king's act was against the law. John Pym (1584–1643) denied that "our sovereign Lord the King" had "sovereign power," but he did not claim such power for parliament either. In the 1620s, a major leader of the House of Commons, Sir John Eliot (1592–1632), acted on the principle that parliament's authority must prevail over that of the king. For his pains he was confined to the Tower. Later, Sir John wrote a book which asserted that the king was subject only to the law of God and possessed absolute authority even against the written law. Even Sir Edward Coke championed the royal prerogative in the first part of his career and later became a champion of the common law. In his own mind, he may have felt that there was less of a distinction between these two positions than we see today. For while believing in the king's prerogative, Coke distinguished between disputable and indisputable issues. In his view, the king is bound by common law in matters affecting disputes over private property. On the other hand, the king's prerogative is indisputable in matters involving war and peace and the security of the realm. Yet from a strictly royalist standpoint, the classification of some issues as "disputable" was null and void, since that denied the king's supreme authority in all matters.

In his own mind, Coke was a conservative upholding the time-honored traditions of his country. Yet the potential radicalism of his position became evident when the Stuart monarchs used reasons of "national emergency" to intervene in domestic affairs. Admittedly, the king alone was entitled to judge what constituted an emergency, but Coke's distinction suggests that there were circumstances under which that sovereign judgment itself had to be limited. The crisis of the seventeenth century was precipitated when Charles I (1625–1649) used his "indisputable" prerogative in order to intervene in the "disputable" matters subject to the laws of the land.[49]

"THE COUNTRY"

This label was a term of political discourse in the seventeenth century most commonly applied to the opposition to the crown between 1620 and 1640. Originally, the term had been used as a synonym for "county," but by the time of Queen Elizabeth this meaning was fused with the general idea of representation and the public interest. Also, the "country" was frequently and invidiously contrasted to the court as a mode of existence denoting sturdy honesty and independence as distinguished from the refined and corrupt manners of court society. Hence,

> The term, 'Country', suggested that the men it designated were persons of public spirit, unmoved by private interest, untainted by court influence and corruption—representatives, in short, of the highest good of their local communities and the nation in whose interest they, and they alone, acted.[50]

The term referred to an amorphous but very real concentration of influence in the hands of a group of landed aristocrats in parliament united by their common religious persuasion, legal doctrines, and opposition to the court and the king.

Many writers refer to England's great crisis of the seventeenth century as the English civil war; others do not hesitate to speak of the English revolution. This uncertain terminology is due in part to the restoration of the monarch in 1660, only eleven years after the civil war ended with the execution of King Charles I. Uncertainty may be due as well to the essential conservatism of the Puritan divines who opposed the doctrine, liturgy, and organization of the Anglican church, and of the common lawyers who opposed royal absolutism. These men wanted to purify and maintain but not overturn the best religious and legal traditions of their country, as they understood them. However, divines and lawyers would have had little political effect by themselves. Their intellectual leadership of the reform movement in church and state was effective only because they received the support of "the country."[51]

Politics in sixteenth-century England centered on ministers of the crown who attracted prominent aristocratic followers and contended with one another for influence on the king or queen. Politics consisted of factional struggles at the court and was little influenced by the bulk of the English aristocracy. As a political factor of consequence, "the country" emerged only in the later sixteenth century when the personal authority of great men at court attracted increasing support from locally prominent gentry; henceforth, the struggle for the ruler's favor involved an increased participation of the ruling aristocracy in the counties. The House of Commons increased in size from 298 members in Henry VIII's first parliament to 467 in the first parliament of James I. Borough representation was extended, competition for seats grew, and education at universities or in the Inns of Court became common among members of parliament. The range of parliamentary activity increased along with the extension of royal power, for parliamentary statutes sanctioned the Act of Supremacy (1534), the dissolution of the monasteries, the creation of new administrative bodies, and the many royal edicts against treason. Under Henry VIII and Mary Tudor, there were occasional instances of parliamentary opposition against the royal will, and such opposition became more pronounced under Puritan leadership in Elizabethan times.

Many segments of the public had become thoroughly alerted to religious and political issues by Catholic conspiracies against a popular, Protestant queen. According to J. E. Neale, the Elizabethan House of Commons was overwhelmingly Puritan in its sympathies. Prominent spokesmen expressed their apprehensions that the rather conservative religious settlement under Elizabeth would once again endanger the Reformation. The Catholic restoration under Mary Tudor was within recent memory. Parliamentary notables agitated for the queen's marriage to secure a Protestant succession to the throne. They advocated penal legislation against Catholics, urged the execution of Mary Stuart, and advised more precautions against Catholic subversion after her death. The civil and religious establishment under Elizabeth had many devoted partisans who did not shrink from personal pressure on the queen. The effect of this agitation was to increase the role of parliament in the public affairs of the realm, but active oppositionists were still a small group and their techniques of opposition undeveloped. Moreover, these critics of the queen's cautious policies were themselves her loyal followers, who did not challenge her personal authority and popularity.

Formal Session of Parliament under Elizabeth I
This picture from Glover's *Nobilitae Politica* shows the presentation of the Speaker of the House of Commons (prolocutor) to the queen, November 1584. He is standing at the rail in the center foreground along with the knights and burgesses who have chosen him at the invitation of the Lord Chancellor. The empty sack directly in front of the throne is for the Lord Chancellor who, in the queen's presence, stands behind the throne to her right and speaks for her, in this case telling the House of the queen's pleasure to accept the choice of Speaker. The core of the parliament is seen in the inner square of four red wool sacks on which are seated the judges and royal counselors. Between the two rows of seated counselors, including the clerk of parliament and the clerk of the crown, are other clerks writing. On the long benches flanking the woolsacks sit the Lords or peers; the lords spiritual or bishops to the queen's left and the lords temporal on the right. (Folger Shakespeare Library)

Procerum   Cancellarius   Pincerna   primogeniti

R Sedes   Rex   Psalt

Cancellarii sedes

Prolocutor

Milites Provinciarum & Burgenses (quos vocant) utrinq, qui Cameram Parlamenti inferiorem constituunt, Prolocutorem conducentes.

Under the reign of James I (1603–1625), these limitations on parliamentary opposition quickly diminished. The Spanish danger and hence the need for unity had passed, while inflation, heavy debts, and the ineptness of the new king readily provoked controversy. The House of Commons had by then developed a corporate consciousness expressed in the declaration that its privileges were not a gift from the crown but a right which could not be abridged without apparent wrong to the "whole state of the realm." In 1607 the House first used the device of "the committee as a whole" by which it could elect its own chairman and thereby evade the rule of the Speaker, who was a nominee of the crown. By these and related procedural innovations, the House won political initiative for itself. This became a source of increasing controversy with the king, finally prompting Charles I to dissolve parliament in 1629 by specific reference to this parliamentary usurpation of authority.

The early Stuart parliaments included an increasing number of men opposing various measures of royal authority, in contrast to the Elizabethan parliaments in which opposition to the queen's policies had gradually diminished. After the dissolution of parliament in 1629, the king exercised personal rule until circumstances forced him to reconvene parliament in 1640, the so-called Long Parliament which sat periodically until 1649. More than a quarter of the members of the Long Parliament had already served as representatives in 1628/29 or earlier; ninety-one or 19.4 percent of 467 had been opponents of the king before the dissolution. Much private consultation among these oppositionists had taken place in the Stuart parliaments since 1604–1610. There were not only complaints against this practice by the king's spokesmen but repeated and explicit defenses of the practice by parliamentary spokesmen. Most important, prominent representatives of "the country" were in illicit communication and met illegally while the king ruled without convoking parliament (1629–1640). Several major leaders of "the country" apparently found a means of continuing their collaboration in the several companies for colonization which held charters from the crown, for under that shelter they could discuss matters other than company business. Militant Puritans were members of these companies, and through intermarriage many of them were related to other opponents of the king's rule. Ties of friendship and a common religious persuasion facilitated a close association with still other opponents. These personal ties among a determined minority help to explain the cohesion of the opposition once the king convened the Long Parliament to help him cope with his rebellious subjects in Scotland. Cohesion of an inner circle of "country politicians" was indispensable for managing the contacts with the Scottish army which were designed to put the king under pressure while preserving the appearance of loyalty to the crown.

During the Long Parliament, the leaders of "the country" engaged in a concerted drive against the monarchy's traditional authority. But these oppositionists were not "progressives" in any modern sense of the word, nor were they prompted by social resentment. On the contrary, they could claim to represent "the country" in the old-fashioned sense that they were pillars of society who had always had the right and privilege to do so. All these oppositionists in parliament were landed aristocrats, justices, lawyers, and other members of England's high society. Among them were prominent peers with strong Puritan sympathies whose political and religious beliefs alone distinguished them from peers loyal to the crown. More surprising still were landed aristocrats who had risen to a middle rank in the service of the king, but were out of sympathy with his policies and apparently felt free to oppose them, since they were not highly enough placed to be directly responsible to the king. In addition, prominent merchants supported the opposition. The leadership of "the country" was clearly in the hands of aristocrats with their contacts in the counties and their many ties with Puritan divines and prominent members of the bar. Without the backing of these aristocratic leaders, divines and lawyers could not have sustained their claim of opposing the "misguided" policies of church and crown in the name of the nation.

CONSENT, EQUALITY, AND LAW

Seventeenth-century England witnessed a major transformation which can be described by several contrasts between the reigns of James I (1603–1625) and George I (1714–1727):

James succeeded by hereditary right, confirmed by Elizabeth's nomination; in 1714 George I owed his throne to an Act of Parliament which passed over many persons with a better hereditary claim. James, like the Tudors before him, chose ministers and favourites as seemed best to him; by the early eighteenth century ministers could not govern without a Parliamentary majority. James was still expected to "live on his own", to finance government from crown lands, feudal dues and the customs: no distinction was drawn between the public and private capacity of the King. Parliament, summoned at the King's absolute discretion, expected to vote taxes only in an emergency (though here theory already lagged behind practical necessity). By 1714 Parliament, in almost permanent session, had complete control of finance. In James' reign members of the landed class themselves admitted to being absurdly undertaxed; in Anne's the gentry paid for Marlborough's wars. By then Parliament had established a degree of control over the executive and over all its actions—including foreign policy, which early Stuart kings had regarded as their private preserve. [In the early seventeenth century] the economy was highly regulated. .... At the end of the period economic policy was formulated by Parliament and *laissez-faire* had succeeded regulation in most spheres.[52]

The Great Seal of England, 1651
The Great Seal was traditionally used to authenticate the most important state documents.
In this case it was struck as a commemorative medal. To show the House of Commons on
the reverse side of the Great Seal of England testified to the ascendance of parliament and
made official the victory of the Commonwealth under Oliver Cromwell over a king who
had wrongfully usurped the authority of parliament. The seal is inscribed, "1651 in the
third year of Freedom by God's Blessing restored." (British Museum)

One way of understanding this transformation is to consider the rein-
terpretation of traditional beliefs by Puritan divines, spokesmen of the
common law, and representatives of "the country."

These reinterpretations had little or nothing to do with modern
ideas of freedom and equality. The freedom of a town, a freehold estate,
a parliamentary franchise, the "liberties of the House of Commons," the
rights and privileges of freemen in the common law courts—these were
the privileges or liberties associated with property. "He that hath no
property in his goods, is not free," as a member of parliament put it in

1624, echoing an earlier statement by Sir Thomas Smith that such men "have no voice nor authority in our commonwealth, and no account is made of them, but only to be ruled."[53] In England, the authority of kings was reinterpreted so as to give greater weight to the mandate of the people. But "people" referred to those who owned property and enjoyed representation in parliament. The main issues of the period arose out of collisions between the king and these propertyholders over the distribution of their respective rights and privileges. Religion was also concerned with property, as, for example, in the titles to former monastic lands, the collection of tithes, or the several livings to which individual church dignitaries were appointed. However, issues of property were secondary to the religious ideas of the Puritan movement which gave the conflicts between king and parliament a broader meaning. For the main challenge to governance by an exclusive hierarchy of dignitaries originated in the religious sphere.

Luther's doctrine of justification by faith alone implied that before God all men were equally sinners, however they might differ in their worldly status. For his part, Calvin based the church on a "communion of saints," in which there was room for elected ministers as interpreters of God's Word, but in which all must share with one another, united in brotherly love. By advancing the claims of Scripture against the primary emphasis on the sacraments, the English Puritans aimed at an administrative revolution of the church. Thomas Cartwright (1535–1603) expressed the main tenets of the Puritan position. As summarized by Haller,

> [the church was to be] the divinely inspired organ of spiritual life in human society, having reciprocal relations with the rulers of this world by acting in complete independence of their authority. Its task was to render men obedient first to God and then under God to Caesar, whose first duty also was to obey God as his Church might direct. . . . Before God all men were equal in sin, equally deserving of damnation. If any were raised above the rest in this world, it was God's doing, not theirs. . . . In the church, the people without distinction of person must choose by whom they were to be taught and served. Parish by parish they should elect their elders and ministers, and the church as a national body should be knit together by a graduated series of representative assemblies drawn from the parishes.[54]

Thus, man's voluntary obedience to the Word of God is the most basic assumption of Puritanism.

Where such voluntary obedience prevails, a proper social order will ensue. Such an order must observe a strict separation between church and state, for Christ's kingdom is not of this world. In making this distinction, Calvin spoke of two worlds "over which different kings and different laws have authority." Cartwright echoed this view when he said that an *ecclesiastical rule under the monarchy* may keep the peace, "yet the peace which is without truth is more execrable than a thousand contentions."[55] A proper organization of the church is separate from the state in that the Word is preached by the *elected minister of a congregation*. Here is the reason for the Puritan opposition to a nonresident clergy, impropriated livings, and stereotyped readings from the Book of Prayers. All this robs the church of a spiritual realm founded on consent and brotherly love. Here also is the reason why ministers must not meddle in civil affairs or hold public office, for in so doing they symbolize the outward force of the state. When men fear the sword, they will question whether their conversion is vouchsafed, as it should be, by the power and simplicity of the Word alone.

Consent or willing obedience is combined in the Puritan creed with the belief in the spiritual equality of men. Social distinctions do not matter in comparison with the inward voice of conscience. Puritans of Cartwright's persuasion did not subscribe to an indiscriminate egalitarianism. They recognized, as Calvin had, that "the gifts of the Spirit are variously distributed." Only those who have made an open profession of the truth are allowed to supervise the examination of a prospective minister and participate in his election. Ultimately, all members of the congregation will know the truth, the world will be free of corruption, and with total obedience to God's word there will be no need for the sword. That time was not yet. Cartwright believed that in the meantime it was the task of the state to serve God's purposes by prompting men to stand before God voluntarily as brothers in truth and submission. This approach implied that the state would lose its reason for being when in the fullness of time the spiritual task would be accomplished. In 1570 Cartwright was dismissed from his Cambridge professorship for seeking to make the state serve as an instrument of the church.

The problem of authority in ecclesiastical affairs was at the heart of the Puritans' "spiritual, serious way of worship" (Richard Baxter, 1642). Preachers of this persuasion wanted to reform rather than challenge the authority of the church. Even a conservative like Archbishop Whitgift (1533?–1604) had conceded that in early Christianity and in free cities a church might well have been governed by elders and elected assemblies. The Puritans wanted to practice now what the archbishop conceded for the remote past. In Whitgift's view, the queen had the last word in all ecclesiastical affairs. He insisted on the superiority of bishops, which derived from the need for order and from the existence of a Christian monarchy.[56] Hence, the Puritan claim that they did nothing against the word of God was null and void, for the Word of God and the word of the ruler were one and the same.

According to Whitgift, there were two kinds of government in the church, the one invisible and spiritual, the other visible and external.

The first is ruled by God alone who directs the hearts and consciences of men. The second is the government executed by man: it consists of external discipline, visible ceremonies, and an order administered by bishops under the authority of the crown. Such an order is indispensable, for there would never be any law if its execution required "every singular man's consent." Such an order is also just because in England royalty governs

> with equity and reason . . . according to the laws that are prescribed for him to rule by. There is neither prince nor prelate in this land that ruleth "after their pleasure and lust", but according to those laws and others that are appointed by the common consent of the whole realm in parliament, and by such laws of this monarchy as never hitherto any good subject hath misliked.[57]

Against this approach, Puritan spokesmen took an exalted view of the ministerial office. They claimed to base their anti-episcopal stand on the eternal decrees of salvation conveyed to the elect by the preaching of the Word. Ministers were spiritually elevated at the expense of bishops. In the Puritan view, the church hierarchy (or episcopacy) represented a human institution not sanctioned by scriptural authority.

Since these preachers of the Word had to order affairs among themselves, their organization of the church was an obvious challenge to established church authority. Strict parity among ministers was a presbyterian principle incompatible with the subordination of one church (or minister) to another. Presbyters had been members of the governing body of the early Christian church, and following that model seventeenth-century Presbyterianism advocated a representative government of the church. (In this view, any hierarchical organization derived from the pope's claim to supreme authority.) At the lowest level the local church would consist of a meeting (*classis*) made up of ministers and elders of the church. Above this, at successively higher levels, synods would be organized. Each meeting or synod would be conducted by a presiding officer selected on a rotating basis so that the principle of parity among ministers and elders would be preserved, in contrast to the Anglican episcopal organization. Yet Presbyterianism held back from full equality. It provided for the subordination of local churches to the ministers and elders of the church, and of their meetings to the synods. Even then, the Presbyterian movement represented a type of religious organization that was bound to conflict with the prevailing views of the Anglican church.

The meetings called "prophesyings" exemplify another challenge. These meetings occurred in market towns where the rural clergy could gather conveniently in the principal church; they were a kind of biblical conference for mutual edification and sociability. Practices at these meetings varied widely. They might involve scholars and students engaged in learned, Latin discourse for mutual instruction. A more popular meeting would permit the public to listen to discussions in the vernacular, or even allow members of the congregation to participate in the discussion of a scriptural passage. Public sermons and discussions were supplemented by private conferences in which the preachers would censure one another's doctrine, life, and manner.[58] Since royal injunctions required the clergy to undertake biblical studies, such conferences were convoked with the approval of the bishop. But such meetings quickly became suspect in the eyes of the church when they came under Puritan influence. Thus, the use of English and public participation exemplified the Puritan belief in the brotherhood of all believers; participation by laymen implied a critique of the church hierarchy with its emphasis on ecclesiastical rank; and the reciprocal edification and control among ministers constituted an exercise of authority outside the channels of the hierarchy.

Cartwright had been dismissed from Cambridge in 1570, and for decades thereafter the preachers of the Word who favored presbyterian principles were in sporadic conflict with spokesmen of the hierarchy like Whitgift, Bancroft, and others. Between the accession of Charles I (1625) and the beginning of the Long Parliament (1640), the Puritan cause, though on the defensive at home, was much invigorated by the example of the American colonies. Moreover, the preaching of the Word had stimulated the rise of a more radical religious movement, culminating in the civil war (1642–1646, 1648). As commander of the parliamentary forces, Oliver Cromwell reorganized the army by giving free reign to the Puritan spirit; and although parliament voiced its misgivings, military success appeared to vindicate the spontaneous religious fervor of the nonconformists fighting the righteous cause.

We have Richard Baxter's circumstantial account of the sentiments to which radical army preachers appealed. They told the soldiers that Christ judges only by the heart and that magistrates have nothing to do with matters of religion. Puritan teaching had already instilled the belief that Christ had entered into the souls of the elect. Now the trouble was

> that there were too many men in the army who, overpersuaded that they had Christ within, were deluded into thinking that they had but to reach forth their hands and retake paradise, . . . just as they had taken Bristol or Basing House or Worcester. That is to say, from Baxter's viewpoint, they were poor simple souls, plunged into mortal error . . . on the crucial point of justification. . . . They jumped to the fallacious and dangerous conclusion that the effect of grace was immediate, absolute, and total, that the coming of Christ was instant or at least proximate, and that the liberation and crowning of the saints was to be looked for not in the indefinite future or upon terms but at once and unconditionally.

Puritan preaching had done its work too well. "Justification by faith alone" helped to win battles in the civil war, but the advocates of a presbyterian church drew back before this radicalization of their own message. Cromwell crushed the agitators in the army. Men like Baxter spent years of anxious pamphleteering in attempts to draw a line between his own hopeful *anticipation* of "the Christian safely landed in Paradise" and this misguided belief that "our Talent, our well doing, our overcoming . . . [is] a *Reason* for our Coronation and Glory."[59] The latter belief modifies the Puritan message by implying a certainty of election based on true faith itself or on secular success. It illustrates an anti-episcopal and egalitarian potential, which had repercussions in the later development of both entrepreneurial and radical political ideologies in English society.

The religious interpretation of consent and equality had an effect on the constitutional transformation of England during the seventeenth century. One reason was the moderation of claims by the political antagonists. England was an intensely conservative country and to many contemporaries the political agitation preceding and accompanying the civil war appeared radical in the extreme. Nevertheless, even radical nonconformists acknowledged some limits to the principle of equality. The Levellers did *not* advocate that equality should be extended below the level of "free" Englishmen to those who were economically dependent on the head of the household.[g] The radicals of the civil war demanded the equality only of those who had a stake in their country.[60] At the same time, the parliamentary leaders of "the country" were more than defenders of their own privileges. In the patriarchal sense that the master is responsible for his dependents, they claimed to represent the interests of the nation.

The champions of "the country" were conservative. They did not set out to alter the established order, but based their stand on the law and the ancient constitution of England.

> What they conceived themselves as contesting, therefore, were those invasions of power that deranged the equilibrium and violated law. For the King to levy impositions on merchandise; to exact forced loans and benevolences; to commit men to prison without showing lawful cause; to lay a direct charge on his people without their common consent in parliament—these things, done by James I and Charles I, they condemned as altogether illegal.[61]

Against this position, spokesmen for the crown did not contend that the king was above the law. Rather, they enunciated the doctrine of the king's prerogative in all matters affecting the general good and safety

[g]*Leveller* is the name of a party that arose in the army of the Long Parliament (c. 1647) and advocated the leveling of the traditional ranks of English society as well as the establishment of a more democratic government.

of the realm. In these matters the king alone was judge of the circumstances in which his "absolute prerogative" applied. Both sides claimed ancient precedent for their positions and thus posed the basic constitutional issue which provoked the civil war.

Zagorin has pointed out that the language of parliamentary debate contained a core of radicalism despite its very real conservatism. The spokesmen of "the country" felt themselves to be the representatives and trustees of "the people" and justified the privileges of parliament on that basis. Phrases like "We are entrusted for our country" or "Let us remember that England sent us" became common. Emphasis was added when various parliamentary leaders noted the fate of continental assemblies under absolute kings: the estates-general of France had held their last meeting in 1614, and the taxing power was conceded to the French king. Charles I had dissolved parliament in 1629 because the exaltation of a representative body jeopardized the exaltation of the king's crown under God.[62]

During the seventeenth century, the supreme authority of the "king-in-parliament" replaced the medieval dualism of kingship. In medieval times, legitimate authority was vested in the king and the great magnates, both claiming rights justified by immemorial custom. Max Weber has recognized the tension implicit in these claims, for immemorial custom endorses the view that what is ancient must remain unaltered, whether it is the king's right to exercise his prerogative and hence use his judgment or the time-honored rights of the magnates who descend from ancient families and offer their counsel and aid at the king's court. However, custom also legitimizes the king's time-honored prerogative of disregarding custom when he deems this necessary for the welfare of the realm as he interprets it.[63] By the second and third decade of the seventeenth century, English constitutionalism had come to embody both principles. Parliamentary spokesmen had specifically justified the rights of parliament on the ground that parliament represented "the country," and they claimed that the king had overstepped his *rightful* prerogative when he denied these rights. To explore this aspect of constitutional reform, we must look at the legal champions of consent who were the architects of constitutional monarchy based on a contract between the people and their king.

Common lawyers, like Puritan divines, sought a new foundation of authority in response to what they conceived as external and internal threats to their country. Puritans had used the ideal of the primitive church of early Christianity in their effort to base religion on an elected minister preaching the Word to his congregation. Lawyers used the fiction of England's ancient constitution in their effort to limit the royal prerogative and raise parliament as the highest judicial and legislative body of the realm. Lawyers, like Puritans, claimed to uphold tradition when they argued in terms of immemorial custom and scriptural truth.[64]

Sir Edward Coke was the most influential interpreter of the common law under Elizabeth and the early Stuarts. He served as solicitor general, attorney general, chief justice of common pleas, and of the king's bench between 1592 and 1616, when he was abruptly dismissed by James I. Thereafter he was active in parliament and played a key role in the Petition of Right of 1628. For Coke, the common law was the ancient and fundamental law of the realm which possessed a pervasive coherence or concordance derived from the "unity and consent" among judges and courts "in so many successions of ages." Ultimately such unity proceeds from God and men should do nothing to disturb it.

> It is a maxim in policy, and a trial by experience, that the alteration of any [fundamental point of the ancient common law] is most dangerous; for that which hath been refined and perfected by all the wisest men in former succession of ages, and proved and approved by continual experience to be good and profitable for the Commonwealth, cannot without great hazard and danger be altered or changed.[65]

With this maxim as a basis, judicial decisions of the past are the proper key to disputed cases in the present. Inconsistencies or contradictions are only apparent and can be readily dispelled by those whose "legal reason" derives from "long studie, often conference, long experience, and continuall observation." For Coke, there was a direct link between his view of the antiquity of fundamental law and the key role of judges and lawyers as expert interpreters of that law. The principle that a previous judicial decision should have authority in deciding a later case (the rule of precedent) came to the fore in the sixteenth century along with the rising prominence of common law.

Such judge-made law contrasts with law enacted by king or parliament. Judge-made law is identified with custom or customary law, consisting of acts repeated again and again because they have been found good and beneficial. A succession of cases having ancient origins acquires the force of law. By contrast, written laws are made by the edicts of princes or councils; they are imposed on the subject without having been tested by experience, which alone can show whether they will fit the circumstances of the people. Thus, enacted laws may grow obsolete, while custom is always up-to-date, or else it would have been abandoned. Statutes may violate fundamental law, they may be copied from foreign sources, and they may have to be repealed because of many inconveniences. On the other hand, custom is indigenous and grows out of the people's experience. Also, statutes are but the wisdom of one man or generation, while custom embodies the wisdom of untold generations, and its retention proves its wisdom and utility. On this basis, Coke concluded that "no man ought to take it on himself to be wiser than the laws."[66]

A fundamental and indigenous English law was almost universally accepted in the sixteenth and seventeenth centuries. Royalist spokesmen argued that the king's sovereign prerogative formed part of immemorial law, much as Coke rested his case for the common law on the ancient constitution. This way of thinking was in accord with the rising nationalism of the period in which an argument gained weight by analogues to ancient precedent, like the king's prerogative to declare war or the Norman conquerors' promise to uphold the old laws of Edward the Confessor.[67] But while everyone rested his case on this type of argument, the spokesmen for the common law tended to shift the discussion in favor of parliament.

The common law, used synonymously with customary law, was judge-made and required the power of "legal reasoning." But it also reflected the wisdom of the people. By associating judicial decision-making with antiquity, the common lawyers linked custom with the idea of consent. For precedents had proved their worth over time by their fitness under changing circumstances, and these precedents embodied innumerable judgments of what was reasonable in specific cases. Custom was constantly adapting but also immemorial, at once flexible and constant. Custom was thus linked with fundamental law, antiquity, native origin, the people's consent, reason, and truth. All these equivalences testified to the glory as well as the continuity of England's ancient constitution.

This ideological structure was bolstered at the same time by a purely negative argument: "For a truly immemorial constitution could not be subject to a sovereign: since a king could not be known to have founded it originally, the king now reigning could not claim to revoke rights rooted in some ancestor's will."[68] In the great agitation leading to the Petition of Right (1628), Coke used this argument with telling effect. Parliament was a court of law, consisting of the king, the Lords, and the Commons. He claimed that this highest court of the realm had existed long before the time of William the Conqueror. Hence, no act of parliament is valid unless it results from the consent of the king, the Lords, and the Commons. There is no appeal from the judicial acts of parliament as the highest court, and in a sense no appeal is needed. For by means of concurrence in parliament, consent is achieved at the highest level of the realm. Coke considered that this consent reflected the ancient customs of the realm. If it did not, it would prove inconvenient to the commonwealth and the law would adjudge such acts null and void. He did not resolve the questions raised by contradictions between judicial decisions and parliamentary statutes. But it is clear that in his hands

> assertions that the law was immemorial tended to be replaced by assertions that parliament, and especially a house of commons representing the property-owners, was immemorial. One of the underlying themes in the history of seventeenth-century political thought is the trend from the claim that there is a fundamental law, with parliament as its guardian, to the claim that parliament is sovereign.[69]

The common denominator of parliamentary arguments was the defense of property rights. For centuries these rights of the freemen of the realm had been defended against encroachments by the crown. The sixteenth century had witnessed the extension of governmental authority into many spheres of life, as in the case of the dissolution of the monasteries, but these were assertions of the king's authority based on the ancient principle of royal sovereignty over the whole realm. In that context, James's theory of the divine right of kings was not as exceptional as later writers have made it seem. Assertions of royal sovereignty were commonplace, and "to call a right divine in the seventeenth century meant no more than that you attached importance to it."[70] The burden of proof was on the side of parliament. For when Coke attacked the royal prerogative by using the great tradition of the common law, he was challenging lawyers for the crown who were using the same tradition to defend the prerogative.[71] Shortly before his dismissal by James I in 1616, Coke had rejected the king's claim to be the highest judge of the realm. Coke quoted Bracton to the effect that the king was under God and under the law and claimed that "the king hath no prerogative but that which the law of the land allows him."[72] Sovereign power, he said, was "no parliamentary word" and would weaken "all our statutes," though he acknowledged nonetheless that "prerogative" is part of the law.[73] When the Protestation of 1621 stated "that the liberties, franchises, privileges and jurisdictions of Parliament are the ancient and undoubted birthright and inheritance of the subjects of England," the assertion obviously benefited from the myth of an ancient constitution. By 1628, in arguing for the Petition of Right, Coke already rejected any reference to the "sovereign power" of the king. Hence, Coke's erratic use of precedents, extravagant language ("Magna Carta is such a fellow that he will have no sovereign"), and panegyrics of common law were weapons in a struggle for power.

The ambiguity was finally resolved only in the revolution of 1688. The Tories, bound by the legal tradition Coke had done so much to establish, were unable to find an argument against James II (1658–1688) consistent with their own recognition of his legitimate title. It remained

The 'Protestant Grind-Stone .

Queen   *King*   *Schomberg*

Old Holy Father, there was once a time
When Clemency was thought a mortall Crime
For Hereticks no pitts you could find;
But most severely did their Faces Grind.

The times now turn'd, harsh Stripes upon you fall.
Too well deserv'd, and this is done that all
Who see the Whore of Babylon may Say.
Shees poxt, because her nose is worn away .

The Protestant Grindstone
This political cartoon of 1690 symbolizes the end of serious Catholic contention for the English throne. James II had been deposed and William and Mary had been elevated to the throne by the "Glorious Revolution" of 1688. In the cartoon, William and Mary look on while the archbishop of Canterbury and the bishop of London grind the pope's nose. The ditty below the cartoon conveys the anti-Jacobite sentiments of the time. (British Museum)

for the Whigs to break with this tradition and claim that the king had forfeited the crown by breaking the *contract* between king and people. If the king violated his oath of coronation, the people were released from their oath of allegiance. Although the hereditary claim of James II was unimpeachable, the nation had a right to expel a king who had broken the "original contract," thereby violating the "fundamental law." In these resolutions of 1689, the old arguments based on history were superseded by appeals to reason and natural law. In the Whig interpretation propounded by John Locke, it was no longer a question whether the law was derived from the will of an ancient sovereign *or* from the people's consent embodied in ancient custom and judicial decisions. Henceforth, law was to be derived "from the natural rights of every individual and from his will, as a rational and sociable being, to set up machinery to secure them."[74]

Little room was left for the principle of equality where so much emphasis was put on a consent reflecting the interests of property owners, as represented by the king, Lords, and Commons. Nor did the idea of an original contract between king and people advance equality. It is true that in these seventeenth-century debates a kind of equality was recognized in the individual's freedom to trade. Legal interpretations buttressed that freedom by defending the rights of property and the rights of labor against the restraints of trade resulting from royal patents of monopoly and from guild restrictions.[75] But seventeenth-century England knew little of equality in the modern sense. The exclusion of all dependents from the "political nation" was taken for granted in a society in which religious spokesmen considered "civil equality morally impossible."[76] Indeed, the very elitism of landed aristocrats and wealthy commoners was the psychological basis on which the challenge of the royal prerogative had been mounted.

Divines and parliamentarians of the seventeenth century lived in a society in which any stronger emphasis on equality seemed to them contrary to nature and the divine ordinance. Yet their development of a church and a state based on consent bore within it the possibilities of a much more radical egalitarianism. Through agitation in the parishes and in parliament, the Puritan movement combined religious with patriotic zeal. Its egalitarian message appealed to the conscience and self-confidence of the people against the hierarchic organization of the church, though the Puritans remained within the Anglican church. But the egalitarianism of Puritan preaching was established primarily in the spiritual sphere and was paradoxically associated with elitism. For this "equality of believers is an equality in their superiority to other men. . . . Considered in relation to the world in which it subsists, [the congregation] is an aristocracy of grace."[77] But within this "aristocracy of grace," some are more equal than others. In this, the Puritan movement exemplified a dilemma which has beset intellectual leaders in "modernizing" societies ever since.

Puritan divines had more scriptural knowledge than their parishioners. As servants of their Lord, these men of the cloth were solely concerned with imparting the truth of the Scriptures to the laity, though this could lead to controversies over the vestments which distinguished the minister from his flock. It is true that the tendency was to reduce the organization of the church to the simple relation between the preacher and his congregation. But this anti-organizational attitude was ambivalent, because the equality derived from doctrine did not square with the inequality of function. Humble as he was before the Lord, the preacher was still His chosen instrument. At his best, the Puritan preacher was singled out by the capacity to search his heart for signs of false pride and by a conscience so exacting that its severity made him a leader among men.[78] Thus, an elitism of conscience lay at the heart of this "brotherhood of all believers," and the same paradox has bedeviled subsequent revolutions.

It is a paradox which occurs in representative institutions as well. The political agitation in the English parliaments of the sixteenth and seventeenth centuries was not egalitarian at all. For these representatives of the shires and boroughs were notables of the realm, accustomed to having access to public affairs from which the bulk of the population was excluded. At the beginning of parliamentary ascendancy, these men expressed their concern for the personal safety of Queen Elizabeth and for the political and religious integrity of the realm with such vigor that their actions often verged on the idea of a parliament coequal with the queen in guiding the fortunes of the nation.[79] This suggested an equality (if one may stretch the meaning of the word) among the property-owning rulers of the country. The queen frequently considered the demands of her parliaments as unprecedented encroachments on her authority, and her Stuart successors certainly considered the claims made in the name of the common law a challenge to their sovereign authority. In the end, the men of parliament began to speak more directly in the name of the country, first in the events leading up to the revolution of 1640, and more firmly after the revolution of 1688 established a constitutional monarchy. But once the king-in-parliament was supreme, elected representatives faced the paradox of being both populist and elitist. For as populists they spoke in response to the opinions and wishes of their constituents, while as elitists they used their judgment in speaking for the country as a whole.

The idea of a government by consent, ultimately derived from a mandate of the people, was advanced during the seventeenth century through challenges of authority in church and state. At the time, the demand for consent did not seem to imply equality in any mundane sense, since in the religious sphere the congregation constituted an "aristocracy of grace," while in the political realm parliament constituted an elite of the titled and the wealthy. The egalitarianism implicit in the demand for consent had to await the further developments of the eighteenth century. The ideal of equality became one hallmark of the French revolution.

10

TOWARD THE
NATION-STATE:
FRANCE

ABSOLUTIST RULE AND ENTRENCHED PRIVILEGE

T HE FRENCH revolution of 1789 was the principal turning point in the transition from the authority of kings to the mandate of the people. Because I have considered French kingship only in the Merovingian and Carolingian period, I wish to begin here with a direct contrast between French and English kingship and the fate of the Reformation in the two countries.

The Norman conquest achieved the political unification of England under one ruler. One-fifth of the land belonged to William the Conqueror and most of the rest of the land was appropriated by the new Norman aristocracy. The holdings of the French kings of that time were small by comparison. All but one of the French king's vassals had lands larger than royal domains. France consisted of five duchies (Brittany, Normandy, Burgundy, Aquitaine, Gascony) and six shires (Comté of Anjou, Flanders, Blois, Champagne, Toulouse, Barcelona) which made up the bulk of the country. The French king was an elected overlord of France rather than an hereditary monarch and had direct authority only over his own domains. When Henry II (1154–1189) was king of England, he was also duke of Aquitaine and legally a vassal of the French king as far as Aquitaine was concerned. In terms of resources and power, the English ruler was much the stronger of the two. But although the resources of the French king were limited, his domains were centrally located around Paris. French royal authority was gradually enlarged either by direct territorial acquisitions or by increased authority over the vassals through the customary devices of feudal rule. The Hundred Years' War with England (1338–1453) assisted this process of

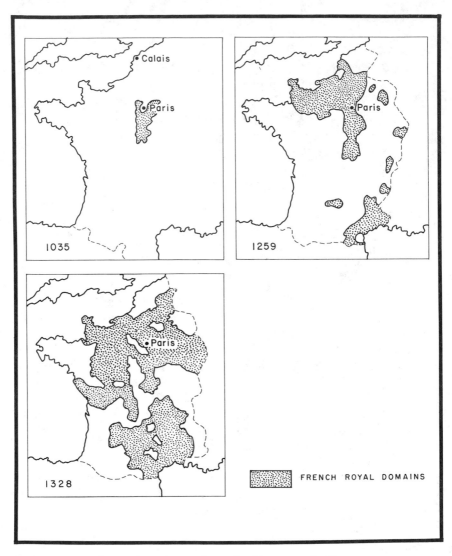

10. France from the Eleventh to the Fourteenth Century

royal ascendance, in part through impoverishing the French nobility. The gradual imposition of the *taille* (a property tax on non-nobles) and the *gabelle* (a sales tax eventually limited to a tax on salt) permitted the French crown to establish a standing army in the fifteenth century. By then the French king had acquired sufficient land and resources so that the great dukes and counts of France were no longer his rivals. The royal court became the center of French society much as it had in England. The gradual enlargement of royal authority in France thus contrasts with the royal supremacy achieved by conquest in the case of England.

The Reformation of the sixteenth century presents a second major contrast between the two countries. The English Reformation preserved some doctrinal and liturgical continuity with the Roman Catholic faith. In France the movement for church reform was inspired by the Lutheran doctrine of justification by faith alone. Indeed, in the first part of the sixteenth century French reformers were known as Lutherans, though after 1550 they came to be called Huguenots.[1] Protestantism was popular since it rejected the cumulative abuses of the old church. But whereas the English Reformation began with the legitimation of the new faith by Henry VIII's royal edict (the Act of Supremacy), the French Reformation was initiated by religious leaders whose popular appeal led to religious conversions. The French government supported the Catholic church. Serious conflicts ensued as the movement of reform spread, and several true believers became martyrs to the Reformed faith in the 1520s. In 1534 placards condemning the Catholic mass were found on the city walls of Paris and even outside the king's bedroom. An edict of 1535 ordered the extermination of heretics and resulted in a general emigration. John Calvin, who settled in Geneva, was one of these religious refugees.

Calvin formulated a constitution of the Reformed church, which declared that ecclesiastical authority resides ultimately in the people, with the faithful selecting the elders who are charged with supervision of the church and the choice of pastors. The higher levels of this Reformed church were organized on the English presbyterian principles discussed in Chapter 9. Inspired by this doctrine, Huguenot communities began forming in France in the 1540s, assembling for their first synod in 1558–1559 (the year of Elizabeth's accession to the English throne). Only fifteen Huguenot churches were represented at this synod, but two years later there were over two thousand. This rapid spread of the movement and its official persecution produced an atmosphere of agitation in which some Huguenots formed a conspiracy in 1560 with the intention of kidnapping the king. The plotters were executed, and a new edict formally prohibited the practice of the Protestant religion. Nevertheless, efforts at reconciliation continued and another edict (1562)

The St. Bartholomew's Day Massacre, 1572
Religious conflicts marked much of the sixteenth century. In France they led to intermittent
civil war between 1562 and 1598, while England under Elizabeth achieved a tension-filled
accommodation after the religious persecution of Mary Tudor's reign. Mass killings like
the St. Bartholomew's Day Massacre weakened France's position and probably contributed
to a legacy of anticlericalism. (Bibliothèque Nationale)

confirmed the religious liberty of the Huguenots. But the agitation
could no longer be stayed by edicts.

A number of Huguenots, assembled for worship in 1562, were massacred by leaders of the Guise family, and when the duke of Guise subsequently staged a coup d'état, the Huguenots under the leadership of
Condé organized for war. The resulting civil war lasted intermittently
until 1598, when the Huguenots at last obtained their charter of religious
and political toleration, the Edict of Nantes. The famous St. Bartholomew's Day massacre (1572) of some 20,000 Huguenots was a major episode in this destructive struggle. The forty years of religious wars coincided with the years of Queen Elizabeth's religious settlement; thus,

England could consolidate its position while France was divided. One consequence of the struggle in France was the elaboration of Huguenot political doctrine in the writings of François Hotman and in the anonymous tract, *Vindiciae contra tyrannos* (1579). These writers postulated a government by consent of the governed and a right to rebel against tyranny. Thus, the French doctrine of consent was entirely identified with the Huguenots, a Protestant minority in an overwhelmingly Catholic country. In England, by contrast, a more moderate doctrine of parliamentary representation of the country was formulated by leading aristocrats in the House of Commons, who were nonconformists but very much part of the English governing class in local and national affairs.

France was split into a Huguenot "party," intent on gaining civic recognition for the Reformed faith, and the "party" of the Counter-Reformation led by the dukes of Guise, who were related by marriage to the French and Scottish royal houses. The French king negotiated and fought with both parties. French religious policy was ambiguous, for the country fought the Protestants at home on religious grounds while also fighting Catholic Spain abroad for political reasons. But this antagonism toward Catholic Spain was temporary. The peace of Cateau-Cambrésis (1559) cemented a new Franco-Spanish friendship by Philip II's marriage to the daughter of King Henry II of France (1547–1559). This clearly made France an anti-Protestant power abroad as well as at home. We saw earlier that dynastic relations supported this Catholic front against Protestant England. Mary Stuart was the daughter of Mary of Guise, the queen-regent of Scotland after 1542. Mary Stuart had married Francis II of France, and her uncle, the duke of Guise, had defeated the English at Calais in 1559. For a short time it appeared that France and Spain would launch a crusade against the English heresy. But suddenly, France's reigning house was weakened by two deaths in quick succession: Henry II died in 1559 and Francis II in 1560. Their reigns were followed by the minority of Charles IX (1560–1574), whose reign commenced at the age of ten, and by the weak rule of Henry III (1574–1589). Throughout these decades, the struggle continued between the Catholic League under the Guise family and the Protestant faction. Strong personal rule was restored only by Henry of Navarre, who was a descendant of the Bourbon family and became king of France in 1589 as Henry IV.

The religious "settlement" under Henry IV (1589–1610) is a convenient starting point for surveying the dilemmas of French "absolutism." I put both terms in quotation marks since relations with the Huguenots were not settled either by the Edict of Nantes in 1598 or by its revocation in 1685, and since this partial resolution of the religious issue reveals the limitations of French royal authority. The Huguenots represented a religious minority of one million in a population of eighteen million Frenchmen. Henry IV's accession to the throne seemed to support the Huguenot position, since he was the rightful heir and he was a Calvinist. But Henry's succession was disputed by the Catholic League because of his religious beliefs, and in 1593 Henry abjured the Reformed faith; he was crowned at Chartres the following year. The Catholicism of France was ensured, as was the crown's supremacy in ecclesiastical affairs. The king's conversion to Catholicism appeared to facilitate a settlement of the religious issue. In 1598 the Edict of Nantes granted the Huguenots a recognized, though second-class, status. Huguenot communities were allowed a separate synodal organization as well as a number of locations which they could fortify and administer under their own jurisdiction. Under specified conditions, the private and public worship of the Reformed faith was permitted. But the Huguenots were obliged to observe Catholic marriage laws and pay tithes in support of the Catholic church. Thus, the Huguenots were treated as a second-class group, tolerated and segregated in a fashion which was typical of the *ancien régime*. The conflict between the Catholic majority and the Huguenot minority was settled through a grant of circumscribed rights to the minority.

In the early seventeenth century, French royal authority was limited by a variety of institutions which largely represented vested interests. A comparison with England and Russia will put the French regime in perspective. Under Elizabeth, the English parliament was composed of leading notables from the shires and boroughs who claimed to represent the interests of the queen's realm. Although parliament received setbacks under the Stuarts, it was clearly establishing itself as representative of "the country." In Russia, the Muscovite dynasty had risen at the expense of independent princes and boyars, and landed notables had become a class of high-ranking servitors. Their assemblies of the seventeenth century (*zemskii sobor*) wanted to restore rather than limit autocratic rule. France possessed neither a parliament in the English sense nor the Russian servitor assemblies. Instead, the French monarchy had become preeminent by successive arrangements between the French king and various sociopolitical groups and institutions. Additional revenues of the crown were obtained through entitlements to revenues, privileges, exemptions, and the like. The French ancien régime of the seventeenth and eighteenth centuries reflected that earlier equivocal ascendance of the French kings over their mighty vassals. For that reason, the term *absolutism* is not easily applied to a monarchy which in its period of greatest power did not achieve control over what Montesquieu was to call the *corps intermédiaires* of society. A system of government in which the ruler has unlimited powers is not practicable in any case, though he may be extremely arbitrary and impose his will on many. But while "absolutist rule" was not the practice in the literal sense, the aspiration to extend monarchical authority and the claims to "absolute" authority were evident in the seventeenth and eighteenth centuries. The central control of major functions of government was actually achieved only in the nineteenth century.[2]

The ancien régime possessed a great diversity of "representative" institutions. Like the English parliament, the institution of the *États Généraux* (Estates-General) originated in the king's council, which was called together on special occasions to give counsel and financial assistance. But the Estates-General did not develop into a national representative body. Its existence depended on royal summons, and strong rulers dispensed with it. Under Henry IV, the institution languished without being formally abolished. The last meeting, which occurred in 1614, exemplified both the impasse of entrenched interests and the limitations of "absolute" monarchy.

The Estates-General were composed of representatives of the clergy (the First Estate), the nobility (the Second Estate), and propertied commoners (the Third Estate).[3] The Third Estate refers to the middle strata which comprised a wealthy patriciate often with hereditary title to municipal office, members of guilds or corporations (also mostly hereditary), bankers and financiers, as well as commercial and smaller merchants. Families of patricians and financiers often intermarried with the nobility.[4]

The three estates met separately in 1614 (as they had before) and voiced their several grievances. With declining land revenues, the nobility faced increasing financial difficulties and used the opportunity to curb the pretensions of the Third Estate. The clergy and the nobility formally asked the Third Estate to petition the king for abolition of the *paulette,* a measure which allowed officials from families of commoners to make their posts hereditary in return for annual tax payments. The Third Estate complied, but under two conditions. The First and Second Estates should reciprocate by petitioning the king for a reduction of the property tax (*taille*) and of the king's expenditures on pensions which largely benefited the nobility. Despite such conflicts, the meeting of the Estates-General proved embarrassing to the government. As a recent study concludes,

An Estates General . . . served to focus the complaints of the people. The Estates General of 1614 failed because it had no means of imposing its will on the government and because the unity of its *cahiers* frightened the upper-echelon bureaucrats. For the first time sensible men from the provinces had united and shown the way to reform, but the reform seemed too dangerous. That could not be permitted to happen again. If it did the bureaucrats . . .

might be forced to try reform which if it worked would lessen their growing power and if it did not might plunge France into civil war. The continuation of the process of strengthening the central government and of ignoring abuses that could not be easily uprooted seemed to be the only sensible choice.[5]

The Estates-General of 1614 were dissolved. They had shown that the monarchy could assert its central authority but could not easily encroach on the rights and privileges it had granted.

The royal or sovereign courts of law (*parlements*) were much more important than the États Généraux. They had extensive judicial duties and were entitled to register and promulgate royal decrees and to issue administrative edicts. A parlement could also refuse registration if the proposed decrees were inconsistent with previous legislation, and in this connection it had the right to address remonstrances to the king. Such an adverse ruling could be countermanded by a special session (*lit de justice*) in which the king could personally command the registration. On occasion, a parlement would resist even that command and would be exiled in consequence. Such confrontations occurred primarily in Paris and became more frequent when the king's position weakened. The parlement of Paris was the oldest and most prestigious of these bodies, setting the tone for the several parlements in the provinces. The Paris parlement had jurisdiction over a large part of France. Some eleven hundred members of the parlements constituted the powerful *noblesse de robe*. Members were neither elected nor appointed. Instead, membership depended on wealth and birth, and parliamentary seats were available for purchase from owners or heirs as a free, hereditary property, provided the purchaser was of noble birth. In this way, the parliamentary nobility could defend its monopoly against other claimants and against the king himself.

By the seventeenth century, most provinces were centrally administered (*pays d'élection*) from Paris, and taxes were assessed without consultation with the estates. But on the periphery, the estate-assemblies of the locally administered provinces (*pays d'État*) had important governmental functions, though these were to decline in the course of the eighteenth century. Membership in these provincial assemblies was by estate, the relative weight of each depending on the mode of election and the social conditions of the province. In Britany and Languedoc, where

A French Parliament

In France as in England, representative institutions originated in assemblies called by the king to help him dispense justice. In this miniature by Jean Fouquet, King Charles VII, seated above the others in the rear, presides over a special session of the parlement (1485). This highest court was called to judge the duke of Alençon, who had been accused of high treason. (Bayerische Staatsbibliothek) estate-assemblies still functioned in the eighteenth century, the assemblies developed permanent committees and officers that remained at work between meetings and handled the increasingly complex business of government (like conscription, road-building, and relief of the poor). But the Estates-General, the small number and diminishing functions of the pays d'État, and the parlements in the pays d'élection do not yet give an adequate picture of French "governmental" institutions.

That picture emerges only when one recognizes that in practice the monarchy rested on a series of contracts

> [made] with the different units of which France was composed: provinces, cities, ecclesiastical foundations, social classes and even economic groups such as the trade guilds. All these contracts left to each group its own liberties and privileges and no one saw anything out of the way in their existence side by side with submission to the king. Provinces, cities, foundations, groups, orders and states were all faithful subjects of the king, but with their own privileges.[6]

The basis of 'this arrangement was either a family's ancient title or the purchase of title and office. The hereditary magistracy of *parlementaires* was based securely on landownership, going back three or four generations. Most parlementaires had a legal education, participated actively in public affairs, and had regular access to the king and his officials. With their facility for meeting privately, the parlementaires assumed leadership over the French nobility as a whole; and conversely, the older nobility obtained through the parlementaires a professional leadership it had not had before. The leadership of the other "intermediate" bodies was perhaps not as well-trained as the parlementaires, but every town, foundation, or order had an elite of its own, highly conscious of its rights or privileges and quite prepared to put up a stiff fight in their defense. During the seventeenth century, and especially under the reign of Louis XIV (1643–1715),[a] the French monarchy was in the ascendant over this multitude of intermediate bodies. One can assess the rise of absolutism by the degree to which the monarchy superimposed its centralized administrative system on entrenched and highly diversified elites.

But before sketching the ascendance of monarchy, two circumstances of seventeenth-century France must be described. One is economic. Holland, not France, was the foremost economic power of the period, its eight to nine thousand vessels represented about half of the world's shipping. Amsterdam was the principal international market and warehouse, and Dutch commercial practices and financial facilities were the most advanced of their time. By comparison, France did not

[a]Louis XIV was born in 1638, became king of France in 1643 at the age of five, and began his effective rule in 1661 at the death of Cardinal Mazarin.

have a developed economy. It had no national bank or budget, French currency had to compete with foreign coins, waterways and roads were often impassable, French coalfields lay dormant, its ironworks were technically backward. The list of economic deficiencies is long and includes the condition of French agriculture. Yet seventeenth-century France had the reputation of being the foremost political power of Europe as well as its main cultural center. The country was engaged in foreign wars for almost fifty years between 1600 and 1700, and in addition the government had to put down a large number of internal rebellions. Demographic strength was the basis of this great outward success, since with the exception of Russia, France had two or three times the population of any other European country. Of almost twenty million people, some twelve million were productive and taxable, and the country's population may have been near that level since the mid sixteenth century. France had the unusually high average of one hundred inhabitants per square mile, at a time when population density was a source of military and economic strength.[7]

The other circumstance is political. The rise of monarchical power at the expense of local jurisdiction depended on personal rule at the center of affairs, and that rule was strong under Cardinal Richelieu (1624–1642), Cardinal Mazarin (1642–1661), and Louis XIV. It is true that Henry III and Henry IV were assassinated in 1589 and 1610, and Louis XIII (1610–1643) was first under the influence of his mother, Marie de' Medici, and her confidants, and then under that of Richelieu. But two strong regents and Louis XIV's strong personal rule after 1661 counted for more than these vicissitudes. Richelieu's influence rose in the midst of a revolt by the Huguenots (1625–1628). The cardinal also had to defeat a conspiracy of the king's brother and the duke of Montmorency in 1632 while directing France's participation (1631–1648) in the Thirty Years' War. His successor, Cardinal Mazarin, reaped the benefits of French gains from the Peace of Westphalia (1648), though the same year witnessed the outbreak of the Fronde (1648–1653), the last attempt of the French nobility to oppose the king by armed resistance.

Louis XIV's concern with his dignity, greatness, and reputation was expressed above all in his military undertakings. In fairness one should add that France had reason to fear encirclement by the Austrian and Spanish branches of the House of Habsburg.[b] The 1660s witnessed the

[b]In the Mediterranean, the Spanish Habsburgs controlled not only Spain but the Balearic Islands, Sardinia, and the kingdom of Naples (including Sicily). In addition, Spain controlled the province of Milan, Franche Comté (an area adjoining the Western border of modern Switzerland), and the Spanish Netherlands to the north. Farther east, the Austrian Habsburgs controlled an area extending from the south of Berlin to the Adriatic coast and from territories adjoining the Rhine just north of Basel to a section of the kingdom of Hungary.

king's forays into the Spanish Netherlands, the 1670s his war against Holland (1672–1678), and 1683 another invasion of the Spanish Netherlands.[c] The revocation of the Edict of Nantes in 1685 resulted in a massive emigration of French Huguenots. Following the revocation, Louis was engaged in a war with the League of Augsburg from 1689 to 1697, a Protestant coalition against France which had been organized by William, Prince of Orange, who had become king of England (1689–1702). From 1701 to 1714, Louis was engaged in the War of the Spanish Succession. The first eleven years of Louis' effective rule were marked by great success abroad and at home, but after 1672 his military successes were outweighed by defeats arising from various European coalitions against France. France was at war for twenty-five out of the last thirty years of Louis XIV's reign. How does this record of foreign involvement based on a sturdy if old-fashioned economy relate to the internal policies of the ancien régime?

An older view, partly inspired by Tocqueville, held that a centralized bureaucracy had been established long before the French revolution and indeed had prepared the way for the nation-state, but more recent studies suggest that central administration often remained on paper.[8] The substitution of royal for local authority was a protracted and uneven development. The record of Richelieu makes this clear. The cardinal had been ruthless in defending the king's interests against the Huguenots and various conspiracies by the queen mother, the king's brother, and leading members of the nobility. But Richelieu did not create a centralized form of government. The members of town councils and the parlementaires retained their authority more or less unimpaired. Richelieu raised revenue by the old methods of selling useless public offices as well as the very lucrative right to collect taxes. He did appoint provincial governors (*intendants*) to supervise regional and local affairs, but their missions were temporary and limited to a few provinces. Still, the intendants were beginning to encroach on the rights of the parlements. The civil war, known as the Fronde (1648–1653), was in part directed against this interference, since leaders of the revolt demanded the abolition of the intendants as well as the reconfirmation of the parlementaires and their well-established rights.[9]

The ascendance of absolutism may be dated from the effective rule of Louis XIV, as long as the term is understood with the proper reservations. The companies of officers organized in the Fronde were abolished. In 1673 the parlements were instructed to register royal

[c]The Netherlands' declaration of independence from Spain in 1581 (see Chapter 9, p. 275) referred only to the independence of the United Provinces (roughly, modern Holland). Spanish forces reconquered the south (roughly, modern Belgium), which remained part of the Spanish branch of the Habsburg empire under the general designation of the Spanish Netherlands. Spain lost these possessions in the Treaty of Utrecht of 1714.

edicts forthwith. They could still address their humble petitions to the king, but he would then end the matter by saying yes or no. There was some resistance, but it was put down. The emasculation of the officers of finance was effective. These men had participated in the Fronde but were not suppressed by force. Instead, the less important ones were bought out by the government, while the more important ones were replaced by the intendants, who took over the assessment of the taille. The highest ranks of the nobility, including the princes of the blood, were shoved aside by creating for them splendid-sounding posts which conferred no power. Some nobles who held provincial governorships had their terms reduced to three years and were forbidden to reside in the area of their official duties. Louis XIV's lavish court society had the political purpose of forcing the nobility's personal attendance. They could win favors only by personal petition, often impoverishing themselves in the process. Nobles who stayed at home were subjected to searches of their titles, a calculated subordination of recalcitrants which could lead to their demotion and provided an indirect method of taxation besides. The creation of many new titles as well as the sale of titles and coats of arms provided further revenue and served to degrade the nobility.

In the beginning of Louis XIV's reign, France's position seemed assured. The country was wealthy enough to support the massive expenditures of the king's foreign undertakings without compelling a reorganization of domestic affairs. Administration was in the hands of Jean-Baptiste Colbert as controller general of finance (1662–1683). The crown's income of 60 million livres a year was unmatched by any other country except Holland. In addition, Colbert promoted the construction and purchase of ships. The French army was organized along the new lines adopted by the main European powers after the 1560s. The emphasis was on discipline, inspections, maneuvers, the storage of arms, ammunition, and supplies; strategic military positions were repaired and garrisoned; and morale was bolstered through periodic public reviews.[10] The French army with 70,000 men and some 1,800 cannon was the largest in Europe.

Savings on expenses was Colbert's most successful device for financing the king's ambitious undertakings. Half the annuities payable by the crown were simply abolished and the remainder was cut substantially. The savings achieved were worth 4 million livres to the royal treasury. Thousands of new offices had been created and sold after 1630, costing more than 8 million a year in salaries. By repurchase, Colbert relieved the annual drain of these payments by more than 2 million. By these and other methods, he succeeded in reducing the permanent charge on the annual budget from 52 to 14 million livres over a ten-year period. Some of Colbert's positive measures were equally successful. He increased the revenue from the property tax (taille) in the pays d'État by 50 percent. Income from the royal estates increased from virtually nothing to 5 million by 1671, and the revenue collected from the peasants from 37 to 60 million. Between 1661 and 1671, Louis' *net* income had doubled, and a substantial surplus of income over expenditures mounted from year to year.[11]

Governmental administration was still rudimentary. Colbert and his associates accomplished a great deal during the first, rather peaceful period of Louis XIV's reign (1661–1672). But a few men at the top, some thirty councillors, less than thirty intendants, perhaps a hundred masters of requests, and all the attendant scribes and servants made up an administrative corps of less than one thousand persons trying to reorganize a country of twenty million people. Although quite a bit was accomplished, a centralized administration of provincial and local government was *not* achieved. Instead, new privileges were added (even when old privileges were curtailed), largely in order to raise more revenue but also because the monarchy respected, and depended on, the institutions of privilege.[12]

Colbert's intention to establish a centralized administration had been shared by a number of his predecessors. Royal intervention in the relations between landlord and peasant dated back to the fourteenth century. Appeals could be addressed to royal officials for relief from the abuses of landlords. Also, urban communities emancipated themselves from their feudal overlords and thereby came under the control of royal magistrates. In theory, royal authority became the guarantor of justice, an idea developed in Jean Bodin's doctrine of royal sovereignty (*Six Livres de la République*, 1576). In practice, royal officials assumed administrative and judicial authority over some peasants and collected taxes from them, while others continued under seignorial jurisdiction. The royal call to arms had originally been addressed to the nobility, and was only gradually extended to some of the tenants of landowners.

Many of these measures were poorly administered, but conditions of war generally favored the extension of royal authority. The provincial estates, where they still existed, were rendered powerless by official supervision of their discussions and the alternate use of bribes and threats. The major cities saw their franchises undermined little by little, as one right or exemption after another was curtailed or eliminated. In 1667 the king created a lieutenant general of the police for Paris. By 1699 lieutenants of police had been appointed in the majority of cities, their duties comprising in rudimentary fashion the various functions we associate with municipal administration. The exigencies of war probably were the most important causes of administrative centralization and reorganization.

The aggravation of old burdens and the imposition of new ones had the curious effect of giving the royal administration a more settled, effective and authoritative place in the kingdom. Military organization, supplies, troop movements, coastal defenses, new taxes, letters patent of nobility or offices for sale, all these were added to the work of the *intendants*. . . . [From the 1690s on] each *intendant* had his own offices which were becoming increasingly organized, and a fair number of assistants whose usefulness no one dreamed any longer of disputing as Colbert had once done. An administration with increasing powers and influence was developing within the kingdom.[13]

But the policies of war which furthered administrative centralization entailed financial burdens in excess of France's still considerable wealth. Between 1672 and 1676, France's deficit reached 24 million livres. Colbert was forced to resort to "extraordinary measures." Tax exemptions were first sold to minor officials, and then the intendants were instructed to impose new taxes on these clients of the government at exorbitant rates. Some 8 million were obtained in this way, and although the policy was suspended as unwise, it was resumed later. Half the tax exemptions on freeholds were sold for 7 million. The sale of offices and licenses reappeared, the purchasers simply adding their cost to the price of the goods they sold to the public, thus increasing the indirect tax on commodities. Half the royal estates which had been repurchased were sold off once again. Old taxes were revived and regular ones increased. A whole series of new taxes were imposed on the mastery of a craft, on pewters and tobacco, and on all acts of ecclesiastical administration. The clergy was required to increase its "voluntary donations." But the costs of war kept rising and the government fell back on borrowing. Municipal bonds were sold at steadily increasing rates of interest. In 1676 Colbert borrowed from Genoese bankers and the king's financiers in France at rates of 10 percent on the anticipated income for 1677.

Colbert died in 1683, and his work of financing the king's wars by ever more extraordinary measures was taken up by his successors. It is sufficient to state the overall effect in Goubert's words:

Year by year, the cost of the war, of financing the war and of the war time economy had affected the people of the kingdom: taxes and the depredations of tax collectors and soldiery alike, the militia and the continual hunt for deserters; scarcity and famine, made worse by the war, poverty and profiteers; monetary difficulties, the dread of counterfeit coin and "notes" of all descriptions, all devalued by 80 or 90 percent; the growing burden of debt placed on the peasantry and the impossibility of finding farmers to collect the king's taxes or private revenues; demographic crises of a mild or catastrophic nature; swine fever, typhoid, scarlet fever, dysentery and measles affecting everyone from the court to the remotest countryside; bands of beggars, brigands, and deserters lurking in every forest in the land and emerging to ravage everything in sight; sudden panic uprisings in rural communities precipitated by a new tax, whether real or imagined, a new government agent, a load of grain, troop movements or the rumour that brigands were massing in the region; the army, as it had in the previous century, putting down disturbances. . . .[14]

Everything suggests, as Goubert states, that when Louis XIV died in 1715, every subject of the king experienced a profound sense of relief.

There are indications that after 1715 a fairly rapid economic recovery was made possible by many of the same factors which had accounted for France's preeminence in European affairs two generations earlier. But the political difficulties of "absolutism" persisted despite recovery and the return of peace. Where the king's officials took over the functions of seignorial rule or municipal government, peasants and town residents were separated from their earlier affiliations and became direct subjects of the king. But royal officials appeared only occasionally, whereas landlords and urban patricians were ever-present. The point is that the ancien régime did *not* destroy existing privileges or dispense with the delegation of authority. Rather, the government withdrew from the existing system of inequality the earlier association between status and authority. Louis XIV abolished authority as a right associated with other privileges. Even the most distinguished families were deprived of their political rights. But except in periods of great emergency, most nobles were exempt from ordinary taxes, military service, and the necessity of quartering royal troops. They enjoyed judicial privileges al-

Peasant Bearing a Priest and a Noble on His Back
This eighteenth-century caricature symbolizes the crushing tax burdens imposed on the peasantry while clergy and nobility were largely exempted from taxation. Rabbits and doves, protected by law for the sport of the upper classes, are shown eating the peasants' grain. These same laws also allowed aristocratic hunting parties to follow the chase even if they trampled and devastated the peasants' fields. (Bibliothèque Nationale)

lowing easy access to a parlement as well as a myriad of special rights which varied from one locality to another.[15] These privileges were extended to royal officials so that their noble status would correspond to their official function.[d] But the chances for ennoblement increased more rapidly than the functions of government.

> When there was a shortage of available posts, the office seekers were quick to think up new ones. . . . To a man of some education and with a little money of his own it seemed unbecoming to go to his grave without having held an official post sometime in his career.[16]

Offices also multiplied because the government—though it destroyed the right to authority as an inherited privilege—did not dispense with the creation of privileges as a source of revenue. Tocqueville cites the example of towns which had enjoyed their municipal liberties for centuries. Louis XIV destroyed these liberties but restored them to all towns in a position to buy them back. Seven times in a period of eighty years "the towns were invited to buy the right of electing their executive officials; then, after they had tasted for a while the pleasure of self-government, the right was withdrawn and sold back to them once more."[17] Similarly, ennoblement through the issuance of letters patent had become the vestige of earlier, verbal grants of honor and privilege. In the past, such grants had been revoked only on rare occasions. But under Louis XIV, letters of nobility were revoked by the government on nine separate occasions, forcing the holders of such letters to buy letters of confirmation or other forms of exemption.[18] In addition, the king sold his authority anew through various franchises, immunities, or corporate liberties in order to fill his coffers and perhaps also to get the work of government out of the hands of the ancient nobility.[19]

Ultimate royal authority was assured. But its exercise was divided haphazardly among the royal intendants, the parlements, the old "intermediate bodies," and the newly privileged individuals and communities for whom public offices were a source of income and prestige. Royal officials often proved to be recalcitrant agents of the royal will.[20] Administrative centralization stood side by side with privileges bought and sold for a price, and these privileges provided their incumbents with income that more often than not stood in no relation to the functions they performed.

In the seventeenth and eighteenth centuries, everyone considered

---

[d]In a population of some 20 million people, approximately 190,000 were nobles. This group was divided between the ancient nobility of the sword, the nobility of the robe based on judicial office (some 2,300 in the high offices and perhaps ten times that number in the lower), and a small group of ennobled town magistrates. The nobility as a whole was very heterogeneous, since a tax assessment of 1695 distinguished nineteen classes of nobles, with incomes ranging from 2,000 down to 6 livres.

monarchies a strong form of government. Monarchs seemed to become all-powerful as the authority of parlements and estate assemblies were curtailed. Kings could rally the resources of their country in support of their goals, and frequent war emergencies were a significant cause of administrative centralization. Success was measured by military victories and territorial expansion which added to the royal treasury. "A king could declare war and make peace, conclude alliances, send and receive ambassadors, levy taxes, administer justice and appoint subordinate officials."[21] To put these broad claims into effect it was necessary to unify the central government and develop a clear division of labor among administrative agencies. The central government laid down rules for the implementation of laws or edicts. The king's personal servants became royal officials. In the process, the ruler encouraged a direct relation with his people, rallying them to support the royal cause over and above the petty tyrannies of church and nobility. To an extent, the self-proclaimed glory of the king, and through him of France and its people, was meant to transform the universal submission to the king into fervor for his great designs.

Yet absolutism was beset by paradox. In the name of the king, officials assumed control of affairs formerly in the hands of local institutions. The claims of authority were certainly absolute, and the result was a proliferation of duties imposed on the intendants and their subordinates. But the scope of these duties went far beyond what royal officials could accomplish by themselves. In practice, then, authority was delegated anew, and local jurisdictions or individuals appointed to the task now exercised authority in the name of the king rather than their own. In all these activities, the government did not infringe systematically on the rights of property in offices and land. Thus, the prescriptive authority of government existed side by side with the structure of existing privileges now bereft of their former judicial or administrative autonomy.

In theory, all adult householders were of direct concern to the highest authority, and the king and his officials were informed of all public affairs and exercised absolute authority. In practice, they had to rule without knowing the conditions of the country or the effects of their own measures. No representative institutions existed through which their impressions could have been checked. Two generations after the death of Louis XIV, Turgot would write in his *Mémoire sur les municipalités* (1775) that neither the king nor his ministers, nor the intendants of the provinces, nor yet their subdelegates, could acquire a knowledge of the country. The root of the evil was the lack of a constitution, of any real unity, "with the result that there prevails a perpetual conflict of competing and particularistic interests." Pierre Goubert has described this condition based on the research which has accumulated since Turgot's day. The kingdom of France was made up of a collection of "nations," *pays*, *seignories*, fiefs and parishes. . . . Each of these entities was accustomed to living independently, with its own customs, privileges and even language, snug in its own fields and within sound of its own bells. The king consecrated at Rheims was a priest-king to be revered and almost worshiped, but from afar. When someone sent by him turned up in the village accompanied by an escort of armed or black-clad men, or merely bearing an order in writing, he was met, on principle with suspicion or even open hostility. What "newfangled" idea had he brought with him? A blow struck at local custom? Or a levy of money, horses, or men? . . . Making the king's voice heard in the depths of the countryside was easier said than done when the curé, who was the only means of spreading it, garbled, scamped or merely forgot a task which was clearly no part of his duties; when courts of law were far off, costly, unreliable and even less respected, the forces of law and order never there, the intendant a mystery and his assistants powerless. We have only to look at poor Colbert, trying to establish his manufactures, his tentative regulations and his companies. No one wanted them because all had their own traditions, habits and interests and clung fiercely to their own independence. . . . We have only to stress the rash of desertions prevalent in the regular army and still more in the militia (where it may have been as high as 50 percent) at a time when parishes and even whole provinces were ready to condone, hide and feed the deserters.[22]

In the France of Louis XIV these seething undercurrents and the massive inertia of the population made the task of the king and his ministers extremely difficult, if not impossible.

FRENCH REACTIONS TO ENGLAND AND AMERICA

In *The Old Regime and the Revolution*, Tocqueville assessed the public reactions to the dilemmas and abuses of absolutism. He felt that a cynical egoism was all-pervasive though it was associated, however erratically, with a spirit of independence. The government made money by selling its offices. Purchasers could do what they wished with them, but the government was in a position to exact additional payments from the incumbents. Offices had become private property and were exploited at the public's expense. Though officials were "perniciously estranged from the common people" and had become a "pseudo-aristocracy," on occasion they displayed "the spirit of resistance of a true aristocracy."[23] Increasing exploitation and the demise of public spirit were also true in other contexts. The provinces and towns lost the substance of their ancient franchises, and nobles could not assemble for common deliberation without express permission from the king. Every private right was superseded by the right of royal officials to regulate public affairs. Nevertheless, in practice privileges remained, permitting men of rank to enjoy the liberties of their high station.

The nobility had the utmost contempt for the administration properly so called, though now and again they addressed petitions to it. Even after the surrender of their former power they kept something of their ancestral pride, their traditional antipathy to servitude and subordination to the common law. True, they gave little thought to the freedom of the populace at large and were quite ready to let the authorities rule those around them with a heavy hand. But they refused to let that hand weigh on themselves and were prepared to run the greatest risks in the defense of their liberties if and when the need arose. . . .[24]

Nobles now used their rank to overawe royal officials and defy the government, whereas at an earlier time their pride and privileges had been synonymous with the exercise of authority. In Tocqueville's view, the old regime was not an era of servility and subservience, but the freedom of the nobility had become illegitimate. Immunities and privileges dangerously widened the division between rich and poor when men of privilege exploited their offices for private gain in lieu of serving their public functions.

As penetrating as this famous analysis is, it treats the problems of the ancien régime in isolation from its international setting. In the course of the seventeenth century, France became the foremost power of Europe and maintained that position for much of the eighteenth century. Meanwhile, domestic problems cumulated, and Frenchmen of conservative and liberal persuasions reflected on the nature of these discontents, frequently by comparing French conditions with those of other countries. Among these reflections, those dealing with the political and moral conditions of England and the American colonies are of special interest. The following discussion deals with France's international position and the development of French opinion concerning England and America.

In the sixteenth century, Spain had been all-powerful, whereas France was on the defensive. The treaty of Cateau-Cambrésis (1559) marked a turning point, for it established a temporary alliance between the two powers. In 1659 France concluded the Treaty of the Pyrenees with Spain, which followed twenty-four years of intermittent war. Now conditions were reversed, with Spain in decline and France beginning its dominance over much of Europe. During the reign of Louis XIV, French policies precipitated a great European coalition against France, first in the war of 1689–1697 and then in the War of the Spanish Succession (1701–1714). In the eyes of the anti-French alliance, France's policies had raised the spectre of the same ruling family (the Bourbons) on the French *and* the Spanish throne. These wars marked the ascendance of England and the arrest of French advances on the Continent, but rivalry between the two powers continued. Frederick II of Prussia (1740–1786) observed that both countries sought to be arbiters of all

Europe, France because of its armies and resources and England because of its navies and commercial wealth. Despite its setbacks, France remained the major European power. During the eighteenth century, its population increased from 18 or 19 to 25 or 26 million, figures which were matched only by Austria and, at the end of the century, by Russia. Indeed, through its colonizing ventures in India and North America, France was in competition with England on a global scale. For much of the century France was prosperous, and on the Continent no one disputed the country's cultural preeminence. French superseded Spanish and Italian as the international language. Frederick II observed that whoever knew French could travel throughout Europe without interpreter.

The Seven Years' War (1756–1763) involved all the European powers, combining a many-sided territorial war on the Continent with colonial struggles ranging from India to North America. The Franco-British conflict in the Seven Years' War had broken out in the colonies before 1756, and one can consider the French campaigns against electoral Hanover (dynastically united with England) and the Hanoverian allies as a by-product of the colonial rivalry. (The Seven Years' War was also an Austro-Prussian war in which France, Russia, and Sweden were committed to Austria while Britain was allied with Prussia.) The outcome of this war was important, for in the Treaty of Paris (1763) France ceded to Great Britain all the mainland of North America east of the Mississippi (excluding New Orleans and its environs), some West Indian islands, and all French conquests in India or in the East Indies since 1749. In turn, Great Britain restored to France several islands in the West Indies and the Atlantic, the West African colony of Gorée (Senegal), and the island off the coast of Brittany, Belle-Ile-en-Mer. In the competition for empire, England had won a clear victory over France. The country which the whole European world and the French themselves considered the supreme power and the center of civilization had suffered its first major defeat in several generations.

It is more difficult to assess French public opinion during the eighteenth century than it is to assess public opinion in England two centuries earlier. English antagonism toward Spain together with the coalescence between Protestantism and nationalism under a highly popular queen provide us with clues to the coalescence between educated opinion and popular feeling. By contrast, eighteenth-century France possessed no single focus of educated opinion and popular sentiment, perhaps because of its dominant position on the Continent. But this dominance did not make the country impervious to foreign influences.

The ideas emanating from England are of special interest among the many currents of opinion during the eighteenth century. French-English relations had been marked by interdependence and rivalry ever since the Norman conquest. During the seventeenth century, England settled its Protestant allegiance and its partnership between king and parliament, as well as extended its colonial and mercantile empire. English parliamentary institutions were anathema to conservative Frenchmen but attractive to Frenchmen with commercial interests and enlightened ideas. It was glibly said by Louis XIV that all would be well if the English would content themselves with being the greatest merchants of Europe and leave to the French king as his share whatever he could conquer in a "just war."

But this disingenuous statement meant little in practice.[25] The king himself actively supported the cause of the Stuarts; England in turn intervened in European affairs. The two countries were colonial rivals. The most prominent political judgments in France reflected these complex realities. The French feared English commercialism and criticized its cultural effects, but they realized that English industry and political institutions gave the country a dynamism that was missing in France. In 1753 the *intendant du commerce*, Vincent de Gournay, commented that English merchants saw to the quality of their merchandise because they advanced a way of life respected by the whole country, while French merchants made their fortunes as quickly as possible in order to escape business life through purchase of an official position. A few years later, the French foreign secretary, the duc de Choiseul, went even further in his appreciation of English institutions. Choiseul was a royalist with an authoritarian frame of mind; he deplored the factionalism and near-anarchy of English political life. But his main concern was to make France strong and efficient enough to compete successfully with England. He was prepared to copy English practices, from industrial techniques even to its representative institutions, if that was what it took to rival or exceed England's political and mercantile achievements.[26]

This dual evaluation of England was similarly true of educated opinion. Frenchmen recalled the expulsion of James II of England in 1688 and the conditions under which William of Orange had become king of England. Parliament had successfully challenged the absolute prerogatives of the king; religious toleration and individual liberty seemed secure or could be defended successfully. As French opposition to absolutism surfaced after 1715, it became pertinent to consider the reasons for England's freedom at home and strength in world affairs.[27]

But it was not England alone which was used by eighteenth-century writers to put France in perspective. Perhaps the most striking, and certainly one of the most famous, national assessments is contained in Montesquieu's *Persian Letters* (1721). Supposedly written by two Persian travelers, the book mocks the reign of Louis XIV, makes fun of Parisian civilization, repeatedly compares Christianity with Islam, and satirizes Roman Catholic doctrine. It was a vigorous, iconoclastic satire which reflected the relief felt at the easing of royal autocracy as well as the fact that in its seemingly secure position France's nobility felt free to make light of what most of Europe admired.

Charles Louis de Secondat, Baron de la Brède et de Montesquieu (1689–1755), had inherited title, property, and a parliamentary seat in Bordeaux. He set out to make his way in Parisian society and, despite the opposition occasioned by the *Persian Letters,* was elected to the Académie Française in 1728. Subsequent travels to Austria, Italy, Hungary, Germany, and England broadened his education, and on his return to France in 1731 he settled on his estate and devoted himself to wide-ranging studies which eventuated in his *Espirit des Lois* in 1748. The book went through thirteen editions in eighteen months. Though its great vogue declined after 1767, ten more editions appeared between 1751 and 1789. The work combined comparative studies with the genre of national evaluation, or what we would call the study of political culture. Among its most influential ideas was Montesquieu's elaboration of the contrasts among a monarchy based on honor, a despotism based on fear, and a republic based on virtue.

These elaborations arose directly from the author's reflection on the political experience of his time. Republics like Holland or Switzerland are by nature small. They have to give up all idea of expansion if they want to survive. In some instances, small republics like the Italian cities are afflicted by internal corruption, for they encourage a free attitude toward the laws which can quickly turn into license. And they face the dilemma of either falling into the hands of an oligarchic nobility or undergoing a popular revolt resulting in dictatorship. When Montesquieu spoke of virtue as the basis of a republic, he referred to a people's capacity to choose their representatives and submit to their wisdom. In republics, political decisions are made by constituted bodies, whose foremost task is to prevent despotism.

Monarchies, according to Montesquieu, also face the problem of despotism. The constituted bodies of their aristocracies are hereditary rather than elected, but a monarchy will be incorruptible only if these bodies obey the laws (that is, if they abide by the principle of honor). Corruption begins when this regard for constitutional law declines. Montesquieu apparently believed that under the conditions of the eighteenth century, only mixed forms of government were viable.

[The problem] could be solved only within the context of the difficult but fruitful compromise between the structures of the nobility, of the citizens, of the judiciary and the sovereign. This compromise might take the French form, or, undoubtedly better, the English. In the former the constituted bodies became intermediaries. In the second, they were the very base of the separation and equilibrium of the three powers [legislature, executive, judiciary].

Montesquieu described (Book XI, Chapter 6) this balance of powers. He favored the English constitution but was careful to add that most European kingdoms enjoy a moderate government because although the prince is invested with legislative and executive functions, he leaves judicial authority to his subjects. Montesquieu underscored this cautionary comment when he pointed out (Book III, Chapter 3) that those favoring democracy had been devoid of virtue in the English civil war, that as a result the government had been continually changing, and that finally the people—after "undergoing many violent shocks"—had been obliged to return to the monarchical government they had previously destroyed.[28] Montesquieu's balanced judgment was forgotten because only his favorable view of the British constitution was generally remembered.[e] This favorable assessment was partly incorporated in the *Encyclopédie* (to which I refer later) and furthered French admiration of a political structure which appeared best suited for the defense of liberty.[29]

This view of the English constitution declined temporarily during the Seven Years' War (1756–1763), but the years following the Treaty of Paris witnessed an outpouring of pro-English sentiment in France. French nobles admired the brilliant role played by English aristocrats in parliament, the limited power of the king, the absence of arbitrary imprisonment, and the balance achieved by the separation of powers. Philosophers like Claude Helvétius (1715–1771) believed that the British parliament had the happy effect of associating enlightened men with the conduct of government. English public affairs were better arranged than the French because they were freely discussed in parliament. Many others praised the reconciliation of liberty with order, the respect for property, and the safeguarding of individual rights which provided protection against servitude as well as anarchy. To scientists and men of letters, England was the home of Newton and Locke. Voltaire contrasted Descartes, who had to leave France to "philosophize in liberty," with Newton, who lived a tranquil, happy and honored life in a free country.

These sanguine appraisals were challenged by conservative critics. To French royalists, the English revolution of 1688 meant that the people had the right to take the throne away from the king if, for example, he converted to Catholicism. The Frenchmen who thought this principle contemptible and dangerous to neighboring monarchies tended to support James II and his heirs. Moreover, England seemed unreliable to them, for no English king could keep his word under the capricious pressures of parliament. There was the further danger of heresy. After the revocation of the Edict of Nantes in 1685, French Huguenots

---

[e]Other admirers of England were less restrained than Montesquieu. Diderot excoriated English commercialism and Voltaire, who had championed English liberty, included a devastating comment on English justice in his *Candide*.

flocked to England, where they were often commercially successful and began to exert their influence in English politics. French Catholics particularly feared that this influence would affect French domestic affairs, for the Huguenot refugees retained many ties in France. These fears were intensified when English supporters of the dethroned James fled to France and recounted cases of English insubordination and irreligion. Just as England harbored French Protestants, so France became a haven for English Catholics (Jacobites).[f]

French apprehensions concerning England's commercialism and representative institutions increased during the decades following the death of Louis XIV. A supposed anglophile like the Abbé Leblanc thought the English political system was falling apart because of the conflicting private interests to which it was subjected. A journal sponsored by the marquis de Mirabeau asserted in the 1760s that the English constitution encouraged constant civil war between landed proprietors and capitalists. At an earlier time, the marquis d'Argenson (1694–1757) had commented that the English were incapable of putting the public good before their petty private interests, a rather typical judgment that was often contrasted to the legendary public virtues of the Romans. The abuses of English politics were vigorously denounced, such as the corruption of parliament, the divisiveness of political parties, diplomatic duplicity, mercantile imperialism, and moral corruption. French conservatives were not alone in making these judgments. The English Tory Lord Bolingbroke lived in France from 1715 to 1723 and from 1735 to 1751. To many, he was an enlightened philosopher in the age of reason. But in his politics, Bolingbroke longed for the days of untrammeled royal authority, when the English constitution had not been undermined by corruption and party strife. Like Leblanc or d'Argenson, Bolingbroke believed that the English constitutional system militated against patriotism by encouraging parties, and that in this respect the French system was superior. In the judgment of Derek Jarrett, "For every Frenchman who saw England through the admiring eyes of a Voltaire or a Montesquieu, there were probably four or five who knew it from the soured recriminations of exiled Jacobites."[30]

The critical view of English institutions received additional impulses from French assessments of England's colonies in North America.[31] Early in the eighteenth century, some note had been taken of the British colonies, both favorable and unfavorable. America was a new and primitive land, with the Indians considered as "good savages" by some and as an inferior breed by others. The American climate was believed unfavorable to human life. Attractive only to settlers motivated by avarice

[f]Jacobites are the Catholic followers of James II and his descendants and should not be confused with the Jacobins of the French revolution.

(an obvious defamation of the British colonists), the country was thought incapable of producing any notable cultural achievement. The Dutch writer De Pauw, publishing in French in 1768, considered the discovery of America the most important and disastrous event in the history of civilization. His idea of the degeneration of man in the New World has its place in the history of evolutionist thought, and it was influenced by his sojourn at the Prussian court, which actively discouraged emigration. But he obviously appealed to French royalists with his declaration that a second catastrophe like the discovery of America would bring mankind to extinction.

In the conservative view, the American rebellion against the legitimate sovereign was deplorable and the prospect consequently dark. Appealing to these sentiments, Simon Linguet predicted that the colonies would soon be divided by factional struggles and degenerate into a despotism ruled by petty local tyrants. Disorder would increase as vices were magnified by a horde of restless emigrants from Europe. There was also the possibility that America's wealth and power would grow. Both prospects were threatening to European civilization. Fostered by news from America transmitted by the English press, a number of French writers elaborated an anti-American ideology. The abbé Mably expressed serious doubts about the wisdom of the common man and the prospects of American democracy (1784). Other writers questioned the patriotism of Americans during the war of independence and pointed out that 700,000 slaves lived in that land of liberty. Also, a large number of complaints arose from businessmen engaged in French-American trade and from unsuccessful ventures of emigration to America. These and related arguments appealed to French conservatives, who were made uneasy by an alliance with an America demanding independence.

But there were counterarguments appealing to liberal sentiments, and for a time these came to dominate French opinion. Some French writers had noted the accomplishments of the Quakers in Pennsylvania toward the end of the seventeenth century. One writer remarked that in New Jersey there were no lawyers, doctors, or theologians, which seemed a very good thing to French critics of their own country. These pamphlets were addressed to French Huguenots in order to encourage their emigration to America. Similar ideas were included in several articles of the *Encyclopédie*, which noted the principles of religious toleration and enlightened government in the colonies.

Following the Treaty of Paris of 1763, interest in America gradually increased. A number of American artists and scientists visited France. When Benjamin Franklin came to Paris (1767) as the American colonists' representative in London, his scientific and political reputation won him ready acclaim.[32] With the Declaration of Independence in 1776, the

French fad for America turned into widespread enthusiasm. Although the French government was suspicious of American republicanism, even conservative royal officials welcomed the attack on England, which promised to open the American market to French trade. In this sense, French conservatives also championed American independence. For a time, the French government furnished secret aid and then, in 1778, joined in a military alliance with the Americans and declared war on England. Among the French public, this move was very popular. Revenge for the humiliation suffered in 1763 was one reason; participation in the war by prominent French soldiers like Lafayette was another. During the war and in the years following, information about the emerging nation was supplied in increasing quantity, with French writers issuing books on America and newspapers devoting considerable space to reports on American affairs, including copious translations of contemporary American writers and documents. In this setting, Franklin became a pivotal figure, skillfully exploiting the situation and his own popularity in a propaganda campaign favorable to the American cause. As a scientist, moralist, and politician, Franklin preached the gospel of American prosperity and progress and personified the ideals of liberty and equality.

The championship of American independence soon broadened into the philosophic and political idealization of America. To the leading representatives of the ancien régime, France's alliance with America probably appeared as old-fashioned power politics: England was the enemy and here was a chance to defeat it. Once France had joined the American war of independence, a critical approach to English institutions became widely accepted among liberal writers as well.[33] The *Journal encyclopédique* noted in 1782 that the prestige of the British constitution diminished as sympathy with the American colonies rose. England had not merely the imperfections to be found in other governments, but a rather large number specific to itself. Fiscal impositions and corruption were suffocating English liberty, a point on which Frenchmen of many persuasions could readily agree. At one time, the English parliament had led that nation against the king, but now parliament itself was hostile to the colonists, a point seemingly confirmed by the list of grievances in the American Declaration of Independence. Thus, the liberties of Englishmen were defended more energetically and effectively in the colonies than in the mother country, a point of some weight with those Frenchmen who identified themselves with the libertarian elements of the English constitution. Many arguments were advanced to supplement this position, like the right of the colonists to self-taxation which all other Englishmen enjoyed, or the oppressiveness of English colonial trade. These and related specifics were probably overshadowed by nationalist sentiments in which most Frenchmen could join even though they differed in other respects. After all, France had been defeated by Britain in the Seven Years' War.

France's participation in the American war of independence opened a pandora's box of liberal sentiment. Enthusiasm could be openly expressed for the liberty, equality, and constitutionalism of America, and by praising America and condemning England, Frenchmen could attack monarchical absolutism and demand the thorough reform of their own society without saying so explicitly. Turgot called America the "hope and model of the human race." An anonymous writer justified the war of independence on the ground that England had broken the social contract. Brissot extolled the principle that in the American republic all power emanates from the people. Diderot called America "an asylum from fanaticism and tyranny." Mandrillon praised the spirit of tolerance and emphasized the political maturity of the Americans. America was transformed imaginatively from a number of English colonies overthrowing British political and economic domination into a symbol of an entire people opposing the tyranny of absolute power, asserting the inalienable rights of man. Transferred to France, the pragmatic realities of English settlers in America became the ideal qualities of a popular revolution. At the same time, American political literature was published extensively in France. The basic constitutional documents elicited wide interest and demonstrated that "American liberty" had specific content: representative government, religious toleration, trial by jury, freedom of speech, and freedom of the press.

A number of cultural features were associated with these specifically political ideas. Franklin made a great impression with his estimate that the population was doubling every twenty-five years. America was an agricultural society in which people lived a peaceful, happy life. Liberty was made secure by the equal distribution of landed property and the absence of great wealth. At the same time, prosperity was in evidence, though there was the danger that luxury would lead to corruption and inequality. Since the standard of living of the American farmer was much higher than that of the French peasant, some writers saw evidence for their advocacy of a free agricultural economy, while others saw their belief confirmed that liberty and enlightened legislation produced economic prosperity. America provided evidence that through reason and experience men could attain material well-being and freedom from superstition. French writers on America emphasized the scientific, artistic, and educational achievements of the country. Franklin, Jefferson, and the other "founding fathers" made it seem that the ideal of a society governed by philosophers was realized at last. The hope that the arts and sciences could flourish without the corruptions of an aristocratic and urban society was inspired by the image of a high civilization emerging from a rustic setting at the edge of the wilderness.

To many Frenchmen of the 1770s and 1780s, America had become the promised land in which man's power to create an ideal society was manifest. Basic philosophical doctrines together with French aspirations in public affairs were projected onto a scene that was distant enough to sustain a myth and real enough to lend it credence. Many literary works together with much social and political writing seemed to confirm that the Americans were doing what John Locke had taught to his many French disciples. This symbolic representation of America could encompass a conservative *and* a progressive vision. In his *Letters from an American Farmer* (1782–1784), de Crèvecoeur proclaimed that in America men were making a new start, combining the sciences of a modern nation with the simplicity and virtue of a rural society. In 1786 the marquis de Condorcet published an essay, "L'Influence de la révolution de l'Amérique sur l'Europe," which stated that America had provided a singular object-lesson to Europe. Men can exercise their rights only when prejudice and ignorance are destroyed; people can achieve happiness only where wealth is distributed equally. Both conditions were approximated in America, thus demonstrating that the rights of man are a practical possibility rather than merely philosophic speculation. In the 1770s and 1780s texts of American state constitutions, bills of rights, and eventually the new federal constitution became available in France. In this way, the earlier equation between virtue and enlightenment (as Crèvecoeur described it) was given political significance in a program of popular sovereignty, representative government, and the guarantee of individual rights.

In the early eighteenth century, French noblemen had admired England because its aristocracy had acquired dominant political influence. French men of letters had idealized the division and balance of powers that had been achieved among the three branches of government. By the 1770s, attention shifted to the American struggle for independence, and writers like Turgot, Raynal, and others accompanied that struggle with a stream of encouraging and cautionary letters and pamphlets. In 1784 news reached France of a Society of Cincinnatus which had been created under the sponsorship of General Washington in order to perpetuate the military tradition of the revolutionary war and to constitute the officers and their descendants as an hereditary brotherhood. Franklin and his friends in Paris saw in this development the danger of a new aristocracy in the making. They suggested to the comte de Mirabeau that he compose a pamphlet attacking the Society of Cincinnatus and its sponsors, General Washington and the marquis de Lafayette. Both men were prominent Freemasons, as were Franklin and many members of his circle. Washington withdrew his support of the Society (even before the pamphlet was published), and the Society in turn deleted from its bylaws the clause concerning hereditary membership. Still, here was a pamphlet by a French noble directed against the dangers of hereditary nobility in America. Prominent aristocrats and Freemasons like the duc d'Orleans, the marquis de Lafayette, the Noailles family, the La Rochefoucaulds, the Bouillons, and others joined in this attack on their own position. I turn now to the nobility and men of letters in French society who helped to promote such prerevolutionary sentiments.

WRITERS, PARLEMENTAIRES, AND FREEMASONS

Tocqueville states in *The Old Regime and the Revolution* that French society in the eighteenth century presented a spectacle of "many absurd and unjust privileges," of "many ridiculous, ramshackle institutions," which no one had attempted to harmonize or adapt to new needs. Faced with this spectacle, the *philosophes* or men of letters came to "loathe everything that savored of the past," thinking that "what was wanted was to replace the complex of traditional customs governing the social order of the day by simple, elementary rules deriving from the exercise of the human reason and natural law."[34] Tocqueville was right when he declared that these "simple and elementary rules" helped to turn diffuse discontents into a social and political force. Prerevolutionary France contained the classic example of an intelligentsia as defined by *Webster's Dictionary* (1961): a "class of well-educated articulate persons constituting a distinct, recognized, and self-conscious social stratum within a nation and claiming or assuming for itself the guiding role." The most successful philosophes of the eighteenth century defended property and distinctions of social rank and were quite eager to be accepted by high society. Yet they espoused the principle of Reason, and their ideas came to influence members of the French nobility.

Revolutions occur more readily when ruling groups within a society begin to embrace views that conflict with the rationale of their own existence. Tocqueville states that the French nobility engaged in the "delightful game" of lightheartedly talking about the "absurdity" of all the old French customs, while clinging to their immunities and privileges.[35] How was this possible? Under the reign of Louis XIV, the French nobility had been excluded from participation in public life, and Tocqueville felt that this exclusion contributed to the spread of rationalist ideas among the nobility. Yet conditions changed after the death of Louis XIV in 1715. The parlements of France played a rather active role in public life between that date and the outbreak of the revolution in 1789. The agitation by the members of parlements (*parlementaires* or *noblesse de robe*) centered on the defense of their privileges. But members of the nobility and especially the parlementaires were quite prepared to clothe the defense of privilege in the rhetoric of humanity, even apart from the individual noble who actually put a conception of social responsibility above his private concerns. This potential for a coalescence of views between the philosophes and the nobility helped to create a climate of opinion favorable to the revolution. The following discussion considers French men of letters as a social group, the growth of opposition to royal government (especially among the noblesse de robe), and one instance of coalescence between writers and nobility in the gatherings of the Freemasons.

French writers of the eighteenth century came to form a social group as men of letters and as an oppositional vanguard. They were sensitive to the fate of their country, aware of what went on elsewhere, and capable of formulating ideas that appealed to an increasing number of readers. They were versed in many fields rather than specialists in any one. Voltaire wrote that their philosophical spirit, their "searching and purified reason . . . has greatly contributed to instructing and refining the nation."[36] Yet such a sense of importance was only gradually established. In 1726 Voltaire was beaten up by hired thugs. He had offended the chevalier Rohan-Chabot and was sent to the Bastille for daring to seek revenge. In 1734 Voltaire noted the lowly position of writers in France in pointed contrast to the consideration they received in England. But by the 1770s, an English observer wrote that French men of letters "have considerable weight on the manners and sentiments of people of rank, of the public in general, and consequently are not without effect on the measures of government."[37] In 1778, after an absence of twenty-eight years, Voltaire returned to Paris in triumph (from his home in Ferney on the Swiss border) and was treated with adulation at the Académie, at the Comédie Française, and in the streets. Voltaire's case was unusual, but not unique. Between the 1720s and the 1770s, prominent French writers had acquired social recognition, a certain notoriety, and a sense of importance, despite the economic insecurity of many individual authors.

Two conditions help account for this transformation: one is the improvement in the social and economic position of *some* writers; the other is the continuation of religious controversy.

The transition from the writer's dependence on private patronage to the development of a marketplace for literature was a general phenomenon of the period. In 1760 Oliver Goldsmith wrote that the man of letters could bravely assert the dignity of independence. This statement applied more fully to England than to France, where the larger reading public was offset by the absence of an international copyright agreement which meant that many French books were published abroad

Philosophers Dining

The leading philosophers of the Enlightenment are pictured at dinner; among them are Voltaire (with hand raised) and the two editors of the *Encyclopédie,* Diderot (at Voltaire's left) and d'Alembert (left foreground). Bold and witty conversation was almost as important a part of eighteenth-century sociability and culture as the written word. (Bibliothèque Nationale)

without compensation to the authors. Writers for the theatre were in a better financial position if their plays were really successful. But success was sporadic. Many prominent writers still depended on private patrons; others had inherited property and did not wholly depend on income from their writings. The copyright laws favored publishers rather than writers until the late 1770s, though for prominent men of letters that legal disadvantage was made up by their increasing acceptance in the circles of high society. Thus, the economic and social position of well-known writers improved, especially in the last decades of the century, though as a whole the profession of writing remained economically insecure.

Religious controversy contributed to the writer's insecurity as well as to his sense of importance. France suffered from wars of religion in the sixteenth and seventeenth centuries and from religious controversy in the eighteenth. The revocation of the Edict of Nantes (1685) was followed by a royal declaration of 1724 which further strengthened punitive measures against Huguenots who remained in France. The monarchy fully supported the Catholic church, and the church sought to monopolize the control of religious beliefs. Furthermore, the church imposed its interpretation of philosophy and history against all attempts to espouse the cause of science and reason. The church held firmly to the position of religious uniformity, which required that the secular power must intervene when an individual deviated from orthodox belief. In practice, the government did not go as far as the church desired, but in a few spectacular cases its persecution of Huguenots went far indeed and left an indelible impression of utter intolerance. Church authorities condemned various writings, and the Sorbonne faculty of theology expounded the religious duties of secular government. All manuscripts had to be approved by the censor; even with approval, however, the author still ran the danger of his book's suppression or proceedings against his person if on publication the book aroused the hostility of the university or the parlement. In practice, many uncensored books were published in, or smuggled into, France. But censorship exacerbated the condition of writers already beset with economic insecurity, at the same time that it made even mediocre writers notorious for their defiance of authority.[38]

High society had treated writers with utter contempt in the seventeenth century, but Voltaire's experience with hired thugs (1726) was one of the last instances of this kind. As the writer's social and economic condition improved, the intolerance and censorship by church and government were frequent sources of both irritation and the sense that writing really mattered. The relation between men of letters and the leaders of society became a favorite theme of philosophical reflection, which mirrored the old fear of impotence and the new feeling of importance. At one point, Diderot speaks of philosophy as the opium of the passions, suggesting a painful awareness of the discrepancy between the idea of Reason and political reality. A certain tension developed between literati and activists over the relative emphasis on style and propaganda. Since he favored high literary quality, Voltaire voiced his skepticism to the two editors of the famous *Encyclopédie*.[g] He addressed them occasionally as "Atlas and Hercules who carry the world on their shoul-

---

[g]The *Encyclopédie, ou Dictionnaire raisonné des sciences, des arts, et des métiers* began publication in 1751 under the editorship of the philosopher Denis Diderot and the mathematician d'Alembert. The widespread distribution of the *Encyclopédie* should be noted. Estimates put it at 15,000 copies between 1751 and 1789. The various editions ranged from 17 to 36 volumes of text and 3 to 11 volumes of plates. Even 15,000 copies of the whole work would come to between 255,000 and 540,000 volumes of text and between 45,000 and 165,000 volumes of plates. The *Encyclopédie* was sold all over France and its readers consisted not only of the literary elite, but of the lawyers, doctors, and other professionals in the provinces who later made their literary and revolutionary careers in Paris. I am indebted to Professor Robert Darnton of Princeton University for information on this point.

ders, the Department for the instruction of mankind."[39] As Robert Darnton has shown, the familiar figures of the Enlightenment were an elite. In their view taste belonged "to a very small number of privileged souls. . . . It is unknown in bourgeois families, where one is constantly occupied with the care of one's fortunes." Yet a host of lesser writers flocked to Paris in the wake of these famous men. Desiring to make their fortune, they were often forced to eke out an existence by hack work, and these *déclassé* men of letters were instrumental in turning the main ideas of the Enlightenment into a revolutionary ideology.[40] The successful writers, on the other hand, cultivated their contacts with the nobility in fashionable salons and the other meeting places of high society. If the ancien régime allowed the moderate expression of libertarian ideas (or did not succeed in suppressing them and their debased versions in the form of political diatribes and much obscenity), this was due in part to the prominent nobles who embraced and protected the philosophy of humanity.

In the eighteenth century, Paris boasted a fashionable society in which brilliant writers gave expression to myriad discontents and were applauded and rewarded for their efforts. Discontents had built up during the reign of Louis XIV and, as Tocqueville pointed out, were transformed rather than allayed by the renewed prosperity of the country during the eighteenth century. For as conditions improved, pressures increased to oppose the onerous effects of a regime which claimed to govern the country but in practice left much provincial and local rule in the hands of those who made a comfortable living from the financial exploitation of officeholding. Opposition was rife among nobles who resented the abrogation of their political rights. Entrepreneurs and financiers resented the arbitrary and secretive handling of state debts because this often resulted in major financial losses for them. Many bourgeois officials and judges developed a critical attitude toward the royal edicts which they themselves were obliged to implement. Finally, some 400,000 Huguenot refugees had left France following the revocation of the Edict of Nantes (1685), and these Frenchmen abroad formed clubs and propaganda centers favoring a constitutional monarchy.

By the middle of the eighteenth century, all these groups provided a ready audience for men of letters who "wished to replace traditional customs . . . by elementary rules deriving from the exercise of reason" (Tocqueville). These intellectual leaders appealed to many groups. But they acquired a special resonance by virtue of the disaffection spreading in the circles of high society. The old regime was weakened by the disloyalty of its leading strata long before the revolution of 1789. Courtiers and other aristocratic men of affairs met with writers in the salons and literary clubs organized by ladies of fashion, in various academies, and

even in the popular gatherings of occult science. This ideological activation of the nobility can be understood by noting the increasing participation of the parlementaires in public affairs.

Louis XIV had begun his effective rule in 1661 by silencing the
Paris parlement in the matter of registering royal edicts. Thereafter, the
king reduced parlements' rights of registering royal edicts and of remonstrance to an empty formality. After the king's death, however, the
situation changed abruptly. Goubert states that "every parlement in the
realm was to spend the eighteenth century getting its revenge for fifty
years of captivity."[41]

In his will, Louis XIV had limited the powers of Philip of Orleans,
the regent during the minority of Louis XV (1715–1723). The Paris
parlement set aside the late king's will in return for the regent's recognition of the parlement's right of remonstrance. But the regent then
opposed the use of that right. From 1716 to 1720, the Scotsman John
Law was financial advisor to Philip of Orleans. Law aroused the opposition of parlement when he repudiated financial claims arising from
the War of the Spanish Succession, devalued the currency, and put war
contractors on trial for malpractice. This opposition took the usual form
of a remonstrance to which the regent responded in the customary fashion by meeting with the parlement (lit de justice, 1718), personally prohibiting the remonstrance, and, when opposed, sending the parlementaires into exile from Paris. Law remained in favor until his schemes
collapsed in 1720, when *he* had to flee into exile while the Paris parlement returned.

A second aspect of the struggle between the Paris parlement and
the French monarchy concerned religious issues. The French Catholic
church and the papacy had been engaged in intermittent controversy
over the relation between royal and papal powers since the thirteenth
century. The general tendency of the French church had been to support the French kings' authority over ecclesiastical appointments and to
accept papal teaching as infallible *provided* it was approved by a council
of the whole church (*Gallicanism*). This position was never accepted by
the papacy, but it became the quasi-official posture of the French
church, though some French Catholics, especially the Jesuits, bitterly
opposed Gallicanism. In addition, Jansenism became associated with this
intra-Catholic struggle during the seventeenth and eighteenth centuries.

Jansenism was a nonorthodox, Catholic religious movement, initiated by the Flemish theologian Cornelius Jansen (1585–1638), who exalted the all-powerful character of grace made available by Christ the
Redeemer. This traditional Catholic doctrine appeared suspect in the
eyes of the Jesuits, particularly by its emphasis on the inviolable rights
of individual conscience. The papal bull *Unigenitus* (1713) condemned
a Jansenist devotional work and the idea that Bible reading was a reli-

gious duty of laymen. In his last year, Louis XIV enforced registration of this bull as a royal edict by the Paris parlement. The parlementaires may not have been Jansenists themselves, but their Gallican hostility to the influence of Rome was outspoken. In 1714 the Paris parlement declared its opposition to *Unigenitus*. In 1720 the parlement secured the crown's agreement to modify the bull and bring it in line with Gallican principles. In 1730/31 parlement defined Gallican principles in intransigent terms, defying Cardinal Fleury's attempt to silence the parlementaires. And in 1752 the conflict flared up again when the archbishop of Paris, a strong partisan of the papal position, ordered his clergy to refuse the last sacraments to all persons suspected of Jansenism. In response, the parlement forbade any priest to refuse the sacraments on such grounds and in 1753 added the Grand Remonstrance, which demanded "that the king should not exercise his authority in an unrestricted manner." Louis XV (1715–1774) rejected the remonstrance, parlement declared a judicial strike, and the magistrates were ordered into exile. But two years later they returned, having largely won their point. By 1764 the Gallican parlementaires had won a clear victory with the expulsion of the Jesuits from France.[42]

A third aspect of this rising opposition by the Paris parlement, and the provincial parlements allied with it, involved the perennial tax issue. The century witnessed many projects for financial reform which miscarried because of opposition by the parlements. The struggle over the *vingtième* is a case in point. In 1749 the finance minister Machault had proposed that this tax on income be imposed on all proprietors. The parlements initiated opposition and were joined by the clergy, who succeeded in obtaining exemption from the tax for church property. This precedent was quickly taken up by others, and before long the vingtième was so riddled with exemptions that it became little more than still another tax on the unfortunate peasantry.[43] The argument over taxation, old though it was, received a new impetus from the Seven Years' War. The French defeat in the Treaty of Paris (1763) was made still more galling by the huge debts of the government, and it was popular to make a scapegoat of the financiers with their exorbitant profits and high interest rates. In fact, corporations of every kind, many wealthy people, and even the king himself had lent money to the government during the war. But in 1763 the pamphleteers of the parlements launched the attack on "the financiers," just as the Paris parlement was forced to register two new tax edicts. It should be noted that this renewed agitation coincided with the final controversy leading to the expulsion of the Jesuit order.

These examples suggest that by the middle of the eighteenth century, the parlementaires *were* participating in public life. Indeed, in the Grand Remonstrance of 1753 the Paris parlement advanced a constitutional view of the monarchy. Its declaration that "if subjects owe obedience to kings, kings for their part owe obedience to laws" came close to the idea of contract between the king and the people previously articulated by the English parliament in 1688. To be sure, the parlements remained primarily courts of law; therefore, the starting point of their agitation was the seemingly innocuous one of wishing to preserve the integrity and continuity of the laws. The parlements were the officially recognized depositories of all laws; but repeated insistence that the parlements must verify all new enactments on behalf of the nation tended to transform the custodial functions of the parlements into the claim that some dozen parlements were as one body defending the rights of the nation. Local conflicts between the crown and a parlement, and particularly the repeated conflicts involving the parlement of Paris, came to be interpreted as matters of principle involving the whole country. As Robert Palmer has stated,

> Protesting against modernization of property assessments, they had banded together in a *union des classes,* or a super-parlement claiming to be representative of the whole kingdom. On the one hand, a royalist pamphleteer denounced the parlements as a "monstrous hereditary aristocracy". On the other hand, the parlements, as early as the 1760's, put a good deal of incipient revolutionary language into wide circulation—*citoyen, loi, patrie, constitution, nation, droit de la nation, cri de la nation.* It seems likely that the parlements had more positive influence than the *philosophes,* especially among lawyers and other makers of public opinion, to whom they spoke out as weighty and reputable bodies in Paris and a dozen provincial capitals.

In this way, the effort to preserve the law gradually blended with Montesquieu's idea of the *corps intermédiaires,* the intermediary powers between the king and the country, which had the right and duty of representing the people as a whole. It remains true, however, that the parlementaires were engaged in an excess of rhetoric when they used the language of the philosophes in describing what was primarily a defense of their own vested interests.[44]

The parlementaires were the most politically active segment of the French nobility and were perhaps most influential among "lawyers and other makers of public opinion." At the same time, there is evidence that the philosophes, with their rational and humanitarian ideals, exerted considerable influence on other segments of the nobility and on wealthy commoners. This is the reason why I conclude this part of the discussion with some attention to Freemasonry. The idea that the Freemasons were at the heart of a conspiracy leading to the revolution against the ancien régime must be attributed to the myths of a plot which proliferated during and after the French revolution. The only relationship between Freemasons and the revolution worth taking seriously is an indirect one. As J. M. Roberts observes, [the Freemasons] can hardly have failed to contribute to the short-lived atmosphere of philanthropic, libertarian, egalitarian and constitutional progressiveness which inspired much of the early work of the National Assembly. They no doubt served to generalize and disseminate the basic ideals of the humanitarian elite of eighteenth-century France.[45]

My discussion of the spread of enlightened ideas by the Freemasons among the ruling groups of French society is meant in this sense.

Freemasonry had begun in England in the late seventeenth century and was introduced in France in the 1730s by noble Scotch refugees loyal to the House of Stuart. Masonic meetings became a generally accepted setting for the encounter between writers and leaders of French society, who ranged from the highest ranks of the nobility down to well-to-do merchants and craftsmen of some standing in their local communities. Members of the French clergy also entered the order in considerable numbers, though the church disapproved and much hostility existed at the parish level. Membership in the order allowed all these men to meet and enjoy one another's fellowship free from religious or political controversy and without challenging the social and political order. As men all Masons were equal. Through its social structure as a secret and hierarchical society and through its humanistic appeals, Freemasonry combined the ideals of liberty, equality, and fraternity in a France of little liberty, much inequality, and bitter class antagonisms.

There are several clues to the paradox that an organization attractive to nobles would nevertheless sponsor ideals of equality. The order made a deliberate effort to attract members of the nobility, putting them at the head of its lodges and having them lead its processions and parades. From the standpoint of the order, noblemen could give valued financial and political support; and through their prestige and personal authority they could dampen the fires of controversy within the order. From the standpoint of the nobility, Freemasonry was attractive because it provided an accepted form of escaping the artificialities of high society and the burden of affairs. There seemed nothing suspicious about an organization that engaged in a mixture of drinking, singing, lectures, philanthropy, religion without orthodoxy, benevolence, vague mysticism, and a brotherhood that allowed the noble to enjoy his superior status anyway.

The Freemasons were a secret society only in the sense that on entering each member had to swear a solemn oath to keep the secrets of Masonry. Violators of the oath were threatened by extreme penalties which were almost certainly symbolic. The detailing of these penalties in the oath presumably expressed the social pressure to which the individual exposed himself if he violated his commitment.[46] On the other hand, membership in the order was openly declared. The oath of secrecy made the order suspect, and Freemasonry took special care to assure the authorities of its religious and political probity. The Masonic order stood for science, and in the early eighteenth century that meant Newtonian physics. Newton himself was a devout Christian, but as a Protestant he was hardly reassuring to French Catholics. Moreover, English Freemasonry had been founded by a disciple of Newton's, John Theophilus Desaguliers (1683–1744), a French Huguenot whose family had fled to England after 1685. These were damaging associations, and although in France the Catholic church did not prohibit the order, the Masonic attitude toward religion was a critical issue.

Desaguliers formulated that attitude by expounding Newton's theories to Christian laymen. Newton had reduced innumerable and contradictory phenomena to a single doctrine and explained the mysterious movement of the heavenly bodies and of all other bodies by a universal law. Desaguliers' God, like Newton's, appealed to the mind rather than the heart, substituting observations of nature and experiments for divine revelation. Under Desaguliers' influence, the Masonic constitution incorporated what we would call an ecumenical approach to religion:

> A Mason is obliged, by his Tenure, to obey the moral Law. . . . But though in ancient Times Masons were charg'd in every Country to be of the religion of that Country and Nation, whatever it was, yet 'tis now thought more expedient only to oblige them to that Religion in which all Men agree, leaving their particular Opinion to themselves; to be *good Men and true* or Men of Honour and Honesty, by whatever Denominations or Persuasions they may be distinguish'd; whereby Masonry becomes the *Center of Union,* and the Means of conciliating true Friendship among Persons that must else have remain'd at a perpetual Distance.[47]

Masonry thus constituted itself as an institution capable of working for the social and mental unity of mankind. Under the influence of a spiritualized interpretation of Newtonian science, the Masons abandoned revelation and dogmas as well as the earlier subordination of all private association to the prevailing religious dispensation.

The Masonic attitude toward the state was similar. All initiates were enjoined to obey the moral law and civil authority. In England, the order was sponsored by the Hanoverian dynasty and loyalty was taken for granted. But in France, where the order was barely tolerated, failure to pledge loyalty to the king was an act of some defiance. In the Masonic pledge of obedience, references to the civil power are very general. The pledge refers to "ancient Kings and Princes" under whom Masonry had always suffered war and bloodshed. Nevertheless, ancient royalty had encouraged the order because it was known for its peacefulness and loyalty, and eighteenth-century Freemasonry likewise declared its peaceful intentions. The order wanted to be as free of political involvement as it was of organized religion. In the Constitution of 1723, the pledge reads as follows:

If a Brother should be a Rebel against the State, he is not to be countenanced
in his Rebellion, however he may be pitied as an unhappy man; and if convicted of no other Crime, though the loyal Brotherhood must and ought to
disown his Rebellion, and give no Umbrage or Ground of political Jealousy
to the Government for the time being; they cannot expel him from the
Lodge, and his Relation to it remains indefeasible.[48]

One may wonder why the French government, anxious to maintain its
authority, would countenance such transparent reservations. Perhaps
the answer is that the Masons remained completely aloof from public
affairs and included among their members some of the most distinguished names of French society, including the king's brother. Royal
officials would hardly proceed against such personalities, and one may
say that official toleration of Masonic secrecy was simply one more grant
of exemption to men who enjoyed many such grants already.

The rules of the order stipulated that no candidate may be asked
his religious convictions or political opinions and that discussion of these
matters is excluded from all lodge meetings.[49] Free from the bonds of
the outside world, the Mason is a man among men, engaged jointly with
them in the cultivation of morality.

> Le cri de la nature, ami, c'est Liberté!
> Ce droit si cher à l'homme est ici respecté.
> Egaux sans anarchie et libres sans license,
> Obéir à nos lois fair notre indépendance.[50]

In the seclusion of the lodge meeting, man's right to freedom is respected. Here men can be equal without anarchy and free without license, for by following their own laws they have achieved independence.
By accepting, though not endorsing, such an order, the civil authorities
permitted Freemasonry to establish a realm of morality *outside of church
and state*. "In a nation teeming with officials" the order provided the
meeting ground for men who either did not hold posts of any kind or,
even if they did, wanted to meet with others "keeping steadily aloof from
the political arena."[51]

This ostensibly nonpolitical stance was spurious. Masonic secrets
allowed for a critical confrontation between morality and politics, just
as freedom of expression for writers permitted a critical assessment of
history and religion.[52] In their relation to the world, both Masons and
men of letters promoted the ideal of equality but asserted their superiority over others. For the Masons, the philosophy of humanity was
embodied in the human fellowship made possible by their secret organization and was supported by the distinguished nobles participating in
it. For men of letters, taste was for the privileged few rather than for
those concerned with making a living. Writers like Duclos, Voltaire, and

d'Alembert believed that enlightenment should begin with those whose "superiority of birth and position commands our deference and our respect."[53] Masons and writers criticized church and state from this standpoint of a higher morality.

Nobles and men of letters met on an equal footing in the Masonic lodges. In France, Freemasonry developed rapidly in the 1770s, the number of lodges increasing from 104 in 1772 to over 600 in 1789. Among these, the 65 lodges in Paris were the most important. The philosopher and banker Helvétius and the astronomer Lalande helped to found the Loge des Neuf Soeurs (1769), whose roster of participants reads like a cross-section of the French elite.[h] Benjamin Franklin was elected master of the lodge in 1779–1781. Under his leadership, the lodge became a center of propaganda for humanitarian causes, American independence, and the ideals of brotherhood. In the last year of his life (1778), Voltaire was solemnly initiated into the Loge des Neuf Soeurs, sponsored by Franklin and Lalande.

The Masonic members and prominent men of letters were elitists in terms of their social composition and their aspirations. But in terms of their appeal to fraternity and their philosophy of humanity they were also populists. Ambivalence about elitism and populism as well as tacit assumptions about the relations among virtue, ideas, and power are archetypical ingredients of an ideology that breaks with tradition. The pursuit of ideas by men of letters sets them apart from ordinary folk. But these men of letters also seek a responsive audience in their own society. They sense their isolation and realize the defects or backwardness of their country in comparison with others. The resulting perspective is exacerbated by a sense of impotence. Men of letters typically do not have access to positions of power commensurate with their sense of mission and anxiety for their country. Thus, powerlessness is experienced most acutely just when men of letters develop a group consciousness. They are confronted with the tragic discrepancy between what is and what ought to be, between their political impotence and the significance of ideas in their own lives. In this setting, it is a great temptation to implicitly attribute to theory, to principle, to ideas a potential impact, a power to move men. For men will seek mastery where they can find it, and when ideas are their only weapons they will attribute special power to them.

[h] A partial listing includes the scientists Lalande, Lacépède, Berthelot, and Fourcroy; the financiers and noblemen Bailly, Prince de Rohan, duc de la Rochefoucauld, and the marquis de Condorcet; the parliamentarians Duval d'Esprémesnil and President du Paty; the philosophers and writers Montesquieu, d'Alembert, Abbé Sieyès, Cabanis, and other important artists and journalists; and finally later revolutionaries like Danton, Desmoulins, Brissot, and Rabaut-St. Etienne.

AN EQUALITY OF RIGHTS

During the eighteenth century, French society was marked by the paradoxes of absolutism, by a national awareness articulated in part through reflections on England and America, and by the mobilization of intellectual, social, and political elites. The affirmation of rights and the ideal of equality emerged in each of these contexts. By reflecting on the English and American constitutions, intellectual leaders were encouraged to adapt a libertarian constitution to their own situation. By their association with the leaders of French society, men of letters helped to catalyze the diffuse disaffection aroused by the ancien régime. Unwittingly, they also encouraged the radicalization of aspiring literati who flocked to Paris. And, finally, the parlementaires in Paris and the provincial capitals became increasingly obstreperous defenders of their vested interests, using a rhetoric of law, citizenship, and rights of the nation which had more radical implications than were probably intended.

The main purpose of this concluding section is to consider equality of rights as the foundation of the mandate of the people. Some of the circumstances of the immediate, prerevolutionary period are crucial for an understanding of these ideas. By 1783 France had incurred an enormous governmental debt due to its participation in the American struggle for independence. Drastic tax reforms were proposed to settle the debt, but instead these reforms precipitated the crisis which culminated in the revolution. Royal edicts such as the tax proposal had to be registered and promulgated by the parlement of Paris, but for decades the parlements had opposed royal edicts in defense of their privileges. In the process, they had thwarted much-needed administrative and fiscal reforms, while asserting their function as representatives of the nation.[54] The contest between the parlements and the crown had stirred public opinion, while the rhetoric in which that contest was expressed had aroused expectations of reform.

In 1787 and 1788 ministers of finance repeatedly attempted to secure agreement on a tax reform and a new tax on land. These measures were extremely unpopular. Attempts to bypass the parlements by ad-hoc assemblies of notables proved in vain and provoked considerable popular agitation. By August 1788 the national exchequer was so depleted that the finance minister agreed to a convocation of the Estates-General, which had not met since 1614. In September the parlement of Paris was called back into session amid great acclaim. But when the royal decrees convoking the Estates-General were registered, parlement added the stipulation that the electoral provisions of 1614 should be observed. Clergy, nobility, and the Third Estate should meet and vote separately; each estate should have an equal number of representatives; and the rights of the Third Estate to deliberate should remain limited. This declaration aroused a storm of protest, and in the ensuing agitation the whole struggle was transformed from a contest of the parlement with the monarchy into a struggle of the Third Estate against clergy, nobility, and the entire royalist regime. There was a sense of betrayal when the parlement, which had stood for decades as a symbol of liberty against despotism, proved to be what in fact it had always been—an upholder of privilege.[55] This sense of betrayal still echoed in the assertions of 1787–1789 that only when the three estates met in the Estates-General as one body could the nation give the necessary consent to the imposition of a permanent tax.

Under the rules for the election of the Estates-General, some 40,000 meetings were held to debate the issues. The organization of the electorate and the extension of the franchise were at the heart of this debate, and the royal government did its part, however unwittingly, in mobilizing the Third Estate.[56] In the official view, the convocation of the Estates-General was a measure of last resort. But it was important that the government hear grievances, for traditionally the deputies to the Estates-General had stated the grievances of the electors to the king. From a conservative standpoint, it was plausible to think of the forthcoming elections as an opportunity for the people to voice their complaints and affirm their loyalty to the king who had granted them this opportunity.

The Three Estates
After an interval of 175 years, the Estates General were convened at Versailles on May 4, 1789. Resisting the old procedure of separate voting, the Third Estate declared itself the only true representative of the nation (June 17). Ten days later the king's opposition collapsed and the Third Estate together with 170 clerical deputies and 50 nobles met in a Constituent Assembly to "hammer out" a new constitution, as shown in this contemporary cartoon. (British Museum)

Recourse to the old procedures could be seen as an appeal to royalist sentiment. It was largely taken for granted that the general population was loyal to the king.

From the standpoint of reform, this proposed return to an abandoned institution stood for the accumulation of ills in French society. By recourse to precedent, the monarchy and the parlement of Paris merely defended their privileges. The revolutionary ideas of the Third Estate as well as the idea of equality were formulated in protest against this recourse to the past. In 1775 Turgot had stated to the king that "the rights of men gathered in society are not founded on their history, but in their nature." In the past, laws were made either out of ignorance or through compromises with "the very powerful self-interests of parties." The king was not bound by such precedents, for "there can be no reason to perpetuate establishments which were made without reason."[57] Turgot's statement shows how far a loyal but reform-minded member of the royal government had come in recognizing history as the embodiment of ignorance or ill-advised compromise. Opposition to vested interests sustained by precedent was symbolized by the appeal to reason and nature, and from this symbolic contrast emerged the ideal of an equality of rights.

For the men of the eighteenth century, privilege and equality were contradictory ideas. The philosophes based their opposition to privilege on the idea that in their human nature all men are equal. In his article on "natural equality" in the *Encyclopédie*, the chevalier de Jaucourt rejected the most common misinterpretation of that idea:

> Let no one do me the injustice of supposing that with a sense of fanaticism I approve in a state that chimera, absolute *equality*, which could hardly give birth to an ideal republic. I am only speaking here of the *natural equality* of men. I know too well the necessity of different ranks, grades, honors, distinctions, prerogatives, subordinations that must prevail in all governments. And I would even state that *natural* or *moral equality* are not contrary to this. In the state of nature men are truly born into equality but do not know how to remain so. Society forces them to lose it, and they only become equal again by laws.[58]

In practice men are unequal in their gifts and possessions, but let the state not add "an unjust inequality of rights alongside this actual inequality of means."[59] Jaucourt's understanding of the term *natural equality* is that each person should value and treat others as "naturally equal to himself." From this he concludes that those who have risen above others should avoid insults to their inferiors, demand nothing beyond what is required, and be humane in demanding what is their due. Men must not claim more than others unless they have acquired a right to preferential treatment. And certain universal rights to humanity and justice should be equally enjoyed by all or enjoyed in some distributive manner that removes all suspicion of contempt or partiality.

In this discussion of equality the initial accent was on injured pride. The pamphlet "What is the Third Estate?" by the Abbé Sieyès is the most representative expression of this view. As a cleric, Freemason, and active participant in the National Assembly of 1789, Sieyès was in close touch with the prevailing currents of opinion. He succeeded in putting the belief in a mandate of the people in suitable terms; his principles were those of the revolution in its initial phase. In his pamphlet, Sieyès drew up a list of grievances which had been provoked by the denial of status to the Third Estate.

The parlement of Paris had opted for the old procedures in electing the new Estates-General, but then tried to soften the blow by declaring in favor of fiscal equality among the three estates. To Sieyès this seemed to add insult to injury, for it served as a reminder that clergy and nobility had been tax exempt. "We expect you to submit to the common laws, not to offer a token of insulting pity for an order which you have treated mercilessly for so long." If all are to be equal in the field of taxation, why deny to the Third Estate its emergence from political incapacity? The Third Estate has been excluded from all offices of distinction. In the payment of taxes, it has been discriminated against. In legal matters, there has been no redress against oppression, for a commoner's lawsuit is regarded as insubordination. The police are terrified to act against a man of privilege, but paupers have been maltreated merely on suspicion. What of the judicial privileges of the nobility while the members of the Third Estate have suffered personal humiliations from tax agents and petty officials? How does the nobility justify the exclusive privilege of bearing arms? Why do the privileged escape the penalty for the most horrible crimes? And if they do not, they are first deprived of their title before they are punished.

> With what ridiculous and ferocious contempt do you dare to relegate the criminal of the first two orders to the third, in order, so you proclaim, to *degrade* him and apparently, to render him, in such company, *liable* to be executed! What would you say if the legislator, before punishing some scoundrel of the Third Estate, proposed to rid his order of him by giving him letters-patent of nobility.[60]

In the light of such invidious privileges, an offer of fiscal equality appeared to make matters worse, for it implied that the nonprivileged people of France cared only for money while thinking nothing of "liberty, honour or equality before the law." Clearly, Sieyès spoke not for the lower classes on whom the economic burden of the system fell. He spoke for the lawyers, merchants, and other occupations of the Third Estate who were moved by a "deeply wounded self-respect," by a sense of outrage at the privileged orders deliberately humiliating men of true merit who spoke for the vast majority of the French people.[61]

In this atmosphere of mounting exasperation, Sieyès formulated the idea of citizenship by using the argument of the privileged in reverse. What has the Third Estate been until now? Nothing. What is the Third Estate? Everything. In numerical terms, the clergy and nobility together comprise some 200,000 individuals in a nation of 25 to 26 million persons. In legal terms, the clergy has rights because it performs a function, but the nobility does nothing. Since the privileged consume without producing, they are an alien element in the nation. Moreover, because of its civil and political prerogatives, the nobility is not subject to the common laws and thus stands apart from the nation. The moment a citizen is granted special privileges, he is no longer part of the common order, for his new interest conflicts with the general interest; he has become incompetent to vote in the name of the people. Since the privileged man stands outside the nation, he is not entitled to be represented; only if he divests himself of this unjust usurpation can he be represented as a citizen. For the right to be represented is enjoyed by all citizens by virtue of what they have in common. True, there are many inequalities which divide them, including wealth, ability, age, and sex. But these do not alter the equality of citizenship, and the rights inherent in citizenship should not be attached to these differences. It is the common interest of citizens which is protected by law, and the law "protects what exists until what exists begins to be harmful to the common interest."[62]

Here Sieyès's attack on privilege merges with the idea of popular sovereignty which Diderot had formulated succinctly in his article on political authority (1751)—ten years before Rousseau's *Social Contract*.

> No man has received from nature the right to command others. Liberty is a gift from heaven, and each individual of the same species has the right to enjoy it as soon as he enjoys the use of reason. If nature has established any *authority*, it is paternal control; but paternal control has its limits, and in the state of nature it would terminate when the children could take care of themselves. Any other *authority* comes from another origin than nature, . . . either [from] the force and violence of an individual who has seized it, or the consent of those who have submitted to it by a contract made or assumed between them and the individual on whom they have bestowed *authority*.

Reliance on force depends on how long the force of one can prevail over that of another, and whoever wins has only the right of the strongest on his side. Diderot clearly favored authority by consent, and he made interesting use of the idea that communities governed by kings are still under the law of God. No man can give himself entirely to another, because in his entire being he belongs only to God. For the common good, God permits men to establish a system of subordination among themselves; this must be done with reason and proportion, not blindly or without reservation. God does not care about such external ceremonies. But to "deliver one's heart, spirit, and conduct without any reservation to the will and caprice of a mere creature, making him the unique and final reason for one's action," is a "veritable crime of idolatry."

It took courage to write this in 1751, and there were many attacks on this article. Yet Diderot was no revolutionary. He merely elaborated the contract theory of government which had been propounded in the remonstrances of the parlements. In his view, the prince has bound himself to the people, and the people in turn are bound to obey him according to the laws. The prince and his ministers are repositories of authority.

> Everywhere the nation has a right to maintain against all forces the contract that they have made; no power can change it; and when it is no longer valid, the nation recovers its rights and full freedom to enter into a new one with whomever and however it pleases them. This is what would happen in France if by the greatest of misfortunes the entire reigning family happened to die out, including the most remote descendants; then the sceptre and the crown would return to the nation.

Here radical principles were still compatible with support of the status quo.[63]

But in Sieyès's hands the same premises led to revolutionary conclusions. He argued that a privileged class has special advantages which place it outside citizenship and hence deprive the nobility of the right to be represented. Nor is there need to call on the nobility, since the Third Estate has an ample number of men sufficiently affluent and educated to take an interest in public affairs. "Such classes have no interest other than that of the rest of the People. Judge whether they do not contain enough citizens who are educated, honest and worthy in all respects to represent the nation properly." Sieyès wished to vindicate not only the intelligence but the virtue of the people. "While the aristocrats talk of their honor, but pursue their self-interest, the Third Estate, i.e., the nation, will develop its virtue, for if corporate interest is egotism, national interest is virtue."[64]

In this emphasis on popular sovereignty, the idea of the nation played a key role. To reach this result, men like Sieyès posited a series of contrasts: virtue against vice or abuse, equality against privilege, common rights against special advantages, citizenship and the national interest of the vast majority against the separate status and corporate interest of the few. If one chose one side or the other, one could derive a series of identities: virtue = equality = common rights = citizenship = national interest. Take any of these terms and the others were sure to follow. Despite their conflict with the king, the parlements stood revealed as the spokesmen of a narrow, corporate interest. To oppose their pretensions, it was logical to appeal to the nation as the source of morality and law. The Freemasons had anticipated the identification of morality with humanity and brotherhood. Sieyès followed in their footsteps when he declared,

> The nation is prior to everything. It is the source of everything. Its will is always legal; indeed it is the law itself. . . . The power exercised by the government has substance only insofar as it is constitutional; it is legal only insofar as it is based on the prescribed laws. The national will, on the contrary, never needs anything but its own existence to be legal. It is the source of all legality.[65]

A generation earlier, Diderot had pointed the way with the statement, "the nation recovers its rights and full freedom to enter into a new [contract]" once the old contract is no longer valid. By 1789, this was no longer a theoretical issue.

The common will of the nation is the ultimate source of legality and

A Scene from the French Revolution, August 10, 1792
Louis XVI (behind the barred window at right) takes refuge in the hall of the legislative assembly, to jeers from the Paris mob fresh from sacking the Tuileries. Later that day the king was deposed. (Musée du Louvre)

cannot be delegated. But a nation cannot meet in solemn assembly; therefore, the people elect extraordinary representatives who substitute for the whole nation in framing its constitution. Sieyès anticipated that no agreement would be reached on the organization of the newly convoked Estates-General. The nation could speak only with one voice, and Sieyès saw no difficulty if the representatives of the Third Estate assumed the title of National Assembly and deliberated for the entire nation, "minus a trivial two hundred thousand heads."[66] The Third Estate would form a National Assembly *by itself*.[i]

In what way does this system of national sovereignty guarantee the equality of rights? In a sense, the question is rhetorical. Popular sovereignty means popular participation in the process of formulating the constitution of a country.

> Political rights derive from a person's capacity as a citizen. These legal rights are identical for every person, whether his property happens to be great or small. Any citizen who satisfies all the formal requirements of an elector has the right to be represented, and the extent of his representation cannot be a fraction of the extent of some other citizen's representation. The right to be represented is single and indivisible. All citizens enjoy it equally, just as they are all equally protected by the law which they have helped to make.[67]

In the thought of the revolutionary period, the ideas of freedom and equality were closely linked. All men have certain needs and drives and certain capacities of feeling, acting, and expressing themselves. Surely men differ in their natural endowments; but all men have endowments of some kind, given at birth and developed thereafter. Freedom refers to the right of each to bring his capacities or endowments to fruition as much as lies within him. Hence, the differences among men are considered legally irrelevant. Whether a man owns much or little, each is free to own property just as each is free to develop his capacities, however great or small they may be. In these respects he enjoys the protection of the law. By saying that *everyone* has the right to develop and express himself, personal freedom is given a general application. The law must protect the whole range of moral and esthetic values since all men have the right to develop their capacities. But the law can allow the fullest scope to each man's self-development *only because it does not evaluate*. All men possess the same legal rights. To ensure this result, the law asks only whether or not a man's actions prevent another from developing to the full his own natural capacities. Thus, a great diversity of ideas and actions enjoys legal protection, as long as each man can do what he

---

[i]Sieyès conceded that this approach was perhaps too abrupt and suggested alternative procedures more in line with conventional thinking concerning the three estates. I cite his most extreme alternative here in order to suggest how far the thought of a moderate spokesman had moved at the beginning of the revolution.

will with his person and property. This freedom defines his value as a human being, and it is the function of law to uphold that value.[68]

The Declaration of the Rights of Man and Citizen of August 1789 states that "the aim of every political association is the preservation of the natural rights of man." The purpose of the declaration was to put before all members of the social body "a perpetual reminder" of these rights. At the same time, its formulations revealed a distinction between legal and political rights, between a *passive* and an *active* aspect of citizenship. Each man's enjoyment of "liberty, property and security" is to be protected by law.

> The enjoyment of the natural rights of every man has for its limits only those that assure other members of society the enjoyment of those same rights; such limits may be determined only by law. . . . Whatever is not forbidden by law may not be prevented, and no one may be constrained to do what it does not prescribe.

This law is to be "the expression of the general will"; that is, "all citizens have the right to concur personally, or through their representatives, in the formation of the law," because they are active members of the nation, which is the ultimate source of sovereignty. Also, "all citizens . . . are equally admissable to all public offices, according to their capacity, and without other distinctions than that of virtues and talents."[69]

But the citizen's right to concur in the "formation of the law" and to stand for public office proved more controversial than the right to equal protection under the law. As the principle of equality was implemented, inequalities reasserted themselves. We saw that the Abbé Sieyès had opposed voting by estates with the assertion that the Third Estate was identical with the nation and hence had the right to formulate its fundamental laws. But this populist position of a liberal reformer was egalitarian only within limits. Sieyès believed that in a large state representation is indispensable. The great majority of the people are too preoccupied to be "available" for public office. Certainly, citizens have the right to concur in the formation of laws which they must obey, as in voting for a constitutional assembly. The nation retains an ultimate authority which it cannot delegate. But the multitude can only increase its freedom by delegating a limited authority, much as in private life that man fares best who has people working for him rather than does everything himself. Nothing in the idea of popular sovereignty precludes such delegation. Rather, the national will is reflected by a proper representative assembly. Elected representatives should enjoy a free mandate to deliberate on the common good. When such deputies are bound by instructions from their constituents as they had been in the old Estates-General, they can only reflect partisan interests. If they have a free mandate, they can speak on behalf of the interests of the whole nation.[70]

To support this view of representation, Sieyès relied in part on his option for a restricted franchise. Within the Third Estate, he distinguished between the mass of the population and that segment which enjoyed a degree of economic security. Only those have an "active right" of citizenship who can afford to take a large view of affairs. In the debates of the National Assembly, Sieyès stated that women, children, foreigners, or those who pay no taxes are excluded from active influence in public affairs. To be sure, all of them may enjoy the advantages of society. But only those who contribute to the "public establishment" are proper shareholders in the great social enterprise. They are in truth active citizens, members of the political association, and hence qualified to stand for public office.[71]

In the debates on the *Declaration of the Rights of Man*, these ideas were opposed by men who saw in these restrictions and the safeguards provided for property a defense of monopolists and speculators. But the majority thought a restricted franchise advisable, because those who do not own property are also not part of society, as Dupont de Nemours put it. They are too preoccupied with making a living, their assemblies would be tumultuous, and they could be bribed easily by aristocrats, thus becoming a danger to the state. On the other hand, property was part of the established order, and those who owned it had a vested interest in that order. The propertyless would not respect the rights of property and hence the public interest. Direct democracy was impossible as long as Frenchmen lacked a more equitable distribution of goods and hence a sufficient harmony of interest.[72]

How could the men who endorsed a limited franchise still claim they believed in equality? The answer is that they believed only in an equality of legal rights. They were quite aware of the inequalities in wealth, talent, and rank which would remain. But they were combating a social order in which—over and above such "natural" differences—those who were specially privileged enjoyed the protection of the law. Property and equality appeared compatible because the defeat of privilege meant that any man's rights to his property would be equal to the property rights of everyone else. As they saw it, the sole function of the law is to ensure that each man can dispose of his property as he sees fit, so long as he does not curtail the freedom of others. By considering men only in their equal capacity as legal agents, the law ignores all other distinctions.

In France, the electoral system was to become a weapon in the struggle between rival political camps; thus, only once since 1789 has the same system survived for as long as thirty consecutive years.[73] Nevertheless, subsequent constitutions have consistently reaffirmed that the right to vote should depend on a certain level of interest and judgment. To this end, minimum age, sex, residence, and tax payments have all been used in various combinations. None of the constitutions has recognized the rights of economic dependents. In its majestic impartiality, the law forbids rich and poor alike to sleep under bridges, to use Anatole France's famous simile. The unifying theme of the revolution was the equality of *legal* rights in opposition to legal privileges. Such equality meant a direct relation between the individual citizen and the state in contrast to the earlier importance of "intermediate bodies." In conclusion, it will be useful to describe some aspects of this emerging conception of national citizenship.

In eighteenth-century France, legal recognition of individual rights meant, in the first place, hostility to associations. We saw that the government had substituted royal magistrates for elected municipal officials. In addition, the government used corporations or guilds as agents implementing its own administrative edicts.[74] The Jesuits were a teaching order and in a Catholic country preempted the field of education. They came under attack and in 1763 La Chalotais argued against their control of education and particularly against the exclusion of laymen from the teaching profession.

> I claim the right to demand for the Nation an education that will depend upon the State alone; because it belongs essentially to it, because every nation has an inalienable and imprescriptible right to instruct its members, and finally because the children of the State should be educated by members of the State.[75]

The Jesuits were suppressed in 1764. The hostility to associations continued through the French revolution, which abolished trade guilds in 1791, religious bodies in 1790 and 1792, academies and literary societies in 1793, and financial associations in 1794. Note the comment by Sieyès that "the major difficulty springs from the interest by which a citizen allies himself with just a few others. This type of interest leads to conspiracy and collusion; through it anti-social schemes are plotted; through it the most formidable enemies of the People mobilize themselves."[76] In a speech before the Constituent Assembly of 1791, Le Chapelier argued against mutual benefit societies among workers in terms that reveal the broad policy behind these measures, not just the hostility to organizations of workers.

> It should not be permissible for citizens in certain occupations to meet together in defence of their pretended common interests. There must be no more guilds in the State, but only the individual interest of each citizen and the general interest. No one shall be allowed to arouse in any citizen any kind of intermediate interest and to separate him from the public weal through the medium of corporate interests.[77]

This opposition to corporate interests was aimed also at the Catholic church. Revolutionary spokesmen advocated a civil constitution of the clergy, substituting the authority of the nation for that of the king. Henceforth, ecclesiastical offices were to be elective. In this view, all qualified electors—regardless of their own religion—were entitled to vote for eligible candidates. The principle of civil marriage pointed in the same direction and had far-reaching consequences. According to the constitution of 1791, marriage was a civil contract under state control; a year later, marriages were declared legal if concluded before a municipal official, even in the absence of a priest. At the same time, all transactions affecting the civil status of persons were secularized; that is, the written registers of births, marriages, and deaths were taken from the clergy and entrusted to municipal officials. The measure was defended on the ground that it would overcome the divisions among religious groups. As matters stood, only priests, ministers, or rabbis could prove the civil status of a person, and this despotism of the different sects divided men from one another. To overcome such divisions, it was necessary to separate civil from religious transactions so that all Frenchmen could enjoy the same civil rights. Frenchmen were born as citizens before they became Catholics, Protestants, or Jews.[78]

In the case of the Jews this approach presented special difficulties because the revolution sought to abolish rather than curtail Jewish communities. Throughout the Middle Ages, these communities (like the municipalities of which they were a subordinate part) performed a variety of duties for the government, including the collection of taxes. Also, the Jewish community maintained its own legal order with respect to marriage, inheritance, and related matters. The revolution opposed such "corporate autonomy." In 1789 de Clermont-Tonnerre declared in the National Assembly that "all should be refused to the Jews as a nation, but everything should be granted to them as individuals."[79] Revolutionary leaders did not want to interfere with religious beliefs and were often sympathetic to Jews as a persecuted minority. But they gave little consideration to the Jewish tradition. Jews should be banished if they refused to dissolve their communities, because this was tantamount to a self-willed exclusion from citizenship. On the other hand, they would enjoy the same rights as citizens if they abandoned their communities except for strictly religious purposes. This position was echoed among the Jews themselves. A petition of the Jews from Avignon stated,

> Will the Jews again be treated as before, i.e., as citizens only in matters of paying taxes, but as foreigners in matters of rights? . . . No! French legislation will not be thus insulted. A contradiction that would disgrace our laws shall not be tolerated. . . . When a system is fundamentally just, then it is necessary to accept the consequences. . . . It is not possible to have abolished the *corporations* and yet to admit the existence of one of them. The National Convention cannot recognize the Jews. There are no more Jews in France. There are no more Catholics, Protestants, Jews, sectarians of any kind, there are only Frenchmen.[80]

This appeal to principle had economic implications. Jewish communities demanded that on dissolution their debts be assumed by the government, as was done with the debts owed by other religious bodies. But the revolutionary government refused to accept financial responsibility. As a consequence, Jewish communities were maintained for purposes of taxation, though in other legal respects the revolutionary government required their dissolution. Contrary to what the Avignon petition had anticipated, Jews became citizens in their civil status, but not in matters of taxation.

The special treatment of the Jews helps to clarify the general revolutionary principles from which it deviates. The most widespread and onerous burden of French agriculture was the private appropriation of tax collection. Taxes on land varied widely, and the reasons for these differences had become obscure over time. The demand for equal citizenship was in part an attack on this private appropriation of a public function and on the cumulative inequities of assessment. Citizenship should mean a new nationwide assessment of tax liability which was owed to the state rather than to privileged individuals. In this respect, the special treatment of Jews with regard to their tax payment continued the old discrimination against them.

Questions of personal status were also connected with the law of land tenure. By the eighteenth century, serfdom had long been abolished, but the heirs of a serf were more restricted in their rights than the heirs of a freeman, and such distinctions rankled. In the decades preceding the revolution, agitation against these and related practices mounted as the abolition of the "feudal system" became the demand of the day. A decree of August 4, 1789 abolished without compensation all "feudal" duties including those associated with serfdom, while other duties could be abolished against payment of an indemnity. But the effort to distinguish different types of property produced paradoxical results. One family would be relieved of all charges without indemnity while an adjacent one was still obliged to pay rent. Everything hateful came to be condemned as "feudal," but legal implementation required that rightful claims be distinguished from those that were "feudal" and hence illegitimate, a source of much controversy and confusion.[81]

The opposition to "feudal" privilege was expressed in many ways. In March 1790 the Assembly proclaimed that "all honorary distinctions, all power and superiority, resulting from the feudal system, are abolished." Later that year, the Assembly abolished all hereditary nobility, titles of rank, liveries, and armorial bearings. The Convention abolished the law of primogeniture (1793), bestowing on all descendants the right to an equal part of the property. These edicts affected all families of wealth, not only noble families.

The attack on privilege extended also to paternal authority in domestic relations. Under the ancien régime, fathers possessed the right of correction over their children under the age of twenty-five. Before his majority, any man could be put in prison on his father's orders. Even beyond that age he could be imprisoned if his father obtained a *lettre de cachet* from the king. In 1790 the lettres de cachet were abolished, and later that year the father's right to imprison his children was restricted. The age of minority was reduced to twenty, the time of detention could not exceed a year, and the penalty could be inflicted only by a family tribunal. In the relation between spouses, the revolution also diminished the authority of the husband. Divorce was permitted along with the secularization of marriage. The age-old disability of married women was reduced, though not eliminated. In this field, even radical spokesmen like Mirabeau and Robespierre drew the line. A woman should reign within the house, but everywhere else she was out of place. In particular, women were denied political rights, the right to be a guardian, and the right to take part in the council of the family. Under the laws of the revolution, then, the legal status of women improved, but political status was denied them.[82]

Opposition to "feudal privilege" was thus a unifying theme of revolutionary legislation. With regard to the law of property, the land was liberated by prohibition of perpetual and irredeemable rents. The principle of equal inheritance was instituted in opposition to testamentary freedom: revolutionary legislation "fortified the proprietor during his lifetime, [but] it weakened his influence after death."[83] (Subsequently, a reaction in favor of paternal authority set in. By 1800 the head of the family could again dispose of a considerable part of his property and favor one of his children, although primogeniture and entail were never restored.) With regard to the law of persons, the changes were even more sweeping. The division of the population into three estates with their corresponding fiscal and legal inequalities was abolished. Rules of inheritance based on differences of status as well as privileges and penalties based on religious affiliation were eliminated. In these and other ways (already described), a secular state was instituted in which individual property was given equal legal protection and the law of persons was emancipated from religious and patriarchal control.

This legislative enactment of individual rights in opposition to inherited privileges was buttressed by the revolutionary attack on church property. The revolution opposed all corporations intervening between the nation and the individual citizen. The church was such a corporation. French kings had expropriated church properties in times past. The auctioning of these properties was a ready means of meeting the deficit incurred by French support of American independence. Moreover, the leaders of the revolution were haunted by fear of an aristocratic counterrevolution, and they knew that such a cause would be aided by the church. There were many municipalities and private families anxious to buy church lands. When the sales opened in December 1790, the purchase of church lands was initiated by prominent members of society, including members of the royal family. Most church properties were bought by wealthy members of the Third Estate and the richer peasants who became the mainstay of the new order. The sale of church lands thus gave rise to a multitude of proprietors whose interests were indissolubly linked with the revolution, much as the sale of monastic properties in England more than two centuries earlier had created a vested interest in the English Reformation among the landed gentry.[84]

Some of these revolutionary achievements were undone under the Restoration and in the subsequent developments of the nineteenth century. Eventually, hostility toward "corporations" made way for the reemergence of "intermediate bodies." The measures which facilitated the

Symbols of Privilege Destroyed
In this contemporary cartoon the mitres of bishops and the swords and insignia of the nobility are destroyed by four young men representing the revolution and the people. Similarly, the commemorative medal struck to celebrate the National Assembly of August 4, 1789 shows the delegates swearing an oath on the pillar inscribed to the fatherland under the slogan "Abandon all privileges." (Mansell Collection, London)

subdivision of property and the diminution of the father's and husband's authority were partly reversed. But the old structure of estates had been destroyed and with it the division of the population on the basis of legally protected privileges. To an important degree, the nation-state had emancipated the individual from his previous subservience to the master of the house. Henceforth, the "inequality of means" rather than the "inequality of rights" still provided a basis for the unequal distribution of opportunities. Social solidarity would arise from the interest by which a citizen allies himself with others rather than from alliances built on kinship and inherited prerogatives. It would arise also from nationalist appeals which spoke directly to the individual citizen. The nation-state introduced a formal equality of citizenship, albeit hedged by restrictions based on property and sex, and these restrictions would provide the basis for agitation in the future. The ultimate paradox is that the nation-state introduced the very juxtaposition of the individual citizen and the central powers of government which the ancien régime under Louis XIV and Colbert had proclaimed, but had never achieved. It was the French revolution rather than "absolutism" which destroyed the "intermediate bodies" based on grants of privilege or exemption.

11

NATION-BUILDING: GERMANY

THE HOLY ROMAN EMPIRE: PROVINCIALISM AND INTELLECTUAL MOBILIZATION*

EUROPE WAS the scene of a great struggle for power during the first half of the seventeenth century, from which France emerged as the dominant state. About a dozen wars were fought in different parts of Europe. The Thirty Years' War (1618–1648) centered on German territories and was part of that struggle. Since this area did not have great political significance, it provided a convenient battleground for contentions among the French monarchy, the Dutch Republic, Sweden, and the Austrian and Spanish branches of the House of Habsburg. Several treaties were signed in 1648; one of them was the Peace of Westphalia which ended the Thirty Years' War. Among the settlements was the end of the eighty years' war between Spain and the United Provinces of the Netherlands. Another was the end of the war between France, Sweden, and Germany's Protestant rulers on one side, and the Habsburg emperor and the German Catholic princes on the other. The Franco-Spanish war continued for eleven years until 1659 and ended with the defeat of Spain and the European ascendance of France. Hostilities also continued among Russia, Poland, Denmark, Sweden, and Brandenburg, which ended in treaties assuring the rise of Russia and Brandenburg at the expense of Poland and Denmark. In this general setting, France had a strong interest in preserving the territorial divisions and political and military weakness of the Holy Roman Empire, for it provided a buffer zone against Austria. Sweden and Germany's Protestant rulers shared this interest, because they feared not only Catholic Austria but the German Catholic princes as well.

*A much abbreviated version of this chapter was first published under the title "Province and Metropolis: The Case of Eighteenth-Century Germany," in Joseph Ben-David and T. N. Clark, eds., *Culture and its Creators, Essays in Honor of Edward Shils* (Chicago: University of Chicago Press, 1977), pp. 119–49.

The contrast between Germany's fragmentation and the unity of England and France was of long standing. England was politically unified through the Norman conquest in the eleventh century. France achieved political unification under kingship more gradually and several centuries after England; the process through which the French kings established their supremacy left a legacy of jurisdictional particularism. The German territories of the Holy Roman Empire were fragmented from the period of the Saxon emperors of the tenth century to the dissolution of the empire in 1806. Germany achieved political unity only in 1871. The following section discusses Germany during the seventeenth and eighteenth centuries, and specifically the political disunity and cultural ferment of the country.

Under the terms of the Peace of Westphalia, the Holy Roman Empire continued to exist as a loosely organized confederation of sovereign territories. Austria, Bavaria, Prussia, and Saxony were the most important of the eight electoral states (*Kurfürstentümer*) within the empire. In addition, more or less scattered but sovereign territories belonged to twenty-seven spiritual members of the College of Princes (archbishoprics, bishoprics, prince-abbots' lands), thirty-seven lay princes (*weltliche Fürsten*), ninety-five imperial counts (*Reichsgrafen*), forty-two imperial founders (*Reichtsstifter*), and fifty free or imperial towns (*Reichsstädte*).[1] Although the office of emperor was formally elective, he was usually the head of the Habsburg house and the power of that house was formidable. The emperor was the leading Catholic ruler in Germany. The coronation oath obliged him to protect the rights of the small sovereign territories. In practice, all these territories survived through their link with the imperial office, for the emperor used his legal powers and political influence to prevent the constituent units of the empire from encroaching on one another's jurisdiction. By upholding the conditions laid down in the Peace of Westphalia, the emperor ensured the security of every petty territory and other jurisdiction despite its political and military impotence.

But while the German emperor could preserve the status quo under the Peace of Westphalia, the powers of his office were very circumscribed. He was entitled to issue patents of nobility and to urge certain ecclesiastical appointments. His revenues were limited to customary presents received on his coronation and to "protection money" collected from the Jews. Earlier he had possessed other powers and revenues, but on successive coronations the electors had imposed restrictions (capitulations) which limited the powers of the imperial office. This weakness of the emperor in taking any political initiatives of his own was reflected in the other institutions of the empire.

The Imperial Diet (*Reichstag*) was a congress of ambassadors rather than a legislature, since in practice it was incapable of enacting laws.

Some 160 "states" had the right to be represented at the Diet in Regensburg, but only about 25 delegates were active at any one time. Only those delegates attended whose territories were likely to be affected by the business on the agenda. Procedures were cumbersome and delays interminable, because the delegates were strictly bound by instructions and there was frequent need for consultation with the home territory. The agenda included such items as disputes between princes, between princes and their estates, or certain religious issues. Periodically, various states would refuse to pay the taxes which a Reichstag majority had endorsed, thus revealing the weakness of the empire. Analogous difficulties were to be found in the imperial courts and the imperial army.

Strong states like Austria or Prussia ignored or bypassed the emperor and the Imperial Diet with impunity. They would not subordinate their interests to the empire, but at the same time they remained within it because they would not risk violating the stipulations of the Peace of Westphalia. All the smaller sovereign territories were in a different position. Imperial knights, bishoprics, and towns depended on the empire for their survival, as did an additional four thousand hometowns—small towns which for various historical reasons possessed certain rights of self-government.[2] The Peace of Westphalia had stipulated that all self-governing territories of the empire might freely make or change alliances in defense of their liberties. This made for continued political fragmentation in the center of Europe, and as France and Sweden were guarantors of this settlement, they did nothing to promote unification.

Every independent territory—even the smallest hometown—was preserved in its weakness:

> [For] where one's own appetite for political power was frustrated and smothered, the obvious policy was to help smother and frustrate the aspirations of others; and this applied not only to a rival's efforts at territorial expansion but also to any effort a ruler or estate might make to impose full control over his individual or corporate subjects.[3]

One can learn much about the political conditions and cultural consequences of German disunity by examining the institutions through which even small towns preserved their autonomy. In a typical hometown one would find a council consisting of six to twelve life members. The composition of the council was achieved by informal agreement among the most active heads of households, even when all heads of households formally elected the council. Heads of households together with leaders of guilds and districts constituted a citizenry which interacted on a daily basis with the members of the council. Chief of the council was the mayor, who was chosen by collegial consent and often held his office for life. The mayor ran the day-to-day affairs of the hometown, and he, together with members of the council, appointed lesser town officials. The council formulated and the mayor executed community policies with regard to town properties, police powers, taxes, and fees as well as the issuance of residence permits to new citizens of the community. Members of the council also frequently held judicial posts, but most disputes were settled out of court so as to preclude adjudication by outside authorities.

> Certain families tended to persist in community leadership over the generations, and older families had an advantage over newer ones. But their positions were not prescriptive, or only vaguely or partially so; they could be lost in a generation. . . . The base of a hometown leader's influence was with the community, and depended in the end on the possession of qualities— family tradition included—that his fellow townsmen respected and needed more than they envied or mistrusted them, and that is a long way from hereditary right.
> . . . For the hometown leader was a *Bürger*, and could not think of his place in terms other than those of his own town and its Bürgerschaft.[a] The Bürgerschaft were his acquaintances or his relatives; a great many of his acquaintances *were* his relatives, and almost every Bürger had a relative or a close acquaintance in a position of political influence. Social, political, and economic relations intertwined, giving the community great strength even as it gave great local power to the "uncles." That was the situation that written constitutions and electoral schemes sought to embody and assure.[4]

Hometown leaders and citizens like guild-masters and guild-members controlled one another by the thousand devices of mutual suspicion and affection arising from familiarity.

To be the citizen of a hometown was a communal status granted by one's neighbors. It involved all aspects of life, not just one's civic status. And as it tied the individual to his neighbors through his life, honor, and property, so it deepened his separation from all outsiders and his hostility toward them. Membership in the community was the issue on which patronage, familial influence, and considerations of economic advantage converged, and the gradation of membership fees reflected this shared concern. To enter a guild, an outsider had to pay six times as much as the son of a guild-member and three times as much as a citizen's son from another trade. The sons of citizens would obtain citizen status without fee when they reached their twenty-fifth year, married with council approval, or were accepted as masters in a guild. For the same privilege outsiders paid fees of 120 to 300 Gulden for a man, 60 to 100

---

[a]*Bürger, Bürgerschaft, Bürgertum,* and *Bürgerstand* may be translated townsman, townsfolk, citizenry, and commoner estate. In the eighteenth century, these terms referred to the town practice of allowing or denying the *Bürgerrecht* or municipal citizenship (the right of the citizen to reside in the community), based on a community judgment of his financial and moral standing. These terms also convey the sense of being below the aristocracy but above peasants and laborers, not to speak of domestic servants.

Gulden for the wife, and 20 to 35 Gulden for each child.[b] Marriage outside the community meant either abandonment of citizenship and residence or a special grant of residence to the outside partner on payment of an appropriate fee. Admission to the community was refused if a new resident's trade would result in competition within a crowded occupation. Moreover, membership in the community was lost by entry into an occupation that involved outside ties, like the army or the civil service.

> To be without citizenship meant to have no right to pursue a citizen's trade, usually no marriage and no right to an established home, no vote, no eligibility for office, no communal protection against the outside (or against citizens), and no share in community property.[5]

The *Bürgerschaft* was content with a moderate level of living and used its powers of exclusion to maintain the status quo. (The cleavage between the patriciate and the artisan class was more pronounced in towns of larger size with more outside involvement.)[6] The strongly conservative *Bürgertum* of the hometowns cultivated a localism that is not unique to Germany. But only there did it enjoy strong, if indirect, institutional support through the political fragmentation of the empire.

A basic condition of the hometowns was that there was almost no penetration into their internal affairs from the outside. This privilege of self-rule was based on each sovereign's acceptance or formal acknowledgment of customary jurisdiction, which by its complexity shielded each community against the outside. The towns always appealed to their ancient customs, consisting of local usage or statutory compilations, much as the common lawyers had done in seventeenth-century England. In both cases, ancient custom was invoked against the arbitrary acts of sovereign rulers. But in England this appeal to a legal fiction had been used to assert the rights of parliament to represent the country, whereas in Germany the same appeal was used to assert the separate jurisdiction of each town.[c]

[b]These are Walker's figures for the town of Rottweil. It should be added that renunciation of citizenship involved an emigration tax and that contracts, especially those involving real estate, between residents and outsiders were subject to elaborate regulations.

[c]In an estimate for 1800, Walker calculated that in a total German population of about 28 million (including Prussia and German-speaking Austria), two-thirds were rural and one-third urban. The distinguishing characteristic of the urban community was the existence of some rights of self-government. About 7 percent of the total population lived in three dozen "large" towns (15,000 and above), while 25 percent lived in the four thousand hometowns (from 750 to 15,000 inhabitants). In the German territories under the empire the hometown population comprised some 7 million people. Hometowns were more frequent in the western and southern parts of Germany and less frequent in Prussia and Hannover.

Local rule was quite similar in the other small territorial enclaves —those of imperial knights, the bishoprics, and numerous petty principalities—which were as insistent on their autonomy as the hometowns and also used their jurisdiction for defensive purposes. Thus, the familial and neighborhood control of the hometowns and the oligarchic paternalism of the rural areas were characteristic of German society until well into the nineteenth century. When conservatives of the period extolled the virtues of traditional authority, they had in mind the hometowns and small territorial domains where oligarchic and personal domination prevailed. They idealized the autonomy and freedom of provincial living and applied their model to all the territorial enclaves threatened by absolutist regimes and enlightened thought. In the process, they disregarded the fierce, if often tacit, coercion typical of familial and neighborhood interdependence.[7]

This personal local rule prevailed even in Prussia, the best organized state of the empire. The earlier discussion of Prussia briefly traced the ascendance of monarchical authority over the estates as an aspect of administrative centralization in military affairs. Yet this centralization was as compatible with local autonomy as it was in France. The Prussian government did not seek to abolish municipal institutions, though the Prussian towns were less strongly organized internally than other German towns. Under the supervision of the Prussian government, local affairs continued to be administered in accordance with traditional local practices. From the standpoint of absolutist *rule*, the General Legal Code (*Allgemeine Landrecht*) of 1794 was a major step in strengthening the state. But from the standpoint of law and administrative practice, the code did not supersede the customary legal practices of towns, guilds, and corporations. The code endorsed these practices, but turned agencies of self-government into instruments of state administration.[8] Thus, even the Prussian autocracy remained an intermediate phase between an estate or corporate society and a modern state which attempts to regulate society directly.

Political particularism can mean different things in different countries. In France, the ancien régime consisted of a multitude of jurisdictions which the king had created (more often than not) to raise revenue, and which the monarchy defended as a right of property and a potential source of future revenue. In Germany, the empire prevented the separate and sovereign jurisdictions from interfering with one another. German particularism had a territorial basis which had been so entrenched that it prevented the rise of royal supremacy, and in this respect the Peace of Westphalia only endorsed conditions which had existed from the time of the Saxon, Salian, and Hohenstaufen rule.

The empire's balance of power through political fragmentation was disrupted by the War of the Austrian Succession (1740–1748), involving the conflicting claims of Bavaria, Saxony, Prussia, and France. The war was precipitated by Prussia's occupation of Silesia and its military ascendance over Austria. In the course of this conflict, successive alliances occurred between Austria and England, Russia and France, and between Prussia and France as well as England. In the end, Prussia's alliance with England and unprovoked invasion of Saxony led to a coalition among Austria, Russia, France, and Sweden against Frederick II in the Seven Years' War (1756–1763). The peace of Hubertusburg (1763) between Austria, Prussia, and Saxony restored the previous balance of power, except that Silesia remained in Prussian hands. That balance was preserved until the French armies under Napoleon began their conquest of Europe in 1798. Napoleon reorganized the German states and allowed a number of them to seize ecclesiastical territories, imperial cities, and the territories of the imperial knights.[9]

In August 1806 the Holy Roman Empire was formally dissolved, and the last emperor, Francis II of Austria (1792–1806), abdicated. In the same year, Prussia, in alliance with Russia, challenged the French seizure of Prussian territories, but in October Prussia suffered a disastrous defeat at Jena. In the peace settlement that followed, Prussia lost half its territories; its population was reduced to some five million inhabitants. Much of this loss was made good after Napoleon's defeat in 1815. The Congress of Vienna of 1815 created a German Confederation of thirty-nine sovereign powers in the territory of the old Holy Roman Empire, consisting of the Austrian empire, five kingdoms, one electorate, seven grand duchies, ten duchies, eleven principalities, and four free cities. By the standards of the modern nation-state, this political consolidation of the old empire was still only the beginning of a development which would result in political unification in 1870–1871, and which was to be lost again in 1945 at the end of World War II. The whole background of political particularism of the Holy Roman Empire and the German Confederation had important repercussions for the country's reorganization of authority on a constitutional basis. In order to assess Germany's equivocal transition from the authority of kings to a mandate of the people, the consequences of the country's political particularism for its economic and cultural developments must be considered.

From the thirteenth to the sixteenth century, German trade flourished under the aegis of the Hanseatic League, an association of north German towns and of German merchants abroad which combined a monopoly of the Baltic trade with vigorous trading in the Low Countries and England. But in the era of European expansion overseas, Germany became an economic backwater, and in 1632 the Hanseatic League was dissolved. Its place was taken by the Dutch, who occupied the lower

Rhine and preempted the Baltic trade with Scandinavia, Russia, and Poland. On the lower Elbe, Denmark and Hanover (under English sovereignty) imposed various tolls and interfered with the trade of Hamburg. The bad effect of external competition on German trade was further aggravated by the proliferation of internal customs barriers. On the Rhine from Strasbourg to the Dutch border, ships had to pay thirty-two separate tolls. Mainz and Cologne also claimed staple rights—the right of a local jurisdiction to demand that commodities in transit must be offered for sale for a certain period before further shipment is allowed to proceed. On land, staple rights involved prescribed routes into towns. Violations of that right entailed confiscation of the ship, horse and wagon, or shipment as well as fines or jail terms for the boatmen or drivers. These tolls and rights were abolished when the French occupied the Rhineland, and after 1815 the Rhine became the greatest transport facility of Germany. Negotiations with Holland concerning Dutch rights on the lower Rhine were completed only in 1831, with further concessions coming twenty years later. Much the same was true of the Elbe River, where nineteen tolls were levied between Magdeburg and Hamburg. In 1821 Prussia agreed not to impose tolls on goods in transit. Danish tolls were abolished in 1857, and Hannoverian tolls in 1861.[10]

Other obstacles to economic development were also slow to be removed. Political particularism produced a multiplicity of currencies and of weights and measures until well into the nineteenth century. Every territory had its passport controls, its transport restrictions, and its special currency. As Goethe said in a conversation with Eckermann in 1828,

> I am not concerned if Germany is not unified; our good roads and future railroads will have their own effect.[d] . . . Let [Germany] be one in that the German *Taler* and *Groschen* have the same value in the whole *Reich*; one in that my travel bag can pass unopened through all thirty-six states. Let it be one in that the urban passport of a Weimar citizen will not be considered insufficient like the passport of a foreigner by the border officials of a large neighboring state. Among German states there should be no further difference between natives and foreigners. Furthermore, Germany should be one in her weights and measures, in commerce and traffic, and a hundred similar things.[11]

The economic consequences of political particularism greatly impeded the German economy. Here the comparison with France may be instructive, for in many respects France suffered from similar difficulties.

The French government repeatedly tried to replace the tangle of provincial and local levies as well as the old system of public finance through private enterprise by a national customs union and a centrally

---

[d]In 1828, the first railroad had been opened in England; in Germany this was to occur in 1835.

administered system of public revenue. None of these efforts succeeded until the French revolution abolished the private appropriation of public offices for profit and replaced it by a bureaucratic organization, in which officials performed their public duty for a salary.[12] Similar conditions occasionally existed in Germany as well. But in Germany the private appropriation of public offices probably did not thrive, because it occurred in some 250 sovereign territories (before 1815) and only a few of these could compete as European powers. Of course, there was petty corruption and a mushrooming of offices, but given their restricted economic and military base, the sale or purchase of offices was not a lucrative field of public revenue or private investment.

Most German sovereigns of the eighteenth century took it for granted that they must promote the economy as well as strengthen their military and political power. These impulses meant a good deal in large states like Prussia or Austria, but they turned into travesties in the smaller territories. In spirit, the economic policies adopted were modeled after those of Colbert. The government promoted trade and industry, supervised the conduct of economic enterprises, and generally regulated social and economic life. A burgeoning officialdom was the inevitable accompaniment of monarchical rule. In eighteenth-century Germany, every sovereign territory down to the smallest imperial knight required a corps of officials! In the electoral state of Mainz, some 900 officials were employed for a population of 224,000, not counting court personnel and clergy. There was 1 official for every 250 inhabitants. Moreover, many constituent units of the empire were composed of scattered rather than consolidated territories. Even under the same sovereign, each separate territory possessed its own administration and judiciary. Biedermann estimates that there were some two thousand separate jurisdictions.[13] This multiplicity of jurisdictions necessitated a large number of officials, though we have no overall figures. The ranks of the bureaucracy were swelled further by the general practice of treating all teachers and—in Protestant territories—all clergymen as employees of the state. Unlike the tolls on the Rhine, this large and heterogeneous officialdom did not disappear later. In Germany, bureaucratization is a legacy of political fragmentation and absolutist economic policy, as well as a by-product of advanced capitalism and complex organization.

Ever since the eighteenth century, officials, teachers, and clergymen have represented an important segment of the German *Bürgertum*. No appropriate English equivalent is available, and the French *bourgeoisie* is a literal but inappropriate translation. *Bürgertum* and related German terms came to be associated with a level of education, and this association is absent from "middle class" or "bourgeoisie." The term *Bürger* also evokes connotations of "financial and moral standing" that have been transferred from the context of a self-governing small community to the larger society. It is a symptom of these linguistic and cultural differences that after another half-century of economic development and at a high point of German liberalism in the revolution of 1848, 58 percent of the delegates to the German National Assembly at Frankfurt (the so-called *Paulskirche*) consisted of civil servants, teachers, and clergymen, while another 24 percent comprised lawyers, writers, and other free professionals. Only 9 percent of the delegates were merchants, manufacturers, artisans, and landed proprietors of non-noble origin.[14] By contrast to England and to a lesser extent France, the culturally and politically most active segment of the German middle class consisted of state employees. In Germany as elsewhere, free professionals and entrepreneurial types in many walks of life played an important role. But since the eighteenth century, the German Bürgertum included a disproportionately large number of state employees. Under the influence of this group and of the free professionals, education became so important a feature of the Bürgertum as a whole that special phrases (*Bildungabürgertum* or *gehobene Schicht*) were occasionally used to distinguish this class from persons who lacked education. For this reason I use the phrase *educated commoners* in the discussion here.

Perhaps the rapid increase of intellectuals in the late eighteenth century was as important a phenomenon as bureaucratization. There is no simple, causal relation between this "intellectual mobilization" and the proliferation of officials. Literacy was certainly not confined to officials, teachers, and clergymen. Yet in terms of status and education, this stratum stood clearly above the common people. Contemporary descriptions of officials idling away their time or attending to business in desultory fashion also mention that they read newspapers. Government officials and clergymen may have been narrowly provincial, status conscious, and negligent of their duties, but they relied on the printed word, and in relatively well-governed states like Prussia, military discipline and reformist zeal saw to it that the servants of state and church did their duty.[15]

The eighteenth century witnessed the sporadic development of education at several levels. Commerce, administration, and an effective military force called for elementary literacy as well as for education in law, finance, and higher administration. But the establishment of schools and universities depended on funds that were often unavailable and a general interest in education that was often lacking. Spokesmen for the status quo feared that education—even the teaching of reading and writing—would prompt people to aspire above their station. The enlightened rulers of the period shared such misgivings, though they often called for the establishment of schools in the interest of military training, administration, and commerce. They had learned that increased trade and industry would lead to increased revenues, but educational development was impeded. Each of the 250 sovereign territories required a school system of its own, and funds for educational development were limited. At the highest level, student enrollment in the universities actually declined during the course of the century. Average annual enrollment seems to have reached a high of 4,400 in 1720, sunk below 4,000 after 1755, and increased to above 7,000 after 1820.[16]

This record of simultaneously promoting and restraining educational development reflects the interest of German rulers. Education would help make soldiers and officials into better instruments of the royal will but could also lead to reactions against autocratic rule. No education could be insulated against the free thought of the Enlightenment. University training had provided preparation for teachers and clergymen, and after 1740 it also became a condition of public employment. Three-quarters of the students were enrolled in the fields of law and theology. Academic teaching was often antiquated, though the universities of Königsberg (founded in 1544), Jena (1558), Halle (1694), and Göttingen (1736) were notable centers of innovation. However, higher education served the strictly limited purpose of training teachers, clergymen, and public officials. German rulers generally sought to achieve a balance between maintaining the status quo and furthering the intellectual mobilization needed for more effective government.

The development of journals and newspapers was of special concern to them. Under Frederick the Great, Prussia had a relatively enlightened attitude toward the press, though Frederick publicly disparaged German literature. His successors reverted to a more restrictive policy toward the press. However, the center of German cultural life was in the south and west rather than in Prussia. Early in the eighteenth century, the rulers of both Saxony and Saxony-Weimar issued decrees prohibiting "untruthful newspaper writings," declaring that they did not want "reasoners for subjects."[17] At the same time, Leipzig with its book fairs was an economic asset, and this made the authorities rather lenient in their censorship of publications, although they still forbade debates on religious questions in the newspapers. Similarly, the duchy of Württemberg witnessed both an intensification of intellectual life and the arbitrary suppression of individual writers. Later in the century, Saxony-Weimer was exceptional as the most famous center of high culture under the aegis of Goethe and his patron, Grand Duke Carl August.

Thus, autocratic rule could intervene in, but could not control, a burgeoning cultural life owing to the political fragmentation of the country. With so many sovereign territories in which people spoke the same language, it was relatively easy to escape censorship by moving the place of publication to a neighboring state. Under these conditions writers made invidious comparisons between German disunity and powerful countries such as France and England, and thereby promoted the "intellectual mobilization" of the educated public. Despite political and economic fragmentation, there was a virtual springtide of cultural interest in the second half of the eighteenth century.

Since 1564 semi-annual catalogues of newly printed works had appeared, and book publications provide a rough index for the growth of the reading public. During the eighteenth century, the Leipzig and Frankfurt book fairs were the two centers for the distribution of books. Most publications were in Latin, German, and French. In 1701, 55 percent of the books were written in Latin, but by 1800 that proportion had declined to 4 percent. During the same period, works in German and French became the prevailing languages of books published in all German-speaking territories. This shift in language signifies a shift in audience, for the Latin works were addressed to scholars and clergymen exclusively, while French and German works appealed to the general educated public.[18]

TABLE 3

NUMBER OF BOOKS IN LEIPZIG BOOK FAIR CATALOGUES
BY YEAR AND FIELD

Field	Total Number of Books Listed by Year					
	1700	1720	1740	1760	1780	1800
Theology[a]	430	374	436	269	389	241
Law	85	86	172	52	149	143
Medicine	63	79	101	70	191	198
History[b]	157	209	221	277	469	631
Philosophy[c]	197	198	334	392	968	1,590
Poetry[d]	46	33	62	138	476	1,209
TOTAL	978	979	1,326	1,198[e]	2,642	4,012

SOURCE: Gustav Schwetschke, ed., *Codex Nundinarius Germaniae Literatae Bisecularis, Mess-Jahrbücher des Deutschen Buchhandels* (Halle: G. Schwetschke's Verlagsbuchhandlung, 1850, 1877), pp. 78, 198, 218, 238, 273, 313.

[a]Theology includes both Protestant and Catholic writings, but the former predominate throughout.

[b]Based on the more detailed breakdown in 1801 and subsequent years, one can assume that "history" includes biography, classics, politics, geography, and travel.

[c]On similar assumptions "philosophy" includes education, philology, natural science, economics, "cameralistics," technology, mathematics, military science, and business.

[d]"Poetry" also includes music, novels, plays, and art books.

[e]The numbers for 1760 would have been higher if book publishing had not been affected by the Seven Years' War (1756–1763).

The data in Table 3 indicate only the general trend in book publications, not their absolute magnitude. For example, the listings for the
Leipzig fair show 2,642 publications for 1780, but a contemporary book-
seller estimated a total of some 5,000 German books and pamphlets, not
counting foreign language books or miscellaneous publications. An estimate for 1783 suggests that some 2,000 separate publications were issued in editions totaling 2 million volumes. The number of writers living
in Germany is supposed to have doubled from 3,000 to 6,000 between
1773 and 1787. Estimates of the number of writers in specific areas or
individual towns are probably more reliable, but all such estimates are
approximate.[19] In any case, there is little doubt about the general trend.
This profusion of reading matter was obviously a mixed lot: novels,
plays, travelogues, biographies, religious tracts, and historical and scientific literature at one end, and encyclopedias, almanacs, cookbooks,
household manuals, calendars, and a profusion of lurid and occasionally
pornographic booklets at the other.

Books were often serialized in the various journals which also proliferated in the last decades of the century, and here the figures seem
to be quite reliable. According to the most comprehensive study available, 2,191 new journals were published between 1766 and 1790 (248
in 1766–1769, 718 in the 1770s, and 1,225 in the 1780s). The total for
1766–1790 was three times as large as the corresponding total
for 1741–1765. Thirty-four percent of the new journals in the period
1766–1790 were light reading or fiction (*Unterhaltungsliteratur*). In other
subjects, new journals for the twenty-five year period were distributed
as follows:

history	10.0 percent	science	4.9 percent
literature	10.0	economics	
theology	7.3	(cameralistics)	4.0
pedagogy	5.0	popular science	8.5
medicine	5.5		

The remaining 10.8 percent were distributed among military science,
music, and philosophy. This sudden increase in the publication of journals and a rather high degree of specialization went together. There
were fifty-six towns, many of them quite small, in which at least three
new journals were published between 1766 and 1790. In the minds of
contemporaries, this whole intellectual mobilization represented a major
change, and concern was frequently expressed at this proliferation of
"scribblers." But whatever the evaluation, all parts of Germany underwent a major intellectual mobilization in the last decades of the eighteenth century.[20]

These facts present a paradox which has reappeared many times.
During the eighteenth century, the great majority of the German pop-

ulation lived in the countryside and in self-contained hometowns. People were preoccupied with, and took pride in, local affairs. This positive well-being and sense of community was given artistic expression in Goethe's *Hermann and Dorothea* (1797), a poetic celebration of the parochial spirit which regards refugees from the French revolution with sympathy and detachment in the happy thought that one is not involved in these world affairs.[21] But even in this quiescent population there was an occasional rebellious spirit who railed at the confining world in which he had to live. In 1799 Hölderlin wrote a famous outburst which castigated what Goethe had held up to admiration.

> It is a harsh statement and yet I say it, because it is the truth: I cannot think of a people more torn apart than the Germans. You see artisans, but not men, thinkers but not men, masters and servants, youths and established people but not men—is it not like a battle field where hands and arms and all limbs lie about dismembered, while the spilt lifeblood melts into the sand?[22]

The vast majority of rural folk and hometownsmen would have found Hölderlin's statement very strange. Eighteenth-century German society was deeply provincial. Yet it produced a Goethe and a Hölderlin who, for all their differences, were part of an intellectual mobilization which sought to cultivate in a docile, parochial population a concern with the larger issues of humanity. The paradox is that so much intellectual mobilization occurred in the midst of a society that was far from the mainstream of contemporary history.

COURT SOCIETY AND THE CULTURAL IDENTITY OF COMMONERS

In the eighteenth century, French cultural influence on the courts of Germany's many sovereign territories was overwhelming. "Germany" was open to foreign influences, because the country had no unity of its own. Each of its many sovereign territories was a separate social enclave, in which educated commoners were aware of the larger world and had to come to terms with their own social position and with the provinciality of their little land. Once the courts with their French manners and the responses to them are described, we can get a better understanding of the eighteenth-century German reaction to the French revolution.

Under Louis XIV, France had become the most powerful nation in the world. The French monarch overwhelmed his enemies at home and abroad not only in the military field, but by the exemplary magnificence of his buildings, the works of art he sponsored, and the elaborate ceremonial which distinguished his court at Versailles. The ruling circles of German society responded with alacrity to the latest French fashions.

Versailles in 1668
Louis XIV turned a hunting lodge into a vast palace with extensive gardens laid out in geometric designs. As nobles, officials, and retainers moved into the buildings adjacent to the
palace, the community grew to 150,000 persons. The design of this royal establishment
was copied on a smaller scale by many German courts of the eighteenth century, as were
the entertainments. For example, a three-day festival of 1664 had as its central theme the
legend of a mythical island on which brave knights enjoyed wondrous pleasures with the
aid of an enchanted ring. The first day included a concert tableau extolling the four sea-
sons and employing animals from far-off lands. The second day saw the presentation of a
comedy and a ballet performance. The third day witnessed great festivities on the enchanted isle guarded by strange and fearsome water monsters. The whole affair was concluded with elaborate fireworks. (Giraudon)

The import of French luxury goods contributed largely to the fact that
between 1700 and 1790 the German territories had a negative trade
balance with France of some 18 million Marks annually.[23] In actuality,
most German courts could produce but a sorry imitation of their model,
because the economic resources of these territories were small and their
political power negligible. Yet in their little worlds, many German rulers
expressed their aspirations through buildings, festivals, liveried ser-

vants, and ceremonial displays. Outward splendor made up for the lack of political substance. Such magnificence was seen as the necessary attribute of a ruler who represented God on earth. If the maintenance of such a court meant the cruel exploitation of the people, then this was also considered part of the divine order.

The German courts received encouragement from France. French emissaries frequented the residences of German rulers and these in turn (or their representatives) were received at Versailles. The German cultivation of the French manner was encouraged by the 30,000 French Huguenots who had fled to Germany after 1685. Dependent on the powerful among their German hosts, these refugees promoted French fashions by means of the luxury trades in which they were engaged. Frenchmen replaced Germans as private tutors at courts and in aristocratic households, and young aristocrats made a special tour of the French capital part of their education. Even after the Seven Years' War, many sons of German ruling houses (not allied with France) volunteered for service in the French army! In some court circles, French conversation became so customary that native German was looked on as a vulgar, provincial dialect, and persons of low rank were referred to as those who could not speak French. The children at court were first taught French, and outsiders sometimes wondered whether people at court still knew German. Even early German classics—plays by Lessing, for example—had to be translated into French to be performed (in the electorate of Brunswick). Naturally, the veneer often cracked even at court: German was frequently spoken with interspersed French phrases. Imitation of French fashion, use of French as the language of high society, and demonstrations of homage to the French monarch seemed a small price to pay for an unofficial, but seemingly unchallengeable, verification of sovereign status at the German courts.

The French model was not confined to language, fashion, and culture. At Versailles, young German aristocrats could observe the seamier side of court life: sexual license seemed to be an attribute of high rank. The French hardly invented the practice, but Versailles gave it the stamp of cultural approval. The exclamation of a resident in the capital of a small German principality when he witnessed the wedding procession of the reigning sovereign illuminates a general condition: "Now our prince lacks nothing but a beautiful mistress!" He had seen the father and grandfather with their mistresses and saw this as an attribute of princely dignity.[24] These petty rulers often vied with one another, the number of their "conquests" sometimes taking on an obsessional quality, as if they could make up by "love" what they could not achieve in politics. There was much visiting back and forth among the various courts: in 1721 some four hundred foreign aristocrats spent time at the Saxon court at Dresden in an eight-month period. Many of these cavaliers were foreign-born aristocrats like Casanova who set the tone by their prodigal manner. They would spread the word from court to court concerning the customs and splendor they had witnessed elsewhere.

There was much to tell not only about illicit, if eminently public, love affairs, but also about the round of activities of high society. Lavish and long-drawn-out meals with a multitude of guests were staged; in the evenings, a French comedy or an Italian opera was performed. For persons of standing, entry to these entertainments was free of charge. Visits to neighboring courts and longer journeys to the fairs at Leipzig or Frankfurt or to the many famous spas required a large entourage and much display. Many special festivals were held to celebrate the birthday of the prince or his mistress, or the special days of the princely family, or the presence of a visiting dignitary. For that matter, some festivity might be arranged simply on the spur of the moment. These events were given a baroque style through various allegorical devices.

It was taken for granted that the ruler was free to call not only on his own resources but on the people of "his" realm with all of their possessions to serve the needs of his court. The preparations for the festivals, the events themselves, and the reminiscences they left behind could bring commotion to a whole area for weeks or even months. These activities were most conspicuous at the small courts with their discrepancy between pretense at home and the world outside. But even at the Prussian court the French fashion prevailed. With his contempt for German language and literature, Frederick II designed his Academy of Science on the French model, with Maupertius as its first president. Frederick hired an obscure French librarian at twice the salary he was willing to pay to Winckelmann, the famous German classicist. Voltaire was surprised to find that everyone at the Prussian court spoke French. But Frederick combined French fashion and culture with personal austerity and strict discipline which he imposed on his entourage. Little of that Prussian spirit was to be found elsewhere in German court society.[25]

By imitating the model of Versailles, the German courts and courtiers were separated by an unbridgeable gulf from the people at large. In Saxony, the aristocracy demanded that its sons be entirely segregated from the sons of bourgeois families, because a common education would unfit them for their social role. Religious ceremonies such as christenings were to be conducted in aristocratic homes, because it would be demeaning to christen aristocratic babies with the same water as ordinary children. Men of standing preempted high offices while the actual work was done by bourgeois menials. Any social contact with persons of lower status was granted as a special favor or regarded as altogether demeaning. But the bastard children of a ruler's mistress or cavalier adventurers with aristocratic manners and pretensions were readily accepted as equals. In such a setting, affairs of court and state were in the

Frederick the Great Visits Voltaire in His Study
Voltaire was the guest of Frederick II from 1750 to 1753 and in this picture remains seated
while the king is standing. In the view of the Enlightenment, the philosopher and this
enlightened ruler were colleagues in the Republic of Letters. Voltaire was showered with
honors at the Prussian court but eventually fell into disgrace. (Potsdam-Sanssouci)

hands of rulers and their confidants, while commentaries on such affairs
by persons outside that circle were a social presumption that was rejected
out of hand. A public was absent in the specific sense that no one outside
the ruling circle had the right to an opinion. Frederick II was relatively
permissive in matters of censorship, yet his edict of 1784 stipulated that
no private individual had the right to make critical judgments concerning the activities of sovereigns and their courts, or to publish news of
these activities and distribute them by means of print. "A private person

is quite incapable of making such judgments, since he will be lacking in the complete understanding of circumstances and motives."[26]

Defenders of the status quo supported this hierarchic view of society. As employees of the state, clergymen, teachers, and officials were hardly in a position to dissent from an interpretation which legitimized their own role in society. But the same view was shared by the people at large, especially by those middle strata of society—entrepreneurs of various kinds and professionals like lawyers, doctors, and writers—who in France stood in the forefront of intellectual and political mobilization. As a contemporary observer put it, "Every nation has its [own] great impetus: in Germany it is obedience, in England freedom, in Holland commerce, in France the honor of the king. It would take very great transformations, in order to alter the whole direction of a way of thought."[27] Obedience toward established authority was a stronger force in Germany than "the honor of the king" was in France. German reactions to the English and French revolutions reflect that obedience.

The English revolution and the execution of Charles I in 1649 marked the overthrow of an old social order. German writings on this event were unanimous: They condemned the execution of a crowned head in the strongest terms, excoriated the Cromwellian regime which followed, and then welcomed the restoration of Charles II to the English throne.[28] This acceptance of every legitimate ruler's sovereign authority remained the prevailing opinion in the eighteenth century. To see such acceptance in proper perspective, it is necessary to refer back to the German Reformation. Luther had rejected the monastic ideal of medieval Catholicism and demanded that every Christian believer prove himself in this world. But Luther considered man both intellectually incapable of achieving knowledge and morally incapable of achieving virtue. In his view, man can be reborn by faith alone, each in the calling in which God has placed him. This doctrine proved highly suitable for aristocratic rule and mercantilist practices. Everyone is called to do his best in his appointed role, with due regard for the traditional modes of work and profit. Competition and striving after wealth are dangers to the soul, but with faith as his guide the Christian believer may have a modest living. At the same time, the ruler and his officials have responsibility for the country's welfare, which is of no concern to the ordinary citizen. The horizon of artisans and merchants is confined to their calling and their religion. It is the task or calling of rulers and aristocrats at court to know diplomacy, the practices of court life, and the affairs of the world. In this religious construction of the social world, intellectual interests belong to high society, not to the socially confined circle of commoners.

This widespread attitude is reflected in the Moral Weeklies (Moralische Wochenschriften), a type of eighteenth-century publication modeled after such English journals as the *Tatler* and the *Spectator*. Predominantly moralistic and didactic in tone, the Moral Weeklies lacked any news content and used a variety of entertaining literary devices to carry their message. An estimated 110 weeklies appeared in the half-century between 1720 and 1770. Most of them had editions of a few hundred up to a thousand copies, and most lasted only a few months or years. However, editors and publishers often started new ventures, because when bound together the weeklies served as books in private libraries, and this seems to have made them profitable. The majority originated in Protestant territories, primarily in large towns like Hamburg, Leipzig, Berlin, Hannover, and Nuremberg. Though a good many were published in small towns, few appeared in towns of princely residences.[29]

The Moral Weeklies provide the best available evidence for the reactions of persons who were educated and had leisure to read, but who were excluded from all political participation. The journals make little reference to occupations or estates but give considerable attention to a middle level of education and interest. They were written so as to be understandable to everyone of ordinary intelligence—"neither too bad or vulgar for the scholar, nor too lofty and incomprehensible for the unlearned," as the Hamburg *Patriot* put it. They wanted to be useful and attractive to all estates, but in practice they counted officials, clergymen, professionals, merchants, and above all women among their readers. The households depicted in them have servants, the sons travel and go to universities, while the daughters learn French. There is leisure for reading and conversation. Men of middle rank have some aristocrats for friends, but do not befriend artisans, peasants, or servants. The Moral Weeklies never portray the virtues of common people who live by proven rules and do not have either leisure or background for a life of principles derived from reason. The weeklies did not begrudge these people their due respect if they were an asset to the community. However, one cannot expect them to be "virtuous," as defined by the Enlightenment. The laws of the time drew a distinction between the status of educated commoners (*Bildungsbürgertum*) who constituted the "nation," and common folk (*Pöbel*, literally rabble) who comprised the subject population. The Moral Weeklies were not likely to be egalitarian when even progressive writers called artisans and peasants "half-men" who were not ready for Enlightenment.[30]

The great majority of subscribers were state employees; only a few aristocrats figure in the two or three subscription lists which have survived. One may speak of many subscribers as *Beamtenbürgertum* (literally "officials as townspeople"), which shows how remote this eighteenth-century social world is from the more familiar connotations of "bourgeoisie."[31]

The Moral Weeklies of the eighteenth century made an effort to instill a sense of purpose and self-assurance among the middle strata of society. Their message of virtue certainly included the demand that everyone promote the common welfare, especially in large towns like Hamburg with civic traditions of their own. Still, this message was addressed primarily to questions of fashion, child-rearing, and proper conduct in all phases of life. The cultivation of virtue itself was considered a way of promoting the common good. The object of these discussions was to suggest in what ways the common man—*by staying within his proper sphere*—contributes to the welfare of the whole. To be concerned with politics is not his task, and ridicule is heaped on those who presume to judge affairs of state which require a higher level of knowledge than is compatible with the circumstances of private persons. Accordingly, the Moral Weeklies had nothing to say about the rights of man, but a good bit about his duties. When "rights" are mentioned at all, they refer to the ways in which a man can maintain his happiness and his peace of mind by being sociable, living up to his contractual obligations, and obeying the authorities, for if he fails in these respects he will be punished and his peace disturbed.

There is no mention of the injustice and arbitrary tyrannies that were rampant in the eighteenth century—not even in Moral Weeklies published in the imperial towns that prided themselves on their freedom. Here is an example from the *Alte Deutsche,* published in Hamburg. Just one essay in one issue deals with the freedom of the city, and it emphasizes the duties which freedom entails. Disorderly conduct is condemned, as is any willful opposition to authority. One contributes to freedom in this way:

> I do not meddle in public affairs, I do not have the proper calling for that. But still I possess love and honesty for the general welfare. As I see it, freedom is therefore nothing else than the opportunity and the effort to promote the general good according to one's own fitness [*nach seinem Masse*]. As I see it, he is not worthy of freedom, who grumbles when he is called upon to contribute his due share to the support of the general good. . . . To be bound by laws is not slavery; to resist the laws is not freedom, but wickedness.

Just as the common man has his duties, so indeed do those in authority. Moral Weeklies never question or challenge kings or princes. They express only the wish that rulers be fatherly, surround themselves with honest advisors, and act for the welfare of their subjects, and in these terms they criticized the courts.[32] They state that commoners have their proper and important position in the social order. This self-definition in relation to the high ranks of society and to those below provides the most general background for the German reaction to the French revolution.

The Moral Weeklies gave *no* direct attention to the affairs of the courts. Other papers reported the rampant gossip about luxuries, intrigues, and scandals in over two hundred sovereign residences. But for the Moral Weeklies the world of the courts was a dangerous or disquieting sphere which the honest man would be well advised to avoid. To achieve power and wealth through a career at court was a matter of luck and took place in a setting that was hazardous to one's conscience and one's life. Courtly splendor was a false veneer, service at court empty of purpose, and the rational and capable man could do far more useful things elsewhere. But while the Weeklies denounced fawning and deceiving courtiers and with them the whole courtly way of life, the political implications of that critique were never mentioned. There was no challenge to the institution of the court or to the legitimacy of sovereign authority. Rather, the discussions of court society served as a background before which the ethical outlook of the educated commoner— the emphasis on virtue, general welfare, diligence, family happiness, sociability, and contentment—could be displayed to good advantage.

Seventeenth-century writings on the courtly arts had advised the man of fashion and good breeding how to conduct himself in order to achieve his personal ends.[33] In practice, this amounted to advice on the personal manipulation of others and an iron-willed control over one's own emotions—all under the outward guise of personal grace and an elaborate etiquette. This is the type of conduct which the writers in the Moral Weeklies called political.

> I understand here by the term *political man* someone who loses sight of faithfulness and honesty in order to realize his unjust intentions; who perjures himself, lies and knows how to dissemble, not in order to achieve something good in secret, but in order to do an evil deed that much more securely. Such politics is attributed to courtiers who are told that they must not have a conscience, that they must not hesitate to violate the holiest alliance or covenant [*Bündnis*], and that they must be adroit enough always to invent a pretext. But one meets with such politics also very frequently in ordinary life and in all kinds of commerce. It is undeniable that this politics is an invention of hell and the most shameful vice in that it destroys entirely the good faith [*Treu und Glauben*] which is the soul of society. Nevertheless, this vice has found its admirers, defenders, and even preachers, who have made out of it an art and science and laid down its rules and laws. And in this way the art of being unfaithful appears under the name of politics.[34]

Writers in the Moral Weeklies did not want such politics; rather, they wished the court would attract honest men so that the virtues of the educated commoner could flourish there. One should add that these writings do *not* attribute such virtues to some ancient and pure German tradition, nor do they attribute the vices of court life to the evil influence of French culture. In the spirit of the Enlightenment, virtue is accessible to every reasonable man and vice the result of unreason and lack of faith.[35] Hindsight may suggest that the identification of politics with deception had very dangerous implications for the future of German society. But as it appears in the Moral Weeklies of the time, the definition was a means of rejecting court society and raising the self-assurance of the Bürgertum.

In the course of the eighteenth century, the number of German commoners with social aspirations increased. Free professionals, artisans, merchants, manufacturers, and the "civil service intelligentsia" acquired an education and were exposed to a considerable intellectual mobilization. Yet these educated commoners were confronted with the French culture and personal arrogance of aristocratic courtiers who themselves lacked stature in the provincial setting of the small German courts. Still, most commoners doubted that they were capable of forming relevant opinions. They might enjoy a level of comfort or even a degree of affluence, but they were content not to come to the attention of autocratic rulers and their officials. Moreover, in thousands of hometowns, commoners took pains to keep this petty official world above them from intruding in their affairs. Commoners generally, but especially those with some education, tended to search for some sense of value in their own sphere.

The personal worth of the individual in society is a major theme of German classical literature. In the *Sorrows of the Young Werther* (1774), Goethe portrayed the demeaning exclusion of his hero from an aristocratic gathering as a searing experience—and his novel was a great popular success. In his *Wilhelm Meister* (1795–1796), he drew a telling contrast between the nobleman and the citizen (or commoner):

> Personal cultivation is only possible for the nobleman . . . a certain dignified grace in common things, a sort of easy delicacy in serious and important ones, becomes him well, for he lets it be seen that he is everywhere in equilibrium. He is a public person, and the more cultivated his movements, the more sonorous his voice, the more restrained and measured his whole being, the more perfect he is. . . . He may be cold, but with a clear head; playing a part, but clean. . . . Everything else which he has in him and about him—capacity, talents, riches—all seem to be only extra gifts.
>
> Now imagine a citizen only thinking of making some claim to these advantages; he must absolutely fail and he must be all the more unfortunate the more Nature may have given him of impulse and capacity to that mode of being. . . .
>
> If the nobleman by his personal carriage offers all that can be asked of him, the citizen by his personality offers nothing and can offer nothing. The former has a right to seem, the latter only to exist, and what he wishes to seem becomes ridiculous and in bad taste. The former is to ask and make, the latter is to effect and procure—he is to cultivate individual capabilities so as to become useful, and it is already presupposed that there is no harmony

in his manner of existence nor can there be, because he is obliged to make himself useful in one direction and must, therefore, neglect everything else.

Goethe did not expect major changes in the condition he diagnosed nor did he think the changes desirable. Eventually, Meister finds personal fulfillment under the educative influence of a company of aristocrats. Ironic detachment was one of the ways in which great writers like Goethe distinguished themselves from the sentimentalism of the Moral Weeklies.[36]

Most writers of the classical period shared Goethe's skeptical esti-mate of Germany's educated commoners, but these writers were never-theless close to the scene to which the Moral Weeklies addressed them-selves. One novel or play after another contrasted the world of the courts and its occasionally good but predominantly evil and always mas-terful men to the world of commoners who were moved by ideals of feeling and piety, of diligence and rectitude. The world of commoners was inevitably narrow, and the greatness of German classical literature consists in part in the effort to break out of this identification of passivity as the virtue of the Bürger, although the scene is frequently and sig-nificantly set outside Germany. The courts may be places of vice, but they are also centers of power; the commoner may be virtuous, but he is without power to achieve his ends. Until the middle of the nineteenth century, novels and plays tended to counter this impotence of common-ers by idealizing equanimity and contentment. Man should not quarrel with God, but accept the fate which befalls him as part of divine dis-pensation. Indeed, the dramatic heroes of this literature are almost always aristocrats—even when their actions idealize the typical virtues of the educated commoner. This approach precludes all subjective claims on life, any idea that by his personal intervention a man can change his fate. In Lessing's *Emilia Galotti* (1772), virtue is preserved by the father killing his own daughter rather than allowing her to be vio-lated by the evil designs of the prince—passivity is overcome but at an enormous price, for action results in the death of the daughter, not of the prince. Many subsequent plays show the great difficulties besetting the virtuous man of action. The inward struggle over the problem of self-assertion provided the classic writers with one of their major themes. Schiller's *Wilhelm Tell* (1804) is one of the few plays in which a com-moner's right to individual assertion is finally vindicated, but the setting of the play is Switzerland many centuries earlier.[37]

With an outlook on life as portrayed by the Moral Weeklies and the classical writers, how did German commoners respond to the French revolution? There can be no single or simple answer to this question, but I believe that Friedrich Schiller's work may be taken as represen-tative in a symbolic sense. Schiller (1759–1805) directly confronted the questions raised by the French revolution. In a letter of 1793 addressed to Duke Friedrich Christian von Augustenberg, he justified his own preoccupation as a poet and philosopher—but only after giving full consideration to the political concerns of the day. The revolution in France seemed to require the attention of every thoughtful citizen. In ancient Athens, Solon had condemned citizens who failed to take a stand for or against rebellion, and Schiller approved of Solon's judgment. Surely, the same principle applied to the French revolution,

> in which the great destiny of mankind is called into question, and in which it appears that one cannot remain neutral without becoming guilty of the most unpardonable indifference towards the most holy concerns of man. A spirited, courageous nation which had been considered exemplary for a long time, had begun to take violent leave of its established social order and return to the state of nature in which reason is the sole and absolute law-giver. An affair which ordinarily only opportunism and the right of the stronger would have decided, has been brought before the judgment-seat of *pure reason* and at least makes some pretense of being decided in accordance with *principles*. Every thinking person may consider himself . . . an associate judge in this court of reason, although as man and world-citizen he is also a party to the case and involved in its success.[38]

But in Schiller's judgment, the revolution had failed to fulfill its great promise. Lawmaking had not become rational, the new state was not founded on true freedom, and man was still manipulated rather than respected. The attempt of the French people "to institute the holy rights of man and achieve political freedom has only revealed that the people are incapable and unworthy." Elsewhere he says "that a moment so prodigal of opportunity finds a generation unprepared to receive it." The "moral opportunity is lacking," because the lower classes only want to satisfy their base desires, while the cultivated classes offer a repugnant spectacle of a lethargic and deprived character.[39]

In Schiller's view, the task was to reform the character of the people without recourse to the state, for under existing conditions the people were incapable of reforming the state.[40] He claimed that by cultivating the arts he was addressing the political issues of his day, not evading them. Whatever one's assessment of Schiller's view, he was surely right that the people to whom the Moral Weeklies appealed were not prepared to undertake the political reconstruction of their country. These people were separated, psychologically and culturally, from their aristocratic rulers, and nothing constructive could be accomplished politically until that gap was overcome. The poet's task was to make one people out of a socially divided society:

> Our's is no longer the Homeric world, in which all members of society were at approximately the same stage in their feelings and opinions, and hence could recognize themselves readily in the same description and meet one another in the same emotions. Today, a large gulf is visible between the elite

and the mass of the nation, due in part to the fact that moral ennoblement and the enlightenment of ideas is a coherent whole, but nothing is gained by mere fragments [of this process]. In addition . . . the members of the nation have become extremely unlike each other in their feelings and expressions. . . . In our times, a poet of the people has to make a choice between the easiest and the most difficult [course]. Either he accommodates himself exclusively to the comprehension of the large crowd and forgoes the applause of the educated class. Or he pursues both purposes in combination and by the greatness of his art vanquishes the enormous distance existing between the two.[41]

Thus, Schiller explicitly defined his artistic task as educational and used his superb poetic gifts to present his audience with an understanding of the tragic realities of political power.[42]

Along with other writers of his day, Schiller emphasized the ideal of *Bildung* or self-cultivation at the cost of any direct involvement with public affairs. He denounced the "all-pursuing demon of criticizing the state."[43] He believed that a higher interest in truth and beauty would lead men beyond the narrow tensions of the day and help unite a politically divided world. Men of good will and liberal sentiment like Schiller and his friends saw little prospect of revolution in a politically fragmented country, and before long they witnessed the terror of the French revolution and became doubtful about revolutions altogether. They had little taste for politics where politics was defined as court intrigue, and they had no access to it in any case. Yet as spirited men they had high aspirations, and under the circumstances the appeal to Bildung appeared as a constructive alternative. For they believed that self-cultivation was worthwhile in its own right and, in the long run, of political significance as well. The ideal of Bildung defined a specifically German contribution to an enlightened age. With such a contribution as a seemingly viable alternative, many men would not opt for a political struggle that appeared hopeless. This is not to argue the case of German idealism, but to show what sense it made to the believers. The ideal of Bildung was a positive alternative in a world of court intrigue and crass commercialism, even though it is also true that this idealism fostered a neglect of political concerns and skills which proved pernicious to institutions based on popular sovereignty.

To aim at greater unity among classes in a hierarchic society and contribute to the cultivation of moral and intellectual qualities are worthy goals in any country. But education is a long-run process, its results are always incomplete, and its relation to the political process equivocal. Art has educational implications, but one suspects that the ideal of self-cultivation simply asked too much of ordinary people. One wonders how much Schiller kept the public of his plays in mind when he idealized classical Greece as the model for the artist and the political analyst. Perhaps he had an inkling of this difficulty when he wrote,

> Kaum hat das kalte Fieber der Gallomanie uns verlassen,
> Bricht in der Gräkomanie gar noch ein hitziges aus.

> Hardly has the cold fever of Gallomania departed,
> Than a hotter fever, Grecomania, erupts.[44]

This ironic couplet describes an important shift from the idealization of French culture at the German courts to a new idealization of classical Greek culture, which had a lasting impact on German secondary education.

Wilhelm von Humboldt (1767–1835) declared that no people could rival the ancient Greeks in combining "so much simplicity and nature with so much culture," and Humboldt was to play a major role in reforming Prussian university education. This approach was given public sanction when F. A. Wolf was called to the University of Halle in 1783. During the momentous years of the French revolution, this classical philologist justified ancient Greece as the principal subject of general education by pointing out that no other people could serve so well as a model. In Wolf's view, the most glaring defect of *all* other cultures was their tendency to subordinate high culture to the most urgent needs of daily existence. Wolf considered it proper enough to use German in writing on "political, economic, medical, military, mathematical and other useful subjects," which to him were "voracious demands of civilization"; but only classical Greek could reveal the "manysidedness and depth of culture."[45] An antipolitical and antiutilitarian attitude of writers and academics had been espoused earlier when the Moral Weeklies sought to boost the self-assurance of educated commoners. The trouble was that in the hands of vulgar men, Bildung (of the kind espoused by Wolf) could become a means of social and national self-assertion. It is an ironic reflection that perhaps the fault lay in the very talents of writers like Schiller, Goethe, and Humboldt. Psychologically and artistically, their aspirations were simply too esoteric for the ordinary German public which in the late eighteenth century had to come to terms with the French revolution.

Among the many reactions to that revolution it is possible to find a common theme, aptly suggested by one of Goethe's Venetian epigrams. Gallomania had prevailed at the courts, and educated commoners lacked self-assurance and political judgment in their relations with an aristocratic governing class. With this background in mind, Goethe wrote,

> Lange haben die Großen der Franzen Sprache gesprochen,
>   Halb nur geachtet den Mann, dem sie vom Munde nicht floß.
> Nun lallt alles Volk entzückt die Sprache der Franken.
>   Zürnet, Mächtige nicht! Was ihr verlangtet, geschieht!

Long have the Great spoken the Frenchies' language,
    Little regarding those who did not master the tongue.
Now, delightedly, all people babble the language of France.
    Mighty ones, do not rage! What you have demanded, occurs![46]

The ruling groups of German society had taken the French monarchy as their model and had exploited the people (though Goethe does not say so) to support the luxuries of a French court life. Now suddenly, the French revolution had replaced the old model with a new one. With subtle irony Goethe suggests that the "mighty ones" should not object if people still followed the model that had been set before them. However, he did not think the positive response to the French revolution evidence of a new self-assurance among educated commoners. He disapproved of their political awakening, thought it misguided, and considered the ideal of self-cultivation irrelevant to the rise of political awareness.

The several phases of the French revolution set off responses in Germany ranging from a conservative rejection of the revolution root and branch to democratic and socialist proposals for a constitution and the equalization of property. Each response had its liabilities. A complete rejection of French revolutionary ideas also meant support of the German status quo with its political particularism at a time when France was advancing the cause of nationalism. A good many conservatives feared revolution in their own country and hence accepted the necessity of reforms, albeit holding fast to the principles of a hierarchic social order and monarchic rule.[47] At the other end of the political spectrum, German radicals did not want to depend on French precedent and support as the German courts they detested had done, even though they completely accepted the ideas of the French revolution. In some circles, the credibility of German radical democrats was impaired by their identification with French revolutionary excesses.[48] The revolution and its Napoleonic aftermath thus tended to undercut both the unyielding defenders and the radical critics of the status quo.

The French revolution did change German politics despite these unresolved ambiguities. It showed that reform through enlightened but autocratic rulers was not the only way of effecting reform, and this presented German critics with a great dilemma. Many crucial issues of the French revolution were caused by the same abuses which had aroused personal indignation and sporadic protest in Germany for almost two generations. Should all German critics of such abuses automatically identify themselves with the revolution? Or, if they rejected the revolution, how could they continue as critics of the German status quo?

Conservatives like the publicist Schloezer and the historian Johannes von Mueller deplored aristocratic privilege, the immoralities of high society, and specific abuses like excessive taxation, hunting rights, as well as the infamous dragooning of men for military service in foreign countries. Schloezer was a highly respected and staunchly monarchist publicist who had strongly opposed the American revolution. Yet this man cursed the despots who had made the French revolution necessary. Cancerous lesions could not be healed with rose water, he maintained. For his part, Mueller was a skeptical critic of the Enlightenment and greatly feared radical change. Yet he thought it was a good idea that kings and magistrates learn they were also human. In his view, censorship was useless because news of the revolution would spread anyway and carry its own message.[49] Thus, even conservatives were prepared for a favorable reaction to the French revolution because of the policies of enlightened absolutism—especially those of Frederick II and Joseph II. When relatively conservative men greeted the revolution so warmly, more liberal spirits responded even more eagerly.

Yet this ready acceptance of an emancipatory ideal was matched by a very widespread rejection of the revolution itself. Many liberal Germans who had been enthusiastic about the revolution turned against it when Louis XVI was executed in 1793 and a regime of terror followed. With the fall of Robespierre in 1794, France experienced a retrenchment under the Directory, allowing German sympathizers of the revolution to maintain their liberal attitudes as well as their traditional acceptance of authority. Moreover, as their scepticism toward revolutionary methods turned into outright condemnation, German liberals turned for inspiration to the English experience with constitutional government and to the doctrines of the English classical economists.[50]

As a model for German aspirations, France had become tarnished. The artificiality of French culture at the German courts had become repugnant. German intellectual mobilization had preceded the French revolution for decades, and with the change from revolutionary ideals to the terror France no longer appeared as the citadel of liberty. The need of German writers to look to France for cultural and political inspiration had diminished. To be sure, nothing could be done about Germany's political fragmentation, but considerable progress had been made in reforming the abuses of autocratic rule. A system of laws had been established. Enlightened rulers had begun to protect the common people against the privileged, to promote elementary and higher education, to clear swamps, and to develop the economy. Governments had become relatively free of corruption, and the better rulers employed trained officials to check on the execution of commands. Oppressive religious orthodoxy had been alleviated in the interest of toleration. There was no call for a revolution in the face of such promise, even if as yet only half-fulfilled. On the contrary, there was a belief that the

German territories were finding their own way of reforming the old regime.[51]

By the end of the eighteenth century, then, educated commoners and civil servants had acquired a sense of identity not only in the cultural realm but in public affairs. In 1791 the publicist Schloezer declared that the Germans were more prepared than all other peoples for the "quiet reconquest of the lost rights of man."

> To be sure, the revolution will be slow, but it is occurring. Enlightenment is rising from below, as in France; but it is also meeting with enlightenment in the upper ranks of society: nowhere are there more cultivated sovereigns than in Germany. . . . From all appearances it will be more the work of professional writers [*Schriftstellerei*] than of cabinets, that this [revolution] occurs slowly, without mischief, without anarchy. Princes will remain princes and all Germans will become free men.[52]

That same year, the Prussian finance minister Struensee despaired of reforming the thousand and one anachronisms of autocratic rule, but by 1799 he declared that "the beneficial revolution which . . . Frenchmen have conducted violently from below, we Prussians will conduct gradually from above."[53]

Later, Goethe articulated the same idea in the manner of "enlightened absolutism."

> It is true, I could not be a friend of the French Revolution, for its horrors touched me too directly and revolted me daily and hourly, whereas its beneficial consequences could not yet be envisaged at that time. Nor could I be indifferent when in Germany one sought to introduce in an *artificial manner* similar scenes, which in France were the consequence of a great necessity.
>
> But neither was I a friend of an arbitrary autocracy. I was also completely convinced that a great revolution is never the fault of the people, but rather of the government. Revolutions are quite impossible whenever governments are perpetually just and alert so that through timely improvements they meet [the revolution] half way and do not resist until the necessary [reforms] are forced upon them from below.[54]

In Goethe's view, successful reform must grow out of a nation's own circumstances, rather than by imitation of another country. He resented being labeled a defender of the status quo. He was no friend of what was antiquated or unjust under existing conditions. But he wanted the good to be recognized where it existed, though he was convinced that even good institutions require constant attention and reform.[55] Goethe was not only Germany's most illustrious poet; he had been the highest paid official in the service of Grand Duke Carl August of Saxony-Weimar-Eisenach. By virtue of his extraordinary gifts, Goethe was a unique figure, and his outlook tended to the conservative side of the political spectrum. Nevertheless, his combination of official duties and the ideal of self-cultivation was typical of the reform intelligentsia of the early nineteenth century.

A REVOLUTION FROM ABOVE?

In the German society of the late eighteenth and early nineteenth centuries, there was no well-defined group of "leaders in opposition" comparable to the lawyers, religious dissenters, and parliamentarians of England or the philosophes and parlementaires of France. One reason was that Germany lacked a cultural center like London or Paris. The consequences of this fact are vividly described in a review article by Goethe:

> Nowhere in Germany is there a center of social life and education [*gesell-schaftlicher Lebensbildung*], where writers can congregate and develop, each in his own field, but in a unified fashion. Born dispersed, educated very differently, mostly left only to themselves and to impressions from very different situations; swept away by the preference for this or that example of native or foreign literature; impelled to all kinds of dabbling attempts in order to test their powers without guidance; only through gradual reflection convinced of what one should undertake; instructed by practice in what one can accomplish; led astray time and again by a large public without taste, which devours the bad and the good with just the same delight; then again encouraged through acquaintance with the educated multitude scattered through all parts of the *Reich*; strengthened by contemporaries engaged in collaborative endeavors; thus the German writer finally finds himself in the age of manhood, in which worry about his livelihood and a family forces him to look around. Often he is forced with the saddest feeling to obtain his living through works he himself does not respect, in order to be allowed to create what his mature mind would solely wish to be occupied with. What respected German writer will not recognize himself in this picture and confess with humble sadness, how often he has sighed for an opportunity to subordinate the peculiarities of his creative genius to a national culture, which unfortunately did not exist? For the cultivation of the higher classes through foreign fashions and a foreign literature prevented a German from developing as a German early on, however much advantage such cultivation has brought us as well.[56]

In our context, Goethe's description is best read as an account of the peculiar stamp which these conditions put on cultural life. In a fragmented country like Germany, the petty circumstances of daily life were not relieved by larger public preoccupations as in London or Paris. Perhaps it was as a way of countering (or compensating for) the provincial particularism surrounding them that German writers came to focus on humanity as a whole. Citizenship of the world (*Weltbürgertum*) was a favorite slogan of the period.

Circumstances did not favor impulses for reform, although the number and importance of publicists increased considerably during the late eighteenth century. Most of these writers were staunch monarchists who expected reforms from the enlightened rulers. Their concern with reform was manifested in publicized views that were read by public officials and educated commoners, the Beamtenbürgertum as well as the Bildungsbürgertum. But it is not clear what either officials or commoners could do. Officials were called royal servants and treated as such. Frederick William I of Prussia said, "One must serve the ruler body and soul, with all one's possessions, with honor and conscience, indeed with everything but one's salvation: that is from God, but everything else must be mine." Frederick II acted on this precept. He concentrated all decision-making in his hands, denied all initiative to subordinates, and distrusted everyone who served him—an attitude that inevitably made his officials conceal the truth and work in an atmosphere of universal suspicion.[57] Everywhere in the German states, the chances for constructive reforms depended on the will and enlightenment of the ruler. Although no state of the eighteenth century could achieve the complete regulation of society called for by the ideology of the "well-ordered police state," Prussia came closer to this objective than most. Its militarization of society established many direct relations between the state and the individual. The people were a resource of the state, and this approach prepared the way for the idea that people who serve the state are entitled to services by the state. This is another basis for government in the name of the people.

Between Frederick II's accession to the throne in 1740 and the defeat by Napoleon in 1806, Prussia's population increased from 2.2 to 10.7 million people, and its total land area from 2,186 to 6,023 square miles. Total exports and imports more than quadrupled between 1752 and the end of the century. Between 1740 and 1806, income from royal domains increased by a factor of three, total state income by four and a half, military expenditures by four, and the size of the standing army from 72,000 to 250,000 men.[58] All these changes required an expanded civil service. Even Frederick II, with his preference for the aristocracy, could not hold the line against the administrative advancement of commoners, especially after the Seven Years' War (1756–1763) had decreased the supply of qualified aristocratic candidates. Frederick intervened in the administrative process without warning, and under his successors personal autocracy continued. Prussian rulers insisted on personally making even low-level appointments, partly because they wanted subordinate officials recruited from retired noncommissioned officers and disabled soldiers, and partly because they wanted to make every official a personal servant of the king.[59]

But gradually the Prussian rulers became less capable of personally directing all public affairs and had to rely on nominees recommended by leading courtiers and officials. As a result, the role of professional administrators increased and attempts at management on the old pattern declined, especially after Frederick's death in 1786.[60] By the 1770s top administrators controlled admissions and promotions through entrance examinations and the establishment of a civil service commission. Standardized qualifications for appointment and promotion were a remarkably efficient method of reintroducing discipline and coping with graft and unauthorized exercise of power which had increased during the Seven Years' War. At the same time, entrance examinations served to exclude many nonaristocratic university graduates from competition, because they lacked the resources to pay the high examination fees and to become in-service trainees without pay. Moreover, candidates for the examination had to be nominated by ranking superiors who injected standards of social acceptability in the selection procedure. Such practices protected the privileged access of aristocratic youths to the civil service, hardly a propitious basis for independent thought and institutional reform. Many officials responded to the opportunities of a greatly expanded state by a determined exploitation of the advantages accruing to their privileged position in state and society.[61] Nevertheless, Hegel was right when he singled out civil servants as "the greatest part of the middle class, the class in which the consciousness of right and the developed intelligence of the people is found."[62] Several factors contributed to this intellectual leadership of high government officials.

Frederick II and his successors employed educated commoners and aristocrats from other German states in top positions when qualified Prussians were in short supply. High social status and experience outside Prussia contributed to the outlook of these men. Under a strong ruler, they were more dependable in the autocrat's struggle with recalcitrant subordinates or with the landed estates. They were likely to be at odds with the self-serving cliques of native aristocrats in the provinces and in the civil service. However, origin, education, and experience made these men impatient with autocratic interference and rather independent in approaching the problems of administration. The entrance examinations to the civil service could provide them with a check against royal arbitrariness, and as non-Prussians they could leave the service in protest. One reason for the intellectual leadership of the Prussian civil service, then, was the fact that at the center of affairs freedom from local ties and declining autocratic interference afforded officials of non-Prussian origin an opportunity to innovate.[63]

Another reason was the importance of educational qualifications. Universities were increasingly organized to prepare young men for their official duties in government, church, and school. Among the faculties, law had the highest prestige because it was usually attended by students from aristocratic families. Commoners tended to enroll in theology and philosophy and prepare for a clerical or teaching career.[64] The standard training was state controlled and narrow in purpose, but by the last decades of the eighteenth century universities were losing some of their earlier antiquated character. The teachings of Adam Smith became an important, liberalizing influence. Published in England in 1776, the first volume of the *Wealth of Nations* appeared in German translation in the same year, with the second volume following two years later. Universities such as Göttingen, Königsberg, and Halle taught the doctrines of economic liberalism; free trade and opposition to guilds and other monopolies became important subjects of writing and instruction. Civil servants who became leaders of the Prussian reform movement had attended these universities and had specifically studied under professors who were teaching "Adam Smith." There is ample evidence that among high officials in Denmark, Schleswig, Holstein, and Berlin in the 1780s and 1790s, the doctrine of free trade and of opposition to guild monopolies was a major topic of interest.[65]

Journals began to contain more direct discussions of cultural and political problems. Though classification of journals by content is uncertain, one compilation indicates that the number of cultural-political journals increased from seven in the 1770s to twenty in the 1780s and twenty-four in the 1790s.[66] Some of these journals were shortlived, although a good many appeared for a decade or more. Many articles were published anonymously, but fifty-nine writers could be identified: Nineteen were aristocrats and forty educated commoners. While there were some conservatives among them, the great majority of the writers favored reforms and came from families of civil servants and clergymen.[67]

This quickening interest in public issues among German civil servants was paralleled by much cultural ferment in the Prussian capital of Berlin, the nearest approximation to a cosmopolitan city then existing in Germany. In 1747 the city had 107,000 inhabitants, and by 1798 that number had increased to 142,000—not including the military garrison. In the decades around 1800, Berlin was a center of cultural activities with its large number of journals (including a plethora of scurrilous pamphlets), its privately organized lectures, and its fashionable salons.[68] In our context, the so-called Wednesday Society (Mittwochgesellschaft, 1783–1800) is of special interest, since it provided a meeting ground for higher civil servants and the literary intelligentsia. Lectures were held in the houses of participants and dealt with political questions of all kinds, especially with problems of administration and political philosophy. The participation of officials as prominent as Svarez, Klein, and Dohm suggests that for a minority of highly placed civil servants the ideals of Bildung reinforced their efforts of coping with the mounting problems of state administration.[69]

What kind of intellectual leadership could reform-minded civil servants provide? Most of them had shared in the initial enthusiasm for the ideals of the French revolution and in the subsequent disenchantment—a reaction which once again endorsed the enlightened absolutism that most of them had never really abandoned. Yet this endorsement was a contradiction from which German liberalism could never free itself. Reforms under absolutist auspices are state directed, whereas enlightenment means "to use one's intelligence without the guidance of another" (Kant). The desire to promote both state-directed reforms and enlightenment is paradoxical. Hegel's description of civil servants exemplifies that paradox. He calls civil servants the class which is politically conscious and

> [the one in which education] is most prominent. For this reason it is also the pillar of the state so far as honesty and intelligence are concerned. A state without a middle class must therefore remain on a low level. Russia, for instance, has a mass of serfs on the one hand and a mass of rulers on the other. It is a prime concern of the state that a middle class should be developed, but this can be done only . . . by giving authority to spheres of particular interests, which are relatively independent [civil society], and by appointing an army of officials whose personal arbitrariness is broken against such authorized bodies.[70]

On the one hand, civil servants are said to be the greatest and most educated part of the middle class, the pillar of the state. Yet the state, as administered by these officials, is also called on to develop "spheres of particular interests, which are relatively independent." (This idea probably reflects both the practice of giving state assistance to private enterprises and Hegel's recognition of civil society as the sphere of independently acting individuals which he adapted from English political economy.) Under the direction of an absolute ruler, then, one part of the middle class (civil servants) is to help create another independent part of the middle class (particular interests). Hegel adds that the officials will be prevented from using their "education and skill as means to an arbitrary tyranny" by the sovereign working on them at the top and "corporation rights" working on them at the bottom.[71]

Hegel's assessment of the civil service accurately describes the outlook of reform-minded civil servants themselves. They understood that reform is the task of state action and that its aim must be the protection of individual rights. The two principles were most readily applied to the legal position of the officials themselves. As servants of the king they are subject to arbitrary dismissal, but as servants of the state they must be protected against royal arbitrariness. Here state action itself must be reformed by laws which regulate the legal position of civil servants. The ruler would then be obliged to conform to the requirements of the law. Some of these changes were incorporated in the General Prussian Code (*Allgemeine Landrecht*) of 1794, which substituted the phrase "officials of the state" for the earlier "royal servants" and provided some legal safeguards against arbitrary dismissal. But these safeguards were limited and did not provide for the permanent tenure of civil servants during good behavior.[72] The legal protection of all civil servants against both arbitrary dismissal and compulsory removal to another post had to await the further legislation of the 1820s and 1840s. Nevertheless, the Prussian civil service of the early nineteenth century promoted the view that state action through legal reform and the protection of individual rights are compatible goals.

This idea did not remain confined to the civil service. With prominent officials in the forefront of the reform movement and "enlightened absolutism" the most widely accepted political principle, it was natural to extend the idea to society at large. The need for reforms was generally accepted, especially after the catastrophic Napoleonic victory over Prussia in 1806. By means of law, the state could initiate reforms and define its own limits; thus, "particular interests" would be both encouraged by the state and protected in their rights by law, even from the state. The promotion of industry is a case in point.

Disillusion with the French revolution intensified the long-standing interest of German liberals in English culture. German travelers were impressed by the economic prosperity of the country. It was natural, therefore, to visit England with the idea of learning its industrial technology. The Prussian government sent a number of officials, and private entrepreneurs went as well. At the same time, German travelers, officials, and entrepreneurs noted with apprehension the seamy side of industrial progress—the poverty, ill health, and premature death of many workers. These observers came from a country in which the economic role of government was prominent. In Prussia the state had its own salt mines, collieries, iron works, and armament factories; and the other German states pursued a similar pattern. So there was no incentive to follow England's example of leaving industrialists and merchants to their own devices. On the contrary, it was assumed that by means of state sponsorship, the advance of German industry could be achieved more rapidly and the gap between Germany and England narrowed.[73]

Leonard Krieger has observed, "The general rule of reform was the extension of monarchical authority by destroying the remnants of aristocratic and administrative autonomy, by establishing the equality of all citizens before the royal law, and by conceding an economic and social mobility which would undermine local and provincial attachments."[74] The general rule was implemented under Napoleonic auspices with the abolition of serfdom, the legal protection of religious differences, and the loosening of the guilds' stranglehold on trade and industry. The great reformers of the period were Stein, Hardenberg, and Humboldt. All three were aristocrats and high civil servants who adhered to the German liberal creed of maximizing both state power and individual freedom. Indeed, they believed that the first was a necessary condition of the second. Karl Freiherr Vom und Zum Stein (1757–1831) repeatedly juxtaposed the sanctity of personal freedom with the need for a powerful governmental administration and the duties of patriotism, which would prompt the people to sacrifice property and life for king and fatherland. During the reform period, Stein was naturally preoccupied with revitalizing the Prussian state; thus, he conceived of the free activity of individuals as a contribution to the strength of political authority. Here freedom appears as a constituent element of state power, not a constraint on it.

Freiherr Karl August von Hardenberg's (1750–1822) outlook was very similar. Like many others, he endorsed the ideals of the French revolution but rejected the revolution itself. He desired a more centralized German constitution and a federation of princes under Prussian hegemony. He wanted to see the realization of "true freedom": equal application of the laws, free competition based on merit, security of property and person, and the equal distribution of burdens. If Prussia was to survive as a state, it must adopt these "democratic principles in a monarchical government."

> The revolution has been promoted to an ever increasing extent by the illusion that one could counteract the revolution most effectively by adherence to the old and by the severe persecution of revolutionary principles. [But] the power of these principles is so great, they are recognized and disseminated so generally that the state which rejects them must accept its own demise or face up to their enforced adoption. Even Napoleon and his favorite aides with their craving for domination, their pride and their plundering are subject to the power of those principles, and will remain so. There is no denying that Napoleon adheres to those principles in many essentials, or is at least obliged to abide by them to save appearances, despite the iron despotism of his rule.
>
> Our aim and our guiding principle is a revolution in the good sense, one that will lead to the great goal of ennobling mankind through the wisdom of government and not through violent impulses from within or from the outside. Democratic principles in a monarchical government: to me this seems the appropriate form for the spirit of the present age.[75]

On this basis, Hardenberg advocated unlimited freedom in economic and social activities, proposing the emancipation of the peasant and the abolition of estate distinctions and of tariffs and guilds—though he remained very cautious with regard to intellectual freedom and the extension of political rights. However such policies worked in practice, their goal was again a strengthening of state power *and* of individual freedom.

Wilhelm von Humboldt (1767–1835) went farthest in opposing state power on theoretical grounds. He is best known for his essay "Ideas for an Attempt to Determine the Limits of the Power of the State," which was written in 1792 but not published during his lifetime. In this essay, Humboldt accepted the political system, but sought to exclude the state from all spheres in which politics would hinder the development of the human spirit. When these convictions were put to the test, Humboldt tended to compromise. As Prussia's minister of education, he was concerned with the cultivation of the individual's personality. But in that position he also recognized the necessity of state action on the ground that the state makes the social arrangements which individuals need for their many-sided development. He meant to restrict the legal competence of the state, but he also called for state action when men were not sufficiently mature for a free development of the self. Thus, even the foremost German spokesman of an antistatist liberalism did not in practice deviate from the simultaneous endorsement of state action and individual liberty.[76]

It remains for us to consider what a "revolution from above" accomplished for the mandate of the people. The answer is not much, and this answer is related to the social and political position of the bureaucratic elite which headed the Prussian reform movement.

LIBERTY AT THE KING'S COMMAND

The mandate of the people presupposes some idea of equality, if only because such a mandate requires a larger popular participation in politics than the authority of kings permits. Participation and equality are ideals with many facets. In England, religious dissenters opposed the hierarchy of church office and advocated a more egalitarian organization in which the congregation could participate. The modes of that participation varied from the Presbyterian emphasis on elders to the Quaker emphasis on the brotherhood of all believers. At the same time, civil lawyers appealed to an ancient constitution and the supremacy of law to which all authority should be subordinated. The lawyers' principle of equality under the law arose from a narrow guild-spirit, though this was compatible with congregational equality. In France, still a third meaning of equality came to prevail. The philosophes defied the authority of crown, church, and nobility in the name of reason. A new equality of citizenship was asserted in place of the old inequality of privilege. Henceforth, the nation alone possessed sovereign authority, and all men were equal participants in that nationwide constituency. The representatives of that constituency would issue the laws under which men would live in peace. All three meanings of equality—under God, under the law, and in the name of reason—were incompatible with Prussian traditions.[e]

The principle of monarchical legitimacy proved to be the basic obstacle. The French revolution had challenged that principle by its overthrow of the monarchy and the election of a constituent assembly, thus replacing the old principle of legitimacy with the new one of the sovereign nation under law. Was it possible or desirable to reconcile monarchical rule with popular representation? Between 1807 and 1822, the struggle over constitutional reform in Prussia turned on this question. Impulses for the reform of political institutions antedated Prussia's defeat by Napoleon in 1806, for there was dissatisfaction with the exclusion of commoners in a society of commercial and intellectual mobilization. Reform-minded civil servants were specifically dissatisfied with two glaring defects of the old order: the multiplicity of overlapping jurisdictions and the multiplicity of guild monopolies, tax exemptions, hereditary privileges, and other vested interests.

Both preoccupations were evident in the administrative career of Hardenberg long before he played a leading role in the reform movement. In 1776, as councillor of the exchequer (*Kammerrat*) in Hannover, he advocated that the management of royal domains be put in the hands of private entrepreneurs who could profit from increasing agricultural productivity. Such a measure would have separated the economic sphere, based on capitalist principles, from the centrally organized administrative staff, paid by fixed salaries and solely charged with governmental responsibilities. This proposal was rejected. Later, as minister of the Prussian state of Ansbach-Bayreuth (1790–1798), Hardenberg addressed himself to the task of overcoming the crazy-quilt jurisdictions of a territory with 400,000 inhabitants extending over 116 square miles. The borders of this little land were broken up by more than twenty different jurisdictions consisting of dukedoms, imperial cities, principalities, ecclesiastical estates, and various jurisdictions of imperial knights. In combating these conditions, Hardenberg made use of the centralized administrative devices that had been developed in France. As a result, he acquired the reputation of a radical reformer, possibly a Jacobin, in the eyes of those whose established rights his measures violated.[77]

In practice, the Prussian reformers faced an insoluble dilemma. Military defeat and foreign occupation had discredited monarchical authority, whose conservative spokesmen were on the defensive against the populist ideas emanating from France. But a strong monarchical au-

---

[e]As in Chapter 5, the last two sections of this chapter deal mostly with Prussia in contrast to the earlier sections which deal—albeit broadly—with "Germany." At a few points, this focus on Prussia must be supplemented by reference to all-German events.

thority was required to simplify jurisdictions and curb vested interests. Under the circumstances, reformers like Stein, Hardenberg, and others concluded that the monarchy had failed to engage public interest and initiative. They favored popular representation largely in the sense of enlisting the populace in defending the fatherland and providing stronger support of the monarchy. They believed that society must be brought into closer cooperation with the state. The reformers addressed this appeal to the king in the interest of making his rule more effective. But spokesmen of the restoration called on the king to grant greater authority to the old estate assemblies and hence restore the political particularism which the Hohenzollern rulers had overcome in the seventeenth century. Such arguments regularly conjured up the spectre of a popular uprising which was imminent if any concessions were made to popular demands for representation. In the end, the forces of restoration won out—supported as they were by similar forces in France and Austria. The Prussian king's rejection of any form of popular participation was made still more galling by public promises of a constitution on three separate occasions (1810, 1815, and 1820). Unilaterally given, these promises were as unilaterally withdrawn. Each time, the fear of revolution provided the most effective arguments in defense of established privilege.[78]

Still, many conservatives were ready to accept reform once the legitimacy of monarchical rule was assured. For the monarchy had been defeated at Jena, its resources were strained to the utmost, and popular disaffection could become dangerous if no reforms were undertaken. Reformers like Stein and Hardenberg were themselves conservative men who wanted to make the established order more effective. Thus, a good many conservatives accepted reforms that aided the mobilization of economic resources, even if these reforms had to be pushed through against diehard defenders of the old particularistic jurisdictions. "Liberty yes, popular representation no!" would have been an apt summary of the spirit in which the Prussian bureaucracy promoted institutional reform.[79] By introducing liberties at the king's command, the Prussian reformers saw to it that these new liberties would not enhance political liberty as well.

Prussia was predominantly agricultural, and serfdom was its most glaring denial of liberty. With the accession of Frederick William III in 1797, the king himself took the initiative in sponsoring the removal of restrictions, beginning with the emancipation of peasants on the royal domains. The worsening international situation temporarily halted this effort, but in 1807, following the defeat at Jena, it was declared that serfdom should be abolished on private estates throughout the country, the measure to take effect in 1810. At the time, owners of large estates in East Prussia were increasingly using landless laborers, and agricultural estates were changing hands at a brisk rate. The decree of 1807 also removed all restrictions on the sale of land; thus, landed estates hitherto reserved for the aristocracy could now be acquired by middle-class or peasant purchasers, while the aristocracy in turn was now allowed to engage in industry and commerce. But while these last measures effectively removed the legal basis of the existing estates, the emancipation of the serfs proved more troublesome because of landlord resistance.

The basic problem of abolishing serfdom (as later in Russia) was the effect of abolition on the rights of property. Those who opposed emancipation on these grounds typically did not stop to consider that the rights over the peasant as a person had often been established by usurpation generations earlier. Past violations did not diminish the claims of those who currently held title to the peasant's services. Hence, legislation had to come to terms with the question of how the earlier obligations of peasant-serfs toward the knightly estate owner (*Rittergutsbesitzer*) were to be handled. The rights of peasants ranged from those of the hereditary leaseholder through claims of peasants to portions of the harvest down to the low status of the temporary leaseholder. It became necessary to define these several rights of peasants, assess their remaining service obligations, and determine compensation for the "purchase of freedom" appropriate to each level of obligation. Inevitably, the estate owners claimed to be shortchanged, especially where settled peasants rather than landless laborers provided the bulk of the work force. Under the edict of 1816, which assessed the rent payments due from each peasant, many peasants proved unable to keep up the payments required of them. They had been freed only in the sense that they were now direct subjects of the king rather than personal subjects of their landlords. Unlike the peasants on the royal domains, they had not been relieved from the duty to provide services which were incumbent on them if they were given the right to till the land.

These were the difficulties of transition from a rural economy in which land was encumbered by various rights often of long standing, to one in which land was a commodity freely traded on the market. In the earlier economy, the rights and duties attached to personal status could not be readily distinguished from those connected with the land, and the new legislation did not make that distinction any clearer. For example, the noble estate owners lost their inherited claims to the personal service of the peasants on their estates. But neither the legal freedom of peasants nor the commercialization of land destroyed the old aristocratic rights of jurisdiction, exemption from the land tax, and exclusive control over local self-government in the country districts. (These rights of the landed aristocracy were lost only in 1848/49, 1861, and 1891, respectively.[80]) In the thirty years following the 1816 edict, 1 million hectares (1 hectare = 2.47 acres) and well over 100,000 peasant holdings came into the possession of the aristocracy.[81] The peasants who were forced off the land and now constituted an agricultural proletariat were still subjected to a patriarchal regimen by law (*Gesindeordnung* of 1810, a code regulating domestic master-servant relations). Economic liberty had been introduced into the countryside by the legal abolition of serfdom and the commercialization of land, but the privileges of the landed aristocracy were reinforced.

The result was that the new inequalities of the free market were compounded by the old inequalities of hereditary privilege. In accord with the principle of the free market, the peasants had been granted their "liberty" which exposed them to the risks of unemployment and deprivation, unrelieved by whatever protection the old patriarchal system may have provided. In addition, the dispossessed peasants were injured psychologically. Their new personal liberty made continued social inferiority more galling because patriarchal authority under the new order was in practice indistinguishable from the old serfdom. As Max Weber was to observe later,

> Domestic servants flee the household of the master. Threshers want to sever their close tie-in with the economy of the estate. The laborer on annual contract relinquishes his secure position, in order to make his precarious way as a "free" day laborer. The peasant with very little land would rather starve than accept a job and work for someone else. Innumerable workers prefer to pay any price to a jobber for a piece of land and to live in abject dependence on creditors who charge usurious interest rates, all this for the sake of the "self-dependence" which they crave, i.e., for the sake of independence from personal subservience to a master.[82]

We saw that the edict of 1807 permitted aristocrats to engage in trade and commoners to purchase a knightly estate (*Rittergut*). By 1810 other decisive steps toward a free economy were taken. Henceforth, every adult worker was allowed to practice any trade on obtaining a license, though some occupations were made dependent on a proof of proficiency as well. A year later, the old guilds with their monopolistic restrictions were abolished. Anyone could now hire apprentices or journeymen, and most qualifying examinations were rescinded.[83]

The effects of these measures were far-reaching. Until the mid-nineteenth century, craftsmen made up a majority of the urban population. With guild monopolies removed, the crafts were soon teeming with artisans who had little training and no capital. In a city like Berlin, principles of economic individualism had found their spokesmen well before 1800, but by the early nineteenth century the municipality was alarmed at the deterioration of workmanship, the "speculation and irresponsibility" among artisans, and increasing unemployment. By 1838

the handicrafts had deteriorated, the number of bankruptcies increased, and expenditures for poor relief quadrupled in less than twenty years. Other cities showed similar developments, and the hometowns had a further incentive for their exclusionist policies.[84] As a result, sentiments favoring the old protective, if monopolistic, system were widespread, even in the large towns.

The old order of many sovereign territories impeded trade by its many customs barriers. The Prussian customs law of 1818 abolished all internal imposts and levied duty only at its external frontiers. In addition, between 1828 and 1836 the German customs union (*Zollverein*) under Prussian leadership abolished duties throughout the German Confederation. Only the states of northwestern Germany remained outside the union, though local resistance throughout Germany was often considerable. Abolition of internal customs barriers meant increased competition and the encroachment of the factory system on local craft guilds and markets.[85] Great strides in taxation were made in 1810 when luxury and consumption taxes were applied generally, distinctions between urban and rural taxpayers abolished, and an occupational and a

The Congress of Vienna, 1815

In this formal picture by Jean-Baptiste Isabey, the figures in the foreground (from left to right) are Hardenberg of Prussia (seated), Metternich of Austria (standing), Castlereagh of Britain (seated, partially hidden by the back of a chair), Talleyrand of France (seated, full face), and Stackelberg of Russia (seated, in profile). The assertion of monarchical legitimacy and religious orthodoxy gave the "Holy Alliance" the appearance of unity which it did not possess. A contemporary caricature gives another version of the Congress, showing (from left to right) Talleyrand observing events from the sidelines; Castlereagh deliberating whether to join the merry dance of England's allies, Frederick William III, Metternich, and Alexander I. Meanwhile, the king of Saxony fears the loss of his crown and the Republic of Genoa plays up to the other powers in the hope of keeping its independence. (Albertina, Vienna) general income tax levied. Even a general land tax was introduced which did away with the previous tax exemptions of the aristocracy. But these initial successes of the reform movement did not last, and during the 1820s and 1830s many of the old privileges were reintroduced. In the field of taxation, lasting reform had to wait until the second half of the nineteenth century.

The leaders of the Prussian reform movement claimed to have made a "revolution from above," for these and related measures were generally similar to those enacted by the constituent assembly of the French revolution. However, Prussia suppressed all moves toward constitutionalism. Even when privileged jurisdictions were destroyed, privileges were frequently reasserted in another form. Moreover, German liberalism itself departed very early from the principle of laissez-faire when it became apparent that a free market would create many intractable social problems.[86] These tendencies toward restoration were part of an international reaction to the threat of revolution. Hence, the Prussian development must be related to German and, indeed, to European developments which directly affected Prussian internal affairs.

The final defeat of Napoleon in 1815 was followed by the Congress of Vienna, convened by the victorious powers of Austria, Russia, and Prussia. The political order established under Napoleon was replaced by the German Confederation (*Deutscher Bund*) of thirty-nine sovereign territories (including four cities). The Congress (dubbed the "Holy Alliance") endorsed the principle of patriarchal government, based on the solidarity among throne, altar, and nobility. On the whole, the policy of restoration was successful throughout Germany. After more than two decades of war and revolution, large segments of the population were eager for peace. In Prussia, even the leaders of the reform movement endorsed the general effort to stabilize conditions under monarchical rule. But they believed such stability could be achieved only by moderate constitutional reforms, not by mere appeals to law, order, and loyalty. This modest constitutionalism became the main point of controversy in Prussia as well as in the other states of the German Confederation.

Napoleon's conquests had spread the nationalism and constitutionalism of the French revolution throughout the Continent. The nationalist aspirations for a unified Germany were dashed by the Congress of Vienna, but constitutionalist principles were not rejected. The Congress had an interest in helping the new states of the German Confederation consolidate the legitimacy of their several territorial possessions. The adoption of a constitution was a means to that end, though in the spirit of the restoration these constitutions tended to combine explicitly conservative precautions with a token acceptance of liberal principles. In any event, nationalism and constitutionalism were in the air, reverberations of a revolutionary tradition which the Napoleonic era had heightened rather than diminished.

After 1815, small groups inspired by revolutionary nationalism sprang up in all parts of the German Confederation, brought together by common opposition to the restoration with its political particularism, its domineering bureaucracy, and its legitimist defense of monarchical absolutism. Service in the wars of liberation against Napoleon had mobilized German youths politically. In contrast to their fathers, they were no longer content with the promises of enlightened rulers. The ideals of liberty, equality, and fraternity were widely extolled, and nationalist agitation was influenced by romantic notions of the German folk community. In student circles and in the general population, the conviction grew, especially in the southwestern states of the Confederation, that a constitutional guarantee of individual rights could be achieved only in a unified nation-state, based on general elections and a national representative assembly. Demands for individual rights and national unity were voiced in a multitude of literary societies, Masonic lodges, athletic clubs, and student associations (*Burschenschaften*), which were fluctuating in membership, often temporary, and frequently on the borderline between innocent social gatherings and politically oriented, secret organizations.

Conservative governments looked on these patriotic-libertarian associations with grave suspicion and denied them public recognition. As a government spokesman in Nassau put it (in words similar to those already used by Frederick II), "It is as unreasonable as it is in violation of the law, if private individuals should believe themselves to be called upon or empowered to participate independently or directly in the great national affairs of Germany, either individually or in association with others, either now or in the future."[87] Oddly, this was a bureaucratic echo of those anticorporatist slogans which in France had resulted in the expulsion of the Jesuits, the expropriation of church properties, and the suppression of guilds. In France, this approach had furthered the destruction of the privileges enjoyed by the nobility, but in the states of the German Confederation the same principle was used to support the absolutist claim that public affairs were the exclusive concern of the privileged classes.

Prohibitions and declarations did not dampen the growing enthusiasm for nation and liberty. At the Wartburg festival of 1817, the German student movement, gathering for the first time from all parts of Germany, proclaimed its support for "honor, freedom, fatherland." In the eyes of the dynastic governments of the period, such mobilization was ominous. The Wartburg festival was taken as a warning at meetings of the European powers, which included France and England. The confrontations that followed quickly assumed a symbolic character. While conservatives saw the Wartburg festival as presaging revolution, the national liberals regarded the writer August von Kotzebue as a symbol of reaction. Kotzebue had held up liberal and national ideals to public scorn and ridicule, and his notoriety increased when it was learned that he was employed by the Russian diplomatic service. In 1819 he was assassinated in Mannheim by Karl Sand, a student who on his execution became a symbol of agitation against the status quo. This political assassination was promptly seized on by conservatives. By pushing through the Karlsbad edicts in the year of Kotzebue's assassination, the Austrian chancellor Metternich succeeded in coordinating policies of restoration in all sovereign territories of the German Confederation. Under the edicts, all German universities were subject to strict supervision, the *Burschenschaften* were dissolved, censorship of the press was introduced, and a commission was appointed to investigate all radical agitation.[88]

In Prussia, this conservative reaction went further than in the other states of the German Confederation. In 1821 a national constitution was rejected outright by Frederick William III (1797–1840) less than a year after it had been promised for a third time.[89] But this assertion of the Prussian ruler's prerogatives did not satisfy the spokesmen of the restoration. Under the leadership of the Prussian crown prince, it was proposed that instead of a national representation the provincial estates be restored so as to ensure the desired relation between king and people. But the old estates and their corporate jurisdictions had been abolished. When the laws of 1823–1824 established provincial assemblies, existing inequalities were reconfirmed while the principle of *popular* representation was evaded. The 584 seats in all the assemblies were distributed in rough proportion to the population, two-thirds of the delegates representing rural and one-third representing urban areas. But among the delegates, decided preference was given to landowners; even the 182 delegates from the towns qualified only because they owned land. It may not seem unusual if in the early nineteenth century day-laborers, small peasants, and domestic servants were excluded from voting for delegates to these provincial assemblies. But every urban resident who did not own land was also denied the right to vote, including businessmen, professionals, and other educated and often wealthy commoners. Landownership as the prerequisite of the right to vote exacerbated the old division between privileged and second-class status.[90]

A series of paradoxes resulted. Typically, landowners depended on government loans, but these debtors of the government were represented prominently. At the same time, many creditors of the government such as bankers and industrialists, who ranked highest in terms of wealth and tax payments, were excluded from representation when they did not own land. Also, the law deprived town residents of the intellectual leadership typically provided by notables from the professions and the university, because they rarely owned land. The towns of the period included many agricultural proprietors among their residents, and these were not only eligible but counted as urban representatives. In other words, the provincial assemblies were turned into bodies which primarily represented local, landed interests because these interests were considered "politically reliable" from the standpoint of the Prussian monarchy. And even then, the functions of the assemblies were restricted to the right of petition and of consultation on questions posed by the government. In effect, the provincial assemblies were token concessions to the demand for representation.

The position of the Prussian monarchy was contradictory. The civil service had promoted a market economy and the growth of an entrepreneurial class. The German customs union promoted economic interests which were national rather than local. Every step along the way toward a free market gave fresh impetus to demands for political representation. Yet encouraged by his circle of intimates, Frederick William III brusquely and repeatedly denied any right of self-government even to the provincial assemblies whose one-sided composition was supposed to ensure loyalty and submission. Yet these carefully selected assemblies voiced demands for greater jurisdictional rights because the delegates responded to the pressures resulting from economic competition.

Eventually, the anxiously conservative temper of Frederick William III and his court party also clashed with the civil service itself. The liberal orientation of Prussia's leading officials had been fostered by the emergency conditions of the Napoleonic era, the aspirations of German idealism, and moral appeals to a national regeneration.[91] Hegel was accurate when he noted that in a civil service "busy with the important questions arising in a great state . . . the habit is generated of adopting universal interests, points of view, and activities."[92] After 1815, Prussia's territorial acquisitions in Saxony, Westphalia, Pomerania, and elsewhere had increased the country's legal and geographic diversity, and the educated civil service provided whatever unity Prussia in fact achieved. However, the monarch himself claimed to symbolically represent the whole people. This was his warrant for subjecting the universities, the clergy, and the teaching profession to an increasingly severe surveillance under the formal authority of the Karlsbad edicts. The conservative reaction reached the civil service by 1823, initially in the form of new rules governing the proceedings leading to dismissal. A secret ordinance of 1826 declared that officials could be dismissed because of moral failings or deficient conduct in office, even though these grounds "are *legally insufficient* to sustain an application for transfer or dismissal." In 1833 this ordinance was published to give it added weight. This openly extralegal procedure aroused much comment. It took the monarchy eleven years to provide civil servants with legal protection against arbitrary dismissal (1844), and this protection was still half-hearted. The difficulty was largely symbolic: The Hohenzollern ruler did not wish to accept any limitation on his authority over officials whom he regarded as his "royal servants."

Naturally civil servants reacted to the distrust shown them by the reigning monarch. In practice, they were the only people directly concerned with public policy on a day-to-day basis, since no effective representative system was permitted and the monarch reigned and interfered but did not rule. Many civil servants did not own land and so were excluded as electors to the provincial assemblies. Many of them favored liberal policies, but in the restoration after 1815 they had to maintain a very conservative official position. In effect, the governmental actions of civil servants helped to justify a monarchy which abridged their legal protection against arbitrary dismissal. The question was how long these officials would maintain their liberal outlook in economic affairs without being won over by the agitation for popular representation which spread in part through the public implementation of that liberal outlook. Some officials found it impossible to remain politically inactive. As one civil servant put it (in 1844), "I resign as an official, in order that I may remain a citizen [*Bürger*]."[93]

Civil servants who wanted to be citizens were elected to the representative assemblies of the 1848 revolution in large numbers, after the requirement of landownership for elective office had been removed. In that year, revolutionary events in France had precipitated political upheavals throughout central Europe. Each of the thirty-nine sovereign territories of the German Confederation was affected internally, and to this was added a national-liberal agitation for a united Germany, culminating in the German national assembly in Frankfurt, the so-called Paulskirche. The deliberations of the assembly need concern us here only in their bearing on Prussia. The Paulskirche formulated a constitution purporting to replace the German Confederation with a unified Imperial Germany, combining the monarchical principle with an Imperial Diet, elected on the basis of a general, equal, and direct franchise. This constitution was accepted by the Paulskirche in 1849. Imperial Germany was to be under Prussian leadership and was to exclude Austria. The Frankfurt assembly elected Frederick William IV (1840–1861) of Prussia as hereditary emperor, and a delegation went to Berlin to offer the imperial crown. The Prussian king rejected the offer because he rejected the principle of popular sovereignty on which the Frankfurt assembly had been based.

In these proceedings of the Paulskirche, liberal civil servants played a large role. In practice, they were the only class of persons with some direct involvement in public affairs. In the Paulskirche, civil servants along with free professionals comprised the vast majority of the delegates, making it clear that throughout the German Confederation "educated commoners" rather than landowners or entrepreneurs were in the forefront of political mobilization. The proportion of civil servants in the Paulskirche was 58.3 percent, and the proportion of civil servants among the Prussian delegation was still higher (67 percent). An additional 24.2 percent of the delegates were free professionals; thus, perhaps some 70 percent were educated commoners.[94] Accordingly, the German idea of freedom was shaped in close association with the state and the ideal of Bildung.

By the time the proposal of the Paulskirche was submitted to Frederick William IV, the forces of the Prussian restoration had rallied once again. Prussia had not escaped the revolutionary agitation of 1848. Indeed, the upheavals of that year in Berlin led to a fourth royal promise of a constitution, specifying the main liberal objectives in outline (proclamation of March 22, 1848), including the destruction of patrimonial jurisdictions, the independence of the judiciary, the rights of free assembly, and trial by jury in political cases and those involving censorship of the press.[95] In the ensuing events, liberal agitation increased in the Prussian national assembly, as did the conservative intransigence of Frederick William and his intimates. The elected assemblies insisted on the fundamental tenets of constitutionalism. But the king made it clear that he would accept a constitution only if his right to veto any law and his authority over army and administration were preserved intact. No compromise was possible between these two positions, and in the end the Prussian constitution of 1850 with the king's provisos was imposed by royal fiat and remained in force until 1918.

However incongruously, this Prussian constitution institutionalized all three principles: the absolute royal prerogative, the liberal conception of fundamental human rights, and the hierarchic conception of society (anticipated in the provincial assemblies under the law of 1823/24). The person of the king was "inviolate." He was the supreme head of government and the armed forces, responsible to no one. Laws could be enacted only through the concurrence of the two Houses and the king. At the same time, the king retained the absolute right to veto any enactment, and he alone was empowered by the constitution to issue emergency decrees or impose martial law. Second, the constitution contained a full list of basic individual rights—freedom under the law, personal freedom, religious liberty, freedom of opinion, freedom of association and assembly, the protection of property, and the right to justice. This bill of rights was basically flawed because the constitution and its interpreters declared these rights to be conditional. Nothing in the consti-

tution prevented the legislature and the king from enacting laws which interfered with any of these rights; and once this was done, administrative abridgement of such rights was legal. In this way, the bill of rights was made compatible with the absolute prerogatives of the king. Third, the constitution introduced an electoral law (*Dreiklassenwahlrecht*) which provided for indirect, unequal, and open elections. Voters chose electors who in turn chose the delegates of a district. The voters of each district were divided into three classes based on the level of taxation. Each class chose a third of the electors, but the classes were of very unequal size. Classes I and II, comprising the wealthy and middle segments of the population, contained only 4.7 and 12.6 percent of the voters, but chose two-thirds of the electors. Class III, comprising the poorest segment of the population, contained 82.7 percent of the voters, but chose only one-third of the electors. Finally, the elections were open so that the voting of the economically dependent population was not only deprived of proportional participation but was supervised directly by employers and their agents.[96]

Liberty at the king's command was without safeguard against the king's prerogative. Public affairs remained preempted by the privileged few. The Prussian constitution of 1850 institutionalized the monarchy's basic distrust of a popular mandate, though it included a bill of rights. But by the second half of the nineteenth century, the population had

The Imperial Crown Denied and Accepted

In 1849, the *Paulskirche* in Frankfurt voted to make the king of Prussia hereditary emperor. The first picture shows this National Assembly in session and the second depicts a middle class deputation of that assembly in Berlin, informing the Prussian king of his election. Frederick William IV renounced the election, which he considered a revolutionary act of the people. Contrast this with the third picture, a genre painting of a scene in 1871 at the conclusion of the Franco-Prussian war: William I of Prussia is proclaimed German emperor at Versailles by a company of his generals and officers led by Chancellor Bismarck and General von Moltke. (Historisches Museum, Frankfurt) become mobilized, and it was no longer simple to ignore the idea of a popular mandate. When the constitutions of the North German Confederation and the German Empire were enacted in 1867 and 1871, respectively, they did not contain a bill of rights, but instead extended voting rights to all males twenty-five years or over. These constitutions, like the Prussian constitution before them, were dictated from above and protected the absolute authority of the king and emperor. While the Prussian constitution safeguarded the king's authority by the three-class suffrage system, the constitutions of 1867 and 1871 did so by freeing him from the financial control of the legislature. All three constitutions stipulated that the army remain outside the competence of the legislature and that each soldier must swear his oath of loyalty solely to the Prussian king and, after 1871, to the emperor of the *Reich*.

Nevertheless, the idea of a bill of rights and of popular sovereignty had been at least verbally embraced, and the question was how long the people would remain under the political tutelage of the monarch and his court party. We know today that Germany was unprepared for the advent of popular sovereignty when that tutelage was destroyed in 1918. The history of the Weimar Republic demonstrated that the mentality of hometownsmen, a legal order primarily upheld by officials, and the idealization of Bildung and duty had provided a weak foundation for national citizenship. Few people had internalized the "rules of the game" of democratic politics and without that internalization a mandate of the people cannot function.

12

NATION-BUILDING: JAPAN

THE TOKUGAWA SHOGUNATE[a]

CIVIL WARS had marked the history of the Ashigaka shogunate since the fourteenth century, as well as the reigns of Oda Nobunaga (1559–1582) and Toyotomi Hideyoshi (1582–1598). When Tokugawa Ieyasu won the battles of Sekigahara in 1600 and of Osaka in 1614, he terminated this long period of internal wars and initiated a regime which was to last for the next two and a half centuries. Japan had never been conquered; it had no territorial possessions on, or dynastic ties with, the mainland. The country had been secluded long before it adopted a policy of exclusion.

If the rise of central authority in Japan had a European analogue, it was France. The French kings and Japanese shoguns of the sixteenth and seventeenth centuries achieved supreme authority after generations of weak rule. The central location of the domains of both rulers (the Paris region and the Kanto plain) aided political unification. Both the ancien régime and Tokugawa Japan combined supreme authority at the center with considerable autonomy in the provinces. Each regime exercised central control through nationwide administrative and police measures.

The details of these similarities, of course, differ. The French kings established their supremacy primarily through the use of royal prerogative in wars with foreign powers, whereas Nobunaga, Hideyoshi, and Ieyasu established their supremacy primarily in wars with internal enemies. Japan's geographic location and exclusionist policies prevented any immediate outside threat to the country's political integrity; thus,

[a]The title *shogun* derives from *Seii-tai-shogun* (barbarian-quelling generalissimo) which was bestowed on Minamoto Yoritomo, the first Kamakura ruler, in 1192. After that, the military government of the shogunate came to be called *bakufu,* as distinguished from the civil government in Kyoto.

unlike France, even prolonged periods of civil strife did not entail the danger of foreign invasion. In Japan, central authority and local autonomy were largely complementary, whereas in France these two levels of authority tended to be mutually exclusive. The foundation of local autonomy in France was privilege based on a grant or purchase, whereas in Japan it was territory based on service and loyalty. Japan achieved administrative consolidation under the central authority of the Tokugawa shogunate, but the long tradition of regional autonomy was preserved.

In what sense can the term *feudalism* be applied to Tokugawa Japan?

> [In Japan] the force of authority which united the system was at the top feudal, particularly as it applied to the relationship between Shogun and daimyo. Yet within the administrative subparts, within the direct jurisdictions of the Shogun or daimyo, authority was increasingly exerted through bureaucratic means. . . . The regime kept alive a dynamic tension between feudal and bureaucratic techniques and between centralized and decentralized authority.[1]

This tension may account for the phrase *centralized feudalism* which is often applied to Tokugawa Japan, though the phrase is a contradiction in terms. The evidence for centralization is massive: the shogunate controlled a large portion of the land, monopolized the coinage, maintained a nationwide espionage system, prevented internal customs barriers except for toll stations under central control, and moved daimyo about at will. A large patrimonial bureaucracy was required to administer these central controls, even though the daimyo's personal liability for wrongdoing or disobedience assisted governance and gave it a feudalistic appearance. I have suggested (in Chapter 7) that patrimonialism and feudalism coexist and that a specific historical situation will show the prevalence of one or the other. It is doubtful that Western European feudal structures ever achieved a balance between centralizing and decentralizing tendencies that is comparable to those of Tokugawa Japan.

I will refer to the Tokugawa regime, then, as *absolutist* in the same sense as I refer to the absolutism of regimes of seventeenth- and eighteenth-century Europe. For neither was the term *absolutism* strictly applicable to Western Europe, since absolutist regimes claimed complete control while in practice contending with considerable local autonomy. Sansom stresses this parallel when he notes,

> Late Tokugawa Japan can be described as a feudal state only if the word "feudal" is employed in a very loose way and without any medieval connotations. It bore a close resemblance to the less highly centralized states of Europe in the eighteenth and early nineteenth centuries and was undergoing a process of change similar to that through which most European countries had passed or were passing in the same period. These developments were not a part of feudalism, though they might be, and frequently were, outgrowths of a particular feudal institution.[2]

Though absolutist regimes varied within Western Europe, the pattern of governance—especially in France and Prussia—tended to be bureaucratic at the center and "feudal" in the provinces. The royal government of Louis XIV and his successors sought to introduce centrally organized controls through the *intendants,* whereas at the local level many quasi-feudal elements of seignorial jurisdiction and patriarchal rule remained. Much the same can be said of Prussian central government and local administration.[3] Though conditions were broadly similar in Japan, they differed in at least one significant respect. Tokugawa regional institutions—the administration of many *han*—achieved considerable efficiency in contrast to the frequent immobility of European local administration.

Contrasts between Tokugawa Japan and Western European absolutism are most clearly marked in their political cultures. In Western Europe and especially in France, the earlier patriarchal ideology lost its appeal because of the commercialization of land and labor and the sale of offices. In Japan, the ideology of master-servant relations and of personal loyalty continued to pervade the whole society. In Europe, very large expenditures for military preparedness and imperialist policies were a main factor in the bureaucratization of the central government. Rulers enlisted young aristocrats in the officer corps and thus involved the aristocracy in their own pursuit of military glory abroad. In Japan, there was no need for a large military force at the center. In a population of 20 million, some 12,000 men were on police duty, and only in wartime was that force increased to 35,000. The shogunate relied on the principle of the master-servant relationship which was compatible with patrimonial administration at the center and a bureaucratic administration in the daimyo domains. European militarism was directed outward and was highly centralized. In its more secluded setting, Japanese militarism was most important as a code of honor and obedience, thereby ensuring internal peace.

Local vendettas as well as larger struggles occurred throughout Japanese history. But by the sixteenth century, civil war had become so endemic that historians call this period the Age of the Country at War (*sengoku-jidai*). The victory of the Tokugawa put an end not only to the intensified hostility of the preceding era, but also to military feuds as the principal means of righting wrongs. During the early seventeenth century, the Tokugawa shogunate proceeded to buttress its preeminent position.

Initially, the Tokugawa destroyed the power of only 87 out of 245 daimyo, but by 1651 the landholdings of 131 other houses had been confiscated, redistributed, or reduced for lack of succession or for disciplinary reasons. In this process, a cumulative total of some 18.6 million

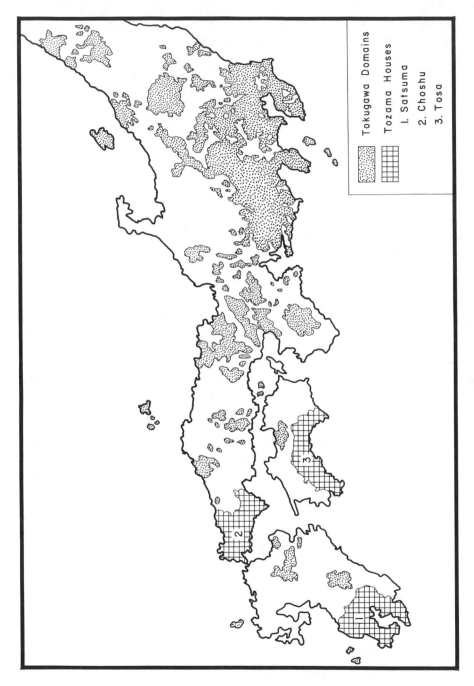

11. Tokugawa, Satsuma, Choshu, and Tosa Domains in 1664

koku[b] changed hands to the advantage of the Tokugawa and their closest allies, representing a very thorough change in the distribution of wealth and power among the country's landed aristocracy.[4]

Within this *bakuhan* system (from *bakufu* = tent [military] government and *han* = daimyo fief or domain), power was distributed strategically. By the middle of the seventeenth century, the shogun's own domains had risen from 2.0 to 6.8 million koku. These lands supported about 23,000 direct retainers, or samurai, including 5,000 "bannermen" (*hatamoto*), who were senior retainers, the more important of whom held fiefs and also possessed audience privileges, and 17,000 "honorable house men" (*gokenin*), who received hereditary salaries but did not have audience privileges. In addition, the shogun administered the important mines, which facilitated his control of the currency (precious metals), and the cities which were the main centers of trade and production. The largest daimyo after the shogun, the Maeda house, possessed only 1,023,000 koku, or less than one-sixth of the Tokugawa landholdings.

Nor was this the full extent of shogunal power. Ieyasu built a hierarchy of graded loyalties, based on proximity and obligation to the Tokugawa house. Twenty-three directly descended and collateral Tokugawa families known as "related han" (*shimpan*) formed an outer line of defense. The three major ones were founded by Ieyasu's sons at Mito, Nagoya, and Wakayama. The domains controlled by all the collateral houses totaled 3,370,000 koku. The shogunate next directly controlled the house daimyo (*fudai*), who eventually came to number 145 and whose total holdings came to 6.7 million koku, although many individual domains were quite small. Added together, these figures show that the shogunate had direct or indirect control over land yielding 16.1 million koku, or about 65 percent of the country's total assessed yield of rice for 1602.

At the same time, 97 of the largest daimyo were called "outside lords" (*tozama*), both in the geographic sense that they occupied lands distant from the central stronghold of the Tokugawa (the Kanto region), and in the sense that these houses were descended from former enemies or recent allies of Ieyasu at the time of Sekigahara. With a total yield of 9.8 million koku, the tozama daimyo would have been a formidable power had they ever united against the shogunate. Ieyasu and his successors took elaborate precautions against this eventuality. Evidently, these were prudent precautions, for at the time of the Meiji Restoration

---

[b]One koku equals five American bushels of rice. Landholdings were assessed in terms of the area needed to produce a given quantity of rice. In 1602 the total assessed revenue of the country was 24.5 million koku; thus, the total area redistributed between 1600 and 1651 represented some 75 percent of the 1602 figure, a rough index only because it includes an unknown amount of double counting. At any rate, the extent of redistribution was massive.

(1868) most leaders of opposition to the Bakufu came from these areas, notably Satsuma, Choshu, Tosa, and Hizen.

The Tokugawa regime managed to preserve the distribution of power achieved after 1600 for a period of two and a half centuries, in good part because internal power relations were insulated from extraneous influences. By 1641, after a century of Christian missionary effort in Japan, Christianity was banned and all contact with European foreigners was confined to a small, rigidly controlled Dutch colony in Nagasaki. This policy of exclusion facilitated "a civil government administered by a professional military caste"[5] which retained many of its traditions of militancy but in the absence of internal feuds and foreign wars.

The Tokugawa shogunate forbade military feuding among territorially based lineages in much the same way as England, France, and Germany had done in the sixteenth and seventeenth centuries. But unlike these European powers, the Tokugawa established special internal controls as a counterpart to their policy of exclusion to ensure that the powerful tozama lords would continue to accept Tokugawa supremacy. To this end, the Bakufu regulated the position of the emperor and the daimyo.

The Tokugawa deferred to the prestige of the emperor, but they also controlled and isolated him. In theory and by custom, the shogunate governed with the consent of the emperor, and each successive shogun assumed his position in accession ceremonies symbolizing this consent. No shogun ever attempted to claim the throne, and the fiction of imperial supremacy was scrupulously observed in the language of loyalty by which the advice or requests of the shogun were submitted. The imperial court was assisted in rebuilding its palaces, and the lands put at its disposal yielded a total of 187,000 koku. But this was somewhat below half the income of the largest fudai daimyo and very much below the income of many tozama daimyo. In terms of wealth, the emperor and his entourage were placed in the lower half of the country's aristocracy. Moreover, the emperor and his court were controlled by a shogunal military governor and by a large garrison force stationed immediately adjacent to the imperial palace in Kyoto. No daimyo was allowed to approach the imperial court except through the shogun's representatives at the capital. The military governor worked through two court officials who transmitted the shogunal will, specifically regulating all appointments, including that of the shogun and his successor. These direct controls were supplemented by a code for the Kyoto nobility which restricted the emperor and his court to literary pursuits and ceremonial functions and regulated the relations between the imperial family and the great temples.

All daimyo were vassals of the shogun. By the mid-seventeenth century, only some ten to fifteen daimyo still remained on their original land. Control of the daimyo began with the formal grant of investiture by which the shogun confirmed them in office. Although in theory the grant was hereditary, the practice of confiscation and transfer made daimyo landholding precarious. Each daimyo swore a private oath of loyalty to the shogun, promising not to enter into collusive alliances with other daimyo and to serve the shogun wholeheartedly. Furthermore, the shogunate imposed on the daimyo a code regulating their private conduct, including dress, marriage, and ceremonial tokens of submission at the shogunal court. Perhaps most importantly, the system of alternate residence (*sankin-kotai*) was made compulsory after 1635. The daimyo were obliged to build permanent residences in Edo (Tokyo), with their wives, children, and appropriate retainers in permanent attendance. The daimyo themselves lived in Edo for required periods every other year and remained at their domain headquarters the rest of the time. A high degree of political conformity was achieved, because the daimyo could be kept under personal surveillance, and because the safety of family hostages at the shogunal court was at stake. Moreover, the system was extremely effective in two other ways. The constant coming and going helped to stimulate local economic development by requiring heavy expenditures by the daimyo, and this in turn increased their dependence. The system also helped to center all communications in Edo, while the shogunal police controlled communications among the daimyo away from the capital.[6]

Officially, the sankin-kotai system was interpreted in Confucian terms, extolling the loyalty men in each rank owed to their superiors, from the shogun's obeisance to the emperor down through the ranks of the daimyo and samurai to the obeisance each son owed to his father. In the *Hundred Articles* or the *Legacy of Ieyasu,* a severe code of conduct was laid down which emphasized the unquestioning performance of duty to superiors as the highest goal in life—at the expense of personal desire or even familial obligations. The code also extolled as inviolate the laws of the first Tokugawa shoguns.[7] The desire to preserve the hierarchic structure established after 1600 produced a reawakening of Confucian doctrine:

> The Imperial Way which was the ideal of Confucianism was virtually identical to the spiritual foundations of the Japanese state—namely, the descent of the first emperor from the national deities; the divine origin of the realm was a guarantee of righteousness. This Imperial Way, practiced in antiquity, had suffered progressive degeneration since the Nara and Heian periods of the eighth to twelfth centuries. This decay was caused by the spread of an alien religion, Buddhism, which eclipsed the national spirit (*kokusui*) and caused degeneration. The political consequences were spread across history: loss of imperial virtue, weakening of the imperial policy, takeover by the Fujiwara

Daimyo Procession
The Tokugawa requirement of alternate residence involved great expense for the daimyo domains. The river crossing of a feudal lord and his escort gives an impression of the size of these biannual expeditions. As the feudal lord's escort enters the outskirts of Edo, the artist Hiroshige depicts the military bearing of the retainers and the deference shown by the town residents as long as they are within sight of the procession. (Historiographical Institute, University of Tokyo)

regents, the insidious superstitions promoted by the Buddhist clergy to acquire political influence, disruption of political tranquillity, hardships among
the people. . . . The triumph of a military polity, the theory continues, re-
minded the Japanese of the true tradition. The establishment of the *bakufu*
rescued the Imperial Way (*odo*) from the decaying court government and
restored the legitimate principle of political authority. The military estate
restored the only possible political organization, the *jinsei*: an ethical realm
based on the righteousness of the Imperial Way. The political organization
ultimately adopted by the Tokugawa—the bakuhan system, a balance of centralized and decentralized elements—became the concrete manifestation of
this "benevolent polity" operating under imperial sovereignty.[8]

This ideology helped to combine effective central authority with a
high degree of local autonomy. By contrast, European absolutist regimes
such as Prussia became centralized at the expense of the estates, while
in France centralized administration was all-encompassing in theory but
not in practice. Tokugawa absolutism achieved its more effective combination of central controls and regional autonomy in part through the
policy of exclusion. Japan's external security stands in obvious contrast
to the European powers during the seventeenth and eighteenth centuries. In the 250 years between 1600 and 1850 France was at war 115
years; Austria, 129.5; Great Britain, 125; Spain, 160.5; Prussia, 97; and
Russia, 142.5. Japan was at peace during the entire period.[9] Aided by
Japan's seclusion, the Confucian code of conduct could counteract the
disintegrative effects of local autonomy; greater contact with the outside
world would have meant greater exposure to foreign cultural influences,
jeopardizing loyalty and hierarchy. Seclusion also made it easier to increase the political and economic dependence of the daimyo on the shogunate, since it precluded all alliances with foreign powers against the
Bakufu. The daimyo were compensated for these deprivations by their
own extensive authority, which was as absolute locally as the shogun's
controls over the court and the daimyo were nationally. These were important assets of the policy of exclusion; its drawback was technological
backwardness. The very stability of Tokugawa rule also increased the
rigidity of shogunal administration.

The shogunate encouraged local authority in part for practical administrative reasons. The daimyo was not taxed directly, but certain contributions were expected from him on a fairly regular basis. Among
these were military and logistic assistance in times of emergency. In an
era of peace, economic aid was more important, especially for the building of castles, roads, bridges, and palaces. Such assessments in kind were
called "national service" (*kokuyaku*) and were equally useful in strengthening the shogunate and weakening the prosperous daimyo economically. Gigantic fortifications in the strongholds of the Tokugawa were
erected on this basis.

Under the Tokugawa shogunate, the daimyo domains varied greatly in size, ranging from the largest, Maeda, with over 1 million koku, down to over half the daimyo who held territories of less then 50,000 koku. In addition to an average of 265 daimyo, there were 5,000 minor fiefs of the hatamoto and many thousands of jurisdictions of temples and shrines, not to speak of still more thousands of subjurisdictions within the shogun's own domains. Since many of these territories were non-contiguous, the administrative map of Japan was very complex. Nevertheless, considerable administrative uniformity was introduced by moving many daimyo and their retainers from domain to domain so that they acquired some characteristics of an administrative class. Japan's population increased from roughly 20 million in 1600 to 30 million in 1721, the year of the first census. The administrative class, which included everyone from the shogun down to common foot soldiers of samurai status, comprised 6 percent of the total population. Since France under Louis XIV had only about 1,000 administrators for a population of 18 million, it is clear that Japan with its over 1 million men of samurai status was an intensively administered country.[10]

This contrast between Japanese and French "administrators" should be understood in context. The thousand administrators under Louis XIV estimated by Goubert were all officials in the literal sense, which cannot be said of 1.2 million samurai. In France, there were far more officeholders then officials of the central government, but that large number of officeholders did not carry out the orders of the government. Office was property and administered or disposed of at will. By contrast, Japanese samurai carried out orders of the shogunal or daimyo government, although many of their duties were nonadministrative, and no doubt many had no regular duties at all. But the ideology of the master-servant relation made all of them *ready* to obey whatever orders were issued to them, and nothing comparable can be said about officeholders in France.

The daimyo exercised full rights of government over his own territory under a shogunal grant. At his castle headquarters he assembled his retainers, who swore an oath of loyalty to the daimyo and were entered on his register of men (*samurai cho*). At the highest level of this administrative class were so-called "elders," usually independent vassals who formed the daimyo's council of advisors. In peacetime, they acted as the daimyo's deputies and/or judges; in wartime, they served as his generals in the field. Next in the hierarchy was a more numerous group of high-ranking retainers charged with civil administration such as finance, security, and liaison with the shogunate. Below them were retainers of middle rank who handled such civil functions as the administration of the castle town, the villages, tax collection, the civil police, household affairs of the daimyo, military procurement, civil engineering, education, and temples or shrines. Still lower in rank was a body of foot soldiers, pages, and servants who performed a variety of menial tasks. Each of the villages, towns, and temples had self-governing units of farmers, urban residents, and priests or monks who lived under the authority of their own superiors.

The shogunate had a more complex administrative apparatus, but it operated in the same basic pattern. In addition to managing a domain about seven times larger than the largest daimyo, it had a multitude of governmental functions. For his staff, the shogun relied on his "house daimyo" and direct retainers rather than on the tozama or shimpan houses. Most administrative activity pertained to the shogun's domains. But "this territory by reason of its size—roughly a quarter of the country —and its resources, which included the major cities of the land, placed the greater portion of the Japanese population within the scope of the shogun's personal rule."[11] Beyond this, the shogunate controlled all contacts with foreigners, supervised national defense, and generally policed the conduct of local affairs.

Despite the large degree of autonomy allowed to each daimyo, the Tokugawa regime upheld the idea of a nationwide social order, formed by a hierarchy of status-groups. Laws were applied in terms of the social division to which the individual belonged. The bulk of Tokugawa legislation was directed toward defining the behavior appropriate to each rank and maintaining the boundaries between different ranks, especially the distinction between samurai and commoner. The population was divided into (1) warrior-bureaucrats, including different groups of daimyo, richly enfeoffed house elders, and bannermen down to foot-soldiers, (2) peasants or primary producers, (3) artisans or secondary producers, and (4) merchants. In this "national hierarchy," the merchants were the most despised, although economically they were the most successful. The laws upholding this hierarchy still applied to the family (the individual existed only as a member of his family and in terms of his rank within the family). But under the Tokugawa regime, the status of the individual was no longer the result of personal submission and preferment alone. By legal means, the Tokugawa introduced a "rule by status . . . [which was] considerably more impersonal in its application to the individual than the exercise of direct personal authority" had been in the past.[12] With the legal system and the ideology of neo-Confucianism upholding this hierarchic structure, it was uncommonly difficult for any individual to exist outside the accepted categories. *Ronin* or samurai without a lord and hence without status were particularly troublesome for the regime, and it tells us something about the status of priests, doctors, and teachers when we learn that only these occupations were open to the ronin.

The samurai were transformed from landed warriors into a class of urban administrators and rentiers in the course of the sixteenth century. This transformation was part of the process by which the daimyo superseded the earlier proliferation of petty fiefdoms, each with a castle of its own, and consolidated their landholdings, increased their income, and strengthened their military position.

Castles were a means of military and political unification in addition to providing a stimulus toward urbanization. Twenty-five major Japanese towns were built up around castles in the brief period between 1580 and 1610. The shogunal edict of 1615 ordered the destruction of all but one castle in each province. Sansom estimates that toward the end of the seventeenth century Edo, Kyoto, and Osaka had between 350,000 and 500,000 inhabitants, while nine cities had more than 50,000, eleven cities more than 20,000, and about a hundred other castle towns more than 5,000 residents. The construction of massive fortifications, residences, and temples, together with the maintenance of a large resident population, required the wholesale supply of produce from the hinterland as well as the continuous commercial linkage of each daimyo economy with the major trading center of the region. It is estimated that on the average, half the population of the castle towns consisted of samurai, their families, and retainers, while in some towns like Sendai and Kagoshima the proportion went up to 70 or 80 percent.[13]

Independent, landed, and self-equipped warriors had done the bulk of the fighting for centuries. Now, in the early decades of the Tokugawa regime, they were transformed into an estate of urbanized, aristocratic retainers. The agony of that transition was marked by the appearance of large numbers of ronin who had lost their previous position due to the massive confiscation and redistribution of land by Ieyasu and his successors. Sansom gives a cumulative estimate of 400,000 ronin during the seventeenth century. Still, the transition was eventually accomplished, and a new political structure was established along the lines sketched previously. The samurai were now maintained as urban retainers on a rice stipend provided by their master, the ruler of the han:

> In the cities the gentry warriors of the earlier days became increasingly removed from the actualities of the countryside both in their way of life and in their legal relationship to the land. By the eighteenth century, except for a few locations, the *bushi* [warriors] had been stripped of any direct jurisdiction over their fiefs by the expanding power of the daimyo. Though as a class they nostalgically clung to the concept that they were a landed aristocracy, they had been converted, in reality, to little more than salaried officials of the daimyo. . . . Separated from their duties of land management, they became a thoroughly urbanized group living increasingly in sedentary style.[14]

The massive expropriation of the samurai was probably the major reason why Tokugawa absolutism could combine its highly centralized authority with so large a degree of autonomy in the daimyo domains. The daimyo were forced to subordinate themselves to the shogunate, but they remained masters of their own han. Hence, the real burden of subordination fell on the samurai who had lost wealth and power under the Tokugawa regime, as well as much of their earlier identity as the fighting men of the feudal order.

Within decades of Sekigahara, the samurai were leading a peaceful civilian existence. As rentiers, they supplemented their meagre rice stipends by working as craftsmen or teachers of fencing. Others became peasants or even merchants.[15] They had lost what little independence and authority they or their fathers had earlier possessed. And as rentiers the samurai were typically exploited, since the sankin-kotai system forced lavish expenditures and heavy debts on the daimyo, who "supplemented" their regular revenues by appropriating nearly half of their retainer's income. The practice of forced appropriations of samurai stipends was widespread since the samurai were in no position to resist their master, on whose good will they depended and to whom they were bound by personal loyalty. From about 1700, more than a hundred han were heavily in debt.[16] Only the samurai's high status seemed assured, symbolized by the exclusive right and duty to wear two swords.

Samurai Warrior
This samurai warrior with two swords and a lance is depicted in the Edo style of the 1660s. The warrior is anonymous and the posture and expression stylized, but both the strut and the fierce expression were very much "in style," the norm of conduct appropriate for a samurai proud of his status and conscious of maintaining it by his bearing. (Honolulu Academy of Arts, Gift of James A. Michener)

The dilemma facing these men is illustrated by the Law of the Military Houses (*Buke Sho-Hatto*), promulgated by Ieyasu in 1615, which decreed that the samurai must devote themselves equally to arms and polite learning. The fact is that there were no important calls to arms after the suppression of the Shimabara rebellion of 1637. Moreover, the growth of a settled urban population after 1615 and the conspicuous consumption imposed on the daimyo gave rise to a class of tradesmen and artisans (*chonin*) that did not fit easily into the traditional class structure. Prosperity allowed new types of sensibility to flourish which were responsive to the tastes of the chonin. In the Tokugawa era, the earlier aristocratic monopoly of culture was broken.[17] Accordingly, the Tokugawa regime put the samurai under special psychological pressure by encouraging military skills while prohibiting combat and by calling on men of the sword to acquire learning at a time when the arts were becoming increasingly responsive to the plebeian tastes of merchants.

Within this general context the samurai were supposed to remain attached to their traditions of ceremonious conduct, intense pride of rank, and the cultivation of physical prowess—a most unlikely outcome:

> They were to serve as models of virtue and frugality for the entire nation. But as time went on, the samurai proved themselves unworthy of their high responsibilities. They did not devote themselves in time of peace to the study of the literary arts, but since they were compelled to spend much of their time in Edo, indulged in all the pleasures the capital afforded. . . . Their extravagant habits frequently caused them to run up heavy debts with the city merchants. . . .
>
> Most samurai could see no way out of their predicament. Not schooled in the practical realities of business life, they were taught to despise everything that savored of trade as a low seeking after profit. Thus, though they might be so heavily in debt as to feel it necessary to address the merchants they met in the street in terms of great politeness (instead of the brusque tones of the superior), the samurai were convinced by training that all their difficulties were the result of the businessmen's striving for profit; if only everyone would follow their example of placing righteousness before other considerations, all problems would soon be solved.[18]

The samurai were not the only ones affected by the commercialization of land, labor, and capital. The whole hierarchic structure of Tokugawa society was in danger of being eroded, and the shogunate took strong measures in order to preserve that structure.

Japan faced special problems because of its policy of exclusion. For example, the supply of basic foodstuffs always fluctuates from natural causes, and ordinarily this fluctuation can be offset by imports or exports. But this safety valve was less available to Japan because exclusion militated against foreign trade, just as it was less available to several European countries because mercantilist doctrine argued for national self-sufficiency in food production. Hence, in Japan and in Europe, governments sought to counter the fluctuations of harvests, by improvements in agricultural productivity. Under the Tokugawa regime, the area under cultivation doubled between 1600 and 1730 and could sustain a steady growth in population. Yields per acre were increased by improved tools and seeds, draft animals, iron plows, hoes, and the use of fertilizers. Areas of double cropping expanded, cereal production doubled between 1600 and 1730, and the government provided farmers with instruction on the improvement of agricultural techniques. By 1721 the country's population had increased to 30 million, but some time thereafter population leveled off, reaching only 32 million by the middle of the nineteenth century. Part of the explanation is that with complete dependence on a rice diet, periods of acute crop failure led to widespread famine. Between 1675 and 1837, several great famines brought more than a million people to the edge of starvation. The shogunate and the daimyo provided what relief they could, but the evidence of infanticide suggests that such relief often proved inadequate.[19]

During the eighteenth century, Japan's agricultural economy was undergoing a process of commercialization. Conditions in the villages changed as sharp price fluctuations led to increased sales of land despite edicts prohibiting such sales. The result was pauperization and a class of landless laborers on the one hand, and the accumulation of surpluses and a class of wealthy farmers on the other. The benefits arising from increased agricultural production largely accrued to the upper strata of Tokugawa society. The peasant was the only regular taxpayer, and he was hard pressed even in good times. When his crop was good, he had to turn in more bushels than ordinarily; when it was bad, he had little left over for his own needs. From the shogun down to the samurai, the upper strata of Tokugawa society exerted pressure on the peasantry to meet the rising cost of government at central and local levels. The peasants suffered most as taxes were increased and repeated manipulations devalued the currency. From about 1700, the number of peasant uprisings increased. Between 1750 and the 1860s, both the frequency and the size of these riots, sometimes involving 100,000 men, were a source of constant concern. The issues in these riots were special levies in money or labor, unfair officials, or unjust methods of assessment. The riots were brutally suppressed, but the sources of unrest remained.[20]

Transport and communication facilities grew with the rising importance of cities and of commercialized agriculture. Most of the important cities could be reached by water, bulk commodities were handled by boat, and the development of shipping lines became a major industry. A highway system was also developed to handle commercial transport and overland travel, as people of all levels went to and fro in response to shogunal demands. Along the highways, post stations and small settlements prospered by catering to the needs of travelers. In addition, runners operated a regular postal service. The maintenance of the highways was a responsibility of shogunal and daimyo authorities, who in turn put owners along the road in charge of building and maintenance for the stretch of road passing their property.

As communication increased and government became more bureaucratic, there was widespread attention to education. Ieyasu's admonition of 1615 that the samurai acquire military skill *and* polite learning was followed to a considerable extent. In 1703 only nine daimyo domains had schools, though by then samurai families which could afford it hired private tutors for their sons. By 1791 the advocate of "Dutch learning," Hayashi Shihei, gave his opinion that a soldier without literary attainments was no better than a barbarian.[21] By 1814 about half the domains, and almost all the large ones, had schools. In addition, a significant proportion of tradesmen and well-to-do farmers sent their sons to temple schools or private schools where they learned the rudiments of reading, writing, and arithmetic. Even farmers could use the manuals on improved agriculture techniques sent to them. Figures for the number of private tutors and writing schools are uncertain. But by the time of the restoration in 1868, 40 percent of Japanese boys and 10 percent of the girls were receiving formal education. It seems clear that schooling had increased steadily, if gradually, for at least a century and a half.[22]

The growth of transport, communication, and education resulted from the changing position of the merchant and the growth of urban centers in Tokugawa society. Although merchants stood at the bottom of the social hierarchy and as mere "movers of goods" were considered unproductive, the whole governing class from the shogun down to the samurai became dependent on the merchant's services. The urban concentration of shogunal and daimyo administration meant that the governing elite of the country required supplies for their headquarters and hence took procurement merchants into their service. In the large cities and the more numerous castle towns, merchant quarters were laid out adjacent to the castle headquarters of the local ruler. Here, under close supervision, merchants were encouraged to serve the needs of the authorities, albeit under the shadow of continuous social discrimination.

The extent of the resulting commercial activities is impressive. Though prohibited for a time, monopolistic guilds and other licensed organizations developed quickly to handle a multifarious trade in silk threads, gold, silver, copper, lime, and vegetable oils. Before 1700 Edo had ten and Osaka twenty-four wholesale guilds. During the eighteenth century, the licensing of such organizations expanded because the government relied on them to stabilize prices and assure adequate distribution. Annual license fees also added to the public revenue. Increasingly, the commercial and fiscal operations of shogunal and daimyo domains came into the hands of merchant houses. Rural wholesalers bought commodities to sell in the castle towns and the commercial centers of Edo and Osaka, and such sales were often handled by urban wholesale guilds. Since the large cities served as distribution centers for the different daimyo territories, it was convenient to establish domain warehouses supervised by domain financial representatives, whose functions were turned over from the daimyo's retainers to financially influential business houses.

Soon, Edo and Osaka had exchange houses as well as rice and commodity markets. By 1750 Osaka had over 130 han warehouses, and the annual flow of rice into its docks was about one million koku. By 1761 Japan had over 200 commercial houses, whose total capital worth had become equivalent to that of many daimyo. The great business establishments of modern times originated during this period. By 1690 Mitsui had become the financial agent for the shogunate and the imperial house, while Konoike handled the financial affairs of nearly forty daimyo, thereby earning an annual income in excess of most of the daimyo he served. Under the Tokugawa shogunate, the process of commercialization was thus well advanced. In the field of manufacturing it was supplemented by the beginnings of mass production and of a modern labor force in such branches as silk-weaving, paper-making, lacquer work, and sake-brewing.

This large expansion of commerce and industry altered the relations between samurai and merchants. In practice the samurai suffered most from the dislocations of economic expansion. The Bakufu and many daimyo met their financial difficulties time and again by reducing the allowances of their retainers. When such precipitous cuts were aggravated by decreases in the money value of rice, samurai families were in dire straits, and their poverty-stricken life stood in stark contrast to their acknowledged social prestige. In these conditions, a good many samurai either became ronin or abandoned their status by taking up commercial pursuits. Still others adopted sons or daughters from families of prosperous merchants or farmers, conferring on them the status of samurai. Bakufu officials and daimyo were aware of these conditions and sometimes took steps to relieve distress, including the repudiation of debts. But such emergency measures did not alter the basic situation.

Meanwhile, the merchants and artisans had grievances of their own. While a good many of these townspeople suffered from poverty and occasionally from shortages of food, the more prosperous among them chafed under the discrepancy between commercial success and inferior social status. Even the richest merchants and bankers suffered from official interference in their commercial dealings. In the absence of national loans, the bakufu met its recurrent budget deficits by special levies on the mercantile community. With foreign trade down to a trickle and the peasantry already overtaxed, there was no other source of cash available, since for political reasons the daimyo could not be asked for contributions too frequently. The merchants were "invited" to lend large sums, but frequently these debts were not repaid because by so-called acts of grace the authorities would repudiate debts contracted by daimyo and their retainers. The sums involved were often enormous, whether these "loans" involved the bakufu directly or benefited his or the daimyo's hereditary followers. Sansom cites an instance of 1760 in which the sum "borrowed" from the trading guilds equaled the total expenditures of the government for one year.[23] None of this changed the official attitude, according to which the merchant's contribution to society was insignificant *and* pernicious. Such prejudice was a convenient justification of the forced loans or confiscations of property imposed on the mercantile community.

Throughout the Tokugawa period the official attitude of contempt for the chonin was at odds with the nationwide commercialization of the economy. The merchants came to occupy a remarkably favorable economic position. According to the house laws of the Mitsui clan,

> the merchant was obliged to understand his place and acknowledge the fact that he was a servant in the samurai's world. But in his own world he was master. Relieved of the temptation to strive for noble status either by purchase or infiltration, the Japanese merchant could concentrate his energies on the struggle for business success. It was perhaps this feature of the Tokugawa system which more than any other induced the *chonin* to press for the economic growth which so marked the latter half of the Tokugawa period.[24]

This account may suffice to explain why merchants were ready to join the movement against the Bakufu in the years preceding the restoration of 1868.

We must turn now to a consideration of the nationalism and class consciousness of the samurai in the eighteenth and nineteenth centuries. The economic position of the samurai deteriorated rapidly during this period, but significant numbers (perhaps a majority) retained their militancy and social pride. It will be seen that the policy of exclusion and its accompanying xenophobia contributed to this retention of the "samurai spirit." Following the analysis of "reference societies" and Japan's rising nationalism, the third section analyzes the growth of an anti-bakufu movement among daimyo and samurai. The concluding section deals with the policies of restoration and the constitutional redefinition of the Japanese social order.

REFERENCE SOCIETIES AND NATIONAL IDENTITY

Attempts to invade the Japanese islands were few and unsuccessful so that the country enjoyed exceptionally long periods of safety from aggression. But foreign influences on Japan were, nevertheless, pervasive. The formative phase from the Yamato dynasty to the Heian period (ca. 300–1185 A.D.) was marked by the preponderant prestige of Chinese civilization. Sansom notes that in a list compiled at the end of the seventh century, over one-third of the Japanese aristocracy claimed Chinese or Korean descent. Monks, doctors, and artisans had crossed over from the mainland, bringing with them treasures of learning and religion that were highly prized in Japan.[25] The skills and ideas thus transmitted helped to form Japanese culture, though they became vehicles in struggles for power as well. The high point of Chinese political influence was the adoption of the Taika reforms in 646 A.D. (noted in Chapter 3). Chinese cultural influence persisted long after the methods of Chinese administration had lost their hold. By 838 A.D., the Japanese prohibited further cultural missions to China, which suggests that by then the country had attained a sense of identity which combined Chinese models with indigenous developments.

This early precedent is recalled here because a somewhat similar pattern recurred in the sixteenth and seventeenth centuries. Portuguese adventurers reached Japan in 1542, and between 1549 and 1551 Father Francis Xavier initiated the Jesuit mission which flourished for half a century. At first, Western traders were welcome. The Portuguese and the Dutch brought with them expertise in navigation and the use of firearms. A civil war pervaded the country, and local overlords exploited such novel skills and resources to gain advantage over their opponents. Since traders accompanied the Jesuit mission, tolerance toward the Jesuits and adoption of the Christian faith also appeared to some local rulers as a means of achieving trade benefits. The Christian mission received its most important official endorsement under Oda Nobunaga and Toyotomi Hideyoshi, for the Jesuits represented a convenient counterforce to Buddhism. Both leaders were engaged in a major struggle against Buddhist monasteries which doubled as military bases where warrior-monks and mercenaries stood as a major obstacle to political unification.

But quite suddenly in 1587, Hideyoshi reversed his earlier toleration of the Christian mission by condemning Christian teaching and ordering the missionaries to leave within twenty days. He feared that Christian propaganda would undermine native traditions and thus impede his drive for military and political supremacy. Probably he also wanted to forestall hostile alliances with foreign powers. The main

Portuguese in Japan
A Portuguese trading ship arrives in Nagasaki, awaited by Western and Japanese merchants on the quay. Detail (three panels) of a six-leaf Namban screen, Momoyama period, from the end of the sixteenth century. (Asian Art Museum of San Francisco, Avery Brundage Collection)

grounds for an anti-Christian policy were political rather than religious and doctrinaire, and for that reason persecution remained sporadic and some missionary activities continued. Official persecution of Japanese Christians became severe in 1596, when the missions were interpreted as an advance guard of a Spanish invasion, launched from the Philippines. The anti-Christian edicts of 1616 and 1624 were inspired by renewed fears of Spanish intervention. Peasant uprisings also caused fear of foreign intervention and led to the expulsion of Portuguese priests and traders in 1638. At the same time, foreign travel by Japanese nationals was prohibited; eventually the death penalty was imposed for attempts to leave the country or to return to it after travel abroad. An embargo on Japanese foreign trade with Europeans followed, and as noted earlier only a small colony of Dutch merchants remained in Nagasaki, under strict surveillance. The shogunate feared that powerful regional rulers like the Mori and Shimadzu families might conspire with foreigners to obtain artillery, ships, and even outright military support. Ieyasu had established the hegemony of the Tokugawa house, but its national authority remained precarious for several decades.[c]

Japanese history thus presents two examples of contact with what was seen as a culturally or technically superior civilization. Both contacts are noteworthy for the readiness with which the Japanese adopted foreign ideas and practices and for the determined rejection which followed. The seventh century witnessed an unsuccessful attempt at centralized state-building through adaptation of Chinese bureaucratic institutions; later these institutions of the Taika reforms were abandoned. The sixteenth and seventeenth centuries witnessed a successful political unification which terminated centuries of feuding among locally powerful clans. At first this drive for unity was aided by the trade and technology of the West; later the policy of exclusion curtailed or prohibited contact with Europeans and their ideas.

Paradoxically, Japan's intellectual mobilization occurred at a time of heightened seclusion from the rest of the world. In this respect, the preceding chapters on England, France, and Germany have dealt with "intellectual mobilization" in quite different terms. In all three countries, the period from the sixteenth to the eighteenth centuries witnessed a burgeoning of education, literature, and science, as well as an overall intensification of efforts to cope intellectually with each country's position in the world. Typically, these efforts displayed a more or less cosmopolitan sensitivity to challenges from abroad and a more or less nationalist striving to meet these challenges in a manner conducive to a personal and collective sense of worth.[27]

In turning to Japan, one must understand that the Japanese experience differs significantly from the Western European one. A pattern of complete cultural receptivity followed by an increasingly selective approach to foreign ideas followed by the almost complete rejection of them appears to be a very distinctive attribute of Japan's insularity and

---

[c]Ieyasu's succession to the shogunate remained questionable until he eradicated the Toyotomi house in 1614, and Tokugawa legitimacy remained in some doubt even after the conquest of Osaka in that year. According to the prevailing doctrine, shogunal legitimacy depended—in addition to the imperial sanction—on unification of the country, a succession of rulers for three generations, and official recognition of shogunal supremacy by foreign powers. Victory at Sekigahara and Osaka established the first, and Ieyasu's formal retirement of 1605 in favor of his son Hidetada aided the second criterion. Equally important was Japan's international position in East Asia. During the 1630s, the shogunate increasingly declared its independence from the sinocentric world order which Japan had previously accepted in order to maintain its trade relations with China. By 1645, Japan had made itself diplomatically independent of China both through adoption of a Japanese era name (Kan'ei) and the shogun's adoption of the new title Grand Prince of Japan (Nihonkoku Taikun). This declaration of diplomatic independence in relation to China greatly aided the legitimation of Tokugawa rule.[26]

cultural history. Unlike many countries challenged by Western expansion since the sixteenth century, Japan did not have to cope with the consequences of colonialism. In the sixteenth century, it readily received Western traders and missionaries, but by the 1590s a nativist reaction had set in. In this respect, Japan resembles Germany and Russia in the eighteenth and nineteenth centuries. But Japan is unique in that it had to come to terms with the ideas and institutions of an advanced foreign civilization from the beginning of its history. There may be no other country in the world in which thinkers have been preoccupied throughout with what could be learned from another country and how such lessons might be useful to their native land. From the middle of the sixteenth to the middle of the seventeenth centuries this age-old pattern led from Christianity to exclusion, from neo-Confucianism to Japanese nativism, and from Dutch learning to nationalism in its xenophobic or pragmatic variants.

As indicated earlier, Japanese political leaders of the sixteenth century thought in terms of expedience when they tolerated the Christian missions. However, Japanese converts to Christianity applied the exacting standards of true believers. In 1579, after thirty years of missionary work by some 50 members of the Society of Jesus, the number of Christians in Japan was about 130,000. By 1600 that number was put at 300,000 in a population of 20 million, and by 1614 there were approximately half a million Christians.[28]

In the early years, most Japanese converts were simple peasants, whose hard life was made still more burdensome by almost constant civil war. For such people, neither Buddhism nor Shinto offered much personal consolation, while Christian observances provided scope for activity and an emotional outlet. Indeed, Japanese converts were noted for the intensity of their new faith. At times they subjected themselves to such merciless flagellation that the Jesuit fathers had to intervene. Vigorous preaching against suicide also appeared necessary, since the converts' love for the crucified Christ and their devotion to the cross made it difficult to "moderate their spirit of love and penitence." The Japanese Christian literature exalted the spirit of martyrdom and exhorted the faithful to be steadfast in the face of persecution. A tabulation for the period 1614–1650 shows over 2,100 Christian martyrs.[29] The passionate commitment of these converts probably owed much to the idealization of duty and self-sacrifice, which was a central tenet of Japanese neo-Confucianism.

In 1610 Ieyasu appointed Hayashi Razan (1583–1657) as his personal advisor and official scholar at the shogunal court. Hayashi was the outstanding Confucian scholar of his day and with the shogun's approval established the neo-Confucian philosophy of Chu Hsi (1130–

1200) as the norm of samurai education. According to Chu Hsi, the subject was duty-bound to render loyal service to the sovereign, and in an analogous manner so should the son obey his father, the wife her husband, the younger brother his older brother, and a friend his friend. The social order is secure when each person recognizes his proper station in life and thus upholds the idea of righteousness. In their daily behavior, men must observe "social discrimination"—that is, they must express their full loyalty and filial piety toward their immediate superior rather than to any higher authority. Those who "exceed discrimination" are committing "the crime of usurpation and rebellion." Such an approach provided the new Tokugawa regime with a suitable justification of the lord-vassal relationship.[30]

Appropriate interpretation also provided a justification of usurpation. In China's legendary past, T'ang and Wu had overthrown their lord. That act was bad, but the resulting unification was good. In a dialogue between Tokugawa Ieyasu and Hayashi Razan, Ieyasu argued, not surprisingly, that what mattered was the norm of conduct once power is seized, not the means by which it is seized. For Hayashi the issue was more complex. He could not relinquish the Chinese conception that men are good only insofar as they practice the principle of loyalty. But neither could he relinquish the precedent of T'ang and Wu. Hence, he argued that these two usurpers, knowing the principle of loyalty, had been justified in claiming that they obeyed the mandate of Heaven; and indeed their act had not revealed any private selfishness.[31]

The "Mandate of Heaven" theory had to be adapted to Japanese conditions of shogunal power. The belief in the divine descent of the imperial house and its unbroken continuity through the ages was a central Japanese tradition. Accordingly, Japanese thinkers were bound to reject the Chinese view that under certain conditions the sovereign might be removed or a dynasty overthrown. Yet, by emphasizing a dynastic continuity which preserved the divine charisma of the Sun-Goddess (*Amaterasu*), Japanese thinkers left the shogun's position in doubt. No one questioned either the ceremonial supremacy of the emperor or the actual authority of the shogunate. But there was room for argument whether

(1) the emperor is the true sovereign and the shogun his rightful deputy; or

(2) the shogun is the legitimate ruler in his own right, while the emperor is above him as an object of reverence, but without actual connection with the government; or

(3) the emperor *is* the Supreme Deity in contrast to other countries where the decree of Heaven is above the ruler's decree. Hence, the shogun's actual supremacy and use of force are legitimate only as long as

they are in accord with the wishes of the emperor to whom all reverence is due.[32]

Under the Tokugawa shogunate, commentators of the neo-Confucianist tradition moved gradually from the first to the second and—toward the end of the period—increasingly toward the third position. This last position had been formulated by writers in the seventeenth and early eighteenth centuries, who cast their imperial loyalty in religious terms. Eventually elaborations of their views inspired the restoration movement leading to the overthrow of the shogunate in 1868.

For our purposes it is sufficient to note the growing ambivalence over Chinese models. One writer (Kumazawa Banzan, 1619–1691) noted that in China all people are equal under heaven, and anyone who takes control can become sovereign. By contrast, the divine emperor of Japan is different from an ordinary mortal. Another writer (Yamaga Soko, 1622–1685) reasserted the true beauty of Japan against the neo-Confucian idolization of China. The unbroken descent of the imperial house from the Sun Goddess was the token of Japan's preeminence. A third (Yamazaki Ansai, 1618–1682) went so far as to question the "Mandate of Heaven" theory, raising doubts about the legitimacy of T'ung and Wu, who—in overthrowing their lords—had violated their duty as subjects. The Tokugawa rise to power was not mentioned.[33] But in a culture imbued with hallowed precedents from Chinese history, such questioning of the model country evoked uneasy feelings, to say the least—especially under the Tokugawa who relied on neo-Confucian doctrine for the legitimation of authority.

A writer like Yamazuki Ansai seems to have been genuinely unaware of the antishogunal potential of his views, although some of his disciples were punished severely by the shogunate. Apparently, the Tokugawa regime was divided in the matter. At home it encouraged the neo-Confucian tradition with its emphasis on hierarchic authority, at least for awhile, and writers continued the citation of Chinese precedents as binding. Occasional mavericks even extolled China at the expense of Japan. But in its foreign policy the shogunate took a much more independent position toward China, and the main trend of thought seems to have been that of a growing ambivalence toward this age-old model of Japanese culture. Various writers began to "discover" affinities between neo-Confucianism and Shinto, attempting to incorporate the prestige of Chinese culture into the native Japanese tradition. Before long, many of the same writers asserted the unique superiority of Japan over all other countries, China included, even while they used Chinese traditions to define their new sense of Japanese identity.

National learning (*kokugaku*) was the watchword of this reaction against the dominance of the Chinese classics and of the related desire to derive all guidance from Japanese tradition. In its early modern form, kokugaku was the work of two scholars, Motoori Norinaga (1730–1801) and his self-styled disciple, Hirata Atsutane (1776–1843). Motoori was the son of a wholesale merchant. He became a physician and then turned to classical Japanese studies. Sponsored by a member of the Tokugawa family, Motoori became a private tutor who attracted nearly five hundred students from all walks of life and all parts of the country. His most important writing consists of a forty-eight-volume commentary on the *Kojiki*, the Japanese classic least affected by Chinese influence. The main theme of this work was the elaborate elucidation of the "Way of Japan as the Way of the Gods," based on the conviction that Japan is inherently superior to all other countries.

> In summarized form, Motoori's argument was as follows: the Way of the Gods is the course of existence of the Japanese nation; land and people came into being through the agency of Izanagi and Izanami; Amaterasu was established as ruler to the end of time. Therefore, the ancient and eternal Way of Japan can be nothing else but the Way of the Gods. This is not to be taken in the narrow sense of religious worship alone, but rather as the fundamental source of government and of all moral and social relations: as the unchanging character of the Japanese nation is fixed for all ages, it must be expressed in the daily life of the people. There is no reason whatsoever for the Japanese to be influenced by inferior foreign doctrines such as Confucianism and Buddhism.[34]

In political terms, Motoori's main message was that the individual has no choice but to submit to the gods and hence to the emperor as their direct descendant. The task of preserving the Way of the Gods and hence the Way of the Sovereign was of such overriding significance that temporary evil deeds by the sovereign have no importance by comparison. The prevailing Tokugawa shogunate was not merely the rightful deputy of the emperor: such delegation was justified in accord with the original instructions of Amaterasu. And since foreign countries (particularly China) are not the domain of the Sun Goddess, they have no fixed rulers like the divinely descended imperial house. The forces of evil have corrupted foreign rulers. By focusing attention on the descent and continuity of the imperial house, Motoori discredited Confucianism and the Chinese historical tradition. China had been conquered repeatedly by barbarians, and the Mandate of Heaven had been exploited time and again to justify usurpations of the throne. By comparison with the Way of the Gods embodied in Japan, the Chinese Way commended by Confucianism was clearly faulty.

To these ideas, Hirata Atsutane added not only literary elaborations, but a religious emphasis. If the emperor is descended from the gods who founded the nation, then duty toward the emperor is indistinguishable from worship. From this position it was a short step to the idea that Japan as the original creation of the gods was the ancestor of all countries, while the emperor was destined to be the sovereign of the world. Therefore, the great task was to recover the truly Ancient Way of the country before its traditions were totally corrupted by foreign influence.[35]

The defenders of the Tokugawa shogunate had taken a major step when they extolled the native Japanese tradition at the expense of the Chinese model. In this about-face, they rejected the age-old identification with China as the ideal civilization. As if to compensate for what had been given up, the kokugaku scholars proceeded to depict Japan in terms of its divine mission as the very center of human culture. We have encountered this new search for old roots before. In seventeenth-century England, the great conflict between king and country was debated with each side appealing to the "ancient constitution." In the eighteenth century, French as well as German writers and political activists sought to construct viable political and cultural models by references to classical antiquity. It may be that the formation of national identities requires this link with an ideal past which has been lost, but is now found to be of the highest value. Japanese thinkers of the late eighteenth and early nineteenth centuries were faced with an unusually difficult problem. Because China had been the only viable model for so long, claims for the native Japanese tradition had to be especially strong.

One would think that this xenophobic attitude would be incompatible with a positive view of Western learning. The only thing in favor of that learning was its utility; the massive argument against it was its total incompatibility with the new Japanese nativism. Nevertheless, many writers found ways of combining national and Western learning, foreshadowing the attitude prevailing among the political leaders of the restoration. To provide a context for understanding this union of different cultural elements, we must say something about the Japanese discovery of Europe.

After 1641 the European presence in Japan was confined to the tiny Dutch settlement in Nagasaki. The Dutch were friends neither of Catholicism nor the Portuguese, and this attitude made them acceptable to the Japanese. Moreover, the Dutch were simply traders and hence did not appear as menacing to the Japanese as the combination of trade, religious mission, and military conquest. All the same, Japanese suspicions of foreigners were acute. The Dutch were subject to detailed surveillance and more or less deliberate indignities at the hands of Japanese officials. But the Dutch presence, though miniscule, served the Japanese interest in European goods and skills. Western learning was another matter. Private scholars could obtain it only by special and devious effort, since the study of Dutch was painfully difficult and Chinese books on European religion and science were banned. To the Tokugawa censors, any passing reference to Christianity or Europe even in Chinese books on subjects other than religion was sufficient ground for confiscation. Restrictions on the import of foreign books were relaxed only in 1720, and the study of Dutch was not officially encouraged until 1740, under Shogun Yoshimune (1716–1745). Not until 1774 was a translation from the Dutch circulated openly.[36]

By the 1770s, interest in Dutch learning had increased markedly. In 1783 Otsuki Gentaku published his *Ladder to Dutch Studies*, and by 1789 he established the first Dutch language school in Edo. In the following decades, similar schools were established elsewhere. In addition to grammatical instructions, Otsuki's book contained a spirited defense of Dutch studies, declaring them to be as worthy of the superior man's attention as the Chinese classics. At about this time, the Japanese term for foreign studies changed from *bangaku* (barbarian learning) to *rangaku* (*ran* derived from "Oranda" or Holland), suggesting that Otsuki was not alone in his views. It might appear simple to add Dutch studies to the Chinese classics and Japanese lore, but in fact the rangaku scholars challenged Chinese intellectual supremacy. Spokesmen of neo-Confucianism were already breaking away from tradition whenever they combined the Chinese classics with an emphasis on Japanese spiritual values. By introducing Dutch studies on an equal footing with Chinese culture, the rangaku scholars in effect challenged the Japanese to choose

An Early Japanese Use of a European Invention
An illustration from Ihara Saikaku's novel *The Man Who Spent His Life in Love* (1682) showing the nine-year-old hero training his telescope on a maidservant in her bath. This whimsical episode exemplifies the incongruities of cultural diffusion, but is hardly representative of the deadly seriousness with which the use or misuse of European inventions was debated a century later.

between Chinese and Western knowledge as a complement to their native heritage. The clash between rangaku and Confucianism lasted for many years and was embittered by governmental measures endorsing the teaching of Chu Hsi and placing severe restrictions on Western learning.

Dutch learning emphasized utility, science, and modernity, while national learning emphasized Japan's ancient cultural tradition. Nevertheless, the rangaku and the kokugaku scholars had in common the desire to preserve and enhance their native land. Many Japanese writers of the late eighteenth century saw that European science was a source of power which could help protect their country against invasion and make it economically sound. In finding ways of reconciling nativism with Western learning, these writers ranged from rather pragmatic considerations to the extremes of xenophobia. A few examples will illustrate this range of attitudes; I begin with the "pragmatists."

In the 1770s there were indications that Russian infiltration threatened from the south as well as the north. This suggested a resumption of the dangers which the policy of exclusion had averted since 1641. Hayashi Shihei (1738–1793) was one of the first Japanese to respond to this new challenge by linking the development of science with the needs of national defense. His book, *Military Talks for a Maritime Nation*, appeared in 1791. Hayashi left no doubt that reliance on Chinese texts was responsible for the neglect of the proper coastal defenses.[37] Although defenses were strengthened as Hayashi had advised, he was punished for insubordination. His transgression consisted in appealing to the public by publishing a book dealing with affairs of state, and this constituted a violation of existing laws.

In late-eighteenth-century Japan, neither public opinion nor politics was tolerated because both were incompatible with the Confucian emphasis on duty to the superior. Yet the same shogunal regent (Matsudaira Sadanobu, 1759–1829) who had ordered both the strengthening of shore defenses and the punishment of Hayashi Shihei also initiated a collection of Dutch books for governmental use. His justification of this collection fully displays the ambivalence of officials pulled in different directions by nationalism, the desire for security, the importance of Western learning, the fear of its implications for domestic tranquillity, and the need to keep affairs under tight official control.

> I began about 1792 or 1793 to collect Dutch books. The barbarian nations are skilled in the sciences, and considerable profit may be derived from their works of astronomy and geography, as well as from their military weapons and their methods of internal and external medicine. However, their books may serve to encourage idle curiosity or may express harmful ideas. It might thus seem advisable to ban them, but prohibiting these books would not prevent people from reading them. There is, moreover, profit to be derived

from them. Such books and other foreign things should therefore not be allowed to pass in large quantities into the hands of irresponsible people; nevertheless it is desirable to have them deposited in a government library. If there is no one to read them, however, they will merely become nests for insects. I informed the Governor of Nagasaki that if such works were acquired by the government, they would not be dispersed throughout the country, and could thus be consulted if there were any official need of them. This is how it happened that foreign books came to be purchased.[38]

In a statement like this, the potential benefits of European learning—while recognized in principle—recede into the background, as both the threat of "harmful ideas" and the impossibility of preventing people from reading dangerous books are realized. And while the statement adopts a middle course by endorsing a government collection of Dutch books with access limited to officials, it also reveals the cultural nationalism, caution, and fear prevailing in official circles. The "considerable profit" to be derived from Dutch books is overshadowed by the notion that they *could* be consulted in a restricted government library "*if there were any official need of them.*" When the leading statesman of the day expressed himself in this manner, one would hardly expect shogunal officials to become eager students of Dutch learning.

These attitudes were not shared by everyone. Some bakufu officials (like Takashima Shuhan, 1798–1866, and Egawa Tarozaemon, 1800–1855) who were in touch with local affairs became pioneers of Western science, especially in its military aspects. Their work was an uphill struggle, since Confucianism and suspicion of "barbarian learning" prevailed in Edo. Hence, the initiative for combining nationalism with Dutch studies tended to shift to the domains, especially to Satsuma, Mito, Echizen, Hizen, and Choshu.[39] As Shimazu Nariakira of Satsuma put it in 1856:

> At this time when defence against the foreign barbarians is of crucial importance it is the urgent duty of all samurai both high and low to cooperate in learning of conditions in foreign lands so that we may adopt their good points to supplement our deficiencies, reinforce the military might of our nation and keep the barbarian nations under control.[40]

Shimazu did not see any contradiction between Western technology, Japan's wealth, and the preservation of shogunal and daimyo authority.[d] For him and the other reforming daimyo, European science used to

[d]Shimazu was unusual for the personal interest he took in such novelties as photography, the telegraph, gas lighting, the manufacture of glass and agricultural implements in addition to cannons and rifles. Other reforming daimyo stressed the political aspects while allowing their retainers to pursue Western studies. The convergence of interest between reforming daimyo and bakufu officials broke down after 1857 when the daimyo became critical of official negotiations with foreigners while the bakufu became suspicious of daimyo self-interest in the promotion of internal reforms.

advance Japan's economy and military technology was entirely in harmony with Confucian ethics stressing the obedience of each man to his superior.[41]

But the interest in Western learning was not confined to a few bakufu officials and reform-minded daimyo. Paradoxically, it was taken up by the more fanatic spokesmen of Japanese nativism—for example, the kokugaku scholar, Hirata Atsutane. He began his studies of Shinto in 1801, and his first major work was entitled *New Discussion of the Gods* (*Kishin Shinron*, 1805).[42] For Hirata as for other writers of the kokugaku school, Japan was the land of the gods and superior to all other countries because of its unbroken line of god-descended emperors. These views were a standby of Shinto doctrine. But in Hirata's work they were combined with the idea that in acquiring foreign learning the Japanese should select the good points of such studies and thereby make them part of Japanese culture. This approach was attacked bitterly by advocates of ancient Japanese learning who wanted to protect the old simplicities from defilement by Western rationalism. However, for Hirata, who was a physician, there was no going back to the innocence of ancient ways, and he turned the argument around. Only "beginners unsure of themselves or self-satisfied people like the Chinese would refuse to profit from the worthwhile parts of Western learning."[43] But his attitude was not one of tolerance at all. He dismissed out of hand scientific findings at odds with national superiority. For example, Hirata acknowledged that foreign medicine was far in advance of its Japanese counterpart. But then he argued that in ancient Japan the medical arts had been unnecessary, since serious diseases had commenced only when Japan engaged in relations with China and other foreign countries. It was only proper to cure foreign diseases by recourse to foreign medicine. Another example is the use Hirata made of his knowledge of geography and economic relations to "demonstrate" Japan's unique position in the world. Other countries were larger, but Japan was superior in all respects. Witness its self-sufficiency: other countries were urging Japan to trade with them, but Japan enjoyed the special favor of the gods and did not require trade! In other words, Hirata's admiration of Western learning did not imply esteem for Europeans. Perhaps he feared that the rangaku scholars would be as deferential toward the Dutch as Confucian scholars had been toward the Chinese. At any rate, he combined his acceptance of Western learning with a denunciation of the Dutch which ran the whole gamut of prejudiced rumors and quasi-racist slogans.

Hirata's bigotry may have been atypical, but his impulse to link the use of Western knowledge with extreme Japanese nationalism was shared by Yoshida Shoin (1830–1859), among others. A samurai of Choshu, Yoshida encompassed in his short life the whole range of attitudes which inspired the young men of spirit (*shishi*). His and their loyalty to the national cause (*kokutai*) had the intensity of the true believer who wants to sacrifice his life for his ideal.[e] In 1858 Yoshida wrote,

> In studying the learning of Europe and America, to adore and idolize the barbarians . . . must be rejected absolutely. But the barbarians' artillery and shipbuilding, their knowledge of medicine, and of physical sciences, can all be of use to us—these should properly be adopted. . . .
> When I was desirous of going to America, my teacher [Sakuma] Zozan said to me: "If this duty were to be undertaken by one who was not possessed of a firm aspiration for loyalty, one who did not recognize the obligation resulting from the benefactions of the nation, it would unfailingly lead to great harm. Truly you are fitted for this responsibility."[44]

Men like Sakuma and Yoshida apparently did not feel troubled by the necessity to once more follow a foreign model. The Westerners might hold a temporary advantage in science and technology. But once Japan adopted these techniques, it would regain its rightful place in world affairs and fulfill its destiny "as the source of civilization and center of an eternal world empire."[45]

One can discern a certain pattern in the preceding discussion. First, the Japanese accepted Christianity and then had recourse to Chinese precedent as a counterpoint to the expulsion of the Christian missions. Next, Japanese thinkers reacted against the age-old reliance on Chinese precedent by their idealization of the ancient Japanese tradition. Finally, Japanese political and intellectual leaders discovered that Western learning was useful for the national cause; thus, advocates of Dutch learning found common ground with the spokesmen of kokugaku. The paradox of the country's history was reenacted. Since its beginning as a political entity, Japan had always been indebted to cultural models taken from abroad. During the eighteenth and early nineteenth centuries, the simultaneous emphasis on national and Western learning was to demonstrate that the tension between cultural dependence and self-assertion was as central to Japanese nation-building as it had been throughout the country's cultural history.

Yoshida Shoin was twenty-three when Commodore Perry arrived at Uraga in 1853 and presented the country with its most severe challenge since the Christian missions three centuries earlier. The debate elicited by that challenge marked the decline of the Tokugawa shogunate and the beginning of modern politics. For the first time, affairs of state became the concern of a public outside the ranks of government.

[e]*Kokutai* had a range of meanings including honor or avoidance of disgrace, dignity or prestige, influence or authority in action, the ideals of the spirit. Yoshida was executed in 1859 for his part in planning the assassination of a high bakufu official. His attitude toward Western learning was only a small part of his concerns, but it is cited here as typical of the leaders opposing the Tokugawa regime.

Instruction in a "Temple School" for Commoners
Sons from families below the aristocracy were given instruction in reading, arithmetic, and calligraphy in *terakoya* schools. This picture of a schoolroom in action gives some impression of the youngsters' reactions. The task of maintaining standards of excellence was correspondingly great. (Kodansha International)

The debate on how to meet this new challenge was indeed agonizing. But it is worth noting that the debaters, whether Yoshida and his loyalist[f] friends or the officials and neo-Confucianists defending the Tokugawa house, had the same vision of Japan's god-given superiority. The great controversy of the restoration movement concerned the means by which the nation's goals could best be achieved.

THE RESTORATION MOVEMENT: EMERGENCE OF PUBLIC DEBATE

In the preceding chapters on England, France, and Germany, I have referred to an "intellectual mobilization" that was more or less separable from social and political action. In England this mobilization included lawyers and Puritan divines as well as members of parliament;

---

[f] The term *loyalist* became a catchword for all those who used "loyalty to the emperor" as a basis for attacking the policies and, in the end, the existence of the Tokugawa shogunate.

in France, the philosophes and Freemasons as well as the parlementaires; and in Germany, writers and journalists as well as civil servants. In some cases, the political activist and the writer were the same person —Goethe and the Abbé Sieyès are outstanding examples; but on the whole, the two activities are separable in the European context. This separation seems inappropriate to Japan. Certainly, the daimyo and samurai who took up Dutch studies in the interest of national defense were engaged in intellectual pursuits. But they are distinguished from "intellectuals" in nineteenth-century Europe by the extraordinary singleness of political purpose with which they pursued these studies. Moreover, in Europe the divergence between conservatives and radicals implied a conflict over goals as much as over the means to achieve them. This was not the case in Japan. An arch-conservative like Tokugawa Nariaki (see further on) and a fanatic like Yoshida Shoin both wanted to use European science for strengthening Japan against the dangers of Western penetration. In dealing with the restoration movement, then, I shall be concerned with the way in which members of the Japanese aristocracy became prepared to act politically in a social structure which was based on the suppression of politics. This movement also provided a training for leadership in the period of reconstruction which followed the restoration of 1868.[g]

The culture of the Tokugawa period encouraged regional loyalties and pride of rank over national concerns; it also militated against self-discipline. The samurai had been demilitarized. Employed as daimyo officials, many could be expected to develop a bureaucratic mentality. The urbanized, rentier existence of others offered countless opportunities for corruption. The official emphasis on rank together with the discouragement of competition fostered social parasitism. Finally, many lower samurai families were forced to supplement their rice stipends by work they considered degrading. In one form or another, many samurai yielded their traditional posture, yet the weakening of "moral fiber" was also intensely resented and resisted.

Comparison with other aristocracies makes this moral resilience of a good many samurai somewhat puzzling. Negative cases are hard to interpret, but Thomas Smith has pointed out that some samurai retained their traditional posture in part because under the Tokugawa shogunate their privileges were not challenged by a rising "democratic" movement. Japanese merchants never raised their private grievances to "a great principle of struggle between right and wrong," despite their increasing wealth, experience in affairs, and intense resentment of an inferior position. In the absence of a challenge from below, samurai

---

[g]Daimyo officials and samurai provided the active political and intellectual leadership of the nation and pioneered in modern entrepreneurial activities as well. This leadership role is reviewed in the following section.

could retain a positive view of their position, however jeopardized in fact, and thus avoid the rigid defensiveness so typical of aristocratic responses to populist movements.

We may cite other reasons for the ultimately constructive activism of the samurai. At the beginning of the Tokugawa period, the samurai had been removed from their land, losing the main anchor of their inherited privileges. For more than two centuries, they had depended on government service or rice stipends as their means of sustenance. Consequently, they had an interest in supporting a government which functioned effectively in their behalf. At the same time, the Tokugawa regime and many samurai retained an ideology of militancy and service, even after the samurai had turned into rentiers and engaged either in administrative work, demeaning occupations, or simply dissipation. This discrepancy between an ideology of militancy and administrative routines or between claims to high status and the actuality of degradation brought the ideals of the samurai into frequent conflict with their way of life and thus imparted much tension to their collective experience. Such tension is missing from the life style of European aristocrats who enjoyed their privileges and merely defended their entrenched position.[46]

Education under the Tokugawa provides an important clue to this tension and helps to explain the moral resilience of many samurai, as well as their leading role in the restoration movement. In 1786 Hayashi Shihei formulated the aims of this education as follows:

> With the eight virtues as your basis [his list is filial piety, respect for elders, loyalty, trust, courage, justice, straightforwardness, and a sense of honor] cultivate a boldness of spirit without losing self-discipline; acquire wisdom and wide learning without despising other people. Do not become weak and feeble; do not lose your dignity; do not sink stagnantly into mere logic-chopping nor allow yourself to be carried away by prose and poetry. Do not lose your courage; do not become introverted. Do not become an admirer of China who sees no good in Japan. Do not fall in love with novelty or with pleasures of the eye. Practice your military skills with devotion and at the same time learn something of astronomy and geography, of the tea ceremony and of No drama.[47]

Hayashi's statement was representative of advanced opinion in his time. A number of writers combined the Confucian code of conduct with the activist ethic of the samurai, the nationalist rejection of the Chinese model with the praise of military skills, modern science, and the traditional Japanese arts. This set of ideas became increasingly common in the late eighteenth century and spread to the education of commoners as well.

In the fief schools and in schools for commoners, instruction became a highly formalized affair. While it was intrinsically dull and meaningless, reading and writing were used as media through which the student learned proper behavior and the right frame of mind. The student's bearing and attitude were subjected to the most detailed scrutiny, and tedious repetition was the method by which self-discipline was taught.[h] This educational system helped to maintain the ideals of the samurai. The teachers had a vested interest in these ideals, and the daimyo and bakufu officials encouraged their educational endeavors because they considered these ideals suitable supports of domestic stability.

Many samurai students did not accept with alacrity admonitions of self-discipline, filial piety, and an activist way of life. Fief edicts frequently deplored the lack of diligence and urged samurai students to show greater effort. Although the ideology and practice of swordsmanship were continued, personal militancy was discouraged and all contests or simulated combat among the pupils was prohibited. One result of this double-edged policy was that, as Dore comments, "combat was less and less practiced, and swordsmanship and the use of the lance became increasingly a matter of formal gymnastics, and disciplined choreography."[49] This presumably applied to those pupils who put dignity and respect for elders above the cult of action. There were others, however, whom circumstances and temperament prompted to make the opposite choice. As ronin or masterless samurai, they lived by the sword at the expense of most other tenets of the samurai ethic. Yet some of the ronin made up by ascetic rigor what they had lost in wealth and status; they came to believe that they alone upheld the old standards. One can gauge the tensions inherent in Japanese culture before the restoration when one observes that the Tokugawa regime did not abandon its praise of militancy despite its policy of pacification and the apprehensions aroused by the activities of the ronin.

The famous story of the forty-seven ronin exemplifies many of these themes. At the shogunal court a daimyo has drawn his sword and wounded a high court official to avenge an insult. As a penalty, the daimyo is asked to commit suicide because he has jeopardized Tokugawa supremacy and the policy of pacification on which it rests. The daimyo's retainers are now without a master; they acknowledge that he had to die, but out of loyalty to him they make every effort to preserve their lord's fief for the members of his family. This effort fails. For two years the forty-seven ronin (the original number is larger, but many withdraw) secretly plan to avenge their lord. After successfully eluding the ubiquitous Tokugawa police, they kill the court official who had provoked their master. As a penalty for this violation, the shogun demands that the forty-seven commit suicide in turn. The conduct of these men exemplifies unconditional loyalty to their master, self-discipline in guard-

[h]Sons of commoners learned the art of writing in temple schools and through private tutors in a manner that is strikingly reminiscent of certain Puritan and Victorian precepts of conduct. Literacy was linked to the ideology of self-discipline.[48]

Admiral Perry is Greeted by the Governor of Uraga in 1853
(U.S. Naval Academy Museum)

ing their secret plans, and perseverance until their plan is executed. The story epitomizes the priorities and contradictions of Tokugawa culture. The ronin divorce their wives or have their wives and daughters turn to prostitution for their livelihood so that as samurai they can fulfill their pledge of loyalty to their dead master. For these men, the hierarchy of rank and action to fulfill their pledge are more important than family; for the shogunate, control of violence is more important than the hierarchy of rank or the cult of action. These priorities are exemplified by the ronin who sacrifice their families and themselves to avenge their lord, and by the shogunate which protects the peace of the realm even though this necessitates punishing those who by their loyal action uphold the ideals of hierarchy and militancy which the shogunate itself espouses.

This true story of 1702 instantly became the cultural epitome of the samurai ethic; in retrospect it reads more like a tragic epitaph than an apotheosis. One would suppose that many of these men, for whom militancy was the mark of rank, were aware at times of its emptiness. While the story of the forty-seven ronin certainly upheld the ideal, did it not also underscore the pretensions of a militancy without war? Under the Tokugawa regime the peaceful existence of most samurai was at odds with their militant stance, a condition hardly conducive to the vigor and self-discipline the samurai displayed during the Meiji Restoration. Historical instances are numerous in which such conflicts between theory and practice lead to the decline of an ideal. Why did this not occur in Japan?

Some allowance must be made for the accident of timing. We will never know whether the samurai ethic would have become a sham if the Western challenge to Japanese independence had come much later. All we know is that when the Tokugawa regime was jeopardized after 1853, the samurai displayed a capacity for self-disciplined action that had been jeopardized (and may well have been diminished) by the discrepancy between ideal and conduct in their life before 1853.

Bakufu officials had always upheld the *ideal* of samurai militancy while in practice insisting on the pacification of the country. The best elements among the samurai probably tolerated such inconsistency, as long as the shogunate itself appeared to act decisively. But even conservative samurai turned against the regime once its capacity for action waned. For then it appeared that the shogunate was putting Tokugawa interests ahead of the interests of the country at a time of national emergency.

One should also consider that the cult of action found some outlets in Tokugawa society and in sublimated form had constructive results. Dore has shown how the militant ideal of self-disciplined action was "domesticated" through the educational system, especially in the teaching of calligraphy. Gradually, samurai ideals became ideals for commoners as well. In contrast to Europe, there is hardly any evidence in Tokugawa Japan suggesting that commoners should be barred from the acquisition of literacy on the ground that this would make them unruly. At the same time, samurai who became important daimyo officials naturally used their education to improve the economic and administrative affairs of the several domains.

Broadly speaking, it is probable that the top and middle strata of the samurai benefited from the Tokugawa system. Beasley characterizes daimyo officials as the top of the samurai class, comprising some 5,200 retainers with the right of audience (hatamoto) in the Tokugawa domains and much smaller numbers of comparable rank in the daimyo domains. A middle stratum of "ordinary" samurai (*hirazamurai*) was more numerous: in Satsuma they numbered 3,900 families, in Choshu and the Tokugawa domains of Owari about 2,500 each. No total count of the top and middle ranks of samurai officialdom appears to be available, but these figures suggest that the two ranks comprised probably between 5 and 10 percent of the samurai class as a whole.[i] The moderate leaders of the restoration movement, those who had the greatest stake in making the existing system more effective, were recruited from these ranks of Tokugawa or daimyo officialdom. At the same time, many of these high officials were time-servers and corrupt, exploiting their status and title to hide their incompetence and lord it over their inferiors. In the last decades of the Tokugawa era, neo-Confucianism with its emphasis on hierarchy was used increasingly as a rationalization of bureaucratic pathologies. At the same time, a large number of educated samurai and commoners found that nepotism and corruption barred them from employment as shogunal or daimyo administrators. Indeed, the lower samurai were exploited, often cruelly. Many of the younger and more radical leaders of the anti-Tokugawa movement were recruited from the ranks of these frustrated office seekers who chafed under incompetence in high places and strained to put their ability at the service of the nation. The firebrands who pushed longest for expulsion of the "barbarians" and resorted to assassination as a political weapon probably came disproportionately from these lower ranks of the samurai class as well as from the ronin, whose lack of a master placed them outside the system.[j]

The restoration movement and the period of reconstruction which followed provided the opportunity to overcome the long-standing, internal contradictions of the Tokugawa regime. Having endured these contradictions between ideological militancy and a peaceable rentier existence for so long, a significant minority of the samurai at last found an outlet for their ambitions after 1853. As Dore puts it in a telling summary,

[i] Estimates put the number of samurai households at 570,000 or a total of 2 million persons of samurai status at the time of the restoration in 1868. The number of officials varied among the domains, with the top ranks being more numerous in the Tokugawa and the middle ranks more numerous in the outside daimyo domains. A total of 57,000 in the top and middle ranks is not improbable, since there were some 250 daimyo domains in addition to the many subdivisions of the Tokugawa holdings. The lower samurai were divided into foot soldiers, retainers of subvassals, and rural samurai; they comprised the bulk of the class, say between 80 and 90 percent.[50]

[j] If roughly 10 percent of the samurai class were officeholders of high or middle rank, while in 1868 some 40 percent of Japanese boys were literate, the group of frustrated office seekers must have been large. Crude as this estimate is, it points to an important problem of the Tokugawa regime.[51]

Sensitive pride and fear of shaming defeat, the strength of which probably led the majority of samurai to avoid competitive situations and certainly prompted most educators and teachers of military skills deliberately to refrain from creating them, also meant that—once competition was declared and the race was on—the self-respecting samurai really did go all out to win.[52]

This release of pent-up energies was decisive. During the critical period from 1853 to 1868 (the so-called *bakumatsu* period), the goal of strengthening the country and diminishing the danger of foreign intrusion was shared by all. Spokesmen for the various approaches shared a belief in filial piety, self-discipline, and an activist way of life as the model of righteous conduct. They differed, often violently, as to the best means of achieving the national goal. The suggested means ranged from genuine accommodation through evasive tactics to a politics of violence. Nevertheless, the task of reconstructing a country has rarely been confronted with so much underlying unanimity. But then, only Japan has confronted that task after a millennium of experience in dealing with foreign cultures and more than two centuries of seclusion from the outside world.

Restoration means renewal, or else the return to a former condition, whether viable or moribund. The reestablishment of the English monarchy in 1660 was a restoration. So was the European defense of monarchical prerogatives which were threatened by constitutional and nationalist movements mobilizing the people. The Japanese restoration movement also sounded conservative, demanding obeisance to the sacrosanct wishes of the imperial house which had not played a political role for more than a thousand years. But the accent of the Japanese movement was on national renewal, not on the defense of established privilege as in nineteenth-century Europe.

The Tokugawa regime had been founded on the suppression of politics. The restoration movement made it legitimate to discuss political issues outside the circle of appointed officials. To see this contrast, it is necessary to outline the precipitating events which undermined the Tokugawa settlement from the 1830s to the 1850s.

In the first decades of the nineteenth century, the social and economic situation of the samurai deteriorated rapidly. Rising prices, currency manipulations, and imposed reductions of stipends undermined their livelihood and degraded them socially. Between 1819 and 1837, the currency was debased nineteen times, yielding profits to the bakufu amounting to one-half of the government's annual expenditures. Crop failures, famines, and sporadic peasant uprisings are other evidences of acute distress in this period. In response, messianic religious movements proliferated, as did debates expressing national apprehensions. In the daimyo domains, financial conditions deteriorated. One domain (Owari) borrowed one-half of its annual rice income in 1801 and more than seven times its total annual income between 1849 and 1853. Another (Satsuma) had a debt of almost twice its annual income in 1807 and about six times that income in 1830. By 1840 the economic decline of the Japanese aristocracy was manifest. In that year, Osaka merchants held daimyo debts equivalent to 60 million koku. Interest on these debts amounted to a quarter of the country's tax revenue. But it was paid very irregularly, if at all. With bakufu support, powerful daimyo used their social and political privileges to evade financial embarrassment—at least for a time.[53]

A sense of urgency led to attempts at reform. In 1841 senior bakufu officials dismissed a thousand Tokugawa employees. New edicts were issued to preserve the hierarchy of rank. Dangerous literature was censored. Rural poverty had led peasants to move to the towns; now bakufu officials attempted to force them to return to the countryside. Officials sought to counteract the declining fortunes of the Tokugawa government by recoinage and forced loans in unprecedented amounts. Since debts were mounting precipitously, the government prohibited licensed monopolies and wholesale trading organizations in line with the anti-mercantile ideology of neo-Confucianism. The effect was to throw the supply of commodities into confusion and to provoke still more inflation. A decade later, the edict was canceled. Such measures had been tried before and failed. But this time they exacerbated divisions among Tokugawa supporters, even provoking outspoken disagreement with official policy among the daimyo and the collateral houses of the Tokugawa.

Meanwhile, the large han also attempted reform, and a few were more successful than the bakufu. Some resorted to neo-Confucian propaganda campaigns, others tried aid to agriculture and drastic reduction of expenses. Among the most successful were Choshu and Satsuma, the two tozama houses which were to become major centers of the restoration movement. Choshu had been shaken by a peasant uprising in 1831. Six years later, internal reforms of the han were put on an emergency basis, starting with a resurvey of the land for the purpose of a more equitable tax system. Han monopolies were converted into protected merchant enterprises, and debt payments were regularized on a long-term basis. Profits were increased by providing for better transport of goods. At the same time, military organization was improved, based on the purchase of Western equipment. Similar measures were undertaken in Satsuma. Debt payments were reformed, and the production of sugar cane was increased, as was the domain's commerce, especially with the Ryukyu Islands. On balance, the record of han reforms was mixed. Failures in one domain were matched by successes in another.

Some benefit was derived from regional decentralization, which allowed the different han to experiment with remedial measures. But the country continued to be in serious domestic trouble with no solution in sight.

Meanwhile, foreign pressure for Japanese trading concessions compounded the domestic problems. The Western powers wanted the harbors open to foreign trade, supplies provided for merchant vessels, protection of shipwrecked sailors, and the admission of official representatives on a regular basis. The Russians attempted to get such concessions in the eighteenth century but were diverted by Napoleon's invasion of Russia in 1812. British explorations in the eighteenth century reached Japanese coastal waters in 1808, but Britain was diverted by its preoccupations in China. In the end, the main pressure came from the Americans. Gold drew them to California in 1848, and shortly thereafter prospects of trade turned them toward Canton and Shanghai. Commodore Perry arrived in Uraga in 1853. In the following year, a treaty was signed with the United States. But this provoked such a storm of protest in Japan that for political reasons bakufu officials were unable to enforce the limited provisions of this first treaty. Meanwhile, American pressure for enforcement and further concessions mounted. Only the appointment of a virtual dictator (Ii Naosuke, 1858–1860) led to a regular commercial treaty with the United States in 1858. Even so, intense controversy followed, and after two years Ii was assassinated. The authority of the bakufu was waning: by 1862 shogunal control over the daimyo through required residence in Edo was relaxed. Domestic controversy continued for another five years, and in 1867 the Tokugawa shogunate was replaced by the enthronement of the Meiji emperor. After a thousand years, the absolute political control by regents and shoguns had come to an end.

An unusual combination of central control and local autonomy in the Tokugawa system as well as the policy of exclusion had facilitated the pacification of Japanese society. But these achievements were obtained at a price. Officials or leading Japanese aristocrats were unable to acquire any experience in foreign relations. When contacts became unavoidable, the result was xenophobia, epitomized by the slogan "Revere the emperor, expel the barbarian" (*sonno-joi*). Exclusion also facilitated the suppression of internal politics. Neo-Confucian precepts instructed each person to show loyal obedience to his superior, so that all public affairs were naturally managed by officials of the highest rank. No one outside the ranks of Tokugawa officialdom could acquire experience in managing internal conflicts when even the daimyo were excluded from participating in the decision-making process. Hence, when external pressures destroyed the policy of exclusion and demonstrated the incompetence of Tokugawa officialdom, they also destroyed the pos-

sibility of insulating administrative actions from the opinions and interests of leading strata in Japanese society.

Commodore Perry's arrival in 1853 sent shock waves through the
country, though such an event had been anticipated for decades. Bakufu
officials temporized when they could neither reject nor accept the demands presented by the Americans. But temporizing was an obvious
sign of weakness in a regime claiming absolute authority. When that
claim proved invalid in practice, conservative daimyo allied with the
Tokugawa house began to criticize shogunal policies in the interest of
making them more effective.

Tokugawa Nariaki was a conservative critic of this kind. Sansom has
called him a "self-indulgent, tempestuous man," but perhaps it took such
a man to break through the bureaucratic rigidities of the shogunate. In
1842, as lord of Mito, Nariaki opposed a shogunal plan to relax the policy of exclusion. In the same year, he wrote, "If the Shogun takes the
lead in showing respect for the throne, the whole country will naturally
be united, but it is vital that in this each should preserve his proper
place. The samurai shows respect for his lord, the lord shows respect
for the Shogun, the Shogun shows respect for the Emperor."[54] The lord
of Mito was an important figure who came to differ *publicly* with the
official position of the shogunate—despite these neo-Confucian principles. In 1855 cannon were cast in the Mito domain on his instructions,
but without the required shogunal permission. As a result, Nariaki was
ordered to retire as daimyo in favor of his son, and for five years thereafter he was barred from active participation in han affairs. But this
formal exclusion did not prevent his continued role in Mito or his intermittent participation as self-appointed advisor to the shogunate. Here
was an outstanding representative of the regime who tried to fortify the
shogunate by timely internal reforms.

In 1846 Nariaki urged a senior bakufu official to arrange for the
translation and wide circulation of Dutch works on military subjects. In
the 1850s, he made the Mito domain a model of "modernization"
through financial and administrative reforms and through the establishment of Western-style shipbuilding and an iron industry. From 1853,
he consistently opposed diplomatic concessions, even in the face of Japan's certain defeat by the Western powers. All these positions were exemplary demonstrations of Mito's opposition to foreigners, reverence
for the emperor, and concern for a strengthened Japan. At the same
time, Nariaki's role involved not only factional struggles within the Mito
domain, but a more or less running battle for influence in bakufu councils, direct defiance of some bakufu decisions, and specifically a complex,
changing relationship with Abe Masahiro, a senior shogunal councillor.
Nariaki was a senior member of the Tokugawa house and a relative
through marriage or adoption of leading members of the imperial court

and of several tozama lords. His opinions and actions could not be ignored, even when they were proscribed. By pressing these opinions on the basis of so strategic a position, Nariaki contributed inadvertently to the emergence of political debate outside the circles of bakufu officialdom.[55]

In initiating the debate of public issues in contravention of past bakufu practice, Tokugawa Nariaki and the other "reforming lords" were anxious to make the shogunate more effective.[56] They had to come to grips with their own domain problems and in doing so became aware of Edo's growing inability to govern effectively. They did not anticipate that the events they helped to set in motion would lead eventually to an overthrow of the entire bakuhan system. Foreign pressure, bakufu indecision, and the agitation of their own samurai in the end pushed these daimyo leaders beyond administrative reforms to debate and conflict over public issues.

A first official step along that road was taken by Abe Masahiro. It had been shogunal practice to deal with foreign challenges arbitrarily. Now, in 1853, Abe recognized that it was impossible to drive off the Americans. Accordingly, he decided to send out letters requesting the daimyo to give their opinions. Responses to the request were sharply divided.[57] Nevertheless, a report was made to the imperial court. For the first time in more than two centuries, the shogunate had made a policy issue a matter of public discussion—at least among ranking members of the aristocracy. For the first time in over five hundred years, the shogun submitted preliminary findings to the emperor, abandoning his own absolute authority as the "barbarian-subduing generalissimo."

Under these circumstances, Abe sought to minimize concessions to the Americans while pushing military preparations at home. But each step led to complications. Whatever its provisions, any treaty would terminate the Tokugawa policy of exclusion. Abe's substitution of consultation for authoritarian leadership antagonized the fudai daimyo who opposed any policy discussions outside bakufu official circles; access to these discussions was among their most important prerogatives. Conciliation toward the foreigners antagonized those who wanted expulsion even at the risk of defeat. With the foreigners, bakufu officials were evasive. But temporizing merely provoked the foreign representatives and did not satisfy the Japanese whose desire for decisive action ranged from the advocacy of war to the promotion of foreign trade. Bakufu efforts to strengthen the defenses of the country came too late to protect the shogunate against foreign pressures. Meanwhile, its internal position was weakened through military preparations in the daimyo domains.

When the treaty of Kanagawa (Yokohama) was signed in 1854, all these conflicting pressures resulted in a storm of protest throughout the country. In response, Abe's successor, Hotta Masayoshi (1810–1864), turned to Kyoto for imperial sanction of a policy of compromise. Abe's consultation of the emperor had brought the throne into the arena of foreign policy-making. Now, in the 1850s, bakufu officials, daimyo, and samurai put pressure on influential court nobles and the emperor for support of their conflicting causes. A thousand-year tradition of having elevated only the religious and artistic prestige of the imperial house was suddenly exploited to facilitate, by its hallowed prestige, the resolution of an intractable political controversy. Then, in 1858, matters were complicated further by the sudden death without heir of the incumbent shogun, Tokugawa Iesada (1824–1858). Senior councillors and fudai daimyo, led by Ii Naosuke, favored Tokugawa Yoshitomi. Tokugawa collateral houses and tozama daimyo, led by Tokugawa Nariaki, favored Hitotsubashi Yoshinobu (or Keiki), Nariaki's son. The dispute over foreign policy was compounded by a dispute over the shogunal succession. In this context, Nariaki appealed to the emperor for support, breaking with the tradition of excluding the court from intervening in the succession of regent or shogun.

For the moment, uncertainty was overcome when Ii Naosuke became Great Councillor. He signed the American treaty of 1858 without imperial sanction, settled the succession in favor of Yoshitomi, and punished members of the "Hitotsubashi party" with penalties ranging from the execution of Yoshida Shoin to the house arrest imposed on important daimyo like those of Mito, Owari, Tosa, and Satsuma. But these actions only delayed the crisis. The succession dispute had helped to forge an alliance among the daimyo who had lost out in the struggle over the shogunal succession.[58] When even these conservative daimyo had become politically mobilized, other and less conservative men were sure to follow. Two years after the 1858 treaty, Ii Naosuke was assassinated by a group of Mito samurai who resented his treatment of their lord and bitterly opposed his conciliatory foreign policy. In the following years, sporadic violence against foreigners and bakufu or daimyo officials further increased internal and external tensions. Bakufu officials remained indecisive in the face of Western pressure, while daimyo and samurai leaders became increasingly aware that time and institutional change were needed to preserve the country, even if this meant a temporary accommodation to foreign demands.

The gathering restoration movement comprised all persons outside Tokugawa officialdom who were becoming actively concerned with the public affairs from which they were formally excluded. Tokugawa officials could not suppress the efforts to obtain the emperor's sanction for one policy or another after Abe Masahiro had initiated that effort. Moreover, for the first time in a millennium, a leading shogunal official had called on the daimyo to submit their opinions. It is this mounting controversy and the conflicting appeals to the emperor's sanction that I have called the emergence of public debate.

The restoration movement culminated in the overthrow of the Tokugawa shogunate in 1868, the installation of the Meiji emperor as the supreme head of government, and the conduct of affairs by an oligarchy of Meiji leaders who had become prominent in the restoration movement. The result was a transformation of the social structure, and under the Meiji constitution of 1889 the supreme authority of the emperor was combined with appeals to a popular mandate.

A REVOLUTION UNDER OLIGARCHIC LEADERSHIP

On January 3, 1868, armed contingents from Satsuma and Choshu seized the imperial palace in Kyoto. A council was called from which Tokugawa partisans were excluded and a formal return of governmental authority to the emperor was announced. Strictly speaking, the Meiji Restoration of 1868 consisted in the dissolution of the shogunate and the formal transfer of authority to the emperor. But under the Meiji dynasty, the emperor remained a ceremonial figure just like his predecessors. In what sense, then, was the Japanese state reconstituted in 1868? Did the "return of authority" to the emperor have any realistic, political meaning beyond its legitimation of the new Meiji government? In practice, the Meiji leadership answered these questions by measures directly affecting the imperial house and the social and political position of the Japanese aristocracy.

Tokyo (Edo) was established as the national capital and the residence of the emperor. The change ending the age-old separation of the residence of the emperor from the seat of government was more than symbolic. Henceforth, all specific acts of government were announced by, and implemented in the name of, the emperor. In the past, shoguns had received their mandate to govern from the imperial house, but then acted in their own name. Their formal submission to the emperor had been confined to the inception of their rule or to specific emergencies. Thereafter, invocation of the imperial mandate was a sign of weakness in a shogunate. By contrast, after 1868, each governmental edict was issued in the name of the emperor, now a sign of strength. The government was identified with the imperial court, and the emperor resided in the palace formerly occupied by the Tokugawa shoguns. The court was no longer a center of potential opposition that had to be controlled, as had been the case in Kyoto in times past.

The leaders of the Meiji government established new relations with the domains. Their first move was to issue an imperial edict which expropriated all the lands belonging to the Tokugawa house, made them the property of the emperor, and subjected them to an imperial administration. By this action, the emperor became the wealthiest of the country's landed proprietors. Moreover, imperial appropriation of Tokugawa domains clarified the purpose of the Meiji leaders who were clearly not enlarging their own domains at the expense of the Tokugawa. By the end of 1868, the emperor's household was administratively separated from the management of the imperial domains. This separation quickly became the model for the country. All the daimyo domains were reorganized in similar fashion. At all levels, senior posts in estate management were filled by men chosen for their ability, not because of their birth. A majority of the daimyo favored this approach which seemed to reform the old bakuhan system now under imperial auspices, but also preserved the prerogatives of the old daimyo families. These men thought that total abolition of the old domains and prerogatives would destroy the unity of the new Meiji government.[59]

This was precisely the reason why some Meiji leaders decided to go much further. The first reforms still perpetuated regional subdivisions and the old, inherited privileges. In their view, total abolition of the domains was the precondition of national unity. Accordingly, a few of the Meiji leaders presented all the daimyo with a fait accompli. In March 1869 a memorial addressed to the emperor put the lands of Satsuma, Chosu, Tosa, and Hizen at his disposal. Formulated in the language of a "feudal submission," the memorial cited as its warrant the shogunal usurpation of imperial authority some seven centuries earlier. The outcome of this bold move was uncertain. There was considerable opposition from samurai conservatives, and the principal Meiji leaders made military preparations in the event of a head-on clash. But by July 1869 an imperial decree announced the court's acceptance of the proposal and ordered all other daimyo to follow suit. Clearly, this was a genuine "return of authority" to the emperor. For it marked a decisive break with the "privatization of authority" in the hands of the daimyo which had characterized Japanese society for a millennium.

Under the new system, the daimyo became governors of lands which were transformed from domains into prefectures. As governors, they would retain one-tenth of the former domain revenue as their household expenses. In the end, the daimyo fell in line because the new system appeared to preserve their distinguished social and economic position. Nevertheless, the abolition of the domains turned relatively autonomous local hierarchies with regional loyalties into factions struggling for influence at the center. This movement toward national unification was paralleled by decrees which simplified the existing hierarchy of social rank. Court nobles and daimyo were transformed into a single order of aristocracy (*kazoku*), and all samurai were divided into two broad categories of gentry (*shizoku*) and foot soldiers (*sotsu*).

It was soon evident that the abolition of domains would have far-reaching repercussions. In a policy statement of 1870, Iwakura Tomomi (an important Meiji leader of the court nobility) declared that tax collection must be unified under a central authority to ensure financial stability and an equality of burdens among the regions of the country. Samurai privilege should be brought to an end since stipends from public funds were not warranted in the absence of military and administrative service. Iwakura also advocated a national system of education divorced from the Confucian tradition and a modern national army based on conscription.[60] These influential views foreshadowed the measures which were eventually adopted.

Abolition of the domains involved half a million samurai. Inducing samurai compliance was a critical problem, since the burden of change fell disproportionately on them. When the domains were abolished, the government had to assume responsibility for collecting the land tax throughout the country as well as for paying stipends to the samurai. As a first step, the imperial government urged the prefectures to reduce samurai stipends. In loyalist areas like Satsuma, Choshu, and Tosa, reformers responded by cutting stipends to the bone, while rewarding men of ability with increased stipends in return for administrative or military service. The highest stipends were cut to some 10 percent of their former value, while samurai families of the middle and lower ranks were often reduced to a bare subsistence. Consequently, between 1870 and 1873, the amount required for stipends was reduced from one-half to one-third of the land tax. Further reductions could not be accomplished without causing real hardship.

Abolition of the domains also jeopardized the symbolic position of the samurai. Commoners received permission to intermarry with members of the newly established peerage (kazoku). At the same time, samurai lost the right to use their swords on commoners to avenge an offense. In 1871 they were permitted to go about without wearing their swords, and in 1872 they were officially permitted to engage in trade or farming.

Under the Tokugawa system, military units were loyal to the daimyo in each domain, and the daimyo, in turn, was bound in loyalty to the shogun. In 1870 Iwakura Tomomi suggested that units should be detached from their local affiliation so as to make them part of a truly national army. Okubo Toshimichi, the main Meiji leader from Satsuma, urged military reviews by the emperor so that the men would "become soldiers of the court."[61] Such proposals were highly controversial; the first proponent of national conscription (Omura Masujiro) was assassinated at the end of 1869. Nevertheless, in 1873 an imperial edict established a conscript army in which all men, regardless of social background, were made liable for three years of active military service, followed by four years in the reserves. This was probably the most revolutionary step of the Meiji leaders. Commoners had been denied the right even to possess swords for almost three centuries; the distinction between samurai and commoners had depended on the privileged military status of the former. Now, suddenly, the masses were furnished with arms. This was a drastic change toward equality a mere five years after the overthrow of the Tokugawa and was, therefore, circumscribed by strict military discipline.

The Meiji leaders were much more cautious about other moves toward equality, but they were determined to put an end to samurai privileges. While the 1873 edict sought to placate samurai opinion by its national appeals, the executive council of the Meiji government used the occasion for a slashing attack on samurai pretensions. A separate declaration called the samurai of the Tokugawa period obstinate and turbulent, living at the expense of others. Now, after the abolition of domains and the establishment of national conscription, samurai like commoners were "subjects of the Empire."

> After living a life of idleness for generations, the samurai have had their stipends reduced and have been authorized to take off their swords, so that all strata of the people may finally gain their rights to liberty. By this innovation the rulers and the ruled will be put on the same basis, the rights of the people will be equal, and the way will be cleared for the unity of soldier and peasant.[62]

It is symptomatic of the Meiji Restoration that perhaps the first *official* reference to the rights of the people occurred in this military context. The equality of the samurai and the commoners consisted in their equal liability to render military service under the emperor.

Beasley has shown that by 1873 stipend payments by the government to the samurai still amounted to one-fourth of total revenue, or one-third of the land tax.[63] If the government had accepted this situation, a large part of its revenue would have become a fixed expenditure. On the other hand, abolition of the stipends meant a direct attack on the livelihood of the samurai. The Meiji leaders understood the plight of the samurai whose background they shared, but they were determined to proceed in the spirit of service with which that background had imbued them. In 1873 the higher stipends were taxed for the first time. Samurai receiving 100 koku or less were allowed to receive cash payments in lieu of rice stipends. This measure provided capital for middle and lower samurai who could then engage in farming or trade. By 1876 the commutation of rice stipends into cash payments was made compulsory at the same time that a law was passed banning the wearing of swords.

Thus, the main burden of Japan's national revolution had been imposed on the samurai. In the initial period, the great majority of samurai felt almost as excluded from the new ruling group as they had from the shogunate. They had expected that overthrow of the Tokugawa would be followed by prompt expulsion of foreigners, only to find that the new government sought accommodation with foreign powers and proceeded to destroy the domains as well as samurai privileges. But while its measures provoked great anxiety among the samurai, the Meiji government also depended on them for political support. The points of friction are apparent from a memorial left by a samurai of Kagoshima who committed suicide in August 1870 as an act of public protest. His grievances were that appointments went to careerists rather than men of true merit, that expediency prevailed everywhere, that high prices, high taxes, railways, and treaties with foreign powers violated the spirit of the loyalist movement. These complaints reflect not only the disappointment of antibakufu samurai, but the continuation into the Meiji period of problems that had been at the root of samurai debts, peasant protest, and antiforeign sentiment during the Tokugawa era.[64]

In the words of one Meiji leader, the samurai were "absurdly misinformed about the world at large."[65] But the government had to deal with the more fanatic "men of spirit" all the same. Those imprisoned by the Tokugawa were released and pardoned. The men were rewarded and honored, but rarely given responsibility. More positively, provision was made early in 1868 for the domains to send delegates to a samurai assembly. Reorganized several times during its brief existence, this assembly permitted the debate of such issues as the abolition of domains, the wearing of two swords, forced loans, and the prohibition of Christianity. But this airing of "feudal opinion" was terminated in July 1869, presumably because the government felt strong enough by then to do without such consultation. Exploitation of the emperor's prestige was probably a more important means of legitimation. In the past leading samurai had called on, and manipulated, the ruling daimyo to endorse policies which they had devised. Now, the government manipulated the emperor's symbolic endorsement of all decision-making in much the same way. But appeals to this new imperial legitimacy did not silence controversy within the ruling oligarchy. The leaders of reform were apprehensive. Some suggested the idea of a war against Korea in order to rally people to a national cause and divert their attention from the grievances provoked by the reforms. But senior officials such as Iwakura, Okubo, and Kido opposed this Korean project and secured the emperor's concurrence, whereupon five members of the Meiji government resigned.

The initial unity of the ruling group was destroyed. Eto Shimpei of Hizen and Saigo Takamori of Satsuma, who had resigned over the Korean issue, withdrew to their home territories. Eto raised the flag of revolt in 1874 and was quickly crushed by government forces. Saigo worked for local reform until the mandatory commutation of stipends in 1876 aroused the desperation of conservative samurai who rejected trade or farming as incompatible with their privileged status. In the end,

Saigo's loyalties were with these samurai, whose ideals he shared, even though he thought their plans for a revolt ill-advised. He could not refuse them when the men put themselves under his leadership in a campaign which the government suppressed only with difficulty. Saigo's death by suicide on the battlefield in 1877 was avenged in the following year by the assassination of Okubo Toshimichi, the leading figure of early Meiji reform.

A politics of violence had accompanied the restoration movement after 1853. Attacks against foreigners and some Meiji leaders also followed the overthrow of the shogunate in 1868, when it became apparent that the new government would not expel foreign representatives. Sporadic violence against high officials accompanied the reforms of the 1870s and 1880s. Such protest originated in the "loyalist" circles of middle and lower samurai, especially those of Satsuma, Choshu, and Hizen. The violence aroused by temporizing foreign policies and social degradation also symbolized the more diffuse commitment to a cult of action with which centuries of idealization had imbued Japanese life. This samurai legacy outlasted the disappearance of the samurai as a class.

The leaders of the Meiji government undertook drastic reforms in the interest of national survival. Voluntary sacrifice to fulfill a personal duty to the emperor was an act of filial loyalty. Samurai leaders causing the sacrifice of personal interests of the samurai were of critical importance in the restoration. To assess that importance one need only imagine what would have happened if the same burdens had been imposed by leaders representing the despised class of wealthy merchants. In the 1860s, the samurai comprised about half a million households and two million persons in a population of thirty million (1872). By contrast, European aristocracies numbered in the thousands or at most tens of thousands, representing less than 1 percent of the population, not 5 or 6 percent as in Japan.[66] Separation from the land was the other unusual feature. The samurai provided a ready reservoir of qualified personnel available and eager for public employment. The Meiji government had no need to go outside the ranks of the samurai and also no incentive to do so.

Hall has identified twenty-seven individuals as the most prominent leaders of the Meiji Restoration. Twenty-one of them were from the four tozama han of Satsuma, Choshu, Tosa, and Hizen. Three others came from two more tozama han (Echizen, Kumamoto), one was a bakufu official, and two were court nobles from Kyoto. In 1868 the average age of this group was slightly over thirty. For the most part, these men were lower samurai who had begun their careers in their respective domains, often in military service. All members of the group were highly educated, and a good many had specialized training as well as contact with Western culture. Despite their youth, they had been advisors to their daimyo, agents on diplomatic missions, and organizers of military units. Brought up in the samurai code, they had been subject to military discipline and indoctrinated in the Confucian virtues of loyalty and dedication. Many of them knew one another from their days together at fencing school, or through negotiations in which they had engaged on behalf of their domains.[67]

A study of the larger Meiji elite is of interest here, because it shows that court nobles and younger samurai were the leaders who transformed their own class socially and economically. Bernard Silberman's study of the Meiji ministers is based on a sample of 253 individuals and includes 80 percent of those who held "high office" in the Meiji government from 1868 to 1873. This was clearly a very distinguished group, since of those who remained in office until 1900, between 70 and 80 percent occupied ministerial or vice-ministerial positions. The Meiji leadership represented a shift brought about by the restoration. Under the Tokugawa government, neither court nobles (kuge) nor lower samurai had held high administrative office, these being reserved for daimyo and upper samurai. Members from these previously excluded groups had become active politically between 1853 and 1868, and after 1868 they comprised 65 percent of the Meiji administrative elite.[68]

The different groups within the Japanese aristocracy did not enter the race for advancement under the Meiji dynasty with equal chances of success. Much depended on the type of education they had received before 1868. Court nobles, daimyo, and upper samurai had had a traditional, Confucian education, and most of them were unsuccessful after 1875. However, some of these men had also acquired Western learning, and they had more successful careers in the Meiji era. Among lower samurai, the proportion of those who had received a Western education was highest, and so was the proportion of those with successful careers after 1875.

Regional origin and social status also affected careers under the Meiji. Daimyo and samurai from the tozama domains as well as the Kyoto nobility had been subject to special controls by the Tokugawa, and the Meiji government reversed this tendency. Of the 253 persons in Professor Silberman's sample, 124 came from tozama domains, 75 from Kyoto, 34 from fudai or Tokugawa houses, and 6 from Edo.[69] During the first few years after 1868, the Meiji leadership was largely recruited from those who had prominently participated in the restoration movement, but this criterion became obsolete. The marked consensus on goals among the leaders seems to have extended to the personnel policies of the new government. For almost a generation after 1868, Meiji officials were recruited from samurai families, albeit with an increasing emphasis on ability rather than social origin. But by the 1890s, public employment came to be based on formal education and civil service examination.[70] It is as if successive Meiji governments had decided to give the samurai an advantage in public employment as recompense for their sacrifices. But after about twenty years, standards of performance rather than social and regional background were to be the main criteria. By the 1880s, Japanese society had been transformed, as had the foundations of samurai existence.

Did the reforms undertaken by the Meiji leaders constitute a revolution? It is conventional to identify all revolutions with lower class movements, and there was no widespread popular uprising in the overthrow of the Tokugawa regime. Rather, it was a "revolution from above" such as some Prussian reform ministers had had in mind, but did not accomplish. The Meiji Restoration was accomplished by members of the ruling class who had been disadvantaged under the Tokugawa shogunate. Tokugawa officials were ousted summarily after 1868, and higher government positions came into the hands of those court nobles and samurai who had previously been excluded from political participation. If the restoration had been confined to this change of personnel, one would be entitled to speak only of a coup d'état. In fact, the Meiji government went on to restructure the whole social and political order, and the change it accomplished should therefore be considered revolutionary. Should this restructuring be called a revolution, even though it was undertaken in the interest of national survival and quickly entailed the imposition of new restraints? It should because both nationalism and the reassertion of authority are found in many (possibly in all) modern revolutions. (For that reason Beasley's suggestion of the term *national revolution* seems to me less apt than Thomas Smith's *aristocratic revolution*.) A revolution occurs when the social order it seeks to overthrow is drastically transformed, and this was the case in Japan in the years following 1868.

The leaders of the restoration movement had struggled to expand public debate in order to make the Tokugawa shogunate more effective. In the end increased participation was denied them, the regime itself became helpless, and they succeeded in overthrowing the shogunate by recourse to the traditional symbol of the emperor. Once they had achieved control of the new government, the Meiji leaders were determined to effect major changes in the political and social structure of the Tokugawa order but to prevent the "democratization" of Japanese society. They were aware of the major deprivations imposed on the samurai with whom they identified. Hence, they took measures to make the drastic changes they introduced psychologically acceptable. The charter oath of 1868 is an example of such symbolic legitimation. It combined reverence toward the emperor with a kind of representation which publicly favored the aristocracy. At the same time, it contained the main points of the new governmental policy which imposed sacrifices on that aristocracy.

Henceforth, the imperial court would decide matters of public policy in the interest of the country rather than of a particular faction like the Tokugawa. The oath committed all classes to the promotion of national goals, a marked departure from the earlier emphasis on samurai loyalty to each daimyo and his domain. The oath refers to "people," and this wording may have been borrowed from the language of Western constitutionalism. But the Japanese reference was to people who counted, that is, members of the aristocracy who preempted participation in politics under the Meiji government. Rich farmers and merchants were added only later. Under the Tokugawa shogunate, policy discussions had been confined to bakufu officials and a select group of daimyo. Under the new Meiji government, the "people" legitimately concerned with politics were only those men of samurai background who were properly qualified to participate. The charter oath referred to the common people, but emphasized that "a widely convoked assembly" shall be established and that "all civil and military officials shall be allowed to fulfill their aspirations." Revocation of the policy of exclusion ("base customs from the past") and commitment of the country to observance of treaty obligations ("principles of international justice") were just as telltale and roundabout. The oath also endorsed the search for knowledge "throughout the world" in order to strengthen the country, thus ending by imperial sanction the long debate over Western learning.[71]

The Meiji government, like the Tokugawa earlier, had to contend with samurai who upheld the Confucian ideals and expected more radical measures against foreigners, as well as samurai who expected more radical internal reforms. All negotiations with foreign powers were suspect in conservative circles. Appeasement of samurai conservatives was also complicated by the necessity of abolishing samurai privileges. At the same time, official proposals for a constitutional regime were suspect to Japanese reformers who anticipated various safeguards of imperial authority. Moreover, foreign advisors expressed conflicting Western expectations regarding a proper constitutional system, and some of them had to be fulfilled if Japan was to gain international recognition. The Meiji leaders realized that "popular" participation would jeopardize their own oligarchic control and would probably conflict with their capacity for decisive action.

Many of these cross-currents are reflected in the following comments by Ito Hirobumi (1841–1909), the principal figure in the second generation of Meiji oligarchs and the main author of the Meiji constitution of 1889. Reflecting on the movement for a constitution in the 1870s, Ito observed,

We were just then in an age of transition. The opinions prevailing in the country were extremely heterogeneous, and often diametrically opposed to each other. We had survivors of former generations who were still full of theocratic ideas, and who believed that any attempt to restrict an imperial prerogative amounted to something like high treason. On the other hand there was a large and powerful body of the younger generation educated at the time when the Manchester theory was in vogue, and who in consequence were ultra-radical in their ideas of freedom. Members of the bureaucracy were prone to lend willing ears to the German doctrinaires of the reactionary period, while, on the other hand, the educated politicians among the people having not yet tasted the bitter significance of administrative responsibility, were liable to be more influenced by the dazzling words and lucid theories of Montesquieu, Rousseau and similar French writers. . . . The virtues necessary for the smooth working of any constitution, such as love of freedom of speech, love of publicity of proceedings, the spirit of tolerance for opinions opposed to one's own, etc., had yet to be learned by long experience.

It was under these circumstances that the first draft of the Constitution was made and submitted to His Majesty. . . .[72]

Ito's comments describe the situation very well, but do not describe the dilemma of reconciling constitutionalism with the maintenance of strict authority. The overthrow of the Tokugawa regime and the institution of Meiji reforms required strong leadership. The preference for central authority was apparent in the use of "public opinion" as a synonym of national unity against the "private opinion" of shogunal or han officials. Similarly, the memorial initiating the abolition of domains had as its major aim the preservation of "one central body of government and one universal authority."[73] The imperial edicts on the code of education and national conscription (1872) transformed education and military service from a samurai privilege into a duty of citizenship and hence strengthened central authority further. In the long deliberations leading up to the Meiji constitution, this emphasis on authority was deliberately identified with the imperial house. As Ito observed, constitutionalism had ancient and specifically religious antecedents in Europe. There were no such antecedents in Japan: "The one institution which can become the cornerstone of our constitution is the Imperial House. . . . For this reason the first principle of our constitution is the respect for the sovereign rights of the emperor."[74]

Nevertheless, all members of the Meiji oligarchy favored a *constitutional* regime. In the statement just quoted, Ito explains that checks and balances must be established, ministers must be held responsible if "the danger of abuse in the exercise of sovereign powers" is to be prevented. He thus agreed with all his colleagues that a properly Japanese constitutional system would safeguard both "the principle of monarchical rights and the principle of joint rule of sovereign and subjects."[75] In fact, Ito gave a fine account of the reasons why he and his colleagues favored constitutionalism despite their authoritarian tradition.

> The present political disturbance [of the 1870s] is symptomatic of a general trend sweeping the whole world and is not limited to a single nation or province. About a hundred years ago the revolutions in Europe started in France and spread gradually to other European nations. The momentum of these revolutions gained strength and has come to constitute a tremendous force. Sooner or later practically all nations . . . will feel the impact of this force and change their form of government. The change from old to new was accompanied by violent disturbances. The disturbances have lasted to this very day. An enlightened ruler and his wise ministers would control and divert the force towards a solidifying of the government. To achieve this, all despotic conduct must be abandoned, and there can be no avoiding a sharing of the government's power with the people. . . .

But while these general trends were "sweeping the whole world," Ito made clear that in Japan they would be adopted deliberately and very gradually:

> Even as we control the trends, there will be no violence, and even when ideas are given free reign they will not lead [people] astray. Progress will be orderly and we will set the pace of progress, and the passage of time will bring about the normalization of the trends.[76]

This statement speaks with confidence of control and orderly progress. But how could a constitutional regime, responsive to the demands and rights of the public, be made compatible with the sovereign authority of the emperor?

The Meiji leaders were aware of this dilemma. Only three years after the restoration, the Iwakura mission to Europe and America was charged with the task of studying "foreign laws, customs and institutions and of recommending those which should be adopted by the Japanese."[77] Members of the mission like Kido Koin, Okubo Toshimichi, and Iwakura Tomomi returned with tentative proposals for gradual steps toward constitutional reform.

Meanwhile, a group of more radical constitutionalists had formed within the Meiji government. When they resigned after their proposal of war against Korea was rejected, they submitted a memorial (1874) calling for the immediate election of a popular assembly. The memorial stated that, as matters stood, the governing power did not lie either with the imperial house or the people, but solely with the officials. The authors of the memorial were junior councillors under the leadership of Itagaki Taisuke, a Tosa loyalist of middle samurai background. They challenged the argument of more gradualist reformers, like the members of the Iwakura mission. In their view, the Japanese were ready for a constitution.

Iwakura Mission, 1871
A group portrait of this mission which includes (from left to right) Kido Koin, Yamaguchi
Hisayoshi, Iwakura Tomomi, Ito Hirobumi, and Okubo Toshimichi. The four men from
tozama han have adopted Western clothing whereas Iwakura, the court noble, still appears
in the traditional attire. (Kodansha International)

> The reason why foreigners were so slow and gradual in developing a con-
> stitutional form of government was because they did not have any example
> before them. But now the Japanese had such an example before their eyes
> and could imitate it. Just as in the technical sphere Japan was not waiting to
> invent all the new machines and use new methods of research but was adopt-
> ing what had already been invented in other countries, so also in the political
> sphere Japan could without any gradualism adopt systems perfected in other
> nations.[78]

Yet these "radicals" were no democrats. They were concerned with the
strength of the country, not the liberty of its citizens. They accepted
without question that political rights would be given only to samurai,
rich farmers, and merchants. Pittau has examined the ensuing debate
in the years 1874–1878 and concludes that much of it revealed "a mixture of liberal ideals and despotic methods."[79]

By 1878 the Meiji government had prepared the first draft of a
constitution which reflected the widespread study of Western parliamentary models. At the time, Iwakura Tomomi remained as the principal survivor of the original Meiji leadership. Alarmed at the agitation

for radical reform and the government's own draft proposal, he petitioned the throne in 1879 to order the junior councillors to present their views on a constitution. Such presentations were duly submitted. Through the supreme authority of the throne, the debate was removed from the public forum and made a matter of policy determination at the highest level. To be sure, public debate continued. But the effect of Iwakura's initiative was to place constitutional reform on the agenda of the government itself. As Inoue Kowashi pointed out (in 1881), the Meiji government must assume leadership on the constitutional issue. If this opportunity was left unused for two or three years, "public opinion will cast aside the draft of a constitution presented by the government, and the private drafts of the constitution will win out in the end."[80]

By the end of 1881, the outlines of the official position had been fixed. On October 12 of that year, the main spokesman for constitutional reform along British lines (Okuma Shigenobu) was ousted from the government, and an imperial decree promised the establishment of a parliament by 1890. Shortly thereafter, a committee was appointed under the chairmanship of Ito Hirobumi, charged with the preparation of a constitution.[81]

In March 1882 Ito was ordered to lead another study mission to Europe. He returned in August 1883, and the final text of the Meiji constitution was promulgated from the throne in 1889. The debate on a constitution had been a main focus of Japanese politics since the early 1870s. It had turned on the suitability of Western precedents for Japan. The Meiji government desired its own principles, but did not want to forego available sources of knowledge and legitimation. In 1878, four years prior to Ito's mission, the government had hired the German constitutional lawyer Hermann Roesler. And in 1881, Iwakura Tomomi defined the government's position, based on the preparatory work of Roesler, Inoue, and Ito. This "Opinion on the Constitution" represents the consensus of those principally responsible for the Meiji constitution of 1889. The guidelines incorporate what the second generation of Meiji oligarchs understood as a proper blend of imperial supremacy with the constitutional protection of liberty, property, and personal security— that is, between Japanese tradition and European institutional models.

The Japanese had several models from which to choose. In England, sovereignty was nominally shared between king and parliament. In fact, the king entrusted all political authority to the prime minister who depended on a parliamentary majority. Hence in practice, parliament was supreme, while the king's position was similar to that of the Japanese emperor prior to the restoration. By contrast, the Prussian system put all executive power in the hands of the king. The Prussian prime minister was appointed by the king without any consideration of parliamentary majorities. Under this system, all ministers were directly and solely responsible to the king. As Iwakura's statement puts it,

> If we plan to establish a constitutional government in our country and open a parliament, we will be creating something new. The problem is: shall we follow the English model and establish a party government, making the parliamentary majority responsible for the administration? Or shall we, following the principle of gradualism, grant only legislative power and reserve the executive power to the Emperor, according to the Prussian model?[82]

The English constitution presupposed a two-party system with a sufficient supply of persons in both parties capable of taking over the administration of affairs. Such conditions did not exist in Japan. Hence, the Prussian system seemed more appropriate.

As in Prussia, the constitution should be created as a gift of the emperor to the nation. Like the Prussian king, "the Emperor shall have supreme command over the army and navy, declare war, make peace, conclude treaties, etc.; moreover, the Emperor will direct the national administration."[83] Thus, the emperor would have the power to appoint and dismiss ministers and high officials. To ensure that the cabinet would not be controlled by parliament, a provision should be adopted for continuation of taxes from the previous year in case the assembly and the cabinet could not agree on the annual budget. Finally, with regard to the rights of citizens, Iwakura's "opinion" stated that "constitutional provisions of other nations should be consulted," but care should be taken to ensure a gradual approach toward constitutional government. The Prussian model appealed to the Meiji leaders because it made the king (or emperor) the father of his people. His power and sanctified authority permitted no diminution, stood above all controversy, and was justified by the care he bestowed on all his subjects. In the Japanese version, this outlook was tied directly to the mythological origin and age-old tradition of the imperial house.[k]

Yet this acceptance of the Prussian model created a major problem as well. Earlier, Ito had made it clear that a constitution *meant* safeguards against the abuse of sovereign power. But immediately after the emperor issued the Meiji constitution, he declared,

> Although it is impossible to avoid the rise of political groups in any parliament or society, a government party is most improper. . . . The emperor stands above the people and apart from every party. Consequently, the government cannot favor one party above the other. It must be fair and impar-

---

[k]To a legal rationalist like Roesler, this transcendental legitimation of imperial authority was unacceptable—despite his unqualified justification of monarchical authority in Wilhelmian Germany in other respects.

tial. And the prime minister . . . who assists the emperor, must not allow the government to be manipulated by the parties.

Even Ito's own followers were confused. Inoue stated that apparently Ito intended "to apply completely the Bismarckian absolute state to Japan." Ito responded by asking whether state ministers must then be responsible to the Diet. Inoue answered "absolutely not," but then continued, "There is no justification for the emperor to place confidence in a cabinet that has nothing to do with public opinion. Therefore, I believe that, though from the point of legal theory the state ministers are responsible to the emperor, actually they are responsible to the people through the Diet."[84]

This confusion was an integral part of the Meiji Restoration. To a man, the Meiji oligarchs favored authoritarian rule under the mantle of imperial sanction. But that position depended on the homogeneous outlook of the restoration movement, and unity disappeared once the Tokugawa shogunate was overthrown. Against a background of centuries of absolutist rule, it was agonizingly difficult to accept political parties and parliamentary responsibility, the two institutions which were implementing the mandate of the people by the end of the nineteenth century. The Meiji constitution of 1889 sought to protect authoritarian rule under the emperor against the growth of parties and their influence on public affairs, but this attempt did not succeed. Ito Hirobumi, the architect of the constitution, finally accepted the inevitability and even the utility of political parties. Just as the Tokugawa shogunate had clothed absolutist rule in the language of feudal loyalty, so Meiji governments came to clothe a government of elite groups in the language of constitutionalism and imperial supremacy. Indirectly and reluctantly, Japanese leaders began to accept the view that ministers formally responsible to the emperor must in practice be responsible to an elected Diet representing the people. Once its isolation was ended, Japan did not escape the momentum of the European revolutions.

13

NATION-BUILDING: RUSSIA

EﾠNGLAND, France, Germany, and Japan each went through its own transition from an old to a new system of authority. Where once kings had ruled and the people were excluded from public affairs, new structures of authority emerged. The transition from the authority of kings to a mandate of the people is a protracted process which was centuries in the making. One can examine these transitions at any time and attempt to distinguish between the legacies from a country's past (tradition) and the signs of change which point to the future (modernity). The distinction is useful for analytic purposes, but one should remember that every historical development is continuous. Legacies from the past are the ever-present context in which changes toward the future occur.

Russia emerged as a unified state only after long wars against enemies to the east, the south, and the west. The early Byzantine influence and the impact of Mongol overlordship reinforced Russia's cultural isolation, which was also increased by the Orthodox church and its hostility to foreign ideas. Russia's transition from the seventeenth to the nineteenth centuries involved a mobilization of resources, people, and ideas through trade, manufacture, and population increase as well as through war and literacy. Autocratic rulers attempted to develop their country by means of a "well-ordered police state," creating not only a great European power but a rising cultural and national awareness of the people. This transition of Russia was perhaps more strongly influenced by foreign cultures and empires than the development of any other country considered here.

In England, a long period of invasions ended with the Norman conquest, and although English relations with the Continent remained close, the country developed a strong autonomy. The sixteenth and seventeenth centuries in particular witnessed an intense period of nation-building which was stimulated by a fear of Spanish and Catholic dominance. In medieval Germany, political fragmentation was institutionalized by the Peace of Westphalia (1648). Then, under the stimulus of French absolutism and the French revolution, this fragmentation coincided with an extraordinary cultural flowering in the age of Lessing, Schiller, and Goethe, of Kant, Fichte, and Hegel. Japan was politically unified at an early time and was not conquered until 1945. Despite this very prolonged seclusion, the country had to cope from the beginning with the cultural influences of the highly sophisticated civilization of China. Japan has a longer history than any other country of developing an indigenous culture through a process of adapting the ideal models of another culture. The imperial court at Kyoto never lost its pattern-setting influence on the Japanese people; thus, after 1600 the country could begin its political consolidation with an ancient and highly stylized culture virtually intact.

A country such as Japan, effectively free of conquests for more than a millennium, which preserves its territorial integrity despite internal conflicts, is clearly distinguished from a country such as Russia which is exposed to invasions from all sides for some nine centuries and which emerges as a unified state only after some seven centuries. The cultural contrast is more difficult to make, though it may be as important as the political. How does one compare the Japanese imperial court and the Russian Orthodox church, which were both influenced by military and political forces? Both became centers of pervasive and enduring cultural influence. The Japanese court involved an aristocratic elite surrounding the divinely descended emperor, while the Orthodox church involved a hierarchy of ecclesiastics from the Metropolitan down to a mass of illiterate priests. The Japanese court culture provided a ritual and esthetic elaboration of sensibilities inspired by the nature worship of Shinto, whereas Russian religious culture developed a ritual and esthetic elaboration of sensibilities inspired by the worship of God and Christ. The possibilities of such comparison lie outside the framework of this study. They are noted here, nevertheless, because they underscore that Japan's seclusion and resistance to change were fostered by prolonged cultural autonomy and the absence of conquest, whereas Russia's isolation and resistance to change developed despite repeated conquests and massive influences from abroad.

The following discussion begins with Russia during the seventeenth century, when France was at the height of its continental influence. The great religious schism, the early influx of foreigners and alien ideas, and incipient economic changes suggest that Russia was slowly coming out of its cultural isolation. The autocratic transformation of Russia began with the draconian measures of Peter I (the Great, 1682–1725). Peter's impact on Russia had particular importance for the Russian aristocracy. Further autocratic reforms occurred under the reigns of Peter III (1762) and Catherine II (the Great, 1762–1796). All these initial steps toward a break with long-established traditions were undertaken under the influence of Western ideas. These eighteenth-century developments were continued by the tsarist reigns from Paul I (1796–1801) to Nicholas I (1825–1855), which sponsored Western ideas and education to provide needed skills. The story of Western models and Russian responses can best be told consecutively, for the gradual transformation of Russia's "backwardness" is indistinguishable from its responses to the West.

AUTOCRATIC TRADITIONS, WESTERN MODELS, AND NATIVE RESPONSES

In the sixteenth and seventeenth centuries, Russia was an inward-looking, provincial society on an imperial scale, undeveloped economically and isolated culturally. At the same time, the late Renaissance and the Reformation, with their individualism and cultural efflorescence, marked the countries of Western Europe.[1] Russia's isolation was guarded by the church through its control of education. Learning hardly went

Reception of Foreigners at the Court of Alexis (1645–1676)
Russia had great need of foreign skills, but when foreigners arrived in Moscow they were permitted to live and conduct their affairs only in rigidly segregated areas. In this scene the tsar has surrounded himself with boyars, and after each foreigner is introduced the tsar performs a ritual ablution to cleanse himself of contamination. (Olearius, *Voyages,* 1662)

beyond elementary skills of reading and writing. Biblical and liturgical texts were memorized, and a considerable part of the clergy remained illiterate. The country lacked secular schools and a leisure class of educated people who could pursue ideas or scientific work free of church control. Russia did not possess a single university, which meant that there was no formal training in jurisprudence, medicine, and astronomy —with the addition of theology, the established subjects of training in Western universities. Moreover, Russians were usually forbidden to travel abroad, because relations with other people were considered a profanation, and the Russian church strongly opposed any learning that detracted from religious worship. As a consequence, the church controlled almost the entire cultural life of the country. Secular knowledge was regarded as equivalent to heresy, arithmetic and geometry were treated as magic arts, and science generally was seen as the work of Antichrist.

Western European cities had been centers of trade and cosmopolitan contact for centuries, but this was not true of Russian towns. Instead, the merchants and artisans were organized by the government so as to ensure the payment of taxes and the performance of services. This did not preclude individual initiative and success even on a large scale, and the government encouraged such success by grants of monopolies and special honors. But men of wealth who were thus distinguished also had to pay the highest taxes, account for their receipts, and be personally liable for various services. Applications for exemption from such duties were denied, causing merchants typically to resort to subterfuge. A contemporary report on their attitude describes not only the merchants but also a rather general reaction to government.

> The more they have, the more danger they are in, not only of their goods, but of their lives also. And if they have anything, they conceal it all they can, sometimes conveying it into monasteries, sometimes hiding it under the ground, and in woods, as men are wont to do where they are in fear of foreign invasion. . . . I have seen them sometimes when they have laid open their commodities for a liking [for approval] . . . to look still behind them and towards every door; as men in some fear that looked to be set upon and surprised by some enemy. Whereof asking the cause, I found it to be this, that they have doubted lest some nobleman or *syn boiarskii* of the Emperor's had been in company and so laid a train upon them to prey upon their commodities per force.[2]

Entry in the roster of wholesale merchants (*gosti*) had certain advantages, such as the permission to travel and the right to invest in land. But merchants were in a precarious position and would even discontinue their commercial activities if the government obliged them to provide special services. Under these conditions the merchants did not acquire a cosmopolitan outlook.[3]

Yet there were signs of change even within the framework of Muscovite Russia. Between 1500 and 1700, the country was at war for 136 years, and during the seventeenth century its armed forces were greatly enlarged and reorganized, with firearms providing a new military technology.[4] The country's territories were expanded through conquest of borderlands and expansion into Siberia at the same time that defense headquarters were established against Poland, the Crimea, and Sweden. In the beginning of the seventeenth century, maintenance of the army required almost 250,000 rubles, and by 1680 that amount had tripled, absorbing half the state budget. Such a burden could not have been sustained without some development of the country's resources. Contacts with foreign powers expanded. Trade and production for the market increased, as did the number of specialized markets for grains, salt, furs, leather goods, cotton, and metal products. By the middle of the seventeenth century, Moscow had become one of the largest cities in Europe with 200,000 inhabitants and many more suburban and temporary residents. The city retained regular marketing relations with some 150 towns and 40 districts. In addition, specialized markets existed in many places which provided temporary centers of economic activity. A detailed study of "manufactories" in the seventeenth century (iron mills, glass and leather factories, paper mills) records 57 such establishments, most of them built after 1620 by foreigners or under state auspices. The tsars increased the number of ministries and appointed more officials in order to cope with the expanding tasks of government. Even a regular postal service was established with several European countries. During the eighteenth century, economic development further increased. Under Peter I there were only 98 factories in Russia; by 1762 there were ten times that number; and at the death of Catherine II (1796), a total of 3,161. The last three decades of the century witnessed a fourfold increase of exports and imports.[5]

Demographic factors account for much of Russia's rise as a major European power. The first census of the taxable male population (1719) showed a total of 7.8 million. By the seventh census of 1815, that figure had increased to 21.5 million. This increase was partly due to the substantial territorial acquisitions in the intervening century. Another set of figures indicates that between 1762 and 1796 Russia's total population rose from 19 to 29 million.[6] Census-taking was rudimentary and the units counted varied, but there is no doubt that the country's population increased substantially. Until well into the nineteenth century, more than 90 percent of the people lived on the land, and the bulk of state revenue and of the income of the aristocracy came from agriculture.

There were also signs of cultural change in Muscovite Russia. By the seventeenth century, Kiev had become a center of growing intellectual activity. Located in the Ukraine, in a frontier area between Moscow,

Lithuania, and Poland, the city was under Polish rule and inevitably involved in the struggles for territorial supremacy. Polish power over the Ukraine declined in the 1660s, and in 1667 Muscovy annexed the left bank of the Dnieper.

> [But] the balance of cultural forces did not shift accordingly. Though the Muscovites grew strong enough to annex much of the Ukraine, their intellectual strength had not increased. When Kiev became a Muscovite city, from the cultural standpoint it was Kiev which was increasingly influencing Moscow, not the reverse. . . .

The reason for Kiev's cultural dominance was that the city had become a center of learning. In the Monastery of the Caves, Peter Mogila, the metropolitan of the Orthodox church (from 1633), used the method of Roman Catholic education and taught in Latin. This meant that the cultural level of religious instruction was significantly raised, even though no doctrinal change was contemplated. Moscow soon adopted these innovations in the technique of instruction.[7]

In Moscow itself, Kievan and other influences led to an incongruous mixture of cultural elements, best exemplified by Tsar Alexis (1645–1676). The tsar was interested in medicine and astronomy, but he was also a deeply religious man who gathered around him a group of young priests eager to rejuvenate the Orthodox church. These were moderate reformers: Many came from Kiev and all were dedicated to increasing the range of learning, so long as there was no challenge to Orthodox beliefs. Even so, Kievan learning was suspect in the eyes of those who opposed *all* reform of the Orthodox church, because for them the original Doctrine of the Lord was a spiritual treasure that must not be diminished. Such suspicion became more pronounced when one of the reformers, Nikon, was appointed patriarch (1652–1666). Nikon's reforms no longer seemed moderate when he revived the old controversy over printed ecclesiastical books.

These books with all their idiosyncrasies, errors, and interpolations were the token of Russian Orthodoxy from 1500 onward, and any change was considered tantamount to heresy. Nevertheless, Nikon ordered a revision of the texts and instituted the Greek practice of making the sign of the cross with three fingers and three "hallelujahs" in lieu of the Muscovite practice of two fingers and two "hallelujahs." In the Orthodox church, icons portraying saints making the sign of the cross were venerated as holy images; thus, a change of making that sign appeared literally as desecration. In a council of 1656, Nikon even declared that although he was a Russian he had the faith and ideas of a Greek, and he proceeded to buttress his position by endorsements from church councils, other patriarchs of the church, and Tsar Alexis himself. Despite these endorsements, the reforms were rejected by the Old Believers or Old Ritualists, who were willing to die for the traditional faith, thus accentuating a division between nativism and receptivity to "foreign" ideas. According to one estimate, over 20,000 Old Believers burned themselves alive between 1672 and 1691 in thirty-seven communal conflagrations. Nikon was eventually deposed for political reasons, although Tsar Alexis decided in favor of the reforms Nikon had sponsored. The Great Schism of the mid-seventeenth century thus led to the defeat of both Nikon and the Old Believers, the supremacy of the tsar over the church, and the opening of the country to the spread of learning.[8]

At the time, learning referred to the Greek traditions of the Orthodox church and borrowings from Latin sources through which the methods (not the content) of Catholic instruction had become influential in Moscow. The Nikonian reformers and the Old Believers were divided only over the question of how best to preserve the Orthodox church. Both groups shared an anti-Western orientation. The charter which Fedor III (1676–1682) gave to the Slav-Greek-Latin Academy at the Zaikonospasskii monastery shows the strength of this opposition in the highest circles. The academy was permitted to teach the traditional, scholarly subjects. But it was also assigned the task of censoring imported books, supervising the ideas of foreigners employed by the government, and keeping all secular knowledge out of its curriculum. Fedor's charter ordered that teachers of the academy who disseminated scientific knowledge be condemned as magicians and burned to death.[9] This basic suspicion of all foreign influences was quite similar to the exclusion policy of Tokugawa Japan. But Russia was a Continental power and isolation was difficult to maintain.

In a country where all political decisions originated with the tsar or his confidants, contacts with the West had to be initiated from the very top. Ivan IV (1533–1584) had sent young Russians to study in Germany and had encouraged foreigners to come to Russia. Boris Godunov (1598–1605) had hoped to establish European schools in his country and had tried to attract foreigners. A select group of tsarist officials became interested in Western customs and ideas. Boris Morozov, A. L. Ordin-Nashchokin, V. V. Golitsyn, and others ranked high at the tsarist court and could afford to take a larger view of affairs—despite the general cultural inertia and definite hostility to foreign ways. Men like these had traveled widely, criticized Russian backwardness, and cultivated contact with foreigners. A few leading court officials also changed their lifestyles, including their dress and the interior decoration of their houses, as well as sponsored various leisure-time activities such as theatrical entertainments. Rich Muscovites began to accumulate libraries and hire foreign-language teachers despite the edicts of 1672 and 1675 prohibiting possession or trading of foreign books. Between 1550 and 1700, some 150 translations appeared, of which only 37 were works on

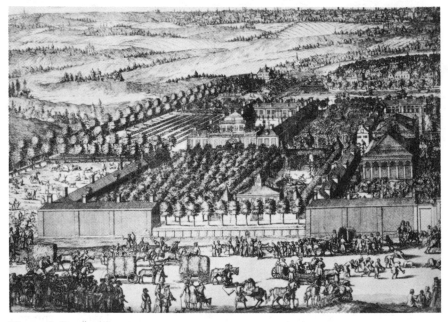

Moscow's Foreign Quarters
Foreign professionals were required to live in a segregated but comfortable section of
Moscow. The foreigners comprised the young tsar Peter's "university." One of his most
congenial companions was General Lefort, whose mansion is shown at the center of the
engraving. This mansion was the scene of many evenings filled with conversation and high-
spirited entertainment. (New York Public Library)

faith and morals; the others dealt with literature, history, geography,
medicine, astronomy, and natural science and included various reference works. Significantly, nearly all these were disseminated by manuscript rather than through publications controlled by the state-church.[10]

The employment of foreigners was one way of resolving the conflict
between an economy demanding skills and an orthodox religious culture
inimical to secular learning and all things of Western derivation. As early
as the fifteenth century, tsarist rulers had contracted for the services of
foreign specialists needed for trade and military preparedness. Some
were employed as tutors of children in aristocratic households; others
were physicians, military officers, and translators, as well as assorted
craftsmen and technicians. Initially, these foreigners were allowed to
reside in Moscow. But when antiforeign feeling ran high, they were assigned to a "German" suburb (*Nemetskaya Sloboda*) in Moscow as well as
in other cities. Aside from the few who adopted Russian ways and converted to the Orthodox faith, the bulk of the foreign residents constituted a cultural enclave of their own. Permission to worship their several

faiths was granted, but they were not allowed to administer their own affairs. About 1672 (the year of Peter the Great's birth), some 18,000 foreigners were estimated to reside "in the Muscovite empire."[11] A few leading aristocrats were in contact with foreigners and receptive to foreign ideas. In his youth, Tsar Peter shared in these contacts and developed a taste for new ideas, especially in the military field.

THE REIGN OF PETER I AND ITS LEGACIES

The interest in Western ideas and institutions became a dominant motif of the Russian government under the influence of the young tsar. Though formally enthroned at the age of ten (1682), Peter replaced the regency of his half-sister Sophia in 1689, at the age of seventeen. Early in his reign, the young tsar traveled to Western Europe (1697–1698) where he combined his interest in technical skills and innovations with first forays in European diplomacy. In his travels, he became acquainted with the academies of science in London, Berlin, and Paris, which provided information and advice. His educational reforms stemmed from this experience. At the elementary level, Peter ordered the establishment of "ciphering" schools and tried to make attendance compulsory. He founded military academies at which foreign instructors taught Russian officer-candidates. At the highest level, he established an Academy of Science, and he curbed by edict the church's opposition to secular learning. Under these conditions, foreign scientists as well as students had to come to Russia since there was no Russian university from which Russian scientists could be recruited, and Russian secondary education in the early eighteenth century did not prepare students for advanced work. Vasilii Tatishchev, one of Peter's emissaries to Sweden, suggested to the tsar that an academy without educational institutions on which to build would be a waste of money.[a] Peter replied that he knew "a Russian academy would resemble a watermill without water, but that [this] beginning would compel his successors to complete the work by digging a canal that would bring in the water."[12]

Peter abruptly returned from his European travels in 1698 to put down a revolt of the guard regiments in Moscow (*streltsy*), prepare for a war against Sweden, and launch an attack on the backward customs of his country. Many earlier tsars had imposed savage punishments on

---

[a]Only foreigners who did not know Russian were involved in the academy, and its proceedings were published in Latin. A gymnasium and university were attached to the academy in 1727, but only a few Russians attended the former and eight German students were brought to the latter so that it could pretend to function. Even a century later a Russian critic of education wrote, "The professors have been invited before there were students to hear them and though many of these scholars are prominent, few are really useful; for the students, being but poorly acquainted with Latin, are unable to understand these foreign instructors."

their opponents, and Peter's actions were hardly exceptional. Nevertheless, his reign represented an autocratic coup d'état against the old regime. Peter's travels abroad, his active interest in foreigners and their ideas, his German mistress, his casual regard of religious symbols (though not of religion)—all these were outrages to the eyes of the pious. Personal humiliations were added. At a reception, Peter seized a scissors and cut the beard of a leading citizen. To believers, this action and the edict against beards which followed were further heretical abominations, since the beard was the pious man's simulation of God's image, while shaving made him the equal of animals. The tsar had taken to wearing foreign clothing, and in 1700 an edict made such clothing incumbent on all servitor aristocrats, while exempting clergymen and taxpaying commoners. In the following years, a graduated tax was imposed on all those who still wore beards and native costume. Soon, tax-exempt and clean-shaven court aristocrats and soldiers in foreign clothes or uniforms could be distinguished from the rest of the population who wore native clothes and beards, and paid taxes.[b] Popular indignation against Peter focused on these willful and sacrilegious changes of native customs; thus, nationalism, defense of the faith, and popular hatred of the tsar coalesced at the very beginning of the Northern War (1700–1709) and of the country's first period of major reforms.[13]

The Cutting of Beards

In this contemporary cartoon an old believer and boyar protests futilely as the barber, probably Peter the Great himself, prepares to cut his beard. In the eyes of the orthodox, a beard meant a man's likeness to the image of God. Foreigners reported that many believers saved their shorn beards and were buried with them. (New York Public Library)

[b]Similar distinctions between court and country existed elsewhere in Europe, but without the religious significance Russian Orthodoxy and popular feeling attributed to beards and clothing.

To outrage native sentiment just after suppressing a revolt at home and just before a major military campaign abroad meant that Peter, like his predecessors, was not especially concerned with the reactions of his people. The tsar's extensive military involvements naturally resulted in extraordinarily heavy tax burdens. The police or military force were often needed at home to collect these taxes, even in the midst of military campaigns abroad. Yet Peter's initiative to reform Russian society had arisen from the desire to increase the country's fighting capacity.

Before 1689 the total budget of the tsarist government had amounted to 1.2 million rubles, of which 700,000 went for the army, 224,000 for the court, and 300,000 for all other needs. More than half of these outlays were raised through customs dues on imported goods and a tax on liquor, the rest through direct and special taxes obtained by leasing lands belonging to the tsar. By 1701 the tax burden had doubled to over 2.2 million rubles, and by 1710 it had risen to 3.1 million. While the proportion of the regular budget going to military expenditures remained roughly the same, the budget tripled in a period of twenty years, and the measures used to raise additional revenue became more extreme. The tsar obtained cash through forced loans from monasteries, rich merchants, and moneylenders, as well as by doubling the tax burdens of the towns. Special levies were imposed. The currency was debased, and state monopolies of especially lucrative trades were created. By 1709 the cost of maintaining the army had made the financial situation desperate. The tsar ordered a new census in the expectation that the taxpaying population had increased in the last thirty years, but instead the 1710 census showed a decline of 20 percent. The government ignored the census and in effect raised the tax assessment on each household in order to maintain its tax receipts despite the loss of population.[14]

This record of Peter's fiscal measures during the Northern War suggests that his wartime government continued the tradition of collecting tribute (taxes) and recruits from a population whose only alternatives were compliance, bribes, deception, or flight. For centuries past, this "system" of government had worked by the overwhelming weight of the autocrat's presence and the awe he inspired in his subordinates. Pressure from above had been "answered" by fear below and, whenever possible, by bribes and the hiding of resources. Such tactics could stabilize the relations between rulers and ruled, and to a degree such stabilization could make life tolerable for the people. By prompting superiors to look the other way bribes facilitated evasions, false reports, hoarding, illicit profits, and the like. In that way, subjects could appear to comply and still retain some margin of resources on which to live — and to comply to a degree on the next occasion, when exactions would be even larger.[15]

The first inroads on this network of bribes and deceptions had been made in Russia's military organization, when regiments were created under foreign mercenary officers. These regiments performed no civil functions in contrast to military units recruited from the villages, led into battle by their peacetime administrators, and returned to their villages on the cessation of hostilities. Peter's reforms began by assigning all recruits to regiments under centrally appointed officers. Peasants were separated permanently from their villages, and the sons of aristocratic landowners had to serve for life. The newly created regiments were composed of men from different areas, so that servitors who spent their lives together in military service developed a regimental allegiance. By 1725 the tsar had created the largest standing army in Europe, with 200,000 regular soldiers and about 100,000 irregulars. The great success of this military force made the country a formidable European power.[16]

At the same time, Russia lacked the local institutions on whose cooperation the tsar's military undertakings could depend. The underdevelopment of provincial society in Russia was directly related to the administrative weakness of the tsarist government. There were no "established rights" of estates which the tsar had to combat, and by the end of the seventeenth century even the old princely and boyar claims had largely disappeared. In practice, the government monopolized all initiative in public affairs. But in so doing, it lost touch with the people in society on whose experience and energies other European governments could draw for the achievement of public ends.[17]

Peter repeatedly tried to inculcate a sense of corporate responsibility in aristocrats and merchants, demanding that they act for the "common good," which in his view was identical with the interests of the state. But prominent merchants hardly appreciated the "freedom" of self-administration granted to them when it entailed a doubling of their tax payments and other onerous services to the state. Local gentry hardly enjoyed a right of representation when they were compelled to elect delegates to provincial assemblies which had no autonomous functions to perform. Nor could repeated census counts inspire public confidence when they were apparently ordered to "find" more people for purposes of taxation. Peter eventually used soldiers to collect taxes, even though his own military reorganization had sought to separate civil from military functions. Thus, in 1722 a census was completed under military pressure, and for five years soldiers were stationed in the villages to collect taxes. Thereafter, centrally appointed civil officials resumed control. But soldiers continued to help with the collection of taxes until 1763, and civil officials were for the most part retired army officers.[18]

Peter's policies of "Westernization" were based on government by emergency decree and large-scale military engagements. From the defeat at Narva in 1700 to the victory over the Swedes at Poltava in 1709,

Peter was preoccupied with the Northern War. He also initiated Russia's dominance over Poland, annexed Estonia and Livonia, and established his influence in the Baltic through the marriage of his niece, Anna, to the duke of Kurland (or Courland). An unsuccessful, but rather brief, military engagement with the Turks in 1711 involved Russia on another major front. Further military actions against Sweden ensued in the following years, leading to the withdrawal of Sweden from the Continent and its replacement at many points by Russian troops. Further marriage alliances with the German states of Braunschweig and Holstein followed, as did simultaneous military engagements against Persia. Peter's vast and almost continuous military and diplomatic involvements suggest the tremendous burdens he imposed on the whole society.

The founding of St. Petersburg as the new capital became the great symbol of that imposition, though canal construction by forced labor and the massive conscription of serfs were also important. The new city provided access to the Baltic and facilitated Russia's rise as a European power as well as enhanced its receptivity to Western ideas. But the city exacted an enormous price in capital, labor, and lives. It also exacerbated the antiforeign sentiment strongly entrenched in the church. Orthodox believers regarded Peter as the incarnation of Antichrist. These sentiments coalesced into a growing opposition to St. Petersburg and the court as "foreign" enclaves, filled with deceit and corruption and dominated by foreigners.[19]

These anti-Western sentiments were greatly reinforced under Peter's niece, Empress Anna Ivanovna (1730–1740). Foreigners had been the obedient agents of the tsar before 1725, but now they began to have direct influence on government policy. The empress appointed men of Baltic or German origin to important positions. New guard regiments under foreign commanders were created. Eventually, Ernst Johann Biron, as the closest advisor to (and lover of) the empress, became the symbol of oppression (*Bironovshchina*), because his name was linked with widespread terror. These Russianized officials of German origin were probably no more corrupt than any of their predecessors or less loyal to their adopted country. Nor were autocratic practices under Anna harsher than they had been under Peter. But resentment against this "government of German foreigners" became a rallying point among courtiers and palace guards, whose intrigues followed Anna's death in 1740. Biron, Muennich, and Osterman lost out in the ensuing struggle over the succession, and the daughter of Peter I, Empress Elizabeth (1740–1762), was hailed as a liberator from a foreign yoke. In practice, only German influence declined while European influences continued —this time under French auspices. Elizabeth retained men of foreign birth among her advisors and St. Petersburg as the capital. By mid-century, the influence of Voltaire and the Encyclopedists had begun to replace the earlier importance of Leibniz, Christian Wolff, and the pietism of Halle University. The rising anti-German sentiment and the turn toward French models corresponded with the ascendance of the French Enlightenment in Western Europe.

As the service obligations of the Russian gentry were lightened, individual courtiers discovered "that the acquisition of French culture was a factor of social distinction welcomed at court and in society, and that it supplied those elements of *bon ton* which characterized most of the European nobility." Western education acquired from foreign teachers was no longer the compulsory activity it had been under Peter's reign, designed to prepare young aristocrats for their military or governmental careers. Now "dancing, the French language, drawing, theatrical performances, and fencing occupied as important a place in the curricula of most educational institutions for the young gentry as did mathematics, history, political science, fortification, and other subjects useful in the military or civil service."[20] Inevitably, this imitation of French culture was satirized and morally castigated, much as Gallomania was denounced in eighteenth-century Germany. Yet reactions were quite different in the two contexts.

In Germany, Gallomania was replaced by a cosmopolitanism that modeled itself on the ancient Greeks. Self-cultivation (*Bildung*) of the individual was the new ideal in contrast to the empty grace of the aristocrat or the French manner affected by the German courts. But the self-cultivation of the individual was not a viable ideal for eighteenth-century Russia. There was no rapid proliferation of educated readers which in Germany was a by-product of education for state service. During the eighteenth century, the annual production of printed publications ranged in Russia from a low of 12 to a high of 366 in contrast with Germany where it ranged from a low of 978 to a high of 4,012.[21] Russian officials often remained as uneducated as the clergy. With little education and little demand for literature, interest in such matters was confined to relatively few aristocratic families. Russian men of letters were either foreigners or the first of the *raznochintsy* (that is, men who had become estranged from the groups to which they belonged by the standard legal categories of the day). A number of these writers protested the evil influence of foreigners by cultivating the Russian language and Russian traditions. Such efforts helped to develop a national consciousness, but Russian culture remained under the pervasive influence of Western ideas until well into the nineteenth century.[22]

The subordination of Russian society to dynastic and military exigencies was nothing new, but Peter's adoption of foreign models and the bureaucratization of government were deliberate innovations. The obligation to serve the tsar personally was made into an impersonal system through reorganization of the aristocracy. A Table of Ranks was established in 1722, which was to enable people to achieve aristocratic status by means of professional and economic success as well as by public and military service. In principle, a commoner could be ennobled once he achieved the civilian equivalent of the lowest officer rank, or of the eighth rank in the civil service. Peter's main objective was to make rank an accurate reflection of service. In practice, some ambitious and successful commoners were elevated, but claims based on a family's length of service rather than on qualification alone continued to predominate.

Peter died in 1725, but his new dispensation had altered the aristocratic way of life. In place of the old rotation between military and civilian service, the tsar introduced a separation. Both types of service were now to be preceded by a suitable, compulsory education. In order to achieve the complete recruitment and control of the aristocracy, a register was established of those eligible for service plus a record of their performance. One third of the males in every aristocratic family were assigned to civilian duty; all others were obliged to enter military service. Each young aristocrat had to enter service at the lowest rank at the age of fifteen. He was obliged to serve between twenty-five and thirty years, and his career advanced through fourteen parallel grades in the military, the administrative, or the imperial court service.

Through the Table of Ranks, rulings by officials had replaced the tsar's personal favor. No doubt his rule was harsh, but the psychological gain of the tsar's personal recognition also had had a compensatory effect. Now, rank had become a matter of seniority and bureaucratic intrigue, while decisions on promotion rested with superior officers or officials.[23] This systematized service exacerbated ill will among the gentry. One can infer their resistance to the Table of Ranks from the edicts issued to enforce the new rules. Under Peter, evasion by aristocrats was to be punished by confiscation of property; evaders could be robbed and even murdered with impunity; informers who denounced malingerers were to be rewarded with the culprit's property; public disgrace was to be visited upon the guilty. Aristocratic youths who failed to do well in the schools preparing them for service were not permitted to marry or inherit landed estates. The very proliferation of these edicts suggests their limited success, but also shows how extreme was the burden of required service.[24]

In the interest of an unprecedented military build-up, Peter systematized the subordination of the servitor aristocracy and completed the conscription of the peasantry as recruits, taxpayers, and state laborers. He sought to compensate the aristocracy for their sacrifice by making *pomestie* holdings hereditary and indivisible (1714).[c] When all landholding became service-bound in perpetuity, the old distinction between he-

[c]I shall use *aristocracy* in the sense of "servitor aristocracy" in preference to *nobility*, because Russian aristocrats governed, albeit in a subordinate capacity, and they owed their rank to tsarist preferment. *Gentry* seems most appropriate as an alternative designation, especially after 1762.

reditary patrimony (*votchina*) and service land (*pomestie*) was abolished, one more instance in which the grant of a right was indistinguishable from the duty to serve the state. The government also accepted the practice of landowners who sold their peasants without land. Although this practice was formally prohibited, the tsar himself encouraged the sale of recruits to the army. Other changes instituted by Peter, such as the promotion of industry, the building of St. Petersburg, and the institution of required schooling, were all designed to develop Russia as a great European power. In the process, the people were decimated by war, forced labor, famine, and repression. There was also a mass exodus to the interior.

In the tradition of autocracy, Peter regarded the people as children who would not learn anything without compulsion. As Kliuchevsky has observed,

> The Petrine Reform was a struggle . . . between despotism and the people's torpor. He hoped by means of harsh governmental measures to evoke initiative and enterprise among an enslaved society, and through the agency of a slaveholding nobility to install European learning in Russia. He wanted the slave, while remaining a slave, to act consciously and freely. To achieve the joint action of despotism and liberty, of education and slavery—this is the political equivalent of squaring the circle, which we have been trying to solve for two centuries, since Peter's day. It is still unsolved.

Tibor Szamuely, who quotes this comment, remarks that Peter's reign evoked two incompatible reactions in Russia. Although he felt closer to the people than any other European monarch, Peter was personally hated by conservative writers and the public at large. At the same time, liberal and radical writers admired Peter as the great reformer of their backward country. This division of opinion made Russia the first in a long line of modernizing countries which have been bedeviled by a similar division between nativists who resent the disruption of established ways, and reformers who are prepared to force the pace of change.[25]

Peter is among the most tragic rulers considered in this study. A physical giant endowed with enormous vitality which made it seem possible to undertake single-handedly the modernization of his country, Peter was excessive in everything he undertook, including his conception of tsarist authority. An army regulation of 1716 proclaimed, "His Majesty is an absolute monarch who is not responsible to anyone in the world for his deeds; but he has the right, and the power to govern his realm and his lands, as a Christian sovereign, according to his will and wisdom." Peter extended this exalted conception of monarchy to the question of succession. In the Muscovite tradition, the crown usually passed to the oldest son, but Peter's son Alexis had been tortured to death in his father's presence on a trumped-up charge of conspiracy

(1718). Four years later, Peter proclaimed the emperor's right to appoint his own successor so that he might eliminate any member of the dynasty he considered unfit. Yet this extreme assertion of authority proved futile; in 1725 Peter died without having named a successor.

After 1725 dynastic instability weakened tsarist rule, and the aristocracy was relieved of the worst burdens Peter had imposed. An imperial manifesto of 1736 provided that in every family one son would be exempt from service to manage the estate while the other sons were obliged to serve for twenty-five years with the right to resign thereafter. Subsequent edicts relieved other burdens. The sons of prominent gentry families were enrolled in the service at birth, so that they already possessed considerable seniority under the Table of Ranks by the time they came of age. Servitors were given special leaves of absence, or their service duties were reduced on an individual basis. In addition, sons of distinguished families were given privileged access to one of the three Moscow guard regiments and, after 1731, to the Corps of Cadets.

Military units attached to the palace together with prominent courtiers had played a major role in the infighting typical of court and bureaucracy since the sixteenth century. Now, after Peter's abolition of a succession based on primogeniture (1722), it was still easier for courtiers and the Moscow regiments to take decisive action when a successor to the throne had to be chosen. During the eighteenth century, Peter's reign was followed by eight monarchs: Catherine I (1725–1727), Peter II (1727–1730), Anna (1730–1740), Ivan VI (1740–1741), Elizabeth (1741–1762), Peter III (1762), Catherine II (1762–1796), and Paul I (1796–1801). Only two of these monarchs achieved the throne without military intervention (Peter III and Paul), and both were subsequently murdered.[26]

All these rulers played leading courtiers against one another in order to exercise autocratic rule, but in this context some prominent personalities and the Moscow guard regiments found opportunities for advancing their careers and increasing aristocratic control over the peasants. Here is a partial list of the relevant imperial edicts:

In 1741, peasant serfs no longer had to swear an oath of loyalty to the monarch;

in 1747, the custom of selling peasants without land was lawful;

in 1760, aristocratic landowners had the right to exile offending peasants to Siberia;

in 1765, landowners at their own discretion had the right to sentence peasants to convict labor;

in 1767, any attempt by serfs to lodge complaints against their masters was punishable by forced labor.[27]

None of these edicts touched the aristocracy's own obligation to serve the state. The Petrine reforms of periodic census-taking, levies of serfs for the standing army and for public works, and collection of the head tax had been implemented increasingly by the army. When these military forces were moved to the front during the Seven Years' War (1756–1763), the provincial government of Russia was very nearly paralyzed. Landed aristocrats were needed as never before to administer local affairs, and the compulsion under which unqualified as well as qualified aristocrats had to serve in the central government was becoming counterproductive.

PETER III AND CATHERINE II

The aristocracy's service obligation had been relaxed after the reign of Peter I primarily because under less demanding rulers exemptions increased and personally lodged complaints found an occasional hearing. Peter III's edict of 1762 freed the aristocracy of its universal service obligation, a move that was popular among aristocrats and probably convenient from the standpoint of the government. The edict, however, did not mean either a diminution of autocracy or a grant of rights to the aristocracy. Rather, aristocrats were granted freedom from the compulsory service obligations of the past. Henceforth, the government could dispense with the service of those who preferred to mind their estates or live a life of leisure. The edict decreeing the "emancipation" at the same time appealed to the aristocracy to continue its service.

> We hope that the whole noble Russian gentry, appreciative of our generosity to them and their descendants, will be inspired by their most dutiful loyalty to Us and their zeal, not to absent or hide themselves from service, but to enter it with pride and enthusiasm, and continue it in an honorable and decent manner to the extent of their ability.... Those who have not been in service anywhere, but spend all their time in sloth and idleness, and do not subject their children to any useful education for the benefit of the fatherland, these We, as they are negligent of the common good, command all Our obedient and true sons to despise and scorn, and they will not be allowed to appear at Our Court, or at public meetings and celebrations.

Aristocrats who availed themselves of their legal freedom were to be ostracized. Moreover, the edict of 1762 said nothing about the desire of aristocrats for freedom from corporal punishment, for a guarantee of serf-possession, and for the immunity of their estates from confiscation. The new freedom from compulsory service obligation was hedged by important reservations.[28]

The Russian aristocracy comprised between 1 and 2 percent of the population. The number of aristocratic families had been about 3,000 in 1700, but as a result of tsarist largesse increased to a little under 200,000 families in 1800.[29] Even after 1762, more than 80 percent of this landowning aristocracy continued to serve the state, often leaving the management of their estates to bailiffs who put their own interests first. Only the wealthiest families, comprising perhaps some 12,000 households, turned to the direct management of their estates. During the last decades of the eighteenth century, they could increase their income from export of agricultural produce, from the distillation of alcohol, and to some extent from industrial production.

In 1795 some 193,000 aristocrats owned 9.9 million serfs. The distribution of serfs among gentry households is difficult to estimate, but figures for 1834 indicate the great disparities of wealth among the gentry (see Table 4). These percentages mean that the leading 2,300 aristocrats (those with more than 500 serfs each) owned just over 3 million serfs. Of these, some 2 million serfs belonged to 870 households, averaging 2,342 serfs per owner.[30] During the years 1830–1835, the total Russian population stood at about 48 million, and the total number of aristocrats at about 720,000. In 1831 some 43,000 lived in Petersburg and another 16,000 lived in Moscow. Thus, only about 8 percent, or 1 out of every 12 aristocrats, lived under the direct supervision of the court and the central government. The vast majority of this upper class lived in the provinces, and although the figures cited pertain to 1834, the same conditions had prevailed earlier.[31]

The aristocracy was not the sole owner of the serf population. According to statistics for 1796, 9.7 million males belonged to landed aristocrats and the church, while 7.2 million males belonged to lands owned by the state and members of the imperial family.[32] The government and the aristocracy depended on the rural population for the bulk of their income. Prior to 1762, the local management of estates and peasants consisted of little more than tax collection and military recruitment by officials of the government, often supported by military force. The peasants worked the land according to their own custom. The typical problem had been peasant flights when burdens became too heavy. In dealing with these flights, the government wanted to preserve the revenue derived from the productivity of the land, but it also wanted to settle newly colonized areas of the empire. A consistent policy was difficult to achieve under these circumstances.

TABLE 4

DISTRIBUTION OF GENTRY SERF-
OWNERS (HEADS OF HOUSEHOLDS)
BY SIZE OF HOLDINGS IN GREAT RUSSIA, 1834

Number of Serfs per Gentry Household	Percentage of Owners	Percentage of Serfs
Fewer than 100	81.5	19.6
101—500	15.1	35.2
501–1000	2.1	14.9
Over 1000	1.3	30.3

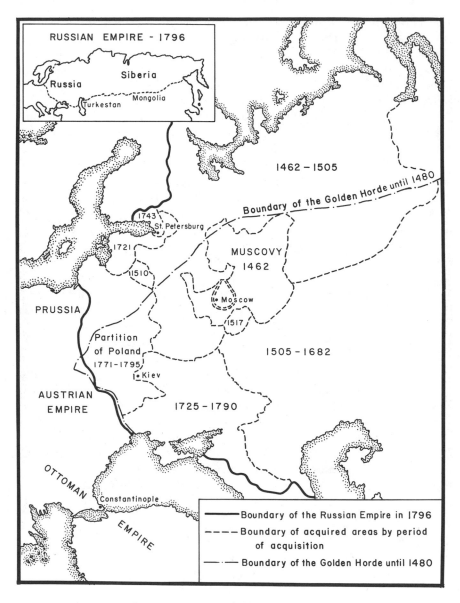

A number of eighteenth-century rulers were weak, but the principle of autocratic supremacy remained in force. When Catherine II ascended the throne, albeit with the aid of courtiers and the Moscow regiments, she restored autocracy to its former strength. Catherine II was born in 1729 as princess of a petty German principality (Anhalt Zerbst). At the age of fifteen, she was brought to St. Petersburg to marry Grand-Duke Peter, who was the son of the duke of Holstein and a Russian mother. Converting to Greek Orthodoxy four months after her arrival, she married in 1745 and a son was born to her nine years later (the future Emperor Paul). Between the ages of sixteen and thirty-two, Catherine cultivated good relations at court. Punctilious regard for amenities, demonstrative loyalty to her adopted country, and study of the enlightened literature of the age marked those years, as did a growing estrangement from her husband. After a reign of only seven months (1762), Peter III was forced to abdicate, and Catherine was proclaimed empress. Peter's murder followed only a few days later, probably with Catherine's consent.

The circumstances of her accession to the throne, the length of her reign (1762–1796), and her handling of foreign affairs leave no doubt of Catherine's own sense of power politics. Russia had become a great European state during the eighteenth century. Territorial acquisitions were one reason. Through the peace of Abo (1743), Sweden had ceded the Baltic countries and the territories adjoining the eastern shores of the Gulf of Finland. Under Catherine II, one main objective of Russian policy was territorial gains at the expense of Turkey (Russian-Turkish war, 1768–1774). The treaty of Kuchuk-Kainardji (1774) brought the territories adjoining the northern and eastern shores of the Black Sea and the Sea of Asov under Russian domination. But through pressure from the Western powers Russia was forced to return to Turkey its conquests of Moldavia and Wallachia. The first partition of Poland (1772) also falls into this period: Russia gained some eastern territories but major parts of Poland were annexed by Prussia and Austria. The Russian annexation of the Crimea followed in 1783 as well as a second war with Turkey (1787–1792), in which Russia obtained additional coastal areas on the Black Sea. In the second and third partition of Poland (1793, 1795) Russia obtained further territories in Lithuania, Volhynia, and elsewhere. In the Swedish-Russian war of 1788–1790 Russia retained its earlier annexations in the Baltic.

The empress probably had a genuine interest in the ideas of her age, but she also used her contacts with luminaries like Voltaire, Diderot, and others to buttress her own legitimacy and enhance Russia's good name in Western Europe.[33] Both impulses are evident in her free adaptation of ideas taken from Montesquieu. In 1764–1766 she drew up a series of instructions that were to guide the deliberations of the Committee of Deputies, convoked for the purpose of drafting a new code of laws. Montesquieu identified autocracy with despotic government, but the empress sought to prove that autocracy was compatible with the separation of powers, the observance of laws, and the other objectives of enlightened rule. Montesquieu had also advocated political privileges for the aristocracy in a limited monarchy, because such privileges would protect a country against the possible despotism of the sovereign. By contrast, Catherine thought of the privileged aristocracy as an aspect of the autocratic system, for under Russian conditions privilege was matched by the aristocracy's obedience to the sovereign.

In practice, that obedience had waned in the course of the eighteenth century, largely due to the combination of weak rulers and the rising power of the Moscow guard regiments. The aristocracy's authority over the serfs had become absolute, and by the 1770s the peasants were at the end of their endurance. In 1773–1775 the Pugachev revolt engulfed a large part of southern Russia. The revolt was ruthlessly suppressed, but then Catherine turned her attention to the "undergoverned" provinces. The Pugachev crisis had shown that local abuse of authority was rampant, and the autocratic response was to strengthen and reform provincial government, presumably in the expectation that this would correct the abuses which the central government itself had facilitated. Local authorities were to be made up of tsarist officials and landed notables elected by the local aristocracy, probably in the hope that the two groups would check each other's excesses. Also, provincial courts were to be separated from administrative agencies so that the adjudication of local disputes would not be misused as a means of implementing governmental edicts.

> Relying on these principles, [Catherine] borrowed theoretical arguments from the treatise on law that Blackstone had published in Oxford in 1765–68 and that had been translated into French in 1774. (In 1780–82 she commissioned Desnitsky to make a Russian translation.) She was fascinated by the constitution of the English county, which was based on a broad autonomy for the local administration and on the dominant role of the landed nobility in the dispensation of justice and the control of the police.[34]

The resulting *Ordinance on Governments* (1775) reduced the size of each provincial government and local district. It decreed both administrative decentralization and representation by elected deputies from each jurisdiction. Courts for each class of free men (aristocrats, merchants, artisans) were to be composed of a presiding judge appointed by the state and associate judges elected by the respective classes. By the end of Catherine's reign (1796), the number of provincial officials had risen to 27,000 (from 12,714 in 1774), and expenditures for provincial administration had risen to over 10 million rubles (up from 1.7 million in 1774). Even with these increases, the limits of the country's administrative capability are suggested by the fact that Prussia, with 1 percent of Russia's land area, employed 14,000 civil servants.[35]

These and related measures were supplemented by the Charter of 1785. The aristocracy was now legally freed of its liability to corporal punishment (the token of its servitor status for centuries); it had free disposal over its estates, could engage in trade, and was protected under due process of law. Assemblies were instituted with the right to debate governmental proposals and to establish schools and hospitals through voluntary contributions. Yet an aristocrat had to attain the rank of junior officer before he had the right to vote in the election of assembly delegates. Members of the aristocracy might be free from compulsory state service, but they were ineligible for elective office if they did not perform such service. In practice, governmental restrictions on local activities remained severe, but initiative was not wanting when the occasion seemed promising. Witness the flood of grievances and proposals submitted to the legislative commission of 1767, although these submissions merely continued in altered form the age-old right to petition the tsar. Few remedies were forthcoming in response to such grievances.

Ultimate jurisdiction remained in the hands of the provincial governor-general. Catherine believed that autocratic rule did not allow for any significant local autonomy, although she admired the principle of local rule as practiced in England. In her view, such principles were not applicable in Russia. Enormous resources were needed to sustain Russia's military and diplomatic efforts in the European concert of nations. As long as the supreme position of the landed aristocracy and the serfdom of the peasants continued, the state was supplied with the service and revenue it required. Centralized administration and the necessary use of force buttressed the prevailing system of exploitation and could control the uprisings which recurred from time to time.

Yet coercion could not provide either the skilled work force or the teachers, administrators, and engineers which Russia needed to safeguard its status as a European power. During the 1780s, Catherine was concerned with organizing a school system that could provide her government with educated officials at the middle rank. After careful preparations based on the study of Western models, a statute of 1786 proposed the establishment of a two-year "minor school" in every district and a four-year "major school" in every provincial capital. Under Catherine's sponsorship, useful learning was emphasized and the education of girls was encouraged. Rote learning and discipline were to be replaced. The guiding idea was that children must be separated from their families at an early age so that they might receive the full benefit of a teaching uncontaminated by the surrounding society.

In 1786 there had been only 40 schools with 136 teachers and some

4,400 pupils; by 1796, the last year of Catherine's reign, there were 316 schools with 744 teachers and some 17,340 pupils.[36] But this outward success was deceiving. The ambitions of the autocrat were at odds with the educational conceptions prevailing in the society at large. In the major schools, less than half the students were children of aristocratic families and the rest were commoners. The parents of both groups were dissatisfied. For the aristocracy, association with social inferiors seemed demeaning as well as dangerous to the established order. For the commoners, schooling in the absence of employment opportunities was a dispensable luxury. As a town council stated in 1790, "Schools are not necessary for the children of merchants and craftsmen. Therefore, we do not intend to send our children to school. We have no desire to support the schools and we see no value in them for us."[37] Both attitudes were reinforced by the educational practices of the day. Teachers were held in low esteem and paid next to nothing. Many children from the aristocracy were kept home and given private instruction. As for the children of commoners, only a small proportion of those attending ever graduated. A first step had been taken, but major educational advances had to await the second half of the nineteenth century.

On balance, the reforms of Catherine II did not change Russia's social order. Even the charter of 1785, which actually formulated rights of the aristocracy, declared that "at the first summons from the autocratic authority" every aristocrat "is bound to spare neither labor nor life itself for the service of the state."[38] The bulk of the aristocracy was in practice so poor that they were eager for government service and could not claim the exemption to which they were now entitled. Moreover, in the borderlands of the south, the Ukraine, and the west, the fortune of aristocrats depended on the state; though they might want more freedom for themselves, they thoroughly identified with the tsarist regime.[39] Although a few aristocrats could afford to take their ease after centuries of personal subservience and readily ignored the admonitions to serve voluntarily, neither this nor related reactions altered the close interdependence between the tsarist government and the aristocracy.[d] Since Catherine's accession to the throne was of doubtful legitimacy, she maneuvered carefully by adding to her European reputation and by favoring prominent aristocrats with her largesse. Her determined suppression of peasant uprisings and her support of greater aristocratic dominance over the serfs do not suggest that she feared challenges to

---

[d]Perhaps the most pathetic combination of abject subordination with pride was the repeated request that aristocrats who had committed acts deserving corporal punishment be formally divested of their title before the penalty was inflicted on them. Note the moral outrage with which the Abbé Sieyès commented on a similar "demotion before punishment" in eighteenth-century France.

her reign. At any rate, she firmly rejected constitutional limitations on her supreme authority.[40]

From the standpoint of the aristocracy, it was a reasonable compromise. Their own preeminence was assured, the burden of personal service lightened, and their rights over the serfs enhanced. Meanwhile, they felt the threat of peasant uprisings, not only in the great Pugachev revolt but in sporadic violence against individual landowners. This internal hazard necessarily loomed larger at the time of the French revolution. A strong autocracy seemed the best guarantee of peace and order at home, and it also proved to be effective in foreign affairs. The aristocracy was hardly averse to benefiting from the successful military campaigns against Turkey, the three partitions of Poland, the secularization of church estates (1764), and the occupation of the Crimea. Nor were the highest circles of the aristocracy disinclined to follow the court's lead in adopting French culture as the model of refinement. With an annual rent payment of 5 rubles from each peasant-serf, the aristocracy had an annual income from its serfs of 50 million rubles, of which Professor Kahan estimates that over 35 percent was spent for imported goods, education, and travel.[41] To purchase these foreign amenities and thus support an aristocratic sense of well-being, a family required a minimum work force of one hundred male serfs. A majority of aristocratic households lacked these amenities but still depended on what serfs they possessed. Even where their status was combined with indigence, aristocratic families rarely wavered in their support of autocratic rule.

FOREIGN POLICY, MILITARISM, AND EDUCATION

Tsarist governments taxed the Russian population ever more rigorously in order to pursue their foreign policies and many military undertakings. At the same time, the autocracy sponsored the development of education in order to improve the country's productive, administrative, and military capability. But the second undertaking also involved contact with ideas from the West which called Russian autocracy into question. Indeed, Russia's aristocratic society in Moscow and Petersburg was educated in the language and thought of France and Germany; thus, the leaders of society were affected by such trends of the time as Protestantism, pietism, Freemasonry, and French socialism. Accordingly, the following discussion considers the foreign involvements and educational policies of the successive reigns of Paul I, Alexander I, and Nicholas I. The changing interplay between foreign affairs and education exemplify the peculiar brittleness of Russia's political tradition, seemingly centralized and all-powerful, and yet exposed to every current of opinion from abroad.

The five-year reign of Paul I (1796–1801), which followed the thirty-four-year reign of his mother, Catherine, illustrates the ease with which autocratic rule could change foreign models and revoke "liberal" concessions. Catherine's models had been France and England; her son's model was Prussia. Paul thought of laws as if they were military commands and tended to adopt policies which reversed those of his mother. Participation of estates in local government did not suit a military model. Local bodies were reduced in size, and henceforth representatives of the aristocracy were appointed rather than elected. More serious was Paul's decision to tax the aristocracy in order to pay the costs of local administration, a direct contravention of the 1785 charter. Still, these provincial matters probably did not count for as much as the tsar's despotic measures at the center of affairs. One edict followed another in chaotic profusion. The import of foreign books was banned; certain words were prohibited; curfews were imposed; officials were dismissed; officers were sent to Siberia for trivial reasons; a dead general was disgraced posthumously; an admiral was imprisoned one day and ordered to head a squadron a few weeks later.

Russia's international position was also precarious. The French revolution had been followed by Napoleon's rule, and his series of conquests had provoked a European alliance against him. Under Paul's direction, Russia joined the second coalition against Napoleon, largely because of Napoleon's conquest of Malta. The tsar was a Freemason and Grand Master of the Knights of Malta. These were strange preoccupations for a head of state, but the military significance of Russia's war against Napoleon was considerable. Its Baltic fleet joined the British fleet near the Dutch coast, the Russian Black Sea fleet together with Turkish naval forces operated in the Mediterranean, and Russian land forces defeated the French in northern Italy. But Russia then left the coalition as erratically as it had joined when Britain occupied Malta as a move against the French and refused to yield the island to the tsar. Paul's despotic treatment of the highest ranking officers and officials as well as these mystically motivated ventures in foreign policy were among the causes of an aristocratic conspiracy against his reign. In 1801 Tsar Paul was murdered and his son, Alexander I (1801–1825), was installed on the Russian throne.[42]

The new tsar had known of the conspiracy to dethrone his father, but very early he had learned to disguise his feelings in coping with the greatly strained relations between his grandmother Catherine II, who had seen to his liberal education, and his father Paul, who had conspired against his own sons. On Alexander's accession, which was greeted with a wave of popular enthusiasm, the tsar declared that he would follow the spirit of Catherine's reign and his first edicts quickly undid the worst features of his father's rule. Ousted officials and officers were authorized to request reinstatement; amnesty was declared for political prisoners; the institutions of local government were restored; the police was ordered not to overstep its authority; the borders were reopened to travelers and the import of foreign books; the Charter of 1785 was restored; the government promised not to impose new taxes; the secret political police was abolished.[43] By these and related measures Alexander seemed to express the liberal ideas he had absorbed from his grandmother and from his tutor Laharpe, a Swiss educator strongly influenced by the ideas of the French Enlightenment.

The tsar surrounded himself in the early years of his reign with friends who represented a cross-section of the country's "reference societies." Prince Adam Czartoryski and Count Nicholas Novosiltsov had stayed in Paris during the beginning of the French revolution. Count Stroganov had even been a member of the Jacobin Club and had had extensive contact with Condorcet's educational ideas. When a Ministry of National Enlightenment was established in 1802, its first director was Count Zavadovsky, who had a strong liking for German academic models. Condorcet's scheme of public education was closely followed by the Russian statutes of 1804, emphasizing the utilitarian approach to teaching and the principle of equal access based solely on qualification. Under Alexander's leadership, conservatives and reformers agreed that by anticipating demands for culture and progress, a major cause of public unrest could be averted. Between 1801 and 1825, the number of universities increased from 1 to 6, the number of gymnasia from 12 to 57, and the number of district schools from 44 to 370, while parochial and private schools increased from 180 in 1805 to 960 in 1825. The total number of students during Alexander's reign more than tripled.[44]

These early liberal measures, the very rapid development of educational institutions, and the liberal sentiments expressed by the tsar himself on a number of occasions encouraged the most hopeful expectations for reform. Through his committee of friends, Alexander had become acquainted with Michael Speransky (1772–1839), the son of a country priest who had made a brilliant administrative career and prepared several memoranda for the committee. In 1808 the tsar put Speransky in charge of preparing a new codification of Russian laws. Speransky quickly became the leading constitutional reformer of Alexander's reign and its outstanding statesman from 1809 to 1812. His ideas for reform were modeled on French precedents, and this became the basis of his downfall. Speransky's position depended entirely on the favor of the tsar, whose moves toward a more liberal conception of autocratic rule were beset very early by the difficulties of Russia's international position and by conservative tendencies at home.

The new tsar had inherited a secret treaty with Napoleon and a policy friendly to France, although Russia's economic interests called for closer relations with England. In the circle around the tsar, ideas derived from France had to compete with the suspicions aroused by the revolution. For a time, Alexander only dabbled in foreign affairs, but by 1805 an English-Russian alliance was concluded which was joined by Austria and led to the third war of coalition against Napoleon. Napoleon remained in ascendance. In less than two years, Russian policy veered toward a division of spheres of interest between France and Russia, initiated by the Peace of Tilsit (1807) and officially proclaimed after a meeting of Alexander and Napoleon in 1808. This new alliance led to Russian moves against Sweden and Turkey, which allowed Napoleon freedom of action against Austria. But both rulers were evidently wary. Napoleon avoided involvement against Sweden and Turkey, while Alexander avoided involvement against Austria. Napoleon's conquests in Northern Germany and his support of Polish claims aroused Russian suspicions, while the Russians in turn appeared unreliable to Napoleon because they evaded joining the Continental blockade against England.

Alexander knew that the alliance with France was unpopular. Russian conservatives saw Napoleon as a symbol of the revolution, while Russian liberals saw him as the conquering tyrant. In this context, several courtiers accused Speransky of undermining the country with foreign ideas in a period of national emergency. In addition, Speransky had become inconvenient to Alexander as a critic of autocratic rule at a time when Napoleon's invasion of Russia (1812) called for national unity under the personal leadership of the tsar. Speransky was dismissed from his post and exiled (1812), though later he was rehabilitated; however, his major work of constitutional reform was terminated.[45]

Napoleon and Alexander I meet at Tilsit. (Bibliothèque Nationale)

Napoleon's retreat from Russia with decimated troops and much diminished power was the great turning point in Russia's relations with Europe. Alexander had become the savior of his people. He became the leader of the final coalition against Napoleon, culminating in the entry of Russian troops into Paris in 1814. Following the Battle of Waterloo and the reorganization of Europe at the Congress of Vienna (1815), the tsar initiated the Holy Alliance among Russia, Austria, and Prussia. This ideological compact was addressed to all European sovereigns as fathers of their people and sought to consolidate the political and moral foundations of authority. To this end, foreign and domestic policies were linked. War became an instrument of international defense against revolutionary and popular national movements everywhere, while domestically a reinforced absolutism was to reign supreme. The Russian tsar had become a mystic. His European interventions came to little in comparison with the strategies of the Austrian chancellor Metternich. But the tsar's change of heart from his earlier, liberal convictions was echoed at home by a gathering of conservative forces. Napoleon's invasion of Russia and his subsequent defeat had given a powerful boost to Russian patriotism and the rising hostility toward all things French.

The early liberal and later conservative phases of Alexander's reign were reflected in Russian education. The education act of 1809 (sponsored by Speransky) provided that promotion above a certain level of government service would depend on a university certificate or on passing an examination in the knowledge required for the position. The universities were to control the civil service examinations, and Speransky envisaged that the requisite instruction would be oriented toward Western constitutional ideas. However, these plans foundered on internal opposition. It proved impossible to unify military academies, private schools for the aristocracy, seminaries for priests, and special institutes for young ladies. The aristocracy retained its preference for foreign tutors or foreign schools, while lagging enrollments in public schools raised awkward questions about large educational expenditures. Nor was it possible to extend the system downward to the village level. Moreover, the education act of 1809 aroused the indignation of many aristocrats who could not attack the tsar directly and instead turned on Speransky.[46]

Alexander's and Speransky's early policies had been inspired by the Petrine tradition. For a century, educated Russians had taken the ideas and institutions of Western Europe as their model. Russia's chances of success in a military showdown with France were considered negligible during Napoleon's hegemony. Hence, the miracle of the Russian victory over Napoleon in 1812 and the ascendance of Russia as a leading European power brought about an upsurge of nationalism and Orthodoxy. Even during Alexander's liberal phase, there had been conservative warnings against the dangers arising from liberal ideas and too much education.[e] This conservative spirit came to prevail in court circles and ministries once the tsar himself abandoned his earlier liberal views.

As a result, a joint Ministry of Education and Religious Affairs was established in 1817, and two years later Prince Alexander Golitsin was appointed as its head. Golitsin was president of the Bible society. Gradually, the principle of utility which had determined the earlier curriculum (based on Condorcet's ideas) was replaced by catechism lessons on religious and national precepts. In addition, the principle of equality which had allowed the sons of commoners and even of peasants to attend schools and universities on the basis of state scholarships was abandoned.[48] In 1824 Admiral Alexander Shishkov was appointed minister of education. He believed that universal literacy would do the nation more harm than good, and his views were seconded by the chief of police who thought that educated people would seek to curtail the power of the monarchy.

Nevertheless, Western models retained some of their attraction. Officers of Alexander's armies had spent several years as young adults campaigning in Europe, and they returned to a homeland in which serfdom, poverty, and autocratic rule seemed appalling in comparison with Western freedom, prosperity, and constitutionalism. When Alexander I died suddenly in 1825, leaving some confusion over the succession, groups of these Westernized army officers (the so-called Decembrists) staged a brief and futile attempt to introduce a constitutional monarchy. Nicholas I (1825–1855) came to the throne, and the spirit of his reign is well expressed in the manifesto of 1826 in which the death sentences of the Decembrist leaders were announced. These leaders had stood for ideas taken from the constitutional provisions of England and France. To the tsar and his ministers, this was ideological poison. Admiral Shishkov had warned his subordinates that young people who lack reverence for God, Emperor, and Fatherland, who have no "love for justice and mankind and a sense of honor, will be infected by pseudo-philosophizing, flighty dreaming, puffed-up pride and pernicious self-esteem." In announcing the execution of five officers, the tsar himself stated,

> Let parents turn all their attention to the moral education of their children. The absence of firm principles . . . has produced this fanaticism which has aroused violent passions, this pernicious luxury of half-assimilated knowledge, this urge toward visionary extremes which starts by debasing morals and ends in perdition.[49]

[e]Russian conservatives were joined by a number of Europeans. Among them was Joseph de Maistre, the famous Catholic critic of the French revolution, who served in Petersburg as minister plentipotentiary of the king of Sardinia. De Maistre warned the tsarist court in 1804 that its educational reforms would lead to a "Pougatchev d'université" (that is, a revolt of the intellectuals). When Alexander's policies became conservative, de Maistre's friend, Count Alexei Razumovskii, was appointed minister of education in 1810.[47]

The new regime reversed what remained of liberal educational tendencies. The admission of serfs to secondary schools and universities, though never large, was prohibited. Access to some schooling was preserved for all other strata, but courses of study were adapted to the probable future careers of students. Curricular reforms sought to neutralize the revolutionary potential of Western ideas. Requirements were increased, and courses were confined to strictly scientific and academic subjects. Faculty and students were supervised by district inspectors, who were usually recruited from former military personnel. The emperor himself acted as the supreme inspector, traveling unannounced and making spot-checks to ensure conformity. The new educational statutes of 1828 were drawn up not under French or Polish influence, but under that of Prussian legislation. The Prussia which Nicholas I considered an appropriate model was that of Frederick the Great, not that of Wilhelm von Humboldt.[50]

But taken as a model, Frederician Prussia implied that the king is the first servant of his country and that his objective is the development of its resources and people. Although the Russian population doubled between 1801 and 1855, the number of students in all schools increased almost tenfold. More of this growth occurred in the elementary schools and those controlled by the Holy Synod than in the secondary schools, while at the universities student enrollments increased markedly only under Alexander I and then fluctuated between a low of about 2,000 and a high of 4,000 under the reign of Nicholas I.[51] The conclusion must be drawn that under Nicholas I educational advance was generally encouraged. The Ministry of Education spent large sums on new buildings, laboratories, libraries, and teachers' salaries. Moreover, the government evidenced interest in the educational standards of the country, especially under the leadership of S. S. Uvarov, minister of education from 1833 to 1849. The emperor himself gave special encouragement to technical education and professional schools.

Under Nicholas I, the state also imposed a centrally controlled system of uniform requirements and detailed supervision which would eliminate every trace of intellectual opposition or subversion. The aim was not to eliminate the influence of ideas from abroad, but to use only what was sound and safe. In the words of an historian of Moscow University,

[the aim of education was] to stimulate in all estates, but especially in the gentry, the spirit of patriotic competition . . . to provide for [our youth] all the means necessary to follow the achievements, inventions, and discoveries of the worldwide enlightenment and to transmit these benefits to the fatherland, eliminating harm and evil which are inevitable in all affairs of men; for that purpose to raise the universities and to place them on a level with contemporary European scholarship; . . . to stimulate the development of the practical sciences, useful to society, trade, and industry, in order to develop the material forces of the state and thus to keep pace with the better aspects of the progress of scholarship in the West; in another sense, to oppose its materialism, to sanctify the entire temple of popular education by the Lord's altar, the cross, and prayer—these are the problems which have been solved in the course of the last thirty years in the history of education of our fatherland, according to the thought and the will of our indefatigable monarch.[52]

This statement brings out the full paradox of the official position. Even its most conservative leaders realized that Russia could not dispense with Western ideas, provided of course that these ideas were safeguarded against the political contamination of Western constitutionalism.

Russia had acquired the status of a great power. The Russian population more than doubled between 1800 and 1860, reaching 74.1 million people. Between 1804 and 1860, the number of enterprises increased by a factor of six and the work force by a factor of five. To be sure, half a million industrial workers in a population of 74 million did not indicate very speedy progress, but the economy was beginning to move. Total exports and imports increased tenfold between 1802 and 1860. In the Baltic ports, the number of ships almost doubled, while in the Black Sea ports, that number increased by a factor of six. Urbanization between 1811 and 1863 gives a similar picture of slow but definite growth, with population increase in selected Russian cities ranging from a low of 1.2 to a high of 15.4 percent. Urban population in European Russia doubled between 1811 and 1863, reaching 6.1 million or about 10 percent by the latter year.[53]

To develop and maintain the position indicated by these figures, Russia had to develop a skilled work force, literacy, and an educated elite. A vigorous educational system was needed as a source of technical personnel. Such a system could propagate approved beliefs and suppress heretical or subversive views, even as it strove to combat the profound ignorance of the population and helped narrow the great divide between a Europeanized gentry and an illiterate peasantry. Nevertheless, education is a mixed blessing in an autocracy, however much it may be shielded against subversive influences. When the student is introduced to the physical and intellectual world around him, his analytic capacity is improved. The schools and universities facilitate the state's search for qualified personnel, but they also give larger segments of the population an opportunity to improve themselves. The higher education of commoners antagonized the traditionally privileged and caused discontent among the newly educated if they could not then seek or find employment commensurate with their new qualifications.

An expanding educational system tends to increase the students' expectations and jeopardize their ready compliance with prevailing conditions and, among a few, even the unquestioning devotion to the throne. Although leading officials were well aware of these risks, the government had no choice but to seek the desired results of education while avoiding or deflecting its potential dangers. That seemed a feasible undertaking as long as Russia's military preeminence remained intact. The state of Nicholas I invested a great part of its resources in the military establishment; hence, the foundations of tsarist society were shaken when that establishment went down to defeat in the Crimean War of 1854–1856.[54]

AUTOCRATIC REFORMS AND CIVIL SOCIETY

Of the countries examined here, eighteenth- and nineteenth-century Russia is a special case, for in comparison with Western Europe and Japan its civil society was very weak and developed only after 1861. In Russia, tsarist autocracy implemented the principle of a direct confrontation between government and the individual which in Western Europe was a basic tenet of the French revolution. With the rise of Muscovy, the functions of government had become concentrated, leading to a centralized system of taxation, adjudication, and conscription. Many other spheres of life also became subject to governmental regulation. In a nation of subjects or of citizens, *civil society* refers to all institutions in which individuals can pursue common interests without detailed direction or interference from the government.[f] The municipal corporations and parlements of eighteenth-century France are examples of civil society. In Prussia, where the Hohenzollern rulers suppressed the estate-assemblies, landed aristocrats still associated with one another to conduct their local affairs. In Japan, which had no institutions resembling the estate-assemblies of Europe, many daimyo domains were large enough so that deliberations and the formulation of common interests took place on a regional basis. In the case of Russia, a number of assemblies (*zemskii sobor*) had been convened under the early Romanovs, but their main purpose was the restoration of stable government, and they lacked the will to oppose autocratic rule; they came to an end after 1653. Villages and landed aristocrats on their estates also had a degree of autonomy (buttressed by the Charter of 1785), but they were isolated from other villages and estates. Western European regimes and Japan possessed civil societies because they had inherited a tradition of local privileges or liberties. Russia did not enjoy a comparable inheritance.[55]

The rise of the Muscovite state had left as its enduring legacy a servitor aristocracy, servitor municipalities, and an enserfed peasantry.

---

[f] The term *civil society* corresponds to Montesquieu's *corps intermédiaires*. See the earlier discussion of civil society under the ancien régime and of the opposition to civil society under the inspiration of the Enlightenment and the French revolution (Chapter 10, "An Equality of Rights").

All concerted action depended on commands by the tsar and his officials. "Modernization" in eighteenth- and nineteenth-century Russia is in good part the story of the tsarist government trying to rule the huge country from the center. When measures were adopted which required some action below, it was a matter of local "independence at the tsar's command," to be exercised in the interest of the state. The tsar's subjects had no rights. Peter III's edict of 1762 and Catherine's Charter of 1785 abolished the earlier obligation of the aristocracy to serve the state, and allowed occasional meetings of consultative assemblies of the aristocracy. But these measures did not establish representative institutions with a jurisdiction of their own. The development of some independence from an omnipresent bureaucracy belongs only to the period after 1856, when autocratic reforms had given the initial impetus toward the emancipation of the serfs and the meeting of assemblies (*zemstvos*).

The Russian development of the nineteenth and twentieth centuries set a precedent for plebiscitarian types of domination which differ from the movements toward a mandate of the people considered thus far. *Plebiscitarian domination* is my term for modern, one-party dictatorships in which governments typically rule in the name of the people. The extension of this term to nineteenth-century Russia may be awkward, since the tsars ruled over the people in the name of God; but the patriarchal claim of being the father of his people implies quasi-plebiscitarianism in the sense that the tsars periodically appealed to the people for declarations of loyalty by acclamation. The idea of the tsar as God's representative on earth was among the most venerable traditions of Russian culture. Tsarist ministers, conservative journalists, members of the aristocracy, large segments of the peasantry, and—as we shall see—the Soviet regime after 1928 adhered to the view that *any* organization of interests in civil society constitutes a usurpation of sovereign authority.

The principle of autocracy required that the tsar initiate all government policies personally. The consequences of this claim to omnipotence were very real, although omnipotence is a chimera. Max Weber has pointed out that "the Russian tsar of the *ancien régime* was rarely able to put across permanently anything that displeased his bureaucracy and violated its power interests."[56] Weber attributed this inability to the expert knowledge of the officials and to bureaucratic infighting over issues of policy. In each ministry, different proposals on how to deal with the issues were naturally interlaced with personal intrigues and organizational ambitions. Each ministry depended on its leading officials to be on good terms with the tsar, or with those select few who for a time had access to him. Each sought to present certain proposals as the only appropriate means of executing the tsar's wishes and maintaining his authority.

Faced with difficult policy questions and beleaguered by competing officials, the tsar would seek the counsel of his confidants. In 1809 Alexander I initiated his project of legal reform after discussion with a circle of friends who had been the companions of his youth. Such confidants might or might not be called on to serve in an official capacity. As long as these advisors retained the tsar's trust, they constituted a shadow cabinet on which he would call for counsel or assistance in any manner he deemed appropriate. This created uncertainty at the very center of affairs because the members of the shadow cabinet would often acquire great, even decisive influence over decisions, but nevertheless remain hidden behind the tsar's person.

Further uncertainty was created by the disjunction between authority and responsibility. The tsar announced all major decisions as his own, and he appointed the ministers responsible for the implementation of his policy. But policies are formulated in general terms, while the difficulties and ambiguities lie in the details. The tsar would often vacillate in view of the conflicting advice he received. He frequently delegated responsibility to ministers representing incompatible points of view who sometimes served concurrently in different fields of policy and sometimes consecutively in the same field. Between 1802 and 1917, Russia's six tsars appointed among them thirty-six ministers of the interior, twenty-seven ministers of education, twenty-five ministers of transportation, twenty-one ministers of justice, nineteen ministers of war, eighteen ministers of finance, and fifteen ministers of foreign affairs.[57] This simple index suggests that the most difficult problems facing the autocracy concerned matters under the jurisdiction of the minister of the interior, especially serfdom and self-government. Tsarist policies concerning these two problems illustrate the relations between autocracy and civil society.

Between the 1780s and 1850s market considerations affected the management of landed estates as opportunities of selling agricultural products increased at home and abroad. Whenever serf owners found it profitable to produce for the market, they preferred the use of forced labor (*barshchina*) to the collection of a head tax (*obrok*). On the whole, forced labor was preferred in fertile areas and the head tax in less fertile ones, or where serfs could earn wages that could be taxed. The overall growth of commercial agriculture is suggested by the fact that the percentage of serfs who were obliged to render their dues in the form of labor on the owner's land rose from about 50 percent in 1790 to 70 percent in the 1850s.[58]

Total agricultural output increased with the growth of the serf population. But increases in output per man-hour, while needed for increased income and revenue, were difficult or impossible to obtain as

Russian Serf Owners
About 100,000 Russian aristocrats owned some 25 million serfs, though such ownership was very unequally distributed. When hard pressed for cash, some of the masters would bet their lands and their serfs as stakes in poker games. (Paul Gustave Doré, *Histoire pittoresque, dramatique et caricatures de la sainte Russie,* 1854)

long as serfdom continued. To achieve more productivity, serfs would have had to abandon their primitive farming methods and consolidate the lands they tilled. Such consolidation would have disrupted the rural social order based on the three-field system and the periodic repartitioning of fields among members of the community. For their part, the owners supported village practices in the interest of maintaining law and order. Nor had many serf owners an interest in improvements. They were reluctant to invest capital in new methods of cultivation when they often had more land than they could farm and, besides, an abundance of cheap labor which could be exploited without apparent cost to themselves. The official attitude reinforced resistance to change by emphasizing that the serfs did not engage in agriculture for their own profit, but as an obligation to serve the sovereign, the estate owner, and the whole society.

Yet the government could not remain passive when social stability was threatened by peasant uprisings, the high debts of the aristocracy, and the collection of taxes by force. Regulations were issued to curb abuses of local authority. Credit was extended in the hope that it would be put to productive use. Attempts were made to achieve better agricultural practices by experimenting with model villages. More freedom was granted to state peasants and peasants on tsarist lands in the hope of increasing agricultural productivity. All these measures were so many efforts to undo the effects of serfdom *without* disturbing the privileges of the aristocracy or the established practices of peasant serfs in their villages.[59] But any attempts at local reform under central direction depended on the will to act and the means to do so. In this respect, the tsarist government was underfinanced and understaffed and could not rely on local cooperation. Until well into the nineteenth century, local affairs were controlled by serf owners and village communities.

From a conservative standpoint, serfdom appeared as the cornerstone of Russian society, though from Catherine II to Nicholas I Russia's rulers had mentioned on occasion that something needed to be done about serfdom. Pride in the established order, the growth of agricultural production, and the alarmed reaction to the Decembrist revolt of 1825 put this question aside until the utter collapse of Russian forces in the Crimean War (1854–1856).[60] That defeat brought the faults of the country's social organization to the surface, particularly the institution of serfdom.

That institution was linked directly to Russia's military position. Most European states maintained a small standing army in peacetime to hold down costs, but kept a large trained reserve in case of war. Russia alone maintained a large standing army which in time of need could *not* be greatly or rapidly expanded. The Crimean War had shown that the army was unequal to the task. When the outcome of the war hung in the balance, the Russian high command could muster only 100,000 men for the purpose (out of a total of 2.25 million men under arms), because substantial forces were needed on the western frontiers. At that point, even the enlistment of another 1 million raw recruits did not help, because the necessary officers and equipment were unavailable.

The Crimean War absorbed more than three times the empire's annual revenue and removed more than one million men from the economy for three years. Serfdom was the specific reason for the absence of a trained reserve corps, for Russia's inordinately large military budget in peacetime, and for its manpower difficulties in time of war.

> Under serfdom the army was recruited from the tax-paying population (peasant and *meshchanin* or urban poor) on the basis of five or six per thousand for a period of twenty-five years. Every serf who fulfilled his service obligation left the army a free man, but few were lucky enough to survive the long term and those who did were hardly fit for further military service in any capacity. In other words they could not be expected to form the nucleus of a trained reserve.

The obvious alternative of reducing the term of service and building up a trained reserve was considered too dangerous. It would have greatly increased the annual recruitment, freed serfs at a rapid rate, and left a mass of landless rural laborers trained in the use of firearms.[61]

Great political decisions like the emancipation of the serfs have complex origins and neither the Crimean debacle nor Russia's problems of military manpower were alone decisive. There had been talk of emancipation since the Prussian reform legislation early in the century and the antislavery campaigns in England and America in the 1840s. Under Nicholas I, some high government officials were sensitive to foreign opinion and aware that serfdom symbolized Russia's backwardness. But the fact remains that emancipation was initiated by Alexander II (1855–1881) just after the Crimean defeat and that the tsar gave the highest priority to military considerations. The military reforms adopted between 1867 and 1870 also show the close relation between serfdom and military questions. The minister of war, D. A. Miliutin (1861–1881), more than doubled the effective reserve of the Russian army. With the backing of the tsar, but against heavy opposition, Miliutin worked successfully to introduce universal military service and reduce the term of service to six years. This recruitment policy put newly emancipated peasants on a par with members of the aristocracy, for now both had equal obligations. It is probable, therefore, that Alexander committed himself to emancipation because he wanted to preserve Russia's position as a great military power, and the Crimean defeat had put that position in question.

Before an audience of the Moscow gentry, Alexander II declared in 1856,

> You yourselves know that the existing order of ruling over living souls cannot remain unchanged. It is better to abolish serfdom from above than to await the day when it will begin to abolish itself from below. I ask you, gentlemen, to consider how this is to be accomplished. Convey my words to the gentry for their consideration.[62]

The tsar thus attached some importance to the cooperation of the gentry. He wrote that "it was up to the nobles to figure out how all this can best be carried out."[63] But the tsar did not await the deliberations of the aristocracy. On returning to Petersburg, he immediately instructed the Ministry of the Interior to elaborate the principles of the reform and the methods of putting it into effect.[64]

In fact, there was little reason for the tsar to count on the wealthy gentry to cooperate, for emancipation meant a direct threat to their accustomed way of life. Moreover, tsarist officials had reason to distrust the leading members of the local gentry, who did not relish the attempts of the central government to administer local affairs. During the preceding reign of Nicholas I, the staff of provincial and district governments had increased between two and eight times. It is estimated that the staffs of all central agencies increased four times between 1801 and 1851. Administrative expenditures naturally soared. Still, Russia remained an "undergoverned" country, especially at the local level, although complaints about the burdens of officialdom were legion. Various partial studies have led scholars to the conclusion that around 1850 the country had about 1.2 civil servants per 1,000 population. Such a proportion becomes significant when it is contrasted to 4.1 public officials per 1,000 in Britain (1851) and about 4.8 officials per 1,000 in France (1845).[65]

Russia's great increase of taxes during the first half of the nineteenth century largely benefited the military budget, interest payments on foreign loans, and an expanded finance ministry. Between the defeat of Napoleon in 1812 and the outbreak of the Crimean War in 1854, the country remained a nation at arms, with debts from military expenses mounting rapidly even during the periods of peace from 1832 to 1849. In 1854, France had one soldier for every sixty-two inhabitants, while Russia, with its much greater poverty, had one soldier for every seventy-five inhabitants.[66] Between 1812 and 1854, local government received hardly any additional funds, though the number of clerks increased. That paradox is explained by low pay. Provincial governors had to re-

A Provincial Administrator in Tsarist Russia
Unlettered persons from the rural areas were given administrative responsibilities. This lithograph by P. M. Boklevsky for Nicolai Gogol's comedy *The Inspector* (1863) shows a low functionary decked out in a uniform and shining leather boots "barking" at the well-fed merchants standing humbly before him. "You scoundrels, rascals, and swindlers, you want to bring a lawsuit against me?!" The servants carrying the wares and the ladies in the background are silent witnesses to the merchants' humiliation. (P. M. Boklevsky, *Byurokratichesky Katakhezis*, St. Petersburg, 1863)

cruit nearly uneducated rural folk; few educated persons were either available or willing to serve in provincial administration. With funds short and the military successfully pressing its claims, the low pay of provincial officials was justified by their lack of qualification. Provincial government was thus chronically understaffed, unqualified, or both. It was frequently this need for staff at the local level which prompted the government to attempt the corporate organization of the provincial gentry. The object was to improve local administration, not to encourage local political activity. But the coopted notables were reluctant to serve and reacted to the flood of central directives by tacit resistance.

Accordingly, the tsar's declaration of 1856 accentuated a basic dilemma of autocratic rule. To emancipate the peasants without consulting the gentry would have needlessly affronted the principal supporters and beneficiaries of the regime, as well as jeopardized the fiction of the gentry as the "first estate" of the realm. But to consult the gentry presupposed a tradition of constructive participation in questions of public policy which did not exist. Consultation also ran the risk of finding the majority of wealthy aristocrats opposed to emancipation, or at any rate to any specific implementation of the policy. However, not to consult the gentry meant that the government deliberately ignored local information and issued decrees in a vacuum. Hence, the logic of the situation demanded that the tsar and his ministers retain the initiative for reform but obtain local cooperation by a type of consultation that was clearly distinguished from political participation and all forms of constitutionalism. Expressions of opinion on the emancipation issue were dangerous for autocratic rule, and yet indispensable for its exercise. This paradox is worth analyzing because it reveals what may be called a quasi-civil society (that is, the kind of politics that was still compatible with personal autocracy).

The tsar's Moscow address seems to have opened the floodgates of public opinion. Between 1825 and 1855 the number of newspapers and journals founded per annum had averaged 8.3, but between 1856 and 1863 that annual average increased to 33.4. In addition, in the 1850s various government ministries made their house organs a forum of discussion on matters of policy. A latent public opinion was ready to play its part, once the signal had been given from above. Moreover, the tradition of referring to Western models was quickly felt. In 1855 only 97 articles on European countries appeared in Russian publications, but in the two succeeding years that number jumped to 269 and 300, respectively. Self-help organizations in the provinces also were proliferating to an astonishing degree. The Imperial Free Economic Society of Petersburg became a clearing house for schools of trade and agriculture and for small public libraries opening in provincial towns. Primary schools were opened as were Sunday schools, a Petersburg conservatory, and commissions on literacy and political economy as part of the Imperial Geographic Society. Professor Starr, from whose study these data are taken, speaks of a "political effervescence" among members of the provincial gentry which was matched by reform-minded officials in the capital.[67]

But the tsar's initial declaration elicited little coherent response. He toured the provinces in person to goad the gentry into action and receive the grateful thanks of the serfs. Recalcitrants were admonished to be grateful for their loving sovereign's benevolence. Meanwhile, the ministries in St. Petersburg worked out the details and inevitably came to incompatible conclusions, one group favoring the gentry and another the serfs. Officials on both sides subjected the tsar to a barrage of proposals, each making his case more persuasive by the "public" support he could elicit for his side. This appeal to the parties concerned was unavoidable. No case could be made without the opinions of the gentry, the provincial governors, and others. Indeed, the tsar himself had called for their opinions. Nevertheless, every unofficial opinion was viewed with the deepest distrust, since no one outside the government could act in the matter. Alexander complained that there was no one he could trust and no one who took this burden from his shoulders. He was indeed a lonely man, for under autocracy the ultimate decision rested with him.

In effect, the tsarist government took the lead in formulating its policy of emancipation and then attempted to elicit expressions of opinion in support of that policy. Lanskoi, the minister of the interior, urged a plan relatively favorable to the peasants and urged that it be tested in Lithuania where (with the consent of the tsar) instructions had been issued to Governor-General Nazimov to prod the gentry into responding to the imperial policy. Yet Nazimov arrived in St. Petersburg with proposals from the Vilna gentry which, contrary to government policy, favored emancipation of the serfs *without granting them any land*. This proposal had been approved by a secret advisory committee which the tsar had appointed. Thus, even in a committee of his own choice, a majority of the advisors were indifferent or hostile toward the reform which the tsar favored! Consequently, Alexander intervened personally, rejecting the principle of landless emancipation. He instructed Lanskoi to draft an imperial edict for Nazimov which would *direct* the gentry to set up provincial committees in Lithuania to prepare precise proposals. These proposals were to include the following principles:

> The landlords were to remain owners of the land, but the peasants were to acquire ownership, by purchase over a definite period of time, of their house and the surrounding lot, and were also to be assured the use of further land, sufficient for their needs, in return for *obrok* or labor services. The peasants were to be allotted to village communities, but the landlords were to retain

police powers and there were to be arrangements to ensure the payment of taxes and the discharge of local services.[68]

Subsequently, this program was published as an imperial directive in 1857. The existence of the tsar's secret committee was made public, but its members continued to disagree, and different ministries submitted conflicting plans of administrative implementation.

It was difficult to choose among these conflicting schemes, with their main intent often obscured by details. Publication of the edict also led to lively discussions in the press, so lively and radical that censorship was imposed in April 1858 to confine the discussion to "learned, theoretical, and statistical articles." During that year committees were set up in most provinces of Russia; these were as evenly divided between opponents and advocates of reform as the tsar's own committee. To deal with the mass of material that was coming in from the provinces (often consisting of majority and minority views), editorial commissions were appointed in 1859.

Two main questions were at issue. First, how much land should be given to the peasants and on what terms? Second, what local administrative authority should replace the authority the landowners had exercised over their serfs? The details of these many-sided issues do not concern us here, but it is relevant to observe the overlapping conflicts which surfaced in this debate over emancipation. First, there was the conflict between serf owners eager to retain their privileges and tsarist officials eager to emancipate the serfs. However, some landowners voluntarily freed their serfs and acted as advocates of emancipation, while some government officials (like the ministers of state domains and of finance) continued to oppose emancipation at the risk of incurring the tsar's displeasure. Second, there was the conflict between officials in the central government at St. Petersburg and the provincial governors, with most officials at the center and some governors advocating (or appealing to) central decision-making on all issues while some officials and most governors advocated the devolution of authority. Third, there was the conflict within the camp of the reformers between bureaucrats who were convinced that emancipation could be realized only by a benevolent autocracy, and landowners who coupled emancipation with the idea of an elected local government, and ultimately with some form of a national assembly.[69]

The whole process involved the tsarist regime in half-directing and half-soliciting the expression of opinion on the question of emancipation. In effect, the autocracy had initiated a degree of public participation which was ultimately incompatible with personal autocracy. Nor could it be expected that the provincial gentry, so long habituated to receiving commands through a rigid hierarchy from above, would necessarily abide by the terms of the debate as the government conceived of them. Eventually, the gentry lost their accustomed reticence and raised larger issues, especially those of representation, self-government, and judicial reform. Elements of a civil society were emerging.

In 1859–1860 deputies from the provincial assemblies were called to St. Petersburg. This was the first instance in which the government had called on the aristocracy for consultation since Catherine's legislative commission of 1767. A good many deputies apparently believed (or wanted to believe) that they had been invited as legislators to plan the reform. Lanskoi and other high officials were apprehensive that the expression of opinion could lead to the fusion of "like-thinking parties" and the formation of harmful oligarchies. The tsar himself proceeded on the assumption that the deputies from the provincial committees understood that they had been invited to clear up points of detail, not to discuss the basic principles of reform which were his exclusive pre-rogative. The clash came when one group of deputies submitted a pe-tition directly criticizing the editorial commissions, while another group put forward a whole democratic political program. The two petitions were isolated instances. But the government severely rebuked both groups of deputies and issued a ban on all further discussion of gov-ernment projects. Nevertheless, further discussions ensued when the deputies returned to their provincial assemblies, and by 1860 the gov-ernment relented by stipulating five questions on which it would wel-come the opinion of the gentry. Significantly, these questions referred to problems of local administration and excluded the emancipation is-sue. The imperial decree on the emancipation of the serfs was issued in 1861, an amalgam of reformist and conservative impulses.[70] Many of the controversial issues were left for future decision by specially ap-pointed arbitrators.[g]

The emancipation of the serfs was ultimately achieved on terms agreeable to the government. Consultation with the gentry had taken place, but without political discussion. Petitions for participation in pol-icy decisions, or for a legislative assembly, were rejected out of hand and "proper" penalties meted out to the petitioners. In the years after 1861, this conservative impulse was greatly reinforced by the constitutional demands of the Tver' assembly under the leadership of A. M. Unkovsky in 1862, the Polish insurrection of 1863, increasing student agitation, and the unsuccessful attempt on the tsar's life in 1866. These events almost eliminated whatever generous impulses toward the former serfs

---

[g] The debate I have described concerned only about one-half of the serf population. The other half belonged to the state, the tsarist family, and the church. Their freedom from serf law depended on actions of the central government which preceded or paral-leled the "emancipation period" from 1861 on.

existed in the highest circles, where it was perceived that the tsar's un-limited personal authority must be maintained at all costs. The regime depended on the tsar's right of ultimate decision and of preemptive in-tervention in all affairs of the realm. Professor Starr has pointed out,

> In crisis situations Russia's top bureaucrats needed the broad principle of autocracy even if in daily practice they did not need the autocrat himself. This truth helps to explain the anxiety which all local initiatives, administra-tive or public, aroused in Petersburg during every crisis from the Crimean War to 1917.[71]

Autocratic rule did not allow for peaceful ways of limiting its authority, whether personally exercised by the tsar or by his officials. The up-heavals of the 1860s and 1870s reinforced this conviction and over-shadowed the whole debate over local self-government.

From the standpoint of civil society at the local level, conditions had deteriorated markedly by the middle of the nineteenth century. The gentry did little to improve agricultural productivity, but instead sought to increase output and their own income by more severe exploitation. Their serfs were forced to work the owner's land (barshchina) to such an extent that it encroached on their ability just to subsist from working the plots assigned to them. At the same time, the numbers of the Russian aristocracy increased, and so did their conspicuous consumption. Two consequences followed. On the one hand, the gentry resorted to state credit to meet their increasing "needs." One way of doing so was to mortgage the future production of their serfs: The number of serfs mortgaged to the state rose from 1.8 million in 1820 to 7.1 million in 1859, the latter figure representing 66 percent of all serfs and the equiv-alent of 425 million rubles.[72] On the other hand, peasant unrest in-creased, and peasant uprisings in the midst of the Crimean War com-plicated matters still further.

Clearly, social stability in the countryside was in jeopardy. We know of these difficulties at the local level primarily through the reactions of officials. In Russia (as in France after 1800) even minor provincial affairs had to be brought to the attention of the central government for its consideration and decision. By 1851 the costs of that centralization had become so prohibitive that ministries were instructed to cut down on procedures and correspondence so as to reduce their staffs. In the two decades prior to the Crimean War various publicists and officials had studied the Western European experience of local administrative re-forms, and this study resulted in the establishment of a Committee on Reducing Correspondence. Its deliberations became urgent as the gov-ernment's financial situation deteriorated in the 1850s. Yet the com-mittee could accomplish nothing as long as the tsar and his officials distrusted every sign of local initiative. As one Petersburg censor and senator pointed out in 1856, any reduction of centralization and hence of governmental expenditures *meant that more power and appropriate spheres of action must be surrendered to subordinate and local agencies.*[73]

The proposal to decentralize authority met with very determined opposition in several Petersburg ministries, but found widespread support among provincial governors. For decades, the latter's work had been hampered by close supervision and arbitrary interference from the center. Hence, the case for decentralization and local self-government orginated when liberal bureaucrats at the center coopted a carefully selected group of provincial governors. The efforts of this group of officials were ultimately successful. But this success only concerned the decentralization of authority to the provincial governors. Even if it had been carried out fully (and it was not), it would have meant that the tsarist government could exert its *own* authority more effectively at the regional and local levels. That would have been a considerable achievement, given the bureaucratic mores in the provinces. But more decentralized authority was still an *administrative* reform. It made no allowance as yet for more independence and initiative in provincial society itself. Indeed, there was little chance for the initiative of private persons or of local associations as long as the central government distrusted even its own agents. Administrative decentralization was a necessary condition for more local independence, but it was not sufficient.

While the issue of emancipation was being debated, it became clear that administrative decentralization could not be pushed too far. Landowners had possessed virtually absolute power over the serfs, and that power had to be abolished if the serfs were to be free. How, then, was local government to be administered? The answer was that the police power of the landowners was replaced by the police power of district and local officials, appointed by the Ministry of the Interior. That meant more centralization, not less. Reform-minded officials believed that the abolition of serf law required the initiative of enlightened authority, since officials would protect the interest of peasants against the avarice of the landowners. This belief was shared by Russian liberals who feared that even if a national representative assembly could be established, it would be dominated by landed interests and encroach on the interests of the peasants.

Some sections of the aristocracy continued to demand such an assembly despite the prohibition to do so. They favored local self-government as a first step toward a constitutional monarchy. On the other hand, conservatives opposed provincial self-government as well as a representative assembly, because they thought both threatened autocratic rule. Thus, the reform of local government and hence new opportunities for a civil society at least at the local level were burdened at the outset with a very deep-seated lack of trust. The government's fear of challenges to absolute authority was matched by the fear of reformers that local initiative would enhance entrenched interests and hence perpetuate or even intensify the poverty and exploitation of the rural population. Local self-government developed despite these misgivings because emancipation had provided the necessary impetus, for the problems of local administration it entailed were too numerous to be handled by the government unaided.

In 1864 an edict on local government instituted an assembly (*zemstvo*) at the level of the district (*uezd*) and the province. The district assemblies were elected by three separate electoral colleges, composed of gentry, townsmen, and peasants, respectively. The provincial assemblies in turn were composed of delegates elected by the district assemblies from among their own members. Procedures varied among the three social groups. Most representatives came from the aristocracy, but its previous monopoly of access to authority had been curtailed.

Under the law of 1864, zemstvo institutions were established in nineteen provinces during the following year, then in fifteen additional provinces in the period 1866–1875, and in nine more in 1911 and 1913. By 1914 the Russian empire had zemstvo institutions in forty-three out of seventy provinces. With regard to a number of programs, the advocates of self-government were certainly vindicated. As a whole, district and provincial assemblies were a success in road-building, the supervision of forests, the management of credit institutions, the administration of vaccinations, and the control of epidemics. They also introduced an effective system of fire insurance where none had existed before, and in a country of wooden buildings this was a great advance. Nevertheless, the financial record of the zemstvos also makes clear that from the first they were hampered by the limitations placed on their right to levy local taxes. As zemstvo institutions were established in additional provinces, their aggregate revenue increased from 5.6 million rubles in 1865 to 24.2 and 33.1 million rubles in 1870 and 1880, respectively. But until the 1890s, these district and provincial assemblies were forced to spend between 40 and 50 percent of their funds for nonlocal purposes, such as conscription, relief of families of war casualties, and certain expenses of judicial officials.[74]

Throughout the 1860s and 1870s, conservative spokesmen considered the zemstvo movement suspect because of its association with the earlier gentry agitation for a national representative assembly. Official suspicions were reinforced by the radical agitation of the period. As a result, each assembly had to find out anew how to distinguish between properly local matters and those which, in the shifting views of the government, encroached on the prohibited sphere of politics and public debate. Above all, the zemstvo faced financial and organizational difficulties. In the field of public health, appropriations were nonexistent or chronically insufficient and trained personnel unavailable. Schools faced similar difficulties, and many assemblies tried to pass responsibility for education to local church institutions, or to the arbitrators who had been appointed after 1861 to settle disputes arising from the emancipation edict. Most zemstvo programs were hampered because the collection of taxes remained in the hands of the local police over whom they had no authority. Assemblies could administer local affairs, but were given little financial resources and no police authority to do so effectively.[75]

The assemblies struggled on despite these handicaps, and their efforts represent an important development of civil society in recent Russian history. In the political debates of the time, the work of the zemstvo came to be known as "liberalism of small deeds." It is true that increasing restrictions were placed on them after the unsuccessful attempt on the tsar's life in 1866. Communication among the zemstvo of different areas was prohibited, and all zemstvo publications required the approval of the provincial governor. Supervision of local education was put in the hands of marshals of the aristocracy with minimal zemstvo representation. Local officials elected by the zemstvo were replaced by government officials. Provincial governors were given controlling authority over the membership of zemstvo boards, over zemstvo decisions, and over the selection of peasant delegates whose already small number was reduced further. Perhaps the most damaging restriction was a new law which

> held the presidents of assemblies and directorates to full account for the legality of any measure passed under their chairmanship. Specifically, presidents were expected henceforth to open and close all meetings, approve the agenda, cut debate on unscheduled topics, maintain order, and close the meeting in the event of any action violating the general interests of the state.[76]

Yet controls were easier to decree than to implement. Provincial officials could not be everywhere, their numbers remained inadequate, and the zemstvos continued their efforts.[77]

In practice, the tsarist government of the later nineteenth century did not want to tolerate the independent activity of zemstvo institutions but could not quite control the local aristocrats who had become active in these institutions. Much the same conclusion follows from the record of judicial reform. Enacted into law in 1864, like the zemstvo reforms, the new statutes seemed to establish for Russia the accepted principles of European jurisprudence. Their implementation spread rapidly, but by 1868 a reactionary trend set in with the appointment of Count C. I. Pahlen, an opponent of the reform, as minister of justice. What followed was a cumulative record of administrative exceptions to the established rule of law. An ever-increasing number of cases was transferred to special judicial tribunals which would handle issues of the press, crimes against the state, and related matters in close agreement with the precepts of tsarist autocracy.[78] But these restrictive measures could not undo what the government itself had started—namely, the development of a legal profession with standards of its own.

The record of reform in local self-government and the judicial system indicates that in the last decades of the nineteenth century, the tsarist government could no longer forego the sponsorship of economic growth, education, and new professional activity, each of which stimulated local and individual initiative which in turn clashed with the restrictions of autocratic rule. After 1861 these developments, all under state sponsorship, engendered a civil society (that is, associations intervening between the individual and the state), despite quite determined efforts by the government to control and curtail them.

In 1861 Russia was still a predominantly agrarian country with only the beginnings of industry and almost without railroads, a banking system, or business corporations. Methods of production and distribution were backward in comparison with Western Europe and the average standard of living correspondingly low. Population growth was a main force for change in the postemancipation period, the total increasing from 74 million in 1861 to nearly 170 million in 1916. During this same period the railroad network developed from a mere 1,000 miles to 40,000 miles, a major factor in the development of heavy industry and the marketing of agricultural products. Agriculture continued to be marked by low per-acre yields and low output per man-hour in comparison with more advanced countries. Nevertheless, there was a major expansion of the area under cultivation and a slow growth in yield per acre. Agriculture remained the most important sector of the economy, with nearly one-half of the national income deriving from it as late as 1913. Grain exports rose roughly sixfold between 1860 and 1895 and constituted about 50 percent of Russian exports in the last three decades of the century. The use of fertilizers, machinery, and scientific farming methods was only beginning in a limited way in the years before World War I. Overall, it is estimated that agricultural production increased at the rate of about 1 percent per year, in contrast to industrial production (including manufacturing, mining, and handicraft) which increased at a rate of 5 percent per year.

However, this development started from a very low level in 1860. By 1913 industry employed only about 5 percent of the labor force but contributed about one-fifth of national income. The total volume of output including not only industry and agriculture, but trade, transportation, and services may have increased at an annual rate of 2.5 percent. This exceeded the growth of population by about 1 percent. It should be remembered that the averages given for the period 1860 to

TABLE 5

RUSSIAN CLASS STRUCTURE in 1897

	Numbers	*(Percentage)*
A. Hereditary nobility including		
1. Whole noble landowning class		
2. Highest ranks of the armed forces		
3. Highest ranks of the bureaucracy		
4. Highest ranks of the professions	1,220,169	(0.97)
B. Personal nobles and officials not of the nobility including		
1. Great majority from higher government service (numbers doubled between 1880 and 1914)		
2. Some landowners		
3. Some professionals	630,119	(0.50)
C. Ecclesiastics	588,947	(0.47)
D. Upper classes in towns (other than nobles and officials)		
1. Distinguished citizens (many professionals)	342,927	(0.27)
2. Merchants (business class)	281,179	(0.22)
E. Urban poor (*meshchane*) including		
1. Small shopkeepers		
2. White-collar employees		
3. Artisans		
4. Urban Workers	13,386,392	(10.66)
F. Peasants including		
1. Cossacks (some 3 million)		
2. Large floating population of the casually employed (some 6.6 million)	99,825,490	(79.45)
G. Indigenous peoples	8,297,965	(6.61)
H. Finns	35,585	
I. Other social classes	353,913	(0.37)
J. Unclassified	71,835	
K. Foreigners	605,500	(0.48)
L. Total	125,640,021	

SOURCE: N. A. Troynitsky, ed., *Obshchii svod po imperii rezul'tatov razrabotki dannykh pervoy vseobshchey perepisi naseleniia, Proizve-Dennoi 28 Ianvaria 1897 Goda* (St. Petersburg, 1905), I, pp. 160–1. I am indebted to John Brown of the George Kennan Institute, Smithsonian Institution, Washington, D.C., for assistance with this source. The categories are adapted from Seton-Watson, *Russian Empire,* pp. 534–5.

A Political Caricature of Russia's Social Hierarchy

About three years after the 1897 census the Union of Russian Socialists issued a caricature of Russian society in a clandestine leaflet. At the top of the pyramid the tsar and tsarina are depicted: "We reign over you." Below them are leading representatives of government: "We rule over you." At the third level are the dignitaries of the church: "We brainwash you." The soldiers are at the fourth level: "We shoot at you." At the fifth level are members of the aristocracy in a social gathering: "We eat for you." At the bottom, the people are crushed by the whole superstructure: "We work for you, we feed you." The stanza below reads: "The time will come when the people in their fury will straighten their bent backs and bring down the structure with one mighty push of their shoulders." (Saltykov Schedrin Public Library, Leningrad)

1913 disguise not only considerable fluctuations (including sporadic famines), but also the difference between rather slow growth between 1860 and the 1880s and quite rapid growth after 1890.[79]

The effect of these developments can be summarized by Table 5, a statistical summary of the Russian class structure, based on the 1897 census. This tabulation should be read in the light of developments since 1861, specifically the decline of the landowning gentry and the rise of an independent peasantry as well as the great prominence of professionals as compared with entrepreneurs in the composition of the "middle class."

In practice, the aristocratic landowners did not benefit from emancipation. Their holdings fell from 87.2 million desiatiny in 1862 to 43.2 million in 1911 (1 desiatina = 2.7 acres). They received nearly 600 million rubles for acreage ceded during 1861–1871, but almost half of this reverted to the treasury as payment for outstanding mortgage loans. Little of the rest was invested in agriculture, and by 1880 the gentry's mortgage debt had risen once again to 400 million rubles, exceeding the debt level before 1861. During the same period, the holdings by individual peasants, peasant associations, and peasant communes rose from 5.7 to 30.4 million desiatiny, while the other 19.3 million desiatiny were acquired by merchants and other townspeople.[80]

Along with the growth of industry and the rise of professionals, educational facilities were developed through the foundation of the Academy of Science (1725), universities (from 1755 to 1819), secondary schools (after 1825), and elementary schools (after 1840). Students in elementary schools increased from 400,000 in 1856 to about 2.2 million in 1885, an increase of 450 percent in one generation. Arcadius Kahan has put this development in perspective by comparing the growth of an industrial work force with the development of student enrollments.

> During the period 1860–1913 the number of employed industrial, construction and railroad workers increased about 4.3 times (from 1,960,000 to 8,415,000), while pupils in elementary and secondary schools increased 16 times (600,000 to 9,840,000). In 1860 there were three times as many workers as school attendants; by 1900 the number of students already exceeded the number of workers by about 40 percent. However, during the years 1900–1913 workers increased relatively faster than pupils, and by 1913 students exceeded workers by only 12 percent.[81]

Between 1865 and 1914, the number of students at Russian universities increased from 4,641 to 35,695, almost a ninefold rise which does not include the considerable number of students at higher institutions of learning other than universities.[82]

As in other undeveloped economies, it proved easier for Russia to develop its educational facilities than its industrial plant. By the end of the century, the effect was a notable increase of professionals and white-collar workers. It is difficult to distinguish the two groups in the 1897 census, especially since it is impossible to say how many employees of the central and local government and how many military officers had professional training. Those clearly designated as professionals (teachers, literati, artists, doctors, lawyers, and engineers) numbered 222,703. If one assumes that all white-collar workers had received at least some secondary education, then the total number with higher education comes to 728,106. (The latter figure includes government employees in the military and civilian bureaucracy.)[83] The higher ranks of all white-collar workers and professionals taken together are almost three times the size of the upper business class.

By the 1890s, it had become a stereotype in liberal and socialist circles that Russia did "not have a bourgeoisie in the Western European sense of the word."[84] Peter Struve made the same point more polemically when he stated that "the farther to the East in Europe, the more politically weak, cowardly, and base the bourgeoisie becomes."[85] These negative judgments are true if one considers that in Russia even prominent merchants obtained their often substantial advantages through services rendered to the state. Such businessmen became staunch defenders of tsarist economic policies. However, members of the professions were in a different position than businessmen. Doctors, lawyers, and engineers might be subordinate, but their training prepared them for independence and the cultivation of competence. For that reason, Russia's civil society developed through the associations of professionals.

The Imperial Free Economic Society of St. Petersburg had been founded in 1765 under the sponsorship of Catherine II. Its purpose was similar to that of several dozen agricultural associations, namely, to give assistance on the technical and economic questions of agriculture. But by the 1890s, owing to the developments I have traced, the Free Economic Society had become an expanded cultural center, in which academics, agricultural experts, journalists, and leading spokesmen of the feuding socialist groups argued rather freely about current economic and political issues. In 1863 the Moscow Society of Jurisprudence had been founded, and it too was a center of discussion as was the Pirogov Society of Russian Doctors, founded in 1885. The Economic Society of Petersburg was probably the most important of these associations; it had some eight hundred members comprising the leading members of the moderate intelligentsia in the capital. Government controls curtailed or suppressed both the Petersburg and the Moscow societies by 1900, but these associations were only the most prominent among many others. Writers and journalists developed a network of rather loose organizations, like the charitable Literary Fund, founded in 1859. Committees on illiteracy developed through which adult education, lecture classes, elementary reading courses, and grammar text-books were made available to many parts of the country.[86]

In the 1870s and 1880s, a number of interest organizations in the metal, petroleum, and other industries also developed. The government watched all these activities closely and imposed severe sanctions on "dangerous tendencies," but civil society was astir nonetheless. In the second half of the nineteenth century, voluntary associations were even promoted by the government, simply because they engaged in activities of which the government approved.

> In 1862, there were six private charitable organizations; in 1899, more than 7,000. Six learned societies were started in the eighteenth century, of which only one, the Free Economic Society, survived. In 1856, there were not more than 20 to 25 such societies, but in 1899 there were 340. By 1905, Russia had the beginnings of a network of voluntary associations—social, cultural, economic, scientific, etc.—all of them forbidden to pursue political aims and seemingly harmless.[87]

The author adds that under an edict of 1906 the regulation of these societies was shifted to provincial boards and that this allowed for more freedom than the stricter, central controls before 1905.

Russia's civil society was not destined to flourish in the long run despite promising beginnings. The tsarist government imposed increasingly restrictive measures. Official impulses toward reform were curtailed after the unsuccessful attempt on the tsar's life in 1866. Terrorist actions after 1878 and the assassination of Alexander II in 1881 brought on restrictions of the reforms which had been introduced after 1861. The thrust of this governmental reaction is critical to an understanding of the following developments and eventual revolution. In the European context, the English and French revolutions had preceded the execution of the king (in 1649 and 1793); in Russia, a reigning tsar was assassinated thirty-six years before the revolution. The terrorists were only a tiny splinter group within the Russian revolutionary movement; yet they represented the assassination of the tsar as implementing the People's Will and adopted the name *Narodnaya volya* which means both People's Will and People's Liberty. The tsarist government responded to the increasing violence not only by harsher measures against revolutionaries, but by imposing ever more severe restrictions on the zemstvos, the judiciary, and the professions. In the view of government spokesmen like K. P. Pobedonostsev (principal tsarist advisor, 1881–1905), all liberal movements within civil society (even those the government's own programs had sponsored) were signals of the revolution which must be suppressed at all costs.

At the accession of Nicholas II in 1894 there was little promise of change. Under the influence of Pobedonostsev, the new tsar warned

Assassination of Tsar Alexander II, 1881
(Illustrated London News, April 2, 1881)

representatives of the zemstvos not to engage in "senseless phantasies" such as plans for constitutional reform and specifically popular participation in the government. But by June 1905 the tsar had to reverse himself. The country had suffered an economic depression in the preceding years. In 1904 Pleve, the minister of the interior, had been assassinated. From January to May 1905 Russia suffered a series of disastrous defeats in its war with Japan, accompanied by a succession of strikes, assassinations, and revolutionary upheavals throughout Russia. By June 1905 the tsar declared to another zemstvo delegation that an assembly of elected representatives of the people was his "unalterable will." An imperial manifesto of October 1905 called for the introduction of freedom of speech, assembly, and association, popular suffrage, and the principle of legal enactments by a representative assembly (*duma*).

By then zemstvo and municipal institutions provided a basis for an organized response to this opportunity. Despite all the restrictions placed on them, these institutions had continued their "liberalism of small deeds," and both the professions and an intelligentsia of "legal Marxists" had developed apace. Congresses of these and related groups were held with the consent of the government even during the Russo-Japanese war. But the government was prepared to make only limited concessions once the imperial duma assembled. The first duma meeting of a little over two months was dissolved by July 1906; the second duma meeting of three months was dissolved in June 1907. Thereupon, the government changed the electoral law so that the third duma (1907–1912) would have a less "radical" composition. But despite this manipulation of the law to ensure compliance, much had changed. Political parties had legally recognized organizations and elected representatives in the assembly. Political issues could be openly discussed, and the main political groups had their own newspapers. Under these conditions even assemblies based on a very restricted franchise, like the third duma, were not servile or reactionary bodies. Further reforms were undertaken under Prime Minister P. A. Stolypin (1906–1911), a reformer but also a supporter of the regime, who was quite prepared to cooperate with elected representatives of the people, provided they complied with his policies. But despite the significant reforms introduced under his leadership, only a semiconstitutional politics was permitted. Laws voted by the duma became valid only through consent of the upper house, which was predominantly conservative, and the signature of the tsar. Ministers were responsible to the tsar rather than the duma; thus, no government could be voted out of office. In addition, the army and navy were exempt from the budgetary controls of the assembly. The basic distrust between tsarist ministers and the duma nullified the daily work of the parliamentary system which even these restrictions might have allowed under more favorable conditions. Stolypin was assassinated in 1911, just three years before the outbreak of World War I. The limited developments toward constitutionalism and a civil society were destroyed by the repercussions of that great conflict.

INTELLECTUAL OPPOSITION AS SOCIAL RESPONSIBILITY

In the last few decades of the nineteenth century, high officials frequently expressed the fear that voluntary associations, innocent as their civil purposes might be, would inevitably turn into political challenges. Officials were particularly apprehensive with regard to the free expression of ideas. In societies that are latecomers to industrialization, educated persons, including government officials, typically stress the importance of ideas as a means of effecting social change.

Questions as to what course Russia should follow had stirred intermittent controversy since the middle of the seventeenth century. Spokesmen for the old regime as well as those protesting against it alternated between reasserting Russia's national traditions and looking on various Western countries as exemplars in one respect or another. By the early nineteenth century, educated persons critical of the old regime began to gather in informal groups. In turn, the tsarist government saw the

growing interest in literature and philosophy as a source of danger. Intellectual awakening, an aspect of civil society, was bound to come into
conflict with autocratic rule and in fact was an early antecedent of the
Russian revolutions of 1905 and 1917.

During the nineteenth century, tsarist officials perceived, despite
their misgivings, that education was needed to train officers for the
military and specialists for the development of mining, agriculture, and
the manufacture of armaments. Equally important was the persistent
shortage of qualified personnel at higher levels of the civil service. According to one report, the empire had 80,000 government positions, of
which 3,000 fell vacant annually. But in the late 1850s only about 400
individuals graduated from the universities, lycées, and law schools.[88]
Accordingly, educational opportunities were expanded, especially in the
second half of the century.

As the gentry and leading officials adopted a more positive attitude,
education was advanced at all levels. The number of professionals increased rapidly, as evidenced in the census of 1897. Among the men
entering military service, literacy increased from 22 percent in 1880 to
65 percent in 1910, a 43 percent rise in thirty years. According to data
for factory labor in Vladimir district in 1897, workers age sixty and over
were about 30 percent literate, while young workers under fourteen
were over 60 percent literate. To be sure, the impact of educational advance varied greatly, and school attendance was much higher in urban
than in rural areas. But it is clear that education at all levels took a major
leap forward during the last half-century of the tsarist regime.[89]

Covert social criticism by the intelligentsia antedated the era of
emancipation which began in 1856, but after this year Russia's educational institutions certainly provided the setting in which critical impulses spread quickly. Unrest seemed to be endemic in universities and
secondary schools. It is an open question whether without that congenial
setting the Russian intelligentsia would have acquired its considerable
historical significance. Marx's reasoning about the conditions favoring
working-class solidarity (ease of communication in the work place and
mounting consensus through struggles with a common opponent) applied directly to Russian *students* in their relations with the government.

Elementary education was clearly useful in economic and military
terms, but it also upset Russia's rigid social hierarchy. For the sons of
peasants and the urban poor it was a first step of upward social mobility.
The aspiration to advance beyond primary school increased as educational facilities expanded. It was easy, of course, to regulate the admission of students from different social strata, but it was difficult to maintain a consistent policy. If one just considers boys in high school
(gymnasia), one can observe the effects of official policies during the
nineteenth century. Under Alexander I (1805–1825), many members

of the aristocracy still preferred private tutoring for their children. Hence, a large proportion of high school boys (over 60 percent according to one count for 1801) came from urban and rural taxpaying groups (that is, from families of peasants and the urban poor). Then, under Nicholas I (1825–1855), decided preference was given to sons of the gentry and of high officials, their proportion rising to as high as 80 percent of all pupils. Under Alexander II (1855–1881) and his successors, this policy was reversed. The need for qualified personnel became urgent by the end of the century, so boys in gymnasia from the highest social circles represented probably a bit over 50 percent of the pupils, while most of the remainder came from urban taxpaying groups.[90]

The access to educational opportunities aroused a great deal of class feeling, especially after the debate over emancipation had publicized the problems of inequality. Social unrest among students had been widespread in response to the emancipation declaration of 1861. Students, along with many liberals, expressed their solidarity with the peasants, who strongly disliked the terms of the emancipation settlement and in one case rose in violent protest. Terrorist attacks began in 1866, and unrest became widespread during the 1870s as students flocked to the "populist" movement. Between 1873 and 1879, more than a quarter of 1,665 participants in the movement were under twenty-one and 87.2 percent were under thirty. Another study reports that of 5,664 persons implicated in radical movements during the 1870s, 433 were teachers, 644 came from elementary or secondary schools, 266 from clerical seminaries, 37 from military schools, and 2,023 from institutions of higher learning, a total of 3,403 or 61.6 percent.[91] Conservatives naturally attributed these developments to the expansion of education beyond the circle of the privileged. In addition, tsarist officials became concerned because many students from nongentry families dropped out before completing their studies and because Jews constituted a large proportion of the students in secondary schools and universities. Consequently, provincial officials were advised in 1887 not to admit to university preparatory schools "children of coachmen, menials, cooks, washerwomen, small shopkeepers, and the like. For, excepting occasionally gifted children, it is completely unwarranted for the children of such people to leave their position in life."[92] When this circular became known, it met with public outcry, for by the 1880s the tsarist government had lost much of its former control over the expression of opinion, despite the general reaction against the terrorists. Also, as a practical matter, there seemed no warrant for social discrimination when the children from families of the gentry and of tsarist officials could not fill the growing demand for qualified personnel. Nor were children from aristocratic families immune to revolutionary ideas. Increased education seemed generally to contribute to the unrest the government sought to suppress.

St. Petersburg Police Discovering a Nihilist Printing Press, 1887
(*Illustrated London News,* April 16, 1887)

In 1855 some 17,000 boys were enrolled in seventy-seven secondary schools.[93] The fact that under Nicholas I pupils from gentry families predominated is less important than that the gymnasia were boarding schools, isolated from the family environment and a meeting-ground for students from different parts of the country. These schools were financed and controlled by the state. Usually located in the same district town as provincial government, the gymnasia were centers of civilization in a primitive setting, rather than subordinate institutions in a cultured, urban milieu like secondary schools in Western Europe.[94] Teachers in the gymnasia belonged to the "high society" of these towns, while as civil servants they symbolized the authority and cultural mission of the state. Inside the schools, the students were put in uniforms, reinforcing their isolation from society and, one can presume, their identification with one another.

In many respects, the Russian schools were modeled after the elite schools in other European countries, especially between 1866 and 1880 under the leadership of Count D. A. Tolstoi, minister of education. Tolstoi was a scholar of some note concerned with the high quality of education, but also a staunch monarchist determined to exclude or suppress subversive ideas. His method was a heavy emphasis on Greek and Latin and mathematics, in contrast to his predecessor in office (A. V. Golovnin, 1861–1866) who had stressed natural science and Russian history, language, and literature. Even with regard to the classics, the curriculum emphasized grammar and language rather than literature to reduce to a minimum the intrusion of potentially subversive ideas. Perhaps some of this was a bit extreme even in nineteenth-century Europe, but English, French or German schoolboys were subjected to a comparable regimen. Basically, this was the contemporary ideal of education for those who aspired to study at a university.

Unlike his successors, Tolstoi rejected class discrimination or discrimination against Jews. But in emphasizing the classics he certainly wanted to keep students busy with a curriculum so demanding that they simply had no time for anything else. Nor did he rely solely on the curriculum to keep students in line. Special counselors (*nastaunik*) judged the student's moral and political reliability, and their recommendation was a required part of the certificate needed to enter a university. When student unrest spread in the gymnasia as well as the universities in the 1870s, Tolstoi's answer was more detailed supervision.

> [He] sought to limit the opportunities students would have to proselytize one another and to reduce their contacts with unreliable elements outside the schools: the former by prohibiting students from forming societies and from bringing any books but texts into the buildings; the latter by declaring public places like clubs, coffee shops, taverns, billiard parlors, and, in many instances, theaters off limits and by proposing a rigid work schedule which would give pupils no time for frivolous pastimes during weekday nights.[95]

Nearly all disciplinary matters were withdrawn from the jurisdiction of the individual school councils and placed in the hands of the school directors or the curator of the educational district. Within a short time, even these local officials lost most of their authority to the officials of the central ministry. In the field of education, as in that of self-government generally, the autocratic response to unrest, as to most other problems, was more centralization.

Massive controls imposed on students and the aridity of the secondary school curriculum did not distinguish the Russian schools from boarding schools elsewhere in Europe. But in Russia, students reacted against the state as their most visible and oppressive opponent, and they used the declarations of state officials as weapons in their attack. In the 1850s, the state itself had initiated an era of reforms. When young men and women made reform a matter of principle, it was easy to show that vacillating and conflict-ridden state policies violated principle at every point. The contrast is sharpest with English conditions, where public schools with many of the same features as the Russian gymnasia produced quite different results. The graduates from the English schools could join the elite of a successful empire, whereas Russian graduates had to enter the ruling elite of a starkly backward society or join a revolutionary minority which condemned autocracy and backwardness.

The comparison is closer with Prussian conditions. Some Prussian students certainly resembled their radical counterparts among the Russians, though the many states of German society may have helped to diffuse, while Russia's state consolidation helped to intensify, radical tendencies. At any rate, Russian student reactions exemplify Tocqueville's general maxim that revolutionary fervor rises sharply not when conditions are at their worst but when there are signs of improvement, as in Russia after 1856.

The activism of university students was a direct response to governmental policies. Under Nicholas I, quasi-military controls had been imposed on university students, but this policy was reversed after the Crimean defeat. Military drill was discontinued and limitations on enrollments and auditors removed. Also, the government provided help for many indigent students by more state scholarships. Most important, many student organizations supported needy students by loans, raising money by special performances, providing student libraries, and so forth. Such activities were forbidden by law, but some government officials openly encouraged these philanthropic efforts, while others simply looked the other way. Before long, escalating illegal activities on the part of the students and repressive measures on the part of the government replaced this benign atmosphere.[96]

The tsarist government could not tolerate student activism even during the liberal phase of the 1850s and 1860s, when such activism took the form of philanthropic work or of Sunday schools organized to combat illiteracy. In a memorandum of 1860, the chief of police, Prince Dolgorukov, stated his reasons for subjecting the Sunday schools to official control.

> The government cannot permit half of the population to owe its education not to the state but to itself or to the private philanthropy of any particular class. The middle stratum of society and invisible forces which rely upon its strength have arbitrarily assumed the leadership of this important enterprise. By teaching without payment they have established a solid basis of trust and gratitude on the part of the masses for whom they are the benefactors.[97]

Here again, nothing could be permitted to intervene between the population and the all-powerful tsar, lest his legitimacy be impaired. Not only his officials but the tsar himself needed the patriarchal fiction that the ruler is the source of all benefits to the people and that these benefits justify the controls imposed in his name. Prince Dolgorukov echoed, oddly enough, the radical sentiments expressed in France a century earlier, when Jesuit control of education was opposed on the ground that the nation should have an education "that will depend upon the state alone."[98]

In Russia, the tsar and his officials preempted public affairs. A government like that makes ideas into a public affair by the act of keeping them under surveillance. Also, by censoring ideas and controlling or suppressing all activities that are independent of government, the regime unwittingly endows the world of ideas with a special capacity for expressing human aspirations and the riches of experience.[h] Under the circumstances, the majority of the people were reduced to grumbling about bureaucracy. Yet in any large population there are a few men and women who have the urge to express their aspirations and those of others, come what may. Over the centuries, men of ideas have responded to censorship and oppression in different ways. In nineteenth-century Russia, they hardly thought of challenging the government directly. But they were eager to acknowledge the importance of ideas. In the face of poverty and corruption, of hypocrisy above and sycophancy below, in the presence of tyranny that crushed the individual, they would uphold the dignity of the human spirit. By giving all their passion to the pursuit of truth and beauty, they would realize a better life even under tsarism.

Faced with such single-minded dedication, the tsarist government confronted cruel dilemmas of its own. It was ready to suppress all overt opposition and political opinion, but how was it to deal with the personal independence embodied in cultural expressions without appearing as the enemy of truth and beauty? An episode involving the great poet Alexander Pushkin illustrates the dilemma. Following the Decembrist revolt of 1825, Pushkin had been exiled because some of the active participants had been his friends. When the harsh repression of the revolt was at an end, Tsar Nicholas I wanted to demonstrate his magnanimity. He ordered Pushkin's release from exile, because anything concerning the famous man would achieve maximum publicity. A very frank interview followed. Pushkin acknowledged his sympathy with the Decembrists and the tsar paid his respects to Pushkin's great gifts. But then Pushkin complained about censorship and the tsar offered to be the poet's personal censor. It was the grand gesture of a supreme ruler and Pushkin appreciated it as such. Opposition-minded students at Moscow University, who had flocked to Pushkin on his return from exile, turned against him when they discovered his support of the tsar. Pushkin replied in verse: "He freed my thought. How should I not / Sincerely sing his praise?" This delicately ambiguous response had to be submitted to the censorship of the tsar, who declared, "Let it be circulated, but not printed."[99] Like the censors who kept asking the government for guide-

[h]At least one American writer commented during the 1960s that by its control of literature the Soviet regime gave evidence of taking literature seriously, whereas in the United States official tolerance was indistinguishable from indifference toward culture.

lines which were never forthcoming, the tsar himself was uncertain how to proceed when praise itself somehow bordered on the subversive. Nor was it easy to dismiss praise which so famous a poet offered to authority. Nicholas chose the method of private circulation in preference to an official endorsement, just as Russian writers ever since have circulated their works in manuscript (*samizdat*) when they could not get them past the censor.

Under these circumstances, literature became a substitute for life itself. By its control of all activities independent of government as much as by censorship, the tsarist government had helped to stimulate informal associations among individuals who shared an interest in literature and saw in the expression of ideas an act of social responsibility. The term *intelligentsia* became common only late in the nineteenth century, but the group to which it refers developed earlier. This group was defined by the *civic function* which intellectuals attributed to ideas. Neither the changing social origin of the intelligentsia nor the succession of intellectual fashions (like German idealism, French utopian socialism, or the belief in scientific progress) are as important a constituent of the group as this concept of social or civic responsibility, for it provided a criterion of exclusion. Specific intellectuals, like spokesmen for the church or the autocracy, or liberal government officials, or persons interested in ideas for their own sake, did *not* belong to the intelligentsia, because they had betrayed the "cause." The conception of social responsibility had a common core. A person would be recognized as a member of the intelligentsia if he was concerned with the fate of the people and the nation, opposed to the established order, preoccupied with effecting social change by means of ideas, and most importantly always ready to subordinate all private interests to this conception of social responsibility.

That way of defining the term helps to explain the furious debates of the nineteenth century in which a man could be judged as belonging to the intelligentsia only in part, or only at one time in his life but not at another. With a man like Alexander Herzen (1812–1870), the question might not be put quite this way. But his long exile (after 1848), wealth, and cosmopolitanism cast doubt on his dedication to the cause, even though he had been imprisoned and exiled for his beliefs and devoted most of his energy to the advance of Russian liberty. Novelists like Gogol and Dostoevski underwent similar changes of reputation. Gogol's portrayal of provincial life and Dostoevski's early novels and Siberian exile had "qualified" them. But their ultimate adherence to the Orthodox faith cast doubt on their concept of social responsibility. Turgenev was suspect because of his cosmopolitan dedication to literature.

Isaiah Berlin has followed the Russian critic Paul Annenkov in labeling the period from 1838 to 1848 "the marvelous decade." Preoccupation with philosophy and literature was considered the only possible way of meeting one's responsibility. A case in point is the career and subsequent reputation of Vissarion Belinski (1811–1848). Brought up in a remote provincial town, he was aroused early to an acute sense of injustice by the casual brutality of his father, a retired naval doctor, and by the poverty-stricken student life he was forced to lead as a provincial commoner among the sons of the aristocracy at Moscow University. Ill health and expulsion from the university for a mildly subversive play added to his misery. The rest of his short life was spent as a penniless literary critic. During his lifetime, he was idolized by such diverse figures as Herzen, Turgenev, Goncharov, and Dostoevski. Belinski became "the idealized ancestor of both the reformers and the revolutionaries of the second half of the century."[100] He died of consumption in 1848, apparently just after having received an invitation to visit the police, officially known as the Third Section of the Imperial Chancellory. Gendarmes attended his funeral as they had attended Pushkin's, to keep an eye on his friends and prevent any demonstration.

Belinski brought to his critique of literature a quite extraordinary moral passion. The questions that concerned him were the perennial ones. How do individuals relate to one another and to society, what are the ends of life, and above all what is the proper moral purpose of imaginative literature? So intense was his preoccupation with a truthful answer to these large questions that even the suspicious officials of the Third Section thought of Belinski as wayward and offensive, but for all that concerned solely with questions of taste, not with anything that touched on "either politics or communism."[101] But this was not how Belinski and his friends regarded their interest in ideas.

There is a quality of thought which can transform intellectual preoccupations into partisan struggles in the republic of letters. Belinski himself commented on the Russians' inability to "divorce a man from his thought," on their tendency "to lose time, to ruin their own health and make enemies from attachment to some deeply felt opinion, from love for some lofty, disinterested thought."[102] A sampling of Belinski's opinions conveys the atmosphere of these literary circles, in which sheer passion for truth turned differences of opinion into moral-political commitments.

At age twenty-three, Belinski noted that men of letters discussed every idea imported from abroad but did not create anything of their own. This exploitation of ready-made ideas was "the cause of our incredible instability." Seven years later his lament was still more despairing:

> We are a people without a country, worse than that, we are people whose country is a ghost, and we are ghosts ourselves. Yet we are people who make

enormous demands on life, capable of any sacrifice, though forced to stand still like idle spectators. . . . Without goal there is no activity, and without activity our life withers away.

Yet Belinski could not be inactive and neither could his friends. He was torn, as they were, between the heady attraction of ideas taken from abroad and revulsion at the realities of bourgeois societies; after visiting France, Belinski wrote of the "syphilitic sore running through the French body [politic]." At the same time, all these men were sick at heart when they contemplated their own country. They had "a passionate desire to see in it the realization of human ideals, and to promote them as far as one's strength permits."

At one point in his intellectual journey, Belinski deeply shocked his friends when he suddenly made his peace with the tsarist regime, recognizing the rationality of the real in Hegelian fashion. But the very terms in which he endorsed tsarism reveal his moral fanaticism.

Drown yourself, lose yourself in science and art, love them as the goal and necessity of your life, and not as mere instruments of education and winning success in the world—only then will you be blessed. . . . Without a prior sense of truth in feeling, it is impossible to acquire it in knowledge. . . .

Above all, avoid politics and steer clear of any political influence on your cast of mind. Politics in Russia are senseless and only empty heads can busy themselves with political questions. Love what is good, and you are bound to turn out useful to your country, without thinking or striving to be useful to it. . . .

This passage is followed by a discourse on the Russian tsar-emperors, above all Peter the Great, who alone could safeguard the people and gave them like children what rights they could handle without committing mischief. But then Belinski returned to his theme that men of ideas must be apostles of enlightenment like the early apostles who hatched no conspiracies but boldly preached their doctrine in the face of emperors and judges. Subsequently, Belinski repudiated this position with the same passion with which he had embraced it, saying that he would not make his peace with vile realities.[103]

In his *Thoughts and Notes on Russian Literature* (1846), Belinski gave an assessment of his life's work by contrasting the facts of society with the effects of literature.

There is a prevailing spirit of disunity in our society: each of our social estates possesses specific traits of its own—its dress and its manner, and a way of life and customs, and even its language. . . .

It would be wrong to say that we had no society whatever. Undoubtedly, there exists with us a strong demand for society and a striving toward society, and that in itself is important. . . .

But the beginning of this *rapprochement* among the social estates . . . does not by any means belong exclusively to our times: it merges with the beginnings of our literature. . . .

In speaking of the progress of society's education, we have in mind the progress of our literature, for our education is the direct effect of our literature upon the ideas and morals of society. Our literature has created the morals of our society, has already educated several generations of widely divergent character, has paved the way for the inner *rapprochement* of the estates, has formed a species of public opinion and produced a sort of special class in society that differs from the *middle estate* in that it consists not of the merchantry and commoners alone but of people of all estates who have been drawn together through education, which, with us, centered exclusively in a love of literature. . . .

Pecuniary interests, trade, shares, balls, social gatherings and dances are also links, but they are external, not vital, organic links, though necessary and useful. People are internally bound together by common moral interests, similarity of views, and equality of education, combined with a mutual regard for one another's human dignity. But all our moral interests, all our spiritual life, have hitherto been and will, still for a long time to come, be concentrated in literature: it is the vital spring from which all human sentiments and conceptions percolate into society.[104]

A year later, in his famous letter to Gogol, Belinski followed a passionate denunciation of orthodoxy and autocracy with a further paean to literature, which alone shows signs of life and a progressive movement. That is why the writer in Russia is held in such high esteem, even if he is a man of little talent. Every liberal tendency in literature is rewarded with universal notice by a public which "looks upon Russian writers as its only leaders, defenders, and saviors against Russian autocracy, orthodoxy, and nationality, and therefore, while always prepared to forgive a writer a bad book, will never forgive him a pernicious book."[105] Thus, Belinski touches on the special power which literature has retained in Russian society to this day. Writers take enormous moral and social responsibility upon themselves when autocracy (or dictatorship) makes them the sole spokesmen for human dignity and individual freedom.[106]

In the "marvellous decade," literature had become a substitute for civil society. Belinski said as much when he referred to a "kind of public opinion" created by literature, to "persons simply associating with other persons," to an "internal meeting of social classes." For these are references to ideas and associations independent of government, which yet transcend the concerns of the individual. "The love of what is good . . . as the goal and necessity of life" was considered the only possible way of meeting one's social responsibility. But the European revolutions of 1848, the military defeat of 1856, and Alexander's "promise" of emancipation changed the setting, especially for men of ideas. Between

1856 and 1866, a period of heated debate ensued, even of agitation, in which philosophical and literary argument alone appeared insufficient. The moment it was possible to go beyond the previously prescribed limits of permissible expression, it became imperative to do so. How else could men of ideas meet their responsibility, subordinate private interests to the welfare of the people, and link their "love of what is good" with a search for the forces that could overthrow autocracy and make "truth" a reality? Under tsarist censorship, literature remained important as a means of communicating about social conditions, but now personal commitment to progressive social action loomed much larger.

Nikolai Chernyskevski (1828–1889) exemplifies this change in intellectual opposition from the 1840s to the 1860s.[107] His father, a parish priest, was a comparatively educated man who taught his son himself and borrowed nonreligious books for him from the notables of the area. The boy read Gogol, Belinski, Herzen, and everything else that reached his native Saratov. The family background was orthodox and patriarchal, but evidently benign. At age eighteen, his father encouraged Chernyshevski to leave for St. Petersburg, where he was admitted as a student at the university. Under Russian conditions it was unusual for the son of a priest not to follow an ecclesiastical career, to be admitted to a university, and indeed to move from the province to the capital.[108]

Chernyshevski's birthplace and early experiences left a lasting impression on him. Saratov on the lower Volga was frontier territory, where the rising Muscovite state had battled against Tartar tribes and where Cossacks or free peasants later had owed allegiance neither to landlords nor to the tsar. Many Old Believers (*raskolniki*) and merchants trading with the East had settled in this area. State centralization had left its mark, but so had peasant revolts, the encounter of many ethnic groups, and the corporate interests of international traders. Life on the frontier was a hard struggle against packs of wolves, bands of brigands and horse thieves, nomads who came to seize and enslave Russian peasants, epidemics, and the stark poverty which turned men into lifelong drunkards. Chernyshevski's realism about provincial society remained with him throughout his life.

His career was brief and tragic. After completing his university studies he returned to Saratov to teach in a local secondary school. He seems to have been an exceptional teacher, but he noted in his diary that things he said in class "smell of penal servitude." During his stay in Saratov he married a local socialite, who may have been attracted to him by his championship of women's rights. He warned her that he might be arrested at any time for views he could not change. In 1853, Chernyshevski returned to Petersburg with his family. For two years, he made a precarious living as a journalist and translator, while preparing his dissertation in hopes of an academic career. These hopes were disappointed and in 1855 he accepted an invitation to join the staff of the *Contemporary (Sovremennik)*. By 1859 he had become editor-in-chief and a very prominent figure.

The *Contemporary* was one of the major journals in which the issues of peasant emancipation were debated. Obviously, the government scrutinized the journal and its editor closely and tried to establish links between Chernyshevski and the agitation precipitated by the prospect of emancipation. The journal was suspended in 1862 and its editor arrested. After spending two years in prison waiting for his secret trial, Chernyshevski was condemned to fourteen years of hard labor in Siberia and to perpetual banishment. He had been cautious out of consideration for his family, but his appeal to the younger generation was sufficient reason for the government's desire to silence him. They did not succeed, but Chernyshevski spent all but four months of his remaining twenty-seven years in penal servitude and exile from European Russia.

Chernyshevski's controversial dissertation on esthetics illuminates the generational change in the intelligentsia. Belinski had distinguished between a bad book and a harmful one, thus introducing a social or political perspective into literary criticism. Chernyshevski elaborated this emphasis by stressing the links between the work of art and its historical setting. He turned Belinski's literary commitment into a manifesto of artistic realism. This argument did not appeal to the older generation of writers. One critic upheld Pushkin's pure art against Chernyshevski's exaggerated imitation of Gogol and Belinski. Turgenev initiated a campaign against "this disgusting book" since he "could not long live with this art hating and dogmatic schoolmaster. Tolstoy despised his dreary provincialism, his total lack of aesthetic sense, his intolerance, his wooden rationalism, his maddening self-assurance."[109] Moreover, Tolstoy along with Turgenev made nasty, snobbish references to Chernyshevski's priestly, plebeian origin. It may seem just a literary vendetta with overtones of class discrimination, but Chernyshevski challenged the very idealization of literature by means of which the older generation had expressed its love of truth and human dignity. Tsarist censorship had been responsible for a literature doing double duty as art and social criticism. After 1856, Chernyshevski was no longer satisfied with this conception and stressed the social utility of art. A generation that had achieved much under Belinski's leadership naturally resisted seeing its accomplishments cast aside or even disparaged.

However, Chernyshevski's main concern was journalism, not literature. For a few years after 1856 he was able to discuss public questions as far as censorship permitted. Most of Chernyshevski's critical commentaries dealt with Western Europe, in part because he saw the possibility of profiting from the example and the mistakes of the West. In Russia, "we are still only foreseeing these changes, we must prepare for events, and control their developments."[110] Accordingly, he wrote about social problems that had arisen in the course of industrialization and about ideas for reform which went beyond the usual half-measures. Some of these discussions were cut by the censors, but Chernyshevski was allowed to report news from other countries, and Russian readers knew how to interpret such news in the light of Russian conditions. Chernyshevski's discussion of emancipation could be more forthright since the issue was debated publicly. He strongly advocated that the emancipated peasants be given the land they had tilled.

Throughout his life, Chernyshevski retained a shy manner, doubtful of his courage but adamant in his convictions. He was a secular ascetic whose moral probity and pedestrian manner made him an object of derision among the older literati, but he was venerated by the younger generation. With his customary eloquence, Isaiah Berlin has described Chernyshevski's manner:

> Chernyshevski laid it down that the function of art was to help men to satisfy their wants more rationally, to disseminate knowledge, to combat ignorance, prejudice and the anti-social passions, to improve life in the most literal and narrow sense of these words. . . . This outlook helped to make him the natural leader of the "hard" young men who had succeeded the idealists of the "forties." Chernyshevski's harsh, flat, dull, humourless, grating sentences, his preoccupation with concrete economic detail, his self-discipline, his passionate dedication to the material and moral good of his fellow men, the grey, self-effacing personality, the tireless, devoted, minute industry, the hatred of style or of any concessions to the graces, the unquestionable sincerity, the combination of brutal directness, utter self-forgetfulness, indifference to the claims of private life, innocence, personal kindness, pedantry, moral charm, capacity for self-sacrifice, created the image that later became the prototype of the Russian revolutionary hero and martyr.[111]

All these qualities find expression in the novel *What Is To Be Done?* One need not dwell on its literary failings, since the author himself acknowledged that he did not have "a trace of artistic talent."[112] It is the story of a young woman rescued from the petty tyranny of her parents by a young scholar who marries her. The couple agree to live independent lives, and she sets up a cooperative shop of seamstresses. When she falls in love with her husband's friend, the husband disappears and the lovers marry. Later, the first husband returns in the company of his new wife, and the two couples live together in harmony. Both young men are of lower class origin, tough-minded, scientifically trained, and democrats by conviction. They reject all high-minded precepts like conscience and self-sacrifice, claiming to be moved entirely by rational egoism. But they act by the most selfless standards and are completely devoted to the cause of the people. One high point of the novel is a dream of the young woman which glimpses a future in which people enjoy abundance, freedom, and the equality of the sexes. Another high-point is the portrayal of the minor character Rakhmetov, an aristocrat who has traveled to America and gone over to the people. Rakhmetov leads the life of an athlete in training for the coming revolution, developing his strength and divesting himself of all ties so as not to be deflected from his purpose. In the novel, Chernyshevski extols Rakhmetov as one of the chosen few, but also states that "a man with an ardent love of goodness cannot but be a sombre monster."

He wrote this book in prison while awaiting trial. The novel was published in *Contemporary,* which was appearing again before being banned permanently. Thereafter, the novel circulated in clandestine fashion and remained popular for decades. Chernyshevski thought its merit consisted in its truthfulness. For the younger generation, the book symbolized their idealized dedication to the cause of revolution.

After 1856 members of the intelligentsia and students in the universities flocked to the revolutionary cause as single individuals or in small groups. They were vigorously condemned and subjected to severe penalties. They shared the conviction that industrialization imposed mounting human costs on the vast mass of the peasantry, already victimized by centuries of cruel abuse. With renewed urgency they confronted the question of whether Russia should follow the path of Western Europe or could reach a better social order without incurring the horrors of industrialism, the materialism of bourgeois culture, and the pretenses of a merely formal, legal equality. Alexander Herzen answered this question in a manner that echoed the aspirations of many reformers and revolutionaries: "Human development is a form of chronological unfairness, since late-comers are able to profit by the labours of their predecessors without paying the same price."[113]

In that hope, a minority of true believers took their stand against the ugly realities of autocracy, poverty, and inequality. They did so in part because they felt guilty. Peter Lavrov (1823–1900), a former officer and political activist who escaped from Siberia to Switzerland in 1870, put into words the underlying reasons for the appeal of Chernyshevski's exemplary conduct and for the popularity of his novel:

> Every comfort which I enjoy, every thought which I had the leisure to acquire or work out, was purchased by blood, by the suffering of or by the labor of millions. I cannot correct the past, and no matter how dearly my development cost, I cannot renounce it. . . . Only the weak and intellectually backward person falters from the responsibility weighing upon him. . . . Evil has to be righted, insofar as that is possible, and it has to be done only during one's lifetime. . . . I remove from myself responsibility for the bloody cost of my development if I use this very development in order to lessen evil in the present and in the future. If I am a developed man, then I am obliged to do this. . . .

Lavrov thought this an easy duty, because searching for and disseminating truth and the idea of a just social order would satisfy the individual and potentially help the suffering majority. But his idealism was also demanding:

> Neither literature, nor art, nor science saves one from immoral indifference. By themselves they do not include nor cause progress. They only furnish it with tools. . . . But only that writer, artist, or scholar served progress who did all that he could to apply his energies to the dissemination and strengthening of the civilization of his time, who struggled with evil, embodied his artistic ideals, scientific truths, philosophical ideas, publicistic strivings in creations which were fully infused with the life of his times. Whoever did less . . . [whoever] forgot about the immense amount of evil and ignorance, against which he should have been struggling, might as well have been anything— a skilled artist, an uncommon scholar, a brilliant publicist—but he excluded himself from the ranks of conscious actors of historical progress.[114]

In this spirit, young men and women joined the revolutionary movements of the 1870s.

Education represented a debt which they had to repay by working for the progress of their country. Whatever their specific persuasion, they were all nationalists in that sense. The intelligentsia could repay their debt to the people only if it worked for a future in which autocracy, poverty, and inequality would disappear. If it failed in this duty, unrelieved tyranny and destitution would cause still more blood to be spilled. Motives such as these made the quest desperately urgent. Heated, endless arguments over how to lift the tsarist yoke from the people divided the Russian intelligentsia for decades. The passionate intensity of these arguments reflected the intelligentsia's sense of social responsibility, and Chernyshevski epitomized the socially responsible individual.

These Russian movements of the nineteenth century foreshadowed the movements for reform or revolution in other countries that were also latecomers to industrialization and, possibly, democratization. Such protest movements consist largely of an educated minority of elitists with a bad conscience. Elitism is many-sided, but there is some structure to its diversity. An educated elite in a backward country has the choice between moral and rational means. It can seek to *reform itself morally*

—by an ascetic life style based on the conviction that no reform is possible unless individual men and women live virtuously;

—by exemplary conduct which can symbolize the expiation of guilt, virtues that can redeem others, and so forth;

—by self-discipline which prepares the individual for his role in the coming crisis.

An educated elite can also seek *reform by intellectual preparation*. This would enable the individual to qualify for the necessary leadership through the acquisition of ideas and skills. Here again many ways are possible. An elite can prepare itself

—by its "love for science and art" (Belinski) as the only spheres in which human dignity and freedom can be preserved;

—by the pursuit of science and institutional reform for the immediate good it can do (like medicine or the zemstvo movement);

—by the study of history in the belief that the prior development of other countries has lessons to teach us from which our own country may profit (Herzen, Chernyshevski);

—by the study of social and economic conditions, for without understanding the causes of misery we can do little to remove them (some versions of populism and Marxism).

These are some of the options among which members of the intelligentsia chose during the nineteenth century.

But elitism is never enough. It provokes its opposite—"populism" in the broad sense of that term. Members of the intelligentsia cannot ignore the fact that they constitute an educated minority pitted against an entrenched autocracy in the midst of an indifferent or hostile population. A vast majority of the peasants adhered to the myth of the tsar long after they had become bitter opponents of his officials. When young revolutionaries in the 1870s went to the people not to teach but to learn, they were met with deep suspicion and frequently denounced to the police. With that experience, the so-called populist movement lost much of its earlier appeal, but populism as a doctrinal complement to elitism lived on. The intelligentsia dedicated itself to the cause of the people and hence had to relate to the people in some form. The question was how to conceive of the people: as backward, as a source of virtue, or as a force capable of overthrowing their oppressors.

The intelligentsia could seek to *teach* the people

—before the coming revolution, in order to make the people ready for this great turning point and safeguard justice and equality in the society to come;

—after the coming revolution, because centuries of oppression have barbarized the people and nothing but a cataclysmic overturn can redeem them from their present state.

Or the intelligentsia could *learn* from the people because wisdom and virtue inhere in their accustomed way of life. In Russia, this view always turned on the attributes of the peasant community (*mir*), which were variously seen as

—the foundation of spiritual values inherent in the Russian tradition and hence a protective shield against Western individualism (Slavophils);

—the foundation of spiritual values from which the intelligentsia has become separated through education and to which it must return if it and the country are to be restored;

—the foundation of future cooperatives and hence the beginnings (and no more) of a more equitable society (Chernyshevski);

—the foundation of the collectivism characteristic of a socialist society whereby Russia can arrive at the desired future without having to incur the high costs of capitalism (Herzen).

Or the intelligentsia could *rely* on the people as a source of that strength which alone can overthrow autocracy. So conceived, the people would throw off their chains, either soon or at some point in the future, because

—their burdens and the vileness of their oppressors have become unbearable (Bakunin);

—both their suffering and the spread of advanced ideas have prepared them for the final day on which they would not only overthrow the old regime, but take the reconstruction of the new society into their own hands (ethical and legal populism);

—once the necessary force has been supplied to make a revolution, the people will be guided to effect the desired social reorganization, lest through ignorance or educated deception they would fall victim to revived or new types of oppression (Tkachev, Lenin).

No doubt this listing is incomplete. Even if it could be completed, it would not convey either the sheer welter of opinion in the last decades of the nineteenth century or the profound ambiguity of these ideas. Men like Chernyshevski, Lavrov, and many others did not hold the same views throughout their lives. They probably held most of their views in an ambiguous fashion (however doctrinaire their formulations), for circumstances changed along with the hope or despair that accompanied their search for a way to the new society. The great range of liberal and socialist opinion in the West provided an important resource for the intelligentsia's opposition to the tsarist regime, but was regarded warily by nearly everyone. Westernizers *and* Slavophils were eager to avoid the weaknesses of the Western tradition and build on the strengths of the Russian. A Westernizer like Herzen commented on his "elective affinity" with the Slavophils: "Like Janus, or the two-headed eagle, we looked in opposite directions, but one heart beats in our breasts."[115]

Herzen's comment applies generally to the revolutionary movements of the nineteenth century, not only to the old dispute between Slavophils and Westernizers. There *was* a unity underlying the virulent disputes. All the revolutionaries were concerned with the regeneration of their country. Most revolutionaries and, indeed, a good many of the liberal reformers favored autocratic methods, at least after the failure of the Western-European revolutions in 1848. Some of them worried

about the dangers of a new autocracy: might not a future society under
the direction of the "intelligents" prove as oppressive as the old? An-
archists like Bakunin or morally scrupulous men like Chernyshevski and
Kropotkin were concerned with that question but could not resolve it.
Among most, passion dispelled such scruples. Their overriding concern
was that in the West

> liberal parties and their leaders neither understood nor made a serious effort
> to forward the fundamental interests of the oppressed populations of their
> countries. What the vast majority of peasants in Russia (or workers in Europe)
> needed was to be fed and clothed, to be given physical security, to be rescued
> from disease, ignorance, poverty and humiliating inequalities. As for political
> rights, votes, parliaments, republican forms, these were meaningless and use-
> less to ignorant, barbarous, half-naked and starving men; such programmes
> merely mocked their misery.[116]

All of them agreed further that the urgency of these needs required
unswerving personal dedication.

Driven by a sense of social responsibility, the radical opponents of
the tsarist regime put its abolition above all other considerations. When
peasant hostility and government arrests caused the populist movement
to fail in the 1870s, a minority emerged from this experience more determined than ever. In the clandestine meetings which followed, some
wanted to continue their work for the peasants' needs and aspirations.
Others opted for terrorist blows against the government. Members of
the latter group planned and carried out the assassination of Alexander
II in 1881. In documents made public after the tsar's death, the "executive committee" justified its action by reciting the history of intelligentsia opposition and government repression.

In addressing Alexander III (1881–1894), the terrorists declared
that the whole bloody struggle, including this final terrorist act, sprang
from the failure of the government to realize the will of the people.
"The government has degenerated into a pure camarilla. . . . [Its] intentions have nothing in common with the desires of the people." The government consists of usurpers, the document declares, in contrast to the
revolutionaries who

> have tried in several different ways *to act on behalf of the people.* At the begin-
> ning of the seventies we chose to live like workers and peacefully propagate
> our Socialist ideas. The movement was absolutely harmless. But how did it
> end? . . . A movement, which was unstained by blood and which repudiated
> violence, was crushed. . . . The short time that we lived among the people
> showed us how bookish and doctrinaire were our ideas. We then decided *to
> act on behalf of the interests created by the people, interests which were inherent in its
> life and which it recognized.* Such was the distinctive character of Populism.
> From metaphysics and dreams we moved to positivism, and kept close to
> the soil. . . . Instead of spreading Socialist ideas, we gave first place to our

determination *to reawaken the people by agitation in the name of the interest that it felt. . . .*[117]

This document was written by men and women who expected to die and wanted to justify their action in the eyes of the world. Given their outcast status as revolutionary activists, it was easy for them to denounce the government and deny it popular legitimacy. But it was not so easy to claim an *unequivocal* mandate for themselves, even though they wrote in their own behalf. Inadvertently, they revealed the persistent ambiguity between elitism and populism. They claimed to have acted on behalf of the people and in their interest. But the statement that the people recognized their own interests is qualified. For the determination of revolutionaries to "reawaken the people by agitation in the name of the interest that it felt" means simply that an elite articulates interests which *it* imputes to the people. Action on behalf of the people's interest was confused, perhaps unwittingly, with action that would awaken or reawaken the people by agitation. The intention of the revolutionaries was to act in behalf of the people, but in practice they were not satisfied with what the people themselves desired. Instead, they would represent "interests which were inherent in [the people's] life." This equivocation over what the people want and what a revolutionary elite interprets as the people's interest remained a characteristic of the revolutionary movements which followed.

The history of the movements which intervened between the assassination of Alexander II in 1881 and the revolution of 1917 will be omitted, for my purpose has been to characterize the autocratic suppression of civil society and the early formation of an opposition to autocracy. The declaration of the terrorists of 1881 shows the equivocation concerning a popular mandate which has characterized the Leninist revolution and the later Stalinist collectivization of agriculture.

REVOLUTION AND THE MANDATE TO RULE

Rule in the name of the people was a principle first articulated in seventeenth-century England and eighteenth-century France. Later writers discerned in Rousseau's concept of the general will a potential tyranny of the majority. They hardly anticipated that one day a tyranny of the minority would also be exercised in the name of the people. Yet such a tyranny has been instituted under a Soviet regime which preempts decision-making by the highest authority, delegates all responsibility to the lower echelons, and thoroughly controls or suppresses civil society. The Soviet regime has greatly intensified these characteristics of tsarist autocracy, confirming Merle Fainsod's observation that "Bolshevism as a movement was an indigenous, authoritarian response to the environment of tsarist absolutism which nurtured it."[118]

After 1881 a number of revolutionary movements developed which existed as small, clandestine groups in Russia and as competing groups of Russian revolutionaries abroad. The Russian Social Democratic Labour party was one of these groups, and in the course of an internal dispute in 1903 the radical left wing of the party adopted the name *Bolshevik* (majority) as distinguished from *Menshevik* (minority). These names persisted throughout a long series of internecine disputes. Lenin (born as V. I. Ulyanov in 1870, died in 1924) was the leader of the Bolshevik faction and the greatest single leader of the 1917 revolution. Lenin's brother was executed (1887) for participating in a plot to assassinate Alexander III. Lenin himself was a law student and revolutionary from 1887 to 1895, when he was arrested and deported to Siberia. In 1900 he went abroad, and though he traveled to Russia intermittently for some years, he remained in exile until his return in 1917.

Tsarist Russia participated in World War I on the side of the Western allies against the Central Powers of Germany and Austria. But after three years of war, the tsarist regime was overthrown in the revolution of 1917. Russia's military defeat was caused not only by the devastations of war but by famines, epidemics, and the accompanying breakdown of the economy. The revolution of February 1917 was due to the spontaneous acts of Russian workers and peasants returning from the front, rather than to the actions of the revolutionary leadership. The early constitutionalist phase of the revolution was followed on November 7, 1917 by a radical, Bolshevik coup. Lenin and his followers regarded the war as a capitalist and imperialist venture and favored a peace without annexations and indemnities. Civil war broke out between the new revolutionary regime and its Russian opponents, who wanted to continue the war against Germany. The Western Allies, still engaged in fighting that war, sent some supplies and military assistance to the Russian opponents of the revolution. These chaotic conditions hastened the opening of peace negotiations between the Bolshevik leaders and the Central Powers. Yet the negotiations dragged on because, in contrast to Germany, Russia had lost the will and the capacity to continue the war. When the Treaty of Brest-Litovsk was signed in March 1918, Russia was forced to abandon Poland, Lithuania, the Ukraine, the Baltic provinces, Finland, and Transcaucasia.

In the period after World War I, Russia underwent not one but two revolutions. The first revolution from October 1917 to January 1918 consisted of the conquest of power and the expropriation of land by masses of peasants. The large-scale destructions caused by the war and by military defeat precipitated these violent transformations so that the ruling groups of tsarist society were effectively destroyed. The second revolution from 1928 onwards did not result from military defeat and its ensuing chaos. It occurred rather in an economy that was slowly re-

May Day Parade in Petrograd, 1917.
The slogan on the banner reads: "Down with the old order." (New York Public Library)

covering from cataclysmic decline. And it consisted of a collectivization of agriculture and a political purge which were initiated and driven forward from above by the leadership of the Communist party. The implications of both revolutions for the Communist conception of a popular mandate can be understood only against the background of social and economic conditions in post-1917 Soviet Russia.

In the years after 1917, epidemics, famines, and civil war caused precipitous decline in industrial and agricultural production. The gross industrial output of the Russian economy in coal, oil, and railway tonnage carried declined from an index of 100 in 1913 to 31 in 1921. The production of electricity fell to one-fourth and the production of pig iron, steel, bricks, and sugar virtually disappeared. Russia was still predominantly agricultural, but overall agricultural production fell from 100 in 1913 to 60 in 1921. Between these years, agricultural exports fell to one seventy-fifth (from 1,520 to 20) and imports of finished products to one-sixth (from 1,374 to 208) of their former levels.[119]

Shortages of food and fuel, aggravated by extensive disruptions of the transportation system, created the worst problems. The peasants together with soldiers returning from the war seized and redistributed the land, acts which the Bolshevik regime quickly legalized. Expropriation of the landowning class had been a major part of the Bolshevik program. But because it was accompanied by much destruction of property and livestock, redistribution greatly aggravated the disruption. The concomitant rise of small peasant holdings also tended to lower productivity; implements and fertilizer were in short supply. Between 1916 and 1921, the number of horses and cattle declined by a fourth and the number of sheep and goats by one-third. The consequence was a reduction of the sown area from 79.4 to 58.3 million desiatiny between 1917 and 1921, and of the gross yield of crops from 3.3 to 1.6 million *pudy* in the same period (one *pud* = 36.11 pounds).[120]

As a result, the existing structure of society was overturned on a massive scale. In 1913 industrialists, merchants, real estate owners, and officials in the towns as well as landowners and better-off peasants in the countryside had constituted about 16 percent of the Russian population. Persons in these categories represented the "capitalist class" in the Communist definition of the term. By 1921 "urban capitalists" and former tsarist officers and officials had either perished in the upheavals of the period, emigrated, or been coopted by the new regime in subordinate, white-collar positions and as officers of the Red Army. In the countryside, larger landholdings were expropriated and redistributed to peasants who were allowed one horse and up to 4 desiatiny of land. These smaller holdings accounted for 72.1 percent of arable land in 1921. Due to famine conditions, the number of industrial workers declined by half between 1917 and 1920/21; most of these workers returned to their villages. White-collar workers increased by 60 percent between 1913 and 1920, due to rapid bureaucratization and the shift of former entrepreneurs into managerial positions under political supervision. Population figures measure the impact of the revolution and its aftermath in another way. The main losses occurred in the eight-year period from 1915 to 1923. Emigration accounted for two million people and deaths in World War I for another two million. Disease, famine, and civil war resulted in the deaths of fourteen to sixteen million people. Demographers also speak of a "birth deficit" of some ten million due to the deaths of child-producing adults (that is, a deficit of children who would have been born if those adults had remained alive). The overall loss which these upheavals imposed on the population has been estimated at between twenty-eight and thirty million people.[121]

The Bolshevik leadership sought to cope with these chaotic conditions by its policy of "War Communism" (1920). Alec Nove has identified the main aspects of this policy as follows:

(1) An attempt to ban private manufacture, the nationalization of nearly all industry, the allocation of nearly all material stocks, and of what little output there was, by the state, especially for war purposes.
(2) A ban on private trade, never quite effective anywhere, but spasmodically enforced.
(3) Seizure of peasant surpluses (*prodrazverstka*).
(4) The partial elimination of money from the state's dealings with its own organizations and the citizens. Free rations, when there was anything to ration.
(5) All these factors combined with terror and arbitrariness, expropriations, requisitions. Efforts to establish discipline, with party control over trade unions. A siege-economy with a communist ideology. A partly-organized chaos. Sleepless, leather-jacketed commissars working around the clock in a vain effort to replace the free market.[122]

In a largely agricultural country, the main task was the procurement of foodstuffs to supply the towns and the army.

The principal problem of "War Communism" was the relation between the state and the peasantry which had just benefited from the seizure and redistribution of land. The Soviet regime had endorsed that redistribution and now, to meet an emergency, turned to the forced requisitioning of grain from the peasants. This was a dangerous expedient: "Naked requisitions . . . provoked the two traditional replies of the peasant: the short-term reply of concealment of stocks and the long-term reply of refusal to sow more land than was necessary to feed his own family." Maurice Dobb cites estimates for 1920 according to which peasants concealed between 14 and 20 percent of the sown area and 33 percent of the harvested produce.[123]

The policy of requisitions and the peasants' response recalls the "local government by tribute collection" practiced under the Mongols and the tsars. But the policy of War Communism was more than an echo of things past or an emergency strategy. Nationalization, forced allocation, rationing, the use of record-keeping rather than money as a means of exchange, and state control of manufacture, trade, and trade unions were anticapitalist measures in keeping with communist ideology. The attack on property and money, expropriations, and rationing made it seem that emergency conditions unwittingly favored that substitution of planning for the market and that equality through allocation which were steps toward a socialist society.

As Moshe Lewin has stated,

> In Capitalism the law of value, in its different forms, regulated the economy through an interplay of spontaneous forces in the market, but the socialist economy would eliminate money, prices, wages, profits, and the other capitalist market paraphernalia. Socialism and socialist planning were conceived uniquely in terms of a distributive function in kind, where economic activity was no longer concerned with market categories such as merchandise, value, and cost but with human needs served by products created to satisfy them. Elimination of private property was an indispensable precondition for the elimination of private producers, and the disappearance of private producers exchanging commodities would lead to the elimination of both the market and the category of "commodities." This logic was responsible for the following conception, if not illusion: the more nationalization, the narrower the market, the nearer the advent of socialism, or the larger the socialist sector. . . . When Lenin suddenly found himself in a situation in which all the allegedly "capitalist" mechanisms began to disintegrate under the strains of war, the party leaders fell prey to the illusion that the dream was becoming real.[124]

On the face of it, market mechanisms were replaced by administrative structures, and this seemed to identify the coming of socialism with the growth of the state machinery. Nationalization of the means of production was hailed as a token of the disappearance of classes. With the disappearance of the former ruling class, its agent—the state—would disappear also. As Lewin points out, opposition against an oppressive ruling class had libertarian connotations which "anesthetized the revolutionary Bolsheviks and made them build a Leviathan when they thought they were entering the free world of their dreams."[125]

By 1921 the Bolshevik regime had won the civil war, but conditions had deteriorated badly. Bandits roamed wide areas; in the Kronstadt uprising, sailors protested against miserable conditions and the Bolshevik commissars; in some provinces large armed units were needed to suppress peasant rebellions. Lenin agreed to the substitution of a fixed tax in kind for the earlier requisitioning of agricultural surpluses—the crucial step needed to pacify the peasants. He endorsed the New Economic Policy (NEP), which established a mixed economy in the years from 1921 to 1927.

The results of this policy were notable, especially in the private sector of the economy. To be sure, large-scale industry, foreign trade, and finance remained in the hands of the state; less than 2 percent of these activities were in private hands. But the picture was reversed in small-scale industry and handicraft production. By 1926/27, 77.5 percent of such industry and production was privately owned, and this was down from 89.7 percent in 1923/24. The bulk of this production involved self-employment and assistance by members of the family. During the NEP period, the traders and private entrepreneurs of the towns became important economically and numerically. In agriculture, 98.3 percent of the sown area was controlled by individual peasants in 1927.[126] Private initiative had developed as soon as the combined pressures of the civil war and of the party's policy of War Communism were diminished. In the countryside, party influence declined as emergency conditions abated and privately managed farming became dominant.

This ascendance of private enterprise represented a major reversal of party policy and was the subject of continuous debate throughout the NEP period. In the eyes of many party leaders, NEP constituted a return to capitalism. When the peasants increasingly resisted the policy of requisitions under War Communism, when they threatened the countryside with major upheavals, Lenin had retreated to markets, money, and capitalism. He stated that the increase of productive forces in the rural sector would have to be measured in decades. The country had passed from tsarism to the Soviet system in five years, but now it was necessary to test "the steps forward [which] we proclaim every hour, take every minute, and then prove every second . . . that they are flimsy, superficial and misunderstood." In his Central Committee Report to the Eleventh Party Congress (1922), he made the following argument:

> Our aim is to restore the bond, to prove to the peasant by deeds that we are beginning with what is intelligible, familiar and immediately accessible to him, in spite of his poverty, and not with something remote and fantastic from the peasant's point of view. We must prove that . . . in this period of appalling ruin . . . the Communists are really helping [the small peasant]. Either we prove that, or he will send us to the devil. . . . This is the significance of the new economic policy. . . .

> Link up with the peasant masses, with the rank-and-file toiling peasants, and begin to move forward immeasurably, infinitely more slowly than we expected, but in such a way that the entire mass will actually move forward with us. If we do that we shall in time get such an acceleration of progress as we cannot dream of now.[127]

But Lenin found it difficult to explain the new policy to the party. Was the policy of War Communism a step toward socialism, in which case the New Economic Policy was a retreat? Or was War Communism a mistake, in which case NEP would correct it and facilitate the transition to socialism? As a retreat, NEP was temporary, but as a transition to socialism it could last for generations.[128]

The debates over the fate of the revolution during the 1920s turned on the continuation or reversal of the New Economic Policy, and Lenin died in 1924 before this issue was settled. The Russian revolution had based itself on Marxism, which predicted a proletarian revolution for the advanced, capitalist countries. The paradox was that the Bolsheviks had come to power in an overwhelmingly agrarian country. The party called itself the vanguard of the masses of workers and peasants. How was that party to transform the country economically, once the ravages of World War I and of the civil war were overcome? The main issue concerned the peasantry which made up the bulk of Russia's labor force. In this respect, a moderate and a radical position were articulated in the later 1920s. In view of the frequent factional struggles and "changes of line," it is best not to identify these positions with specific names.[129]

The *moderate* position envisaged the continuation of the New Economic Policy for the foreseeable future. Farm surpluses came from the better-off rather than the poor peasants. Hence, encouragement should be given to the peasants from whom surpluses could be obtained. The NEP goal was to achieve greater prosperity among the peasants and more commercial production. The slogan "get rich" was used for a time to signal this tolerance for private accumulation in the interest of agricultural productivity. The only alternative, as the advocates of this policy saw it, would be to favor the poor peasants and use coercion against the better-off peasants (*kulaks*), as under War Communism. The risk of this alternative was peasant unrest and loss of production. However, the advocates of a continuation of NEP were hard put to remain consistent. Although they favored the better-off peasants, they still wanted the poor peasants to cooperate with the socialist program. Hence, they withdrew the slogan "get rich," continued their appeals to the poor peasants, and advocated that more industrial products should be supplied to all the peasants. The champions of this moderate position saw that more coercion in the interest of accelerating production in the towns and the countryside would promote an all-powerful state apparatus and violate the humanist goals of socialism.

The *radical* position arose from a concern with national security and great misgivings about the New Economic Policy. Western military assistance to the Russian opponents of the revolution had fed fears of further intervention that would aim at destroying the achievements of the

revolution. Such fears lent support to the emphasis on speedy industrialization and helped to justify attacks on NEP as contrary to national
as well as socialist interests. Since industrialization under a continued
NEP would be slowed, this policy had to be abolished. At the same time,
advocates of the radical position realized that a "primitive socialist accumulation" was needed to finance heavy industry and expand the na-
tionalized sector of the economy. The necessary resources had to be
obtained from the private sector, and that meant primarily from the
kulaks. In this impending conflict, it would be necessary "to pump resources out of the private sector and so finance the state's investments
into the expanding socialist industrial sector."[130]

This radical position, under the leadership of Stalin, was victorious.
Stalin, who was born J. V. Dzhugashvili in 1879 (d. 1953), had risen
through participation in clandestine and partisan activities before and
during World War I. In 1912/13 he had been chosen by Lenin as a
member of the central committee of the Bolshevik party and as first
editor of *Pravda*. In 1922 he was appointed secretary-general of the
Russian Communist party and from that position rose to unrivaled leadership with the inauguration of the First Five-Year Plan (1928–1933)
and the drive to collectivize agricultural production. The NEP model
was repudiated. In effect, a new revolution was initiated from above,
directed against private peasant agriculture as well as against private
trade and industrial production. The coexistence of public and private
sectors in the economy under NEP was replaced by the controls of a
central planning organization. The new policy of expropriations and
requisitions resembled the emergency measures of War Communism.
But now the goal was different, however similar the method.

In 1928 Russia was no longer in a state of siege and civil war. Now,
industrial production was pushed forward at a feverish pace. The pressures created conditions of manpower conscription and full mobilization
such as usually occur only in wartime. The Communist leadership
brushed aside the complexity of economic planning. The idea of achieving balanced economic growth was replaced by emergency measures and
special-purpose campaigns. As early as 1921, Stalin had revealed his
distrust of experts when he urged Lenin to appoint "men of live politics,
ready to act on the principle of 'report fulfillment.'" This language of
a civil-war commander proved to be symptomatic of the simulated combat conditions under which the first five-year plans were launched:

> Undoubtedly, this style and approach were unavoidable when the core of the
> economic policy consisted of tempos. "Tempos decide the whole thing!" This
> dramatic slogan was intended by Stalin to mobilize energies and imagination.
> But the leadership used terror in order to make sure that these tempos would
> not be scrutinized nor derived from any principle other than the need to
> rush. To ask the crucial question "how much, and why so much?" was treated

as treason. . . . Stalin understood plans as temporary sets of targets that, however high, had to be surpassed. . . . Hence, the core of Stalin's program was the building of as many factories as possible. . . . Thus, the "unleashing" of productive forces became the guideline and was understood as a prescription for the maximum outpouring of investment into giant enterprises without any regard to coordination, correlation, proportion, and long-term considerations, which were now considered treasonable measures intended to curtail the salutary "unleashing."[131]

Special methods were needed to force the pace of collectivization. The party had a difficult task in the countryside.

As late as 1927, over 98 percent of the sown area belonged to individual peasants. These were kulaks in the official definition, and ideology demanded that poor peasants be the principal agents of the party in the drive toward collectivization. The rural soviet (*selsovet*) was the local unit of the Communist party. The poor peasants were tax exempt, yet as members of the soviet they were charged with the task of tax collection. One of the first steps away from NEP, then, was to activate the soviets manned by poor peasants to collect taxes from the kulak households which NEP had encouraged. But in 1927–1929, the better-off peasants quickly increased their representation in the soviets. These peasants were influential locally, and they naturally sought to protect their interests.

Moreover, peasant proprietors had their own traditional methods of handling community problems. In 1917 the old village community (mir) had been in disarray, with only 50 percent of the peasants belonging to it. But with the encouragement of proprietorship under NEP, the peasants quickly reverted to the old practices and by 1927 95 percent of their holdings were regularly redistributed by the community. The responsibilities of the village assemblies involved the distribution and reallocation of strips, methods of crop rotation, communal use of grazing land and forests, control of membership, as well as the discussion of community problems like schools and roads. The importance of village assemblies (*skhod*) is suggested by the fact that in twenty-three districts of Tula province, some 19,000 assemblies met during 1925/26. When the party sought to activate the rural soviets with the onset of collectivization in 1928, these assemblies had considerable funds and the great advantage of performing functions of interest to the peasants. By contrast, the rural soviets had few funds as well as unpopular administrative responsibilities. Nevertheless, the drive toward collectivization could be accomplished only through the forced activation of the rural soviets at the expense of the village assemblies.[132]

Collectivization thus meant the destruction of civil society in the countryside. In this case, the record literally speaks for itself. The property of 1 million kulak households, which had prospered during NEP, was confiscated. An estimated 4.5 million people were removed from their native area to other parts of the country—the same method the Muscovite tsars had used after their conquest of Novgorod (1565–1572). This campaign against better-off peasant households was (among other things) a means of forcing the rest of the peasants to accept collectivization. Between 1930 and 1936, the proportion of collectivized peasant households increased from 23.6 to 89.5 percent, covering about 95 percent of the crop area by the latter date. The peasants reacted with the only means at their disposal. They reduced grain harvests from a high of 83.5 million tons in 1930 to a low of 67.6 million tons in 1934.[133] They also slaughtered their animals (see Table 6).

This resistance in the countryside was echoed by intensified struggles within the ruling Communist party. Stalin's collectivization drive was followed by the "Great Purge," in which real and imagined opponents of the new policy and all those considered potential opponents of Stalin's leadership were summarily liquidated. Estimates of the number executed and of those who perished in Russian labor camps vary between ten and twenty million persons, with the weight of the fragmentary evidence favoring the higher figure.[134] In this second as well as in the first revolution, the number of deaths amounted to between 12 and 15 percent of the Russian people; emigration played an important role only in the first revolution. Put another way, Russian society underwent a loss of some thirty-four million people in a period of twenty to twenty-five years.[i]

But the two revolutions did not consist of coercion alone. The Soviet regime claimed to represent the laboring masses of the Russian people. This claim is basic for understanding the Communist concept of the mandate to rule.

In the *Communist Manifesto* of 1848, Marx and Engels had distinguished between workers and communists. They made clear that workers' understanding was partial, nationalist, often backward, irresolute, and limited. By contrast, the understanding of communists was com-

---

[i]Krushchev is reported to have given an estimate of eight million purge victims, Andrei Sakharov put the figure between ten and fifteen, while Conquest comes to twenty (which he calls almost certainly too low). If one takes a middle estimate of fifteen for the 1930s and adds the estimate of a loss of nineteen million (deaths or emigrations) during the civil war, one arrives at a minimum loss of thirty-four million. If one takes birth deficits due to the deaths of child-bearing adults into account, the total loss sustained during the two revolutions was much higher.

In citing these estimates, one touches on a trauma of the twentieth century. Earlier instances of mass killings may have been equally devastating: One thinks of the Mongol conquests in Russia and Persia, the Thirty Years' War, the European powers at war on the Continent and overseas, or outbreaks of mass violence as in the partition of India and Pakistan. The special trauma of the Soviet purges (or of genocide under the Nazis) is the use of mass killings as a government policy in peacetime, or so it seems to me.

TABLE 6

	1928 (million head)	1933 (million head)
Cattle	70.5	38.4
Pigs	26.0	12.1
Sheep and goats	146.7	50.2

SOURCE: Nove, *Economic History,* p. 186.

prehensive, internationalist, resolute, and long range. The distinction followed from the role which Marx attributed to reason and science. In his view, workers would provide the political momentum for the revolutionary overthrow of capitalism, while the intellectual direction of this upheaval would be provided by "bourgeois ideologists." While workers react against the inhumanities of exploitation, ideologists respond sympathetically to the intensified class struggle and the underutilization of man's productive potential. Marx allowed that workers would increase their understanding through their experience in the class struggle. He also insisted that communists of bourgeois origin could not provide effective leadership at will, but only where the class struggle was preparing the ground for revolutionary action. Marx did not offer a simple solution. He considered the relations between workers and "bourgeois ideologists" problematic and would probably have said that only practical, political action could resolve such relations in the future.[135]

Equivocation is inevitable whenever an educated elite acts out its *own* sense of social responsibility by claiming to represent the needs and interests of the people. Marx himself made this clear when he wrote that "it is not relevant what this or that worker or even what the whole proletariat *conceive* to be their aim, for the time being. It matters only what the proletariat *is* and that it will be forced to act historically in accordance with this being."[136] In the Russian context, this equivocation preceded the adoption of Marxism as a revolutionary ideology. The terrorists who assassinated Alexander II in 1881 claimed to "act on behalf of the people," but then declared that they were determined to "reawaken the people by agitation," that interests of which the people were unaware were yet inherent in their life. Previously, the terrorists had encountered the people's hostile reactions to their agitation, but they hoped that the assassination itself would bring popular grievances against tsarism out into the open. The intelligentsia's uneasy relation with the people must be emphasized in order to appreciate the radicalism of Lenin's position.

In his pamphlet *What Is To Be Done?* (1902), Lenin abandoned the idea which the populists had shared with Marx, namely, that a radical political orientation would arise spontaneously from the workers' experience in the class struggle.

> There is a lot of talk about spontaneity, but the *spontaneous* development of the labor movement leads to its becoming subordinate to bourgeois ideology . . . for the spontaneous labor movement is pure and simple trade unionism. . . . Hence, our task . . . is to *combat spontaneity,* to *divert* the labor movement, with its spontaneous trade unionist striving, from under the wing of the bourgeoisie and to bring it under the wing of revolutionary Social-Democracy. . . .
>
> The workers can acquire class political consciousness *only from without,* that is, only outside of the economic struggle, outside of the sphere of relations between workers and employers. . . .
>
> The Social-Democrat's ideal should not be a trade-union secretary, but a *tribune of the people,* able to react to every manifestation of tyranny and oppression . . . he must be able to group all these manifestations into a single picture of police violence and capitalist exploitation; he must be able to take advantage of every petty event. . . , in order to explain to *all* and everyone the world-historical significance of the struggle for the emancipation of the proletariat.[137]

The upgrading of what the professional revolutionary can do goes hand in hand with the downgrading of working-class spontaneity.

The nucleus of the party must be composed of persons whose "profession is revolutionary work." They are to receive enough financial support from the party to change their place of work, engage in clandestine activity, and acquire the requisite knowledge and experience. All decision-making of the party must be concentrated in a cadre of professional revolutionaries. To be sure, the broad masses should be enlisted in the movement. But only a party led by tested revolutionaries will create a firm organization that inspires confidence and ensures victory. Lenin formulated this principle of centralized decision-making by a party elite in 1902, long before the Bolshevik revolution.

In *What Is To Be Done?*, Lenin argued for strict centralization of controls in the party. He adopted the title of Chernyshevski's novel which had extolled the sterling qualities of professional revolutionaries, an emphasis natural to a political exile who had to identify with the masses from afar. Lenin returned to Russia in April 1917 after the outbreak of the revolution. Under these circumstances, it was natural to employ the slogan "All Power to the Soviets." Assemblies of workers and soldiers had been formed by left-wing political leaders after the tsar's abdication in March, but they were a familiar organizational form going back to the revolution of 1905 and other antecedents. Lenin had disparaged the spontaneous trade unionism of the working class in peacetime, but he extolled the revolutionary spontaneity of Russian soldiers and workers. He used this mass mobilization as a legitimation of the

Bolshevik seizure of power. Nevertheless, it is doubtful that he abandoned his earlier, elitist view of the central cadres of the party as the leaders in the postrevolutionary period.[138]

The legitimation of a party leadership in exile differs from the legitimation of party authority during a revolution, and that in turn differs from legitimation of a revolutionary government in authority. As the leader of a revolutionary government, Lenin abandoned not only the earlier dichotomy between professional revolutionaries and "trade unionist" workers, but also any simple reliance on the soviets. He was clearly aware that the new regime needed all the popular cooperation it could obtain, but also that in order to survive it must obtain that cooperation on its own terms. This realization is reflected in his design of party organization.

By "democratic centralism," Lenin meant that there would be free and vigorous (indeed, ruthless) discussion among all party members, who were the closest approximation to the public and to popular sentiment which the party would encompass. Party members were the vanguard of the masses, represented their sentiments, and provided the needed cooperation—or so it was maintained. Once discussion had taken place among the members, the leaders made the decision, and then every loyal party member must follow the "party line." In this way, Lenin sought to combine the people's spontaneous cooperation with the leaders' full freedom of action. In practice, his own position was quite flexible. In his statements on the New Economic Policy, Lenin advocated a slow, personable approach so that the mass of the peasants could move forward with the party. He did not explain how party activists could be flexible in their work with the peasants while complying unquestioningly with decisions of the Central Committee of the party. His last anguished writings even argued for a more accommodating approach among party leaders, although earlier he had emphasized toughness as indispensable for the dedicated party leader.

How did the one-party dictatorship of the Bolsheviks claim to represent the people when it first used the spontaneous outbursts of the revolutionary period to apply the old methods of "government by tribute collection" and then reversed itself and restored the capitalist methods of small private enterprises? The answer is that from Lenin down to the present, Soviet leaders have justified these and later policies by reference to the capitalist encirclement which threatens the achievements of the revolution.

Lenin's last article "Better Fewer, But Better" (1923) is symptomatic in this respect. He felt that the revolution had to its credit the destruction of capitalist industry, medieval institutions, and landed proprietorship. Now, however, the Soviet Union had to keep going on its path despite the absence of socialist revolutions in more developed countries.

To be sure, the intervention by the Western capitalist powers had failed to overthrow Russia's revolutionary government. But in Lenin's view, these powers had succeeded in preventing the Bolshevik system

> from *at once taking the step forward that would have justified the forecasts of the socialists,* that would have enabled the latter . . . to develop all the potentialities which, taken together, would have produced socialism; socialists would thus have proved to all and sundry that socialism contains within itself gigantic forces and that mankind had now entered into a new stage of development of extraordinarily brilliant prospects.

These brilliant prospects were delayed *indefinitely,* because timely concessions had retarded the revolutionary movements in the developed countries. On the other hand, capitalist development had begun in countries like China and India, where imperialist exploitation would be the main cause of worldwide revolution in the future. The task of Soviet leaders and the whole Russian people was, therefore, "to hold on" until this future would come to pass, and Lenin had no doubt of the outcome.

> In the last analysis, the outcome of the struggle will be determined by the fact that Russia, India, China, etc., account for the overwhelming majority of the population of the globe. And during the past few years it is this majority that has been drawn into the struggle for emancipation with extraordinary rapidity, so that in this respect *there cannot be the slightest doubt what the final outcome of the world struggle will be. In this sense, the complete victory of socialism is fully and absolutely assured.* . . . To ensure our existence until the next military conflict between the counter-revolutionary imperialist West and the revolutionary and nationalist East, between the most civilized countries of the world and the orientally backward countries, which however, comprise the majority, *this majority must become civilized.* We, too, lack enough civilization to enable us to pass straight on to socialism, although we do have the political requisites for it.[139]

Lenin did not say how socialism could have released "gigantic forces" immediately if the majority of the world population "must become civilized" first. Instead, he linked the brilliant promise of socialism (his article of faith) with the certainty of victory. For now the majority of the world's population had been drawn into the development of capitalism and hence would experience the predicted intensification of the class struggle. This prospect made up for what Lenin acknowledged as an earlier and mistaken assumption—namely, that the revolution would occur in the economically advanced countries. His discussion made Soviet hopes depend on the inevitable class conflicts which would occur as capitalism spreads. These conflicts would provide Russia with the respite it needed to develop its industry and thus defend itself against Western capitalism and imperialism.[140]

Lenin's article of 1923 outlined the siege mentality which facilitated

Stalin's rise to power in the 1920s. Stalin emphasized the role of the Communist party as the general staff which could give "correct guidance to the proletarian millions."

> The Party must be, first of all, the vanguard of the working class. The Party must absorb all the best elements of the working class. . . . The Party cannot be a real Party if it limits itself to registering what the masses of the working class feel and think, if it drags at the tail of the spontaneous movement, if it is unable to overcome the inertness and the political indifference of the spontaneous movement, if it is unable to rise above the momentary interests of the proletariat, if it is unable to elevate the masses to the level of the class interests of the proletariat. The Party must stand at the head of the working class; it must see further than the working class; it must lead the proletariat. . . . The Party is the political leader of the working class.[141]

Stalin conceived of the party as a quasi-military instrument of rule against civil society. Instead of waiting until a worldwide revolution would provide a more favorable setting, as the New Economic Policy and the moderate wing of the party had suggested, he used the permanent emergency induced by "capitalist encirclement" to advance the idea of "socialism in one country."

Ordinary methods of administration do not suffice when the political leaders of a country undertake the task of collectivization and rapid industrialization. Max Weber called an ideally functioning bureaucracy the most efficient method of solving large-scale organizational tasks. But this ideal type can be approximated only where there is orderly administration under the rule of law. Such conditions did not exist after the revolution of 1917 when the country faced internal chaos, nor did they exist after 1928. The norms governing conduct cannot remain stable for any length of time when a government must cope with the aftereffects of war and revolution, or for political reasons wishes to force the pace of collectivization and industrialization. Under these conditions, officials are faced with an unremitting drive for prodigious achievement. They are likely to employ all the maneuvers of concealment not only to escape pressure and make their lives more tolerable, but also because the party leadership makes demands on them which are "irrational," that is, incompatible with expert knowledge and systematic procedure. The party, on the other hand, must try to prevent such concealment. It will put executive officials under maximum pressure in order to utilize their expertise to the fullest extent. From this standpoint, it is "rational" to place a party functionary at the side of every major official in order to prevent concealment and apply pressure.[142]

Russia has become an industrial world power by means of emergency decrees. The use of terror in factional struggles or as a means of applying pressure is no longer what it was at the height of the Stalinist purges or at the end of World War II, though the incalculable use of severe, punitive measures remains a prominent feature of Soviet life. Rapid industrialization, military victory in World War II, and Russia's position as a superpower appear to justify the claim of representing the Russian masses and laboring people everywhere. The Communist one-party state has made this claim, backed by dictatorial power, ever since the 1917 revolution. This together with unquestioned achievements at whatever price have shaped the categories of thought in which both the leaders and ordinary Russians think about the world. Enforcement of ideological conformity has been a principal means of inducing the people to cope with the ever-recurring impediments to the achievement of targets set by the party leaders. The determination to overcome such obstacles by subjective effort and ardor are evidence of Lenin's and Stalin's emphasis on the decisive importance of belief and action rather than favorable conditions for the attainment of a socialist society.[143] In this view, subjective factors can outweigh the disadvantages of backwardness, an approach which underscores the crucial importance of the party and its correct political leadership for overcoming not only obstacles to economic growth but to cultural development as well. Capitalist encirclement and the danger of foreign military attacks further justify the lasting importance of the state in a socialist society. They also account for the punitive and terrorist methods the state uses—in the long-run interest of workers and peasants.

Western leaders have repeatedly been told by their Russian counterparts that on this ideological front there will be no relaxation of tensions. The reason is that Marx's distinction between communists and workers, Lenin's distinction between professional revolutionaries and the spontaneous "trade unionism" of the working class, and Stalin's concept of the party as the general staff of the proletariat remain the model of the Communist concept of authority. The party is the guardian of the collective interests of the masses, and all "immediate interests" must be subordinated to the decisions of the Central Committee. Article 126 of the USSR constitution of 1936 (as amended in 1965) ostensibly guarantees the right of all citizens to "unite in mass organizations—trade unions, co-operative societies, youth organizations, etc."; but it then adds,

> the most active and politically-conscious citizens in the ranks of the working class, working peasants and working intelligentsia [are] voluntarily united in the Communist Party of the Soviet Union, which is the vanguard of the working people in their struggle to build communist society *and is the leading core of all organizations of the working people, both government and non-government.*

In other words, no organization in civil society is permitted which does not have its coordinate party cell exercising functions of control, agitation, and education.

The rights guaranteed by the constitution are indistinguishable from duties. People who refuse to vote will be told that their right to vote is the "honorable duty of a citizen." And this is the perspective not only for the present. Current Soviet writings about a utopian communist society of the future make clear that the party's guidance of the masses will become ever greater until the day when "all members of society are raised to the same level of consciousness and organization as the members of the Party." The party can fulfill its mandate to rule only by using all the means at its disposal to raise the consciousness of the people. On the day when these efforts are fully successful, the party will not have "withered away"; it will have become an all-inclusive organization merged with all aspects of the life of the people.[144] In this conception, government in the name of the people will reach its final goal only when the people have come to agree with the party.

14

FROM ROYAL AUTHORITY TO POPULAR MANDATE: TWENTIETH-CENTURY PERSPECTIVES

OUR INQUIRY into structures of authority and their transformations in different societies has taken us on a long journey through time. The study has placed the particularities of each country within a general movement of history. In this concluding chapter, the same guidelines are briefly applied to contemporary societies, and it seems appropriate to round out an earlier discussion (Chapter 2) by focusing on China and the Arab world.

THE CHINESE REVOLUTION

Modernization has been marked by recurring conflicts between nonindustrial and industrial ways of life and between monarchic and populist authority. Such conflicts have been intensified through the demonstration effects that are faciliated by modern communication. Major advances toward industrialization and a popular mandate in one country have had consequences in others, a process which is still continuing. The history of China in the nineteenth and twentieth centuries provides us with a recent example of this phenomenon as well as with a new setting and conception of the mandate of the people.

During the nineteenth century, China was forced into wars with Western powers and with Japan. China's technological backwardness was made evident not only through military defeats but also through the "treaty port" system in which China was forced to grant to Western traders the rights of extraterritoriality and favorable conditions of trade.

The Manchu dynasty (1662–1911) made unsuccessful attempts to cope with these pressures, but was weakened by popular rebellions which were directly or indirectly linked to the effects of foreign intrusion.

Reactions to contact with foreign powers were ambivalent. Chinese scholars assumed that their civilization was the center of human culture and that foreign powers could be expected to pay tribute to the Chinese emperor. Some tried to cope with the Western threat by claiming that the basic principles of science and technology had long been known and previously applied by the Chinese; thus, the mastering of admittedly superior Western techniques in effect merely constituted a return to ancient Chinese practices. Others claimed that the West was no threat because it possessed a strictly material culture, as opposed to the higher spiritual culture of the East. After the overthrow of the Manchu dynasty in 1911, these efforts at reconciling an ancient tradition with the Western ideas of "Mr. Science" and "Mr. Democracy" gave way for a time (1917–1921) to a great cultural ferment in which all the theories then current in the West and in Japan were eagerly debated.[1]

During the period of warlordism under the Chinese Republic (ca. 1916–1937), the Nanking government of the nationalist Kuomintang party was founded under Chiang Kai-shek (1928). The Chinese Communist party was established in 1921, and for a time Soviet Russian representatives attempted to control it. The party eventually came into conflict with the Kuomintang, and after the famous Long March of 1934–1935 northward across Western China, some 20,000 Chinese Communist troops established their base and staging area in Yenan in 1936. During the Sino-Japanese war (1937–1945), the Chinese Communist party joined the Kuomintang and the American forces in the struggle against Japanese occupation. Once the Japanese were defeated in 1945, a civil war broke out between the Kuomintang and the Communists from which the latter emerged victorious. The Chinese People's Republic was proclaimed in Peking on October 1, 1949.

The Chinese Communist idea of a popular mandate combines the centralized mobilization of the people with the spontaneous initiative of the peasant masses themselves. Originating in the years of the Yenan retreat, this idea was developed further during the Communist war-mobilization of North China against the Japanese. In this national mass mobilization, cooperation between peasants and Communists was greatly enhanced by the distinctive structure of the Chinese peasantry.

That structure can be defined in contrast to the Russian peasantry. While Russian landlords and officials primarily considered the peasants as a source of taxes and manpower, the village assembly was capable of collective decision-making in regard to community affairs. When the tsarist regime disintegrated in 1917, the peasants not only expropriated property from the old owners but also continued their accustomed practices of a rural subsistence economy through communal self-government. When the New Economic Policy allowed individual enterprise, it also permitted the continuation of these old communal practices.[2] However, rural traditions were disrupted by Stalin's policies of forced collectivization, beginning in 1928. The Marxist as well as the tsarist tradition contained an antirural bias which reinforced the weakness of civil ties between the towns and the countryside. Under the tsars, autocratic governments had ruled and exploited the provinces from the center, and peasants as well as gentry had evaded that rule by every subterfuge at their disposal. However, provincial administration was very inefficient, and although Russian landowners exacted tribute from the population, they were not otherwise involved in the self-contained affairs of the village. The Stalinist drive of collectivization was much more ruthless than tsarist administration had been in breaking down the isolation of the countryside and overcoming rural resistance to central directives. Yet even after more than four decades of a concerted drive to organize the peasantry, the private sector still plays a significant role in Soviet agriculture.[3]

The Chinese village was never as isolated from centers of authority as the Russian village community. Even in the nineteenth century, Chinese peasants had been linked to gentry, merchants, and artisans by regional market areas. Moreover, the local notables who retained their influential position in the village cultivated their ties with other notables and government officials in the marketing and administrative towns of the region.[4] These differences between the Russian and the Chinese village in part explain differences between the revolutions in the two countries.

The Russian revolution of 1917 was generated by an upsurge of peasant opposition to tsarism and the first World War. The ensuing civil war destroyed whatever was left of the formal political structure of the old regime. The Chinese revolution of 1911 destroyed the Manchu dynasty and resulted in the establishment of the Chinese Republic, but much of the old network of personal relations, albeit badly fragmented, remained. Local warlords and gentry retained power, and neither workers nor peasants were able to overthrow them. Indeed, the 1920s witnessed a resurgence of conservatism under the Kuomintang. The Chinese Communists "were pushed out of the cities (and most administrative towns) of China altogether, forced to pursue a do-or-die strategy of rural guerilla warfare while the now rightist re-oriented Kuomintang was left in control of the most modernized urban centers."[5] In contrast, the Bolsheviks were based in the towns and their military leadership during the civil war was facilitated by the railroads built under the tsars. The Chinese revolution had to base itself on the peasantry as the main revolutionary force, because China's urbanization was much less advanced than that of Russia. When the Nanking government was actually joined by the Chinese Communists in the struggle against the Japanese (1937–1945), the Communists expanded the rural areas under their control at the expense of the Japanese. Thus, by 1945 they controlled some nineteen "liberated areas" with a total of 70 to 90 million persons. In North China, they were clearly the most effective leaders of peasant resistance to Japan.

In Russia, military defeat in World War I led to revolution and then to civil war. In China, by contrast, military victory over the Japanese led first to civil war between the Chinese Communists and the Kuomintang and then to revolution. During the civil war (1946–1949), the Chinese Communist armies used their long experience of organizing the peasants in defeating and overthrowing the Nanking government. Thus, the way was prepared for a new Chinese version of what Marxists, Leninists, and Stalinists had grappled with before—namely, the relations between town and country and between the Communist party and the masses.

Mao Tse-tung was exceptionally skilled in combining the Chinese tradition with ideas taken from abroad. In his youth, he studied the "new learning" from the West, but standard Western learning was tainted because of the acts of aggression the Western powers committed against China. Marxism-Leninism was a more useful Western import for Mao. But he was careful to point out that although the study of Marxism was important, it was equally important "to understand our historic inheritance and to evaluate it critically by the use of the Marxist method."

> Today's China is an outgrowth of historic China. We are Marxist historicists; we must not mutilate history. From Confucius to Sun Yet-sen we must sum it up critically. . . . The assimilation of this (precious) heritage itself turns out to be a kind of methodology that is of great help in the guidance of the revolutionary movement. . . . If a Chinese communist who is a part of the great Chinese people . . . talks of Marxism apart from Chinese peculiarities, this Marxism is merely an empty abstraction. Consequently, the Sinification of Marxism—that is to say, making certain that in all of its manifestations it is imbued with Chinese peculiarities . . . becomes a problem that must be understood and solved by the whole Party without delay. . . .[6]

In 1962, when Mao looked back on the preceding twenty-four years, he acknowledged that the Chinese Communists had copied the Soviet Union during the early years because of their lack of experience in economic construction. But beginning in 1955, "we decided to make self-reliance our major policy," and henceforth foreign aid and ideas would be secondary, a temporary crutch only.[7]

China's collectivization of agriculture is evidence of this independence and provides important clues for the Chinese conception of a popular mandate. The Chinese Communists came to power after three years of civil war during which they had already effected a working relationship with the peasants in the regions they controlled militarily. Chinese collectivization was accomplished between 1954 and 1956, with about 83 percent of farm households collectivized by the latter date. The lands of rich landlords were expropriated and collective farms were set up for land-hungry poor and middle-level peasants. No doubt, many rich landlords were killed, but compared with Russia the cost in human lives was relatively moderate. Though the post-revolutionary expropriations occurred in two years, the whole revolutionary process of expropriating and displacing the rich was a gradual one.

> During over twenty years in the countryside of China, between 1927 and 1949, the Chinese Communists gradually developed tactics to drive the warlords and gentry from regional and local, political-military and economic power. . . . The Chinese Communists both displaced, and in a sense, replaced the warlord-gentry nexus of provincial-local power left over from the collapsing Old Regime; the peasants still remained oriented to non-parochial leaders with a foothold in the localities, only the Party and Red Army hierarchies replaced the landed and official gentry.[8]

By building on their successful mass mobilization in the countryside during the Yenan period and the war against Japan as well as leading the popular attack on the rich peasants, the Chinese Communists were in contact with the masses—an inspiring and, among Communist movements, unique experience.

In Russia, by contrast, the peasants expropriated land on their own initiative. When agricultural production fell and supplies to the towns were disrupted, the Bolshevik regime resorted to confiscation to secure food supplies for the towns. In response, the peasants curtailed agricultural production and slaughtered their cattle. The policies of confiscation during the period of War Communism were reversed by the New Economic Policy which encouraged individual proprietorship (kulaks) and resulted in an increased food supply. But the kulaks later became the target of Stalin's collectivization drive, thus perpetuating the antagonism between town and country. Russia's collectivization drive required a decade, with 93 percent of farm households collectivized between 1928 and 1937. The cost in human lives and the unceasing struggle of the Soviet regime against the peasantry have been noted already.[9]

The contrast between the two collectivization drives was due not only to different circumstances but also to different cultural traditions. Mao Tse-tung's emphasis on re-education rather than liquidation owed something to China's Confucian legacy[a] and to the village collectivism

---

[a]Care should be taken not to exaggerate the continuities between Confucianism and Chinese communism, much as Soviet appreciation of Peter the Great or the "Slavicization" of archeological evidence serves Communist rather than historical or scientific purposes.

of the past. The concept of "renovating the people" by moral inspiration (*hsin-min*) influenced Mao's youth and had been espoused by Mao's hero, Liang Ch'i-ch'ao (1873–1929), who echoed the Confucian belief that it was a gentleman's duty to inspire people by his exemplary conduct. In addition, there were traditional institutions which encouraged collectivist indoctrination. In the sixteenth century, a village covenant system (*hsiang-yueh*) was devised which would rehabilitate rebels by drawing them back into civil society. Evil was an antisocial act produced by degenerate customs and could be abolished only if the inhabitants of a village covenant area (under the guidance of virtuous officials) pledged themselves to "return to goodness." In periodic assemblies, good deeds were praised and bad ones denounced; ideally, every effort was made to help the miscreant rather than turn him over to the authorities. But the accent of this system had been on virtuous officials lecturing to the people, whereas Mao's experience with mass mobilization prompted him to destroy the hierarchy of learning and urge every man to learn for himself.[10]

Mao used the Confucian tradition even in his attacks on it. He chose to be remembered as the "Great Teacher" rather than by any of the other panegyrics heaped on him. Education, he maintained, must break with rote learning and the traditional submission of the pupil to the authority of the teacher. Education must be linked to practice and must not be separated from the class struggle. The great objective was for students and for the masses generally to combine spontaneity and initiative from below with obedience to the correct line laid down from above. Stuart Schram has pointed out that in Mao's view there was no contradiction between his slogan "let a hundred flowers bloom" early in 1957 and his policy later that year when many opinions were reclassified and suppressed as "poisonous weeds." In July 1957 Mao stated,

> Our aim is to create a political situation in which there is both centralism and democracy, both discipline and freedom, both unity of purpose and personal ease of mind and liveliness, in order to facilitate the socialist revolution and social construction and make it easier to overcome difficulties, so that we can build more quickly a modern industry and agriculture in our country, and the Party and the state will be consolidated and better able to weather storms. . . .
>
> A communist must be good at discussing things with the masses, and must at no time be divorced from the masses. The relationship between Party and masses is exactly like that between fish and water. . . .[11]

Mao's view was that the masses would provide the democracy, freedom, and liveliness essential to socialist construction, while the party would provide centralism, discipline, and unity of purpose. Unlike Lenin, and certainly Stalin, Mao used the argument of the masses (the so-called mass line) time and again to oppose the cumulative petrification of bureaucracy in the party and the government, countering the emphasis on discipline and regular procedure by men like Liu Shao-ch'i, Lin Piao, and others. Of course, massive pressures have been used under the slogan of "voluntarism" to support re-education campaigns when necessary.[12] This interplay between mass mobilization and guidance by the party represents what Mao means by the mandate of the people.

> In all the practical work of our Party, all correct leadership is necessarily from the masses, to the masses. This means: take the ideas of the masses (scattered and unsystematic ideas) and concentrate them (through study turn them into concentrated and systematic ideas), then go to the masses and propagate and explain these ideas until the masses embrace them as their own, hold fast to them and translate them into action, and test the correctness of these ideas in such action. Then once again concentrate ideas from the masses and once again take them to the masses so that the ideas are persevered in and carried through. And so on, over and over again in an endless spiral, with the ideas becoming more correct, more vital and richer each time.[13]

Perhaps without knowing it, Mao put into practice Trotsky's old saying that the majority is not counted, but won over in action. Now that Mao Tse-tung has died and memories of the "Yenan way" begin to fade, calls for discipline, controls, and increased productivity become more insistent.

For China after 1949, the Russian revolution became the "reference society," at least for awhile. But Russia's overthrow of an old regime in an economically backward society and its forced collectivization and industrialization were achieved at enormous cost. The Chinese under the leadership of Mao Tse-tung reacted to this model by accepting a slower rate of economic growth and with a positive emphasis on the peasantry, on re-education campaigns, and on the importance of subjective commitment as a major cause of change. By linking these policies with the Chinese tradition, they have created a new revolutionary model. Thus, Communist China has demonstration effects on other countries, which have been added to the demonstration effects of earlier revolutions and restorations.

The Arab states of the twentieth century have also inherited a great tradition which they must combine as best they can with the challenges of today. My remarks on the Arab world, like my remarks on China, are meant to be suggestive for a fuller inquiry into governance and legitimation in the twentieth century.

ARAB NATIONALISM AND SOCIALISM

Muhammad died in 632. A century later the Umayyad caliphate reached from Spain across the North African rim and the Middle East to the Indus valley. By 830, a process of political fragmentation began and has continued to the present. The Arab conquerors of a great empire, the originators of a great civilization, were conquered themselves by invaders from central Asia and elsewhere. Many competing caliphates, emirates, and other political units emerged, but in the midst of this centuries-long fragmentation Arab civilization and Islam achieved a great cultural efflorescence. Until the sixteenth century, Arab spokesmen considered the Northern Europeans as barbarians, but India, China, and others were felt to have great civilizations. To the heirs of the Umayyad and Abbasid caliphates, their own society appeared as having the greatest heritage of all, a sentiment which is retained among Arab people to this day.

Arab contact with Western Europe dates back to 710 when the Muslims landed in Spain. The Crusades of the eleventh century made inroads upon the Near East; Ottoman conquests of the fifteenth century established the Turks in the Balkans. By the end of the fifteenth century the balance of power between the European and Arab worlds began to shift when the Christians ousted the Muslims from Granada (1492) and Vasco da Gama made his successful voyage to India (1498). But while the Europeans initiated their overseas expansion, Ottoman conquests of Syria and Egypt (1517) and subsequent military engagements with Persia established a land empire which was dissolved only at the end of World War I (1918).

Until the nineteenth century, only Austria and Russia made military inroads upon the Ottoman possessions in the Balkans and elsewhere, although European trade with the Middle East had existed for centuries. But in 1798, Napoleon's occupation of Egypt initiated an era of European military penetration on a larger scale, the first Western invasion of the Middle East since the Crusades. The idea of Islamic superiority over the infidel West was shattered. The period following Napoleon's withdrawal (1799) witnessed internal Egyptian reforms under Mohammed Ali (viceroy of Egypt, 1805–1848), greater administrative centralization of the Ottoman empire, but also the increasing commercial and military penetration of the Muslim world by the great European powers. British shipping companies began services to various Arab lands from India, and by 1820 England had established its supremacy on the coasts of the Arabian peninsula. Regular shipping services by various European powers to the shores of the Mediterranean followed shortly thereafter. Native means of transport were soon replaced through road-building and regular boat services on inland waterways in Iraq and Egypt. The first Egyptian railroad was built in 1856, linking Cairo and Alexandria; by 1914 there were over 3,000 miles of railroad track. In 1869, the Suez Canal was opened. (Similar developments in Arab Asia occurred between 1890 and 1914, largely on French and Turkish initiative.) All these means of transport as well as irrigation constructed by modern equipment encouraged the extended cultivation of cotton and sugar in Egypt. The twentieth century has added to all of this cars, lorries, and airplanes and after World War I the vast development of oil exploration and extraction.

European cultural penetration first occurred through the various Christian minorities in Lebanon and Syria which operated printing presses in their own languages. At the time Arabic books were printed in Europe and then circulated in the Near East. Although Napoleon brought an Arabic press with him to Cairo, the first Muslim printing press was established in Egypt in 1822, with Turkish books outnumbering Arabic ones especially on technical and military subjects. These developments were supplemented by the missionary efforts of French Jesuits and American Protestants, who maintained schools and colleges in Syria, established Arabic printing presses, and trained a new generation of Arabs

> at once more conscious of their Arab heritage and more affected by European influence. . . . It was in this period [of the late nineteenth century] that Arab nationalism was born. It was of mingled origin. To the old Arab dislike of Turks and the urgent mistrust of the encroaching and alien West were added the European idea of nationality and a revival of the Arabic language and culture. Nationalism was strongest among the Christians, least affected by the Muslim ideal of unity, most by economic change and Western cultural influence. The Christian could not subscribe to the pan-Islamic idea which was the modern political expression of the old community of Islam. He sought instead to give a new expression, in national rather than religious terms, to the solidarity and resentments of the East against the invading West. For Muslims the two forms of expression were never really distinguished. The basic sentiment of identity was religious and social, the complete society of Islam expressed sometimes in national terms, sometimes in religious terms as synonymous and interchangeable sets of words denoting the same basic reality.[14]

This mixture of quasi-religious and xenophobic nationalisms was greatly enhanced by direct European control. The French occupied Algeria from 1830 to 1962 and Tunisia from 1881 to 1956. British occupation of Egypt lasted from 1882 to 1936 and the Italian occupation of Libya from 1911/12 to 1951. After World War I, mandates under the League of Nations were established in 1920. The French mandate over Syria and Lebanon came to an end in 1941; the British mandate in Iraq ended in 1932, in Transjordan in 1946, and in Palestine in 1948. The state of Israel was founded in 1948 in conformity with a United Nations plan partitioning Palestine into separate Jewish and Arab states.

The Arab states as well as China were subject to increasing European penetration during the nineteenth century, and both areas entered this period in political disarray. In China, the Manchu dynasty was declining and increasingly subject to internal and external attacks, but the country retained its territorial integrity even when the overthrow of the Manchu was followed by the warlordism of the Chinese Republic (ca. 1916–1937). By contrast, the Arab states of North Africa and the Middle East retained many of the political divisions that had first appeared at the end of the Abbasid caliphate in the tenth century; others were provinces within the Ottoman empire. China suffered periodic European intrusions, but for the most part European occupation was confined to the treaty ports. By contrast, the Arab states were subject to colonization for periods between 40 and 130 years, and were subject to occupation under a mandate of the League of Nations for periods between 12 and 28 years. The Second World War had profound impact in both areas. China joined the Allied powers in the struggle against Japan; internal political divisions were put aside. In the wake of Japan's defeat, China underwent a revolutionary civil war that ended with the takeover by the Chinese Communists. Contrast this to the Arab experience during the war. Much of North Africa and the Middle East were scenes of battle between the Axis powers and the Western Allies. The Arab states took no effective part in the struggle, though their people were employed by both sides and subjected to Allied and Axis propaganda.

Perhaps the greatest contrast is cultural. Even the Communist revolution does not alter the fact that moral teaching specifically concerned with the conduct of government has been a main preoccupation of Chinese civilization for some three thousand years. The emphasis of this tradition is resolutely secular. Islamic civilization has never made a distinction between religious and political concerns; the caliphs were both religious and political leaders of their community. When a choice had to be made the maintenance of religious functions had clear priority. One may relate this priority to the Islamic tradition which obliges all members of the community (umma) and above all its leaders to uphold God's truth as embodied in the Qur'an; one can relate it to the long history of political division in the Arab world which meant that power was in the hands of invaders while the religious conversion of these alien peoples presented a formidable challenge to the caliphs and the ulema. At any rate, there is long precedent for the separation of religion from political affairs as long as the rulers protect the one true faith and its institutions.

During the nineteenth century, Western intrusions into the countries of the Middle East provided a powerful stimulus to the emergence of an Arab intelligentsia, especially in the Ottoman provinces of Syria, Iraq, and Egypt. Eventually, clandestine opposition to the Ottoman regime arose at the Ottoman capital, mainly among young army officers who championed a Turkish nationalism and modernism increasingly at odds with the orthodox Islamic tradition. In the course of this opposition, emphasis shifted in some Ottoman provinces from the use of British or French precedents to German nationalism as a pattern for the development of an indigenous movement of reform or revolution. German models were compatible with the new aspirations, partly because they were not identified with Britain or France, and partly because the theory of the "folk" supported Arab nativist ideals.[15] Outside Turkey, Arab nationalism has taken several forms.

In the period since World War II, eight of the fifteen Arab states are still monarchies (Bahrain, Jordan, Kuwait, Morocco, Oman, Quatar, Saudi Arabia, and the United Arab Emirates). Hence, contemporary Arab variants of "power and the mandate to rule" include several absolute monarchies trying to preserve their established order while attempting to industrialize the country. These states might resemble the regime of Louis XIV were it not for the fact that personal monarchy must today be maintained in a world abounding in revolutionary movements and that these societies encompass both a nomadic way of life and the technology of the twentieth century. Saudi Arabia and the smaller sheikdoms of the Arabian peninsula reject the very idea of a constitution. All power is vested in the king, who is also the country's supreme religious leader. Legislation is by royal decree, and there are no political parties and no elections. All sensitive posts are held by members of the royal family who favor economic development. Because of its oil, Saudi Arabia is an immensely rich country which has engaged in recent years in an extensive program of industrialization. At the same time, leading members of the Saudi clan (which has some 3,000 members) are acutely aware that it is difficult to contain this rapid development within the framework of monarchy and Islam. Some internal dissension evidently exists, for in 1975 King Faisal was assassinated by a member of his clan as a protest against Westernization and modernization.

The rulers of Saudi Arabia give massive support to the maintenance and protection of Muslim holy places, a popular move which combines genuine conviction with an effort to dampen revolutionary tendencies. The country also supports the overall campaign against Israel, though primarily on religious grounds. The Saudis are naturally apprehensive that in conjunction with that campaign revolutionary extremists will jeopardize the monarchy as they have done in countries like Jordan and Libya. Consequently, Saudi Arabia often attempts to mediate among the contending Arab states in an effort to forestall the demonstration effects of extreme political demands.

The monarchy of Morocco exemplifies other aspects of the Saudi problem of combining monarchy with twentieth-century conditions. The Moroccan constitution declares that sovereignty belongs to the nation, that political parties and other voluntary organizations are allowed, and that only a "single party" state is explicitly prohibited.[16] The constitution also lists the political and economic rights of citizenship. These libertarian ideas of the French tradition naturally are at odds with a poor and autocratically governed country, for in practice the Moroccan kings rely on personal rule, army support, and emergency decrees if necessary. It is an open question for how long a personal monarchy can compensate for this discrepancy between theory and practice by economic development and appeals to the Islamic tradition.

Instability also threatens the six countries which are military regimes with a nominally republican constitution and mostly one-party rule. The six are Algeria, Egypt, Iraq, Libya, Syria, and Yemen; the seventh, Lebanon, has been rent not only by its internal divisions but by the use of South Lebanon as a staging area for the Palestinian struggle against Israel. Generally, the ruling parties and military juntas seek to stabilize their regimes by sectarian and kinship loyalties, by military preparedness mostly directed at Israel, and by such economic development as their own resources, appeals for aid, and maneuvers among the big powers can engender.

In addition, these Arab countries use a kaleidoscope of political ideas derived from previous revolutions. Speeches and formal constitutions declare that the people are the source of all authority. A formal bill of rights is included in most constitutions. To these themes of the French revolution are added those of the Russian. The single legal party is variously characterized as representing all the people, as the vanguard party adhering to the principle of "democratic centralism," and as the instrument which will construct a socialist Arab society. Even the Chinese overtones are heard, as when the state is declared sacred only "to the extent that the masses have exercised their choice freely." Arab leaders purport to speak in the name of the masses, whose sentiments they claim to discern and whose consciousness they wish to raise, so that the people will be able to exercise the sovereign rights they are said to possess. The Arab leaders insist, as do the Russian and Chinese, that their mandate to govern derives from the people—with the proviso that the people must first be raised to the consciousness of their interests by the vanguard party.[17] But the Arab countries are politically fragmented, and these verbal endorsements of revolutionary ideas are in practice political liabilities, since they raise quite unrealistic expectations.

Religious and nationalist appeals are added to the ideological legacies of earlier revolutions. All Arab constitutions (except that of Lebanon) declare Islam the religion of the state and Arabic its official language; a number of them add that Islamic sacred law, the Shari'a, is the primary source of legislation. More notable yet are the repeated references to an Arab nation when in fact an Arab nation does not exist, but only the common adherence to Islam. These religious and nationalist appeals began only in the nineteenth century. They express the genuine desire of intellectuals who want to define an Arab identity that goes beyond the present political fragmentation, and there is reason to believe that this "religious" nationalism appeals to the masses as well.

The fifteen Arab states face a great paradox, whether they are conservative, relatively moderate, or revolutionary (at least rhetorically). Appeals to Islam transcend the boundaries among them and evoke historical memories and powerful feelings that at one level join the intellectuals seeking a "national identity" with the masses finding emotional release in the only world of ideas with which they are familiar. At this level, monarchs and military, one-party rulers alike seek legitimacy on the ground that their regimes reflect and promote the underlying solidarity of the Arab people at home and abroad. Such a solidarity may exist only as an ideal, but the appeals to this ideal seek to merge "the Arab nation" with the Islamic concept of the religious community (umma). In this way, nationalism (and socialism as well) can invoke traditional Muslim sentiments, fostering dreams of empire and desires for a restored Muslim community, buoyed by a sense of history, identity, and solidarity.[18]

The concept of the umma is echoed in all Arab countries. Its romantic appeal has a politically destabilizing effect in countries which are already divided along ethnic and religious lines and which are affected as well by a disparity between rich and poor that is embittered by modern economic developments. Even politically stable countries like Egypt and Saudi Arabia are threatened in this way (despite their more homogeneous populations). Arab leaders are torn between appeals to the great Islamic tradition which they know to be popular and efforts to bring about economic change which along with secular political institutions tend to undermine that tradition. These two worlds must meet, as President Boumedienne of Algeria demanded (1974), when he called on the spokesmen of his military, one-party regime to come in contact with the peasants.[19] So far such "contacts" have taken the form of mass meetings with speeches punctuated by acclamations and probably attended by few peasants. Other "contacts" consist of nationalist and anti-imperialist slogans and the advocacy of "Third World" interests. This propaganda probably creates enthusiasm among students, leaves other educated people ambivalent, and fails to persuade the peasants if indeed it reaches them. But Western observers cannot be surprised if an aggressive rhetoric toward the outside world is used to secure political support at home. It is an open question how the Arab states, which hover between national and pan-Arab appeals, will come to terms with the paradox of an Islamic and imperial legacy and their more or less permanent political divisions in a world of alien superpowers and a modern, technical civilization.[20]

A SUMMARY

Kingship and aristocracy represent one type of rule. Authority is exercised by a single person who is typically consecrated in office. If he is only a nominal ruler, a regent will govern in his name. To supplement his personal commands, the sovereign must delegate authority; thus, rulers are always involved in compromises between central direction and local autonomy. These compromises help to account for the various structures of royal authority from one century to another as well as from country to country. Despite these variations, the royal court is the summit of a country's hierarchy of prestige, resulting in underlying uniformities of kingship.

The old majesty of kings was permanently impaired when in England the king-in-parliament became the supreme authority of government. In the early seventeenth century, three groups developed which eventually coalesced in opposition to the rule of Charles I. The first group consisted of Puritan divines, led by men who had been persecuted under the reign of Mary Tudor. After Elizabeth came to the throne, these men wanted to purify the Anglican church of its Catholic legacies in doctrine and ritual, but they wanted to do so from within the church through reform of the church service, the presbyterian principle of organization, and widespread lecturing. The second group consisted of common lawyers, members of a conservative profession, many of whom had a guildlike interest in the common-law courts as against the prerogative courts of the king. In the agitation of the time, some spokesmen of this professional group developed legal principles on the basis of ancient precedent which accentuated the gathering conflicts between parliament and the crown. The third group consisted of prominent landed gentry in parliament, men of great standing in the realm who sponsored Puritan clergy through their control of church benefices and employed common lawyers in their many lawsuits. These aristocratic representatives of "the country" were often legally trained and many were themselves Puritans. In the course of disputes with the king, some of these parliamentary leaders developed techniques of organization which transformed diffuse resentments into a concerted parliamentary opposition. The ties of interest which linked these three groups have been the subject of much controversy. There is less dispute that a combination of religious inspiration, vested interest, and high social standing in the counties and in parliament brought about powerful opposition to the king. In 1688 a new political balance was achieved between king and parliament as well as between court and country; henceforth, principles of religious toleration and of law existed in a society dominated by a landed aristocracy. These achievements of the seventeenth-century revolution were to prove advantageous for the later development of civic equality and law, but during much of the eighteenth century these advantages were difficult to discern. It would have been plausible, though misleading, to conclude that the revolutions of 1640 and 1688 had resulted only in a conservative restoration.

The French revolution was led by the radical philosophes and the conservative parlementaires, the latter promoting their interests increasingly in the language of the former. Paris society, with its salons and masonic lodges, provided a natural meeting-ground for writers and members of the French nobility. These men belonged to the established society, though it is as true of France as it was of England that by articulating their own grievances and ideas they gave direction to the more diffuse discontents in the society at large. By destroying not only royal authority, but also the legally protected privileges of church and nobility, the French revolution established the new principle that all sovereign authority emanates from the nation as a whole and that the central government is the only legitimate executor of that authority. All intermediate bodies of civil society, such as schools, municipalities, the church, private associations, and assemblies, are under the ultimate authority of the nation; thus, in principle nothing is allowed to intervene between the state and the individual citizen. This principle of the nation-state has had enormous appeal, although in practice many forms of private association have developed (in France and elsewhere) which are tolerated as long as they do not interfere with sovereign functions of the national government, such as taxation, conscription, or adjudication. The French revolution and the populist revolutions which followed must be distinguished from the English revolutions of 1640 and 1688. The mainstream of English revolutionary thought was limited by the religious and legal contexts in which the old justifications of authority had been questioned. English theory and practice remained compatible with the restoration of oligarchic rule, though on the new basis of the "king-in-parliament." By contrast, French revolutionary thought went beyond such limitations because it made the people or the nation the basis of all authority.

The English and French antecedents have provided demonstration effects to which educated elites in other countries have responded. Attempts to develop new stable political institutions in the name of the people have ever since involved a *reconsecration* of authority, however ostensibly secular or antireligious the new conceptions have been. The English revolution appealed to the ancient constitution and the country, while the French revolution based itself on the ancient precedents of republican virtue and the ultimately unchallengeable authority of the nation. In these cases, authority was taken from the king and returned to the people from whom kings were said to have derived their authority in the distant past.

As a reaction to these precedents, German rulers of the eighteenth and nineteenth centuries, in an effort to maintain their inherited authority, proposed to do for "their" people—by a revolution from above —what the French people had done at high cost by and for themselves. The king as the "first servant of his people" and the officials' ideals of law, duty, and *Bildung* were the newly consecrated foundation of German governmental authority.

The modern use of the term *revolution* was unknown prior to the end of the eighteenth century, when Condorcet summed up what by then nearly everyone took for granted: "The word 'revolutionary' can be applied only to revolutions whose aim is freedom." The French revolution has since served as an implicit standard by which all other upheavals are assessed. Even today, revolution means progressive forces from below overthrowing an oppressive regime. However, successful revolutions have had outcomes which did not result in greater freedom. Stalin's regime caused a major upheaval in Russian society but was also a human disaster, and some spokesmen of the progressive tradition have therefore denied that Stalin's regime was revolutionary. But revolution simply means that a form of government or social system is overthrown and another takes its place; the term should be applied where such overthrows occur. Most revolutions have had equivocal results: They have enhanced some freedoms and diminished others. In addition, major changes have occurred in the absence of political revolution, and they also have enhanced some freedoms and diminished others. Revolutions are often initiated by dissension among the dominant groups in society rather than by the protest of subordinate groups. Past revolutions do not represent a prototype of future revolutions, because those who come later will try to use the earlier revolutionary experience to their own advantage and in their own way.[21]

Thus, in Germany, restorative tendencies *and* significant transformations prevailed in the nineteenth century. Monarchy preserved its prerogatives not only in Prussia but throughout the German Confederation after 1815 and even in the united Germany after 1871. Moreover, many aristocratic privileges were preserved, which served to buttress autocratic rule. Nevertheless, major changes occurred. The development of the German legal system represented a major advance in the protection of individual rights, which was also a main achievement of the French revolution. A customs union achieved under Prussia's leadership unified a major part of the German Confederation, and Germany as a whole became politically unified under the leadership of Bismarck. Since political fragmentation had prevailed in this Central European area for a thousand years, these transformations of Germany (however transitory) can hardly be dismissed as minor.

It is true of Germany, as it was of England and France, that the changes which occurred had equivocal results. What appeared "pro-gressive" from the standpoint of German national liberation and uni-fication (note that these terms have a more revolutionary connotation in the twentieth century than they did in the nineteenth) also created enormous liabilities for the future. But it will not do to contrast these liabilities of the German transformation with the positive results of the English and French revolutions. The consequences of German autoc-racy and the weakness of German liberalism should be compared rather with the costs of economic individualism in the industrial development of England or France as well as the costs of "free trade" imperialism in the colonial empires of both countries. As a general rule, comparison requires a consideration of assets and liabilities, rather than contrasts between the liabilities of one country and the assets of another.

Japan is a unique case, since for a millennium its governmental and ceremonial authority had been divided. When the governmental au-thority of the Tokugawa shogunate faltered, recourse to the divinely descended imperial house was readily at hand, for its sacred, legitimat-ing function had never been abandoned. But the Meiji emperor was now so exalted that it became difficult to relate his imperial authority to the people without desecration. Where German rulers sought to maintain themselves by now serving the people, the Meiji oligarchs had to find ways of politically combining a godlike emperor with an organized expression of the nation's interests.

The Meiji Restoration has rarely been called revolutionary, but this may not be justified. The term *restoration* suggested that the supreme authority of the emperor had been usurped by the shogunate a thou-sand years earlier, but that now in 1868 the emperor was restored to his rightful position. This interpretation was part of the time-honored Jap-anese tradition which the Meiji oligarchs were eager to preserve intact. Western observers, with the model of the French revolution in mind, readily agreed that the Meiji Restoration was a strongly conservative movement, for it was initiated by members of the Japanese aristocracy. Nevertheless, the changes brought about by the restoration represented a complete transformation of the old social structure. Samurai stipends were reduced drastically and eventually eliminated, daimyo domains were changed into administrative provinces, and commercial and in-dustrial enterprises were officially encouraged and then left to fend for themselves. Merchants had been the most despised class in Tokugawa Japan; under Meiji, the samurai were encouraged to become successful entrepreneurs. These and related changes were achieved under con-servative auspices. The very speed with which a highly disciplined ruling group forced the pace of industrialization left grave liabilities for the future development of the country. But it does not follow that major changes of a society are nonrevolutionary because they are accomplished under conservative and militarist auspices or because they have led to militarism and dictatorship.

Since restorations can initiate important changes and revolutions need not have "progressive" results, how are we to think of the Russian case? One should distinguish between the reforms of the tsarist regime (from the emancipation of the serfs in 1861 to the industrialization drive after 1890), the revolution of 1905, the revolution of February 1917, the Bolshevik coup of October 1917, and finally the "revolution from above" from 1928 onward.[22] Stalin's revolution of forced collectivization under central party directives and his opting for "socialism in one country" represent a daring and vastly costly innovation in the succession of Russian transformations and modern revolutions. We have no reason to think this final development inevitable. If Russia had remained at peace in 1904 and 1914, reforms under tsarist auspices might have had more effect. Lenin might have lived longer and sided with the moderate wing of the party. But these and other possibilities must be set against Russia's fateful legacy of autocratic rule. For centuries, all civil impulses had been subordinated to the service of the state, and since 1928—for nearly half a century—the fiction of a popular mandate has been manipulated to justify a wholly dictated revolution. Now, as previously, the Russian state is directed by a government supported through "tribute collection." The country has been industrialized by means of "primitive socialist accumulation," in which the peasants' surplus above subsistence has been expropriated by force. This is the same peasantry in whose name in part the revolution was made. Tsarist authority was overthrown in the name of "soldiers, workers, and peasants" and ultimately in the name of the "world proletariat." Appeals to the Great Russian people, to Russian nationalism, and to the pioneering role of Russian civilization have supplemented the reconsecration of Soviet authority.

CONCLUDING REFLECTIONS

Authority exercised in the name of the people is a type of rule with at least as many structures of government as kingship and aristocracy. Despite these diversities, the direct relationship between the government and the citizens and the appeal to a popular mandate is characterized by the generic, ever-recurring paradox between elitism and populism. For the thesis that "sovereignty is the property of the people" (Ba'th party constitution) does not preclude government by the few and raises the question of how "the people" are to be defined.

The initial answer of the French revolution was the simplest. The Abbé Sieyès distinguished between 25 million Frenchmen and the 200,000 nobles and clergymen who hardly counted by comparison. More recently, Mao Tse-tung has employed a similar argument. Yet this contrast between the vast majority of the people and the few who hold power poses problems. As soon as an old regime is overthrown, the personnel of the new regime must be selected and difficult questions of citizenship must be answered. "The people" must be classified into minors and adults, into those liable to, or exempt from, taxation and conscription, and—before the days of universal franchise—into those entitled, and those denied, the right to vote and stand for public office.

Such definitions of "the people" have a world-historical dimension.[23] The English and French revolutions liberated their societies from an inhibiting political framework. They redefined the rules under which the people were entitled to participate in public affairs, though the French revolution went much further in this respect than the English. The Russian revolution also destroyed an inhibiting political framework, but one that had allowed major economic developments since the 1890s only to be weakened by defeat in two major wars. After a decade of restoration and policy disputes, the Russian revolution proceeded to its second phase in which the state, under a single-party system, collectivized agriculture and forced the pace of industrialization. In this second phase, the people were defined in terms of the loyalty which they could demonstrate by maximum performance under a regimen of universal civilian conscription. Subsequently, the Chinese attempted to do by mass campaigns of re-education what the Russians had done by coercion. Bending the Confucian tradition in a revolutionary direction, the Chinese Communists have primarily applied moral persuasion and group pressure to all the people, not just to an educated elite as Confucianism had done. This universal application of a greatly altered Confucian tradition also constitutes a definition of "the people." We do not know the results of this approach or how it will be modified in the future. But a universal morality for "the people" is not likely to be considered a viable policy outside China; ultimately, it may not be successful there.

Most states that have won political independence since World War II do not possess either China's territorial integrity or its political tradition of a rather effective linkage between villages and the urban centers of markets and government administration. Even in China, that linkage broke down when dynasties declined. Other old states like those discussed here have grappled for centuries with internal divisions and the problems of political integration. For example, "England" does not include Scotland and Wales and is a misleading name for the United Kingdom of Great Britain and Northern Ireland. Scottish nationalism, Welsh language and culture, and the continuing struggles in Northern Ireland certainly reinforce that point.[24] In other instances, old political divisions do not play a major role in contrast to the new divisions which do. In the Federal Republic of Germany, *Länder* like Bavaria, Baden-Württemberg, or Westphalia were separate political units at one time, but today's divisions among them do not compare in importance with the division between East and West Germany. Oddly enough, this last division is partly responsible for more internal unity within the Federal Republic, because the proportion of Catholics and Protestants in the West is more evenly balanced than was the case in a united Germany. Ethnic, linguistic, and religious divisions pose ever-changing problems of political accommodation, and societies are unified only in the sense that they have learned to handle such diversities. Terms like *state* or *nation* play down or ignore these persistent divisions, but political unity is never complete and serious challenges to it recur to this day even in the old states.

In the new states, the predominance of civil ties over the affinities of language, religion, and ethnicity is a much more recent and precarious development.[25] These new states are typically areas of great poverty. The bulk of their population is agricultural, while a small sector of the economy in a few urban centers consists of enterprises and a government derived from twentieth-century models and still dependent on foreign capital and personnel. My purpose here is to consider three implications of that center-periphery contrast for a government in the name of the people: the conflict between communal and civic loyalties; the absence of a political community; and the universal occurrence of nationalism.

Where poverty prevails and governments are weak, people find what security they can in the protection which kinship affords them, for language, religion, and group identity are transmitted through the family and thus given at birth. Where opportunities are scarce, claims based on such affinities are often effective. All modern states have developed in competition with these communal affinities, for the state directs our attention to the nonfamilial and, in that sense, impersonal exercise of authority. For a people to constitute a political community, the government must impose obligations on the individual, and these civic obligations typically conflict with familial obligations. Through its legal innovations, the French revolution emancipated the individual from such obligations. Henceforth, all persons who had come of age were empowered by law to act in their own behalf, a principle greatly reinforced by the individualism of the marketplace. Through their political innovations, communist and fascist regimes carry this "emancipation" further by obliging the individual to put the claims of the ruling party above the claims of his family. The use of family members as spies on one another or as hostages whose lives depend on the political conformity of their kindred is one typical technique of such regimes. Many new states which are organized as one-party regimes may attempt comparable methods, but in their case the antifamilial drive in the name of the people comes into intense conflict with the communal affinities transmitted at birth.

The direct juxtaposition between the central government and the individual and hence an antifamilial *tendency* is a general attribute of the nation-state, though this common tendency does not diminish the differences among legal, communist, and fascist domination, or the one-party regimes of the new states.

In the twentieth century, the people's ultimate sovereignty in the new states suffers from weak political institutions. In the countries we have studied, the institutions of the state were formed not only over centuries, but specifically through organization for war. Hence, these older states became political communities in the sense that over the generations many of their citizens have faced death in the interest of king and country. The common struggle of life and death creates shared memories and symbols of group identity which greatly facilitate the functioning of political institutions even in ordinary times. Other groups than the state have demanded the individual's sacrifice of his life as the ultimate test of shared obligation. The political community combines this demand with its enduring power over a considerable territory and hence with greater resources and force than privately organized groups have at their disposal.[26] This emotional foundation of a political community is missing in the new states, whose people typically share collective memories only of colonial domination and now of the struggle against it. Sabotage, armed struggle, nonviolent resistance, and all the other devices of independence movements did not help to build state institutions as did the system of vassalage and later the collection of taxes or the control of civilian populations for the organization of military supplies and the deployment of military forces. This weakness of an effective civilian government in the new state is one reason for the frequency of military, one-party regimes, since armies are functioning hierarchies by definition. Such a substitute military government is often unstable, but it is readily available and *seems* to provide a solution for societies which must simultaneously construct a state and develop a modern economy. Yet the armies of the new states cannot build political communities, as some armies of the older states could, as long as the superpowers and their nuclear deterrents prevent the new states from fighting large-scale wars, even if they had the means to do so.

Fifty-one countries founded the United Nations in 1945; from 1946 to 1976 ninety-one additional countries have become sovereign. Most new states have had to establish their governments on a new basis and define "the people" as the ultimate source of authority. In the new states, there are nationalist appeals to legitimacy everywhere—even in the absence of war. But nationalism, while a nearly universal phenomenon in modern history, is not in fact a force that easily unifies countries. England, France, Germany, Japan, Russia, and China underwent long periods of intellectual mobilization and polarization when they had to come to terms with challenges from abroad. In the examples of Englishmen responding to the Spanish and Catholic danger, or more recently of the Chinese to "Mr. Science" and "Mr. Democracy" of the West, certain basic themes recur over and over again. Perception of advances abroad are reminders of backwardness or dangers and weaknesses at home. Men of letters must try to cope with the dilemmas of this recurrent situation: whether to adopt the advanced model and invite its attendant corruptions, or fall back on native traditions and risk their inappropriateness to the world of power and progress. These dilemmas engender heated debates and ever-uneasy compromises which have their common denominator in a shared concern for the native country. Such intensive debates prompted by common concerns are the foundation of nationalism. The result need not be divisive. A traditionalist like Gandhi and a modernist like Nehru could work together in their opposition to British rule. But the debates between "nativists" and "modernizers" remain unresolved more often than not, both during the struggle against an old regime and after it has been overthrown and a new regime established.

Before as well as after the revolution the root causes of nationalism remain. Men want their country recognized and respected in the world, and to this end they cultivate or revive native traditions. The reconstruction of history is an act of resacralizing authority in the name of the people. It is an appeal to civic loyalty and national brotherhood in lieu of more divisive communal attachments, because birth in a common homeland makes all people members of one nation sharing equally in its past glories. But the desire to be recognized and respected in the world also calls for the development of a modern economy and government which focuses attention on the advanced society (or societies) of one's choice. This reference to foreign models has become inescapable since the great intellectual mobilization of the sixteenth century. Several countries have been in the world-historical position of providing demonstration effects. In the twentieth century, old models have been replaced once more. After Spain and Portugal, after England and France, it is now the turn of the United States, the USSR, and China. Any heir of the Western tradition will watch the new states with humility and respect for the personal courage of people who must try to blend restored traditions with the demands of modern development under the conditions of the twentieth century.

NOTES

CHAPTER I. INTRODUCTION

[1]The terms *state* and *nation* and their cognates *state-building* and *nation-building* are troublesome, but unavoidable. *State* refers to the sphere of highest governmental authority and administration, but that is its modern meaning. In the kingdoms discussed in Part 1 the ruler possessed the highest authority but controlled only his own domains; as yet no central executive existed. The emergence of the modern state is synonymous with the gradual concentration of administrative functions in the hands of the central government. *Nation* refers to at least two phenomena: (1) an historically developed community with a distinctive culture and language in common; (2) the juxtaposition of the central government and a citizenry which consists of individuals who are equal under the law, a principle of government introduced by the French revolution. Since there are national movements which transcend the boundaries of several states, nation-states with dissident national minorities, states which lack the capacity to appeal to a national community, states in which the French principle of nationhood is practiced but in the absence of an historically developed community, and so on, even a careful use of the terms cannot achieve consistency. As an approximation, I shall refer to *states* and *state-building* in the period before 1500 while confining the terms *nation* and *nation-building* (and sometimes *nation-state*) to the period since then.

[2]See Gerhard Lenski, *Power and Privilege* (New York: McGraw-Hill, 1966), pp. 190–192, 194–210, and passim for a more detailed discussion of these points.

[3]This is true even of the early modern period. See ibid., and p. 228. However, there were differences between countries and especially between figures for the whole country and for the towns. For England in 1688, Gregory King's estimates suggest that 5 percent of the population controlled 28 percent of the income. Carlo Cipolla reports that studies of one French (1545) and two Italian towns (1427–1429) show 10 percent of the population controlling more than 50 percent of the wealth. Carlo Cipolla, *Before the Industrial Revolution, European Society and Economy, 1000–1700* (London: Methuen, 1976), pp. 9–14.

[4]Marx's statement concerning peasants in nineteenth-century France applies here: "The small peasants form a vast mass, the members of which live in similar conditions, but without entering into manifold relations with one another. In so far as there is merely a local interconnection among these small peasants, and the identity of their interests begets no unity, no national union, and no political organization, they do not form a class." See Karl Marx, *The Eighteenth Brumaire of Louis Bonaparte* (New York: International Publishers, n.d.), p. 109. For a good statement of the Western interpretation of the social rank-hierarchy as part of a consecrated, cosmic order, see Theodor Spencer, *Shakespeare and the Nature of Man* (New York: Macmillan, 1945), chap. 1.

[5]Jean Jacques Rousseau, *The Social Contract* (New York: Hafner Publishing, 1957), pp. 8–9.

[6]The terms *tradition* and *modernity* are also troublesome and difficult to avoid. There are important distinctions between medieval and modern history, and the terms *tradition*

and *modernity* evoke these distinctions. There are also many unwarranted extrapolations from these terms. I have dispensed with the use of quotation marks to suggest my reservations. For a critique of this terminology, see Reinhard Bendix, "Tradition and Modernity Reconsidered," *Embattled Reason* (New York: Oxford University Press, 1970), pp. 250–314.

[7]Adam Ferguson, *An Essay on the History of Civil Society* (5th ed.; London: T. Codell, 1782), pp. 208–9, 305, and passim.

[8]For a review of the literature on modernization and a special emphasis on its self-critical features, see Hans-Ulrich Wehler, *Modernisierungstheorie und Geschichte* (Göttingen: Vandenhoeck & Ruprecht, 1975), passim.

[9]For an analysis of modernization that does not result in modernity, see my essay "Tradition and Modernity Reconsidered," cited in footnote 6. See also Wehler, *Modernisierungstheorie*, for an analysis of the ideological assumptions underlying the idea of a "completed modernity," as for example in American society.

[10]The special problems of European settlements overseas are examined in Louis Hartz, *The Founding of New Societies* (New York: Harcourt, Brace & World, 1964).

[11]Otto Hintze, "Calvinism and Raison d'Etat in Early Seventeenth Century Brandenburg," in Felix Gilbert, ed., *The Historical Essays of Otto Hintze* (New York: Oxford University Press, 1975), p. 94.

[12]Perez Zagorin, *The Court and the Country: The Beginning of the English Revolution* (New York: Athenaeum, 1971), p. 198.

CHAPTER II. SACRED AND SECULAR FOUNDATIONS OF KINGSHIP

[1]The terms *ruler* and *sovereign* are more comprehensive than emperor, tsar, king, or prince, but I shall use kingship and king in the generic sense of sovereign ruler unless otherwise noted. The emphasis of this chapter is on kingship. Chapters 3 through 6 deal with kingship and aristocracy.

[2]See Clifford Geertz, "Politics Past, Politics Present," *European Journal of Sociology*, vol. 8 (1967), pp. 1–14, as well as his forthcoming book on Bali.

[3]For a broad discussion of the destruction of kingship by oligarchic rule and of the eventual displacement of the latter first by plebeian forces and subsequently by imperial rule and by military forces in the provinces of the Roman empire, see W. G. de Burgh, *The Legacy of the Ancient World* (Baltimore: Penguin, 1961), chaps. 7–8.

[4]Max Weber, *Economy and Society* (tr. and ed. by Guenther Roth and Claus Wittich; New York: Bedminster Press, 1968), III, p. 1142.

[5]For this interpretive extension of Weber's general remarks, I am indebted to an unpublished paper by David N. Keightley, "Shang Metaphysics" (presented at the Association for Asian Studies, Chicago, March 1973), which is based on bone inscriptions concerned with divination, dating back to China in the fourteenth and thirteenth centuries B.C. Of course, Professor Keightley is not responsible for my general reading of his specific evidence.

[6]See J. M. Wallace-Hadrill, *The Barbarian West, A.D. 400–1000* (New York: Harper & Row, Harper Torchbooks, 1962), pp. 9–10. Two classic expositions of this material are Max Weber, "The Social Causes of the Decay of Ancient Civilization," *Journal of General Education,* vol. 5 (October 1950), pp. 75–88, and Jacob Burckhardt, *The Age of Constantine the Great* (Garden City: Doubleday, Anchor Books, 1956), chap. 1. The latter contains a vivid account of imperial succession at the bidding of the Roman armies.

[7]I infer this divergence between the Roman and the Germanic perspectives from the evidence presented in J. M. Wallace-Hadrill, *Early Germanic Kingship in England and on the Continent* (London: Oxford University Press, 1970), chap. 1. This divergence is not stated by the author as distinctly as I put it in the text. Some Germanic tribes emphasized hereditary kingship, while others combined the idea of charismatic lineages with that of counsel and election. My point is that the second principle proved inadvertently useful in the era of migrations. See Chapter 6 here for further discussion.

[8]Jan de Vries, *Altgermanische Religionsgeschichte* (Berlin: Walter de Gruyter, 1956), II, pp. 76–80, 348–52, and passim.

[9]William Chaney, *The Cult of Kingship in Anglo-Saxon England* (Manchester: Manchester University Press, 1970), pp. 14–21.

[10]See Fritz Kern, *Kingship and Law in the Middle Ages* (New York: Harper & Row, Harper Torchbooks, 1970), pp. 12–27, for a discussion of "kin-right." The importance of royal magic even after the decline of royal power is discussed in J. M. Wallace-Hadrill, *The Long-Haired Kings* (London: Methuen, 1962), pp. 245–8, and Kern, *Kingship,* pp. 35–6.

[11]These Frankish conquerors of Gaul and of areas east of the Rhine were converted to orthodox Catholicism. The Frankish conversion began with Clovis in 496 A.D. and facilitated the merger of pagan and Christian ideas of kingship, discussed further on.

[12]Wallace-Hadrill, *Early Germanic Kingship,* p. 135.

[13]Modern scholarship concerning these problems is summarized in A. H. M. Jones, "The Social Background of the Struggle between Paganism and Christianity," and E. A. Thompson, "Christianity and the Northern Barbarians," in Arnaldo Momigliano, ed., *The Conflict between Paganism and Christianity in the Fourth Century* (Oxford: Clarendon Press, 1963), pp. 17–37, 56–78.

[14]See H. M. Gwatkin and J. P. Whitney, eds., *The Cambridge Medieval History* (New York: Macmillan, 1911), I, pp. 590–2.

[15]Walter Ullmann, *A History of Political Thought: The Middle Ages* (Baltimore: Penguin, 1965), pp. 36–7.

[16]A. Momigliano, "Introduction: Christianity and the Decline of the Roman Empire," in Momigliano, ed., *Conflict,* pp. 10–11.

[17]See Ullmann, *Political Thought,* pp. 38–51 and passim.

[18]See Wallace-Hadrill, *Barbarian West,* pp. 75, 81, and passim.

[19]For a survey of this Christian conception of kingship in Western Europe, see Eugen Ewig, "Zum christlichen Königsgedanken im Frühmittelalter," in Theodor Mayer, ed., *Das*

Königtum (Vorträge und Forschungen, Institut für geschichtliche Landesforschung des Bodenseegebiets; Lindau: Jan Thorbecke Verlag, 1954), III, pp. 7–73. See also the evidence on the Christian conversion of Anglo-Saxon England in Chaney, *Cult of Kingship*, chap. 5, which shows clearly that the population followed the precedents set by their kings, even where this involved repeated changes between paganism and Christianity.

[20]Kern, *Kingship*, pp. 51–4.

[21]The phrase *popular will* refers to the element of consent reflected in the act of acclamation by the magnates. My interpretation is based on ibid., pp. 28–33. The author refers to a decree of 751 by Pope Zacharias declaring suitability as more important than legitimate descent, to the Council of Paris (829) emphasizing the insignificance of the rights of blood and the importance of *ministerium*, and to somewhat later documents affirming the claims of individual candidates against those of the lineage.

[22]Quoted in Ullmann, *Political Thought*, p. 88.

[23]I have paraphrased the interpretation of the *Ecclesiastical History* by the Venerable Bede, as analyzed in Wallace-Hadrill, *Early Germanic Kingship*, chap. 4.

[24]The greater complexity of this sequence is emphasized by Percy Schramm, *A History of the English Coronation* (Oxford: Clarendon Press, 1937).

[25]The belief in the healing powers of the king is an example of that sacralization. See the study by Marc Bloch, *The Royal Touch, Sacred Monarchy and Scrofula in England and France* (London: Routledge & Kegan Paul, 1973).

[26]W. Montgomery Watt, *Islamic Political Thought* (Edinburgh: Edinburgh University Press, 1968), p. 6.

[27]See ibid., pp. 9–14.

[28]Ibid., pp. 38, 40–41. See also the parallel interpretation in Hans Heinrich Schaeder, *Der Mensch im Orient und Okzident* (Munich: R. Piper, 1960), pp. 312–15. The pre-Islamic experience here described has parallels in the conditions under which authority was exercised in the Germanic tribes in the pagan era. See Karl von Amira, *Germanisches Recht* (vol. 2 of *Grundriss des Germanischen Rechts*; Berlin: Walter de Gruyter, 1967), pp. 44–50, 66–71, 80–1. See further on for comments on this parallel.

[29]Irfan Shahid, "Pre-Islamic Arabia," in P. M. Holt, Ann K. S. Lambton, and Bernard Lewis, eds., *The Cambridge History of Islam* (London: Cambridge University Press, 1970), I, pp. 16–17. See also Schaeder, *Mensch*, pp. 315–22, for material on Mecca.

[30]Max Weber, *Ancient Judaism* (Glencoe: Free Press, 1952), pp. 206–7.

[31]*Cambridge History of Islam*, I, pp. 31–6.

[32]The reference is to "believers and Muslim of Quraysh and Yathrib," the last term referring to the valley in which Medina is located. This statement from the preamble along with the whole text is reprinted in W. Montgomery Watt, *Muhammad in Medina* (London: Oxford University Press, 1956), p. 221.

[33]I use the formulation by G. E. von Grunebaum, "Government in Islam," *Islam, Essays in the Nature and Growth of a Cultural Tradition* (London: Routledge & Kegan Paul, 1961), pp. 127–8.

34See Max Weber, *Economy and Society*, II, pp. 439-40.

35The following account is indebted to H. A. R. Gibb, "Constitutional Organization," in Majid Khadduri and Herbert J. Liebesney, eds., *Law in the Middle East* (Washington: Middle East Institute, 1955), pp. 3-27.

36Quoted from Ibn Khaldun in ibid., pp. 13-14.

37In addition to Gibb's essay on constitutional organization, see Watt, *Islamic Political Thought*, chaps. 6, 7, 9, and Sir Hamilton Gibb, *Studies in the Civilization of Islam* (Boston: Beacon Press, 1962), especially pp. 141-65, where this accommodation of political theory to the facts of absolutism is analyzed in the work of Al-Mawardi. For religious scholars, the main task was the effort to integrate the diverse ethno-cultural groups into a community of faith, an effort that had to be protected from the dangers of involvement in political issues. I owe this point to my colleague, Professor Elbaki Hermassi, who refers to the analysis of H. A. R. Gibb, "Religion and Politics in Christianity and Islam," in J. Harris Proctor, ed., *Islam and International Relations* (New York: Praeger, 1965), pp. 3-23.

38This saying, attributed to the first century after Muhammad's death, is quoted in H. A. R. Gibb and Harold Bowen, *Islamic Society and the West* (London: Oxford University Press, 1950), I, p. 28.

39Quoted in Gibb, "Constitutional Organization," p. 5.

40See ibid., pp. 7-11, for an exposition of the Sunni theory of the caliphate according to Al-Baghdadi (d. 1037).

41Robert Heine-Geldern, "Conceptions of State and Kingship in Southeast Asia," mimeo (Data Paper no. 18, Southeast Asia Program, Dept. of Asian Studies; Ithaca: Cornell University Press, 1958), p. 1.

42Paul Wheatley, *The Pivot of the Four Quarters* (Chicago: Aldine, 1971), p. 436.

43A good descriptive account of these beliefs in their ancient setting is contained in C. P. Fitzgerald, *China, A Short Cultural History* (London: Cresset Press, 1965), pp. 34-54. A detailed, functional analysis of ancestor worship, based in good part on contemporary materials, is contained in C. K. Yang, *Religion in Chinese Society* (Berkeley and Los Angeles: University of California Press, 1967), pp. 28-57.

44The statement is quoted from an unpublished paper by David N. Keightley, "Legitimation in Shang China" (submitted to Conference on Legitimation of Chinese Imperial Regimes, Asilomar, June 1975), p. 4. My discussion of early Chinese religion and kingship is indebted to Professor Keightley's paper and to personal discussions with him.

45Ibid., p. 5.

46Ibid., p. 23.

47These statements by the Duke of Chou date back to the early period of the Western Chou dynasty. They are quoted in H. G. Creel, *The Origins of Statecraft in China* (Chicago: University of Chicago Press, 1970), I, pp. 83-4. Various dates have been given for the beginning of the Chou dynasty. I have retained the traditional chronology. The details of the "Mandate of Heaven" theory are more complex than my brief statement can suggest. Cf. Creel's discussion of the issues in ibid., chap. 5 and app. C with D. Howard Smith,

"Divine Kingship in Ancient China," *Numen*, vol. 4 (September 1957), pp. 171–203, and H. H. Dubs, "The Archaic Royal Jou Religion," *T'oung Pao*, vol. 46 (1958), pp. 217–59, which seem to date the theory rather earlier than Creel. For these and other references and for a critical reading of an original draft of this section, I am greatly indebted to Professor David Keightley.

[48]See Ping-ti Ho, "Salient Aspects of China's Heritage," in Ping-ti Ho and Tang Tsou, eds., *China in Crisis* (Chicago: University of Chicago Press, 1968), I, pp. 1–37, and the ensuing discussion by Arthur Wright, Herbert Franke, Derk Bodde, and Herrlee Creel, with an addendum by Ping-ti Ho on pp. 38–92.

[49]See Creel, *Origins of Statecraft*, chaps. 12–13, and Wolfram Eberhard, *Geschichte Chinas* (Stuttgart: Alfred Kroener Verlag, 1971), p. 30.

[50]See the description of Confucius' native state of Lu in the seventh to fifth centuries in H. G. Creel, *Confucius and the Chinese Way* (New York: Harper & Brothers, Harper Torchbooks, 1960), pp. 17–20.

[51]For details, see ibid., pp. 25-56.

[52]See ibid., p. 196.

[53]My paraphrasing of the Confucian teaching is based on Creel, *Confucius*, pp. 109–72, unless noted otherwise. Though I am indebted to Professor Creel's work, I find his analogies between Confucius and Kant's philosophy or modern democratic theories quite unconvincing—the distinction between ethical teaching, charismatic prophecy, and other types of ethical and religious leadership is worked out in Weber, *Economy and Society*, II, pp. 439–51.

[54]Quoted in Creel, *Confucius*, pp. 130, 158.

[55]Quoted in ibid., p. 84, 86, 121–2. For a fuller discussion of *li*, see Creel, *Origins of Statecraft*, pp. 335 ff., and Henry Rosemont, Jr., "State and Society in the Tzün hsu. A Philosophical Commentary," *Monumenta Serica*, vol. 29 (1970–1971), pp. 50–1 and passim.

[56]Quoted in Creel, *Confucius*, p. 130. In his discussion Creel emphasizes the egalitarianism of Confucius, but does not allow for the kind of "egalitarianism" characteristic of aristocrats. When Confucius says that one should "feel kindly toward everyone, but be intimate only with the virtuous" (ibid., p. 131), he expresses a sentiment entirely compatible with the most glaring inequalities. Indeed, since wealth and poverty depend on Heaven, each man can practice the Way in accord with his proper station in life. And by saying that the people will be attracted by good government, Confucius was commending a benevolent paternalism rather than speaking as an advocate of the people.

[57]My sketch is indebted to unpublished papers by Jack L. Dull, "The Legitimation of the Ch'in" (Conference on Legitimation of Chinese Imperial Regimes, American Council of Learned Societies, Asilomar, June 1975), and by Sebastian de Grazia, "The *Dura Lex* of Legalism and the First Empire" (forthcoming).

[58]Details on the ascendance of Confucianism are contained in John K. Shryock, *The Origin and Development of the State Cult of Confucius* (New York: Century, 1932), chap. 3, and Peter Weber-Schaefer, *Oikumene und Imperium, Zur Ziviltheologie des chinesischen Kaiserreichs* (Munich: Paul List Verlag, 1968), pp. 228–9 ff.

[59]These complexities must be mentioned in order to guard against mistaking Confucianism for a single doctrine. However far they diverged from the original message, most writers came to present their ideas in the name of the sage, thus providing that name with the charismatic aura he repudiated. Only the Taoist literature contains attacks on Confucius.

[60]Chan Wing-tsit, *Source Book in Chinese Philosophy* (Princeton: Princeton University Press, 1963), p. 22.

[61]Quoted from the *Han Fei Tzu* in Arthur Waley, *Three Ways of Thought in Ancient China* (Garden City: Doubleday, Anchor Books, 1956), pp. 159–60. I have followed Waley's account of the relation between the *Han Fei Tzu* and the Legalist or Realist school. See ibid., pp. 156–7 and passim.

[62]See Creel, *Confucius*, pp. 236–48, for details of Confucianism in practice under the Han emperor Wu. Experts differ concerning the political influence of Confucian ideology, and there is little doubt that this ideology was largely addressed to subordinate officials and aspirants to office. Cf. the different views of Ping-ti Ho and H. G. Creel in *China in Crisis*, pp. 59–78, 84–92.

[63]See Rosemont, "State and Society," p. 47. My concluding summary is indebted to the essay by Rosemont.

[64]See Wolfgang Eberhard, "The Political Function of Astronomy and Astronomers in Han China," in John K. Fairbank, ed., *Chinese Thought and Institutions* (Chicago: University of Chicago Press, 1957), pp. 33–70.

CHAPTER III. JAPAN

[1]The Japanese term for clan, *Uji,* is sometimes replaced by the Chinese *Shi*; both refer to extended kinship groups worshiping the same god.

[2]John W. Hall, *Government and Local Power in Japan* (Princeton: Princeton University Press, 1966), pp. 26–7. Yamato refers to an area in the Kinki region of Honshu, a central location on the main island of Japan. Note also the summary volume by John W. Hall, *Japan from Prehistory to Modern Times* (New York: Dell, 1970).

[3]Sir George Sansom, *History of Japan* (London: Cresset Press, 1959), I, pp. 25–6.

[4]Ibid., I, pp. 26, 31.

[5]A fuller discussion of the early religious life of Japan will be found in Joseph Kitagawa, *Religion in Japanese History* (New York: Columbia University Press, 1966), especially chap. 1.

[6]Hall, *Government and Local Power*, pp. 46–52.

[7]I have followed the account in Wolfram Eberhard, *Geschichte Chinas* (Stuttgart: Alfred Kröner Verlag, 1971), pp. 162–4.

[8]See Kitagawa, *Religion in Japanese History*, pp. 33–6 and passim. For a vivid description of religious syncretism and the role of the visual arts in court society during the Heian

period (794–1185), see Ivan Morris, *The World of the Shining Prince* (Harmondsworth: Penguin, 1969), chaps. 4–7.

⁹Sansom, *History*, I, pp. 64, 66, 117; and Hall, *Government and Local Power*, pp. 96, 98.

¹⁰See Hall, *Government and Local Power*, p. 57, and pp. 56–8 for the text of the Taika edict. Related discussions are found in Sansom, *History*, I, pp. 56–9, and Roger Bersihand, *Geschichte Japans* (Stuttgart: Alfred Kröner Verlag, 1963), pp. 71–4 and passim.

¹¹Hall, *Government and Local Power*, pp. 61–4.

¹²Sansom, *History*, I, pp. 104, 151, 163, 169, 256.

¹³Ibid., I, pp. 114–15. It should be added that a branch of the Fujiwara family had played an important role at court as early as the Taika reforms of 646; the dates given here refer to the period of their regency and civil dictatorship.

¹⁴The details of this process are set out in ibid., I, pp. 67–70, 83–9, and Hall, *Government and Local Power*, chap. 4.

¹⁵Hall mentions that the last recorded instance of land redistribution in the home provinces under imperial authority occurred in 844. See his *Government and Local Power*, p. 103.

¹⁶Ibid., pp. 118–19.

¹⁷Cf. ibid., pp. 129–35, for Hall's emphasis on the gradual emergence of a respected warrior class out of the very institutions of the imperial government.

¹⁸Sansom, *History*, I, pp. 234–8. The quotation appears on p. 238.

¹⁹Statement by Ono-no-Yoshifuru quoted in Hall, *Government and Local Power*, p. 130.

²⁰Sansom, *History*, I, p. 311. See ibid., chaps. 8, 10, 12–15, for a detailed narration and a judicious appraisal of the main events.

²¹The terms *nobility*, *aristocracy*, and *gentry* are used here in their generic meanings, which are obscured by the inevitable historical complications. Members of a nobility are illustrious by rank, title, or birth; the term has primary reference to status. Aristocracy means literally "government by the best citizens" and, more broadly, the noble class from which the rulers of state and society are derived; the term has primary reference to rule. Complications arise because the conditions affecting the composition of nobility and aristocracy (that is, the conditions of prestige and rule) change over time. Gentry refers to those who rank below the nobility in title and birth; again the term has primary reference to status. My use of these terms with reference to Japan takes account of the overall tendency to leave the status-superiority of those associated with the emperor intact while the actual government came into the hands of a class of military leaders whose formal status did not match their very real power. The overall use of the term *aristocracy* seems justified in view of the fact that all these people were involved with rule in one degree or another. In a broad comparative study, terminological precision may not be attainable, but a cautionary note here will alert the reader to some of the difficulties along the way. For a rather different use of these terms in the European context, see R. R. Palmer, *The Age of the Democratic Revolution* (Princeton: Princeton University Press, 1959), I, pp. 29–30.

[22]The population of Heian Japan is estimated at 5 million, of which perhaps 50,000 lived in the capital and less than 5,000 belonged to the court nobility. See Ivan Morris, *World of Shining Prince*, p. 93.

[23]Hall, *Government and Local Power*, pp. 131, 136, 139.

[24]See Sansom, *History*, I, p. 243, n. 3, for a compilation of the holdings of the two clans in the several areas of Japan.

[25]Ibid., I, p. 346. Note the striking difference with English feudalism in which a direct oath of allegiance by the vassals of great lords to the king became a regular feature of Norman rule. Cf. this volume, Chapter 6.

[26]Ibid., I, p. 352.

[27]See ibid., I, pp. 345–58, for Sansom's description of feudal government and the class structure under the Kamakura shogunate.

[28]See ibid., I, chaps. 17 and 19.

[29]The following resume is based on ibid., II, especially chaps. 11–12 and 15, and on the work of John Hall cited previously.

[30]See the detailed analysis of this transformation in Hall, *Government and Local Power*, chaps. 7 and 8.

[31]Sansom, *History*, II, p. 243.

[32]Ibid., II, p. 208, and Hall, *Government and Local Power*, p. 275.

[33]Sansom, *History*, II, p. 255.

[34]Hall, *Government and Local Power*, pp. 9, 247. See also pp. 240–1 and 248 for evidence of the increasing number of forts and castles in the three Kibi provinces.

[35]Sansom, *History*, III, pp. 255–7, and Hall, *Government and Local Power*, p. 257 and passim. Note also Sansom's discussion of "House Laws and Civil Administration" in *History*, II, pp. 251–5, which gives impressive evidence of the managerial skill of some sengoku-daimyo.

[36]See Hall, *Government and Local Power*, chap. 11, for a case study of consolidation at the local and regional level. The data on firearms are taken from Delmer M. Brown, "The Impact of Firearms on Japanese Warfare," *Far Eastern Quarterly*, vol. 7 (1947), pp. 236–53.

[37]Sansom, *History*, II, pp. 316–19, 330–3.

CHAPTER IV. RUSSIA

[1]Michael Florinsky, *Russia, A History and an Interpretation* (New York: Macmillan, 1947 and 1953), I, pp. 16–17.

[2] See Nicholas Riasanovsky, *A History of Russia* (New York: Oxford University Press, 1969), pp. 43, 45.

[3] George Vernadsky, *Kievan Russia* (New Haven: Yale University Press, 1973), p. 289.

[4] Ibid., p. 61.

[5] Francis Dvornik, "Byzantine Political Ideas in Kievan Russia," *Dumbarton Oaks Papers*, nos. 9 and 10 (Cambridge: Harvard University Press, 1956), p. 88.

[6] Quoted from the *Izbornik* of 1076 in ibid., p. 93.

[7] Ibid., pp. 94–6.

[8] See Günther Stökl, *Russische Geschichte* (Stuttgart: Alfred Kröner, 1962), pp. 127 ff., and J. L. I. Fennell, *The Emergence of Moscow* (Berkeley and Los Angeles: University of California Press, 1967), p. 32. See also Henri Pirenne, *Medieval Cities* (Garden City: Doubleday, Anchor Books, 1956), pp. 131–51.

[9] Stökl, *Russische Geschichte*, pp. 70–1.

[10] For further details, see Fennell, *Emergence of Moscow*, pp. 16–27. See also the details of the will of Vasily II, Grand Prince of Moscow, in 1462, as described in J. L. I. Fennell, *Ivan the Great of Moscow* (London: Macmillan, 1961), pp. xiii–xiv.

[11] Marc Bloch, "The Rise of Dependent Cultivation and Seignorial Institutions," in J. H. Clapham and Eileen Power, eds., *The Cambridge Economic History of Europe* (Cambridge: Cambridge University Press, 1941), I, p. 254.

[12] Jerome Blum, *Land and Peasant in Russia* (New York: Atheneum, 1964), pp. 90–2, 251–3. Cf. also the contrasting picture of the peasantry in Western Europe and Russia in Otto Brunner, *Neue Wege der Sozialgeschichte* (Göttingen: Vandenhoeck & Ruprecht, 1968), chap. 10. See also Stökl, *Russische Geschichte*, pp. 69–77.

[13] For a description of the intricate relations between secular rulers and the Russian church during the fourteenth century, see the summary in Albert M. Ammann, S.J., *Abriss der ostslawischen Kirchengeschichte* (Vienna: Thomas Morus Presse im Verlag Herder, 1950), pp. 91–106.

[14] Stökl, *Russische Geschichte*, p. 79. Perhaps this was an indication of economic decline, since in thriving towns weights and measures were usually in the safekeeping of their assemblies, or of the merchant guilds where these existed.

[15] Events at Sarai, the capital of the Golden Horde, are less a matter of inference. During the first half of the fourteenth century one Muscovite prince and four princes of Tver' died violent deaths there. Later on, with the succession struggles among Mongol dynasties mounting, the number of *yarlyki* increased rapidly, and consequently their importance for Russia declined. But, by then, the Muscovite rulers were well on their way to preeminence.

[16] See Fennell, *Emergence of Moscow*, pp. 186–90, for an analysis of Ivan Kalita's will.

[17] For a brief description of these complex events see Ammann, *Abriss*, pp. 82–4.

[18]For an analysis of this hagiographic practice, see Michael Cherniavsky, *Tsar and People* (New Haven: Yale University Press, 1961). By the middle of the sixteenth century the church probably owned about one-third of the entire area under cultivation. See Florinsky, *Russia*, I, p. 133.

[19]Quoted in Gerd Tellenbach, *Church, State, and Christian Society* (New York: Harper & Row, Harper Torchbooks, 1970), p. 33.

[20]The titles *tsar* (also spelled *czar*) and *autocrat* came into use in Russia in the reign of Ivan III (1462–1505); at an earlier time Russians had applied these terms to the Byzantine emperor. The destruction of Byzantium and Ivan's marriage to the niece of the last Byzantine emperor were interpreted by some observers to mean that the Russian ruler was heir to the Byzantine tsars. Ivan IV (1533–1584) was officially crowned tsar with the sanction of the Russian church in 1547. See George Vernadsky, *A History of Russia, The Mongols and Russia* (New Haven: Yale University Press, 1953), III, pp. 385–6. See also O. P. Backus, "Muscovite Legal Thought," in Alan Ferguson and Alfred Levin, eds., *Essays in Russian History* (Hamden: Archon Books, 1964), p. 38 and passim.

[21]See Gustave Alef, "The Crisis of the Muscovite Aristocracy," *Forschungen zur Osteuropäischen Geschichte*, vol. 15 (1970), pp. 15–58. The author emphasizes that "partible inheritance" (that is, the division of property among the heirs) made Russian aristocrats rather willing to subordinate themselves to Moscow.

[22]By 1688 Russia included Siberia and comprised 15,280,000 square kilometers. See Richard Hellie, *Enserfment and Military Change in Muscovy* (Chicago: University of Chicago Press, 1971), p. 21, for the source of these figures.

[23]See George Vernadsky, *A History of Russia, The Tsardom of Moscow, 1547–1682* (New Haven: Yale University Press, 1969), V, part 1, pp. 10–14.

[24]Cited in Florinsky, *Russia*, I, p. 79.

[25]The details of the country's relations with the East during the Kievan and Muscovite periods are set out in George V. Lantzeff and Richard A Pierce, *Eastward to Empire, Exploration and Conquest on the Russian Open Frontier to 1750* (Montreal: McGill-Queen's University Press, 1973).

[26]See Vasili Klyuchevsky, *Peter the Great* (New York: St. Martin's Press, 1969), p. 58. Peter reigned from 1682 to 1725, but he was only ten in the year of his accession and the regency of his half-sister Sophia lasted from 1682 to 1689.

[27]Complex motives and strategies were involved in the decisions to side with one or another of the contending powers. See the case study of one area by O. P. Backus, *Motives of West Russian Nobles in Deserting Lithuania for Moscow, 1377–1514* (Lawrence: University of Kansas Press, 1957). See also the analysis by the same author, "Treason and Defections from Moscow to Lithuania," *Forschungen zur Osteuropäischen Geschichte*, vol. 15 (Berlin, 1970), pp. 119–44.

[28]George Vernadsky, *A History of Russia, Russia at the Dawn of the Modern Age* (New Haven: Yale University Press, 1959), IV, pp. 114–16 and passim.

[29]The rest were of miscellaneous Oriental and of unknown ancestry. See Paul Dukes, *Catherine the Great and the Russian Nobility* (London: Cambridge University Press, 1967), pp. 20–1.

[30]Blum, *Land*, pp. 170–1.

[31]Giles Fletcher, *Of the Russe Commonwealth* (Cambridge: Harvard University Press, 1966), pp. 25–6. I have modernized the spelling. According to Richard Pipes's statement in the introduction, modern research suggests the correctness of Fletcher's observation. Fletcher follows the Russian sources in using "Tartar" or "Tatar" as a generic reference to the Mongols though originally Mongols and Tartars were only two of the nomadic tribes participating in the Asiatic invasions of Russia and Europe since the thirteenth century. I have used "Mongol" for the period of Mongol overlordship and "Tartar" thereafter, though a more accurate terminology would be needed in a more detailed account.

[32]See Blum, *Land*, pp. 182–8, on the turnover of pomestie occupants and the declining distinction between pomestie and votchina. For the period from 1580 to 1620, the author cites figures for three districts showing that only 6 out of 30, 10 out of 115, and 5 out of 46 noble families retained possession of their original lands by the latter date. See ibid., pp. 150–1.

[33]There is no good solution to the resulting terminological problem, especially since a broad survey must cover different types of aristocratic status. The term *service aristocracy* is a paradoxical compromise and should be kept in mind, even where synonyms like *aristocracy* or *gentry* are used.

[34]Blum, *Land*, p. 138.

[35]Florinsky, *Russia*, I, pp. 179–80. For descriptive detail, see V. O. Kl[y]uchevsky, *A History of Russia* (New York: Russell & Russell, 1960), II, pp. 44–7 and passim.

[36]See Hellie, *Enserfment*, pp. 22–5.

[37]See Marc Raeff, *Origins of the Russian Intelligentsia: The Eighteenth-Century Nobility* (New York: Harcourt, Brace & World, 1966), pp. 22–3.

[38]Florinsky, *Russia*, I, pp. 102–3.

[39]See Raeff, *Origins*, pp. 45–7, 60–3.

[40]See Florinsky, *Russia*, I, pp. 195–6 and passim. See also the related assessment of the zemskii sobor in Riasanovsky, *History*, pp. 188–9, 208–11, and passim, and in more detail in Vernadsky, *History of Russia*, V, parts 1 and 2 (see index).

[41]Hellie, *Enserfment*, pp. 238–9.

[42]See Stökl, *Russische Geschichte*, pp. 299–307. For further details, see Jack N. Culpepper, "The Legislative Origins of Peasant Bondage in Muscovy," *Forschungen zur Osteuropäischen Geschichte*, vol. 14 (1969), pp. 162–237, and Gustave Alef, "Das Erlöschen des Abzugsrechts der Moskauer Bojaren," in ibid., vol. 10 (1965), pp. 7–74.

[43]See Vernadsky, *History of Russia*, V, part 1, pp. 394–411. See also ibid., V, part 2, pp. 719–23. A further discussion of the changing role of the Russian aristocracy is deferred to Chapter 13 of this volume.

[44]These similarities and contrasts between the Russian and the Japanese aristocracies are explored further in Cyril E. Black et al., *The Modernization of Japan and Russia* (New York: Free Press, 1975).

CHAPTER V. IMPERIAL GERMANY AND PRUSSIA

[1] The following account is based on parts 1 and 2 of Geoffrey Barraclough, *The Origins of Modern Germany* (New York: Capricorn Books, 1963) and by the same author, *The Crucible of Europe* (Berkeley and Los Angeles: University of California Press, 1976). The reader interested in more details would be well advised to turn to these books.

[2] Barraclough, *Origins*, p. 135.

[3] See ibid., pp. 316–19, for this discussion of the Golden Bull.

[4] For details, see the discussion in F. L. Carsten, *The Origins of Prussia* (Oxford: Clarendon Press, 1954), chaps. 3, 4, 7, and 16.

[5] See Otto Hintze, *Die Hohenzollern und ihr Werk* (Berlin: Paul Parey, 1915), pp. 42–3, 66–7. Disputes of this kind were very common. For a comparative discussion of the charters often resulting from them, see Werner Naef, "Frühformen des 'Modernen Staates' im Spätmittelalter," *Historische Zeitschrift*, vol. 171 (1959), pp. 225–43. See also the general discussion of *diffidatio*, or the repudiation of the feudal contract by the vassals if the lord did not fulfill his duties, in Walter Ullmann, *Principles of Government and Politics in the Middle Ages* (New York: Barnes & Noble, 1961), pp. 150 ff., and by the same author, *The Individual and Society in the Middle Ages* (Baltimore: Johns Hopkins University Press, 1966), pp. 64–5.

[6] See Barraclough, *Origins*, pp. 327 ff.

[7] See William R. Shepherd, *Shepherd's Historical Atlas* (New York: Barnes & Noble, 1964), p. 85, which shows the lands lost by Brandenburg between 1320 and 1415.

[8] Barraclough, *Origins*, p. 325.

[9] The Hohenzollern dynasty had originated in the political fragmentation that developed out of the investiture controversy. By the third generation, one branch of the Zollern family had become burgraves of Nuremberg through intermarriage, a position they occupied from the eleventh to the fifteenth century.

[10] Barraclough, *Origins*, p. 329.

[11] Hintze, *Hohenzollern und ihr Werk*, pp. 48–50, and Carsten, *Origins of Prussia*, pp. 95–6.

[12] For details see ibid., chap. 11.

[13] See Otto Hintze, "The Hohenzollern and the Nobility," *Historical Essays* (New York: Oxford University Press, 1975), pp. 35–43.

[14] The contrast between the earlier autonomy and later subjection of the towns is described in Carsten, *Origins of Prussia*, pp. 46–51, 136–48, and passim.

[15] See ibid., pp. 165–78, for an account of the "rule of the estates" in the different territories of the Hohenzollern rulers.

[16] The preceding paragraph paraphrases a characterization by Otto Hintze in his essay "Geist und Epochen der Preussischen Geschichte," *Regierung und Verwaltung* (vol. 3 of *Gesammelte Abhandlungen*; Göttingen: Vandenhoeck & Ruprecht, 1967), pp. 5–8.

[17]Hajo Holborn, *A History of Modern Germany, The Reformation* (New York: Knopf, 1959), p. 189 and passim.

[18]Hintze, *Hohenzollern und ihr Werk,* pp. 186–7, and Hans Rosenberg, *Bureaucracy, Aristocracy, and Autocracy* (Cambridge: Harvard University Press, 1958), p. 33.

[19]Hintze reports (*Hohenzollern,* p. 187) that in the second half of the seventeenth century aristocratic landholdings increased by 30 percent. All these developments should not be attributed to the Thirty Years' War, however, since there is evidence of depopulation and pauperization due to epidemics, emigration, restrictive policies of craft guilds, and religious persecutions prior to the war. See Kurt Hinze, *Die Arbeiterfrage zu Beginn des Modernen Kapitalismus in Brandenburg-Preussen* (2nd ed., vol. 9 of Veröffentlichungen der Historischen Kommission zu Berlin; Berlin: Walter de Gruyter, 1963), pp. 27–37.

[20]See Carsten, *Origins of Prussia,* p. 189 and passim.

[21]Ibid., pp. 266–71.

[22]See Hintze, *Hohenzollern und ihr Werk,* pp. 205–21, for details concerning the struggles between the elector and the estate assemblies in his different territories. See also the related account in Carsten, *Origins of Prussia,* pp. 205–52.

[23]The organization and financing of a standing army was a major factor in this ascendance and the related growth of a unified nation-state. Given the heterogeneity of territories and the particularist tendencies of their several estates until well into the eighteenth century, a step toward the consolidation of centralized rule may be seen in the edict of August 13, 1713, which declared all possessions of the Hohenzollern house indivisible and inalienable. In this way all the territories together with the people residing in them were put on a par with the royal domains as the property of the Hohenzollern dynasty. See Hintze, *Die Hohenzollern und ihr Werk,* p. 281.

[24]On the religious development of the Prussian territories, see Otto Hintze, "Die Epochen des evangelischen Kirchenregiments in Preussen," in *Regierung und Verwaltung,* pp. 56–96.

[25]Hintze, "Geist und Epochen der Preussischen Geschichte," pp. 19–20.

[26]See Peter Baumgart, "Zur Geschichte der kurmärkischen Stände im 17. und 18. Jahrhundert," in Dietrich Gerhard, ed., *Ständische Vertretungen in Europa im 17. und 18. Jahrhundert* (Göttingen: Vandenhoeck & Ruprecht, 1969), pp. 131–61.

[27]Opinion on this point is divided. Carsten, *Origins of Prussia,* pp. 216, 258, 269, emphasizes that only members of the aristocracy were appointed to high positions and specifically rejects the contrary opinion of Otto Hintze. On the other side is the detailed study by Rudolf von Thadden, *Die Brandenburgisch-Preussischen Hofprediger im 17. und 18. Jahrhundert* (Berlin: Walter de Gruyter, 1959), pp. 65–99, which shows that commoners of Reformed faith from outside areas rose to prominence in the service of the Prussian kings. This was a bone of contention between the ruler and the aristocracy with neither side prevailing entirely.

[28]Another comparison for 1740 indicates that when Prussia had 80,000 men under arms, Austria and France with a population ten times greater than Prussia had standing armies in peacetime which numbered 100,000 and 160,000 men, respectively. See Otto

Büsch, *Militärsystem und Sozialleben im Alten Preussen, 1713–1807* (vol. 7 of Veröffentlichungen der Berliner Historischen Kommission; Berlin: Walter de Gruyter, 1962), pp. 1–2; Ernest Barker, *The Development of Public Services in Western Europe* (London: Oxford University Press, 1944), note, p. 43; and J. O. Lindsay, ed., *The New Cambridge Modern History, The Old Regime* (New York: Cambridge University Press, 1957), VII, pp. 179–80, for the sources of these figures.

[29]See Büsch, *Militärsystem,* pp. 80–1, as well as the discussion of these and related measures in Gordon A. Craig, *The Politics of the Prussian Army* (New York: Oxford University Press, Galaxy Books, 1964), pp. 10–11 and passim.

[30]See Büsch, *Militärsystem,* p. 83; Karl Demeter, *Das Deutsche Offizierskorps* (Frankfurt: Bernard & Graefe, 1962), p. 2; Robert Ergang, *The Potsdam Führer* (New York: Columbia University Press, 1941), pp. 78–81; and Jupp Hoven, *Der Preussische Offizier des 18. Jahrhunderts* (Inaugural Dissertation Universität Leipzig; Zeulenrode: Bernhard-Sporn, 1936), p. 58, for the source of these data. For a characterization of eighteenth-century militarism, see Barker, *Development of Public Services,* chap. 2, and Walter Dorn, *Competition for Empire* (New York: Harper & Row, Harper Torchbooks, 1963), chap. 3.

[31]Carsten, *Origins of Prussia,* p. 266.

[32]Büsch, *Militärsystem,* p. 2.

[33]See Hintze, *Die Hohenzollern und ihr Werk,* pp. 295, 297–9, for the source of these data.

[34]Büsch, *Militärsystem,* pp. 95–6.

[35]See Hintze, *Hohenzollern und ihr Werk,* p. 286, for the estimate by Frederick William I of the effect of war on the tax yield of towns. The estimates of the proportion of military to civilian population are from Kurt Hinze, *Arbeiterfrage zu Beginn des Kapitalismus,* p. 171. Hinze's data on some other German towns indicate that the 20 percent military personnel in the civilian population of Berlin was rather low.

[36]See A. Goodwin, "Prussia," in A. Goodwin, ed., *The European Nobility in the Eighteenth Century* (London: Adam and Charles Black, 1953), pp. 93–9, for a review of Frederick's policies and the aristocratic response. The family practices of the Prussian nobility in the Electoral Mark (Kurmark) are documented in Fritz Martiny, *Die Adelsfrage in Preussen vor 1806* (Beiheft 35 of Vierteljahrsschrift für Sozial- und Wirtschaftsgeschichte; Stuttgart: W. Kohlhammer, 1938), pp. 28–30 and passim. One study shows that of 547 *fidei commissa* counted in seven eastern provinces in 1885, 27 percent were founded before 1800, 36.5 percent in the half-century 1800–1850, and the remaining 36.5 percent in the thirty-five years till 1885. See August Meitzen, *Der Boden und die landwirtschaftlichen Verhältnisse des Preussischen Staates* (Berlin: Paul Parey, 1901), VI, pp. 551 (n. 3), 554 (estimated).

[37]Schools for cadets (*Kadettenschulen*) were largely attended by sons of impoverished nobles without landed property. They were financed publicly and the number of places in them equaled about 10 percent of the officer corps in 1800. For data indicating the basis of this inference, see Martiny, *Adelsfrage,* pp. 68–9.

[38]See ibid., pp. 69–73. On the last point the evidence is indirect. But only on the assumption of lapsed titles can we explain the large number of renewed titles from 1790 to 1839. See Reinhart Kosellek, *Preussen zwischen Reform und Revolution* (vol. 7 of Industrielle Welt; Stuttgart: Ernest Klett Verlag, 1967), pp. 676–9.

[39]See Martiny, *Adelsfrage*, pp. 74–80. For later evidence on the distribution of titles, see Kosellek, *Preussen*, pp. 676–9, which makes clear that until 1893 the bulk (over 80 percent) of new titles went to officers and officials serving the monarchy.

[40]Martiny, *Adelsfrage*, p. 113.

[41]Ibid., pp. 65, 110–11.

[42]Cf. the figures for 1800–1806 in Demeter, *Deutsche Offizierskorps*, pp. 4–5, with the figures for 1780 given in P. E. Razzell, "Social Origins of Officers in the Indian and British Home Army, 1758–1962," *British Journal of Sociology*, vol. 14 (1963), p. 253.

[43]See Martiny, *Adelsfrage*, p. 80; Craig, *Politics of Prussian Army*, pp. 22–6; Büsch, *Militärsystem*, pp. 56–61, 67–71; Demeter, *Deutsche Offizierskorps*, p. 405; William O. Shanahan, *Prussian Military Reforms* (New York: Columbia University Press, 1945), pp. 29–30; and Rosenberg, *Bureaucracy*, pp. 58–9.

[44]For a modern discussion of the Prussian reform movement, see W. M. Simon, *The Failure of the Prussian Reform Movement* (Ithaca: Cornell University Press, 1965).

[45]This definition of militarism is contained in Eckart Kehr, "Zur Genesis des Königlich-Preussischen Reserveoffiziers," *Der Primat der Innenpolitik* (vol. 19 of Veröffentlichungen der Historischen Kommission; Berlin: Walter de Gruyter, 1965), p. 54. See also Demeter, *Deutsche Offizierskorps*, pp. 12, 18, 26, and Craig, *Politics of Prussian Army*, pp. 79–81, for the data cited in this paragraph.

[46]See Rosenberg, *Bureaucracy*, pp. 61–4, 67–70.

[47]Ibid., pp. 175–81, for a detailed description of this development.

[48]See ibid., pp. 59, 151, 175–81, for a more detailed description of these points.

[49]See ibid., pp. 182–9.

[50]Martiny, *Adelsfrage*, pp. 114–18.

[51]Kosellek, *Preussen*, pp. 511–12.

[52]In the eastern province 3.8 million hectares belonged to aristocratic owners as against 0.88 million hectares belonging to middle-class owners. See Meitzen, *Der Boden*, VI, pp. 555–6.

[53]See ibid., VI, pp. 552–3, and Max Weber, "Agrarstatistische und sozialpolitische Betrachtungen zur Fideikommissfrage in Preussen," *Gesammelte Aufsätze zur Soziologie und Sozialpolitik* (Tübingen: J. C. B. Mohr, 1924), pp. 323–93.

[54]See Kosellek, *Preussen*, pp. 97–8, 101–3, 107–8, and passim for details concerning this emergence of an amalgamated governing class in Prussia.

[55]Ernst Troeltsch, "The Ideas of Natural Law and Humanity in World Politics," in Otto Gierke, *Natural Law and the Theory of Society* (Boston: Beacon Press, 1957), p. 214 (appendix).

CHAPTER VI. ENGLAND

[1]In what follows, I usually refer to England rather than to Roman Britain, Anglo-Saxon England, Anglo-Norman England, and so on. The context will make clear what period is under discussion.

[2]See F. M. Stenton, *Anglo-Saxon England* (London: Oxford University Press, 1971), pp. 34–7. Cf. the earlier discussion of these tribal conditions in Chapter 2, pp. 25–26, 35–36.

[3]John Morris, *The Age of Arthur* (London: Weidenfeld and Nicolson, 1973), pp. 326–7.

[4]The following discussion is based on Stenton, *Anglo-Saxon England,* pp. 545 ff.

[5]Ibid., p. 552.

[6]See ibid., pp. 351–3, 550–3, for these materials on the king's council.

[7]Ibid., p. 305.

[8]The interplay between the cult of kingship and the claims of kings is examined in detail in William Chaney, *The Cult of Kingship in Anglo-Saxon England* (Manchester: Manchester University Press, 1970).

[9]Stenton, *Anglo-Saxon England,* p. 36.

[10]Ibid., p. 680.

[11]See David C. Douglas, *William the Conqueror* (Berkeley and Los Angeles: University of California Press, 1964), pp. 266, 269, 302.

[12]See P. W. Sawyer, "The Norman Conquest of England," *Conquest and Culture,* mimeo (Past and Present Society, Annual Conference 1971; London, 1971), pp. 6–7.

[13]See G. O. Sayles, *The Medieval Foundations of England* (New York: A. S. Barnes, 1961), pp. 226, 228 ff.; Carl Stephenson, *Medieval Feudalism* (Ithaca: Cornell University Press, 1956), pp. 75–7, and Douglas, *William the Conqueror,* pp. 275–8, 281–3, 295–8, for evidence of the contrast between Norman England and the other countries mentioned. The Norman kings and their successors placed their executive, financial, and judicial business in the hands of personal appointees who had been trained in the king's service. See S. B. Chrimes, *An Introduction to the Administrative History of Medieval England* (New York: Macmillan, 1952), pp. 23–4, 87–8, on the social origins of major officials of the Crown, and pp. 156–8 on the general acceptance of officials as the king's personal agents.

[14]Sidney Painter, *Studies in the History of the English Feudal Barony* (Baltimore: Johns Hopkins University Press, 1943), pp. 68–9.

[15]Ibid., pp. 57, 63–4.

[16]See Frank Barlow, *The Feudal Kingdom of England, 1042–1216* (London: Longmans, Green, 1955), p. 90.

[17]See Douglas, *William the Conqueror,* pp. 281–3.

[18]Ibid., pp. 150–1.

[19]Barlow, *Feudal Kingdom of England,* pp. 109–10.

[20]See the account of the regency during the minority of Henry III in Sir Maurice Powicke, *The Thirteenth Century, 1216–1307* (London: Oxford University Press, 1970), chap. 1.

[21]Ibid., pp. 524–9. The quotation appears on p. 529.

[22]C. H. McIlwain, "Medieval Estates," *The Cambridge Medieval History* (London: Cambridge University Press, 1932), VII, pp. 712–13. McIlwain cites the following landmarks of constitutional development: the Provisions of Oxford (1259), Edward I's concessions in the confirmation of charters (1279), the distinction between king and crown made in the reign of Edward II (1307–1327), the ordinances of the barons (1311), the extension of baronial control over the Exchequer and even over the King's Wardrobe, and the enlargement of parliamentary powers and claims during the Lancastrian reign of the fifteenth century. See the further reference to representation in England in Chapter 7, "Representation," this volume.

[23]Otto Hintze attributes the emergence of representative institutions to that "balance" in England and in some other Western European countries. See Otto Hintze, *Historical Essays* (New York: Oxford University Press, 1975), pp. 302–53.

[24]For the justices of the peace, see the detailed descriptions in Sidney and Beatrice Webb, *English Local Government: The Parish and the County* (London: Longmans, Green, 1906), I, pp. 305–10, 372–3, and passim. The Webbs discount the formal coordination by the government because of the wide discretion enjoyed by justices of the peace. For Prussia, see Otto Büsch, *Militärsystem und Sozialleben im Alten Preussen, 1713–1807* (vol. 7 of Veröffentlichungen der Berliner Historischen Kommission; Berlin: Walter de Gruyter, 1962), pp. 84–9, and Otto Hintze, *Die Hohenzollern und ihr Werk* (Berlin: Paul Parey, 1915), pp. 286–8. For the military origin of the *Landrat,* see Otto Hintze, "Der Ursprung des preussischen Landratamts in der Mark Brandenburg," *Regierung und Verwaltung* (vol. 3 of Gesammelte Abhandlungen; Göttingen: Vandenhoeck & Ruprecht, 1967), pp. 164–203.

[25]Stenton, *Anglo-Saxon England,* p. 303.

[26]Frank Barlow, "The Effects of the Norman Conquest," in Dorothy Whitelock et al., *The Norman Conquest* (London: Eyre & Spottiswoode, 1966), pp. 139–40.

[27]Marc Bloch, *Feudal Society* (Chicago: University of Chicago Press, 1961), pp. 59 ff., 190 ff.

[28]Painter, *English Feudal Barony,* p. 42 and passim.

[29]See May McKisack, *The Fourteenth Century, 1307–1399* (London: Oxford University Press, 1959), pp. 234 ff.

[30]See Powicke, *Thirteenth Century,* p. 516. For the characterization of these conditions up to the sixteenth century, I have relied on Lawrence Stone, *The Crisis of the Aristocracy* (London: Oxford University Press, 1965), pp. 199–234. See Chapter 7 for a further reference to feuds as part of the feudal legal order.

[31]Samuel Finer, "State- and Nation-Building in Europe: The Role of the Military," in Charles Tilly, ed., *The Formation of National States in Western Europe* (Princeton: Princeton University Press, 1975), pp. 114 ff.

[32]On the declining military experience of the peerage, see Stone, *Crisis,* pp. 209–16, 234–9, 265–6; see also pp. 454–8 for a description of aristocratic military service under Elizabeth and the early Stuarts. The declining military capacity of the English army during the early seventeenth century is documented by C. H. Firth, *Cromwell's Army* (London: Methuen, University Paperbacks, 1962), chap. 1. On the development of the duel, see Stone, *Crisis,* pp. 234 ff., and Sir George Clark, *War and Society in the Seventeenth Century* (Cambridge: At the University Press, 1958), chap. 2.

[33]This proportion of entrants was not reached again until after World War I and was exceeded only after World War II. See Lawrence Stone, "The Educational Revolution in England, 1560–1640," *Past and Present,* vol. 28 (1964), pp. 57–69. Stone notes that entrants came from all strata of the population, but that the aristocracy was greatly overrepresented.

[34]Ibid., p. 63. This proportion fell to 45 percent in the years 1734–1761 and then rose again to 60 percent in the years 1818–1831. See Gerrit Judd, *Members of Parliament, 1734–1832* (New Haven: Yale University Press, 1955), p. 37.

[35]See Stone, "Educational Revolution," pp. 69–73; Stone, *Crisis,* p. 673 and passim; and M. H. Curtis, *Oxford and Cambridge in Transition* (Oxford: Clarendon Press, 1959), pp. 265–70.

[36]See the vivid description of this contrast by J. H. Hexter, "The Education of the Aristocracy in the Renaissance," in *Reappraisals in History* (New York: Harper & Row, Harper Torchbooks, 1963), pp. 45–70.

[37]Lawrence Stone and Marius Jansen, "Education and Modernization in Japan and England," *Comparative Studies in Society and History,* vol. 9 (1966/67), p. 221.

[38]For further details on the English militia, see Walter Dorn, *Competition for Empire, 1740–1763* (New York: Harper & Row, Harper Torchbooks, 1963), chap. 3, and Julius Hatschek, *Englische Verwaltungsgeschichte* (Munich: R. Oldenbourg, 1913), pp. 735–40. Hatschek notes that the English militia was organized after the Prussian cantonal administration, but in England this implied the supremacy of the local gentry over the recruits, whereas in Prussia the same administrative device ensured the king's supremacy over both officers and recruits.

[39]See Stone, *Crisis,* p. 53. *Peerage* is the term used in lieu of the earlier baronage or tenants-in-chief.

[40]Ibid., pp. 385–98.

[41]Roger Lockyier, *Tudor and Stuart Britain* (London: Longmans, Green, 1964), pp. 28, 86.

[42]Ibid., chaps. 2–5, provide a convenient summary of modern research and interpretation concerning these topics.

[43]See F. C. Dietz, *English Government Finance* (London: Frank Cass, 1964), I, pp. 35–59, for examples from the reigns of Henry VII and Henry VIII. These liabilities were as

much due to foreign entanglements as to the king's financial dependence on the rising class of merchants. Dietz points to the king's use of foreign complications for his own pecuniary advantage (ibid., I, pp. 53–9), but also to the extension of English rule over Ireland as a major cause of royal appeals for subsidies from parliament (ibid., II, p. 48).

[44]During the forty-five years from 1558 to 1603, 878 families were elevated to the knighthood, 3 were made Irish and 18 English peers. This may be contrasted with the thirty-eight years between 1603 and 1641, during which 3,281 families were elevated to the knighthood, 542 were made English, Irish, or Scottish baronets, and 80 were made Irish and 103 English peers. See Stone, *Crisis,* pp. 264, 755, for the source of these data.

[45]See the documentation in Stone, *Crisis,* pp. 449–586.

[46]The growing prominence of a concern with country and hence an incipient nationalism is suggested persuasively by William Haller, *Foxe's Book of Martyrs and the Elect Nation* (London: Jonathan Cape, 1963), pp. 242–50. Haller refers to the late sixteenth century, while the later development of an imperial ideology is discussed by Richard Koebner, *Empire* (New York: Grosset & Dunlop, 1961), chap. 3.

[47]F. W. Maitland, *The Constitutional History of England* (Cambridge: At the University Press, 1961), pp. 74–5. See also the account of primogeniture in ibid., pp. 37–9, 157–78.

[48]See Ernest Barker, *National Character* (4th ed.; London: Methuen, 1948), pp. 122–4.

[49]This summary is based on the detailed study of medieval London by Sylvia Thrupp, *The Merchant Class of Medieval London* (Ann Arbor: University of Michigan Press, 1962), pp. 236–38, 245–7, and passim. See also Curtis, *Oxford and Cambridge,* chap. 10, and the writings of Stone and Hexter cited earlier.

[50]Lockyier, *Tudor and Stuart Britain,* p. 28. A somewhat different emphasis is provided by Wagner, who states that six dukedoms and eight earldoms were destroyed through death in battle, execution, or forfeiture, but that the common impression of a decimation of the old nobility during this period is mistaken. See A. R. Wagner, *English Aristocracy* (London: Oxford University Press, 1961), p. 43. However, the destruction of fourteen major families is not negligible.

[51]See Stone, *Crisis,* pp. 163–4.

[52]Thrupp, *Merchant Class,* pp. 244, 262–3.

[53]See ibid., p. 280, for a description of the steps by which a city merchant could change his status by assuming the social role of a country gentleman.

[54]The source of these quotations and evidence for the status orientation of English society are contained in Perez Zagorin, *The Court and the Country, the Beginning of the English Revolution* (New York: Atheneum, 1971), pp. 19–30.

[55]R. H. Tawney, *The Agrarian Problem of the Sixteenth Century* (New York: Burt Franklin, n.d.), p. 384.

[56]Ibid., pp. 390, 392, 407–8. Later scholarly revisions of Tawney's interpretation do not affect the points made in the text. See the summary of the literature and a compre-

hensive bibliography in Lawrence Stone's introduction to the Harper Torchbooks edition of Tawney's book (1967).

[57]Statement of the Duke of Wellington, justifying the purchase of army commissions at high prices, quoted in P. E. Razzell, "Social Origins of Officers in the Indian and British Home Army, 1758–1962," *British Journal of Sociology,* vol. 14 (1963), p. 258.

[58]See the documentation of these points in Stone, *Crisis,* pp. 209–16, 234–9.

[59]J. E. Neale, *The Elizabethan House of Commons* (Harmondsworth: Penguin, 1963), p. 22, suggests that the "gentlemanly profession of serving-men" was declining at the end of the sixteenth century. Since the reference here is to adults, this is compatible with the statement by Phillipe Aries, *Centuries of Childhood* (New York: Vintage, 1965), pp. 370–1, that the great families of the nobility retained the old system of apprenticeship long after the schooling of boys had been adopted by families of middle rank.

Neale, *House of Commons,* pp. 22–3.

See ibid., pp. 21–2, 133–4.

[62]See ibid., pp. 24–5 for the quotation and pp. 139–40 for Neale's reference to the several M.A. theses which document the overrepresentation of rural areas in the Elizabethan parliaments.

[63]See F. M. L. Thompson, *English Landed Society in the Nineteenth Century* (London: Routledge and Kegan Paul, 1963), p. 276.

[64]J. H. Plumb, *The Growth of Political Stability in England, 1675–1725* (Harmondsworth: Penguin, 1969), p. 39.

[65]H. J. Habbakuk, "England," in A. Goodwin, ed., *The European Nobility in the Eighteenth Century* (London: Adam and Charles Black, 1953), pp. 2–3. A fuller account of the technical details is contained in H. J. Habbakuk, "Marriage Settlements in the Eighteenth Century," *Transactions of the Royal Historical Society* (London: Royal Historical Society, 1950), 4th series, vol. 32, pp. 15–30.

[66]See H. J. Habbakuk, "The English Land Market in the Eighteenth Century," in J. S. Bromley and E. H. Kossmann, eds., *Britain and the Netherlands* (London: Chatto & Windus, 1960), pp. 154–5 and passim. In France, the old regime had still another residence pattern because of the shift to Versailles. There aristocrats resided at court when in attendance, possessed a townhouse in Paris (*hôtel* or *palais*), and owned various country residences, shifting from one to the other as the king's presence or their own ambition indicated. For a detailed analysis of the French aristocratic life style as reflected in their living arrangements, see Norbert Elias, *Die höfische Gesellschaft* (Neuwied: Luchterhand, 1969), chap. 3.

[67]See ibid., pp. 5–6. For the use of public offices as a source of income for the gentry, see J. Donald Kingsley, *Representative Bureaucracy* (Yellow Springs: Antioch Press, 1944).

[68]See the quotations in Sir Lewis Namier, *England in the Age of the American Revolution* (London: Macmillan, 1961), p. 19. This was the basis also of the pleas of the Continental Congress in 1774.

[69]See Habbakuk in A. Goodwin, ed., *European Nobility,* pp. 7–11, who stresses the extreme variability of family fortunes and the rather special economic improvement of the landed gentry during the eighteenth century. For an illustrative survey of aristocratic economic activities, see S. D. Stirk, *Die Aristokratie und die industrielle Entwicklung in England* (vol. 15 of Sprache und Kultur der Germanisch-Romanischen Völker; Breslau: Verlag Hans Priebatsch, 1933), especially chap. 3.

[70]This statement by W. E. H. Lecky is quoted by Namier, *England in the Age of the American Revolution,* pp. 33–5, together with several other, similar observations concerning the economic sophistication of the gentry.

[71]On the other hand, it is probable that this nonutilitarian education acted as a brake on the gentry's interest in the development of science and technology. See the discussion by Lawrence Stone in Jansen and Stone, "Education and Modernization in Japan and England," pp. 219–32.

[72]The special position of the navy is reflected in its jurisdictional autonomy, comparatively generous parliamentary appropriations in times of emergency, the high proportion of sons from aristocratic families among naval officers, and the early professionalization of navy officer training in the eighteenth century. For documentation, see Hatschek, *Englische Verwaltungsgeschichte,* pp. 524–30; Dorn, *Competition for Empire,* pp. 102–9; and Michael Lewis, *A Social History of the Navy, 1793–1815* (London: George Allen & Unwin, 1960), pp. 31, 36, and passim.

[73]For an empirical analysis of aristocratic dominance throughout the nineteenth and into the twentieth century, see W. L. Guttsman, *The British Political Elite* (New York: Basic Books, 1963).

[74]See the detailed discussion by Thompson, *English Landed Society.*

[75]See the analysis by Rupert Wilkinson, *Gentlemanly Power* (London: Oxford University Press, 1964).

[76]See Walter Bagehot, *The English Constitution* (2nd ed.; London: Oxford University Press, 1958), pp. 263–4, and Hippolyte Taine, *Notes on England* (London: Thames and Hudson, 1957), p. 155. This opinion was not confined to conservatives. For a concurring opinion by Friedrich Engels, see his *Socialism: Utopian and Scientific* (Chicago: Charles H. Kerr, 1905), pp. xxxii–xxxiv.

CHAPTER VII. KINGSHIP AND ARISTOCRACY AS A TYPE OF RULE

[1]For details, see Robert G. Wesson, *The Imperial Order* (Berkeley and Los Angeles: University of California Press, 1967), pp. 123–38 and passim.

[2]Marc Bloch, *Feudal Society* (Chicago: University of Chicago Press, 1961), p. 40.

[3]The discussion of Germanic, Islamic, and Japanese traditions provided glimpses of the process by which more complex political organizations arose out of tribal units based on clans. For a survey of these other types of traditional authority with special reference to Africa, see Lucy Mair, *Primitive Government* (Baltimore: Penguin, 1964).

[4]Niccolo Machiavelli, *The Prince* (New York: Modern Library, 1940), p. 15.

[5]The phrase "governing class" has been suggested by Gerhard Lenski, *Power and Privilege* (New York: McGraw Hill, 1966), pp. 219 ff. I adopt it here so as to differentiate traditional societies with their coincidence of ruling influence and actual government from modern societies with their distinction between *ruling class* and *political class*. See Raymond Aron, "Social Class, Political Class, Ruling Class," *European Journal of Sociology*, vol. 1 (1960), pp. 260–81.

[6]For a discussion of this definition, see Joseph R. Strayer, *Medieval Statecraft and the Perspectives of History* (Princeton: Princeton University Press, 1971), p. 65 and passim.

[7]Wesson, *Imperial Order,* pp. 85–6.

[8]Antonio Marongiu, *Medieval Parliaments* (London: Eyre & Spottiswoode, 1968), p. 21.

[9]Ibid.

[10]Quoted in J. M. Wallace-Hadrill, *The Long-Haired Kings* (London: Methuen, 1962), p. 184, n. 2.

[11]See Max Weber, *Economy and Society* (tr. and ed. by Guenther Roth and Claus Wittich; New York: Bedminster Press, 1968), III, pp. 1070–1.

[12]Ibid., III, pp. 1022 ff., 1072 ff.

[13]Ibid., III, pp. 1074–6. "Western European" refers to Northwestern Europe. In Spain, for example, the element of honor seems to have developed at the expense of fealty. See Ronald Glassman, *Political History of Latin America* (New York: Funk & Wagnalls, 1969), pp. 11–12, 80–2.

[14]See Strayer, *Medieval Statecraft*, pp. 66–72, for a delimitation of the military element in the development of feudalism.

[15]This synopsis and rephrasing of Weber's analysis is taken from Reinhard Bendix, *Max Weber, An Intellectual Portrait* (2nd ed.; Berkeley and Los Angeles: University of California Press, 1978), pp. 363–5. See Weber, *Economy and Society*, III, pp. 1104–9 and passim.

[16]See Norbert Elias, *Über den Prozess der Zivilisation* (2nd ed.; Bern: Francke Verlag, 1969), I, pp. 266–9. (Originally published in 1939.) The discussion following is primarily a summary of this important study.

[17]Quoted from a fifteenth-century German text in ibid., I, p. 272.

[18]See J. Huizinga, *The Waning of the Middle Ages* (Harmondsworth: Penguin, 1955), chap. 1, which contains a vivid portrayal of this atmosphere. The qualities listed are those of the aristocracy.

[19]Elias, *Prozess,* I, pp. 281–2, cites this case from the sixteenth century.

[20]See ibid., I, pp. 110–230. See also Philippe Erlanger, *The Age of Courts and Kings* (Garden City: Doubleday, Anchor Books, 1970), p. 59 and passim.

[21]See Elias, *Prozess,* II, pp. 312 ff. Elias is not always clear how he conceives the relation between such changing patterns and the individual. Violence and cruelty or the refinement of manners may be characteristic of a society for a period, but neither the capacity for instant aggression nor that for etiquette and polite manipulation are distributed equally among the people. I suggest that different patterns of interdependence encourage the personality types which are most effective at aggression or manipulation. See the analysis in Reinhard Bendix, "Compliant Behavior and Individual Personality," *American Journal of Sociology,* vol. 58 (November 1952), pp. 292–303.

[22]Quoted in Norbert Elias, *Die Höfische Gesellschaft* (Neuwied: Luchterhand, 1969), p. 160.

[23]My paraphrase is based on Arthur Schopenhauer's translation of the work. See Balthasar Gracián, *Handorakel und Kunst der Weltklugheit* (Munich: Wilhelm Goldmann Verlag, 1960). The work is divided into numbered paragraphs, and the points cited are found in paragraphs 13, 14, 26, 35, 84, 149, 150, 287, and 297.

[24]See George O. Sayles, *The King's Parliament of England* (New York: W. W. Norton, 1974), pp. 21–6.

[25]See Marongiu, *Medieval Parliaments,* pp. 82–4 and passim.

[26]Ibid., pp. 85–6.

[27]Francis Bacon, "On Nobility," *The Complete Essays of Francis Bacon* (ed. H. L. Finch; New York: Washington Square Press, 1963), p. 36.

[28]Gerhard Ritter, "Das britische Parlament im 18. Jahrhundert," in Dietrich Gerhard, ed., *Ständische Vertretungen in Europa im 17. und 18. Jahrhundert* (Göttingen: Vandenhoeck & Ruprecht, 1969), pp. 423–4.

[29]See Archibald S. Foord, "The Waning of the 'Influence of the Crown,'" reprinted from the *English Historical Review* (1947) in Rosalind Mitchison, ed., *Essays in Eighteenth-Century History* (London: Longmans, Green, 1966), pp. 171–94.

[30]Moreover, the property qualification of candidates for office increased the social homogeneity of the political elite still further. See Ritter, "Das britische Parlament," pp. 416–18.

[31]R. R. Palmer, *The Age of the Democratic Revolution* (Princeton: Princeton University Press, 1959), I, chap. 2.

[32]This conflict did not occur everywhere. Northwestern Germany, for example, consisted of subsidiary principalities, bishoprics, and municipalities without political ambitions, and the same is true elsewhere. In such areas, estate assemblies exercised legislative functions until the repercussions of the French revolution destroyed the foundation of these assemblies. See Chapter 11, "The Holy Roman Empire," for a further discussion of the small German principalities.

[33]See Peter Baumgart, "Zur Geschichte der kurmärkischen Stände im 17. und 18. Jahrhundert," in Dietrich Gerhard, ed., *Ständische Vertretungen,* p. 140.

[34]Ibid., pp. 144–6 and passim.

[35]Nikolai N. Alexeiev, "Beiträge zur Geschichte des russischen Absolutismus in 18. Jahrhundert," *Forschungen zur Osteuropäischen Geschichte* (Osteuropa-Institut, Freie Universität Berlin; Wiesbaden: Otto Harrassowitz, 1958), VI, pp. 7–14 and passim.

[36]Gustave Alef, "The Crisis of the Muscovite Aristocracy," *Forschungen zur Osteuropäischen Geschichte*, vol. 15 (1970), pp. 18–19. See also by the same author, "Das Erlöschen des Abzugsrechts der Moskauer Bojaren," in *Forschungen*, vol. 10 (1965), pp. 7–74.

[37]Alexeiev, *Beiträge*, pp. 15–16, 41–7. M. M. Cherbatov, the most prominent aristocratic spokesman in the second half of the eighteenth century, made a special point of attacking the dishonesty of tradespeople using subterfuge in order to acquire aristocratic rank.

CHAPTER VIII. TRANSFORMATIONS OF WESTERN EUROPEAN SOCIETIES IN THE SIXTEENTH CENTURY

[1]See Otto Brunner, *Land und Herrschaft* (Vienna: R. M. Rohrer, 1959), pp. 1–110. For a detailed analysis of this process in Frankish, Anglo-Saxon, and Norman law, see Julius Goebel, *Felony and Misdemeanor, A Study in the History of English Criminal Procedure* (Commonwealth Fund; New York: Oxford University Press, 1937), pp. 17–18 and passim.

[2]Ernst Kern, *Moderner Staat und Saatsbegriff* (Hamburg: Rechts- und Staatswissenschaftlicher Verlag, 1949), part 2.

[3]See Ernest Barker, *The Development of Public Services in Western Europe* (London: Oxford University Press, 1944), pp. 4–5 and passim.

[4]Rights could be considered invalid even though a ruler had enacted them. See Kern, *Moderner Staat*, pp. 71 ff.

[5]Alexis de Tocqueville, *Democracy in America* (New York: Knopf, 1948), I, pp. 5–6 and passim.

[6]The following discussion is based on Carlo M. Cipolla, *Before the Industrial Revolution, European Society and Economy, 1000–1700* (London: Methuen, 1976), chaps. 4–7.

[7]Ibid., p. 173. See also E. J. Dijksterhuis, *The Mechanization of the World Picture* (London: Oxford University Press, 1961).

[8]A major attempt along this line is contained in Immanuel Wallerstein, *The Modern World-System, Capitalist Agriculture and the Origins of the European World-Economy in the Sixteenth Century* (New York: Academic Press, 1974). Wallerstein states that "idea systems are capable of being used in the service of contrary interests, capable of being associated with quite different structural thrusts" (p. 62), and again "any complex system of ideas can be manipulated to serve any particular social or political objective" (p. 152). However, the universality of manipulation does not really come to grips with the differences among cultures, the persistent interest in ideas, or the question of what social and political interests may be served by a completely manipulative approach to ideas. A history and critique of this reductionist approach is contained in Hans Barth, *Truth and Ideology* (Berkeley and Los Angeles: University of California Press, 1976). My study differs from Wallerstein's materialistic approach as well as from Barrington Moore's earlier *Social Origins of Dicta-*

torship and Democracy, Lord and Peasant in the Making of the Modern World (Boston: Beacon Press, 1966) by a greater emphasis on the political antecedents of the sixteenth century and on the role of ideas in the formation of the modern world.

[9]See Fernand Braudel, *The Mediterranean and the Mediterranean World in the Age of Philip II* (New York: Harper & Row, 1973), II, pp. 666–7. Wallerstein, *Modern World-System,* pp. 41–51, gives an analysis of the factors accounting for Portugal's pioneering role in the overseas expansion of Europe.

[10]Cipolla shows that the Muslims quickly borrowed the technique of producing Western artillery, but that for technical and cultural reasons they were handicapped in its use. The reference to the number of French books dealing with Turkey and the Americas is also contained in Carlo M. Cipolla, *Guns and Sails in the Early Phase of European Expansion, 1400–1700* (London: Collins, 1965), pp. 15, n. 1, and 90 ff.

[11]The text of this bull is quoted in K. M. Pannikar, *Asia and Western Dominance* (London: Allen & Unwin, 1959), pp. 26–7.

[12]Jacques Bernard, "Trade and Finance in the Middle Ages, 900–1500," in Carlo M. Cipolla, ed., *The Fontana Economic History of Europe, The Middle Ages* (London: Collins, 1972), pp. 309–10.

[13]Braudel, *Mediterranean World,* I, p. 419.

[14]See ibid., I, pp. 355 ff., 394 ff., for the details and for the author's repeated cautions concerning the overall figures I have cited. See especially the detailed calculation of speeds with which news traveled between Venice and various cities of Europe on pp. 362 ff. See also Cipolla, *Before the Industrial Revolution,* p. 166, n.

[15]I have used the list of foundation dates in William L. Langer, ed., *An Encyclopedia of World History* (Boston: Houghton, Mifflin, 1968), pp. 1314–15.

[16]See Fernand Braudel, *Capitalism and Material Life, 1400–1800* (London: Weidenfeld and Nicolson, 1973), pp. 289–99; Rolf Engelsing, *Analphabetentum und Lektüre* (Stuttgart: J. B. Metzlersche Verlagsbuchhandlung, 1973), pp. 18–20; and Cipolla, *Before the Industrial Revolution,* pp. 167–8, for information on the early book trade.

[17]Marjorie Plant, *The English Book Trade* (London: Allen & Unwin, 1965), pp. 90–1.

[18]Margaret B. Stillwell, *The Awakening Interest in Science during the First Century of Printing, 1450–1550* (New York: Bibliographical Society of America, 1970). I am indebted to my assistant, Theodore Bogacz, for his compilation of these figures.

[19]Carlo M. Cipolla, *Literacy and Development in the West* (Baltimore: Penguin, 1969), p. 61. The linkages between the Reformation and the invention of printing are explored by Elizabeth Eisenstein, "The Advent of Printing and the Protestant Revolt," in Robert M. Kingdon, ed., *Transition and Revolution* (Minneapolis: Burgess, 1974), pp. 235–70.

[20]I use the phrase "commercialization of land, labor, and capital" in preference to the more familiar "rise of capitalism," following a suggestion of Karl Polanyi. The phrase suggests the extension of exchange relations and monetary transactions to the three main factors of production.

[21] Francis Bacon, "Novum Organum," in E. A. Burtt, ed., *The English Philosophers from Bacon to Mill* (New York: Modern Library, 1939), p. 85.

[22] In a series of articles, Elizabeth Eisenstein has analyzed the ramifications of the change from a scribal to a printing culture, with special emphasis on the changes in world outlook which followed from the easy reproducibility of texts. See Elizabeth Eisenstein, "Clio and Chronos," *History and the Concept of Time* (vol. 6 of History and Theory; Middletown: Wesleyan University Press, 1966), pp. 36–64; "Some Conjectures about the Impact of Printing on Western Society and Thought," *Journal of Modern History*, vol. 40 (March 1968), pp. 1–56; "The Advent of Printing and the Problem of the Renaissance," *Past and Present*, no. 45 (November 1969), pp. 19–89.

[23] See G. R. Elton, *The Tudor Revolution in Government* (London: Cambridge University Press, 1962), passim, and G. E. Aylmer, *The King's Servants, the Civil Service of Charles I, 1625–1642* (New York: Columbia University Press, 1961), especially pp. 429–30, for a summary of the laicization of the English government.

[24] This brief statement is based on the historiographic sketch in Wilfrid R. Prest, *The Inns of Court under Elizabeth I and the Early Stuarts* (London: Longmans, 1972), pp. 1–5, and A. M. Carr-Saunders and P. A. Wilson, *The Professions* (London: Frank Cass, 1964), pp. 7–58.

[25] See ibid., pp. 65 ff., 117 ff., for details on physicians and nursing. The sketch of teaching is gleaned from M. H. Curtis, *Oxford and Cambridge in Transition, 1558–1642* (London: Oxford University Press, 1959), chaps. 2 and 7. For a description of the final crisis of secularization from 1850 to 1870, see Brian Simon, *Studies in the History of Education, 1780–1870* (London: Lawrence & Wishart, 1960), pp. 281–99.

[26] J. B. Black, *The Reign of Elizabeth, 1558–1603* (2nd ed.; London: Oxford University Press, 1959), p. 320. See the detailed survey of schools under Henry VIII and Edward VI in Joan Simon, *Education and Society in Tudor England* (London: Cambridge University Press, 1966).

[27] See the survey of private endowments of educational institutions in Louis B. Wright, *Middle-Class Culture in Elizabethan England* (Chapel Hill: University of North Carolina Press, 1935), chap. 3, and Simon, *Education in Tudor England,* part 3, for surveys of education during the reign of Queen Elizabeth.

[28] See the evidence and discussion in Lawrence Stone, "The Educational Revolution in England, 1560–1640," *Past and Present*, no. 28 (July 1964), pp. 42–7 and 54–7.

[29] Lawrence Stone, "Social Mobility in England, 1500–1700," *Past and Present*, no. 33 (April 1966), pp. 18–20 and passim.

[30] These connections are stressed by Christopher Hill, *Intellectual Origins of the English Revolution* (London: Oxford University Press, 1965), chaps. 2 and 3, where he discusses the links between Puritanism and Baconian science and the remarkable efflorescence of science teaching for merchants and artisans at Gresham College.

[31] See Raymond Williams, *The Long Revolution* (London: Chatto & Windus, 1961), p. 159, and M. G. Jones, *The Charity School Movement* (London: Cambridge University Press, 1938), passim.

[32]Williams, *Long Revolution,* pp. 160-l.

[33]The resulting ambivalence between "elitism" and "populism" is analyzed in Leo Lowenthal and Marjorie Fiske, "The Debate over Art and Popular Culture in Eighteenth Century England," in Mirra Komarovsky, ed., *Common Frontiers of the Social Sciences* (Glencoe: Free Press, 1957), pp. 33-112.

[34]In Chapter 1, note 2, I referred to my critical assessment of the terms *tradition, modernity,* and *modernization* in Reinhard Bendix, *Embattled Reason* (New York: Oxford University Press, 1970), chap. 11. The following discussion is in part based on this earlier publication.

[35]Colin Morris, *The Discovery of the Individual, 1050-1200* (New York: Harper & Row, Harper Torchbooks, 1973).

[36]Wilhelm Riehl, *Die Bürgerliche Gesellschaft* (Stuttgart: J. G. Cotta'sche Buchhandlung, 1930), pp. 312-13. This is part of a larger work which was written from 1847 to 1851.

[37]The composition of this class will vary from country to country, and even in the same country over time. For a more judicious assessment of that composition than Riehl's, see Klaus Epstein, *The Genesis of German Conservatism* (Princeton: Princeton University Press, 1966), pp. 48-58.

[38]For an analysis of the rising voluntarism in the Marxist tradition, see Richard Löwenthal, "Unreason and Revolution," *Encounter,* vol. 33 (November 1969), pp. 22-34. A related issue is the social and cultural distance between intellectuals and workers with which Marxists have had to grapple since the Communist Manifesto. See Chapter 13, footnote e, for a discussion of this issue.

CHAPTER IX. KINGS AND PEOPLE IN ENGLAND

[1]Quoted in Fernand Braudel, *The Mediterranean and the Mediterranean World in the Age of Philip II* (New York: Harper & Row, 1973), II, p. 674.

[2]Richard Koebner, *Empire* (London: Cambridge University Press, 1966), pp. 61-2. See also the following pages for English metaphoric uses of "empire" during this period.

[3]The degree of occupational specialization in the sixteenth century is uncertain since production for the market and for home consumption are difficult to distinguish. In at least one town up to one-third of the residents were still engaged in agriculture until well into the seventeenth century. In other towns, a third of the enumerated population were engaged in the production of textiles and clothing and the remainder in food and drink processing, leather and metal work, transport and building. In the rural areas, the proportion of the work force engaged in agriculture ranged between 50 and 80 percent, which presumably means that between 20 and 50 percent were engaged in craft production of some kind, and no doubt partly for the market. See L. A. Clarkson, *The Pre-Industrial Economy in England, 1500-1700* (London: B. T. Batsford, 1971), pp. 88-9 and passim.

[4]Ibid., p. 155.

[5]Sir George Clark, *The Wealth of England, 1496-1760* (London: Oxford University Press, 1946), p. 55.

[6]See David H. Pill, *The English Reformation, 1529–58* (London: University of London Press, 1973), pp. 75-6, and Christopher Hill, *Puritanism and Revolution* (London: Panther Books, 1968), p. 42.

[7]Clark, *Wealth of England,* pp. 64–5, 74. The author cites one estimate that the lands expropriated and sold by the crown brought in twenty times their annual rental value, which would come to roughly 5 million in terms of the figures cited by Hill and Clark. These figures, as well as those on the costs of war, are approximations.

[8]William Haller, *Foxe's Book of Martyrs and the Elect Nation* (London: Jonathan Cape, 1963), p. 21.

[9]Herbert Schöffler has analyzed the process by which in this setting political vacillation in church policy induced religious anxiety and led to a polarization of religious beliefs. See his *Die Anfänge des Puritanismus* (Kölner Anglistische Arbeiten, vol. 14; Leipzig: Bernhard Tauchnitz, 1932). For a contemporary expression of apprehension arising from a church policy dependent on political authority, see the statement by John Rogers quoted in M. M. Knappen, *Tudor Puritanism* (Chicago: University of Chicago Press, 1939), pp. 107–8.

[10]See the discussion in Louis B. Wright, *Middle-Class Culture in Elizabethan England* (Chapel Hill: University of North Carolina Press, 1935), chap. 2. The book covers the period from 1558 to the 1640s, with some references before and after these years.

[11]Quoted from Philip Jones's *Certaine briefe and speciall Instructions* (1589) in Louis B. Wright, *Religion and Empire, The Alliance between Piety and Commerce in England, 1558–1624* (Chapel Hill: University of North Carolina Press, 1943), p. 37.

[12]James A. Williamson, *The Ocean in English History* (London: Oxford University Press, 1941), pp. 115–16.

[13]J. B. Black, *The Reign of Elizabeth, 1558–1603* (London: Oxford University Press, 1959), p. 27. See the similar assessment in Williamson, *Ocean,* p. 4.

[14]In 1578 England possessed 135 vessels of more than 100 tons, in 1582 it had 223 ships of more than 80 tons, and by 1588 there were 363 such ships. By 1582 English seamen numbered 16,306. See J. Holland Rose et al., eds., *The Cambridge History of the British Empire* (London: Cambridge University Press, 1929), I, p. 116.

[15]See the survey of these arguments in Klaus E. Knorr, *British Colonial Theories, 1570–1850* (Toronto: University of Toronto Press, 1944), chap. 2. See also Williamson, *Ocean,* pp. 122–3.

[16]See J. H. Parry, *The Establishment of the European Hegemony, 1415–1715* (New York: Harper & Row, Harper Torchbooks, 1961), pp. 106–9.

[17]Charles Wilson, *Queen Elizabeth and the Revolt of the Netherlands* (Berkeley and Los Angeles: University of California Press, 1970), p. 22.

[18]Ibid., chap. 2 and passim.

[19]W. T. MacCaffrey, "Elizabethan Politics: The First Decade, 1558–1568," *Past and Present,* no. 24 (April 1963), pp. 26–7.

[20]In this respect, the analysis by Charles Wilson just cited may be compared with the studies by J. E. Neale.

[21]See the discussion by Carol Wiener, "The Beleaguered Isle, A Study of Elizabethan and Early Jacobean Anti-Catholicism," *Past and Present,* no. 51 (May 1971), pp. 27–62. See also Christopher Hill, *Intellectual Origins of the English Revolution* (London: Oxford University Press, 1965), pp. 276–84.

[22]Haller, *Foxe's Book of Martyrs,* pp. 224–5.

[23]Quoted in ibid., p. 87. The phrase *true believers* appears in the sermons of Edward Dering, published in 1576.

[24]Knappen and Hart give different estimates of the intensely religious among the Puritan and Catholic minorities, but agree that these were small minorities. See Knappen, *Tudor Puritanism,* p. 333, n. 24, and A. Tindal Hart, *The Country Clergy in Elizabethan and Stuart Times* (London: Phoenix House, 1958), pp. 17–18.

[25]Ibid., pp. 74–5, 80, 105.

[26]Christopher Hill, *Reformation to Industrial Revolution* (London: Weidenfeld & Nicolson, 1968), pp. 34–38.

[27]My formulation is modeled after Max Weber's definition of social action. See Max Weber, *Economy and Society* (tr. and ed. by Guenther Roth and Claus Wittich; New York: Bedminster Press, 1968), I, p. 4. I am also indebted to Robert Merton's analysis of reference groups in *Social Theory and Social Structure* (Glencoe: Free Press, 1957), pp. 225–386.

[28]See Basil Hall, " 'Puritanism,' the Problem of Definition," in G. J. Cuming, ed., *Studies in Church History* (London: Cambridge University Press, 1965), II, p. 290. Hall's definition is similar to Christopher Hill's suggestion that the term "include[s] all those radical Protestants who wanted to reform the Church but (before 1640 at least) did not want to separate from it." See Hill, *Intellectual Origins,* p. 26. See also the chapter "The Definition of a Puritan," in Christopher Hill, *Society and Puritanism in Pre-Revolutionary England* (London: Panther Books, 1969), pp. 15–30.

[29]Haller, *Foxe's Book of Martyrs,* pp. 35–50, 72–7.

[30]C. H. Garrett, *The Marian Exiles* (London: Cambridge University Press, 1938), pp. 32, 41–2.

[31]My statement is indebted to the analysis of Michael Walzer, *The Revolution of the Saints* (New York: Atheneum, 1970), pp. 96–100, 106, 108–9, and passim.

[32]Haller, *Foxe's Book of Martyrs,* pp. 85–6.

[33]Christopher Hill, *The Century of Revolution, 1603–1714* (New York: W. W. Norton, 1966), pp. 86–7. These problems are examined in detail in Hill, *Economic Problems of the Church* (London: Oxford University Press, 1956), part 2.

[34]Hill, *Reformation to Industrial Revolution,* p. 88.

[35]See Hill, *Puritanism and Revolution,* p. 56 and passim.

[36]William Haller, *Liberty and Reformation in the Puritan Revolution* (New York: Columbia University Press, 1955), pp. 11–13 and passim.

[37]Haller, *Foxe's Book of Martyrs,* p. 97.

[38]Hill, *Century of Revolution,* pp. 82–3.

[39]Paul S. Seaver, *The Puritan Lectureships, The Politics of Religious Dissent, 1560–1662* (Stanford: Stanford University Press, 1970), p. 22. Neither Anglicans nor Separatists gave such significance to lecturing, but for the main body of the clergy a lectureship became a regular phase of their career. See also ibid., pp. 36–54, for an assessment of the lay demand for lecturers.

[40]William Haller, *The Rise of Puritanism* (New York: Harper & Row, 1957), p. 154.

[41]The religious affiliations of lawyers in the Inns of Court reflected the vicissitudes of religious policy under Elizabeth and James I. See the detailed documentation in Wilfred R. Prest, *The Inns of Court under Elizabeth and the Early Stuarts* (London: Longman Group, 1972), chaps. 8–9.

[42]The distinction between law as "craft" and as "science" is developed in Max Weber, *Economy and Society,* II, pp. 784 ff. My references to English legal history are based on T. F. T. Plucknett, *A Concise History of the Common Law* (Boston: Little, Brown, 1956). For English legal education, see also Roscoe Pound, *The Lawyer from Antiquity to Modern Times* (St. Paul: West Publishing, 1953), chap. 4.

[43]Sir Charles Ogilvie, *The King's Government and the Common Law, 1471–1641* (Oxford: Basil Blackwell, 1958), p. 26.

[44]Ibid., p. 23. See also ibid., chapter 4, and Plucknett, *Concise History,* pp. 155–9, for discussions of the disappearance of equity from the common law.

[45]Ibid., pp. 176–8.

[46]See Ogilvie, *King's Government,* pp. 67–78.

[47]See Plucknett, *Concise History,* pp. 176–90, and Ogilvie, *King's Government,* pp. 79–97.

[48]I follow the interpretation of Donald W. Hanson, *From Kingdom to Commonwealth* (Cambridge: Harvard University Press, 1970).

[49]See ibid., pp. 281–308, and Hill, *Century of Revolution,* pp. 62–3.

[50]See Perez Zagorin, *The Court and the Country, The Beginning of the English Revolution* (New York: Atheneum, 1971), pp. 33–7. The quotation appears on p. 37.

[51]The following discussion is based on Zagorin's work. The points mentioned in the text and appropriate citations are found in ibid., pp. 75–83, 100–5, 90–9 of chap. 4.

[52] Hill, *Century of Revolution,* p. 45. See also Sir George Clark, *The Seventeenth Century* (London: Oxford University Press, 1960), pp. 85–90.

[53] Quoted in Hill, *Century of Revolution,* pp. 1–2. The statement by Sir Thomas Smith was quoted in this volume, Chapter 6, p. 212.

[54] See Haller, *Rise of Puritanism,* p. 12.

[55] The quotations from Calvin and Cartwright are taken from David Little, *Religion, Order and Law* (Oxford: Basil Blackwell, 1970), pp. 53, 86, 92. The present exposition follows Little's interpretation.

[56] See Patrick Collinson, *The Elizabethan Puritan Movement* (London: Jonathan Cape, 1967), p. 103.

[57] Statement by John Whitgift quoted in David Little, *Religion, Order and Law,* p. 146. See also pp. 135–147 for an exegesis of Whitgift's position.

[58] Here again practice would range widely between strict episcopal control, on the one hand, and control by the elders of the parishes concerned, on the other. See Collinson, *Elizabethan Puritan Movement,* pp. 101–8, 167–79, and passim for a detailed analysis of "prophesyings."

[59] Haller, *Liberty and Reformation in the Puritan Revolution,* pp. 195–7 and passim. My italics. The phrases from Baxter are quoted in Haller.

[60] See Hill, *Century of Revolution,* p. 131.

[61] Zagorin, *Court and Country,* p. 84.

[62] Ibid., pp. 85–90.

[63] See Hanson, *Kingdom to Commonwealth,* pp. 24–5 and passim, and Weber, *Economy and Society,* I, pp. 226 ff.

[64] This emphasis on the restoration of ancient purity has been stressed as a characteristic which distinguishes the revolutions of the sixteenth and seventeenth centuries from those of today. See J. H. Elliott, "Revolution and Continuity in Early Modern Europe," *Past and Present,* no. 42 (February 1969), pp. 35–6.

[65] Quoted in Little, *Religion, Order and Law,* p. 176. Unless otherwise noted, statements in quotation marks cited further on are quotations from Coke's writings referred to in ibid., pp. 176–89.

[66] This paragraph and the next are based on formulations by Sir John Davies, attorney general for Ireland (1612), and the discussion in J. G. A. Pocock, *The Ancient Constitution and the Feudal Law* (New York: W. W. Norton, 1967), pp. 32–5.

[67] Ibid., pp. 42, 54–5.

[68] Ibid., p. 51.

[69] Ibid., p. 49.

[70] Hill, *Century of Revolution,* p. 64.

[71] See William Holdsworth, *Essays in Law and History* (London: Oxford University Press, 1946), pp. 88–91.

[72] See Little, *Religion, Order and Law,* pp. 188–9.

[73] See J. R. Tanner, *English Constitutional Conflicts of the Seventeenth Century, 1603–1689* (London: Cambridge University Press, 1928), pp. 49, 63.

[74] Pocock, *Ancient Constitution,* p. 236. See also Tanner, *Constitutional Conflicts,* pp. 263–7 for an account of the constitutional debates between Tories and Whigs and pp. 294–6 for a summary of the theory of contract.

[75] See Little, *Religion, Order and Law,* pp. 189–217.

[76] Statement by George Hickes, Dean of Worcester, quoted in Richard B. Schlatter, *The Social Ideas of Religious Leaders, 1660–1688* (London: Oxford University Press, 1940), p. 109.

[77] A. S. P. Woodhouse, "Introduction," in A. S. P. Woodhouse, ed., *Puritanism and Liberty* (Chicago: University of Chicago Press, 1951), pp. 68, 81.

[78] As always, practice was more multifaceted than this paradoxical logic of the situation. For a survey of the different modes adopted, see Collinson, *Elizabethan Puritan Movement,* pp. 333–82 and passim.

[79] J. E. Neale, *Elizabeth I and her Parliaments, 1559–1581* (New York: St. Martin's Press, 1958), pp. 417–18 and passim.

CHAPTER X. TOWARD THE NATION STATE: FRANCE

[1] The origin of the name is uncertain. A Besançon Hugues (d. 1532) led the Genevan movement against annexation by Savoy. Huguenot may derive from a French contraction of that name with the Swiss word for *comrade* (*genoz*). According to another version, Huguenot is a nickname. The Protestants of Tour assembled by night near the gate of King Hugo, whom the people regarded as a spirit. In a sermon, a monk derided the Lutherans by saying that they ought to be called Huguenots, kinsmen of King Hugo, since they went out at night like that mythical spirit.

[2] See Herbert H. Rowen, "Louis XIV and Absolutism," in John C. Rule, ed., *Louis XIV and the Craft of Kingship* (Columbus: Ohio State University Press, 1969), pp. 302–16. See also note 8 here.

[3] In this discussion of seventeenth- and eighteenth-century France, I shall use the term *nobility* because the primary reference is to status. French nobles were illustrious by rank, title, or birth, but their share in government was diminishing during this period. For two accounts of the internal divisions of the nobility, cf. David Bitton, *The French Nobility in*

Crisis, 1560–1640 (Stanford: Stanford University Press, 1969), chap. 6, and John Lough, *An Introduction to Eighteenth-Century France* (London: Longman Group, 1960), chap. 3.

[4]See the case study of financiers by Julian Dent, *Crisis in Finance: Crown, Financiers and Society in Seventeenth-Century France* (New York: St. Martin's Press, 1973), especially chaps. 8–9.

[5]J. Michael Hayden, *France and the Estates General of 1614* (London: Cambridge University Press, 1974), p. 217.

[6]Pierre Goubert, *Louis XIV and Twenty Million Frenchmen* (New York: Random House, Vintage Books, 1970), p. 52.

[7]For further details on French historical demography and economic development, see Pierre Goubert, *The Ancient Regime, French Society, 1600–1750* (New York: Harper & Row, Harper Torchbooks, 1974), pp. 31–77.

[8]See Alexis de Tocqueville, *The Old Regime and the Revolution* (Garden City: Doubleday, Anchor Books, 1955), p. 51. See also Kurt Wolzendorff, *Der Polizeigedanke des modernen Staates* (vol. 35 of Abhandlungen aus dem Staats- und Verwaltungsrecht; Breslau: M. & H. Marcus, 1918), which describes Colbert's regulations in detail and tends to take them at their face value. Nevertheless, the ancien régime's ideology of total regulation was an important element of "modernization" in its own right. See the discussion by Marc Raeff, "The Well-Ordered Police State and the Development of Modernity in Seventeenth- and Eighteenth-Century Europe," *American Historical Review*, vol. 80 (December 1975), pp. 1221–43.

[9]John Lough, *An Introduction to Seventeenth-Century France* (London: Longman Group, 1969), pp. 123–6.

[10]This military reorganization was a European phenomenon. See Michael Roberts, "The Military Revolution, 1560–1660," in *Essays in Swedish History* (London: Weidenfeld & Nicolson, 1967), pp. 195–225.

[11]See Goubert, *Louis XIV*, pp. 116–124 and passim for the figures cited and for a characterization of Colbert's work.

[12]Ibid., pp. 86, 96.

[13]Ibid., pp. 85 ff., 228. The quotation appears on pp. 212–13.

[14]Ibid., p. 267. See pp. 137–9, 179–81, 276, 280–8, for the other points relating to Colbert's fiscal policies.

[15]Franklin L. Ford, *Robe and Sword* (New York: Harper & Row, Harper Torchbooks, 1965), pp. 27–9, 31–3, 53–4.

[16]Tocqueville, *Old Regime*, pp. 91–2.

[17]Ibid., pp. 42–3.

[18]Ford, *Robe and Sword*, pp. 13–14.

[19]See E. N. Williams, *The Ancien Régime in Europe, Government and Society in the Major States, 1648–1789* (Harmondsworth: Penguin, 1972), pp. 28, 167, 197, 210–11, 223. See the bibliography of this work for full references to the studies by Dietrich Gerhard, Martin Göhring, Jacob von Klaveren, K. W. Swart, and others dealing with the sale of offices and honors.

[20]See Ernest Barker, *The Development of Public Services in Western Europe, 1660–1930* (New York: Oxford University Press, 1944), pp. 6–12, and Alfred Cobban, "The Decline of Divine-Right Monarchy in France," in *The New Cambridge Modern History* (London: Cambridge University Press, 1966), VII, pp. 214–40.

[21]J. O. Lindsay, "Monarchy and Administration," in ibid., VII, p. 142. See also Fritz Hartung, "L'État, c'est moi," *Historische Zeitschrift*, vol. 169 (1949), pp. 1–30, for an analysis of the doctrine of kingship under Louis XIV.

[22]See Goubert, *Louis XIV*, pp. 305–6. The quotation from Turgot is taken from Douglas Dakin, *Turgot and the Ancien Régime in France* (London: Methuen, 1939), pp. 273–4. The whole *Mémoire* is translated in W. Walker Stephens, *The Life and Writings of Turgot* (London: Longmans, Green, 1895), pp. 265–72. Turgot's views coincide closely with those expressed in the article on "Representation" in vol. 14 (1765) of the *Encyclopédie*, which was probably written by Diderot. See text footnote g, this chapter, for details about this work.

[23]Tocqueville, *Old Regime*, p. 115.

[24]Ibid., p. 110.

[25]See Derek Jarrett, *The Begetters of Revolution* (London: Longman Group, 1973), chap. 1. The full quotation of Louis XIV's statement appears on p. 5.

[26]Ibid., pp. 33–6.

[27]A detailed analysis of different groups is contained in Lionel Rothkrug, *Opposition to Louis XIV, The Political and Social Origins of the French Enlightenment* (Princeton: Princeton University Press, 1965). The sense of relief following the death of Louis XIV is described in Bernard Fay, *Revolution and Freemasonry, 1680–1800* (Boston: Little, Brown, 1935), chap. 1.

[28]My presentation is indebted to Franco Venturi, *Utopia and Reform in the Enlightenment* (London: Cambridge University Press, 1971), pp. 43–6. The quotation in the text appears on p. 46.

[29]See Gabriel Bonno, *La Constitution britannique devant l'opinion française de Montesquieu à Bonaparte* (Paris: Librairie Ancienne Honoré Champion, 1932), pp. 7–8, 17. The following account is indebted to this study.

[30]Jarrett, *Begetters of Revolution*, pp. 20–3 and passim. The quotation appears on p. 21.

[31]The following account is based on Durand Echeverria, *Mirage in the West* (Princeton: Princeton University Press, 1957), chap. 1 and passim. It may be compared with the American reactions to France before and during the French revolution. See Howard

Mumford Jones, *America and French Culture, 1750–1848* (Chapel Hill: University of North Carolina Press, 1927), chap. 14.

[32]See Echeverria, *Mirage,* pp. 45–61, for an account of Franklin's influence.

[33]See, in addition to Bonno, *La Constitution britannique,* chap. 4, the study by Frances Acomb, *Anglophobia in France, 1763–1789* (Durham: Duke University Press, 1950), especially chap. 5.

[34]Tocqueville, *Old Regime,* p. 140. The last phrase is taken from p. 139.

[35]Ibid., p. 142.

[36]Voltaire, "Men of Letters," in Stephen J. Gendzier, ed., *Denis Diderot's The Encyclopedia* (New York: Harper & Row, Harper Torchbooks, 1967), p. 167. Hereafter cited as Gendzier, *Encyclopedia.*

[37]Quoted in John Lough, *Eighteenth-Century France,* pp. 266–7. See also Fritz Schalk, "Die Entstehung des schriftstellerischen Selbstbewusstseins in Frankreich," in *Einleitung in die Encyclopädie der Französischen Aufklärung* (vol. 6 of Münchener Romanistische Arbeiten; Munich: Max Hueber Verlag, 1936), pp. 45–65.

[38]See Lough, *Eighteenth-Century France,* chaps. 7–8.

[39]Quoted in Schalk, *Einleitung,* pp. 61–2.

[40]Robert Darnton, "The High Enlightenment and the Low-Life of Literature in Pre-Revolutionary France," *Past and Present,* no. 51 (May 1971), pp. 81–115. The quoted sentence is taken from Voltaire's article on "Taste" in the *Encyclopédie.* See also Robert Darnton, "Reading, Writing and Publishing in Eighteenth-Century France," *Daedalus,* winter 1971, pp. 214–56, for a critical survey of the evidence on literacy and the reading public.

[41]Goubert, *Louis XIV,* p. 279.

[42]See Alfred Cobban, "The Parlements of France in the Eighteenth Century," in his *Aspects of the French Revolution* (London: Paladin, 1971), pp. 72–3, and J. H. Shennan, *The Parlement of Paris* (London: Eyre & Spottiswoode, 1968), pp. 309–14.

[43]Cobban, *Aspects,* pp. 73–4.

[44]See R. R. Palmer, *The Age of the Democratic Revolution* (Princeton: Princeton University Press, 1959), I, p. 449, for the quotation in the text. See Jarrett, *Begetters of Revolution,* pp. 47–8; Cobban, *Aspects,* pp. 76–7; and Alfred Cobban, *A History of Modern France, 1715–1783* (Baltimore: Penguin, 1963), I, pp. 129–30, for related materials.

[45]See J. M. Roberts, *The Mythology of the Secret Societies* (London: Secker and Warburg, 1972), p. 165 and passim.

[46]The standard wording of the oath is quoted in Paul Hazard, *European Thought in the Eighteenth Century* (Harmondsworth: Penguin, 1965), p. 289.

[47]Quoted in James Anderson, *The Constitution of the Freemason* (1723) reprinted in Bernard Fay, *Revolution and Freemasonry,* p. 320.

[48] Ibid., pp. 320–1.

[49] See Eugen Lennhoff and Oskar Posner, *Internationales Freimaurerlexikon* (Munich: Amalthea Verlag, 1932), p. 28.

[50] Quoted from Hazard, *European Thought,* p. 291. See Reinhart Koselleck, *Kritik und Krise* (Freiburg: Verlag Karl Alber, 1959), pp. 58–61, who quotes this poem and whose analysis I follow at this point.

[51] Tocqueville, *The Old Regime,* p. 138. This description of French men of letters applies to members of Masonic lodges as well, for they were chosen for membership solely in terms of their education, moral principles, and good name. See Lennhoff and Posner, *Freimaurerlexikon,* p. 29, which gives J. G. Findel's (1828–1905) summary of the duties of the Freemason, formulated originally in Anderson's constitution of 1723.

[52] See the further discussion of this analogy in Koselleck, *Kritik und Krise,* pp. 81 ff.

[53] Quoted from d'Alembert's *Histoire des membres de l'Académie Française* in Darnton, "The High Enlightenment and the Low-Life of Literature," p. 91.

[54] See the account by Alfred Cobban, "The Parlements of France," in *Aspects,* pp. 68–82.

[55] Palmer, *Age of Democratic Revolution,* I, p. 473.

[56] Ibid., I, pp. 475–6. See Eberhard Schmitt, *Repräsentation und Revolution* (Munich: C. H. Beck, 1969), pp. 89–113, for an analysis of the emerging role of the parlements as a national representative body.

[57] Quoted from *Mémoire sur les municipalités* in Stephens, *Life and Writings of Turgot,* p. 266.

[58] See article on "natural equality" in Gendzier, *Encyclopedia,* p. 170.

[59] Quoted from a statement in 1789 of the Abbé Sieyès in G. G. van Duesen, *E. J. Sieyès: His Life and Nationalism* (New York: Columbia University Press, 1932), p. 82, n. 27.

[60] Emmanuel Joseph Sieyès, *What Is the Third Estate?* (New York: Praeger, 1963), p. 101. The points mentioned in the text appear on pp. 99–105.

[61] See Palmer, *Age of Democratic Revolution,* I, pp. 472–4, who uses these phrases in characterizing the revolutionary psychology of the period.

[62] Sieyès, *What Is the Third Estate?,* pp. 57–9, 62–4, 161–2, 164–5.

[63] See Gendzier, *Encyclopedia,* pp. 185, 187–8, for the text of Diderot's statement. In Jaucourt's article on "Sovereignty," the censor deleted a sentence stating that the goal of sovereignty is the happiness of the governed and that when this is forgotten the resulting government ceases to be legitimate. See Douglas H. Gordon and Norman L. Torrey, *The Censoring of Diderot's Encyclopédie* (New York: Columbia University Press, 1947), p. 57. A review of the attacks on Diderot's article is contained in John Lough, *Essays on the Encyclopédie of Diderot and d'Alembert* (London: Oxford University Press, 1968), pp. 440–62.

[64]Sieyès, *What Is the Third Estate?*, p. 78, 145, 164–5. Much the same identification of popular sovereignty with virtue animated Robespierre. See Alfred Cobban, "The Fundamental Ideas of Robespierre," in *Aspects*, pp. 137–58.

[65]Sieyès, *What Is the Third Estate?*, pp. 124–6.

[66]Ibid., pp. 124–5, 130–1, 146–9.

[67]Ibid., pp. 79–80.

[68]This discussion is indebted to Bernhard Groethuysen, *Philosophie de la Révolution Française* (Paris: Librairie Gallimard, 1956), pp. 219 ff.

[69]From points 4, 5, and 6 of the *Declaration of the Rights of Man and Citizen* (August 17, 1789) reprinted in J. H. Stewart, ed., *A Documentary Survey of the French Revolution* (New York: Macmillan, 1965), p. 114.

[70]See Karl Löwenstein, *Volk und Parlament nach der Staatstheorie der französischen Nationalversammlung von 1789* (Munich: Drei Masken Verlag, 1922), pp. 10–38, for an analysis of Sieyès's ideas which differentiates between his earlier and later positions. The summary statement in the text describes the latter, which achieved dominant influence in the National Assembly. Löwenstein's book was republished in 1964 by Scientia Verlag Aalen.

[71]Quoted in Heinz Kläy, *Zensuswahlrecht und Gleichheitsprinzip* (vol. 19 of Berner Untersuchungen zur Allgemeinen Geschichte; Aarau: Verlag H. R. Sauerländer, 1956), p. 107.

[72]See ibid., pp. 74–8, 108–11.

[73]Peter Campbell, *French Electoral Systems and Elections since 1789* (London: Faber & Faber, 1958), p. 17 and passim.

[74]An illuminating discussion of this process is contained in Otto Gierke, *Das Deutsche Genossenschaftsrecht* (Berlin: Weidmannsche Buchhandlung, 1881), III, pp. 763 ff. I do not know of a comparably detailed analysis with regard to France.

[75]See La Chalotais, "Essay on National Education," in F. de la Fontainerie, ed., *French Liberalism and Education in the Eighteenth Century* (New York: McGraw-Hill, 1932), pp. 52–3.

[76]See Sieyès, *What Is the Third Estate?*, p. 159. See also Roger Hahn, *The Anatomy of a Scientific Institution* (Berkeley and Los Angeles: University of California Press, 1971), p. 230 and passim.

[77]Quoted in International Labour Office, *Freedom of Associations* (ILO Studies and Reports, series A, no. 28; London: P. S. King & Son, 1928), XXIX, p. 89.

[78]Quoted in Zosa Szajkowski, *Jews and the French Revolutions of 1789, 1830, and 1848* (New York: KATV Publishing House, 1970), p. 359, n. 4. Cf. Arthur Hertzberg, *The French Enlightenment and the Jews* (New York: Schocken Books, 1970) for a comprehensive treatment.

[79]Quoted in ibid., p. 578.

[80]Quoted in ibid., pp. 584–5.

[81]See Georges Lefebvre, *The French Revolution from Its Origins to 1793* (New York: Columbia University Press, 1962), pp. 163–4 and passim.

[82]See Jean Brissaud, *A History of French Private Law* (Continental Legal History Series; Boston: Little, Brown, 1912), pp. 166, 150–1, 230–1, and passim.

[83]H. A. L. Fisher, "The Codes," *The Cambridge Modern History* (London: Cambridge University Press, 1906), IX, p. 148.

[84]John McManners, *The French Revolution and the Church* (New York: Harper & Row, Harper Torchbooks, 1969), pp. 29–31.

CHAPTER XI. NATION-BUILDING: GERMANY

[1]These summary figures are based on W. H. Bruford, *Germany in the Eighteenth Century* (London: Cambridge University Press, 1959), pp. 333–6. The actual number of sovereign territories and jurisdictions is larger and more complex. The following sketch of the "Holy Roman Empire" is derived from Klaus Epstein, *The Genesis of German Conservatism* (Princeton: Princeton University Press, 1966), pp. 238–44, and Karl Biedermann, *Deutschland im Achtzehnten Jahrhundert* (Leipzig: J. J. Weber, 1880), I, pp. 14–71. My interpretation is indebted to the study of Mack Walker cited in footnote 2. The description of the empire is confined to the eighteenth century. Before that time the number of territorial jurisdictions was larger and imperial institutions not as moribund. For a recent study of these earlier conditions, see G. Benecke, *Society and Politics in Germany, 1500–1750* (Toronto: Toronto University Press, 1974), p. 161 and passim.

[2]See Mack Walker, *German Home Towns—Community, State, and General Estate, 1648–1871* (Ithaca: Cornell University Press, 1971), pp. 27–33. I have adopted Mack Walker's term *hometown,* which refers to the German *Kleinstadt,* but have made it into one word to distinguish it from the American "home town," which has quite different connotations.

[3]Ibid., pp. 16–17.

[4]Ibid., pp. 56–67. Quotation marks have been added.

[5]Ibid., pp. 139–40.

[6]An analysis of this growing cleavage is contained in Christopher R. Friedrichs, "Capitalism, Mobility and Class Formation in the Early Modern German City," *Past and Present,* no. 69 (November 1975), pp. 24–49.

[7]See the analysis of the thought of Justus Möser in Epstein, *German Conservatism,* chap. 6.

[8]See Reinhart Koselleck, *Preussen zwischen Reform und Revolution* (Stuttgart: Ernst Klett Verlag, 1967), pp. 37–8 and passim. For a case study of state support as well as regulation of guilds and corporations in the very center of Prussian rule, see Frederick Marquardt, "The Manual Workers in Berlin under the Old Regime" (Ph.D. dissertation, University of California, Berkeley, 1973).

[9]See Epstein, *German Conservatism*, pp. 616–26, for details. Chapters 12 and 13 of Epstein's book provide a convenient summary of the Napoleonic era in Germany.

[10]See Biedermann, *Deutschland*, I, pp. 273–315; Hajo Holborn, *A History of Modern Germany* (New York: Knopf, 1969), pp. 10–11; and W. O. Henderson, *The Zollverein* (London: Cambridge University Press, 1939), pp. 47, 170, 256–9, 267–71.

[11]See J. P. Eckermann, *Gespräche mit Goethe* (Wiesbaden: Insel Verlag, 1955), pp. 629–30. The date is October 23, 1828.

[12]J. F. Bosher has documented that in eighteenth-century France the private appropriation of offices should be considered a case of "capitalist entrepreneurship" rather than of bureaucracy. In his view, bureaucracy properly so-called is a by-product of the French revolution. See J. F. Bosher, *The Single Duty Project* (London: Athlone Press, 1964), pp. 169–70 and passim, and *French Finances, 1770–1795* (London: Cambridge University Press, 1970), chap. 15. Hans Rosenberg's study of Prussian bureaucracy (cited in note 15) shows some similar conditions, but a comparison with German officialdom in all its diversity remains still to be written.

[13]Biedermann, *Deutschland*, I, pp. 100–2. In the ducal residence of Saxony-Weimar, all civil servants and military and court personnel made up a fifth of the town's adult male population in 1699 and a quarter in 1820. See Hans Eberhardt, *Goethes Umwelt* (Weimar: Hermann Böhlau, 1951), pp. 26–7.

[14]Membership of the Paulskirche is tabulated in Gerhard Schilfert, *Sieg und Niederlage des demokratischen Wahlrechts in der deutschen Revolution* (Berlin: Ruetten & Loenig, 1952), p. 406. The author classifies the first group as a "civil service intelligentsia" (*beamtete Intelligenz*) as distinguished from the "free intelligentsia."

[15]Even in Prussia it was an uphill struggle. For a description of Prussian officialdom in the eighteenth century which emphasizes corruption, nepotism, indolence, and all the other negative attributes of bureaucracy, see Hans Rosenberg, *Bureaucracy, Aristocracy and Autocracy* (Cambridge: Harvard University Press, 1958), chaps. 2–4. However, Rosenberg also shows the emergence of "public law" and the merit system.

[16]Figures on student enrollments in the eighteenth century are beset with difficulties spelled out in a study by Franz Eulenburg. Eulenburg attributes the decline after 1755 to three factors: the gradual increase of economic activities, the greater attraction of a military career for members of the aristocracy, and the improvement of secondary education together with the prolongation of academic studies (all deterrents to university study). See Franz Eulenburg, *Die Frequenz der deutschen Universitäten* (vol. 24 of Abhandlungen der Philologisch-Historischen Klasse der Königl. Sächsischen Gesellschaft der Wissenschaften; Leipzig: B. G. Teubner, 1904), pp. 131–9 and passim. See also Hans Waldeyer, "Zur Entstehung der Realschulen in Preussen im 18. Jahrhundert," in Klaus Hartmann et al., eds., *Schule und Staat im 18. und 19. Jahrhundert* (Frankfurt: Suhrkamp Verlag, 1974), pp. 146–70. A useful collection of data on literacy, reading, and degrees of schooling in the eighteenth century is contained in Rolf Engelsing, *Analphabetentum und Lektüre* (Stuttgart: J. B. Metzlersche Verlagsbuchhandlung, 1973), chaps. 11–12.

[17]Biedermann, *Deutschland*, I, pp. 144–5.

[18]The details of fiction and the reading public in eighteenth-century Germany have been analyzed by Albert Ward, *Book Production, Fiction and the German Reading Public, 1740–1800* (London: Oxford University Press, 1974).

[19]See ibid., pp. 87–8, for a compilation of these estimates.

[20]Data in the preceding paragraphs are derived from Johannes Goldfriedrich, *Geschichte des deutschen Buchhandels* (Leipzig: Verlag des Börsenvereins der Deutschen Buchhändler, 1909), III, chaps. 5 and 9, and Joachim Kirchner, *Das Deutsche Zeitschriftenwesen* (Wiesbaden: Otto Harrassowitz, 1958), I, pp. 115–18.

[21]Goethe was a conservative who opposed only some inconveniences of Germany's political fragmentation which from a cultural standpoint had brought many benefits. Also, he felt personally indebted for assistance and largesse to the benevolence of "his very own" ruler. For his attitude toward Grand Duke Carl August, see no. 34*b* of his Venetian epigrams in *Sämtliche Werke* (Zurich: Artemis Verlag, 1950), I, p. 229. The opening line reads "Klein ist unter den Fürsten Germaniens freilich der meine. . . ."

[22]Quoted in Hans-Georg Hass, ed., *Sturm und Drang* (Munich: C. H. Beck'sche Verlagsbuchhandlung, 1966), II, p. 1545. Goethe's and Hölderlin's attitudes toward the French revolution are examined by Claude David and Lawrence Ryan in Richard Brinkmann et al., *Deutsche Literatur und Französische Revolution* (Göttingen: Vandenhoeck & Ruprecht, 1974), pp. 63–86, 129–48.

[23]Biedermann, *Deutschland,* I, note, p. 285.

[24]Quoted from K. Fr. von Moser, *Der Herr und der Diener* (1759), in ibid., II, part 1, p. 101.

[25]This description of the French fashion in Germany is indebted to Biedermann, *Deutschland,* II, part 1, pp. 54–176. For a modern characterization on which I have drawn as well, see Adrien Fauchier-Magnan, *The Small German Courts in the Eighteenth Century* (London: Methuen, 1958).

[26]Quoted in Jürgen Habermas, *Strukturwandel der Öffentlichkeit* (Neuwied: Hermann Luchterhand, 1962), p. 38.

[27]Quoted from K. Fr. von Moser, *Vom Nationalgeist* (1766) in Biedermann, *Deutschland,* I, p. 158.

[28]See Hermann Waetjen, *Die erste Englische Revolution und die öffentliche Meinung in Deutschland* (dissertation, Heidelberg University; Heidelberg: Carl Winter's Universitätsbuchhandlung, 1900), passim, and Franz Muncker, *Anschauungen vom englischen Staat und Volk* (Sitzungsberichte der Königlich Bayerischen Akademie der Wissenschaften; Munich: G. Franzsche Verlag, 1918), pp. 27 ff.

[29]The Moral Weeklies were notably absent from the southwestern parts of Germany. See Wolfgang Martens, *Die Botschaft der Tugend* (Stuttgart: J. B. Metzlersche Verlagsbuchhandlung, 1968), pp. 108–23, 161–7. Martens considers the influence of English weeklies like the *Spectator* significant, but that influence is minimized in Hans M. Wolff, *Die Weltanschauung der deutschen Aufklärung* (Bern: A. Francke Verlag, 1949), chap. 3.

[30]My characterization is based on Martens, *Botschaft.* The quotation from the *Patriot* appears in ibid., pp. 146–7.

[31]Ibid., pp. 141–61. See also ibid., pp. 370–403, for a more detailed analysis of attitudes toward the aristocracy and the lower classes, as expressed in the Moral Weeklies.

[32]The Moral Weeklies expressed much moral indignation about aristocratic arrogance and about the hard drinking and loose living, the debts and lack of culture, the obsession with horses, dogs, and the hunt which characterized many aristocrats. For examples of these critiques of the courts, in addition to Martens, see Biedermann, *Deutschland,* I, pp. 152–7. The quotation defining the nonpolitical attitude of educated commoners is taken from *Der Alte Deutsche* (1730) in Martens, *Botschaft,* p. 334.

[33]The writings of Balthasar Gracian were cited earlier as an example of this literature. See Chapter 7, footnote 23.

[34]Quoted from *Der Mensch* (1751–1756) in Martens, *Botschaft,* pp. 349–50.

[35]Ibid., p. 353. I return to this universalist aspect of the Enlightenment further on.

[36]For an analysis of Goethe's many-sided attitude toward his hero, Wilhelm Meister, see W. H. Bruford, *The German Tradition of Self-Cultivation* (London: Cambridge University Press, 1975), chaps. 2 and 4. The quotation in the text is taken from [*Goethe's*] *Wilhelm Meister, Apprenticeship and Travels* (tr. by R. O. Moon; London: G. T. Foulis, 1947), I, pp. 250–1.

[37]For a succinct statement of this interpretation and supporting documentation, see Fritz Brüggemann, "Der Kampf um die bürgerliche Welt- und Lebensanschauung in der deutschen Literatur des 18. Jahrhunderts," *Deutsche Vierteljahrsschrift für Literaturwissenschaft und Geistesgeschichte,* III (1925), pp. 94–127. See also the discussion in Roy Pascal, *The German Sturm und Drang* (Manchester: Manchester University Press, 1959), chap. 3 and passim.

[38]Quoted from Hass, ed., *Sturm und Drang,* II, pp. 1537–8.

[39]See ibid., p. 1539, and Friedrich Schiller, *On the Aesthetic Education of Man* (tr. by E. Wilkinson and L. Willoughby; Oxford: Clarendon Press, 1967), pp. 30–43. Schiller's position may be contrasted to that of Wieland; see Bernd Weyergraf, *Der skeptische Bürger, Wielands Schriften zur französischen Revolution* (Stuttgart: J. B. Metzlersche Verlagsbuchhandlung, 1972).

[40]See the letter to Duke Augustenburg in Hass, ed., *Sturm und Drang,* pp. 1541–2.

[41]Friedrich Schiller, *Werke* (Weimar: Hermann Böhlaus Nachfolger, 1958), XXII, p. 248. The passage occurs in a review article on the poems of G. A. Bürger. Note how close Schiller's position is to the precept of the Hamburg *Patriot,* "Neither too bad or vulgar for the scholar, nor too lofty and incomprehensible for the unlearned"—a similarity which can be noted without minimizing the difference in cultural level.

[42]See the instructive articles by Gordon Craig, "Friedrich Schiller and the Problems of Power," in Leonard Krieger and Fritz Stern, eds., *The Responsibility of Power* (Historical Essays in Honor of Hajo Holborn; Garden City: Doubleday, Anchor Books, 1969), pp. 135–56, and "Friedrich Schiller and the Police," in *Proceedings of the American Philosophical Society,* vol. 112 (December 1968), pp. 367–70. Schiller's realism is recognized even in the Marxist view that Schiller's work represents a retreat from politics into a timeless realm of beauty. See Georg Lukacs, *Goethe und seine Zeit* (Bern: A. Francke Verlag, 1947), pp. 106–9.

[43] See the prepublication announcement of his journal, *Die Horen* (1794), in Schiller, *Werke*, XXII, p. 106.

[44] See J. W. Goethe, *Sämtliche Werke* (Zurich: Artemis Verlag, 1953), II, p. 485 (from the *Xenien* of Goethe and Schiller).

[45] For the quotations from Humboldt and Wolf, see Friedrich Paulsen, *Geschichte des gelehrten Unterrichts* (2nd ed.; Leipzig: Veit, 1897), II, p. 200.

[46] Goethe, *Werke*, I, p. 234 (epigram 58).

[47] For a characterization of this reform conservatism within the whole range of conservative reactions, see the excellent and comprehensive study by Epstein, *German Conservatism*, chap. 2 and passim. Epstein emphasizes that reform conservatism antedated the French revolution.

[48] See the analysis of democratic and socialist stirrings in Germany in Fritz Valjavec, *Die Entstehung der politischen Strömungen in Deutschland, 1770–1815* (Munich: R. Oldenbourg, 1951), pp. 180–228. The full range of German responses to the revolution has been studied a number of times. In addition to Epstein and Valjavec, see Alfred Stern, *Der Einfluss der Französischen Revolution auf das deutsche Geistesleben* (Stuttgart: J. G. Cotta'sche Buchhandlung, 1928), which deals with the intellectual elite, and Jacques Droz, *L'Allemagne et la révolution française* (Paris: 1949), which deals with the elite as well as with regional variations in response. Among the earlier studies of this topic in addition to those by Karl Biedermann, mention should be made of Woldemar Wenck, *Deutschland vor hundert Jahren* (Leipzig: Verlag F. W. Grunow, 1887, 1890), especially vol. 2 because of its ample use of fugitive contemporary sources.

[49] Quoted in Wenck, *Deutschland,* I, pp. 202–4.

[50] Valjavec, *Entstehung,* pp. 146–79, 244–54. See also Robert Elsasser, *Über die politischen Bildungsreisen der Deutschen nach England* (vol. 51 of Heidelberger Abhandlungen zur mittleren und neueren Geschichte; Heidelberg: Carl Winters Universitätsbuchhandlung, 1917), chap. 4.

[51] See the instructive article by Rudolf Stadelmann, "Deutschland und die westeuropäischen Revolutionen," in *Deutschland und Westeuropa* (Schloss Laupheim: Ulrich Steiner Verlag, 1948), p. 22. For a more differentiated analysis of this political consensus, see Rudolf Vierhaus, "Politisches Bewusstsein in Deutschland vor 1789," *Der Staat,* vol. 6 (1967), pp. 175–96.

[52] Quoted in ibid., p. 184.

[53] Both statements by Struensee are quoted in Epstein, *German Conservatism,* pp. 391–2.

[54] Eckermann, *Gespräche mit Goethe,* pp. 493–4. The conversation is dated January 4, 1824.

[55] See the conversation of April 27, 1825 in ibid., pp. 518–19.

[56] Goethe, "Literarischer Sansculottismus (1795)," *Werke,* XIV, pp. 182–3.

[57]The statement by Frederick William I is quoted in Otto Hintze, *Die Behördenorganisation und die allgemeine Staatsverwaltung Preussens im 18. Jahrhundert* (vol. 6 of Acta Borussica; Berlin: Paul Parey, 1901), p. 277. For a vivid description of the interaction between personal autocracy and evasive officials, see Walter Dorn, "The Prussian Bureaucracy in the Eighteenth Century," *Political Science Quarterly*, vol. 46 (1931), pp. 403–23.

[58]Gustav Schmoller, *Umrisse und Untersuchungen zur Verfassungs-, Verwaltungs- und Wirtschaftsgeschichte* (Leipzig: Duncker und Humboldt, 1898), pp. 138, 166, 180.

[59]See Hintze, *Behördenorganisation,* pp. 276–88.

[60]See Rosenberg, *Bureaucracy, Aristocracy and Autocracy,* pp. 159–65, for details of personnel practices under Frederick II.

[61]Ibid., pp. 175–82, 190–l.

[62]*Hegel's Philosophy of Right* (tr. and ed. by T. M. Knox; London: Oxford University Press, 1952), p. 193.

[63]See Hans Gerth, *Die sozialgeschichtliche Lage der bürgerlichen Intelligenz um die Wende des 18. Jahrhunderts* (Ph.D. dissertation, University of Frankfurt; Berlin: VDI-Verlag, 1935), pp. 110–13.

[64]See Paulsen, *Geschichte des gelehrten Unterrichts,* II, pp. 124–7 and passim.

[65]The details of this growing interest in Adam Smith among higher civil servants are set out in Wilhelm Treue, "Adam Smith in Deutschland," in Werner Conze, ed., *Deutschland und Europa* (Festschrift für Hans Rothfels; Düsseldorf: Droste Verlag, 1951), pp. 101–33.

[66]Johanna Schultze, *Die Auseinandersetzung zwischen Adel und Bürgertum in den deutschen Zeitschriften, 1773–1806* (vol. 163 of *Historische Studien*; Berlin: Verlag Emil Ebering, 1925), p. 27. In the 1780s thirteen new journals were founded while four were discontinued, and in the 1790s nine new journals were founded but seventeen were discontinued. Censorship became more severe after the French revolution.

[67]See ibid., pp. 16–18, 36–40, for biographical data on the contributors to these sociopolitical journals.

[68]For a vivid description of this scene, see Wilhelm Dilthey, *Leben Schleiermachers* (2nd ed.; Berlin: Walter de Gruyter, 1922), pp. 218–19.

[69]Carl Gottlieb Svarez (1746–1798) prepared the General Legal Code (Allgemeine Landrecht) of 1794 and Klein was his assistant. For a description of the Mittwochsgesellschaft and an example of its debates, see Adolf Stölzel, "Die Berliner Mittwochgesellschaft über Aufhebung oder Reform der Universitäten (1795)," *Forschungen zur Brandenburgischen und Preussischen Geschichte*, II (1889), pp. 201–22.

[70]Knox, ed., *Hegel's Philosophy of Right,* p. 291.

[71]Ibid., p. 193. The most telling passage which describes and to an extent endorses the principle of a free market is found in ibid., p. 268 (addition no. 120 to §189).

[72]Cf. the provisions of the code in G. A. Grotefend, ed., *Das Allgemeine Preussische Landrecht* (Düsseldorf: L. Schumann'sche Verlagsbuchhandlung, 1897), part 2, title 10, especially nos. 94–102, with Hermann Conrad and Gerd Kleinheyer, eds., *Vorträge über Recht und Staat von C. G. Svarez* (Cologne: Westdeutscher Verlag, 1960), pp. 61–2. Svarez and his colleagues did achieve the permanent tenure of judges, however. See part 2, title 17, no. 99 of the *Allgemeine Landrecht*. For the further development of the legal position of civil servants, see the summary by Otto Hintze, "Der Beamtenstand," in *Soziologie und Geschichte* (Göttingen: Vandenhoeck & Ruprecht, 1964), pp. 91–4 and passim.

[73]See Hildegard Pischke, *Die englische Industrierevolution im Spiegel der deutschen Reisebeschreibungen, 1780–1825* (Ph.D. dissertation, University of Breslau; Grone: August Schoenhuette, 1935) and W. O. Henderson, *Britain and Industrial Europe* (London: Leicester University Press, 1965), pp. 139–66. On the contrast between German idealism and specialization, see the instructive summary by Roy Pascal, "'Bildung' and the Division of Labour," in *German Studies Presented to W. H. Bruford* (London: George S. Harrap, 1962), pp. 14–28.

[74]Leonard Krieger, *The German Idea of Freedom* (Boston: Beacon Press, 1957), p. 144.

[75]From Hardenberg's Riga Memorial of 1807 reprinted in Georg Winter, ed., *Die Reorganisation des Preussischen Staates unter Stein und Hardenberg* (Publikationen aus den Preussischen Staatsarchiven, vol. 93; Leipzig: S. Hirzel, 1931), pp. 305–6.

[76]My summary statement on Stein, Hardenberg, and Humboldt is based on Krieger, *German Idea of Freedom*, pp. 147–73.

[77]For a vivid description of these conditions and reactions, see Peter G. Thielen, *Karl August von Hardenberg, 1750–1822* (Cologne: Grote'sche Verlagsbuchhandlung, 1967), pp. 35–6, 59–60, and passim.

[78]See Ernst Klein, *Von der Reform zur Restauration* (vol. 16 of Veröffentlichungen der Historischen Kommission zu Berlin; Berlin: Walter de Gruyter, 1965), pp. 169–208.

[79]A detailed account is readily available in Ernst Rudolf Huber, *Deutsche Verfassungsgeschichte seit 1789* (Stuttgart: W. Kohlhammer Verlag, 1957), I, passim.

[80]See Hajo Holborn, *A History of Modern Germany, 1648–1840* (New York: Knopf, 1968), II, p. 407.

[81]Ibid., p. 409.

[82]Max Weber, *Die Verhältnisse der Landarbeiter im ostelbischen Deutschland* (vol. 55 of Schriften des Vereins fuer Sozialpolitik; Berlin: Duncker & Humblot, 1892), p. 797.

[83]These rules applied only to the old Prussian territories; restrictions continued until 1845 in the territories acquired after 1815. See Huber, *Verfassungsgeschichte*, I, pp. 207–8.

[84]See Theodore S. Hamerow, *Restoration, Revolution, Reaction, Economics and Politics in Germany, 1815–1871* (Princeton: Princeton University Press, 1966), pp. 32, 36, and passim; also Marquardt, "Manual Workers in Berlin," chap. 3.

[85]See Hamerow, *Restoration*, p. 33, for an example of armed attacks in 1832 by the populace of Hesse-Kassel on toll houses as the detested symbol of the customs union.

[86]This other side of German liberalism is examined in Donald G. Rohr, *The Origins of Social Liberalism in Germany* (Chicago: University of Chicago Press, 1963), pp. 102 ff.

[87]Quoted in Huber, *Verfassungsgeschichte*, I, p. 703.

[88]See ibid., I, pp. 696–765, for a detailed account of German national and liberal agitation and of the conservative reaction under the Karlsbad edicts.

[89]Ibid., I, pp. 310–13.

[90]Ibid., I, pp. 168–72.

[91]A characteristic feature of this period was the merger between the ideals of Bildung and every citizen's duty to serve his country in war—a blending that for a time animated the efforts of Prussia's foremost military reformers. See Heinz Stubig, *Armee und Nation, Die pädagogischpolitischen Motive der preussischen Heeresreform 1807–1814* (Frankfurt: Verlag Peter Lang, 1971), especially chaps. 2 and 7.

[92]Knox, ed., *Hegel's Philosophy of Right*, p. 193.

[93]Quoted in Reinhart Koselleck, *Preussen zwischen Reform und Reaktion*, p. 413. See also ibid., p. 408, for the earlier quotation from the secret ordinance of 1826. My discussion is indebted to this detailed study, especially pp. 337–447. The changing subculture of the Prussian civil service during this period is examined in John R. Gillis, *The Prussian Bureaucracy in Crisis, 1840–1860* (Stanford: Stanford University Press, 1971).

[94]The total proportion of civil servants and free professionals was 82.5 percent, but since a good many civil servants were of aristocratic origin the exact percentage of educated commoners among the Paulskirche delegates is uncertain. See Schilfert, *Sieg und Niederlage des demokratischen Wahlrechts*, p. 405, for the source of these figures.

[95]Huber, *Verfassungsgeschichte*, II, p. 579.

[96]See ibid., II, pp. 751 ff.; III, pp. 35–62, 85–112.

CHAPTER XII. NATION-BUILDING: JAPAN

[1]John W. Hall, *Japan from Prehistory to Modern Times* (New York: Dell, Delta Books, 1971), p. 165; hereafter cited as Hall, *Japan*. See also John W. Hall, *Japanese History* (publication no. 34, Service Center for Teachers of History; Washington, D.C.: American Historical Association, 1961), pp. 37–9.

[2]G. B. Sansom, *The Western World and Japan* (New York: Random House, Vintage Books, 1973), p. 229. The book was originally published in 1949.

[3]A comparison and contrast between Japan and Prussia is contained in Reinhard Bendix, *Nation-Building and Citizenship* (2nd ed.; Berkeley and Los Angeles: University of California Press, 1977), chap. 6.

[4]For a detailed tabulation of most holdings in 1598 and 1602, see George Sansom, *A History of Japan* (London: Cresset Press, 1961), II, pp. 3–4, 413–16. A convenient map showing the central location of Tokugawa domains in 1664 is found in Conrad Totman,

Politics of the Tokugawa Bakufu (Cambridge: Harvard University Press, 1967), p. 71. The figures in the text are taken from John W. Hall, *Land and Government in Medieval Japan* (Stanford: Stanford University Press, 1966), pp. 333, 342, 355; and John K. Fairbank, Edwin O. Reischauer, and Albert M. Craig, *East Asia, Tradition and Transformation* (Boston: Houghton, Mifflin, 1973), pp. 400–1.

[5] Hall, *Japan,* p. 172. My sketch of Tokugawa institutions is indebted to this work for its concise summary of recent research.

[6] The details of this system are described in Toshio G. Teukahira, *Feudal Control in Tokugawa Japan* (Cambridge: Harvard University Press, Harvard East Asian Monographs, 1966). The author shows (pp. 98–100) that five tozama and five fudai domains spent between 71 and 81 percent of their annual cash expenditures on costs relating to the sankin-kotai system. The resulting indebtedness of the han was a means of political control, as well as a stimulant to economic growth. For a statement of this "sankin-kotai theory," see Albert M. Craig, *Choshu in the Meiji Restoration* (Cambridge: Harvard University Press, 1967), pp. 27–9 and passim.

[7] See Sansom, *Western World and Japan,* pp. 181–4.

[8] H. D. Harootunian, *Toward Restoration* (Berkeley and Los Angeles: University of California Press, 1970), pp. 13–14.

[9] See Quincy Wright, *A Study of War* (Chicago: University of Chicago Press, 1965), p. 653.

[10] See Fairbank et al., *East Asia,* pp. 406, 417.

[11] Hall, *Japan,* p. 177.

[12] Ibid., p. 178.

[13] See Sansom, *History of Japan,* III, pp. 111–13. His estimates of the urban population are based on the assumption of urban residents as 10 percent of the assessed value of the domain in which the castle towns were located. In another estimate, Hall (*Japan,* p. 210) states that by the eighteenth century urban growth had assumed astounding proportions. By then, Edo may have had 1 million inhabitants, and for the country as a whole perhaps 10 percent of the people lived in cities of over 10,000 population. For the estimate of the proportion of urban residents who were samurai, see John W. Hall, "The Castle Town and Japan's Modern Urbanization," *Far Eastern Quarterly,* vol. 15 (1955), p. 46. Urban growth was not continuous throughout the Tokugawa period, especially in the numerous provincial towns whose population became stationary or declined as commercial and industrial employments increased in the surrounding countryside. For an analysis of this process, see Thomas C. Smith, "Pre-Modern Economic Growth: Japan and the West," *Past and Present,* no. 60 (August 1973), pp. 127–60.

[14] Hall, "Castle Town," p. 52. For the ronin, see Sansom, *History of Japan,* III, pp. 32–4, 54–8, who states that by 1651 measures were taken to alleviate the condition and that by the end of the century the number of ronin was small. Still, the ronin were a continuous concern because the men under arms in the Bakufu domains were a relatively small force, and the number of impoverished samurai was considerable. Craig (*Choshu,* p. 16) estimates the size of the Tokugawa military force as between 20,000 and 30,000. The number of urbanized samurai may have been over 1 million. This educated guess follows

if some 50 percent of the urban population consisted of samurai and the urban population is put at 2 million in a total population of 20 million. For two large and two small han, Craig (*Choshu*, pp. 14–15) gives the actual number of samurai, both above and below the number assigned officially.

[15]Sansom (*History of Japan*, III, p. 51) states that by 1660 most daimyo had implemented the shogunal edict demanding that samurai live in the castle towns on their stipends. By contrast, Craig (*Choshu*, p. 14) states that in Satsuma, Choshu, and presumably elsewhere it was not financially feasible for the daimyo to support all their samurai as castle town residents.

[16]See Craig, *Choshu*, pp. 39–46.

[17]Sansom, *Western World and Japan*, pp. 184, 187–93.

[18]Donald Keene, *The Japanese Discovery of Europe, 1720–1830* (Stanford: Stanford University Press, 1969), pp. 96–7.

[19]The main points in this and the following summary description of economic conditions are taken from Sansom, *Western World and Japan*, pp. 223–43; Sansom, *History of Japan*, III, passim; and Hall, *Japan*, pp. 199–213.

[20]For details, see Hugh Borton, "Peasant Uprisings in Japan of the Tokugawa Period," *Transactions of the Asiatic Society of Japan*, 2nd ser., vol. 16 (1938), pp. 1–219. The transformation of the village is analyzed in Thomas C. Smith, *The Agrarian Origins of Modern Japan* (Stanford: Stanford University Press, 1959).

[21]Quoted in Keene, *Japanese Discovery*, p. 42.

[22]See Ronald Dore, *Education in Tokugawa Japan* (Berkeley and Los Angeles: University of California Press, 1965).

[23]See Sansom, *Western World and Japan*, p. 240. Even these methods were insufficient and the shogunate resorted frequently to debasement of the coinage, reaping large but temporary profits and placing additional burdens especially on merchants and peasants.

[24]Hall, *Japan*, p. 213.

[25]Sansom, *Western World and Japan*, p. 106.

[26]For the analysis of legitimacy in relation to the East Asian foreign policy under the early Tokugawa, I am indebted to an unpublished paper by Ronald P. Toby, "Reopening the Question of *Sakoku*: Early Tokugawa Foreign Policy and Legitimacy," presented to the Center for Japanese Studies, University of California, Berkeley (November 1976).

[27]For these themes in their German setting, see Friedrich Meinecke, *Cosmopolitanism and the National State* (Princeton: Princeton University Press, 1970).

[28]Sansom, *Western World and Japan*, pp. 127, 132, 173.

[29]Ibid., pp. 124, 129, 173–4. See also C. R. Boxer, *The Christian Century in Japan* (Berkeley and Los Angeles: University of California Press, 1951), p. 448. Among the martyrs, seventy-one were Europeans.

[30]The statement in the text by Fujita Toko is quoted in Harootunian, *Toward Restoration,* p. 51. In the doctrine of the Five Relationships, Tokugawa neo-Confucianism gave pride of place to the superior-subordinate relationship. See David M. Earl, *Emperor and Nation in Japan, Political Thinkers of the Tokugawa Period* (Seattle: University of Washington Press, 1964), pp. 3–6. The following discussion is indebted to this study, though much detail must be omitted in the interest of brevity.

[31]See Harootunian, *Toward Restoration,* pp. 19–20.

[32]See Earl, *Emperor and Nation,* pp. 16–17. I have modified Professor Earl's formulation in the interest of simplicity.

[33]Ibid., pp. 25, 37–51, 53.

[34]Ibid., p. 70.

[35]See ibid., chap. 5.

[36]See Keene, *Japanese Discovery of Europe,* passim.

[37]See ibid., chap. 3, for details of Japanese contacts with Russian explorers and traders and of Hayashi Shihei's career.

[38]Quoted in ibid., pp. 75–6.

[39]For a general account of the pragmatic accommodation between Western technology and Japanese nationalism, see the chapter "Forerunners of the Restoration Movement" in Sansom, *Western World and Japan,* pp. 248–74.

[40]Quoted in W. G. Beasley, *The Meiji Restoration* (Stanford: Stanford University Press, 1972), p. 121. My discussion is indebted to this work.

[41]For details, see ibid., chap. 5.

[42]I rely on Donald Keene's discussion of Hirata Atsutane in *Japanese Discovery of Europe,* pp. 156–72.

[43]Quoted in ibid., p. 159.

[44]Quoted in Earl, *Emperor and Nation,* p. 147. I have relied on Earl's account of Yoshida Shoin. See also Sansom, *Western World and Japan,* pp. 269–74, and Harootunian, *Toward Restoration,* pp. 184–245.

[45]Quoted in Earl, *Emperor and Nation,* p. 158. For further details on Shoin's attitude toward the nation, see ibid., chap. 9.

[46]These and related points are discussed in Thomas Smith, "Japan's Aristocratic Revolution," *Yale Review,* spring 1961, pp. 370–83. I have used Smith's analysis for a comparison between Japan and Germany in Bendix, *Nation-Building and Citizenship,* chap. 6.

[47]Quoted in Dore, *Education in Tokugawa Japan,* p. 64. I have used Dore's work in an earlier publication on which the following discussion is based. See Reinhard Bendix and Guenther Roth, *Scholarship and Partisanship* (Berkeley and Los Angeles: University of California Press, 1971), pp. 188–206.

[48]See Dore's translation of the rules posted in the temple schools in his *Education in Tokugawa Japan,* pp. 323 ff.

[49]Ibid., p. 151.

[50]For these figures see Beasley, *Meiji Restoration,* pp. 24–6.

[51]For a probing analysis of this question, see Thomas Smith, " 'Merit' as Ideology in the Tokugawa Period," in R. P. Dore, ed., *Aspects of Social Change in Modern Japan* (Princeton: Princeton University Press, 1967), pp. 71–90.

[52]Dore, *Education in Tokugawa Japan,* p. 212. For a description of this pattern of "sensitive pride and fear of shaming defeat" in the light of evidence from Japanese history, see Edwin O. Reischauer, *The United States and Japan* (New York: Viking, 1957), pp. 99–177.

[53]The figures are taken from Hall, *Japan,* pp. 234–5. The following sketch of the domestic crisis in the so-called Tempo reform era of 1830–1844 is based on Hall's presentation.

[54]Quoted in W. G. Beasley, *The Modern History of Japan* (London: Weidenfeld & Nicolson, 1963), p. 52.

[55]My account is indebted to ibid., p. 53. For further details see Conrad Totman, "Political Reconciliation in the Tokugawa Bakufu: Abe Masahiro and Tokugawa Nariaki, 1844–1852," in Albert M. Craig and Donald H. Shively, eds., *Personality in Japanese History* (Berkeley and Los Angeles: University of California Press, 1970), pp. 180–208, and Fritz Opitz, *Die Lehensreformen des Tokugawa Nariaki nach dem "Hitachi-Obi" des Fujita Toko* (Ph.D. dissertation, Philosophische Fakultät, Universität München, 1965), passim. Sansom's characterization is quoted from his *Western World and Japan,* p. 293.

[56]See Smith, "Japan's Aristocratic Revolution," pp. 370–83.

[57]Hall, *Japan,* p. 255, reports that of some fifty replies that are preserved, thirty-four called for rejection of Perry's request of a treaty, fourteen equivocated but advised conciliation, and two advocated opening the country to foreign trade. Only eight of the daimyo favored resort to military action.

[58]For details, see Beasley, *Meiji Restoration,* pp. 129–39, and passim.

[59]See ibid., p. 328 and chap. 13. The following discussion is based on Beasley's work.

[60]See ibid., p. 352, for Iwakura's 1870 statement.

[61]Quoted in ibid., p. 362.

[62]Quoted in ibid., p. 364.

[63]Ibid., p. 381.

[64]See ibid., pp. 340–1, for this list of grievances from Kagoshima.

[65]Statement by Kido Koin of Choshu quoted in ibid., p. 314.

[66]See ibid., p. 24.

[67]See Hall, *Japan*, pp. 267–70. See also Beasley, *Meiji Restoration*, pp. 318–20, for a more detailed discussion of this group.

[68]See Bernard Silberman, *Ministers of Modernization* (Tucson: University of Arizona Press, 1964), p. 49.

[69]Ibid., pp. 52, 58, 74. For fourteen individuals in the sample, the geographic origin could not be ascertained.

[70]For details, see Robert M. Spaulding, *Imperial Japan's Higher Civil Service Examination* (Princeton: Princeton University Press, 1967).

[71]The text of the charter oath is reprinted in Joseph Pittau, S.J., *Political Thought in Early Meiji Japan, 1868–1889* (Cambridge: Harvard University Press, 1967), p. 11.

[72]Quoted from an essay of 1908 in Wm. Theodore de Bary et al., eds., *Sources of the Japanese Tradition* (New York: Columbia University Press, 1958), pp. 675–6. By implication, Ito's observations may exaggerate his own role as moderator, but his description of the situation need not be discounted for that reason.

[73]Quoted in Pittau, *Political Thought*, pp. 18–19.

[74]Quoted in ibid., pp. 177–8.

[75]Statement of 1872 by Miyajima Seiichiro in a letter to Iwakura Tomomi, as quoted in ibid., p. 38.

[76]Quoted in George Akita, *Foundations of Constitutional Government in Modern Japan, 1868–1900* (Cambridge: Harvard University Press, 1967), p. 29.

[77]From the letter of Prime Minister Sanjo Sanetomi to Iwakura Tomomi as paraphrased in ibid., p. 40. The leading Meiji oligarchs participated in the Iwakura mission. The considerations leading to the Iwakura mission are analyzed in Marlene Mayo, "Rationality in the Meiji Restoration: The Iwakura Embassy," in Bernard S. Silberman and H. D. Harootunian, eds., *Modern Japanese Leadership* (Tucson: University of Arizona Press, 1966), pp. 323–69.

[78]As paraphrased in Pittau, *Political Thought*, pp. 51–2. See also pp. 50–1, and Beasley, *Meiji Restoration*, pp. 373–8, 402–4.

[79]Pittau, *Political Thought*, p. 70.

[80]Quoted in ibid., p. 166.

[81]The oligarchic crisis of 1881, leading to the ouster of Okuma Shigenobu from the government, is analyzed in Akita, *Constitutional Government*, chap. 3. Ito Hirobumi and Inoue Kowashi were the principal leaders of the government's constitutional policies. The ideas of both men had been formed a decade earlier in study tours of European capitals.

[82]Quoted in Pittau, *Political Thought*, p. 88.

[83]Ibid., p. 90.

[84]This exchange is cited in Akita, *Constitutional Government*, pp. 70–1.

CHAPTER XIII. NATION-BUILDING: RUSSIA

[1]The resulting clumsiness and feeling of inferiority by some Muscovite travelers to Western Europe is described vividly in George V. Plekhanov, *History of Russian Social Thought* (translation into English of Foreign Social Science Monographs, Works Progress Administration; New York: Columbia University, Department of Social Science, 1938), pp. 2–14.

[2]Giles Fletcher, *Of the Russe Commonwealth, 1591* (Cambridge: Harvard University Press, 1966), pp. 46–7. Spelling and punctuation have been modernized.

[3]For contrasts between this pattern and the mercantile community in Western European towns, see Otto Brunner, "Europäisches und russisches Bürgertum," *Neue Wege der Sozialgeschichte* (Göttingen: Vandenhoeck & Ruprecht, 1968), pp. 225–41.

[4]See Chapter 4, pp. 119–120, for reference to this military transformation.

[5]See Paul Miliukov, Charles Seignobos, L. Eisenmann, eds., *History of Russia*, vol. I, *From the Beginning to the Empire of Peter the Great* (New York: Funk & Wagnalls, 1968), pp. 62, 150, 158, 177; Reinhard Wittram, *Peter I, Czar und Kaiser* (Göttingen: Vandenhoeck & Ruprecht, 1964), I, p. 70; and Joseph T. Fuhrmann, *The Origins of Capitalism in Russia* (Chicago: Quadrangle, 1972), pp. 243–4, for the source of these figures. Population estimates for seventeenth-century Moscow vary from 200,000 to 524,000 around 1650 and even 658,000 in the 1680s, but these last figures seem too high even if they include the large number of residents in outlying districts and suburbs. See George Vernadsky, *A History of Russia. The Tsardom of Moscow, 1547–1682* (New Haven: Yale University Press, 1969), V, part 2, p. 746.

[6]The two sets of figures are cited in Marc Raeff, *Imperial Russia, 1682–1825* (New York: Knopf, 1971), p. 89, and Miliukov et al., eds., *History of Russia*, II, p. 150, respectively.

[7]See Donald W. Treadgold, *The West in Russia and China* (London: Cambridge University Press, 1973), I, p. 62. The author analyzes the complex intermingling of political and religious influences in the Ukraine during the sixteenth and seventeenth centuries.

[8]See Miliukov et al., *History of Russia*, I, pp. 190–4, where Nikon's statement at the 1656 council is quoted. Treadgold (*West in Russia,* I, pp. 62–75) has another description of the origin of the schism and its results. The estimate of self-immolations by Old Believers is cited in Nicholas Riasanovsky, *A History of Russia* (New York: Oxford University Press, 1969), p. 221. For a sympathetic appraisal of this controversy and of the Old Believers' movement as a desperate protest against the secular state, see Michael Cherniavsky, "The Old Believers and the New Religion," *Slavic Review,* vol. 25 (March 1966), pp. 1–39.

[9]See Alexander Vucinich, *Science in Russian Culture* (London: Peter Owen, 1965), pp. 17–25.

[10]See Miliukov et al., *History of Russia*, I, pp. 182–6, and Vucinich, *Science in Russian Culture,* pp. 27–37.

[11]See Wittram, *Peter I,* I, pp. 63–7, and Vucinich, *Science in Russian Culture,* pp. 16–17.

[12]See ibid., p. 70. My account is based on Vucinich and Wittram, *Peter I,* II, pp. 194–207. See also Treadgold, *West in Russia,* I, p. 104. The quotation in footnote a is from

Richard Pipes, ed., *Karamzin's Memoir on Ancient and Modern Russia* (New York: Atheneum, 1966), p. 158.

[13]See Miliukov et al., *History of Russia*, I, pp. 226–38.

[14]These details are extracted from the account in ibid., I, pp. 243–51.

[15]The discussion of local response to autocratic government is based on George Yaney, *The Systematization of Russian Government* (Urbana: University of Illinois Press, 1973), pp. 21–8, 51–5. I accept Yaney's suggestion that in terms of the impact on the local population there was little if any difference between conquered and native Russian territories. For details of "government by tribute collection," see the case study by Alton S. Donnelly, *The Russian Conquest of Bashkiria, 1552–1740* (New Haven: Yale University Press, 1968).

[16]For data on the size of the Russian army under Peter and the psychological importance of regimental allegiance, see Vasili Kliuchevsky, *Peter the Great* (New York: St. Martin's Press, 1969), pp. 81–2, 102–3.

[17]See Dietrich Geyer, "'Gesellschaft' als staatliche Veranstaltung," *Jahrbücher für die Geschichte Osteuropas*, vol. 14 (1966), p. 24. See also Nikolaj Alexeiev, "Beiträge zur Geschichte des russischen Absolutismus im 18. Jahrhundert," ibid., vol. 6 (1958), pp. 8–16, analyzing the equivalence between right and duty under Peter's reign.

[18]See Yaney, *Systematization*, pp. 55–6.

[19]Hans Rogger, *National Consciousness in Eighteenth-Century Russia* (Cambridge: Harvard University Press, 1960), p. 10.

[20]Ibid., pp. 46–7.

[21]Russian eighteenth-century statistics are unreliable since record-keeping was poor and the categories used quite uncertain. Nevertheless, the contrast is striking. Cf. Valentin Gitermann, *Geschichte Russlands* (Zurich: Büchergilde Gutenberg, 1945), II, p. 480, for the Russian figures on publications with Table 3, Chapter 11, this volume, for the German figures.

[22]For details on the eighteenth-century writers who discovered "native folk," developed the national language, and contrasted Russia's past to her inglorious present, see the study by Hans Rogger.

[23]For details, see James Hassell, "Implementation of the Russian Table of Ranks during the Eighteenth Century," *Slavic Review*, vol. 29 (June 1970), pp. 283–95.

[24]See the description of these edicts in Michael Florinsky, *Russia* (New York: Macmillan, 1947), I, pp. 417–21.

[25]Tibor Szamuely, *The Russian Tradition* (New York: McGraw-Hill, 1974), pp. 93, 104–5. The Kliuchevsky quotation appears on p. 104.

[26]See Florinsky, *Russia*, I, pp. 330–3, 426–7, for an account of Peter's relations with Alexis and for a statement on the succession. The regulation of 1716 is quoted on p. 426.

[27]See Szamuely, *Russian Tradition*, p. 117.

[28]A discussion of these limiting conditions of emancipation and of the origin of the 1762 edict is contained in Paul Dukes, *Catherine the Great and the Russian Nobility* (London: Cambridge University Press, 1967), pp. 38–46. The quotation from the edict appears on p. 43. See also Marc Raeff, "The Domestic Policies of Peter III and his Overthrow," *American Historical Review*, vol. 75 (June 1970), pp. 1291–4, which mentions the founding of military academies and of the university of Moscow as directly related to the government's need for qualified administrators and officers. The interpretation of the 1762 edict as a result of a concerted aristocratic drive for freedom from their service obligation makes too much of aristocratic discontents, while emphasis on the tsarist government's manpower needs is probably too rationalistic. The two statements on this problem in Richard Pipes, *Russia under the Old Regime* (New York: Scribner's, 1974), pp. 130–8 and 249 ff. are rather contradictory.

[29]The first figure is an estimate by Kliuchevsky cited in Jerome Blum, *Lord and Peasant in Russia* (New York: Atheneum, 1964), p. 349. The second figure is an estimate by Arcadius Kahan cited in Raeff, *Imperial Russia*, p. 103n. Part of the increase indicated by these figures was due to territorial acquisitions during the eighteenth century, but part of it was due also to the favoritism practiced by Catherine and her successors. See Gitermann, *Geschichte Russlands*, II, pp. 461–2, 483. The Russian aristocracy comprised about 1.5 percent of the population in contrast to the Japanese aristocracy with 6 or 7 percent of the population. See Cyril Black et al., *The Modernization of Japan and Russia* (New York: Free Press, 1975), p. 78.

[30]For the preceding data I am indebted to Arcadius Kahan, "The Costs of 'Westernization' in Russia," *Slavic Review*, vol. 25 (March 1966), pp. 40–66.

[31]See S. Frederick Starr, *Decentralization and Self-Government in Russia, 1830–1870* (Princeton: Princeton University Press, 1972), pp. 8–9.

[32]See G. T. Robinson, *Rural Russia under the Old Regime* (Berkeley and Los Angeles: University of California Press, 1967), p. 63. The figures for 1835, cited by Robinson, differ substantially from the figures quoted in Miliukov et al., eds., *History of Russia*, II, pp. 250–1, but it seems clear that in the 1730s the state and the imperial family had possessed a much smaller proportion of lands and people. See *History*, II, pp. 50–1. At that time, approximately one-third of the peasants lived on lands belonging to the state, while two-thirds were privately owned.

[33]See Marc Raeff, ed., *Catherine the Great* (New York: Hill and Wang, 1972), pp. 21–63, for accounts of Catherine's intellectual development and of her friendly but detached relations with Diderot. With regard to Russian affairs, she concluded that Diderot did not know what he was talking about.

[34]The statement is quoted from A. Kizevetter's account in Miliukov et al., *History of Russia*, II, p. 116. See also pp. 116–19 for the following discussion.

[35]The Prussian figure is for officials in central and provincial administration, but that hardly diminishes the contrast. See Robert E. Jones, "Catherine II and the Provincial Reform of 1775," *Canadian Slavic Studies*, vol. 4 (1970), pp. 502–3, 511.

[36]For the period between 1782 and 1800, there was 1 student for every 1,573 persons. See Paul Miliukov, "Educational Reforms," in Raeff, ed., *Catherine the Great*, pp. 109–10 and passim. See also Patrick L. Alston, *Education and the State in Tsarist Russia* (Stanford: Stanford University Press, 1969), pp. 15–20.

[37]Quoted in ibid., p. 18.

[38]Quoted in Yaney, *Systematization,* p. 144.

[39]See Marc Raeff, "Staatsdienst, Aussenpolitik, Ideologien," *Jahrbücher für die Geschichte Osteuropas,* vol. 7 (1959), pp. 157–72 for a typology of aristocratic attitudes in relation to their varying frontier experience. Cf. also the survey of aristocratic opinions presented to the legislative commission of 1762 in Dukes, *Catherine and the Russian Nobility,* pp. 158–62, 179–80.

[40]It is noteworthy that Catherine rejected efforts by the Senate to limit her jurisdiction as early as 1764, when her position was still quite insecure. A Senate had been established in 1711 as a central governing body and supreme court of appeal, but under Peter I's successors its governing function became secondary. See Gitermann, *Geschichte Russlands,* II, pp. 198, 202 ff. For a detailed study of autocratic rule in this period of aristocratic emancipation, see Robert E. Jones, *The Emancipation of the Russian Nobility, 1762–1785* (Princeton: Princeton University Press, 1973).

[41]See Kahan, "Costs of 'Westernization' in Russia," p. 46.

[42]See Miliukov et al., *History of Russia,* II, pp. 172–3.

[43]Fuller descriptions of these measures are found in Gitermann, *Geschichte Russlands,* II, pp. 312 ff.

[44]See Nicholas Hans, *History of Russian Educational Policy* (London: P. S. King, 1931), p. 59. For details of organization and the specific influence of Condorcet's ideas, see ibid., chap. 2.

[45]See Gitermann, *Geschichte Russlands,* II, pp. 296–311, 319–30, for details of Alexander's and Speransky's careers. Gitermann reprints (ibid., pp. 498–500) an excerpt of a contemporary memoir by J. J. de Sanglen which recounts Alexander's personal reaction to what he took to be Speransky's effort to undermine autocracy. See also the account in Hugh Seton-Watson, *The Russian Empire, 1801–1917* (London: Oxford University Press, 1967), pp. 101–12 and passim.

[46]For a contemporary, conservative reaction to Alexander's educational reforms and the education act of 1809, see Karamzin's comment cited in text footnote a.

[47]See Alston, *Education and the State,* p. 28.

[48]A detailed description of these policies and their abandonment is found in Hans, *Russian Educational Policy,* pp. 33–91.

[49]The last two quotations are taken from Allen Sinel, *The Classroom and the Chancellory* (Cambridge: Harvard University Press, 1973), p. 13. For the other statements in the preceding paragraph see Alston, *Education and the State,* pp. 30–2.

[50]For details, see Hans, *Russian Educational Policy,* pp. 67 ff., and Alston, *Education and the State,* pp. 32–4.

[51]These trends are inferred from the tables appended to Hans, *Russian Educational Policy,* pp. 234–42, and to William Johnson, *Russia's Educational Heritage* (Pittsburgh: Carnegie Press, 1950), pp. 270–1, 290.

[52]Quoted from Shevyrev, "Istoriya Imperatorskogo Moskovskogo Universiteta" in Nicholas Riasanovsky, *Nicholas I and Official Nationality in Russia, 1825–1855* (Berkeley and Los Angeles: University of California Press, 1967), pp. 213–14.

[53]These figures are taken from William L. Blackwell, *The Beginnings of Russian Industrialization, 1800–1860* (Princeton: Princeton University Press, 1968), pp. 427 ff. See also M. E. Falkus, *The Industrialization of Russia, 1700–1914* (London: Macmillan, 1972).

[54]See Sinel, *Classroom,* pp. 1–3.

[55]Russia's unfavorable heritage is analyzed by Guenther Stökl, "Gab es im Moskauer Staat 'Stände'?" *Jahrbücher für die Geschichte Osteuropas,* vol. 2 (1963), pp. 321–42. Stökl shows that demands by "estates" for recognition of their rights by the tsar occurred only in the exceptional circumstances of 1610–1613, when dissident notables negotiated with the Polish king regarding the election of Crown Prince Wladyslaw to the Muscovite throne.

[56]Max Weber, *Economy and Society* (tr. and ed. by Guenther Roth and Claus Wittich; New York: Bedminster Press, 1968), III, p. 993. My italics.

[57]In the critical period from 1897 to 1917, the appointment of twelve ministers of education indicates an especially rapid turnover in that sensitive field. See Erik Amburger, *Geschichte der Behördenorganisation Russlands von Peter dem Grossen bis 1917* (Leiden: E. J. Brill, 1966), pp. 136–7, 191–2, 266, 171, 298, 208, 130.

[58]See Yaney, *Systematization,* pp. 150–1. A summary of varying conditions is contained in Terence Emmons, *The Russian Landed Gentry and the Peasant Emancipation of 1861* (New York: Cambridge University Press, 1968), pp. 21–6. For more details, see Michael Confino, *Domaines et seigneurs en Russie vers la fin du XVIIIe siècle* (Paris: Institut Études Slaves de l'Université de Paris, 1963), pp. 194–201, and passim.

[59]The preceding discussion of the obstacles standing in the way of agricultural reform is based on Yaney, *Systematization,* pp. 151–68, and Starr, *Decentralization,* pp. 3–50.

[60]See the study of "Official Nationality" by Nicholas Riasanovsky cited in footnote 52. Apparently serfdom was compatible with the growth of agricultural output, though probably not of productivity. See Alexander Gerschenkron, "Agrarian Policies and Industrialization," in H. J. Habbakuk and M. Postan, eds., *The Cambridge Economic History of Europe* (London: Cambridge University Press, 1965), VI, part 2, pp. 706–7.

[61]The quotation in the text and the content of this paragraph are derived from Alfred Rieber, ed., "The Politics of Autocracy," *Études sur l'histoire, l'economie et la sociologie des pays slaves* (Paris: Mouton, 1966), XII, pp. 26, 28, and passim.

[62]Quoted in Emmons, *Landed Gentry and Peasant Emancipation,* p. 51. Reform from above as an alternative to revolution from below had been the slogan of the Prussian reform minister von Hardenberg in his Riga Memorial of 1807. See Chapter 11, p. 414. Speransky's efforts at reform under Alexander I paralleled those of von Hardenberg, which had been a direct response to Prussia's defeat at Jena (1806) at the hands of Napoleon. The statement of 1856 by Alexander II was a similar response to another defeat.

[63]Quoted in Rieber, "Politics of Autocracy," p. 39. The tsar's expectation of aristocratic cooperation in the emancipation project was not as unrealistic as it seems, since many high

aristocratic officials had inherited or acquired only a few serfs or none. On the other hand, wealthy aristocrats with many serfs were likely to be uncooperative or openly antagonistic. The difficulty was that the success of emancipation at the local level often depended on the wealthy landowners. For a preliminary report on current studies of this problem, see Walter Pintner, "The Russian Higher Civil Service on the Eve of the 'Great Reforms,'" *Journal of Social History* (spring 1975), pp. 55–68.

[64]See Emmons, *Landed Gentry and Peasant Emancipation,* pp. 51–2.

[65]Corresponding proportions for modern developing countries are often considerably higher. See Starr, *Decentralization,* pp. 13–14, 47–9, and Hans-Joachim Torke, "Das Russische Beamtentum in der ersten Hälfte des 19. Jahrhunderts," *Forschungen zur osteuropäischen Geschichte,* vol. 13 (1967), pp. 133–7.

[66]For details on Russia's military forces under Nicholas I and for its budgetary problems, see John Shelton Curtiss, *The Russian Army under Nicholas I, 1825–1855* (Durham: Duke University Press, 1965), chap. 5, and Starr, *Decentralization,* pp. 14–17.

[67]See ibid., pp. 56–8, 59, 187–91.

[68]Seton-Watson, *Russian Empire,* p. 337. See also Rieber, "Politics of Autocracy," p. 42.

[69]This summary is too succinct to give a proper impression of the complexity of the issues or the intensity of the debate. For details, see the two studies by Starr and Emmons, cited previously.

[70]My account of the process leading to the emancipation declaration is based on Starr, *Decentralization,* pp. 201–19, and Seton-Watson, *Russian Empire,* pp. 341–48.

[71]Starr, *Decentralization,* pp. 327–8.

[72]See Emmons, *Landed Gentry and Peasant Emancipation,* p. 26, for the source of these figures.

[73]Paraphrased from a quotation in Starr, *Decentralization,* pp. 117–18.

[74]See Florinsky, *Russia,* II, pp. 898–9.

[75]See Starr, *Decentralization,* pp. 293 ff.

[76]See ibid., pp. 332–3 and passim, and George Fischer, *Russian Liberalism* (Cambridge: Harvard University Press, 1958), pp. 12–13 and passim.

[77]For a sympathetic appraisal of the zemstvo movement, see Victor Leontovitsch, *Geschichte des Liberalismus in Russland* (Frankfurt: Vittorio Klostermann, 1974), part 3.

[78]See Florinsky, *Russia,* II, pp. 902–6, for a brief account of this development.

[79]This brief summary is based on Raymond W. Goldsmith, "The Economic Growth of Tsarist Russia, 1860–1913," *Economic Development and Cultural Change,* vol. 9 (April 1961), pp. 441–75. See also Florinsky, *Russia,* II, p. 939, for figures on Russia's grain exports. For circumstantial accounts of agricultural and industrial developments, see Seton-Watson, *Russian Empire,* pp. 506–34, and the two articles by Alexander Gerschenkron and Roger Portal in *Cambridge Economic History of Europe,* VI, part 2, pp. 706–872.

[80]Florinsky, *Russia*, II, pp. 928–9.

[81]Arcadius Kahan, "Social Structure, Public Policy, and the Development of Education and the Economy in Csarist Russia," in C. Arnold Anderson and Mary Jean Bowman, eds., *Education and Economic Development* (Chicago: Aldine, 1965), p. 372.

[82]See Hans, *Russian Educational Policy*, pp. 238–40.

[83]See Seton-Watson, *Russian Empire*, p. 536, and Kahan, "Social Structure, Public Policy," p. 374, for the source of these two figures.

[84]Quoted from *Vestnik Evropy* (October 1895), in George Fischer, *Russian Liberalism*, p. 90.

[85]Quoted in ibid., pp. 104–5. From this Struve and others inferred the "greater cultural and political tasks of the proletariat," but I am concerned here with the first part of Struve's observation.

[86]My description is based on ibid., pp. 57–60.

[87]Jacob Walkin, *The Rise of Democracy in Pre-Revolutionary Russia* (New York: Praeger, 1962), pp. 127–8.

[88]See Alain Besançon, *Éducation et société en Russie dans le second tiers du XIX*e *siècle* (Paris: Mouton, 1974), p. 75 and passim.

[89]See Kahan, "Social Structure, Public Policy," pp. 366–8, for the figures cited in the text.

[90]See Hans, *Russian Educational Policy*, p. 236; Kahan, "Social Structure, Public Policy," p. 370; and Besançon, *Éducation et société*, p. 45, for three sets of more or less divergent figures which, however, do not alter the overall development as stated in the text.

[91]See Philip Pomper, *The Russian Revolutionary Movement* (New York: Thomas Y. Crowell, 1970), p. 114, and Sinel, *Classroom*, p. 254, for the source of these figures. Radical ideas were apparently widespread in secondary schools two decades earlier. At the Tsarskoe-Selo Lyceum, founded by Alexander I, located in one of the imperial summer parks and reserved for young men from prominent families, "there was not a single forbidden book which might not conceivably appear within its walls in the possession of boys of fourteen or fifteen." Quoted from a report by A. M. Unkovsky in Sidney Monas, *The Third Section, Police and Society in Russia under Nicholas I* (Cambridge: Harvard University Press, 1960), note, p. 249.

[92]This so-called "cook's circular" is quoted in Alston, *Education and the State*, p. 129. The special problem of Jewish "overrepresentation" in the student body is related to the high proportion of Jews among urban residents. In a country that was still 90 percent rural, the Jewish minority was 90 percent urban. Under Alexander III (1881–1894), one-fourth of the country's urban residents were Jewish. See ibid., p. 122.

[93]According to Hans, *Russian Educational Policy*, p. 235, sixty gymnasia for boys had 14,000 pupils in 1825. By 1900 some two hundred gymnasia had an enrollment of 71,584.

[94]Besançon, *Éducation et société*, p. 21.

[95]Sinel, *Classroom,* p. 179. My comments on Tolstoi's policies are based on this study.

[96]See William L. Mathes, "The Origins of Confrontation Politics in Russian Universities: Student Activism, 1855–1861," *Canadian Slavic Studies,* vol. 2 (spring 1968), pp. 28–45.

[97]Quoted in Reginald E. Zelnik, "The Sunday-School Movement in Russia, 1859–1862," *Journal of Modern History,* vol. 37 (June 1965), p. 157.

[98]See Chapter 10, p. 372. This parallelism between the radical and the autocratic opposition to civil society underscores the quasi-plebiscitarianism of autocratic rule, as suggested on p. 524.

[99]See Monas, *Third Section,* pp. 203–4, 208.

[100]Isaiah Berlin, "A Marvellous Decade; Belinsky: Moralist and Prophet," *Encounter,* vol. 5 (December 1955), p. 23. My account is greatly indebted to this essay and to E. Lampert, *Studies in Rebellion* (London: Routledge and Kegan Paul, 1957), chap. 2.

[101]Quoted from the report of Count Orlov to Nicholas I in Monas, *Third Section,* p. 192. All references to Belinski's relations with the police are based on pp. 187–93 of this work.

[102]Quoted in Lampert, *Studies in Rebellion,* p. 53, where the author also gives a sample of the literary feuds in which esthetic criticism turned quite regularly into political condemnation.

[103]The quotations in the last two paragraphs are taken from Richard Hare, *Pioneers of Russian Social Thought* (New York: Oxford University Press, 1951), pp. 37–48.

[104]Ralph E. Matlaw, ed., *Belinsky, Chernyshevsky, and Dobrolyubov, Selected Criticism* (New York: E. P. Dutton, 1962), pp. 3–9.

[105]Ibid., p. 89.

[106]See the eloquent statement of this position in Martin Malia, "Mandelstam's Power," *New York Review of Books,* January 27, 1972, which reviews Mme. Mandelstam's memoir *Hope against Hope* and in the process compares the past with the present situation of Russian literature.

[107]For an attempt to put the change from the 1840s to the 1860s in general terms, see Vladimir Nahirny, "The Russian Intelligentsia: From Men of Ideas to Men of Conviction," *Comparative Studies in Society and History,* vol. 4 (1962), pp. 403–35. Although the author refers to much the same contrast as I do in the text, he does not clearly distinguish men of ideas like Belinski from men of conviction (like Chernyshevski). Circumstances had changed, and the two groups consequently thought of their social responsibility in different terms.

[108]My account is based on E. Lampert, *Sons against Fathers* (London: Oxford University Press, 1965), chap. 3, and Franco Venturi, *Roots of Revolution* (New York: Grosset and Dunlap, 1966), pp. 129–86.

[109]Isaiah Berlin, "Introduction," to Venturi, *Roots,* p. *xxiii.*

[110]Quoted in Venturi, *Roots,* p. 150.

[111]Berlin, "Introduction," to Venturi, *Roots,* pp. *xxiii–xxiv.*

[112]See Lampert, *Sons against Fathers,* p. 223.

[113]Quoted by Berlin, "Introduction," to Venturi, *Roots,* p. *xx.*

[114]Quoted in Philip Pomper, *Peter Lavrov and the Russian Revolutionary Movement* (Chicago: University of Chicago Press, 1972), pp. 102–3.

[115]Quoted in Avrahm Yarmolinsky, *Road to Revolution* (New York: Macmillan, Collier Books, 1962), p. 73.

[116]Berlin, "Introduction," to Venturi, *Roots,* pp. *ix–x.*

[117]Quoted in Venturi, *Roots,* pp. 717, 719. My italics.

[118]Merle Fainsod, *How Russia Is Ruled* (Cambridge: Harvard University Press, 1963), p. 3.

[119]Alec Nove, *An Economic History of the USSR* (Baltimore: Penguin, 1969), p. 68.

[120]Alexander Baykov, *The Development of the Soviet Economic System* (National Institute of Economic and Social Research; London: Cambridge University Press, 1947), p. 23.

[121]See Boris Meissner, "Der soziale Strukturwandel im bolschewistischen Russland," in Boris Meissner, ed., *Sowjetgesellschaft im Wandel* (Stuttgart: W. Kohlhammer Verlag, 1966), pp. 28–30. For the estimate of population losses during this period, see Frank Lorimer, *The Population of the Soviet Union* (Geneva: League of Nations, 1946), p. 41 and passim.

[122]Nove, *Economic History,* p. 74.

[123]The quoted statement is from E. H. Carr, *The Bolshevik Revolution, 1917–1923* (Harmondsworth: Penguin, 1966), II, p. 150. For the estimates of concealment, see Maurice Dobb, *Soviet Economic Development since 1917* (6th ed.; London: Routledge and Kegan Paul, 1966), p. 117.

[124]Moshe Lewin, *Political Undercurrents in Soviet Economic Debates* (Princeton: Princeton University Press, 1974), pp. 80–1.

[125]Ibid., p. 82.

[126]Nove, *Economic History,* pp. 104, 106.

[127]See V. I. Lenin, *Selected Works* (Moscow: Foreign Languages Publishing House, 1952), vol. II, part 2, pp. 635–7, 736. Lenin's critical comment on haste (p. 736) appears in his 1923 article "Better Fewer, but Better" to which I refer further on. Lenin emphasized the *long-term* change which could be expected from a small-peasant economy, as quoted in Alexander Erlich, *The Soviet Industrialization Debate, 1924–1928* (Cambridge: Harvard University Press, 1960), p. 8.

[128]See Lewin, *Political Undercurrents,* pp. 85–9, and Nove, *Economic History,* pp. 119–21.

[129]The books by Erlich and Lewin present the details that are omitted here. For an analysis of the struggles and decisions leading to the revolution by forcible collectivization, see Moshe Lewin, *Russian Peasants and Soviet Power* (Evanston: Northwestern University Press, 1968).

[130]Nove, *Economic History,* p. 126. In the main, I have followed Nove's account of the great debate and especially of E. A. Preobrazhensky's statement of the radical position, which dates from his lectures of 1924 before the Communist Academy—four to five years before the policy of forced collectivization was initiated.

[131]Lewin, *Political Undercurrents,* pp. 102–4. The quotation from Stalin's letter to Lenin in 1921 appears on p. 101.

[132]See Lewin, *Russian Peasants and Soviet Power,* pp. 81–93. See chapters 3–6 for much illuminating detail on the position of the party in the countryside.

[133]Nove, *Economic History,* pp. 167, 174.

[134]See Robert Conquest, *The Great Terror* (New York: Macmillan, 1973), pp. 699–713.

[135]For the distinction between workers and communists, see Karl Marx and Friedrick Engels, *Manifesto of the Communist Party* (New York: International Publishers, 1932), p. 22. I have simplified Marx's inferences based on this distinction. A more complete statement is contained in Reinhard Bendix, *Embattled Reason* (New York: Oxford University Press, 1970), pp. 35–40.

[136]See Karl Marx and Friedrich Engels, *Die Heilige Familie* (Berlin: Dietz Verlag, 1953), p. 138. My translation and italics.

[137]V. I. Lenin, *What Is To Be Done?* (New York: International Publishers, 1929), pp. 41, 76–8. An analysis of this work in the context of Russian exile politics and its relations with European labor movements is contained in Dietrich Geyer, *Lenin in der russischen Sozialdemokratie* (Cologne: Böhlau Verlag, 1962), pp. 237–46 and passim.

[138]See Oskar Anweiler, *Die Rätebewegung in Russland, 1905–1921* (Leiden: E. J. Brill, 1958), p. 188. See chapter 4 of Anweiler's study for a detailed analysis of Lenin's and the Bolsheviks' attitude toward the soviets during 1917.

[139]Quoted phrases and page references are from Lenin, "Better Fewer, but Better," in *Selected Works,* II, part 2, pp. 735–52. The quotations appear on pp. 748 and 750. My italics. This article is conveniently reprinted in Robert C. Tucker, ed., *The Lenin Anthology* (New York: Norton, 1975), pp. 734–46.

[140]For a more detailed exposition of Soviet Marxism's "basic self-interpretation," see Herbert Marcuse, *Soviet Marxism* (New York: Random House, Vintage Books, 1961), chap. 2 and passim.

[141]J. Stalin, *Problems of Leninism* (Moscow: Foreign Languages Publishing House, 1940), p. 73.

[142]The preceding paragraph restates my generalized conclusions from an earlier study of industrial relations in East Germany. See Reinhard Bendix, *Nation-Building and Citizenship* (Berkeley and Los Angeles: University of California Press, 1977), pp. 175–211.

[143]See the elaboration of this approach to "rationality" in Marcuse, *Soviet Marxism,* pp. 70–6.

[144]For article 126 of the Soviet constitution, see Amos J. Peaslee, ed., *Constitutions of Nations* (The Hague: Martinus Nijhoff, 1968), III, p. 1005. My italics. The reference to voting as a citizen's duty occurs in Valery Chalidze, *To Defend These Rights* (New York: Random House, 1974), note, p. 22. The utopian vision of the party in relation to the people in a publication by D. I. Chesnokov (1960) is quoted in Jerome M. Gilison, *The Soviet Image of Utopia* (Baltimore: Johns Hopkins University Press, 1975), p. 123 and passim.

CHAPTER XIV. FROM ROYAL AUTHORITY TO POPULAR MANDATE: TWENTIETH-CENTURY PERSPECTIVES

[1]The responses of Chinese scholars to the Western impact have been analyzed with great subtlety by Joseph Levenson, *Confucian China and Its Modern Fate* (Berkeley and Los Angeles: University of California Press, 1968), and the "May 4th" movement of 1917–1921 is chronicled in Chow Tse-tung, *The May Fourth Movement: Intellectual Revolution in Modern China* (Cambridge: Harvard University Press, 1960).

[2]See D. J. Male, *Russian Peasant Organization before Collectivization* (London: Cambridge University Press, 1971), passim, and Teodor Shanin, *The Awkward Class, Political Sociology of Peasantry in a Developing Society: Russia 1910–1925* (London: Oxford University Press, 1972), part 1 and passim.

[3] See Karl-Eugen Wädekin, *The Private Sector in Soviet Agriculture* (Berkeley and Los Angeles: University of California Press, 1973).

[4]See the detailed study by T'ung-Tsu Ch'u, *Local Government in China under the Ch'ing* (Stanford: Stanford University Press, 1969), especially chap. 10. Other aspects of the linkages between village and region are analyzed in Fei Hsiao-tung, "Peasantry and Gentry," *American Journal of Sociology,* vol. 52 (July 1946), pp. 1–17, and W. G. Skinner, "Chinese Peasants and the Closed Community," *Comparative Studies in Society and History,* vol. 13 (July 1971), pp. 270–81.

[5]Theda Skocpol, "Old Regime Legacies and Communist Revolutions in Russia and China," *Social Forces,* vol. 55 (December 1976), p. 303. My discussion is indebted to this essay.

[6]Quoted from Mao Tse-tung's October 1938 report to the Sixth Plenum in Stuart R. Schram, ed., *The Political Thought of Mao Tse-tung* (Harmondsworth: Penguin, 1969), p. 172.

[7]Quoted from Mao Tse-tung's speech of January 1962 in Stuart R. Schram, ed., *Authority, Participation and Cultural Change in China* (London: Cambridge University Press, 1973), p. 8. I have replaced Mao's own date of 1958 with 1955, the beginning of the Chinese collectivization of agriculture.

[8]Skocpol, "Old Regime Legacies," pp. 303–4.

[9]One year after Chinese collectivization began, 90 percent of China's 210,000 government districts had organized party branches, whereas in Russia after three years of collectivization more than half the country's rural administrative units were without organized party members. See Thomas P. Bernstein, "Leadership and Mass Mobilization in the Soviet and Chinese Collectivization Campaigns of 1929–30 and 1955–56," *The China Quarterly*, no. 31 (July-September 1967), p. 11 and passim. Related comparisons are found in Alexander Eckstein, *China's Economic Development* (Ann Arbor: University of Michigan Press, 1975), pp. 251–4, and Skocpol, "Old Regime Legacies," pp. 305–9.

[10]See Frederick Wakeman, *History and Will* (Berkeley and Los Angeles: University of California Press, 1973), pp. 8–13 and passim.

[11]Quoted in Schram, *Authority, Participation and Cultural Change*, pp. 50–1. The significance of this statement is attested by the fact that its first lines have been incorporated in the new party constitution of April 1969.

[12]A telling description of such control measures combined with an ideology of voluntarism is contained in Ezra Vogel, "Voluntarism and Social Control," in Donald W. Treadgold, ed., *Soviet and Chinese Communism* (Seattle: University of Washington Press, 1967), pp. 168–84.

[13]Schram, ed., *Political Thought of Mao Tse-tung*, pp. 316–17. See the full discussion of Chinese Communist ideology in Franz Schurmann, *Ideology and Organization in Communist China* (2nd ed.; Berkeley and Los Angeles: University of California Press, 1968).

[14]Bernard Lewis, *The Arabs in History* (New York: Harper & Row, Harper Torchbooks, 1967), pp. 172–3.

[15]A useful survey of the emergence of Arab nationalism is contained in Sylvia Haim's introduction to her anthology, *Arab Nationalism* (Berkeley and Los Angeles: University of California Press, 1962). For a synthetic view with emphasis on the turn to Germany as a model under the intellectual leadership of Sati' Husri (1882–1968), see Bassam Tibi, *Nationalismus in der dritten Welt am arabischen Beispiel* (Frankfurt: Europäische Verlagsanstalt, 1971). The volume contains a comprehensive bibliography.

[16]Where the context suggests that I am paraphrasing the text of various constitutions and where phrases are put in quotation marks, I am referring to the appropriate section of A. P. Blaustein and G. H. Flanz, eds., *Constitutions of the Countries of the World* (Dobbs Ferry: Oceana Publications, 1971), 12 vols. Detailed citations appear superfluous. I have also relied on the Area Handbooks on Algeria, Egypt and Syria, published under the auspices of Foreign Area Studies, American University (Washington, D.C.: U.S. Government Printing Office, 1972, 1969, 1971).

[17]The references in this paragraph are to the constitutions of Egypt, Algeria, Syria, and Iraq. The quoted sentence suggesting some Chinese influence comes from the 1951 Socialist Arab Ba'th party constitution quoted in Haim, ed., *Arab Nationalism*, p. 235. The Ba'th party is dominant in Syria and Iraq.

[18]See Guenter Lewy, *Religion and Revolution* (New York: Oxford University Press, 1974), pp. 443–61, for an account of the religious overtones of Arab nationalism in Egypt.

[19]Quoted in Colin Legum, ed., *Africa Contemporary Record, 1974–1975* (New York: Africana Publishing, 1975), p. B4.

[20]For explorations of this question, see Malcolm Kerr, "The Political Outlook in the Local Area," in Abraham S. Becker, Bent Hansen, and Malcolm Kerr, eds., *The Economics and Politics of the Middle East* (London: Elsevier, 1975), pp. 41–73, and Elbaki Hermassi, "Politics and Culture in the Middle East," in a forthcoming publication by the University of California Press.

[21]For the meaning of *revolution* and the source of Condorcet's statement, see Hannah Arendt, *On Revolution* (New York: Viking Press, 1965), p. 21. For critiques of the modern concept of revolution, see Perez Zagorin, "Prolegomena to the Comparative History of Revolution in Early Modern Europe," *Comparative Studies of Society and History*, vol. 18 (April 1976), pp. 151–74, and J. H. Elliott, "Revolution and Continuity in Early Modern Europe," *Past and Present*, no. 42 (February 1969), pp. 35–55.

[22]The official *History of the Communist Party*, which has been incorporated in Stalin's *Collected Works*, states that "the distinctive feature of the Russian revolution is that it was accomplished *from above*, on the initiative of the state, and directly supported *from below*, by the millions of peasants, who were fighting to throw off kulak bondage and to live in freedom in the collective farms." See *History of the Communist Party of the Soviet Union— Bolshevik (Short Course)* (Moscow: Foreign Languages Publishing House, 1945), p. 305. Professor Robert Tucker of Princeton University has informed me that although written by a committee, the official history probably reflects Stalin's direct influence on key formulations such as this one.

[23]See Elbaki Hermassi, "Towards a Comparative Study of Revolutions," *Comparative Studies in Society and History*, vol. 18 (April 1976), pp. 211–35, for a suggestive formulation of this perspective.

[24]See the detailed study of these divisions within the United Kingdom by Michael Hechter, *Internal Colonialism* (Berkeley and Los Angeles: University of California Press, 1975).

[25]The contrast between civil and communal ties in the new states has been analyzed by Edward Shils, "Political Development in the New States," *Comparative Studies in Society and History*, vol. 2 (1960), pp. 268–87, and in the essay on "The Integrative Revolution: Primordial Sentiments and Civil Politics in the New States," in Clifford Geertz, *The Interpretation of Culture* (New York: Basic Books, 1973), pp. 255–310.

[26]Max Weber, *Economy and Society* (tr. and ed. by Guenther Roth and Claus Wittich; New York: Bedminster Press, 1968), II, p. 903. The distinction between the political community or the state and privately organized groups diminishes the further back one goes in history.

Glossary

Advowson	Right to appoint to a church benefice (England)
Akzise	Sales tax in seventeenth-century Prussia
Allgemeines Landrecht	Prussian Legal Code (1794)
Angevin	Adjective referring to the County of Anjou ruled by the Plantagenet family. Hence, the Plantagenet dynasty is sometimes referred to as the Angevin kings.
Appanage	Land or other source of revenue assigned for the maintenance of a member of the ruling family
Arianism	Doctrines of the Greek theologian Arius (280?–336 A.D.), who taught that Jesus was not of the same substance as God, but only the best of created beings
Armigerous	Adjective referring originally to the armor-bearer of a knight; used in England to refer to a person ranking next to a knight and entitled to a coat of arms (squire)
Auctoritas	Moral influence (Latin)
Bakufu	Headquarters of the Japanese shogun (used synonymously with shogunate)
Bakuhan	Japanese term contracting *bakufu* = military government and *han* = daimyo fief or domain
Bakumsatsu	Japanese name for the period from 1853 to 1868 just prior to the Meiji Restoration
Bangaku	Japanese term for "barbarian learning"
Barshchina	Labor obligation of peasants in tsarist Russia
Be	Japanese workers, grouped by locale or occupation
Benefice	An ecclesiastical living (England), such as a pastorate
Beneficium	Office or land or any source of income granted as a right
Benefit of clergy	Right of church authorities to try, in an ecclesiastical court, any clergyman accused of a serious crime. Judgments were typically lenient and the legal fiction of "benefit of clergy" was used in England to mitigate the harshness of the criminal law.
Bildung	German ideal of personal growth through self-cultivation

669

Bolshevik	Majority wing of the Russian Social Democratic Labor party under Lenin's leadership, so designated at a party congress in 1903
Boyar	Independent landowners of medieval and early modern Russia
Boyar duma	Council of landed notables in medieval Russia
Burgrave	Hereditary head of a castle or town in medieval Germany (literally: castle count)
Bushi	Mercenaries in medieval Japan
Cahiers (also *cahiers doléances*)	Literally notebooks. General term designating the documents in which the French estates submitted their grievances to the government
Caliph	Successor to Muhammad, title of the head of the Muslim state
Ceorl	Head of rural household in early medieval Wessex
Chantries	English endowments for the chanting of the masses, usually for the founder of the endowment
Chin	Grade in the Table of Ranks in tsarist Russia
Chonin	Japanese merchants and artisans
Clan	An early form of social group composed of several families claiming descent from a common ancestor, bearing the same family name, and following the same chieftain
Comitatus	Germanic war bands
Commenda	A partnership contract developed in medieval Italy which facilitated the investment of savings in a commercial enterprise and regulated the distribution of capital, risk, and profits among the partners
Corps intermédiaires	Montesquieu's general term for the parlements, towns, guilds, foundations and other "intermediate bodies" of the French ancien régime
Cuius regio, eius religio	He who controls the area controls the religion
Daimyo	Regional territorial governor of Japan before 1868
Dei gratia	By the Grace of God
Desiatina (pl. *y*)	Russian land measure = 2.7 acres
Dux (Latin)	Earl (medieval English title)
Dvoriane (*Dvorianstvo*)	Court servitor (court nobility) in tsarist Russia
Ealdorman (Old English)	Earl
(to) *enfeoff*	to invest a vassal with a fief, fee, or other possession
Entail	The rule of descent settled for an estate

Escheat	Feudal rule according to which lands or various rights revert to the lord when there are no heirs to inherit the original grant
Estate	A political and social group as in the English division among the lords spiritual, the lords temporal, and the commons. English term for the German *Stand*
États-Généraux	French general assembly (Estates-General), a council last summoned by the king in 1614
Feorm	Food rent levied to support the households of Anglo-Saxon kings
Fideicommissum	German legal instrument for confining the inheritance of a manorial estate to a single heir
Fudai	House daimyo who was dependent on the Tokugawa shogun
Gabelle	Originally a French sales tax on all commodities which was gradually limited to a tax on salt
Gesith	Member of the war-band of an Anglo-Saxon king
Gosti	Roster of wholesale merchants in Russian medieval towns
Hakam	Arab tribal arbiter of disputes
Han	Japanese daimyo domains under the Tokugawa shogunate
Hundred	An administrative subdivision of a county (shire) in medieval England
Ikki	Defense leagues of Japanese peasants
Imam	Mohammedan religious leader, officiating priest of a mosque
(to) *impropriate*	To place ecclesiastical property in the hands of laymen
Incunabula	Books printed before 1500
Intendants	French provincial administrators under the ancien régime
Jihad	A Muslim holy war, campaign against unbelievers or enemies of Islam
Ji-samurai	Japanese yeomen peasants
Jito	Land stewards under the Kamakura shogunate
Junkers	Aristocratic landowners in the Prussian territories east of the Elbe River
Justiciars	High administrative and judicial officials under the Norman and Plantagenet dynasties
Kami	General Japanese term for ancestral or divine spirit

Kampaku	Japanese civil dictator, an office created in 880 which marks the ascendance of regents or governors over the emperor
Kenin	Housemen of the Kamakura shogunate
Khan (or *Great Khan*)	Supreme hereditary ruler of Mongol empire and of Tartar tribes
Khanate	Dominion of a khan
Koku	One koku equals five American bushels of rice. Japanese measure of land area needed to produce a given quantity of rice
Kokugaku	Japanese term for national learning
Kormlenie	Judicial and civil administrative post in tsarist Russia which rewarded officials out of the taxes they collected for the government (also called tax farming)
Kreistag	County estate-assembly in Prussia
Kugyo	High court nobles in imperial Japan
Kulak	Pejorative Soviet term for better-off or wealthy peasants
Kurfürsten	Electors of the emperor of the Holy Roman Empire of the German Nation
Landrat	Prussian county official, elected by the county estate-assembly from among the local aristocracy, but dependent on instructions of the Prussian government
Landtag	Provincial estate-assembly in Prussia
Lateral succession	Rule of inheritance by which the property passes from an owner to his oldest brother, then the second oldest brother, and so on
Letters patent	A government document issued to a person, authorizing him to perform some act or to enjoy some privilege, so called because the document is not sealed but open
Lettre de cachet	A letter under seal of the French king, usually one ordering imprisonment without trial
Lex talionis	Blood revenge; Latin term for a practice widespread among Germanic, Arabic, and other tribes
Li	Religious ritual; Confucian metaphor for propriety, the right spirit, the "golden mean"
Lineage	Direct descent from an ancestor, hence ancestry, family
Lit de justice	Special session of a French parlement, called by the king for the purpose of personally ordering the registration of a decree the parlement had refused to register

Liudi	Merchants and artisans of Kievan Russia
Living	An ecclesiastical office like a parsonage or rectory with revenues attached for the maintenance of the minister and his household (England)
Mana	God-descended power; old Germanic belief
Mandokoro	Office during the Kamakura shogunate, handling business for the Minamoto clan
Menshevik	Minority wing of the Russian Social Democratic Labor party under the leadership of Martov, Axelrod, and others; so designated at a meeting in 1903
Mestnichestvo	Order of the Russian aristocracy which correlated service rank with genealogical rank of the family
Ministeriales	Medieval administrators and knights ranking below the highest level of the German aristocracy
Ministerium	Latin term for office and duty
Mir	Russian peasant community in which the land is periodically redistributed among the members of that community
Monchujo	Office of the Kamakura shogunate handling disputes among vassals
Nestorianism	Doctrines of the Syrian prelate Nestorius (?451 A.D.), who taught that divinity and humanity existed as two distinct natures in Jesus and were not unified into a single personality
No drama	A highly stylized type of Japanese play
Nuhi	Japanese slaves
Obrok	Head tax (or quitrent) paid by peasants in cash or kind
Oprichnina	Dictatorial police regime; special royal domain created by Tsar Ivan IV
Particularism	The principle of allowing each state (or other subordinate unit) of a federation, kingdom, or empire to retain its laws and promote its interests
Paulette	An edict of Henry IV (1589–1610) of France which permitted officials of non-noble origin to make their positions hereditary in return for an annual tax payment
Pietism	A religious movement of the Lutheran church advocating a revival of the devotional ideal
Pomeshchiki	Holder of land on service tenure in tsarist Russia
Pomest'e (*pomestye*)	Land granted in return for service to the Russia tsar
Popery	Pejorative term for the doctrines and customs of the Roman Catholic church

Prerogative	An exclusive right or privilege attaching to an office or position, especially that of the king
Primogeniture	Principle of inheritance by the first-born, specifically the oldest son
Pud	Russian weight = 36.11 pounds
Rangaku	Japanese term for Dutch studies
Raskolniki	Old Believers, a Russian sect which developed in protest against the Nikonian reforms of the Orthodox church in the seventeenth century
Raznochintsy	Men estranged from the social groups to which they belonged according to the law of tsarist Russia
Regia potestas	Latin term for the executive power of the king
Rittergut	Knightly estate in Prussia, so called because ownership of such estates was for a time the exclusive privilege of aristocratic warriors
Ronin	Masterless samurai, especially frequent in seventeenth-century Japan
Sale of indulgences	Payment to receive a remission of the temporal penalties still due after a sin has been forgiven; a point of controversy especially in the Lutheran reformation
Samizdat	Russian term for clandestine, unpublished literature, usually circulating in handwritten or typed form
Samurai	Japanese fighting men; aristocratic title since the Kamakura shogunate
Samurai-dokoro	Office of Kamakura shogunate, handling military affairs
Sankin-kotai	System of alternate residence of daimyo under the Tokugawa shogunate
Sayyid	Arab tribal chieftain
Scutage	Payment in lieu of service as an armed knight on horseback in medieval England
Seignor(ial) (Seigneur(ial))	French lord of a fee or manor (adjective referring to . . .)
Sengoku-daimyo	Former subordinates of Shugo daimyo whose local power increased over their masters during the later Ashikaga shogunate
Sengoku-jidai	Japanese phrase for "the country at war," specifically the period 1467–1568
Sessho	Regent in Japanese imperial government
Shari'a	Islamic sacred law
Shi	see *Uji*
Shi'at Ali	Party of Ali, the fourth caliph after Mohammad

Shimpan	Collateral daimyo of the Tokugawa family
Shinto	Japanese nature worship
Shires	Counties of Great Britain
Shogunate (Shogun)	Military government (governor) of Japan
Shugo	Military governors under the Kamakura shogunate
Shugo-daimyo	Provincial military governors under the Ashikaga shogunate
Simony	The sin of buying or selling ecclesiastical benefices
Sippe	German term for lineage
Smerdy	Peasants of Kievan Russia
Spiritualities	Properties belonging to English monasteries
Ständestaat	A political order of checks and balances between a prince and the estates of his territory, inadequately translated as "estate society" or "corporate state"
Streltsy	Professional soldiers in seventeenth-century Russia
Subinfeudation	Process whereby vassals of the king grant fiefs to their own tenants and thus remove them from direct control by the crown
Subregulus	Under-king or lesser king in Anglo-Saxon England
Sutra	Buddhist scripture
Syncretism	Attempted reconciliation or union of different or opposing principles and practices, especially used with reference to culture and religion
Taille	General French term for tax in the Middle Ages, equivalent to the English tallage. Many forms of this tax existed since it was levied on income, real property, and so forth and varied with the jurisdiction of those collecting the tax
Temporalities	Privately owned lands belonging to bishops of the English church
Teutonic order	A military and religious order founded (c. 1190) during the Third Crusade for charitable purposes and subsequently instrumental in the eastward expansion of medieval Germany
Thegn	Local freeman, lowest rank of Anglo-Saxon aristocracy
Theocracy	Literally, the rule of a state by God or a god; government by priests, emperors, kings claiming to rule by divine authority
Tithe	The tenth part of the annual produce of a householder paid as a tax for the support of the church and the clergy

Tozama	"Outside lords," daimyo who were descended from former enemies or recent allies of the Tokugawa and who were located in areas distant from the Kanto plain
Uezd	Russian district or county
Uji	Japanese extended kin-group
Ulema	Islamic teachers of sacred texts
Ulozhenie	Russian law code of 1649
Umma	Originally the Arabic tribal community, the term has acquired the larger meaning of the community of all Muslim believers
Veche	Assembly of town notables in Kievan Russia and Novgorod
Votchina	Hereditary landed property in medieval Russia; also landed patrimony of early princes
Vox populi, vox dei	The voice of the people is the voice of God
Wergild	Compensation to be paid to relations of a slain kinsman in Germanic and other northern tribes
Witena gemot	Great council of the Anglo-Saxon kingdoms
Yarlyk(i)	Mongol charter(s) authorizing the governing authority of political subordinates
Zemskii sobor(i)	Estate assembly(ies) in tsarist Russia

Index *

*Check glossary for terms not listed in the index. Index includes only those authors whose
  works are quoted in the text.

DISCARD